EGYPTOMANIA

EGYPTOMANIA

A HISTORY OF FASCINATION, OBSESSION AND FANTASY

RONALD H. FRITZE

REAKTION BOOKS

For Rudi Heinze. Teacher, Mentor and Friend.

Published by Reaktion Books Ltd
Unit 32, Waterside
44–48 Wharf Road
London N1 7UX, UK

www.reaktionbooks.co.uk

First published 2016
Copyright © Ronald H. Fritze 2016

Printed and bound in Great Britain by Bell & Bain, Glasgow

A catalogue record for this book is available from the British Library

ISBN 978 1 78023 639 1

CONTENTS

PART TWO: VARIETIES OF MODERN EGYPTOMANIA

This advertisement for John Courage beer combines Egyptomania and imperialism. An intrepid British sailor has climbed the sublime height of the Great Pyramid to find a nice bottle of Amber Courage waiting for him.

INTRODUCTION

'Why did he name his company *Pyramid*?' asked Trout . . . 'Why would anybody in the business of highspeed transportation name his business and his trucks after buildings which haven't moved an eighth of an inch since Christ was born?'

The driver's answer was prompt. It was peevish, too, as though he thought Trout was stupid to have to ask a question like that. 'He liked the sound of it,' he said. 'Don't you like the *sound* of it?'

Trout nodded in order to keep things friendly. 'Yes,' he said, 'it's a very nice sound.'

KURT VONNEGUT, Breakfast of Champions (1973)[1]

WHAT IS EGYPTOMANIA? While that short question could be answered many ways and at great length, the simple answer is that Egyptomania is a fascination with ancient Egypt in its many aspects. It is a phenomenon that has existed for a long time, possibly for 3,000 years or more. Egyptomania can take a scholarly form, but it is also a widespread and persistent aspect of popular culture. In fact, although many people are interested in the history of ancient Egypt, more people are captivated by the Egypt of myth and legend. The goal of this book is to tell the story of the evolution of Egyptomania from its beginning, starting around 1000 BC with the ancient Hebrews and Greeks, and continuing up to the present. Although Egyptomania is a global phenomenon, this book will largely confine itself to Egyptomania in the West, while paying some attention to medieval Islamic Egyptomania. The focus of this book is on the fascination with both the myth and reality of ancient Egypt; although in the world of Egyptomania, myth reigns supreme. This aims to be a history of Egyptomania, not a history of Egyptology – the academic study of ancient Egypt – of which there are several excellent studies. It will touch only briefly on the Egyptomania associated with interior design and architecture, as these areas have been well covered by excellent scholars.[2] Instead, this book will primarily concentrate on the idea of Egypt and Egyptomania in popular culture.

The term 'Egyptomania' could give the impression of being concerned with a form of mental illness. Some people who go to extremes with their interest in Egypt might well be mentally ill, and the name 'Egyptopaths' has been suggested for them.[3] For most people, fascination with Egypt is just that, an enjoyable interest in a manner similar to the way that other people enjoy golf, period melodramas such as *Downton Abbey* or NASCAR. Most people's Egyptomania is harmless; however, some forms of it can indeed be sinister and even hateful. Nevertheless, when all is said and done, 'Egyptomania' is not a pejorative term.

The phenomenon of Egyptomania also goes under alternative names. One of these is 'Egyptophilia', a synonym for Egyptomania that gets rid of the potentially derogatory term 'mania'. Other terms include 'Egyptian Revival', 'Egyptianizing' and 'Nile Style'. But these terms are limited to discussions of the works of art, architecture and interior design that utilize Egyptian motifs. Another title that has been used is 'Pharaonism', which is a manifestation of Egyptian nationalism and was a movement popular in Egypt during the 1920s and 1930s. The movement was led by various Egyptian intellectuals who argued for a sense of national identity that had its foundation in the most ancient Egypt of the pharaohs. It rejected the idea of Egyptians identifying themselves primarily as Arabs or Muslims. There are also more specialized forms of Egyptomania such as 'Mummymania', a fascination with mummies; 'Tutmania', a fascination with King Tutankhamun (c. 1336–1327 BC) that stems from the discovery of his tomb in 1922 and which reappears whenever an exhibit of Tut arte-facts goes on a world tour; and the less well-recognized 'Amarnamania', the fascination with the heretic pharaoh Akhenaten (1353–1336 BC) and the art and architecture of his era. The German scholar Eric Hornung has coined the term 'Egyptosophy' for the idea that Egypt was the original source of wisdom and the heartland of the mystical traditions known as hermeticism. Fringe or pseudo-historical theories about ancient Egypt also have special-ized terms for that version of Egyptomania. The polite term is 'Alternative Egyptology', but irritated mainstream Egyptologists sometimes prefer the definitely derogatory 'Pyramidiots'.[4]

So what might Egyptomania look like? My wife and I went on a per-sonal Egyptomaniac quest back in the summer and autumn of 2001. That summer we were living in Beaumont, Texas, where I had taught at Lamar University for seventeen years until accepting a position in Arkansas. We were making preparations to move and were trying to lessen the amount of our possessions we would have to transport. At the same time, we were thinking about furniture that we wanted to buy once we got settled. Our new house included a cosy sitting/dining area that had a great view and we decided to put a couple of comfortable chairs in it. While still in Texas we were browsing the furniture department of the Dillard's department store. There we saw just what we wanted: two comfortable wingback chairs. But what made these chairs truly special was the motif of the upholstery with a pattern of pyramids, camels, palm trees and sphinxes – a cornucopia of images from ancient Egypt, what historians and interior design historians call Egyptianized artefacts (the artefact is non-Egyptian; its decor, however, strongly evokes ancient Egypt). Although these chairs, in the 'Cleopatra' line, were what we wanted, we decided to wait to purchase them until after we had moved to Arkansas. Once there, we took a trip to the Dillard's in Little Rock, but unfortunately the chairs were, in this store and others nearby, completely out of stock. Back in Texas, the Cleopatra chairs had also sold out. We never got our chairs. Our Egyptomania went unfulfilled.

What does my failed quest tell us about contemporary Egyptomania? First, Egyptianized artefacts are obviously popular. The Cleopatra chairs had sold out quickly everywhere. They were also distinctive enough that they had caught the attention of the sales people. Why were they so popular? I can only answer for my wife and myself in a manner similar to Kurt Vonnegut's truck driver in our epigraph: we liked the look of the chairs. That begs the question, why did we like the Egyptianized look?

Various scholars commenting on the phenomenon of Egyptomania in popular culture have made the observation that at least some of ancient Egypt's popularity is based on the fact that it is both comfortably familiar and intriguingly exotic at the same time.[5] That certainly explains the attraction of the Cleopatra chairs. But why should ancient Egypt feel so familiar to me? One reason is that I had a religious education in parochial school and Sunday school. There we were regaled with the biblical stories in which Joseph and his brothers, and Moses, held a prominent place, second only to the ministry of Jesus. The stories of Joseph and Moses were nicely complemented with rather romantic and sumptuous images of ancient Egypt (the Bible illustrations of the engraver Gustave Doré are fine examples). Then, of course, there were the epic biblical movies of the 1950s. My parents took me to see *Ben-Hur*, *Samson and Delilah* and *Demetrius and the Gladiators*, but the most lavish and epic of all was Cecil B. DeMille's

The Ten Commandments (1956), set in mysterious Egypt. Television added to Egypt's mystique by showing the Christianized historical epic *The Egyptian* on 'Saturday Night at the Movies'. In the film, the court officials cry 'All hail the living god' whenever the Pharaoh enters the throne room. It just so happened that the neighbouring public elementary school had a vice-principal named Godda, who happened to be bald like the villainous priests of Amun. Thanks to watching the movie, little boys cried out 'All hail the living Godda' whenever he approached. *The Egyptian* was memorable enough that later as a teenager I was inspired to read the novel by Mika Waltari on which the film was based. Late-night reruns of the classic Universal Studios *Mummy* movies familiarized my contemporaries and I with the curse of the mummy and the image of ancient Egypt as a weird and scary place. In this way, the seeds of a mild Egyptomania were planted in me, as they were too in generations before and after.

If one stops to think about it, evidence of popular Egyptomania is everywhere. The obelisk known as Cleopatra's Needle graces the banks of the River Thames in London, guarded by two somewhat whimsical

The original Tombs or Halls of Justice and House of Detention in New York City, which stood 1838–1902.

sphinxes. It has delighted people walking the embankment for more than a century. New York has its own Cleopatra's Needle in Central Park, while Paris has the Luxor Obelisk in its Place de la Concorde. Rome has a virtual forest of obelisks, from St Peter's Square to the Piazza Navona to the Piazza della Rotonda outside the Pantheon, among others. Each was looted from Egypt during the height of the Roman Empire, as were several obelisks associated with Emperor Constantine that still stand in the former site of the hippodrome in Istanbul. The Washington Monument in Washington, DC, is a modern obelisk done in imitation and emulation of the Egyptian originals.[6] Of course, the great museums in the West are renowned for their collections of ancient Egyptian artefacts. Visitors flock to the Egyptian galleries of the Louvre and New York's Metropolitan Museum of Art. The British Museum's visitor statistics continually show the Rosetta Stone to be its most popular exhibit while souvenirs based on the Rosetta Stone are the gift shop's best-sellers.[7]

When people watch episodes of the American television series *Law and Order* or one of its spin-offs, they often hear that prisoners are being taken to the sinister-sounding 'Tombs'. This, in fact, refers to the Halls of Justice and House of Detention in New York City. The original building was designed by the architect John Haviland and constructed in 1838. Haviland's design was based on a picture of an ancient Egyptian tomb that appeared in John Lloyd Stephens's *Incidents of Travel in Egypt, Arabia Petraea, and the Holy Land* (1837). The original building was replaced in 1902 and since that date three larger and more modern prisons have replaced the first, highly Egyptianized building. Although the new buildings show no traces of Egyptianized architecture, the nickname 'The Tombs' has persisted.[8]

While 'The Tombs' were not in fact tombs, Egyptian architecture was frequently used for funerary monuments, mausoleums and cemetery buildings. London's Highgate Cemetery, founded in 1839, is as much a tourist attraction as it is a cemetery; Karl Marx is its most famous resident. Sightseers, however, are also attracted to its Egyptian avenue. Begun in 1859, the avenue includes a covered walkway of tombs that feature Egyptianized architecture. Egyptianized tombs are not confined to the Egyptian avenue, however, and neither is Highgate unique. Many cemeteries across England, the European continent and the United States contain Egyptianized architectural motifs. Grave headstones frequently use the shape of an obelisk, as a visit to almost any large cemetery will show. At various times, people have even attempted to revive the pyramid shape for tombs. The most famous is probably the pyramid of the Roman magistrate Cestius that was built in Rome between 18 and 12 BC. It was a must-see monument centuries after its construction for many wealthy youths who undertook the Grand Tour during the 1700s and 1800s, and today it is still a tourist attraction; its nearby metro stop is called Piramide. Pyramidal funerary monuments were proposed for the graves of William Shakespeare, Isaac Newton and Frederick the Great, but these never came to pass.[9]

During the nineteenth century, World's Fairs became popular forms of entertainment as well as being showcases of industrial and technological prestige and imperial display. They were also significant purveyors of Egyptomaniac delights. London hosted the first true world's fair in 1851. It was known as the Great Exhibition and took place in Hyde Park within a vast, specially built glass-and-steel-frame structure that became known as the Crystal Palace. During the six months the Exhibition was open, it was visited by some six million people. After the fair ended, the Crystal Palace was dismantled and moved to Sydenham, where it served as a massive entertainment centre in which many new exhibits were added, including an Egyptian court graced by massive pharaonic statues. It proved to be a particularly popular destination for delighted Londoners and tourists until fire destroyed it in 1936. Other World's Fairs also included Egyptian exhibitions. The Centennial Exhibition of 1876 in Philadelphia included a rather modest collection of facsimiles of Egyptian artefacts, somewhat to the disappointment of American audiences. It was followed by the Paris World's Fair of 1889, which is most famous for giving France and the world the Eiffel Tower. The Paris fair also had an extensive and very popular Egyptian exhibit. Even the melancholic Vincent van Gogh wanted to visit the exhibit (he was interested in the daily life of ancient Egyptians who were normally 'beings whom we know only as mummies or in granite'). As an artist van Gogh admired the Egyptians for the 'kindness, infinite patience, wisdom, serenity' that their art, in its simple lines but monumental size, conveyed. A few years later, in 1893, Chicago's World Columbian Exposition also contained an equally popular Egyptian exhibit which portrayed both ancient and modern Egypt in a timeless, orientalized manner, including the alluring belly dancer 'Little Egypt'.[10] The golden age of World's Fairs is long over now, but the Egyptomania they helped to perpetuate in Western societies remains very much alive.

Just as nineteenth-century Londoners could savour the wonders of Egypt at the British Museum and the Crystal Palace, their American contemporaries were similarly interested in ancient Egypt. As was true for other Western nations, American interest in Egypt surged significantly as a result of Napoleon's expedition to the country from 1798 to 1801. The pre-existing American interest in the classics and the Bible led them to ancient Egypt. Various travel books focusing on Egypt and the Middle East were popular, particularly John Lloyd Stephens's best-selling narrative of his travels in Egypt and Palestine, which did far more than inspire the design for the 'Tombs'. American periodicals carried news of the latest archaeological discoveries, which their readers followed avidly. The United States was a young nation so associating itself with motifs of ancient Egypt would help rub some of that respectable antiquity off on the new republic and its increasingly distinct culture. As a result, the Mississippi River was referred to as the 'American Nile', while towns sporting Egyptian place names sprung up along its banks – most famously Memphis in Tennessee. Southern Illinois has a small region called 'Little Egypt', which is centred in Alexander County and contains the substantial town of Cairo (pronounced 'Kay Row') and the tiny village of Thebes. Within a few years, exuberant Americans began to refer to the Nile as the 'Mississippi of Egypt'. Over-exuberance also appeared in 1839 when John Delafield suggested that the first people to settle in prehistoric America were Egyptians who had made their way across Asia and the Pacific Ocean to reach the Americas. The Egyptianizing architect Robert Cary Long, Jr, of Baltimore eagerly adopted Delafield's theory and made comparisons between Egyptian and Mayan architecture. Given the state of archaeological knowledge at the time, it was not an entirely outrageous theory, but archaeological discoveries in the following decades proved it untenable and ridiculous.

The continuing progress of Egyptological knowledge also overtook Joseph Smith, Jr, the founder of the Church of Jesus Christ of Latter-day Saints, commonly known as Mormonism. In 1835 Smith bought some Egyptian papyri and mummies from a travelling exhibitor. Due to his work translating *The Book of Mormon*, Smith claimed to be an expert on ancient languages and script. He proceeded to translate the papyri using techniques very different from those of his contemporary the Frenchman Jean-François Champollion (1790–1832), who had deciphered Egyptian hieroglyphs. According to Smith, his papyri were writings of the Patriarchs Abraham and Joseph and they were written in 'reformed Egyptian' script. Smith only translated the so-called 'Book of Abraham', never getting around to the papyri supposedly written by Joseph. The 'Book of Abraham' allegedly contained doctrinal statements that justified discrimination against African Americans and for a number of years the document titled *The Pearl of Great Price* was an important source of Mormon church policy. In fact, when translated using the correct techniques, the two papyri that Smith purchased turned out to be copies of a late version of the *Book of the Dead* and *The Book of Breathing*, the latter an unremarkable document. Mormon scholars have stalwartly rejected the finding of mainstream Egyptologists and their rather devastating implications for the reputation and credibility of Joseph Smith, Jr. Such was the kaleidoscopic milieu of nineteenth-century American Egyptomania.[11]

Ancient Egypt has always had a place in the school curriculum, just as Egyptomania is present in popular culture, at least in a mild form. Harper Lee's beloved novel *To Kill a Mockingbird* (1960) and its film adaptation (1962) both contain a little touch of Egyptomania. The novel's narrator, Scout, is a young girl in second grade who is finding school rather grim. She is way ahead of her class and rather bored. But her older brother Jem reassures her that things will get better. As she tells it,

> the sixth grade seemed to please him from the beginning: he went through a brief Egyptian period that baffled me – he tried to walk flat a great deal, sticking one arm in front of him and one in back of him, putting one foot behind the other. He declared Egyptians walked that way; I said if they did I didn't see how they got anything done, but Jem said they accomplished more than Americans ever did, they invented toilet paper and perpetual embalming, and asked where would we be today if they hadn't? Atticus told me to delete the adjectives and I'd have the facts.

In a scene in the film, the children spend time walking like Egyptians.[12] It has even been speculated that that scene might be the inspiration for the Bangles' popular song and music video 'Walk Like an Egyptian' (1986), which has more than its fair share of Egyptianizing elements. The song's writer, Liam Sternberg, however, denies that his inspiration came from *To Kill a Mockingbird*.[13]

The ever-audacious pop singer Katy Perry ventured into Egyptomania in 2014 with a music video for her song 'Dark Horse'. As far as the song's title and lyrics go, there are no references to ancient Egypt except perhaps in general terms. Otherwise, the only cultural references are to Aphrodite and Karma. The set for the video is typical of many products of Egyptomania – that is, a heavily anachronistic and elaborately jumbled collection of Egyptianized costumes and sets. Katy Perry appears as an Egyptian ruler with magical powers in her outdoor throne room, presented with a series of suitors. All of them prove unsatisfactory and are destroyed or punished. There is a classic Nile boat scene with Katy Perry lying on a dais while her attendents row and serve her. Some of the female attendants are cat-headed. The first romantic suitor is dressed in Egyptian garb but sports a pendant with the name of Allah written in Arabic characters. He is reduced to dust by Katy's magic. This scene aroused the fury of some Muslim viewers of the YouTube video, but you have to look closely to see what they are talking about. The scene was taken as an anti-Muslim jab but in the video she is an equal-opportunity destroyer of men bold enough to try and court her. The second suitor is an overweight man who presents her with an array of junk food, including a pyramid of Twinkies surrounded by cheeseburgers. It is his spicy hot Cheetos, however, that trigger Katy's wrath and he is also reduced to dust. Several more luckless suitors are turned to dust while another is transformed into a dog's body. Obviously the video incorporates a number of stereotypes, associating ancient Egypt with magic, luxury, decadence and sexuality (all of which dominate the sets and costuming). As such it is very much a product of popular culture and a subset of Egyptomania.[14]

Where do modern Egyptians stand in all this Egyptomania? They are generally not Egyptomaniacs. Ninety per cent of the Egyptian population is Muslim. Some of the more radical fundamentalists in the country would like nothing better than to destroy the pyramids and the Great Sphinx because they are pagan relics. Historically, most Egyptians have been too poor and struggling to survive to ponder the mysteries of ancient Egypt. The Egyptian economy benefits greatly from the existence of Egyptomania or Egyptophilia in the form of tourism, and it is this that has caused many modern Egyptians to develop a new respect for the monuments and artefacts of their ancient past. Although Egypt has been a tourist destination since the early nineteenth century onwards, it is only in the last few decades, with the introduction of cheap air fares, that tourism has really boomed. In 1999 tourism accounted for 11 per cent of Egypt's gross national product and employed some 2.2 million people.[15] Turmoil since the fall of the Mubarek government has put a significant dent in the numbers of people visiting Egypt, but if and when relative stability is re-established, travel to Egypt will quickly reach its previous levels and surpass them. As Agatha Christie wrote in 1937:

> 'If there were only any peace in Egypt, I should like it better,' said Mrs Allerton. 'But you can never be alone anywhere. Someone is pestering you for money, or offering you donkeys, or beads, or expeditions to native villages, or duck shooting.'
> 'It is a great disadvantage, that is true,' said Poirot.[16]

That is also a part of the eternal Egypt.

Are there other reasons for being fascinated with things Egyptian besides their being both exotic and familiar or because they look or sound nice? Many scholars confronted with the popular fascination with Egypt or Egyptomania profess to find the phenomenon virtually unexplainable.[17] The very antiquity of Egypt is an element of attraction for Egyptomaniacs and Egyptophiles. For a long time Egypt was thought to be the world's oldest civilization, although the past 75 years of archaeological fieldwork in the Middle East have tended to dethrone Egypt as the source of all the major elements of civilization. Egypt's antiquity gives it a seeming cultural priority that every group or nation in the Middle East, Europe, Africa and the Americas wants to be a part of, and this especially includes disadvantaged and marginalized groups in those societies; being associated with Egypt confers respectability.[18] Egypt has been viewed as a repository of wisdom, the more arcane the better. This image of ancient Egypt has attracted and continues to attract those seeking enlightenment or those who are entertained by highly speculative and even bizarre ideas about the past.[19]

Michael Rice and Sally MacDonald, both museologists and Egypto-logical scholars, have suggested that the early twentieth-century ideas of psychologist Carl Jung (1875–1961) on humanity's collective uncon-sciousness, which consists of archetypes and myths, might provide a more theoretical explanation for the persistence of Egyptomania in popular culture. Archetypes are images that have been present in the human psyche from time out of mind. An example of such an archetype is the wise old man. In Greek mythology, Mentor, who took care of Telemachus in the absence of Odysseus, and Chiron, the centaur who tutored so many Greek heroes, are portrayed as wise old men. So are the figures of Kambei Shimada, the Samurai leader, and Gisaku, the village leader, in Akira Kurosawa's *The Seven Samurai* (1954). Or, for that matter, the charac-ters of Obi-Wan Kenobi and Yoda in the *Star Wars* films or Gandalf the wizard in J.R.R. Tolkien's *The Hobbit* and *The Lord of the Rings* trilogy. The great goddess archetype, of which the Egyptian goddess Isis is an example, stands for the nurturing and supportive woman who appears as a deity in many religions. The sun, serpents and cyclopean monuments and buildings are also archetypes. Archetypes appear in our dreams and nightmares and they recur over and over again in humanity's countless stories and myths. For Jung, myths were the stories that arose out of the archetypes in the collective unconscious. Rice and MacDonald point out that Egyptian culture is a rich treasure-house of such archetypes and myths. That trait is what intensifies the fascination and mythologizing that enthrals all sorts of people who possess even a passing interest in ancient Egypt.

The Egyptologist Charlotte Booth has rightly noted that almost all that popular culture portrays about ancient Egypt is myth rather than history. Therefore Egyptomania is largely a fascination with myth which dovetails with the collective unconsciousness's focus on archetypes.[20]

The chapters that follow trace the evolution of Egyptomania in the West chronologically until the twentieth century. At that point the chapters become topical. Chapter One provides an overview of the history of ancient Egypt, and is intended to provide readers with a basic knowledge of Egyptian history and explain how Egyptomania has distorted or mythologized the historical record. Readers who already understand the basic outline of the history of ancient Egypt can skip this chapter if they so wish. Chapters Two and Three look at how the Hebrews, Greeks and Romans viewed ancient Egypt. The writings of these peoples record their fascination with Egypt and form the foundational texts of the history of Egyptomania. As recorded in the Bible, the ancient Hebrews had a long and sometimes conflicted relationship with the Egyptians. Living in a harsher and more impoverished environment, the Hebrews saw that Egypt possessed a favoured and fertile land that made its people wealthy. It was a granary for the world and the Hebrews remembered its fleshpots with longing. Egypt was also a mysterious land of magic and secret knowledge. Its decadence and idolatry were dangerous temptations to the faith of the Hebrews. As a result of having been slaves in Egypt, the Hebrews most often viewed it as a land of bondage and oppression. On occasion, however, Egypt could be a land of safety for refugees and fugitives such as the prophet Jeremiah and the infant Jesus. Thanks to their long association with Egypt, the Hebrews could take pride in their own antiquity as a chosen people. Chapter Three looks at the Egyptomania of the Greeks and Romans whose relationship with Egypt was much less conflicted than that of the Hebrews. Minoans and archaic Greeks traded with Egypt during the Middle and New Kingdom eras. During the late period, Greek mercenaries formed an important component of the Egyptian army. Egypt frequently appeared in the myths of the Greeks. By the classical era of Greece, Egypt had become something of a tourist destination as the writings of Hecataeus and Herodotus show. The Greeks found Egypt to be a land of marvels both natural and man-made. The size of the Nile and its floods fascinated the Greeks, as did the unsolved mystery of its origin. Egypt's monuments awed the Greeks, especially the pyramids and the great ruin near Faiyum that they called the Labyrinth. These testified to Egypt's immense, impressive antiquity. The Greeks also considered Egypt to be a land of wisdom and secret knowledge. Tales abounded of Greek sages – such as Thales, Pythagoras, Solon and Plato

– studying in Egypt, regardless of whether such journeys of enlightenment really occurred or not. Egyptian religion also fascinated the Greeks as they worked to syncretize its gods with their own. During the Hellenistic era and at the height of the Roman Empire, the cults of the Egyptian gods Isis and Serapis were popular and rivalled early Christianity's appeal. Roman observers tended to be a bit more subdued and even sceptical in their enthusiasm for Egypt but they still engaged in Egyptomania. Significant figures of the ancient world such as Alexander the Great and Julius Caesar visited Egypt and succumbed to the spell of Egyptomania, as did a succession of Roman emperors. Thanks to Alexander the Great and his Ptolemaic successors, Egypt was host to one of the great cities of the Hellenistic and Roman worlds: Alexandria, famous for its massive lighthouse and legendary library.

Chapter Four traces Egyptomania from the last days of the Roman Empire in the West to the Renaissance. The Middle Ages in Western Europe was a dark age for Egyptomania. Little knowledge about Egypt survived except for what could be found in the Bible. The pyramids were transformed into the granaries of Joseph. Pharaonic Egypt had also succumbed to the triumph of Christianity, which was followed in a few centuries by the Islamic conquest. Knowledge of how to read the hieroglyphs was lost and only the vaguest memories of ancient Egypt survived. The lure of Egypt's mysterious civilization, however, soon infected Islamic scholars with curiosity that sometimes crossed over into Egyptomania. Chapter Five traces Egyptomania from the Renaissance through the Enlightenment. In the West, knowledge of Egypt revived with the Renaissance's rediscovery of the Classical world, including the Greek and Roman writers who had written about Egypt. There was also renewed interest in hieroglyphs and the mysticism of hermeticism. Scholars of the Renaissance, the Baroque and the Enlightenment were fascinated by Egypt but despite numerous efforts failed to decipher the hieroglyphs.

Napoleon's invasion of Egypt in 1798 and its consequences for Egyptomania are the subject of Chapter Six. The scholars who accompanied Napoleon to Egypt, 167 in total, came to study that land. When they returned to France, they produced the magnificent *Description of Egypt* that caused a great upsurge in popular interest. The French also discovered the Rosetta Stone, which provided the key to the decipherment of hieroglyphs by Jean-François Champollion and Thomas Young. Deciphering the hieroglyphs lifted the shroud of incomprehension that had covered Egypt's past but hardly dispelled the mystery. The renewed fascination with Egypt prompted a looting of Egyptian antiquities, which soon filled the museum galleries in Europe and North America with artefacts and the parks with obelisks. Chapter Seven looks at the manifestations of Egyptomania that appeared in Europe, from the decipherment of the Rosetta Stone to the discovery of Tutankhamun's tomb. This was the era of Egyptian Revival architecture and interior design, the rise of Western tourism to Egypt and the appearance of popular fiction and other entertainment using Egyptian history and themes. The discovery of King Tutankhamun's tomb and the resultant 'Tutmania' subset of popular Egyptomania are the topic of Chapter Eight. The tomb's discovery was possibly the most dramatic moment in the history of archaeology. When Lord Carnarvon died shortly after the opening of Tutankhamun's tomb, his death prompted all sorts of speculation about a curse on the tomb that tapped into the pre-existing idea of mummy's curses. The treasures that were since removed from Tutankhamun's tomb have kept Tutmania alive, as they have gone on tour in the great museums of the world.

Even as scholars have learned more about ancient Egypt, this new knowledge has not stopped the persistent creation of all sorts of implausible and wild speculation. One such major impact of this, Occult Egypt, is the subject of Chapter Nine. Egypt has been considered a land of secret wisdom and magic from the time of the ancient Hebrews and Greeks. More modern groups such as the Freemasons, the Rosicrucians and the Theosophists have claimed to have their origins in the ancient wisdom of Egypt on the basis of rather thin evidence.

The connection between fringe or pseudo-history and Egyptomania is explored in Chapter Ten. For a long time Egypt was thought to be the first great civilization in human history and the source of all the basic innovations such as agriculture and writing. Many people thought civilization diffused throughout the world from Egypt or else that it started at Atlantis and moved to Egypt with the destruction of the lost continent. The pyramids have inspired all sorts of speculations in terms of how they were built, whether they were prophecies in stone or the suggestion that they were some sort of power plant. Other enthusiasts claim that Egyptian civilization was actually far older than mainstream scholars claim and if they don't credit Egypt's culture to the Atlanteans, they give credit to extraterrestrial visitors from primordial times. Chapter Eleven looks at Afrocentrism's claims about Egypt being a black civilization and the source of all human civilization. How Egypt has been depicted in novels and films since the discovery of King Tutankhamun's tomb is surveyed in Chapter Twelve.

Egyptomania persists as a perennial phenomenon of Western culture. As the archaeologist Brian Fagan has said, 'There is something about the

Facsimiles of Egyptian artefacts on display at the museum shop of the Louvre.

Ancient Egyptians that casts, and has always cast, an irresistible spell over people everywhere.' Egyptomania has several recurring themes that will appear over and over again in the chapters of this book. The interest in Egypt's extreme antiquity – it is fascinating because it is fantastically old – is one of them. Another theme is the awesome monuments: its pyramids and temples. Egypt is a land of mystery and secret knowledge. It is also a land of beauty and riches. On the other hand, it can be a land of oppression, terror and death. There is an ambivalence about ancient Egypt. Is it good or bad, nasty or nice? Or is it all of those things together? As the various chapters of this book show, Egyptomania is not a monolithic phenomenon. As the Egyptologists Rice and MacDonald have rightly pointed out, 'No other ancient society evokes so many responses, at so many different levels as Ancient Egypt.'[21]

PART ONE
EGYPTOMANIA
THROUGH THE AGES

ONE

THE REAL EGYPT

About all of them [the kings of Egypt] the priests had records which were
regularly handed down in their sacred books to each successive priest from
early times, giving the stature of each of the former kings, a description
of his character, and what he had done during his reign.

DIODORUS[1]

POPULAR CULTURE usually portrays ancient Egypt as a land of mystery,
and in fact, accurately so – it is a land of mystery. There are lots of
things about Egyptian history that historians and archaeologists are
not sure about to greater or lesser degrees; for example, scholars are only
able to speculate about the techniques the Egyptians used to build the
pyramids. But this type of mysteriousness does not make Egypt unique.
The same could be said about other ancient societies and large segments of
history before the modern era. The fact is, as ancient civilizations go, Egypt
is relatively well documented in terms of the surviving archaeological and
documentary evidence. In contrast, after the civilizations of the Hittites
and the Hurrians of Mitanni fell, they were largely forgotten for centuries
until archaeologists rediscovered them. Neither of these ancient cultures
lasted as long as Egyptian civilization.

Pharaonic civilization remained largely intact for approximately 3,000
years, which accounts for its survival in the historical consciousness of
humanity. The fact that ancient Egyptians built many big stone monuments that have survived to the present also helps to keep their memory
alive. Writing during the golden age of Egyptology, from 1818 to 1914, the
great American archaeologist James Henry Breasted observed, 'Nowhere
on earth have the witnesses of a great, but now extinct civilization, been
so plentifully preserved as along the banks of the Nile.'[2] Ancient Egypt

was also considered by the ancient Greeks and Hebrews to be an exotic culture, and this opinion has persisted to the present. Hieroglyphs mystify us. The Sphinx beguiles us. Mummies fascinate us and the pyramids leave us awestruck. Those aspects of ancient Egyptian culture may be strange, but they are also intriguing, meaning that interest in the memory and remains of ancient Egypt persists. An accurate knowledge of its ancient history, however, is often lacking. What, then, was the real Egypt?

Environment

Egypt is located in the northeast corner of Africa, but even its location embodies a paradox, for its character is not African. It is the place where the continents of Asia and Africa meet. The paramount physical feature of Egypt is the River Nile. Herodotus, who wrote the first detailed description of Egypt and its surviving history, famously remarked that Egypt was the gift of the Nile. Actually, he said: 'The Egypt to which the Hellenes [Greeks] sail is land that was deposited by the river – it is the gift of the river to the Egyptians.'[3] Without the Nile, there would be no Egypt, there would simply be a larger Libya, the region just west of Egypt, which is chiefly desert because it does not have such a river of its own.

The Nile is the world's longest river at approximately 6,695 kilometres (around 4,100 miles) and flows from south to north. Its three main tributaries are the White Nile, the Blue Nile and the Atbara. The White Nile flows from Equatorial Africa while the Blue Nile and Atbara flow from the Ethiopian highlands region. The famous annual flooding of the Nile is generated by the seasonal rainfalls in Ethiopia, which cause the levels of the Blue Nile and the Atbara to rise. The Nile is easily navigable up to Aswan, where the first of a series of cataracts appear. These cataracts are sections of the river that feature flowing rapids. While not necessarily impassable, they are dangerous hazards to shipping. The ancient Egyptians built trading posts and fortresses at the cataracts to assist or to protect commerce on the Nile. Through most of ancient history, the cataract at Aswan was considered the southernmost extent of Egypt. Beyond it lay the land of Nubia.

North of Aswan, the classic Nile Valley begins. The river runs through a flood plain that is flanked by limestone cliffs. As the river approaches the Mediterranean coast, it fans out into seven branches and forms a huge delta of alluvial soil. The best-known branches are today called the Rosetta and the Damietta. For the ancient Greeks, the size of the Nile delta was astounding and unique. In fact, the Greeks coined the term 'delta' for the alluvial deposits found at the mouth of many rivers, but they initially confined its use exclusively to the great Nile Delta. The term 'delta' derives from the triangular letter 'Delta' in the Greek alphabet: Δ. The Nile Delta was the inverted letter, viewed from a north to south perspective.

Egypt, however, is best viewed from south to north following the direction of the river that gives it life. The land of Egypt is divided into two parts: upper and lower Egypt. Lower Egypt is the area of the Delta going south to the location of ancient Memphis or modern Cairo. Beyond lies Upper Egypt, which continues on to Aswan. Both Upper and Lower Egypt received annual floods that brought fresh soil and much-needed moisture. The soil of the alluvial lands is black in colour, hence the Egyptian term for their land, *kemet* (black land). In contrast, the sandy and rocky desert beyond was known as *deshret* or 'red land'. In many places the transition from the farmlands to the desert is so abrupt that a person can stand with one foot in *kemet* and the other in *deshret*.

Such was the importance of the Nile's annual flood that it even dictated the seasons of the ancient Egyptian calendar. Ancient Egyptians divided the year into twelve months of thirty days with five additional days added at the end of the year. They began their new year with the start of the annual flood of the Nile, which occurs towards the end of July and divided the year into three seasons of four months each. The first season was called *akhet* (inundation), referring to the annual flood. *Akhet* was followed by *peret* (emergence), the time when the flood waters receded and the planting of the crops occurred. The third season was harvest, or summer, and was known as *shemu*.

Compared with other lands of the ancient world, Egypt was favoured by modest geographical isolation. The land of Libya, to the west of Egypt, was largely a desert with a few oases, and inhabited by semi-nomadic or nomadic tribes. To the east of Egypt lay the Eastern Desert, which terminated at the shores of the Red Sea. At the far north is the Sinai Peninsula, also a desert but possessing the land route to ancient Palestine, Syria and Mesopotamia. These desert lands were also thinly populated by nomadic tribes. While the Libyans and the tribes of the Eastern Desert posed chronic threats of raiding and brigandage, they generally were not a serious military threat unless Egypt was badly divided internally. The Sinai Desert also made Egypt more difficult although not impossible to invade from Asia. To the south beyond Aswan and the first cataract was the land of Nubia. The Nile Valley running through Nubia was not as favourable to human habitation compared to the Egyptian section of the valley. The fertile flood plain of Nubia was narrower than Egypt's which limited the amount of potential agricultural land and therefore restricted the human population. The series of cataracts also meant that the Nile was not as useful or convenient as a means of transportation and communication for the Nubians. Still, Nubia had its attractions for the Egyptians and they were eager to control it. The southern land produced prized gemstones and gold from its mines and it served as a conduit for African goods of incense, ivory and exotic animal skins to enter Egypt. Through most of the history of ancient Egypt, it was generally the Egyptians who conquered the Nubians, but there were periods of Nubian resurgence and even a dynasty of Nubian pharaohs (the Twenty-fifth Dynasty). Lastly, in the north, Egypt borders the Mediterranean Sea.

Access to the sea brought Egypt into the emerging trade network of the ancient Mediterranean along with the Cretans, the Phoenicians and others. Because the Nile split into several navigable branches in the Delta, Egypt did not have any major coastal cities until Alexander the Great created Alexandria. Instead, Egypt's trading ports were located well up the river and so were less vulnerable to sea raiders. The border with the sea provided both access to the outside world and a degree of protection. For much of its history ancient Egypt existed in a geographical cocoon of relative isolation. As the Greek historian Diodorus accurately put it: 'The land of Egypt is fortified on all sides by nature.'⁴ This isolation reinforced the Egyptians' sense of their own uniqueness and it protected Egypt from the destructive wars and invasions that plagued so many ancient societies.

The How of Ancient Egyptian History

What do we know about the history of ancient Egypt? The answer is: quite a lot. That is not to say that we know anywhere close to what we would like to, but then that is the case about any aspect of human history. At least in this instance we know quite a bit more about Egypt's ancient history than we know about most other civilizations of similar antiquity. How do we know it? Fortunately a fair amount of material from ancient Egypt has survived for scholars to study and use to recreate a chronology of events.

The ancient Egyptians were not a people who wrote history as modern people would recognize it. Instead, the first person to write a surviving history of Egypt was the Greek scholar Herodotus in his *Histories*. Book Two and part of Book Three of that work deal directly with Egypt, but the factual accuracy within it varies. The material covering the Saite Dynasty and the Persian conquest of Egypt is fairly exact, but the earlier material is a jumble of information, sometimes true but other times false, incomplete or out of order.

The true foundation for the chronology of ancient Egypt is the work of Manetho (*c.* 305–285 BC), of whose life little is known. He was an Egyptian priest living in Heliopolis during the reigns of Ptolemy I Soter, Ptolemy II Philadelphus and possibly Ptolemy III Euergetes. In his day he was well known as a promoter of the cult of Sarapis in Egypt and other parts of the Mediterranean world. For modern scholars Manetho is best known as the author of a history of Egypt, *Aegyptiaca*, which is organized into three books or scrolls that divide Egyptian history into thirty dynasties from its earliest times to 342 BC. To compile it, he used the resources of the Heliopolitan temples, but wrote his work in Greek. This circumstance made Manetho one of the earliest Egyptians to write in the Greek language and it further ensured that knowledge of Egypt would become part of European culture. Manetho may have written the *Aegyptiaca* for Ptolemy Philadelphus to promote the antiquity of his realm over that of his rival Antiochus I of the Seleucid Empire in the Middle East. As an Egyptian who was knowledgeable about the history of his own land, he also wrote it to correct and criticize Herodotus' erroneous history of Egypt. Manetho's chronological framework of dynasties became and remains the foundation of the chronology of ancient Egyptian history. Unfortunately, the *Aegyptiaca* has now been lost and only fragments are preserved in the writings of various Jewish and Christian writers, such as Flavius Josephus and Eusebius. Given the information that survives in the fragments, it is clear that a wonderful source for reconstructing and understanding Egyptian history and religion has been lost.[5]

Manetho's king lists or dynasties have aided Egyptologists but they also present many problems which historians and archaeologists continue to untangle. First, there is inaccurate information in the lists, with omissions and unwarranted additions. The lengths of reigns are sometimes wrong, usually being too long. Second, each list is called a dynasty, which usually means a hereditary succession of rulers from the same family group. In fact, some of Manetho's dynasties contain people who are clearly not related to each other by blood or marriage. In other cases, Manetho lists a new dynasty but other information indicates there was not a significant break in the hereditary succession to justify it as separate. Third, Manetho's king lists seem intended to present the appearance of an orderly succession of dynasties ruling over a united Egypt. In fact, some of the dynasties from the intermediate periods, when Egypt was temporarily not a united kingdom, ruled concurrently over different parts of the country. Fourth, some Egyptologists have suggested the idea of co-regencies for certain kings. In a co-regency, the sitting king would name his successor and then rule jointly with the successor until the first king died. The idea was to assure an orderly succession to the throne and to give the successor some experience before that person became the independently governing king. The problem is that

Egyptologists hotly debate whether co-regencies even occurred, or, if they did occur, when and for how long. All of these things complicate the task of creating a reliable chronology for the history of ancient Egyptian rulers.

Chronology is the bedrock of studying the past; it is essential for understanding when events occurred and in what order they took place. Without that knowledge, any accurate understanding of the past is difficult or impossible. There are two types of chronology – absolute and relative. An absolute chronology establishes reliably accurate dates that can be related to the Common Era (CE), the dating system used by modern society, or for most prehistoric dates of the Before Present (BP) system. Prior to the development of radiocarbon dating and similar techniques in the late 1940s, archaeologists had a difficult to impossible task when assigning dates related to the absolute chronology. That circumstance forced archaeologists to fall back on relative chronology, which was used heavily by necessity in Middle Eastern and biblical archaeology, although not so much by Egyptologists, except in the pre-Dynastic eras.

Relative chronology establishes a sequence of events or eras for an ancient site or culture without being able to connect them to the absolute chronology. The concept of relative chronology is based on stratigraphy. Ancient peoples tended to occupy the same sites of towns or cities for hundreds or even thousands of years. During the time people occupied the site, layers of discarded material and rubble accumulated. Frequently, ancient sites would be destroyed by natural catastrophes or marauding enemies and then reoccupied, which would create dramatic breaks in the layers or strata. Over time mounds of such material, known as 'tells' in the Middle East, would grow on the landscape. Ancient cities and towns would be located on mounds that slowly but surely grew in height the longer the human occupations continued. Archaeologists work on the very reasonable assumption that the oldest layers of an ancient site are located at the bottom and the upper layers are the most recent. Sometimes archaeologists would discover buried in a strata an artefact from another culture that could be dated absolutely. Such chance occurrences would allow archaeologists to assign tentative datings within the absolute chronology for at least one strata of a site. At the very least, this technique using stratigraphy allowed archaeologists to create a chronology relative to a site or surrounding culture without necessarily being able to connect it to the absolute chronology. Close study of the evolution of artefacts such as styles of pottery helped, as this method allowed discrete cultures to be identified and placed in chronological orders known as sequence dating.

Thanks to Manetho's king lists, early Egyptologists had a framework for establishing an absolute chronology. In fact, until hieroglyphics were deciphered in 1822 Manetho was the only chronological source available. After that, when Egyptologists began to explore Egypt's rich archaeological remains, they began to accumulate more and more chronological information in the form of other lists of kings in temples, and other inscriptions and documents. These discoveries revealed the problems with Manetho's king lists and led to a more accurate absolute chronology. The development of radiocarbon and thermoluminescent dating helped to bring further accuracy.

The absolute chronology of ancient history remains tentative, fluid and a subject of continual debate, with the timeline's uncertainty growing the further back one goes (three relatively recent histories date the beginning of the Fourth Dynasty variously as 2649, 2613 or 2575 BC). Despite these problems, the basic chronology commands a strong consensus among scholars. Disagreements generally fall into the category of a few years or several decades, which is remarkable considering that the events discussed occurred more than 3,000 years ago.

A Chronological Overview of Ancient Egypt

Modern scholars have long divided the history of ancient Egypt into a standard set of eras or historical periods, although their exact dating and duration are subject to continuous debate.[6] It is always important to remember that historical eras are usually created by historians. Periods are intended to help classify and organize knowledge about the past into a comprehensible form. But because they are the constructs of scholars, historical periods are subject to debate and revision when new evidence emerges. For example, some scholars in the past merged the Early Dynastic Period and the Old Kingdom into one Old Kingdom era. Some contemporary scholars favour making the same merger. The terminology of the historical periods has also changed over time as new discoveries or interpretations have come to light. The Early Dynastic Period has alternatively been known as the Archaic Period or the Protodynastic Period. Despite these differences, the basic outline of Egyptian history has the overwhelming acceptance of Egyptologists, and the various agreed-upon historical eras follow the timeline listed here:[7]

> Predynastic Period, *c.* 5300–3000 BC
> Early Dynastic Period, *c.* 3000–2686 BC
> Old Kingdom, 2686–2160 BC
> First Intermediate Period, 2160–2055 BC
> Middle Kingdom, 2055–1650 BC
> Second Intermediate Period, 1650–1550 BC

New Kingdom, 1550–1069 BC
Third Intermediate Period, 1069–664 BC
Late Period, 664–332 BC
Ptolemaic Era, 332–30 BC
Roman Period, 30 BC–AD 395

A key criterion for organizing a period of Egyptian history into an era was whether the country was, at the time, unified under native rulers. This condition was true for the Early Dynastic Period and the Old, Middle and New Kingdoms. During the other eras, Egypt was disunited, under foreign domination or both. The only exception was the time of the Saite or 26th Dynasty of pharaohs during the Late Period. They managed to reunite Egypt under native rule for one last time. In the past, scholars have tended to consider the Intermediate Periods of Egyptian history as dark ages. While it might be accurate to describe the Second Intermediate Period or even the Third Intermediate Period as a dark age, the First Intermediate Period appears to have been a time of prosperity, even though political authority was divided.

A superficial glimpse at ancient Egypt can leave the impression of an extremely long-lived civilization that was highly stable to the point of being static. However, the many periods of ancient Egyptian history show that this image of changelessness is simply inaccurate. Egypt enjoyed a high degree of continuity but it also experienced significant changes and developments over the course of its history. Each era of Egyptian history had its own unique ethos.

It has been frequently alleged that Egyptian civilization arose suddenly without antecedents in the Nile Valley, but the archaeological record actually says otherwise. There has been a human presence in the region, accompanied by gradual cultural development, for many thousands of years. Artefacts have been found from the Lower Palaeolithic era of 400,000 to 300,000 years ago. Palaeolithic occupation continued until about 12,000 years ago. Humans during the Palaeolithic did not live on the banks of the Nile, they preferred the lakes or oases in the desert which were larger than they are today due to existing in a less arid climate. The people lived a nomadic existence as hunter-gatherers, fishing in the lakes and marshes. The Neolithic Era began about 8800 BC and lasted until about 4700 BC. It was also a time when the Sahara Desert experienced sufficient levels of rainfall for humans to live as nomadic herders of domesticated cattle. While these Neolithic peoples continued to engage in hunting and gathering, they also developed pottery.[8]

The Nile Valley itself seems to have been very lightly inhabited until 5400 BC when the Faiyumian Culture appeared in the Faiyum region of Lower Egypt between 5450 and 4400 BC. The Faiyum is a depression consisting of lakes and marshes located to the west of the Nile, and so it benefited from that river's annual flood. The Faiyumian people appear to have been the first to engage in agriculture in Egypt: they grew barley and emmer wheat, which appears to have diffused into Egypt from the Levant. This archaeological evidence would tend to undercut the theories that claim Egypt as the mother civilization of all humanity. The Badarian culture, which flourished 4400–4000 BC, engaged in the first agriculture to appear in Upper Egypt.[9]

The foundations of the pharaonic civilization were laid during the Naqada era, 4000–3200 BC. Naqada is an archaeological site associated with this culture and it was located in Upper Egypt less than twenty miles north of Luxor. During this era, Egyptians engaged in herding and agriculture with a shift towards living in agricultural villages strung along the banks of the Nile. Larger urban centres began to appear along with the basic elements of pharaonic iconography and artistic motifs. There was a development of greater social stratification as the society became more complex. After 3500 BC, Naqada culture and influence began to move northwards. By 3200 BC the Naqada culture had superseded the simpler Maadian culture of the Delta.[10]

By the period 3200–3000 BC, known as Naqada III, a large territorial state had developed, and its kings were buried at Abydos. Naqada III was the era of the 0 Dynasty, not recorded by Manetho, and was the time when the so-called Scorpion King or kings, made famous today by Hollywood, ruled. When the great Egyptologist William Flinders Petrie first discovered evidence of a strong territorial state associated with Naqada, he credited the development to an invasion by a 'new race' from outside of Egypt, presumably the Middle East. This new race of conquerors supposedly provided Egypt with an elite ruling class that stimulated rapid developments in political power, social organization and culture. A reasonably sophisticated system of writing first appeared in Egypt about 3150 BC, suggesting to some scholars that this form of communication diffused into Egypt from Mesopotamia. On the other hand, the symbols used in Egyptian writing are definitely homegrown, being rooted in the symbolism and culture of Egypt. So the question of the origins of writing in Egypt remains vexed and contentious. Today, scholarly opinion tends to credit Mesopotamia with the invention of writing.[11] What is certain, however, is that the 0 Dynasty had a useable system of writing and record-keeping accompanied by a bureaucracy for managing Egypt's surplus wealth.

As for the 'new race', Petrie was wrong and subsequent archaeological discoveries have shown that the late Naqada culture was very much an evolution from indigenous roots in Upper Egypt. The same observation applies to suggestions that Egyptian civilization arose to the south in Nubia. Archaeological evidence does not bear this contention out. Nubia, with a much narrower flood plain, was blessed with considerably less agricultural land than Egypt. Less agricultural land in ancient times generally translated into less population, less wealth and less military power.[12]

By 3000 BC Upper and Lower Egypt had been united into one large territorial state encompassing land from the Delta down to Aswan. Its capital was strategically located at Memphis to control river traffic between Upper and Lower Egypt. The details of Egypt's unification have been lost in the depths of time. Herodotus reported that Egyptian priests had told him that the first king of Egypt was named Min, better known as Menes. He was a great drainer of swamps and redirected the course of the Nile, after which he established his capital at Memphis. Manetho later reported the same information that Menes was the first king of the First Dynasty of Egypt.[13] Modern scholars have identified Menes with a king named Narmer, who is also credited with uniting Upper and Lower Egypt into one kingdom. Narmer was either a ruler from the end of the 0 Dynasty or really was the first king of the first dynasty.

The era that Egyptologists call the Early Dynastic Period lasted from around 3000 to 2686 BC. It consists of the Naqada III or 0 Dynasty along with the First and Second dynasties. Egypt's favourable environment allowed for plentiful surpluses of grain to be grown. The rulers of pre-dynastic and early dynastic Egypt undertook the task of managing this surplus, allowing them to become very powerful; these rulers were the root of the institution of god-kings that dominated as pharaohs. The title 'Pharaoh', deriving from the Egyptian term *per-aa*, means 'great house' and refers to the royal residence. It was not until the Eighteenth Dynasty that the term 'pharaoh' was used to refer to the kings of Egypt. The First Dynasty showed evidence of increasingly expensive and elaborate royal burials. During the Second Dynasty, the location of new royal tombs moved from Abydos to Saqqara, near Memphis. It was during the Early Dynastic era that Egypt became a unified and centralized state possessing an official bureaucracy and an efficient system of taxation. Its rulers could afford to build monumental architecture with elaborate artistic decoration. The basic elements of Egyptian religion also coalesced from the various regional deities and an ideology of a god-king developed to justify the highly centralized control of land, labour and crops. This political/religious system defined the

Early Dynastic era and the following Old Kingdom era for eight hundred years. It allowed Egypt to flourish as a larger and longer-lasting state than its Middle Eastern contemporaries.

Royal tombs provide a crucial source of information for reconstructing the history of ancient Egypt. Over time the organization and architecture of the tombs underwent various evolutions. Early in ancient history, royal tombs were public monuments which housed the body of the dead pharaoh and also included a temple complex for the continued worship of the cult of the pharaoh. In pre-dynastic times there was already an evolution from simple to elaborate tombs. Instead of burial in the ground, the royal body was placed in a special structure. The earliest structures were rectangular mudbrick blocks with slightly inwards-inclining walls known as mastabas – because they resemble the type of bench found outside of ancient Egyptian houses. Since early mastabas were made with mud brick few survive today. Both royalty and well-to-do Egyptians built mastabas for themselves. During the Early Dynastic and Old Kingdom eras, royal tombs would evolve from the mastaba into the well-known pyramid.[14]

The Third Dynasty marks the beginning of the Old Kingdom era (*c.* 2686–2160 BC), also known as the Pyramid Age. This iconic era lasted for five hundred years. There is very little to distinguish the Early Dynastic era from the Old Kingdom except for the building of pyramids for royal tombs. It was a stable and prosperous time for Egypt. The first ruler of the Third Dynasty was Djoser, who was assisted by the extremely able royal official Imhotep. Djoser began the Pyramid Age when he had a step pyramid built as his tomb instead of the more simple mastaba. His step pyramid at Saqqara was basically a series of mastabas built on top of each other. In its day, it was the largest stone building in the world. Imhotep is credited with helping to develop this innovation and others, including composing some now lost wisdom literature. These achievements earned Imhotep the status of a culture-hero in ancient Egypt that eventually led to his deification as a god of wisdom. It was under Djoser that Saqqara well and truly became the new royal mortuary replacing Abydos. Other kings of the Third Dynasty followed Djoser's lead and built step pyramids for their tombs.[15]

The Fourth Dynasty (2613–2494 BC) marked the high point of pyramid building and was the apogee of the political and economic power of the Old Kingdom. Sneferu was the first king of the new dynasty, although it was hardly a new dynasty since he was the son of Huni, the last king of the Third Dynasty. It was under Sneferu that pyramid building evolved even further and his activities as a pyramid builder attest to the wealth of Egypt and the power of its kings at that time. Sneferu was associated with

The pyramids of the Fourth Dynasty were renowned for their size and their great age, which helped in the creation of ancient Egypt's mystique. This Italian print from 1610, by Antonio Tempesta, shows the gigantic size of the pyramid but also erroneously uses the steeply sloped Pyramid of Cestius at Rome for a model of the other two pyramids depicted.

the building of three, possibly four pyramids. His pyramids also clearly demonstrate the evolution into a true pyramid form; Sneferu was the first pharaoh to build a pyramid with smooth sides rather than steps. He is said to have adapted the step pyramid at Meidum near Faiyum, but it was not an entirely successful conversion. The sides of the pyramid at Meidum were constructed at too steep an angle to resist the pull of gravity for long; its smooth sides collapsed, revealing the original step pyramid beneath. Sneferu had already begun another pyramid at Dahshur with steep-angled sides, but when the pyramid was partially constructed he switched to a gentler angle. The result was the unique Bent Pyramid, which still stands today. Pyramid building was clearly a process that involved some trial and error. Sneferu built a second pyramid at Dahshur known as the Red Pyramid. It has the classic look of a pyramid and is the third-largest pyramid in Egypt after those of Khufu and Khafra. His fourth pyramid was a step pyramid built at Seila near the entrance to the Faiyum. All of this activity made Sneferu the greatest builder of all the kings of the Fourth Dynasty.

Khufu, called Cheops by Herodotus, was the son of Sneferu. Little is known about this ruler, beyond that he was the builder of the Great Pyramid, the largest of the three pyramids at Giza. This pyramid was unique in having its burial chamber located within the core of the structure rather than beneath it. Herodotus considered Khufu to be a harsh despot who commanded 100,000 of his subjects to excavate and haul stone blocks from the quarries of the Eastern Desert. Once ferried across the Nile, another 100,000 labourers hauled the stones to the Giza plateau to build the pyramid. This process of quarrying and hauling took ten years, while the building of the Great Pyramid took twenty years. To help pay for this project, Khufu supposedly compelled his own daughter to engage in prostitution.[16] Keep in mind Herodotus was anxious to portray Eastern potentates as cruel oppressors along the lines of those great enemies of the Greeks – the kings of Persia. But Herodotus probably got his information from Egyptian informants as well; there was a very old tradition of depicting Khufu as a tyrant in Egypt.

When Khufu died he was succeeded by his eldest son, Djedefra, who started but did not complete his own pyramid – his reign only lasted six years. Djedefra's successor was Khafra, a younger son of Khufu, who built the second-largest pyramid at Giza and was known to Herodotus as Chephren. Khafra is also credited with the sculpting of the Great Sphinx, which is the largest statue in the world. Herodotus also depicted Khafra as a great tyrant along the same lines as Khufu and stated that the Egyptians hated the memory of these two kings so much that they refused to speak their names. The next king was Menkaura or Mycerinus, according to Herodotus. He was the son of Khafra, but unlike his father and grand-father he was a fair and thoughtful ruler who reduced the burdensome demands on his long-suffering subjects. His pyramid was also considerably smaller than those of his father and grandfather. This may very well indi-cate that the massive building programmes of Sneferu, Khufu and Khafra had stretched the resources of Egypt to exhaustion. However, Menkaura built his pyramid with granite, which was more durable and expensive than limestone. Furthermore, the historical record does not bear out the conten-tion that Khufu or Khafra were particularly cruel and ruthless monarchs. Menkaura was followed as king by his son Shepseskaf, who built himself an old-fashioned mastaba for a tomb. He was the only Old Kingdom ruler not to build himself a pyramid, which may provide further evidence that Egypt was at least temporarily exhausted by the strains of pyramid building.

Why the Egyptians built pyramids is unclear and the surviving historical documents from the Pyramid Age provide no reasons. Modern scholars speculate that it was part of the god-king ideology that sustained the highly centralized government of the Old Kingdom. Only the efficient bureaucracy of the state made large-scale pyramid building possible. It also helped that

Egypt in the Third and Fourth Dynasties faced no threats of external invasion, which would have diverted resources away from state building projects.

The Fifth Dynasty of the Old Kingdom (2494–2345 BC) continued to build pyramids for tombs but on a much smaller scale. During this era, the cult of the sun-god Ra arose, and this god became the state god for all of Egypt. Another important cultural advancement of this dynasty was the Pyramid Texts, the earliest surviving religious texts from ancient Egypt, which first appear in the walls of the burial chamber within the pyramid of King Unas (2375–2345 BC), the last ruler of this dynasty. The writings consist of a series of spells related to the resurrection of the king after death. The content of the Pyramid Texts varies over time, indicating that there were differing concepts of the afterlife among ancient Egyptians. They also indicate the growing importance of the cult of Osiris. Over time the resurrection spells, including new compositions, appeared on the coffins of lesser nobles and well-to-do Egyptians and are known as the Coffin Texts. These in turn would be collected into the famous Egyptian Book of the Dead during the New Kingdom. This evolution documents a process that scholars have dubbed 'the democratization of the afterlife', in which resurrection was no longer a royal monopoly but instead was available to all Egyptians who received a proper burial.

With the advent of the Sixth Dynasty (2345–2181 BC), the Old Kingdom began to show signs of decrepitude. The highly centralized control of the earlier kings was eroding as local officials and nobles gained more and more power and autonomy. The god-king status of Egyptian rulers was no longer held in the highest regard. King Pepi I (2321–2287 BC), the third king of this dynasty, managed to weather a plot against his life that originated in the royal harem (apparently one of his queens wanted to put her son on the throne). The relatively short reign of his son Merenra was followed by another son, Pepi II (2278–2184 BC), who came to the throne as a child and ruled Egypt for more than ninety years, the longest reign in Egyptian history. This long reign, however, did not result in stability. There were a number of years of very dry weather and arid conditions that resulted in a dearth of crops. The surrounding tribes of nomads suffered from the same circumstances even more so and entered Egypt seeking food. Pepi II's long reign also meant that he outlived his normal successor and a succession crisis ensued. From 2181 to 2160 BC seventeen kings of the Seventh and Eighth Dynasties ruled, each with a fleeting reign, thus bringing the Old Kingdom era to an end.

The First Intermediate Period (2160–2055 BC) followed. During this period, Egypt was not a single unified kingdom. At least part of the Delta and the part of the Nile Valley down beyond Asyut were weakly controlled by the kings of the Ninth and Tenth Dynasties, who moved the capital south from Memphis to Herakleopolis. Beyond Asyut, the local nobles resisted central control. The rulers of the region around Thebes managed to gain control of Upper Egypt and formed the Eleventh Dynasty. From that base of power, after 2112 BC, they proceeded to attack the Herakleopolitan kingdom. The Theban conquest and reunification was completed by Mentuhotep II (*c.* 2055–2004 BC) shortly after 2055 BC and marked the beginning of the Middle Kingdom era.[17]

The intermediate periods of Egyptian history are traditionally portrayed as dark ages of anarchy and strife. Certainly the kings of the restored Middle Kingdom took great pains to claim that their centralized rule had rescued Egypt from chaos. It provided a very nice justification for their authority. The archaeological evidence, however, tells a different story. The decentralized Egypt of the First Intermediate Period was really quite prosperous. Certainly greater numbers of the graves for common Egyptians survive for this era than had previously been the case. The contents of the graves also show a greater prosperity and the existence of a flourishing popular culture. Monumental construction by the kings ceased during the First Intermediate Period, but that probably came as a relief to ordinary Egyptians and possibly even contributed to the evident local prosperity.

The Middle Kingdom (2055–1650 BC) saw Egypt reunited under the rule of the Eleventh, Twelfth and part of the Thirteenth Dynasties. With its origins in Thebes, the Eleventh Dynasty chose the city as their capital. Under Mentuhotep II there was a renewal of royal building projects and the resumption of military expeditions into other lands. His successor, Mentuhotep III (2004–1992 BC), even sent the first expedition of the Middle Kingdom era to the mysterious but rich land of Punt down the Red Sea. Mentuhotep IV had a fairly short reign and apparently died without heirs.[18]

Amenemhat I (1985–1956 BC) had served as a priest and the vizier of Mentuhotep IV. He succeeded Mentuhotep to the throne and founded the Twelfth Dynasty (1985–1773 BC). Amenemhat I was interested in developing the marshes of the Faiyum into agricultural land. As a result, he moved his capital from Thebes to a place called Itjtawy, near Lisht in the Faiyum, although the actual location of Itjtawy has never been discovered. It appears that another harem plot resulted in the murder of Amenemhat, an act that spurred his son and heir Senusret I (1956–1911 BC) to abandon a military campaign against Libya to fight for his right to be king. Most of the kings of the Twelfth Dynasty conducted military expeditions into Libya, Nubia and Palestine along with promoting peaceful trade. They were also great builders and used a system of corvée labour to compel their subjects to work for them. Senusret II (1877–1870 BC) began the great irrigation system for the Fayium. His son Senusret III (1870–1831 BC) made great progress in restoring centralized government while also reducing the autonomy of the provincial rulers known as nomarchs. He also conducted extensive military expeditions into Nubia and Palestine. These exploits may have contributed to his identification as the inspiration for Herodotus' mythical Egyptian King Sesostris. This connection is disputed by some, however; Sesostris is a composite of several Egyptian kings, including the first three Senusrets of the Twelfth Dynasty and Rameses II of the Nineteenth Dynasty. In contrast, Amenemhat III (1831–1786 BC) was a peaceful ruler whose long reign marked the cultural zenith of the Middle Kingdom.

The Middle Kingdom appears to have been a more balanced and sympathetic society than the rigid and formal Old Kingdom. Literacy was more widespread and forms of popular writing appeared, featuring epic narratives of heroes along with folktales of ordinary people. The rulers of the Middle Kingdom promoted the cult of Osiris with its emphasis on resurrection and the afterlife. Senusret II had a cenotaph for himself built at Abydos. It was the first royal monument constructed at Abydos by a Middle Kingdom ruler. The popularization of the cult of Osiris also encouraged the so-called 'democratization of the afterlife' that was growing in Egyptian society.[19] Prior to the Middle Kingdom, Egyptians believed that all people possessed a *ka* or a soul or life-force, but only rulers possessed a *ba*, which was the individual uniqueness that constitutes a personality. It required the *ka* and the *ba* to be kept united, or at least in close proximity, for immortality in the afterlife. When the people of the Middle Kingdom came to believe that all humans had a *ba* they were conceding that everyone could enjoy the afterlife if the proper burial rituals were followed. The Middle Kingdom also saw the appearance of *shabtis* or funerary statues in tombs. *Shabtis* – as another manifestation of the 'democratization of the afterlife' – were figurines that represented servants who would work for the deceased in the afterlife. They first appeared in the tombs of ordinary people and are not found in royal tombs until the Eighteenth Dynasty of the New Kingdom.

After Amenemhat III, the Twelfth Dynasty came to an end fairly quickly. Amenemhat IV succeeded to the throne but had an undistinguished and relatively undocumented reign. He apparently died without issue and was succeeded by his sister Sobekneferu (1777–1773 BC), who is possibly the first woman to rule Egypt in her own right.[20] Following this reign, the obscure Thirteenth Dynasty – apparently a weak group, which included Merneferra Ay (*c.* 1695–1685 BC), who was the last king to rule at Itjtawy – began to rule Egypt. Ay was also the last member of the Thirteenth Dynasty who had monuments in both Upper and Lower Egypt. After his reign, the capital was moved to Thebes, where the Thirteenth Dynasty had faded away by 1650. The minor Sixteenth Dynasty came to power and ruled the area around Thebes from 1650 until 1580 BC. Meanwhile, Egypt degenerated into turmoil.

During the Predynastic, Old Kingdom, First Intermediate Period and the early part of the Middle Kingdom, Egypt remained somewhat isolated. Foreign trade, however, increased during the Middle Kingdom. More importantly, it was a system of exchange conducted by peaceful traders, both Egyptian and foreign, as opposed to the earlier military-style expeditions that brought back gold and other precious items to Egypt. As a result of this trade, significant numbers of foreigners began to set up residence in Egypt, mostly in the Delta. Most of these foreigners were *aamu*, as the Egyptians called them, which is translated as 'Asiatics' and refers to people from Palestine, Lebanon, Syria and beyond. Over time these foreign residents became at least partially Egyptianized. Some of these Canaanites may have carved out a kingdom for themselves in the area of the Delta that included Avaris. They formed the obscure Fourteenth Dynasty and lasted until about 1650 BC.

Far more traumatic for the Egyptians was the arrival of the Hyksos invaders who conquered and ruled much of Egypt from about 1650 until possibly as late as 1520 BC during the Second Intermediate Period, and formed the Fifteenth Dynasty consisting of six kings. The invaders, riding horses and chariots and wielding curved swords – military technologies unheard of in Egypt – took Avaris for their capital. Hyksos is a Greek rendering of the Egyptian term *hakau khasut*, meaning 'rulers of foreign lands'. It has been suggested that the Hyksos arrived from the region around Byblos in Lebanon and they certainly worshipped the Levantine deities Baal, Anat and Astarte. The Hyksos even equated their Baal with the god Seth, a rather ambiguous god of confusion, chaos and storms in the Egyptian pantheon. In the past some scholars have suggested that the era of the Hyksos is when the biblical patriarch Joseph rose to power and moved his family to Egypt.[21]

While Egyptian accounts tended to portray the Hyksos as uncouth and uncultured nomads, the archaeological evidence from Avaris indicates that they were a sophisticated people. At the height of their power, they ruled the Delta, the Memphis area and as far down the Nile Valley as Cusae or Qis. Memphis served as their secondary capital, while their main area of settlement remained the Avaris region. The Hyksos kings adopted the trappings of Egyptian kings and used the Egyptian bureaucracy and institutions in their government. Control of both Avaris and Memphis allowed the Hyksos to dominate the trade coming into Egypt from the sea and along the Nile. The Hyksos settlement at Cusae served as a toll station for ships travelling down the Nile to the sea.

The Hyksos occupation was a bitter experience and a perilous time for the Egyptians. Rule by native Egyptians survived in the Thebes region where the Seventeenth Dynasty came to power about 1580 BC, but beyond Thebes they were caught between the Hyksos in the north and the resurgent Nubians to the south. Egyptian control to the south had shrunk back to Elephantine Island near the first cataract of the Nile. Hyksos control of Memphis also meant that the Theban rulers were cut off from the font of Egyptian culture and knowledge in Memphis and the Delta. This situation meant that the Thebans were forced to fend for themselves. Without access to the funerary texts descended from the Pyramid and the Coffin Texts, the Thebans created their Book of the Dead, which would become a mainstay of grave goods by the later New Kingdom. Despite their dire situation, the kings of the Seventeenth Dynasty were determined to liberate and reunite Egypt under their rule.

The wars of Thebes with the Hyksos began during the reign of the long-lived and powerful Hyksos king Apepi (c. 1570–1530 BC), who was also known as Apophis. Apepi tried but failed to provoke Taa II, the Theban ruler, into war a number of times, but when war finally broke out Taa II decided that conflict was unavoidable. Unfortunately, the war went badly for the Thebans; Taa II was defeated in battle and killed. This success, however, did not ultimately help the Hyksos. Taa II was succeeded by his son (or possibly younger brother) Kamose who was bent on revenge. Thirty years of war followed. Apepi tried to place the Thebans in an impossible position by making an alliance with the Nubians, but Kamose proved to be an able military leader. He handily defeated the Nubians and restored Egyptian control of the Nile Valley down to Buhen by the second cataract. With the Nubian threat neutralized, Kamose turned his fury onto the Hyksos. It is certain that he pushed the border of the Theban kingdom north to Hermopolis. Some evidence indicates that Kamose also made a raid deep into the Hyksos heartland and threatened Apepi in his capital of Avaris. This event, however, may not have occurred and instead might be an exaggerated boast by Kamose intended to irritate the Hyksos king.

The man who drove the Hyksos out of Egypt for good was Ahmose (1550–1525 BC), the younger son of Taa II. Ahmose's big offensive against the Hyksos occurred between the eighteenth and twenty-second years of his reign. First, he captured Heliopolis, then Memphis, leaving only the Hyksos stronghold at Avaris. Ahmose besieged it, but it seems that he negotiated a surrender rather than taking it by storm. The archaeological evidence and the account of Josephus indicate that the Hyksos were allowed to evacuate Avaris with their possessions. Ahmose's conquests restored a united kingdom of Egypt once again under the rule of a native monarch.

Ahmose's reign marks the beginning of the New Kingdom (1550–1069 BC), ancient Egypt's last sustained era of greatness. He was also the founder of the brilliant Eighteenth Dynasty of pharaohs (1550–1295 BC), which included some of the most famous and successful rulers of Egypt. His son Amenhotep I (1525–1504 BC) succeeded him and during his reign stabilized Egypt, establishing the main features of the Eighteenth Dynasty's style of governing. Thebes again became the capital, and the Thebans promoted the cult of the local deity Amun. They linked the cult of Amun to that of the sun-god Ra and used the cult of Amun-Ra as a way to unify their kingdom further. Amenhotep II also extended Egyptian control in Nubia to the second cataract and beyond to secure Egypt's southern frontier. Pharaohs of the Eighteenth Dynasty also attempted to secure their throne by allowing the royal daughters to only marry a king; they were not allowed to marry prominent nobles and so create rival claimants to the throne. As a result, royal princesses were either married off to foreign kings or to their father or brother pharaohs as royal wives. The genetic havoc of these incestuous marriages was, however, avoided, thanks to pharaohs having many other wives who were not blood relatives and who tended to be the mothers of the crown princes. The Eighteenth Dynasty based their central administration on the local Theban elite. This policy kept the government centralized and allowed the pharaohs to keep a close watch on their highest officials.[22]

Amenhotep I died without issue and was succeeded by Thutmose I (1504–1492 BC), who was either a distant relative or a trusted Theban aristocrat. Thutmose I completed the destruction of the kingdom of Kush in Nubia with his forces reaching the fourth cataract. He also campaigned in Syria, where his army encountered the forces of the Mitannians, who demonstrated a significant superiority in chariot warfare. It was under Thutmose that pharaohs began to build royal tombs in the Valley of the Kings on the west side of the Nile opposite Thebes. He was the father of the half-siblings Thutmose II and Hatshepsut.

Thutmose II married his half-sister Hatshepsut, who held the title of 'great royal wife', but his heir apparent, the future Thutmose III (1479–1425 BC), was the son of a lesser wife. Thutmose II only ruled for three years and when he died Thutmose III was still a child. As a result, Hatshepsut served as regent. It also resulted in one of the more mysterious and interesting interludes in the history of ancient Egypt. As her regency progressed, Hatshepsut decided to make herself pharaoh in her own right based on her royal blood. Her rule as pharaoh took place during the years 1473 to 1458 BC. During that time Hatshepsut took on all the trappings of a pharaoh – including presenting herself to her subjects dressed as a male. Her grasping of the throne made Hatshepsut one of the very few women to hold office as pharaoh and it also made her the most famous of the female pharaohs. Her reign appears to have been largely uneventful, with some limited military campaigns, some monumental building projects such as her memorial temple at Deir el-Bahri, and the resumption of trade with Punt. She was assisted in these efforts by her able vizier Senenmut, who some suggest was also her paramour.

In 1458 BC Thutmose III became pharaoh in his own right. Hatshepsut simply disappears from the records. What happened to her is unclear. Thutmose III, later in his reign, attempted to erase Hatshepsut's name from all monuments. Some have suggested that this action was retribution for Hatshepsut having usurped the throne from him. Others feel that because the campaign to erase all memory of Hatshepsut occurred late in Thutmose III's reign, rather than immediately after he gained the throne, it may have been more an effort to expunge an anomalous figure from the dynasty's history – and supposedly the bad precedent of a female pharaoh from the historical record.

Thutmose III became one of the great military leaders of ancient Egypt. He invaded Syria and inflicted a defeat on the Mitannians at the battle of Megiddo in around 1457 BC. Egypt gained territory from Mitanni and Thutmose III discovered that military campaigns were profitable if they were successful. His campaigns made Egypt a great power and brought it into the international politics of the Bronze Age Middle East. His successor, the vigorous Amenhotep II (1427–1400 BC), who enjoyed sports such as hunting and chariot racing, continued the wars with Mitanni, a state viewed as Egypt's great enemy. Thutmose IV (1400–1390 BC), the son and successor of Amenhotep II, began his reign hostile towards Mitanni, but the two countries eventually ended up allies. The rise of the empire of the Hittites in Asia Minor presented Egypt and Mitanni with a formidable new foe who threatened both countries. The result of this diplomatic alliance was a balance of power that kept Egypt at peace for several decades.

Thutmose IV's successor was his son, Amenhotep III (1390–1352 BC). During his reign, Egypt experienced peace and prosperity, and reached the pinnacle of its power. Egyptians so closely associated Amenhotep III with this prosperity that centuries later he was worshipped as a fertility god who helped crops to produce plentiful harvests. Amenhotep III also began to promote the worship of Aten, the god of life-giving sunlight, a different deity from the long-important sun-god Ra. There is some evidence that Amenhotep III claimed the status and traits of a god in his own lifetime. He was also a prodigious builder, adding to the temples at Luxor and Karnak and constructing a huge mortuary temple for himself near the Valley of the Kings. This temple included the huge statues of Amenhotep III that later became known as the Colossi of Memnon. He took a woman named Tiye as his great royal wife and she gave birth to Amenhotep IV, who would rename himself Akhenaten.

The reign of Amenhotep IV or Akhenaten (1352–1336 BC) formed a period of intense religious turmoil in Egypt, which has been subject to all sorts of speculation – with scholarly debates and interpretive controversies, some quite fanciful – about the nature of the pharaoh's reign. When Amenhotep IV came to the throne, he began to promote the cult of Aten more vigorously than his father. During the fifth year of his reign he changed his name to Akhenaten (effective for Aten). His goal was to make Aten the sole god of Egypt. In other words, he was establishing monotheism. Whether this plan was an evolution of his father's support for the cult of Aten or a radical change in emphasis is unclear. Some scholars have pointed out that while Egyptian religion was seemingly very polytheistic, it was theologically approaching monotheism; the Egyptians were coming to view their many gods as manifestations of characteristics of one great god. At the same time as he changed his name to Akhenaten, the pharaoh moved his capital further north along the Nile from Thebes and built a new capital called Akhetaten (horizon of Aten) in a place now called Amarna. It was occupied between 1350 and 1320 BC. There he built new temples for Aten and a palace for himself and his beautiful principal wife Nefertiti, their daughter and his other wives and children. Akhenaten also granted Nefertiti considerable power in his government. Clearly Akhenaten was a very different sort of pharaoh and a revolutionary one at that.[23]

Under the early New Kingdom kings, Egyptian religion had focused more and more on the sun-god Ra and the pharaoh. The god Amun had been added by the Thebans and a fusion god Amun-Ra, the king of the gods, became the paramount god of Egypt. The priesthood of Amun-Ra and their temple had grown in both wealth and political power. Now Akhenaten was directing wealth and power away from them. The priests of Amun-Ra were not happy and neither were Egyptian traditionalists. When Akhenaten started to suppress the cults of all other gods, he posed an even greater threat of heresy and divine wrath.

Akhenaten reigned during a troubled time internationally. The Hittites had defeated and destroyed the Mitannian Empire, and this upheaval subsequently threatened Egypt's own empire in the Levant. With Akhenaten concentrating on his religious revolution, however, foreign affairs were neglected. Akhenaten died in 1336 and his promotion of Aten died with him. He was briefly succeeded by the shadowy figure Smenkhkara, which may have been a name assumed by Nefertiti so that she could take the throne. Then Tutankhamun, his son by a lesser wife, came to the throne as a boy and ruled from 1336 to 1327 BC. Although today he is probably the best-known pharaoh of all due to Howard Carter's discovery of his intact royal tomb, he was insignificant in his own day. Because he died young and in a time of political turmoil, there are many theories that he was murdered, although the physical evidence does not particularly support such a conclusion. He was succeeded by a senior official named Ay, who was an older man and only occupied the throne from 1327 to 1323 BC. When Ay died, the next pharaoh was the general known as Horemheb, who ruled Egypt until 1295 BC. Horemheb's long reign ended the illustrious Eighteenth Dynasty and fully restored traditional Egyptian religion.

Some scholars consider Horemheb to be the last king of the Eighteenth Dynasty while others classify him as the first ruler of the Nineteenth. He certainly established the Nineteenth Dynasty because he appointed his chief advisor Paramessu as his successor. Paramessu, upon becoming the pharaoh, took the new name of Rameses I. Like Ay, he was an older man and only had a short reign, lasting less than two years from 1295 to 1294 BC. He was succeeded by his capable adult son Seti I (1294–1279 BC) – the pharaoh murdered by the sinister Imhotep in the film *The Mummy* (1999) starring Brendan Fraser. The real Seti I further stabilized Egypt and fought the Hittites. He was succeeded by his son, Rameses II, known as Rameses the Great, who had a tremendously long reign, from 1279 to 1213 BC. Rameses II was certainly great in terms of his building programmes. Besides significant additions to the temples at Karnak and Luxor, he also built a great funeral temple for himself – known as the Ramesseum – at the Valley of the Kings, as well as the famous temple with its colossi of Rameses II at Abu Simbel. As a general, he was perhaps not so great. Marching his army north to fight the Hittites in 1275, Rameses II was fooled into a trap near the city of Kadesh in Syria. Only luck and the bravery of his elite troops saved the day and Rameses's life. Both sides claimed victory in a battle that was definitely a draw, but the Egyptians lost territory to the Hittites. Eventually the warring powers made peace. The Hittite monarchy, however, suffered ongoing disruption, such as considerable infighting over the royal succession and the growing threat from the militarily capable Assyrians.[24]

Rameses II also built the royal residence of Piramesse in the Delta. This project has prompted some biblical scholars to identify him as the pharaoh of

Akhenaten or Amenhotep IV (1352–1336 BC): reformer or heretic? He was erased from history by his enemies, but since his mid-19th-century rediscovery he has become one of the best-known pharaohs in popular culture.

Rameses II (1279–1213 BC) was a great soldier and a builder. His four colossi at the temple of Abu Simbel on the border with Nubia were meant to intimidate his enemies.

the Exodus. In Egypt, his achievements became conflated with the legendary ruler Sesostris. Rameses II had many wives, including a Hittite one, and produced many children, which was a good thing as he outlived twelve sons. Fortunately his son Merenptah (r. 1213–1203 BC) survived to take the throne.

The world of the ancient Mediterranean and the Middle East experienced tremendous upheavals at this time. It was the age of the Peoples of the Sea, as the Egyptians called them. The Sea Peoples were various ethnic groups from Asia Minor and the Aegean along with possibly other bands from the western Mediterranean lands of Sicily, Sardinia and Tyrrhenia (Etruria). The lands of the Hittites, the Levant and Egypt began to suffer from attacks by sea raiders as early as the era of Amarna. These raids increased over time until they became mass migrations and invasions of peoples; the survival of the great empires was thus threatened by a late Bronze Age *Völkerwanderung,* or migration of peoples. Rameses II defeated an attack on the Delta by a group called the Sherden or the Shardana. Their defeated warriors were incorporated into the Egyptian army and fought bravely at the battle of Kadesh. Anticipating future attacks on the Delta, Rameses II built a line of fortresses along the coast to protect Egypt.

Merenptah inherited the throne from his long-lived father at an advanced age. In around 1208 he experienced a more serious invasion of the Sea Peoples, who, with other cities and tribes from the Levant, had made an alliance with the tribes of Libya. Again the Egyptians were able to repel the invaders, who numbered about 30,000 (including women and children along with the warriors). Merenptah commemorated his victory on a stele that contains the earliest-known non-biblical reference to Israel – in this case appearing to have been considered by the Egyptians to be a tribe or people rather than a region or land. After the failed incursion the Sea Peoples left Egypt alone for about forty years, but by then Egypt had other problems. A succession struggle ensued when Tawosret (or Tausret), the great royal wife of the deceased Seti II, tried to rule Egypt through Saptah, a son of Seti II by a lesser wife. When he died in 1190 BC, following in the footsteps of Hatshepsut, she tried to rule as pharaoh on her own. Her reign was short and in 1189 BC the obscure Sethnakht, probably a general, seized the throne.[25]

Sethnakht was the first king of the Twentieth Dynasty (1186–1069 BC). Apparently he gained the throne at an advanced age so his reign was brief. His son Rameses III (1184–1153 BC) succeeded him. Rameses III is considered the last great king of the New Kingdom and he consciously modelled himself on Rameses II. Egypt certainly faced extremely grave threats during his reign. During his fifth year as king, rebellious Libyan tribes tried to invade the western Delta with the aid of Karian mercenary troops from Asia Minor. The invading army numbered 12,000 warriors and was defeated at the Egyptian border. A far greater peril threatened Egypt in the eighth year of Rameses III's reign. The Sea Peoples, in a large coalition, attempted to invade Egypt by land and by sea. They had already destroyed the Hittite Empire and devastated the coast of the Levant. These invaders included the Peleset, who would eventually settle along the Gaza region of Canaan where they would be called the Philistines and give their name to the new land in the form of Palestine. Rameses III proved to be an able and brave war leader. Hard fighting resulted in the defeat of the Sea Peoples, leaving Egypt unconquered although its Asian empire was in shambles. Rameses III went on to have a long reign, including the building of many monuments, temples and mortuary buildings, but his reign ended under somewhat baffling circumstances – another harem plot against the pharaoh. Authorities detected the plot and the conspirators were brought to trial. What remains unclear is whether the conspiracy managed to kill or mortally wound Rameses III or whether he survived the ordeal only to die soon after of old age. The sorry ending of Rameses III's reign serves as an emblem of the final decades of the declining New Kingdom.[26]

The circumstances that set the invasion of the Sea Peoples in motion is unclear. Some scholars have suggested that the seafaring peoples of the Aegean and the coasts of Asia Minor had come to learn that piracy and raiding were more profitable than trade. Others have suggested that adverse climatic conditions resulting in famine forced these people to wander in search of food. Bountiful Egypt made a particularly tempting target. Another theory suggests that devastation resulting from the outbreak of the bubonic plague forced the Sea Peoples to seek out new lands. Whatever the cause, the Sea Peoples transformed the ancient Mediterranean world as much as the conquests of Alexander the Great. The Bronze Age ended; the Iron Age began. Old empires were largely swept away and new powers arose. Egypt survived the tumult, but in a weakened state. The rulers who followed Rameses III were named Rameses in imitation of him but all eight successors were merely pallid imitations. Even more ominous, the priests of Amun-Ra in Thebes were becoming more autonomous from the government of the pharaoh. Ultimately they gained so much power and wealth that they were practically the independent rulers of Upper Egypt. It was under these somewhat pathetic circumstances that both the Twentieth Dynasty and the New Kingdom ended in 1069 BC.[27]

The Third Intermediate Period (1069–664 BC) was a time when Egypt broke into smaller quarrelling kingdoms or succumbed to foreign invaders. Technically Egypt remained united under the Twenty-first Dynasty (1069–945 BC) with its capital at Tanis in the Delta. In reality, the priests of Amun-Ra in Thebes and various local rulers exercised independent control over Upper Egypt. During the latter part of the New Kingdom, many Libyans settled in the Delta and large numbers of Nubians moved into Upper Egypt. The previous ethnic homogeneity of Egyptian society ended even though the newcomers tended to assimilate themselves into the predominant Egyptian culture. Some of the Libyans in the Delta assimilated so well that they took control of Egypt from the Twenty-first Dynasty in 945 BC. The new Libyan king, Sheshonq I (945–924 BC), began the Twenty-second Dynasty (945–715 BC) and continued to use Tanis as his capital. Under Sheshonq I, the fortunes of Egypt briefly revived. The priests at Thebes found that their independence was curtailed. Even more dramatically, Sheshonq I invaded Palestine and restored Egyptian control over the region by defeating the kingdoms of Israel and Judah. He was, in all probability, the Shishak of 1 Kings 14:25–8 and 2 Chronicles 12:1–12, who carried away treasure from Jerusalem during the reign of King Rehoboam of Judah. In popular culture, this would also make him the Shishak of the Indiana Jones adventure *Raiders of the Lost Ark* (1981), who supposedly carried off the Ark of the Covenant from Jerusalem to his capital at Tanis (but who almost certainly did no such thing). Unfortunately for Egypt, the successors of Sheshonq I were nowhere near as capable. By 818 BC a rival Twenty-third Dynasty had arisen in a section of the Delta, along with eventually a very brief Twenty-fourth Dynasty and other regional rulers.

Political authority had become so badly fragmented by 750 BC that Egypt was exceptionally vulnerable to foreign invasion.[28]

The foreign invaders who established the Twenty-fifth Dynasty over Egypt were the kings of Kush in Nubia. King Piye of Kush (747–716 BC) invaded Egypt in about 728 BC, and reached as far north as Heliopolis but then withdrew without establishing permanent control. Shabaqo (716–702 BC) succeeded his brother Piye as king of Kush and proceeded to invade Egypt and make it part of his kingdom. The Nubian Twenty-fifth Dynasty was undoubtedly black. It made Memphis its Egyptian capital and, although they never completely stamped out all locally autonomous rulers in Egypt, the Nubian pharaohs attempted to extend Egypt's control into Palestine and Syria as Sheshonq I had done. This action brought the Nubians into conflict with the Assyrian Empire at the height of its power. In 701 BC Shabitqo (702–690 BC), the nephew and successor of Shabaqo, attempted to thwart Sennacherib of Assyria's invasion of Judah. He was defeated, and furthermore he managed to draw Assyrian attention to Egypt. A series of Assyrian attacks on Egypt began in 674 BC in which control of the country see-sawed back and forth between the Nubians and the Assyrians. Finally in 663 BC Ashurbanipal of Assyria invaded Egypt and sacked Thebes, ending Nubian authority in Egypt for good.

Over-extended, the Assyrians attempted to rule Egypt through local vassals, including Psamtek I (664–610 BC) of Sais. Between 660 and 656 BC, Psamtek I extended his lands, gained independence from Assyria and finally reunified Egypt. He also established the Saite or Twenty-sixth Dynasty (664–525 BC), a period in which many Greeks lived in Egypt or visited the country as traders and mercenaries. The next Saite pharaoh was Nekau II (610–595 BC), the son of Psamtek I. He was also known as Necho. By his reign Assyria was in serious decline and the new threat was the Chaldeans of the Neo-Babylonian Empire. Nekau again tried to re-establish Egyptian control over Palestine and Syria and defeated King Josiah of Judah in 609 BC. But the Egyptians were no match for the Chaldeans, who crushingly defeated Nekau at the battle of Carchemish in 605 BC. The victorious Chaldeans drove the Egyptians back to Egypt but a stiffened resistance prevented them from invading Egypt itself at that point. Future Chaldean invasion attempts also failed. Nekau II is also known for supposedly sponsoring a Phoenician circumnavigation of Africa that took three years and for starting but not completing a canal from the Nile River to the Red Sea. The final years of the Saite Dynasty weakened Egypt and opened the way for an invasion by a new superpower, the Persian Empire.[29]

Cambyses of Persia (525–522 BC) conquered Egypt and made it a province or satrapy of the Persian Empire. Although Herodotus depicted Cambyses as a demented tyrant, other evidence does not bear out that characterization. The Persian great kings formed the Twenty-seventh Dynasty (525–404 BC) and their rule was not oppressive. They generally attempted to rule Egypt through the local elite and Darius I (522–486 BC) actually completed Nekau II's Red Sea canal – it was supposed to have been big enough that two triremes could pass each other in the channel. The proud Egyptians, however, longed for independence, which they gained temporarily in 404 BC. Three native dynasties ruled between 404 BC and 343 BC, the Twenty-eighth, the Twenty-ninth and the Thirtieth. These kings were military rulers whose brief reigns were vexed by many coups and plots. The Persians wanted Egypt back in their empire and Artaxerxes III reconquered Egypt between 343 and 341 BC. The second Persian occupation was brief and was ended in 332 BC by the invasion of Alexander the Great.

Alexander the Great of Macedonia's conquest began the Ptolemaic or Hellenistic era (332–30 BC) in Egypt. As the Macedonian army approached, the Persian satrap of Egypt recognized his situation was hopeless and surrendered without a fight. Egyptians and Greek residents welcomed Alexander and his army as he rid them of the despised Persians. Alexander spent only around six months in Egypt. His first major act was to accept the surrender of Memphis where he respectfully participated in traditional Egyptian religious rites and took up various titles of pharaonic kingship. Travelling up the Canopic branch of the Nile to the sea, he recognized a prime location for a new city and on 7 April 331 BC he set up the boundaries of the future Alexandria, which would soon become one of the greatest cities of the ancient world. From there Alexander made the hard and dangerous trek to the oasis of Siwa, which contained the temple and oracle of Zeus-Ammon. In this way he followed in the footsteps of his ancestor, the demigod Hercules, and also paid respects to the king of the Greek gods, Zeus, who Alexander claimed was his true father. After visiting other western oases, Alexander returned via Thebes where he piously toured the great temples. From there he departed Egypt to finish the conquest of the Persian Empire.[30]

Alexander the Great died at Babylon on 10 June 323 BC at the age of 32. He had created in only twelve years one of the greatest empires in the history of the world. It was a legacy that his generals would bloodily fight over.[31] One of them, Ptolemy, seized control of Egypt; he also hijacked Alexander the Great's body. The original plan was to bury Alexander in Macedonia but Ptolemy took the body to Alexandria where it was prominently displayed for several centuries before disappearing from the historical record. It was not until 304 BC that Ptolemy's troops proclaimed him the king of Egypt. Their action founded the Ptolemaic dynasty, which ruled Egypt until 30 BC. All the male rulers of Ptolemaic Egypt used the name Ptolemy. They resided in their capital of Alexandria, which they turned into a cultural as well as a commercial centre of the Mediterranean world. Ptolemy I Soter founded the Museum, a sort of university or research institute that included the fabled Library of Alexandria. His son, Ptolemy II Philadelphus (285–246 BC), had the great Lighthouse of the Pharos built about 280 BC. According to legend, he also sponsored the 72 Jewish elders who translated the Bible from Hebrew into Greek. Ptolemy III Euergetes (246–221 BC), his son, succeeded him and also reigned successfully. Unfortunately the later Ptolemy's were not such accomplished rulers. A policy of incestuously marrying sisters and daughters poisoned the male side of the dynastic gene pool. Vicious infighting over the throne wracked the dynasty while their rivals, the Seleucids of Syria, grew in power; more ominously, the Romans began to intervene in the affairs of the eastern Mediterranean world. Egypt was a realm that was both rich and weak, and ripe for invasion.[32]

Egypt's last ruler, the renowned Cleopatra VII, attempted to revive the fortunes of Egypt. She came close to succeeding in her goal. Entrancing and marrying the great Julius Caesar, she bore him a child but his assassination ruined her plans. Temporarily sidelined, she next married Caesar's formidable lieutenant Mark Antony as a means to rebuild Egypt as the great power of the eastern Mediterranean. Their romance was one of the great tragic love affairs of history. In the end they lost to Octavian, the nephew of Caesar who established the rule of the emperors over the Roman Empire. Defeated, Antony and Cleopatra chose to take their own lives. At that point, Egypt became part of the Roman Empire, where it remained for centuries until the Arab conquest of AD 639–42. During the Roman and Byzantine eras, Egypt became thoroughly Christianized, although not without pagan resistance. After the conquest by Arabs, it was gradually transformed into a predominantly Islamic society. Christianity and then Islam replaced the millennia-old pharaonic culture. But these developments did not sweep away the monumental remains of the pharaonic civilization or its memory in history and popular culture. Egypt from ancient times to the present has remained a perennial object of fascination, fantasy, mystery and, at times, obsession and madness. The Egypt of one's dreams is often just that, a dream rather than the real Egypt of history. That, however, to a large extent is what Egyptomania is all about.[33]

TWO

ANCIENT EGYPTOMANIA: HEBREWS, PHARAOHS AND PLAGUES

The Lord brought you out with a mighty hand, and redeemed you out
of the house of bondmen, from the hand of Pharaoh king of Egypt.
DEUTERONOMY 7:8 (King James Bible)

The most prevalent report . . . demonstrates that the ancestors of the
so-called Judaeans of today were Egyptians.
STRABO[1]

I T IS NOT SURPRISING that ancient Egypt fascinated its neighbours in
the Near East and Mediterranean. During much of its history, Egypt
was a superpower of the ancient world, and at times it was the only
superpower. Other states sometimes rivalled and even exceeded Egypt's
might, but none had its staying power on the stage of history. Even after
Egypt experienced foreign conquests – by the Assyrians, Persians, Greeks
and Romans – it remained important because of its agricultural wealth. For
much of the Roman Empire, Egyptian grain fed the voracious appetites of
Rome's populace. Egypt's geology, wealth and prosperity meant that many
fine buildings and temples were usually constructed from hard stone, not
mud brick, so Egyptian buildings lasted the test of time. The pyramids have
come to be considered as wonders of the ancient world, yet Egypt was full
of other marvels that attest to Egypt's great antiquity.

Egypt was an exotic land. The Nile was a mighty river – its floods
rejuvenated Egypt annually – and it was legendary, seemingly miraculous and definitely mysterious. Egyptian culture and religions were also
unique. Hieroglyphics – the formal writing system of the Egyptians with
combinations of ideographic characters of animals, plants and symbols –
possessed an arcane allure that has remained potent throughout the ages.

The animal-headed gods and goddesses of Egypt and the rituals associated with them enthralled and mystified foreigners. All of these aspects of Egypt attracted curious tourists as early as 1500 BC. In his time, the Greek historian Herodotus (484–c. 425 BC) told how his countrymen came to Egypt for a variety of reasons: trade, as mercenaries and 'merely to see the sights of this country for themselves'.[2] The Greeks were not the first or the last sightseers to flock to Egypt. Unfortunately only the ancient Hebrews, the Greeks and later the Romans left extensive writings concerning their reactions and feelings about Egypt. These three ancient peoples can be considered the first to engage in Egyptomania.

The Hebrews and Egypt

The peoples of the lands that bordered Egypt had longer and more intense interactions with the Egyptians than the Greeks, who lived much further away. Unfortunately, of the many peoples who inhabited the lands adjacent to Egypt, only the ancient Hebrews left detailed accounts of their relationships and encounters with it. The foundation of all Hebrew accounts of Egypt rests on the events depicted in the Old Testament or the Hebrew Bible. Its centrepiece consisted of the Exodus story. In this narrative, Egypt appears as a land of slavery and idolatry that the faithful needed to reject. This negative depiction of Egypt contrasts with the generally positive image of Egypt that prevailed among Greek writers.[3] The earliest biblical reference to Egypt occurs in Genesis 10:6 as part of its genealogical Table of Nations, which provides a story of the origin of the various other peoples with whom the Hebrews were acquainted. There it mentions the four sons of Ham, of whom the second son is named Mizraim, a Hebrew word for Egypt. Crediting Mizraim with being the second son of Ham served to assign a deserved importance to Egypt in the worldview of the ancient Hebrews.

Egypt was a wealthy land, especially when compared to its neighbours. Its unique and highly favourable environment provided the Egyptians with a surplus of food which they could trade with the less fortunate lands on their borders. Egyptians also had access to gold mines and supplies of luxury goods from the upper Nile and the coasts of the Red Sea and East Africa through Somalia. Ancient Canaan and the Levant lying between Egypt and Asia Minor consisted of various fiercely independent city-states that periodically needed Egyptian foodstuffs. In return, they possessed raw materials that the Egyptians needed, such as the famed timber of the Cedars of Lebanon. As a result, Egyptians travelled to Canaan and the Levant and the people of the eastern Mediterranean came to Egypt to trade.

Archaeological evidence indicates that a growing amount and variety of Egyptian goods were appearing in the Canaanite and Levantine cities over the course of the history of Pharaonic Egypt. It also appears that a goodly number of Egyptians were living in these cities while many West Asian people were dwelling in Egypt, particularly the eastern Delta region. These contacts appear to have been largely peaceful and based on trade during the Old and Middle Kingdom eras, although there may have been some Egyptian military expeditions into Palestine. It was not until about 1550 BC and the beginning of the New Kingdom that Egypt created an empire and asserted control over the lands of Canaan and the Levant.[4]

Certainly the narrative found in the Book of Genesis (12:10–20) supports this picture of Egyptian relations with its West Asian neighbours. Abraham had moved to the land of Canaan as God had commanded him, but after he and his followers arrived there Canaan experienced a famine. So Abraham moved with his wife Sarah and their family into Egypt seeking relief. The Egyptians behaved hospitably towards Abraham's band; in the case of his wife Sarah, too hospitably. Sarah was an extremely beautiful woman and Abraham feared that the Egyptians might kill him in order to take possession of her. To avoid such a fate, he told the Egyptians that she was his sister. Meanwhile certain princes of Egypt had spotted Sarah and reported on her beauty to the Pharaoh. As a result she was taken into the royal palace. Thinking that Abraham was Sarah's brother, the Pharaoh showered all sorts of livestock, servants and goods on him. But God protected Sarah's virtue by sending plagues to afflict the royal palace. At that point the Pharaoh discovered that Abraham and Sarah were actually husband and wife; afflicted and annoyed, he berated Abraham for his deception and sent him out of Egypt, although he allowed him to keep all his newly acquired wealth. The renegade Jewish historian Josephus (AD 37–c. 100) later provided a slightly different account, according to which the Pharaoh was much more apologetic towards Abraham. The Pharaoh also allowed Abraham to be a teacher to the Egyptian wise men and brought them the knowledge of arithmetic and astronomy, which he had himself learned in the land of Ur of the Chaldees.[5] The biblical account of Abraham in Egypt essentially agrees with the archaeological evidence that Egypt was the bread basket of the eastern Mediterranean and that foreigners were readily admitted into the country and even welcomed.

Egyptian resources were clearly well known to the Hebrews and contacts were common occurrences. When Lot chose the Plain of Jordan to be the place he would settle, it was described as 'well watered everywhere, before the Lord destroyed Sodom and Gomorrah, even as the garden of the Lord, like the land of Egypt'. Hagar, the maidservant of Sarah and the mother of Abraham's natural son Ishmael, was an Egyptian. The *Midrash* even credited her with being a daughter of the ruling pharaoh. Conflicts with Sarah led to Hagar and her son Ishmael being compelled to leave Abraham's camp and journey into the wilderness, though God protected them from harm. Islamic traditions state that God ordered Abraham to expel Hagar and Ishmael. Ishmael grew to adulthood and lived as an archer in the wilderness of Paran in the Sinai Peninsula. Hagar arranged for an Egyptian wife for him, and their descendents were the Arabs. Meanwhile, Isaac, the legitimate son of Abraham and Sarah, grew up and married the beautiful Rebecca, from Mesopotamia, the birth-land of his father Abraham. The couple had two sons, Jacob and Esau, who became rivals. Once again famine struck Canaan and Isaac contemplated moving to Egypt, but God forbade it. Why God did not want Isaac to return to Egypt is not stated, but He may not have wanted to expose Jacob and Esau to the temptation of marrying Egyptian women. If so, things did not work out; Esau married not one but two equally objectionable Hittite women, much to the chagrin of Isaac and Rebecca (Genesis 13:10, 21:21 and 26:2).[6] Certainly Egyptian records show that many Semitic peoples migrated to Egypt, particularly its Delta region, from the First Intermediate through the Second Intermediate periods. Many of these people also became Egyptianized the longer they lived in Egypt.

The ancient Hebrews' most intimate and sustained contact with Egypt began with the story of Joseph, the favourite son of Jacob. Jacob's favouritism aroused the jealousy and wrath of Joseph's older brothers. Out in the wilderness with the flocks of Jacob, the ten older brothers were one day joined by the despised Joseph. With Joseph at their mercy, the brothers discussed killing him but Reuben, the eldest of Jacob's sons, talked them out of the bloodthirsty act. Instead, they sold Joseph to a passing Ishmaelite caravan loaded with trade goods and bound for Egypt. There the Ishmaelites sold Joseph to Potiphar, a royal official and captain of the guard. With the help of God's blessing, Joseph proved to be an excellent servant to Potiphar and he soon gave Joseph control of all his wealth. Joseph found favour with Potiphar; unfortunately he also found favour with Potiphar's wife. She made numerous attempts to seduce him but he valiantly resisted her entreaties. Infuriated by Joseph's scruples, Potiphar's wife accused him of attempting to seduce her, first to Potiphar's other servants and finally to Potiphar himself. Her accusation enraged Potiphar and he had the supposed betrayer of his trust thrown into Pharaoh's prison.

God continued to look out for Joseph while he was in prison. The prison's governor recognized Joseph's talents for organization and used him to help run the prison. While incarcerated, Joseph also showed an ability to interpret dreams. His reputation soon came to the notice of Pharaoh, who had been experiencing some disturbing dreams. The anxious ruler had Joseph brought to him. When told about the Pharaoh's two dreams where skinny cattle devoured plump cattle and withered heads of grain devoured healthy grain, Joseph warned Pharaoh about a sequence of seven good years of harvests that would be followed by seven years of famine. He advised the Pharaoh to stockpile surplus grain for the coming time of want. Seeing the

'Joseph interprets Pharaoh's Dream' was one of Gustave Doré's (1832–1883) many illustrations for the Bible. Thanks to the vastly improved knowledge of ancient Egypt in the mid-19th century, Doré's illustrations had an historical authenticity not found in medieval and Renaissance depictions of Egypt.

wisdom of Joseph's plan and his great talents for organization, the Pharaoh freed Joseph from prison and made him the most important of his officials. So Joseph came to rule Egypt on the behalf of the Pharaoh, with no one but the Pharaoh holding more authority.

When the famine arrived, it was universal. Only Egypt, and in particular Pharaoh and Joseph, had surplus grain to sell. Pharaoh became very wealthy as a result of Joseph's sales of the stockpiled grain to his own people and to foreigners. Eventually the Egyptians surrendered all their property to Joseph so that they could eat. Thanks to these skilful transactions on Joseph's part, Pharaoh came to have absolute control over the lands and goods of Egypt, except for those lands in the control of the priests.

Back in Canaan, Jacob and his sons had become worried about their own dwindling supply of food, so Jacob sent his ten oldest sons into Egypt to buy grain. The youngest son, Benjamin, remained with his father. Arriving in Egypt the brothers proceeded to buy grain but were unaware that they were trading with their own brother Joseph. Although they did not recognize him, he recognized them. After testing their characters, a forgiving Joseph revealed himself to his astonished brothers. He then invited Jacob and his brothers' families to join him in Egypt and to live in an area known as Goshen so that they could escape the rigours of the famine. When Jacob died, he was taken back to Canaan for burial. On Joseph's death, however, he was buried in the manner of the Egyptians – although the promise was made that Joseph's bones would be taken home for burial when the Hebrews returned to live in Canaan permanently.

The biblical narrative that follows after the death of Joseph tells of how the ancient Hebrews became a distinct people. It gave the ancient Hebrews an origin and they regarded it as a story based in historical fact. Unfortunately the biblical story has proven hard to correlate with the histories of other ancient peoples mentioned in the Exodus narrative. In fact, the first dateable biblical references all refer to events that occurred after 1000 BC. Some scholars have identified Rameses II as the pharaoh of the Exodus, while others think his son Merenptah was actually Pharaoh. Merenptah erected a victory stele in 1207 BC that mentioned defeating 'Israel'. Other scholars placed the events of the Exodus earlier, to the time of the expulsion of the Hyksos around 1550 BC (claiming that the ancient Hebrews were part of the Hyksos). Alternatively, it has been suggested that the Exodus took place in the aftermath of the collapse of Akhenaten's monotheistic Aten cult around 1336 BC. In this scenario, Moses becomes a refugee follower of Aten or even an incognito Akhenaten himself. This suggestion has been bolstered by the appearance in the diplomatic correspondence known as the Amarna letters of a people known as the Apiru. Earlier translations rendered the word as 'Hapiru' or 'Habiru', which was thought to be an alternative for 'Hebrew'. These interpretations of the archaeological evidence remain highly controversial among biblical archaeologists. Some suggest that the Exodus narrative is a tale based on the experiences of various desert peoples from the region of ancient Palestine moving in and out of Egypt. The bottom line is that there is no scholarly consensus concerning the dating of the Exodus or whether it was an actual historical event at all.[7]

After the death of Joseph, the descendents of Jacob, who was also known by the name Israel, prospered and grew in numbers over a period of three hundred years. As the Book of Exodus describes it, 'the land was filled with them.' Egyptians viewed this developing situation with misgivings. Eventually a new pharaoh came to power, one who 'knew not Joseph' and who also worried that the Hebrews might ally with foreign invaders against their Egyptian hosts (Exodus 1:7–8). Furthermore, while the Egyptians may have allowed foreign peoples into their land, they still had their own xenophobic prejudices. When Joseph and his brothers first sat down for a meal, the Egyptians who were present ate their meal apart, 'because the Egyptians might not eat bread with the Hebrews; for that is an abomination unto the Egyptians.' Later, Joseph related to his brothers that they would live apart from the Egyptians in the land of Goshen because they were shepherds and the Egyptians considered sheep-herding an abomination as well. The later historian Josephus added the additional detail to the biblical narrative that an Egyptian seer foresaw that a man would be born among the Hebrews who would bring Egypt low (Genesis 43:32 and 46:34).[8]

From this point onwards the oppression of the Hebrews or Children of Israel living in Egypt began. The Egyptians enslaved the Children of Israel and forced them to work on various building projects, most notably the treasure cities of Pithom and Raamses, as well as other onerous tasks. In his writings Josephus added that the Egyptians also put the Children of Israel to work on channelling the Nile River and building dykes to protect the Egyptian cities. More dubiously he also claimed that the Hebrews were put to work building pyramids as well. Despite the oppression, the population of the Hebrews grew and came to be regarded as a threat by the Egyptians. In response the Pharaoh ordered the midwives serving the Children of Israel to kill any male children born to the Hebrew women. But the midwives disobeyed Pharaoh and spared the babies. So the numbers of the Children of Israel continued to grow prodigiously. Undeterred, the Pharaoh ordered that the Egyptians should throw any male Hebrew babies into the Nile.[9]

The Victory Stele of
Merenptah (1213–1203 BC)
contains the oldest
reference to 'Israel'
in an Egyptian record.

Moses was born during this dire episode. His parents were both from
the tribe of Levi. After his birth, his mother hid Moses, but after three
months she feared his cries would be heard and give them away to the
Egyptians. She made him a floating cradle in the form of a boat of reeds
which she placed on and set adrift in the Nile. One of Pharaoh's daughters
found the reed boat and took pity on the poor baby, even though she realized it was a Hebrew boy. The princess adopted him as her own child and
named him Moses (Exodus 2:6). He was raised in her household while the

Moses in the reed boat as imagined by William Blake (1757–1827). Although Blake visualized ancient Egypt in his quirky style, he depicted it with reasonable accuracy.

Egyptian princess unknowingly employed his own natural mother to be his wet nurse. Thus, although raised as a royal Egyptian, Moses reached adulthood without forgetting his Hebrew origins. One day he observed an Egyptian beating a hapless Hebrew. Angered by the cruelty, Moses killed the oppressor and tried to hide his crime. Eventually word of his crime reached the Pharaoh and forced Moses to flee to Midian in Arabia to save his own life. There he married Zipporah and herded sheep for her father, Jethro, a priest of Midian. While herding his flock near Mount Horeb on the Sinai Peninsula, Moses encountered a burning bush which contained the presence of God. God's voice sounded out from the bush and called on Moses to bring his people out of slavery in Egypt and lead them back to the land of Canaan that God had promised to Abraham. God promised Moses the ability to perform divine miracles, but eventually had to resort to anger in order to persuade the reluctant Moses to go back to Egypt.

Moses was eighty years old when he returned to Egypt accompanied by his 83-year-old brother Aaron. While the Children of Israel agreed to follow Moses' leadership, the difficult task was getting Pharaoh to agree. God's plan involved humbling the gods of Egypt and Pharaoh himself, so He kept 'hardening' the heart of the Pharaoh. The Egyptian ruler persisted in refusing to permit the Children of Israel to leave Egypt, which resulted in the devastation of his realm by the first nine plagues (Exodus 4:21–3 and 7:1–7).[10]

When Moses and Aaron obtained their first audience with Pharaoh, they simply asked that the Children of Israel be given permission to go into the wilderness and hold a religious feast. The Pharaoh refused and cruelly increased the work demanded of the enslaved Children of Israel. They were to make bricks without straw (Exodus 5). Undeterred, God commanded Moses and Aaron to return to Pharaoh and ask him to let the Children of Israel go. Back in the Pharaoh's presence, they were immediately pitted against the powers of the 'magicians' or priests of Egypt. To demonstrate the might of God for Pharaoh, Aaron threw down his walking staff and it turned into a snake. The Egyptian priests, however, performed the same miracle, although Aaron's snake devoured theirs, which confirmed the superiority of God's power. Still the Pharaoh was unmoved. So the plagues of Egypt began. The first plague involved the Nile's waters turning to blood – which actually may have been some sort of outbreak of red algae. Whatever the red waters were, Egypt's water supply was tainted while the Nile's fish were killed, depriving the Egyptians of an important source of food and a ready supply of fresh water. While the Egyptian priests could perform the same miracle, they were incapable of halting its dire effects. Once more the Pharaoh remained unimpressed. The same royal reaction was repeated when the second plague of frogs afflicted Egypt. Again, the Egyptian priests could duplicate the plague of frogs but they could not reverse it (Exodus 7 and 8:1–15).

By the third plague of gnats, the Egyptian priests were no longer able to match the miracle with a similar one and they conceded that Moses' God was greater than their gods. Pharaoh, however, did not agree. So a fourth plague of flies followed right after. This time Pharaoh offered to consent to the Children of Israel offering sacrifices to God within Egypt. Instead Moses managed to persuade the Pharaoh to let the Children of Israel go out into the wilderness of the Sinai where they were permitted to make sacrifices to God. This concession resulted in the end of the fourth plague. The obstinate Pharaoh, however, promptly went back on his promise. God responded to this duplicity by sending a fifth plague that killed the livestock of the Egyptians but not the animals of the Children of Israel. Despite his subjects suffering this great loss of wealth, Pharaoh continued to refuse to let the Children of Israel go. Next came a sixth plague of boils, which afflicted all the Egyptians including the priests, but still Pharaoh would not yield. So a massive hailstorm accompanied by thunder and lightning fell upon Egypt with such intensity as had never been seen before in that land. People, animals, trees and crops were struck down by the hail. Only the land of Goshen, home of the Hebrews, was spared from the wrath of the storm. It destroyed the Egyptians' crops of flax and barley but the wheat and emmer remained safe. Reduced to desperation, the Pharaoh belatedly agreed to let the Children of Israel go. Once again, however, he rescinded his decision almost immediately. In response a plague of locusts descended upon Egypt and devoured the wheat and emmer. Again the Pharaoh gave in and again he changed his mind once more. So God sent a ninth plague of darkness that covered the land of Egypt for three days. At that point a fearful Pharaoh offered to let the Children of Israel go but only if they left their flocks in Egypt (Exodus 8:16–32, 9 and 10).

Moses refused to agree to such terms and at that point he threatened a tenth plague which would cause the death of all the first-born children in Egypt. Although faced by such a dreadful threat, the inflexible Pharaoh still refused to assent to Moses' terms. So God's power moved across the land and left all the first born of Egypt, both human and animal, dead. No household in all of Egypt escaped untouched except for the homes of the Children of Israel. God had instructed them to follow the rituals that became the first Passover, which began with the sacrifice of a lamb. Its blood was to be placed on the door frames of their houses as a signal to God. That night they were to remain at home and make a meal of the slaughtered lamb. Overwhelmed by the enormity of the tenth plague, the Pharaoh capitulated and allowed the Children of Israel to leave with not only their own property but gifts solicited from their Egyptian neighbours. Obedient to the ancient promise, they brought the bones of Joseph with them when they departed from Egypt (Exodus 11 and 12).

The Children of Israel had lived in Egypt for 430 years and now they were returning to Canaan. God, however, planned one more humbling experience for Pharaoh and the gods of Egypt. True to his previous behaviour, the Pharaoh changed his mind and ordered his war chariots to pursue the Children of Israel. Trapped between the Pharaoh's army and the Red Sea, or the Sea of Reeds, the Children of Israel were faced with slaughter and re-enslavement. They wailed to Moses that their previous slavery in Egypt was better than death at the hands of the vengeful Egyptian army. Despite their lack of faith, God provided them with another miracle. The barrier of the Red Sea was parted by the power of God and the Children of Israel were allowed to cross its floor on dry land, not mud. Pharaoh's army followed after the fleeing Children of Israel but its chariots became bogged down in mud rather than the previous dry land. Finally the parting of the waters of the Red Sea ended and the waters returned to their original location. The entire Egyptian army was engulfed and drowned. The Children of Israel had escaped Egypt, but they faced forty years of wandering in the wilderness before they could re-enter Canaan (Exodus 14).

The story of the sojourn of the Children of Israel in Egypt and the events leading to their Exodus played a huge role in the formation of the character of the ancient Hebrews and their attitudes towards Egypt. Certainly the ancient Greeks noticed a close connection between the Egyptians and the Jews. The Jews entered the consciousness of the Greeks rather late. Diodorus was the first Greek historian to mention Jews although the Seleucid Greek rulers of Syria already had a woeful history with the Jews as a result of the revolt of the Maccabees (168–143 BC). The geographer Strabo (*c.* 64 BC–AD 24) thought that the Judaeans of his day were descended from the Egyptians. He depicted Moses as a renegade Egyptian priest who preached an abstract monotheistic religion and led his followers out of polytheistic Egypt with its animal-headed gods. According to Strabo, the contemporary Jews engaged in circumcision and other child-rearing practices that were both similar to and derived from the Egyptians.[11]

God had led them to Egypt through Joseph. Initially treated as welcome guests, they ended up as the abject slaves of the Egyptians. They had been brought down about as low as a people could go, but God arranged for them to escape their Egyptian bondage under the leadership of Moses. Moses and the example of the Children of Israel became and remains a model to other oppressed people seeking freedom throughout history.[12] As for the ancient Hebrews and Jews, they held various images of Egypt. Besides remaining a powerful neighbour, Egypt served for them as a measure of things both positive and negative.

The Bible contains more than six hundred references to Egypt with over one hundred additional references to 'Egyptian', 'Egyptian's' and 'Egyptians'. Most of these references are located in the Old Testament, as might be expected. The Apocrypha contains another 54 references to Egypt along with three Egyptian references. The references for the Apocrypha are overwhelmingly concerned with the wars between the Greeks of Ptolemaic Egypt and the Greek Seleucid dynasty that ruled Syria, or with the revolt of the Maccabees.[13]

Many of the Old Testament's references to Egypt relate to historical – or purportedly historical – events involving the ancient Hebrews and Egypt. For most of the late nineteenth century until about 1970 most scholars accepted that the historical sections of the Old Testament were for the most part accurate. During the last decades of the twentieth century, great controversy arose when some scholars known as Minimalists asserted that the historical books of the Old Testament were composed during the post-exilic period of Persian domination and in some cases as late as the Hellenistic and Maccabean eras. Minimalists consider the historical books of the Old Testament to be fabricated history that were not based on actual events. The most extreme Minimalist scholarship is based almost exclusively on literary research and literary theory rather than the archaeological record.[14] At the same time as the rise of Minimalism, the archaeological record also became fuzzier rather than clearer as more ancient sites started to be discovered and investigated. Based on new research and findings, some archaeologists, such as Israel Finkelstein, have questioned the historical existence of the Patriarchs, the Exodus, the Israelite conquest of Canaan and even the reigns of David and Solomon.[15] Meanwhile other traditionalist or Maximalist scholars have continued to produce scholarship that maintains the basic accuracy of the Old Testament's historical narrative based on their interpretation of the surviving ancient documents and the archaeological record. Further archaeological finds have since undermined the position of the extreme Minimalists and their reliance on literary theory. Otherwise, a lively debate continues between the Maximalists and the moderate Minimalist archaeologists. The controversy periodically reignites as new discoveries of relevant artefacts reinforce or challenge existing theories within biblical archaeology.

From the point of view of studying Egyptomania, it is not crucially important whether the Maximalists or the Minimalists are right about the relative historical accuracy of the Bible. Either way, the biblical record, whether fact or fable, documents a fascination with ancient Egypt. If the Maximalists are correct, then the fascination of the Hebrews pre-dates the ancient Greeks' Egyptomania. If the extreme Minimalists are correct, the Greeks and the post-exilic Jews developed a fascination with Egypt about the same time.

The formative episode of the Jewish view of both themselves and Egypt involved their sojourn in Egypt and the Exodus from Egypt. As noted above, the Old Testament is peppered with references to Egypt as a place of oppression and bondage. Most of these references to Egyptian tyranny are formulaic, brief and repetitive.[16] In some cases, the complaint about oppression is linked to a condemnation of Egyptian idolatry. Egypt's gods served as a dangerous temptation for the Children of Israel (Joshua 24:14–17, Jeremiah 44:8 and Ezekiel 20:7–8). Egypt was also viewed as a land of many diseases (Deuteronomy 7:15 and 28:60). Later Hebrew prophets and the Book of Revelation associated Egypt with vices (Ezekiel 23:3, 8 and 27 and Revelation 11:8).

On the other hand, Egypt rightly retained its image among the Hebrews as a rich land of plenty. Just a few days into the Exodus and the privations of the wilderness, the Children of Israel began to grumble to Moses that in Egypt, 'we sat by the flesh pots, and when we did eat bread to the full.' Soon after, the scarcity of water caused them to also long for the bounteous waters of Egypt – until Moses struck the rock at Horeb with his staff causing it to gush water (Exodus 16:3 and 17:2–6). Later the Children of Israel grew tired of the monotony of eating manna and called for meat and a variety of food. Increasingly nostalgic and longingly recalling their former life in Egypt, they rhapsodized: 'We remember the fish, which we did eat in Egypt freely, the cucumbers, and the melons, and the leeks, and the onions, and the garlick' (Numbers 11:5). To placate their complaints God sent flocks of quail. When the Children of Israel first neared the land of Canaan, they sent spies to scout out the defences of the land. Most of the spies reported that the cities of Canaan were stoutly walled and the inhabitants were giants. This unwelcome news caused the Children of Israel to contemplate picking a new leader who would replace Moses and lead them back to the safety and security of Egypt (Numbers 13:28–33 and 14:2–4; and Deuteronomy 1:21–8). This episode demonstrated a chronically weak faith in God's power among the Children of Israel. For their wavering, God condemned them to wander in the wilderness for forty years before they would be allowed to enter the Promised Land. During that time of wandering, the Children of Israel would continue periodically to long for the plentiful food and ready drinking water of Egypt (Numbers 20:5 and 21:5).

The ancient Hebrews and Jews also viewed Egypt as a place of refuge from danger, and multiple accounts indicate Egypt as a site of sanctuary. Hadad of Edom fled to Egypt when King David's forces overran the Kingdom of Edom; in Egypt, the Egyptian Pharaoh arranged for Hadad to marry the Pharaoh's sister-in-law. King Solomon faced opposition to his rule from Jeroboam the Ephraimite, and when Solomon tried to have Jeroboam killed, the dissident fled to Egypt and the protection of Pharaoh Shishak. Jeroboam stayed there until the death of Solomon, at which point he returned home to lead the ten northern tribes of Israel into seceding as a separate kingdom; they justified their rebellion by an appeal to the Golden Calf tradition of the Exodus (1 Kings 11:26–40 and 12:1–30; and 2 Chronicles 10:1–13). Hundreds of years later when the Babylonians conquered Jerusalem, some of the survivors fled to Egypt as refugees (2 Kings 25:26). In 609 BC, during the first year of the reign of Jehoiakim of Judah, a prophet named Urijah or Uriah condemned how Judah carried out God's commands. His prophecies aroused the anger of King Jehoiakim, who tried to kill Urijah; Urijah fled to Egypt for safety but this time there was no safety there – Jehoiakim had sent men to Egypt to find Urijah and bring him back to Judah. Upon his return, Jehoiakim killed Urijah with a sword and dumped his body in a common grave (Jeremiah 26:20–23).

The Kingdom of Judah faced terrible danger during the life and career of the prophet Jeremiah, a contemporary of Urijah. In 609 BC the great king Josiah died fighting the Egyptians at Megiddo. The Egyptian threat, however, paled with the rapid rise of the Neo-Babylonian Empire in the aftermath of the demise of Assyria. The Babylonians defeated the Egyptians at Carchemish in 605 BC. This defeat transformed the Egyptians from an enemy into an ally in the eyes of the fearful kings of Judah and their political elite.[17] However, the Hebrew prophets disagreed and decried this and earlier Egyptian alliances as futile and dangerous.[18] They were right. Babylonian armies captured Jerusalem in 598 BC and deported some of the population to Babylon. Zedekiah was left in place as the king of a much reduced Judah. Unrest and rebellion swept the Neo-Babylonian Empire in 594 BC. Seeing an opportunity to regain independence for Judah, Zedekiah joined the rebellion. The resilient Babylonians recovered, however, and prevailed over their subject nations. By 587 BC Jerusalem had fallen for a second time, when the rampaging Babylonian army destroyed the city. King Zedekiah was captured and forced to watch as his sons were massacred. Then the Babylonian king, Nebuchadnezzar, had Zedekiah blinded and taken in chains to Babylon with a second group of deportees (Jeremiah 39:1–9).

The Babylonians then appointed Gedaliah, a cooperative Judahite noble, to be their governor of Judah. Although the Babylonians invited Jeremiah to come back to Babylon in honour as a known advocate of non-resistance to Babylonian rule, he decided to remain with Gedaliah. Soon after, a renegade Judahite prince named Ishmael murdered Gedaliah and had the Babylonian garrison massacred on behalf of the king of neighbouring Ammon. The surviving Judahites under the leadership of Johanan feared a ferocious reprisal by the Babylonians, and so contemplated seeking refuge in Egypt. Jeremiah denounced this plan and offered them a stark choice – stay in Judah and prosper or flee to Egypt and face destruction. Johanan and his people decided to ignore Jeremiah's warning and went to Egypt. In fact, they even forcefully took Jeremiah and his scribe Baruch with them. Avenging Babylonian troops arrived in Judah in 582 BC and deported a third group of Judahites back to Babylon (Jeremiah 39:10–18, 40 and 43:1–7). Meanwhile in Egypt, the nominal host of the Judahite refugees, Pharaoh Hophra, was killed by his rivals and his country descended into chaos. According to Jeremiah's prophecy, 'all the men of Judah that are in the land of Egypt shall be consumed by the sword and by famine, until there be an end of them' (Jeremiah 44:27). Jeremiah's Egypt turned out not to be a land of safety and sanctuary.

The most famous biblical incident of Egypt as a land of refuge was the flight to Egypt by Mary, Joseph and the baby Jesus. Herod the Great had learned of Jesus' birth and feared that the baby would supplant him as king of the Jews in the future. He wanted the newborn child dead and his panic instigated the infamous Massacre of the Innocents in Bethlehem. Before that tragedy occurred an angel from God came to Joseph in a dream. He commanded Joseph to take his family to Egypt and stay there until he heard it was safe to return to Judaea. When the Holy Family eventually returned from Egypt, it also fulfilled the prophecy of Hosea, that God had 'called my son out of Egypt' (Matthew 2:13–15 and 19; and Hosea 11:1).

In the narratives of the Old Testament, the sojourn of the Hebrews in Egypt also taught them some ethical lessons. As Exodus 22:21 commanded: 'Thou shalt neither vex a stranger, nor oppress him: for ye were strangers in the land of Egypt.' Similar injunctions appear elsewhere in the Pentateuch, or Torah.[19] Deuteronomy 2 provides another insight into the place of Egypt in the worldview of the ancient Hebrews. It discusses which neighbouring peoples of the Hebrews could join the congregation of the Lord. The Ammonites and the Moabites were excluded because they did not welcome the Children of Israel when they returned to their promised land of Canaan. On the other hand, Edomites, as the descendants of Esau, were to be welcomed into the congregation, as were Egyptians 'because thou wast a stranger in his land'.

The legendary King Solomon of Israel had close relations with Egypt. He made an alliance with the Pharaoh of Egypt and married an Egyptian princess. For a dowry, the Pharaoh conquered Gezer, killed its Canaanite inhabitants and gave the site to Solomon (1 Kings 3:1 and 9:16; and 2 Chronicles 8:11). What impact having an Egyptian wife had on Solomon personally is hard to say, since he had seven hundred wives and three hundred concubines. The Egyptian princess may have been merely just another face in a rather large crowd. Solomon astutely used his kingdom's location, placed between Egypt and Syria and the Hittite kingdom in Asia Minor, to empower his position as the middle man in the trade of Egyptian horses, linens and chariots.[20]

Like the Greeks, the Hebrews recognized that the Egyptians possessed formidable wisdom; it was said that 'Moses was learned in all the wisdom of the Egyptians' (Acts 7:22). Initially the Egyptian priests had matched Moses and Aaron miracle for miracle, although ultimately they could not last long in a direct competition with the power of God. King Solomon's legendary wisdom, however, exceeded 'all the wisdom of Egypt' (1 Kings 4:30).

The Jews of the Roman world took pride in their long and venerable history based on the biblical narrative, and their connection with the antiquity of Egypt only enhanced their own proud heritage. The Jewish historian Josephus offers an outstanding example of such feeling. He may have switched to the Roman side during the Jewish War of AD 66–73, but he remained immensely proud of his Jewish heritage. Josephus wrote four books on Jewish history: *The Jewish War*, *The Antiquities of the Jews*, an autobiography and *Against Apion*. *The Antiquities of the Jews* was a history of the Jewish people from Creation to AD 65, the eve of the Jewish War. Its initial chapters were based heavily on the Hebrew Bible and therefore contained the expected stories of the various interactions between the ancient Hebrews and the Egyptians. Josephus sought to demonstrate the long and rich history and culture of the Jews. When his effort drew criticism from various Greek historians, he was prompted to write *Against Apion* in reply. This work consisted of two books: the first was a rebuttal of the various Greek historians who had criticized his *Antiquities of the Jews*, the second attacked the anti-Jewish Greek writer Apion. Josephus pointed out that the Greeks were a young and relatively uncultured people who derived most of their knowledge from the Egyptians and the Babylonians.

In *Against Apion,* Josephus used Manetho's history of Egypt to defend the greater antiquity of Jewish society. He quotes a substantial section of Manetho in which the Hyksos conquest of Egypt is described along with the later fall of their rule. For Josephus, the Shepherd-Kings of Manetho's narrative 'were no other than our forefathers', that is, the ancient Hebrews. Manetho appears to be the earliest historian to suggest that the Hyksos and the Children of Israel were closely connected, if not simply two names for the same ancient people. Josephus followed Manetho's account and preserved it for posterity. Modern archaeology and historical research have at the least compelled a far more nuanced and cautious approach to the Hyksos/Hebrew connection; for some scholars, this modern research has completely discredited the idea. Today the Hyksos/Hebrew connection remains a controversial and hotly debated topic of biblical archaeology and history of ancient Egypt. Josephus disagreed with Manetho positing a second quite brutal and brief conquest of northern Egypt by the ancient Hebrews. In this episode, Moses appeared as a renegade Egyptian priest from Heliopolis and a collaborator with the invaders.[21] Josephus was happy to pick and choose from Manetho's writings those elements that suited his purposes – to demonstrate that the history of the Jews was far more ancient than the history of the Greeks. However, Josephus shared with the Greeks and the Romans a fascination and awe of the great age and continuity of Egyptian civilization and its people. The Egyptomania of Graeco-Roman civilization will be the subject of the next chapter.

THREE
CLASSICAL EGYPTOMANIA: THE GREEKS AND ROMANS

Greeks find all Egyptian lore and legend irresistibly attractive.

HELIODORUS[1]

Egypt would not easily have attained the high reputation it enjoys for wisdom, but for its less remote situation, the ruins of its antiquities, and above all the tales of the Greeks.

JOHANN GOTTFRIED VON HERDER[2]

THE GREEKS WERE THE FIRST foreign visitors who attempted to study the Egyptians – the geographer Hecataeus (fl. 500–494 BC) and his successor Herodotus were the first Greek students of Egypt. Hecataeus of Miletus was the first Greek writer to visit Egypt when the country was under Persian domination, in about 500 BC. He was followed by Herodotus (484–c. 425 BC), who used aspects of Hecataeus' now lost writings in the second book of the *Histories*. Later scholars who visited Egypt and wrote descriptions of what they saw were the historian Diodorus who visited Egypt in 59 BC, the geographer Strabo (c. 64 BC–AD 24) who visited Egypt during the prefecture of Aelius Gallus from 26 to 24 BC, and the moralistic biographer Plutarch (c. AD 46–c. 121) who visited the country for an undetermined length of time.[3] Obviously many other people were visiting Egypt but did not leave accounts of their travels or impressions. Some of those travellers ranked among the greats of the Graeco-Roman world.

Trade had developed between Egyptians and the Minoans of Crete by the later third millennium BC. The timing was perfect: it was during the Middle Kingdom that Egypt first truly welcomed foreign goods and ideas. Remains of Minoan pottery dating from the era's Twelfth Dynasty

(1985–1773 BC) have been found at Lahun near Faiyum. A fresco in the Minoan style has been found at the site of Avaris in the Nile Delta, but it is unclear whether the fresco was constructed by Aegean craftsmen or Egyptians imitating Minoan styles. Some scholars have suggested that the pharaoh Ahmose was allied with the kings of Crete and even married a Cretan princess. This Minoan artistic influence, however, did not endure and native Egyptian styles reasserted themselves.

For most of the era of the New Kingdom, contact between Egypt and the Aegean world was sporadic, although diplomatic activity increased significantly during the reign of Amenhotep III (1390–1352 BC). This situation is not surprising since, according to Homer, it was a 'long and terrible voyage to Egypt'.[4] Despite this assessment, however, Greek mythology depicts many instances of contact between the Greeks and the Egyptians.[5] The Greek gods fled to Egypt and disguised themselves as animals during Zeus' struggle with the monster Typhon. Dionysos visited Egypt during the madness inflicted on him by the goddess Hera; when Hera, out of jealousy, transformed the lovely virgin Io into a cow, she also inflicted Io with a gadfly that stung her and induced her to keep wandering the world – it was when Io came at last to Egypt that she was able to regain her human form. It was also in Egypt that Io bore the philandering Zeus a son named Epaphos, who Egyptians worshipped as the human form of the bull-god Apis. Moreover Io later married Telegonos, the king of Egypt, and came to be worshipped as the goddess Isis by the Egyptians. Epaphos himself became the king of Egypt and married Memphis, the daughter of the river-god Nile, after whom the great city of Memphis was named. Memphis gave birth to a daughter, Libya, who in turn gave birth to two sons: Belos and Agenor. Belos succeeded Epaphos as king of Egypt while Agenor founded a kingdom in Phoenicia. Belos also married a daughter of the river-god Nile named Anchinoe. She produced twin sons named Aegyptus and Danaus. The brothers both had many wives who bore them many children. Danaus fathered fifty daughters named the Danaids, while Aegyptus fathered fifty sons. It was quite a feat of genetic improbability.

When the ambitious Aegyptus took over his father's empire he named his realm Egypt, or Aegypt, after himself. He wanted his sons to marry Danaos' daughters so that he could absorb Danaos' kingdom of Libya. To avoid that fate, Danaos and his daughters fled to Argos in Greece, the home of his great-grandmother Io. There, Danaos managed to displace the Argive ruler and made himself king of Argos. But before that occurred, the sons of Aegyptus pursued Danaos and his daughters to Argos. A great debate took place among the Argives about whether or not to protect the Danaids – a tale that later formed the subject of Aeschylus' play *The Suppliants*. Ultimately the Danaids were forced to marry the sons of Aegyptus but, conspiring with their father, they murdered 49 of the sons, sparing only one. These events were significant metaphorically: severing the heads of the sons of Aegyptus, the Danaids also permanently severed their ties to Egypt.

Egypt recurs in many mythic Greek travel narratives, one of the most famous of which is the hero Hercules' journey to the garden of the Hesperides to perform one of his twelve labours. Years earlier, the normally fertile Egypt had suffered from nine years of famine. The Egyptian king Busiris was advised to sacrifice a foreigner to Zeus so that the crops would grow once again. Busiris, a cruel man, began to sacrifice any foreigner who came into Egypt. When Hercules arrived in Egypt, Busiris planned to sacrifice him as well and had the strong man tied up. But Hercules burst his bonds and proceeded to slaughter Busiris, his sons and many other Egyptians. Herodotus considered the Busiris story to be improbable, but it still gave rise to a common Greek misconception that the early Egyptians were hostile to strangers and killed any who entered their land. Busiris also became the subject of an essay by the Greek rhetorician Isocrates (436–338 BC).

Daedalus, the builder of the famous labyrinth of Minos on Crete, was also reputed to have built many great buildings throughout both Greece and Egypt. Memnon, the king of the Ethiopians and ally of the Trojans, was also associated with Egypt by the Greeks. They erroneously connected the Memnoneum temple in Thebes and the colossi of Memnon with this king rather than their actual builders. After the fall of Troy, the victorious Menelaus suffered all sorts of problems due to the malice of the goddess Athena as he tried to return home to Greece with his reclaimed wife Helen. A storm over Cape Malea in Greece blew them to Egypt. There the couple remained for eight years while they accumulated a great treasure. Finally satisfied with their newly acquired wealth, they embarked for Menelaus' kingdom of Sparta. Off the coast of Egypt, however, Menelaus' fleet became hopelessly becalmed. After twenty days, with water and provisions running short, the sea-nymph Eidothea decided to help the stranded voyagers. She suggested that they approach her father Proteus, the Old Man of the Sea, for advice on how to get home. She warns them, however, that Proteus is a shape-shifter and if they tried to force him to help he would try to frighten them into letting him go free. Menelaus and his men managed to hold on to Proteus as he morphed his way through various frightening manifestations, such as a raging lion and a venomous snake. Thanks to Proteus' help, Menelaus and Helen finally make their way home. Another variant of the

Trojan War legends depicted Proteus as a kindly king of Egypt who, during the long years of fighting at Troy, took care of the true Helen over a false one created by the goddess Hera. Egypt frequently served as a destination and stopping point in the tales of Greek mythology – more than any other place in the ancient world outside of the immediate region of Greek culture. Clearly, awareness of exotic Egypt enthralled the Greeks.

Mythology and history ultimately converged during the reign of Psammetichus (Psamtek I, 664–610 BC), who hired large numbers of Greek mercenaries, thus beginning sustained and substantial contact between Greece and Egypt. Around this time, Greeks, possibly including the mercenaries, established the city of Naucratis in the Delta. Herodotus claimed that it was a later pharaoh, Amasis, who allowed the Greeks to settle at Naucratis. Located near the Canopic branch of the Nile, about fifty miles southeast of Alexandria, it became an important port of trade until the establishment of Alexandria caused it to go into decline. Naucratis demonstrated the presence of, and supported the existence of, a substantial Greek trading presence in Egypt. It also served as a convenient and familiar base of operations for Greeks coming to Egypt for education or sightseeing. Given the curiosity of the Greeks and their desire to assimilate new knowledge into their worldview, it was inevitable that some Greeks would seriously study Egypt in order to explain it to their countrymen.[6]

As noted above, the first Greeks to study Egypt were Hecataeus and Herodotus. Unfortunately only fragments of Hecataeus' historical and geographical writings have survived. Some modern scholars, however, claim that the Egyptian material in Herodotus' great work plagiarized Hecataeus, which is only true in a very limited and partial way. Hecataeus came from Miletus and during his career visited Egypt, where he conducted interviews and conversations with various temple priests. His understanding of Egyptian history, however, was deeply flawed; he sought to show that Greece was the source of Egyptian civilization. His more famous successor, Herodotus, came from Halicarnassus and may have started his travels as a self-imposed exile, the result of his having picked the wrong side during the Ionian revolt against Persian rule. Herodotus has been called the 'father of history' due to his *Histories* being the first prose narrative of a historical topic. His goal was to describe and explain the great war between the Persians and the Greeks. To do that, he supplied considerable background material, including detailed descriptions of parts of the Persian Empire, but Egypt got the fullest treatment in book two and part of book three of Herodotus' work. Because Herodotus included many fabulous tales in his history, he has also been condemned as overly credulous or as

Herodotus (484–c. 425 BC) and his *Histories* were a principal source for historical information about ancient Egypt for thousands of years. Jean-Guillaume Moitte, *Herodotus*, 1806, stone relief from the west facade of the Cour Carrée at the Louvre, Paris.

the 'father of lies', but close study of Herodotus' writings actually shows him to have been rather accurate in his accounts. His reputation remains mixed, however: he has been both hailed as the first travel writer and condemned as a mere ethnocentric tourist. Others consider him to be the first anthropologist, although many modern anthropologists, upon viewing his unscientific approach, would deny this. What is indisputable, though, is that Herodotus' writings on Egypt formed the foundational text of Greek writings on Egypt. As such, despite other Greek writers also producing works on Egypt – the most important being Diodorus, Strabo and Plutarch – Herodotus' is the premier document of ancient Greek Egyptomania.[7] Fragments from the works of other Greek writers on Egypt are common, including another Hecataeus – this one from Abdera – and the Egyptian Manetho, who wrote in Greek.[8] Roman authors such as Pliny the Elder and Ammianus Marcellinus (c. AD 330–378) followed the Greeks' lead on Egypt, although perhaps with less reverance and more scepticism.

One thing that immediately impressed Greek and Roman visitors to Egypt, and probably others as well, was the geography of the country. The Greeks regarded the Egyptians as singularly fortunate in their physical environment. Egypt was a land like no other. As Diodorus put it: 'The land of Egypt . . . in natural strength and beauty of the landscape is reputed to excel in no small degree all other regions that have been formed into kingdoms.'[9] Its geographical features made Egypt a difficult country to invade. To the north it is bounded by the Mediterranean Sea. To its west lie the vast deserts of Libya. South along the Nile River, a series of cataracts or rapids rendered navigation difficult, while the Nile valley narrowed and the desert loomed larger in the land of Nubia. East of Egypt was the Arabian Desert which ended on the shores of the Red Sea, except in the far north. There the Sinai Peninsula, a dry wilderness, provided a way to Asia. Trading routes crossed the Sinai but they presented a difficult although not impossible trip for an invading army. The Greeks did not consider the land of Egypt to consist of anything but the cultivated land; for them, the bordering desert lands were not part of Egypt proper.[10]

Egypt was bisected by the Nile River, which flowed northwards to the Mediterranean. As it neared the Mediterranean, the Nile fanned out and created a large delta formed by the silt carried in the Nile's waters. This gradual accumulation of alluvial soil into new land was what Herodotus and others meant when they referred to Egypt as the gift of the Nile. The flood waters of the Nile made agriculture possible in Egypt. Without the Nile, Egypt would just be an even vaster expanse of desert. Each year the Nile flood deposited new soil on its farmlands. Even though it almost

never rained in Egypt, the Nile made Egyptian agriculture extremely pro-
ductive compared to other lands. Strabo complimented the Egyptians on
their efficient use of their land, saying, 'They are commended in that they
are thought to have used worthily the good fortune of their country, having
divided it well and having taken good care of it.' Egypt's cities were also
located along the banks of the Nile. For the Greeks, coming from a land
where good farmland was scarce among the rocky hills while rainfall was
meagre and the rivers were very modest streams, even when they had water
in them, Egypt was a marvel. To their eyes, Egyptian farmers had it easy.
Discussing the farmers of the Nile delta, Herodotus observed that 'they
obtain crops from the earth with less labour than all other peoples, and the
rest of the Egyptians too.' Actually, he was downplaying the amount of
labour needed to farm in the Delta. Since Egypt is less troubled by climatic
fluctuations than other locales, hard work in Egyptian agriculture tended
to yield rich harvests. Those rich harvests not only made Egypt a wealthy
land, but a populous one.

The Egyptians also did not simply rely on nature in the form of the
vagaries of the Nile's annual flood to ensure their harvests. Thanks to their
system of canals and embankments, Strabo observed that the Egyptians
had managed 'to conquer nature through diligence'. It was even thought
that the name 'Nile' derived from an early Egyptian ruler named Nileus,
who 'constructed a very great number of canals in opportune places and
in many ways showed himself eager to increase the usefulness of the Nile',
which had been known previously as the Aegyptus River. As Diodorus
described it: 'In density of population it [Egypt] far surpassed of old all
known regions of the inhabited world, and even in our day is thought to be
second to none other.' The building of the Aswan dam during the twentieth
century changed this pattern of life.[11]

For anyone visiting ancient Egypt, the central role of the Nile in
the prosperity and even the survival of Egypt is manifestly evident. It is
no wonder that Herodotus famously declared: 'The Egypt to which the
Hellenes [Greeks] sail is land that was deposited by the river – it is the gift
of the river to the Egyptians'. Or, for that matter, that succeeding writers,
such as Strabo, echoed him. As the philosopher Seneca put it,

> The character of this river is remarkable, because, while other rivers wash
> away and gut the land, the Nile, so much larger than the rest, far from
> eating away or eroding the ground, on the contrary adds strength to it
> . . . Egypt owes to it not just the fertility of the land but the land itself.

In describing the very bountiful fishing that the Nile River provided the Egyptians, Diodorus judged that 'the Nile surpasses all the rivers of the inhabited world in its benefactions to mankind.'[12]

The Nile is also a great and impressive river in size and length, particularly from the point of view of the Greeks whose own rivers were so very modest in comparison. Herodotus observed that no river in Greece or Asia Minor compared in size to even one of the Nile's many mouths in the Delta. Only the Ister or Danube River could stand in comparison to the Nile, although Herodotus points out that the Nile has a greater volume of water. Besides its size, another trait of the Nile that impressed the Greeks and others was that its rise or flooding occurred during the summer. This phenomenon was very different from how most rivers behaved. Their level would fall during the heat of summer because less rain fell – the Danube River was an exception, as its flow and level remained steady throughout the year. The Nile was also a placid and easily navigable stretch of water; at least in Egypt. One had to travel more than 800 kilometres (500 miles) up the river to the first cataract before encountering an obstruction. It was an additional 300 kilometres (200 miles) to the second cataract. After that point, the source or sources of the Nile became enveloped in a mist of speculation. Even possessing only partial knowledge, the Greeks agreed that the Nile was not only a large river, but a very long one as well.[13]

The reason why the Nile flooded every year was a source of great debate among the Greeks and Romans. Herodotus reported that the Egyptians were unable to give him any answers. Its inhabitants gratefully accepted the blessings that nature conferred on their land. For them, the Nile waters were the tears of the great goddess Isis. Explorations in the eighteenth and nineteenth centuries have firmly proven that the Nile flood is caused by heavy rainfall in the Ethiopian highlands during the spring. These rains swell the Blue Nile and the Atbara rivers and by May central Sudan experiences flooding. Due to the vast length of the Nile River, the flood waters do not reach the Cairo or Memphis area until October.[14]

Initially the ancient Greeks and Romans only had the vaguest information about the upper Nile and their knowledge of its physical geography and hydrology was faulty. As a result many erroneous theories concerning the Nile's flooding developed, which Diodorus catalogued and refuted. One of the earliest theories came from the philosopher Thales of Miletus in the sixth century BC. He theorized that Etesian winds blowing from the north during the summer caused the waters of the Nile to back up as they entered the Mediterranean Sea, thus flooding the countryside of Egypt. Anaxagoras and his pupil Euripides both maintained that the Nile flood was caused by snows melting in the mountains of Ethiopia. Diodorus scoffed at this explanation because he thought it was impossible for snow to build up in the heat of the tropics, even at very high altitudes. Herodotus suggested that the Nile during its flood stage was actually the normal size of the river. The Nile evaporated less during the summer months than during the winter months and the build-up of water created the flood. Again Diodorus rejects this explanation as no other river experienced the same phenomenon of winter-time evaporation. Democritus of Abdera put forward a theory that the melting of winter snow in the northern latitudes created great accumulations of clouds. The Etesian winds blew these clouds south until they struck the high mountains of Ethiopia and there they poured out their torrential rains. Diodorus found this theory wanting because the time of the Etesian winds did not correspond to the time of the Nile floods. Another Greek, Ephorus, speculated that the soil of Egypt was like a sponge which collected vast quantities of water in the winter but in the summer expelled those waters to create the annual flood; Diodorus dismissed this idea as physically impossible. Some wise men in Memphis pointed out that the earth has both a northern hemisphere and a southern hemisphere which experienced the seasons of summer and winter at opposite times of the year. So when it was dry summer in the Nile Valley, winter rains were occurring in the southern hemisphere. The waters of those winter rains flowed up the Nile valley and flooded Egypt. However, Diodorus cast doubt on this theory by arguing that the southern waters could not flow uphill into the north.

Clearly Diodorus and his contemporaries correctly believed the world was a sphere. It was the concept of gravity that eluded Diodorus and bedevilled his refutation. Oenopides of Chios, an astronomer, asserted that the waters under the earth were warm in the winter and cool in the summer. During the winter, the heat of the earth would consume the underground water while in the summer the heat of the air would draw the cool water out of the earth, which would then flood the Nile. The problem with this theory, according to Diodorus, is that no other river behaved this way. The final theory Diodorus responded to is that of the historian and geographer Agatharchides of Cnidus, who attributed the Nile flood to heavy summer rains in Ethiopia. Diodorus found this theory to be the best explanation of the Nile flood and for the most part he was right. His near contemporary Strabo agreed, saying 'Now the ancients depended mostly on conjecture, but men of later times having become eyewitnesses, perceived that the Nile was filled by summer rains, when Upper Aethiopia was flooded, and particularly in the region of its farthermost mountains.' The explorations of East Africa conducted by traders working for the Ptolemaic kings of Egypt confirmed the theory of Ethiopian rains but, instead of heavy downpours in summer, they actually occurred earlier in the spring. The ancient Greeks did not understand the vast distances nor the length of time it took for the flood waters of Ethiopia to reach the Nile and flood Egypt. Neither did the Romans understand the nature of the Nile flood. During his retirement, the politician, playwright and stoic philosopher Seneca, in his *Natural Questions* written between AD 62 and 65, described and debunked all of the theories about why the Nile flooded. But he had no theory of his own to explain the phenomenon and instead concluded: 'Opinions about the Nile are varied, but so far the truth has eluded us humans.'[15]

Greeks and Romans were not just curious about the causes of the Nile flood, they were also fascinated by the origins of the river's waters. What were its sources? The great river made its way through hundreds of miles of parched landscape seared by a blazing sun, yet no tributaries added waters to its stream until the Atbara River entered the Nile a bit beyond the fifth cataract far into the land of Nubia. That was well over 1,600 kilometres (1,000 miles) from the Mediterranean coast of Egypt in a straight line, while following the course of the Nile is in fact a lot longer, since the river does a lot of meandering. The famed Blue and White Niles did not come together until more than another 300 kilometres (200 miles) further south below the sixth cataract at the location of the modern city of Khartoum. Still, the two Niles continued on and on into the unknown lands of the African interior. The solution of the mystery of the sources of the Nile would not be solved until the explorations of James Bruce in the second half of the eighteenth century and John Hanning Speke in the mid-nineteenth century.[16] So when Herodotus inquired into the origins of the great river, he discovered that no one had any reliable knowledge to put forth: 'I consulted Egyptians, Lydians, and Hellenes about the sources of the Nile, but no one I talked to professed to know anything about it.' Well, not quite no one, a priest from the temple of the goddess Neith in Sais claimed that the Nile originated in a bottomless pool of water located between two mountains called Krophi and Mophi near Elephantine Island. It was a patently absurd story; many people including Herodotus had visited Elephantine and its region and would know that no such mountains existed. Herodotus thought the man was joking and the priest was probably merely probing to see if Herodotus was a gullible tourist and if so, how gullible.[17]

The mystery of the Nile continued to fascinate the Greeks, notably Alexander the Great. While he was in Egypt, Alexander sent a small expedition to explore the Nile. Included in its company was Callisthenes (*c.* 360–327 BC), the official historian of Alexander's campaigns. Details of the expedition are sparse, but the group clearly reached the Ethiopian highlands during the summer of 331 BC during its rainy season, so they were able to observe at first hand the rains whose runoff would eventually cause the Nile to flood. The early Ptolemaic kings of Egypt were interested in developing trade with East African coastal towns. At their urging, Ptolemaic merchants also conducted explorations into the interior; these expeditions took them into Ethiopia where they also observed the spring and early summer rains. After that, Greek and later Roman opinion maintained a consensus that Ethiopian rains caused the Nile to flood – but it was not entirely believed, as the epic poet Lucan (AD 39–65) and the later Roman historian Ammianus Marcellinus cast doubt on this theory. Even the great natural historian Pliny the Elder, who should have known better, repeated a story about King Juba of Mauretania who claimed that the Nile began in the mountains of lower Mauretania. From there it wound its way through Africa under various names until it reached ancient Meroe. Accurate facts continued to struggle with erroneous ideas.[18]

When the Romans added Egypt to their empire, they continued the Ptolemaic policy of coastal trade with East Africa. They also negotiated a treaty with the rulers of Kush in 29 BC which allowed them to rule the Nile Valley as far south as the first cataract. Cordial relations later soured when the Kushites sacked Aswan in AD 24. In retaliation, Gaius Petronius invaded Kush the following year; he marched to Napata near the fourth cataract and sacked the city. More fighting followed but eventually the Romans and the Kushites made peace. During the reign of Emperor Claudius, a Greek merchant named Diogenes was driven down the coast of East Africa by a storm. His ship landed near what is now Dar-es-Salaam. From there he ventured inland for 25 days until he came upon two great lakes and a great range of snowy mountains. These were called the Mountains of the Moon or *Lunae montes* and were thought to be the source of the White Nile. The great geographer and astronomer Ptolemy (*c.* 100–170) mentioned them in his *Geography* and they appeared on medieval maps where they beckoned later would-be discoverers of the sources of the Nile. The Roman emperor Nero (AD 37–68) contemplated war with Kush and in AD 66–7 sent some explorers to scout out the regions and possibly discover the sources of the Nile. They reached as far as the Sudd region on the White Nile but its tangled marshland blocked any further progress. Nero's expedition marked the highpoint of European exploration of the Nile until the nineteenth century. To this day, the Nile remains an enduring source of Egyptomania, as an iconic representation of ancient Egypt's landscape and culture, and on which many modern tourists continue to travel, and the source of which many continue to visit.[19]

The Greeks and Romans found the Egyptian people, culture and monuments just as enthralling as they found the physical features of the land of Egypt. Egyptians had a persistent reputation among the Greeks for being inhospitable or downright hostile to foreigners. Herodotus reported that Egyptians had no interest in adopting the customs of the Greeks or anyone else, but such ethnocentricism is hardly unique to the Egyptians. Instead, their bad reputation for inhospitality seems to have been based on the myth of King Busiris, who regularly sacrificed foreign visitors to the gods of Egypt until, according to legend, he tried to sacrifice Hercules, who killed him and stopped this practice. The rhetorician Isocrates and Diodorus both discussed the unfavourable reputation of Busiris as a reality. Strabo, however, expressed scepticism. He quite rightly pointed out that the early kings of Egypt were very suspicious of seafaring peoples. In particular, the Egyptians were wary of the Greeks, who engaged in sea-raiding, and set guards to turn them away. Such Egyptian attitudes may have been the result of their experiences with seaborne invasions during the era of the Sea Peoples, at least some of whom came from the Aegean region. According to Diodorus, it was the pharaoh Psammetichus who opened Egypt to foreign traders. Greek reports, however, are at variance with the biblical accounts of Egypt, which tell of people freely entering and leaving Egypt for trade, except in the case of the Children of Israel who needed divine intervention to escape Egypt.[20]

Greeks and Romans, along with other peoples of the ancient Near East, agreed on one thing – the Egyptian people and their civilization were very ancient. The plethora of ancient ruins in Egypt physically attested to that fact. Herodotus reported that the Egyptians had once considered themselves to be the earliest humans. Their king Psammetichus had an experiment conducted to prove it. The experiment was based on the idea of language acquisition among children and it ended up proving instead that the Phrygians were actually the oldest people while the Egyptians were the second-oldest people. From a modern point of view, the experiment was based on very erroneous scientific assumptions about developmental psychology. In Herodotus' opinion, 'they [the Egyptians] have always existed, from the time when the human race was born.' Centuries later Ammianus Marcellinus was of the same opinion: 'The Egyptian nation is the most ancient of all, except that in antiquity it vies with the Scythians.' (He simply substituted the Scythians for the Phrygians as alternate contenders for being the oldest nation.)[21]

As far as theories about how old the Egyptians were, there was considerable speculation among the Greeks and the Romans. Based on conversations with Egyptian priests, Herodotus learned that there had been 341 generations of human rulers in Egypt. According to Herodotus' calculations, this added up to a span of 11,340 years, a very long history indeed. Diodorus gave Egypt an even longer history. He points out that mythology places the origins of the gods in Egypt. The gods Osiris and Isis were Egypt's earliest rulers and from their reign to Alexander the Great some claimed that 10,000 years had passed, although others placed it at just a bit under 23,000 years of history – a figure based on the claim that the first gods and heroes ruled Egypt for a little less than 18,000 years, while mortal men had ruled for a bit less than 5,000 years. These are the type of numbers that, taken literally, provide grist for the advocates of pseudo-historical theories about a very ancient super-civilization in Egypt. Archaeological, scientific and documentary evidence does not support the veracity of such large periods of time that extend Egyptian civilization's existence so far back into prehistory. Greek and Roman visitors all tended to agree that Menes or Min was the first king, or at least the first human king, of Egypt. Modern historians and archaeologists have identified this Menes with Narmer, a predynastic-era ruler, or Aha, the first king of the First Dynasty. The problem is that neither Herodotus nor Diodorus along with other Greek and Roman writers possessed an accurate knowledge of the chronology of Egyptian history. Both writers' accounts contain serious errors and present events and reigns out of order, while not even being aware of great swathes of Egyptian history.[22]

Greek and Roman visitors considered the Egyptians to be a completely unique people in a number of ways. As Herodotus put it, 'the manners and customs established by the Egyptians are at least in most respects completely opposite to those of other peoples.' From there he goes on to list a number of differences: in Egypt it was the women who worked in the market while the men stayed home and weaved; Egyptian women urinated standing while the men sat; only men were allowed to serve as priests in Egypt, whether the gods served were male or female; and Egyptians did not require men to support their parents in old age, but women were expected to support their elderly parents. Greek and Roman visitors also found the Egyptians' attitude to animals to be strange. The Egyptians actually worshipped certain animals – hawks, ibises, bulls and cats were worshipped by all Egyptians – and some of their gods had the heads of animals on human bodies. While the cult of the Apis bull was especially strong in Memphis, cats were held in high regard everywhere. Egyptians allowed cats to live in their houses and when the cats died, well-to-do Egyptians had them mummified and buried at Bubastis. Diodorus visited Egypt during 59 BC in the reign of Ptolemy XII

Auletes and observed at first hand the deep reverence with which Egyptians observed cats. While he was in Alexandria a Roman diplomatic mission arrived because Ptolemy XII was anxious to gain the status of 'friend' of Rome. One of the Roman envoys accidentally killed a cat, which aroused the murderous fury of the Alexandrian mob. Proceeding to the Roman's house, they killed him despite the efforts of royal officials to save the man by playing on the mob's own well-founded fear of retribution from Rome. On the other hand, Egyptians had mixed feelings about crocodiles. Some worshipped the great reptiles while others made war on them. Greek and Roman visitors simply found the dangerous beasts to be both fascinating and repellent. Seneca told his readers of a great battle in the Nile in which a clever and brave school of dolphins defeated a cowardly troop of crocodiles, much to the statesman's delight.[23]

Greek and Roman visitors found the Egyptian practice of mummifying their dead to be a source of wonder. Egyptians first began to practise mummification at least as far back as 3600 BC and possibly as early as the Badarian culture of around 4500–4100 BC. That said, the Egyptians were not the first people to mummify their dead: the mummies of Chinchorro in Chile have been found to be 7,000 to 8,000 years old. Mummification made good sense in a dry climate. Egyptian concepts and beliefs about burials and the afterlife developed, evolved and diverged, sometimes in ways that conflicted with each other. By the New Kingdom era, the embalming cult had become closely associated with the myths regarding the god Osiris. Both Herodotus and Diodorus provided detailed descriptions of Egyptian burial customs, which were viewed as the way that the living could honour the dead. As Diodorus put it: 'Not least will a man marvel at the peculiarity of the customs of the Egyptians when he learns of their usages with respect to the dead.' Mummies have aroused a sort of compulsive interest among many visitors and devotees of things Egyptian ever since.[24]

Egyptian religion intrigued visiting Greeks and Romans with its magical rituals and its myriads of gods in both human and animal form. Although the differences between Egyptian and Greek religion were profound, the Greeks professed to discern a fundamental similarity. The ancient Greeks frequently attempted to syncretize the religions of peoples they encountered with their own. This was particularly true of the Egyptian gods. Herodotus came to the conclusion that the knowledge of the gods spread from Egypt to Greece in the distant past. Almost all the Greek gods derived from an Egyptian original, except for Poseidon who was brought to Greece by the Libyans. Much later, Plutarch continued to find links between Greek gods and mythical figures and their original inspirations in the various gods of the Egyptian pantheon. Both the Greeks and the Romans found the Egyptian deities Osiris and Isis to be especially engaging. Diodorus suggested that at the beginning of their history the Egyptians identified the sun and the moon as the greatest of the gods. Osiris was the sun and Isis was the moon. Osiris did not simply provide humans with life-giving light, he was the civilizer and culture hero who taught humans farming and law-making. Although in the modern stereotype the Egyptian religion is depicted as mystical, mysterious and magical, Greek and Roman visitors did not see it in this way. Plutarch staunchly defended Egyptian religion as rational and ethical rather than merely superstitious. Herodotus went so far as to credit the Egyptians with the invention of the common practices of ancient religion such as altars, statues and temples dedicated to the various gods. The cult of Isis became so popular that it spread throughout the lands of the Hellenistic kingdoms and the Roman Empire.[25]

Besides regarding the Egyptians as religious and pious, Herodotus also found them to be a clean people as well. Furthermore, he observed that Egyptians were very healthy – only the neighbouring Libyans surpassed them in this regard. To promote good health, Egyptians would purge themselves by vomiting and enemas three days in a row each month, but Herodotus thought the Egyptian climate also helped. Seasonal variations tended to cause illnesses and the Egyptian climate did not have extreme changes in temperature. Furthermore, Diodorus would later praise the Egyptians for having an excellent government throughout their history. The kings of Egypt

maintained an orderly civil government and continued to enjoy a most felicitous life, so long as the system of laws described was in force; and, more than that, they conquered more nations and achieved greater wealth than any other people, and adorned their lands with monuments and buildings never to be surpassed.

Egypt had a large population due to this good government and the prosperity it brought. Thanks to bountiful agriculture and a mild climate, having large numbers of children did not entail a lot of extra expenses for Egyptian families. Greek and Roman visitors also found the Egyptians to be a peaceful people not inclined to revolt against Ptolemaic or Roman rule. This pacific nature may have stemmed from later Egyptians not being a warrior people either.[26]

The Greeks considered the Egyptians to be an inventive people who created or discovered many important contributions to civilization. Egyptians were the first astronomers; the first astronomers among the

Egyptians were the Thebans. Here again, as Diodorus pointed out, climate helped the Egyptians as the dry and cloudless conditions allowed them to observe the risings and settings of the stars more closely and accurately. Egyptians used their astronomical observations to divide the year into twelve months, an accurate division of the year being essential to a society heavily dependent on agriculture for its wealth. Diodorus also thought that those other famous astronomers/astrologists, the Babylonians, were actually descendants of Egyptian colonists who learned their science from the priests of Egypt. Greek visitors all agreed that the Egyptians had invented geometry, the impetus for which, according to Strabo, was to measure and re-measure their annually flooded farmlands. In turn, they taught geometry to the Greeks. Writing was another Egyptian first according to the Greeks, an opinion that stemmed from seeing hieroglyphs inscribed on many extremely ancient monuments and temples. Modern scholars, however, disagree. Although some debate continues on the matter, the academic consensus is that writing first appeared in Mesopotamia – but Egyptian writing was probably a mostly independent development. Some Greeks such as Plato maintained somewhat mistrustful attitudes about the utility of writing for society, but for most Greek commentators on Egyptian civilization, their writing system was an outstanding achievement.[27]

Egyptians also made many contributions to other areas of human endeavour. Herodotus credited them with being the first people to hold public religious festivals and processions that carried the images of the gods. He also credited the Egyptians with the best sense of historical traditions of all the peoples he had encountered. In the ancient world, Egypt was known as a land where the healing arts were especially far advanced. According to Diodorus, the goddess Isis taught the Egyptians much useful knowledge about healing and medicinal drugs. He also claimed she continued to promote healing in his day as her cult spread through the Mediterranean world. This belief about the superiority of Egyptian medicine among the Greeks extended back at least as far as the time of Homer. In the *Odyssey*, he has Helen of Troy pick up various medicinal herbs during the time she and Menelaus spent in Egypt. Diodorus also credited Osiris with inventing the cultivation of the grape – and therefore the production of wine – although the Greeks and other peoples had their own ideas about that.

Greek observers of Egyptian civilization could also be wrong. Herodotus mistakenly attributed the belief in the transmigration of souls to the Egyptians. Still Herodotus clearly thought that some unnamed Greeks, probably Pythagoras, had picked up the idea of transmigration from the Egyptians. Later Roman writers, such as Pliny the Elder, did not automatically consider the Egyptians the first inventors. The Phoenicians, instead, were credited by Pliny with inventing astronomy and by Strabo with inventing navigation, arithmetic and accounting (since, as traders, they required those skills). Despite such later scepticism, Diodorus dismissed doubts about the greatness of Egyptian culture, saying:

> Egypt for more than four thousand seven hundred years was ruled over by kings of whom the majority were native Egyptians, and that land was the most prosperous in the whole inhabited world; for these things could never have been true of any people which did not enjoy most excellent customs and laws and the institutions which promote culture of every kind.[28]

Greeks and Romans visiting Egypt, like other tourists throughout the ages, found the massive and often extremely ancient buildings there to be awesome and enthralling. According to Herodotus: 'this country [Egypt] has more marvels and monuments that defy description than any other.'[29] The presence of so many impressive and often mysterious monuments and temples in Egypt has been one of the prime contributors to the phenomenon of Egyptomania for over two millennia.

Visitors to Egypt, including many Greeks, had undoubtedly been gawk-ing at the pyramids of Giza for millennia by the time Herodotus made his trip to Egypt sometime during the years 465 and 444 BC. Unlike his predecessors, Herodotus wrote down his impressions of Egypt. One of the topics he discussed in detail was the pyramids. When he questioned the Egyptians he encountered, Herodotus was told that in the distant past Egypt had been a well-governed and happy land. Then, the tyrannical Cheops became Pharaoh. After closing down the traditional shrines and temples, Cheops put his subjects to work building the pyramid that would serve as his tomb. The stone for the pyramid came from quarries on the eastern side of the Nile where 100,000 men laboured. At Giza on the western side of the Nile, another 100,000 men constructed the pyramid. These groups worked in shifts of three months. When the stones were ferried across the Nile, they were hauled up a causeway to the building site. The causeway took ten years to build while the pyramid was constructed over a span of twenty years. Herodotus did not spend much time giving a physical description of the pyramid. Instead, he tells how the Egyptians used a mechanism or mechanisms that lifted the building stones up from one tier to the next. Although he claims to have obtained this information from Egyptian informants, his description is probably wrong.[30] His account does, however, show that both the Egyptians and Herodotus believed the pyramids had been constructed using the technology available to the ancient civilizations of the Mediterranean and the Near East – not, that is, by the hands of gods or ancient aliens (see Chapter Ten).

Cheops's pyramid consumed vast amounts of Egypt's resources, including the energies of his people. It was a time of great suffering for the Egyptians. There was a story that he even placed his daughter in a brothel to earn money to help pay for the building of the pyramid. His brother and successor Chephren was just as bad. He built a pyramid almost as big as Cheops's and oppressed his people to support his megalomaniac ambitions. Supposedly these two kings ruled for 106 years, during which time the people of Egypt suffered greatly. Both men were hated by their subjects and later Egyptians refused to speak their names. Relief came with the next pharaoh, Mykerinos, the son of Cheops. Mykerinos reopened the temples of Egypt, stopped oppressing the people with exorbitant demands on resources and ruled with justice. Herodotus reported that Egyptians praised Mykerinos more than any of their other kings. Although he built a pyramid for himself, it was much smaller than the pyramids of his predecessors.[31] Obviously Herodotus held a very mangled version of Egyptian history, which probably reflects the Egyptians' gaps and misunderstandings of their own history. This confusion about the pyramids is not surprising because the time that had elapsed from the building of the pyramids to Herodotus' day was just about as long as the amount of time that has elapsed since Herodotus' time to the present.

Diodorus' account of the pyramids followed Herodotus', although he was more impressed by them. As he put it, 'they fill the beholder with wonder and astonishment'. Diodorus was impressed by the durability of the pyramids; although thousands of years old, their structure remained undecayed. Of course, Diodorus saw the pyramids before some of their stone had been looted by later rulers of Egypt. He repeated Herodotus' assessments of the reigns of Cheops (he calls him Chemmis), Chephren and Mycerinus. But he added the caution that there was no agreement among Egyptians and historians about who actually built the pyramids. Some suggested that other pharaohs built the pyramids. All agreed though that, whoever was responsible for building them, they surpassed the many other monuments of Egypt in their size, costliness and the skills needed to build them. Strabo's account added that the pyramids were rightly considered among the Seven Wonders of the World.[32]

In contrast, the later Roman visitors to Egypt were not as impressed by the pyramids as the Greeks were. Pliny the Elder mentioned the pyramids in his *Natural History*, in which he described their size and stated that it took 360,000 men twenty years to build the Great Pyramid, while the time to build all three of the pyramids of Giza was 88 years and four months. He mentioned that Thales of Miletus had devised a technique for measuring the height of the pyramids by using their shadow at certain times of day. Like Herodotus, Pliny had no doubts that the Egyptians built the pyramids and even listed several speculations as to how they did it. He also listed twelve historians, beginning with Herodotus, who had discussed the history of the pyramids and how they disagreed as to which Egyptian kings had built them. He conceded that the pyramids were 'famous throughout the world', although he also characterized them as 'a pointless and absurd display of royal wealth' and said of the kings who built them, 'these men showed much vanity in this enterprise.'

Pliny was not alone in disparaging the pyramids. The Romans took a very utilitarian attitude towards public works and monuments. Frontinus, the great architect, echoed Pliny's opinion when he described the marvels of the aqueducts of Rome: 'With such an array of indispensible structures carrying so many waters, compare, if you will, the idle Pyramids or the useless, though famous, works of the Greeks.' Later Ammianus Marcellinus took a kinder attitude. Speaking of Egypt, he wrote, 'Many and great things there are in that land which it is worthwhile to see; of these it will be in place to describe a few.' First among those few were the pyramids, which, like Strabo, he pointed out were among the Seven Wonders of the World.[33]

The Pyramid of Gaius Cestius in Rome was built in 12 BC. It influenced European images of the pyramids for centuries, as this 18th-century Italian engraving shows.

Although the Great Sphinx is just as much an icon of ancient Egypt as the pyramids, the ancient Greek writers Herodotus, Diodorus and Strabo do not mention it in their accounts. It is probably because the Sphinx had suffered one of its periodic burials by drifting sands during the Hellenistic and Roman periods of Egyptian history. Pliny the Elder, by contrast, was quite impressed by the Sphinx, more so than he was by the Pyramids. He claimed that the local population worshipped it as a god and that the ancient king Harmais (a reference to the god Horus) was buried inside it. He was also told that the Sphinx had been transported to its present location from another place where it was built, which he doubted since it was carved from the local rock. Pliny also observed that the Sphinx's face had been coloured red for divinity.[34]

While the ancient Greeks found the pyramids a source of awe and wonder they were even more impressed by an Egyptian monument that they called the Labyrinth, a monument few modern tourists would recognize. As Herodotus emphatically put it, 'Of all the wonders I have seen, this labyrinth truly beggars description. . . . The pyramids . . . also defy description . . . but the labyrinth surpasses even the pyramids.' What they called the Labyrinth was actually the mortuary temple of a Twelfth-dynasty pharaoh, Amenemhet III (1831–1786 BC), who had built a pyramid at Hawara after his attempt to build one at Dahshur ran into serious problems with the poor quality of the unstable bedrock of that area. His mortuary temple was full of many small chapels and chambers, a sizeable collection which appeared to the Greeks to be a labyrinth. Herodotus claimed that it had two levels with some 1,500 chambers each. Diodorus believed that it provided the inspiration for Daedalus when he built the Labyrinth for King Minos of Crete, a story that Pliny the Elder would later repeat. Strabo also spoke highly of the Labyrinth. Between the Classical Age and today, the Labyrinth has deteriorated so badly that little of its former grandeur remains.[35]

The Greeks associated the great irrigation system of the Faiyum and Lake Moeris with the Labyrinth and were equally impressed by it, if not more so. According to Herodotus, 'While the labyrinth is truly a wonder, the body of water called Lake Moeris, on whose shore the labyrinth was built, is even more amazing.' The Faiyum is a depression located to the west of the Nile River that contains a freshwater lake fed by a channel of the Nile known as the Bar Yusuf. It was a fertile region that had been inhabited since prehistoric times. The pharaohs of the Twelfth Dynasty during the Middle Kingdom era managed to greatly improve its importance by creating an irrigation system. Many temples and tombs were built there, of which the Labyrinth was the most elaborate. The area remained important throughout the Hellenistic and Roman era; both Diodorus and Strabo repeated Herodotus' original praises of the Faiyum and credited the building of its irrigation system to a pharaoh, Moeris.[36]

Thebes, now modern Luxor, is today a frequently visited tourist destination. The ancient Egyptians called the city Wawet but the Greek name for it was Thebes, after the city in mainland Greece. It is the site of the great temples at Karnak and the Valley of the Kings, which some modern visitors to Egypt consider to be more impressive than the pyramids. As early as the age of Homer, Thebes had long been famous among the Greeks for its wealth. In the *Iliad*, Homer declares that 'Egyptian Thebes . . . is the richest city in the whole world, for it has a hundred gates through each of which 200 men may drive at once with their chariots and horses.'[37] Despite its fame, Herodotus only makes a few passing references to the city. Diodorus echoes Homer's hundred-gated Thebes comment but otherwise he focuses on the debate over whether Osiris or Busiris founded the city. Strabo provides more detail in his account to emphasize Thebes's wealth and calls it 'the metropolis of Egypt'. He also describes the whistling colossi of Memnon (actually Amenhotep III) that so fascinated Greek visitors, although he incorrectly dismissed the idea that the whistling sound came from the statues (the sound probably originated from early morning dew evaporating in cracks in one of the statues). Strabo also visited the Valley of the Kings and commented on the impressive royal wealth that it represented. His count of the tombs was low, at forty, as many more have been discovered since his day. He was also impressed by the astronomical and calendrical knowledge of the priests of Thebes. By Pliny the Elder's time, some people had come to believe that Thebes was a hanging town in the manner of the famous hanging gardens of Babylon, although Pliny dismissed the comparison as false. Thebes still rated a mention two centuries later by Ammianus Marcellinus, who was clearly impressed by the size of the city's monuments, particularly its many obelisks.[38]

The Romans appear to have been more fascinated by obelisks than the Greeks. The obelisk first appeared during the Old Kingdom, but the heyday of quarrying and erecting obelisks was the New Kingdom. Obelisks were dedicated to the sun-god Ra and were intended to provide a working model of the cosmos and Ra's daily role in renewing the world with his sunlight. Pharaohs included commemorations of events and anniversaries from their reigns into the dedicatory inscriptions on the obelisks they erected. They were set up at the entrances to temples, almost always in pairs. The largest obelisks made a breathtaking monument. Carved from a single piece of stone, they were sometimes close to 30 metres (100 feet) tall – the obelisk in Piazza di S. Giovanni in Laterano in Rome exceeds this and weighs hundreds of tons. It took thousands of men to move the obelisks and set them in place. It was also very dangerous work. A crew of over 8,000 men moving an obelisk during the reign of Rameses IV suffered nine hundred fatalities. Obelisks caught the fancy of the first Roman emperor, Augustus, who moved several to Alexandria and to Rome. Other succeeding emperors also moved obelisks, but not to the extent that Augustus did. Pliny the Elder later described some of these moves in his *Natural History* although his understanding of both obelisks and hieroglyphs was deficient. It was the emperor's interest in these monuments that started the fascination with obelisks beyond Egypt's borders, and Augustus initiated the desire by other rulers, nations and individuals to acquire one.[39]

Another great building project that fascinated Greek visitors to Egypt was the canal connecting the Nile River with the Red Sea. It appears that originally the easternmost branch of the Nile River flowed into the Red Sea, not the Mediterranean. That situation was possible because the Gulf of Suez in ancient times extended farther north as well. Like many rivers, the Nile changes its course over time as it silts up in places and the waters find another path to the sea. The branch of the Nile flowing into the Red Sea silted up and changed its course to the Mediterranean Sea, meanwhile it also silted up part of the Gulf of Suez and transformed it into the Bitter Lakes. Having a waterway that connected the Red Sea to the Nile River was as important for Egypt's trade as it was for the modern economy to have the Suez Canal connect the Mediterranean and the Red Seas. The rich land of Punt lay somewhere down the coast of the Red Sea, possibly at the present locations of Eastern Sudan or Eritrea. Water transport would also have been an easier way to bring the products of the mines on the Sinai Peninsula back to the cities of Egypt. Some Egyptologists have suggested that Senusret II or III of the Twelfth Dynasty had a new canal built between the Nile and the Red Sea, others think it was Rameses II who had the canal made. Either man could have been the basis for the tales that the Greeks heard about the great pharaoh Sesostris, an amalgamation of several pharaohs. The canal apparently fell into disuse; Necho II, it seems, attempted to build a new canal. According to Herodotus, the canal was about 183 kilometres (114 miles) in length and was wide enough that two trireme warships could row past each other comfortably. It was also said that some 120,000 workers lost their lives building the canal, which was never actually completed. The story goes that an oracle warned Necho that all his building would simply end up benefiting barbarian rulers who would take his place, so he stopped the project. War with the Neo-Babylonian Empire was probably the real reason

'The Pharos of Ptolomey', the Lighthouse of Alexandria, an English print from *A New Geographical Dictionary* (c. 1760). Little is known about the lighthouse's exact appearance.

behind abandoning it. After the Persian Conquest, the Persian king Darius I resumed work on the canal. Diodorus and Strabo both claim that Darius also abandoned the project because it was feared that the water level was higher in the Red Sea than the Nile River, so opening a canal would cause either Egypt to be flooded, or, if the salt water of the Red Sea flowed into the Nile, it would render the Nile undrinkable and ruin lower Egypt's agriculture. They claim that it was Ptolemy II who successfully completed the canal and included a lock in its construction to avoid problems with flooding or tainting the water of the Nile with salt. They were wrong. Stelae have been discovered which commemorate Darius I's completion of the canal. Archaeological evidence shows that it was about 45 metres (150 feet) wide and 4–5 metres (16–17 feet) deep. Pliny the Elder repeats the same stories as Diodorus and Strabo about the canal. The canal was no longer functional by the reign of Cleopatra due to the silting up of its Pelusiac branch. At some point another canal operated between Old Cairo and the Red Sea near present-day Suez but its architect is unclear. Candidates include the emperor Trajan, the Arab conqueror of Egypt Amr ibn al-'As, or the second caliph Omar the Great. This canal was closed by Caliph Mansur in 767 and only briefly reopened in 1000 by Caliph Al-Hakim. It would be almost a thousand years before the Suez Canal would be built and again give Egypt a water route into the Red Sea. In its day and after, the Nile–Red Sea canal greatly impressed Greeks and Romans alike, even though during much of the late Ptolemaic and early years of the Roman Empire the canal was non-functional.[40]

For people travelling to Egypt during the Hellenistic and Roman eras, the first thing they would have seen was the great city of Alexandria. In 331 BC Alexander the Great picked the location and drew the boundaries of the future city with flour, which the area's seabirds proceeded to devour. It was taken as a good omen. The Egyptian coast needed a port capable of accommodating a large fleet as well as a steady traffic of merchant vessels. Alexandria would serve that purpose as well as being a bridge between the East and the West. Ptolemy I Soter, the first Hellenistic king of Egypt, moved his capital from Memphis to Alexandria and the new city quickly grew into one of the premier metropolises of the Mediterranean world. Besides being a centre of government and commerce, Alexandria came to possess many cultural attractions, including the body of its maker. When Alexander died in 323 BC, the plan was to bury him with the other kings of Macedonia. Ptolemy, however, engaged in some machinations that gained him possession of Alexander's body. It was initially taken to Memphis but was later moved to Alexandria to rest in a magnificent mausoleum known as the Sema. Originally Alexander's sarcophagus was made of gold, but it was replaced by glass. Members of the Ptolemaic dynasty of kings were buried in the same area. At some point in the later years of the Roman Empire, Alexander the Great's body disappeared. Some have suggested it was reburied under a mosque in Alexandria where it remains undiscovered to this day. Others claimed that it was taken to the Oasis of Siwa and buried there. The possible whereabouts of Alexander's body has provided the premise for several archaeological thriller novels.[41]

Alexandria possessed other famous attractions. One of these was the great lighthouse known as the Pharos after the island on which it was built in 297–282 BC. Construction was begun under Ptolemy I Soter and was completed by Ptolemy II Philadelphus, although Cnidus of Sostratus either designed the building or paid for it. The Pharos was included as one of the Seven Wonders of the World and at 100 metres (330 feet) in height it was a very imposing structure for its time. Many exaggerated tales were told about the Pharos: its height was stated to be several times higher than it really was, or its light could be seen at fantastic distances, around 480 kilometres (300 miles) away. Strabo, Pliny the Elder and Ammianus Marcellinus all spoke highly of the Pharos in their writings, although Ammianus mistakenly credited Cleopatra with building it. Alexandria was also a centre of learning with its Museum and its great library. The Museum was a sort of a research institution that attracted scholars from all over the Mediterranean world, as did the hundreds of thousands of books housed in its library. Many famous scholars served as its head or librarian. All of these components made Alexandria an exciting and interesting city to visit. It also helped that Alexandria was renowned for its balmy and wholesome climate. Although it was always sunny at Alexandria throughout the year, sea breezes helped to cool the city during the summer. Sadly the growth of the modern city has covered most of the delights and wonders that made ancient Alexandria famous.[42]

Egypt had many other sites that attracted the interests of curious Greek and Roman visitors. One of the more famous and more difficult places to reach was the Oracle of Zeus-Amun at the Oasis of Siwa. It fatally attracted the attention of the Persian king Cambyses, who lost an army trying to conquer it. Alexander the Great braved the perils of the desert to consult the oracle – the success of his journey was attributed to miraculous intervention. Memphis remained a great city with many temples in Hellenistic and Roman times. One of those temples was dedicated to Serapis, as was a more well-known temple at Canobus, a place supposedly visited by Menelaus and Helen on their way home from the fall of Troy. Herodotus was correct when he said that Egypt was full of 'marvels and monuments'.[43]

Egypt attracted many Greek and Roman visitors, some famous, most forgotten. While some well-known accounts by ancient travellers to Egypt exist, most famously Herodotus' book, most Greek and Roman sojourners in Egypt left no surviving record of their experiences and impressions. Some of these travellers left graffiti on various Egyptian monuments, which serves as a reminder that human nature possesses a lot of continuity over time while providing historians with some rare and unique insights about foreign visitors in Egypt. It is also a commentary on the incomplete nature of the historical records that such an act, if committed today, would be considered blasphemous vandalism that might result in arrest and imprisonment in a vile foreign jail, but when the action is sanctified by the passage of over 2,000 years it becomes a valuable source of knowledge about the past.

As noted earlier, the Greeks had been visiting Egypt for a long time before Herodotus. Mythological and legendary figures such as Orpheus, Daedalus, Hercules and Helen of Troy among others visited Egypt. There is good evidence of trading contact with the Aegean region by at least as early as the Middle Kingdom era in Egypt. By about 1550 BC during the early years of the New Kingdom there may even have been Aegean families from the Minoan culture living in Avaris, the former Hyksos city in the Egyptian Delta.[44] Greek visitors were obviously dazzled by what they saw in

Egypt, and its antiquity, massive monuments, exotic religion and mysterious knowledge inspired their respect. By the sixth century BC, Greek authors were writing enthusiastically about Egyptian culture. Plato, for one, credited the Egyptian god Thoth with the invention of writing, mathematics and astronomy. In his *Timaeus*, an old Egyptian priest tells the Athenian lawmaker Solon (*c.* 639–559 BC): 'you Greeks are all children, and there's no such thing as an old Greek' – meaning their knowledge of history was very short compared to that of Egyptians. Some Greeks started to travel to Egypt to study the great knowledge that could be obtained there. Over time it came to be thought that all great thinkers of Greece spent some time studying in Egypt, even if they had done no such thing.[45]

Even before Solon's journey to Egypt, the epic poet Homer and the Spartan lawgiver Lycurgus were supposed to have travelled there and drank of the cup of its learning. It was claimed that what they learned at that font of knowledge influenced their greatest achievements. Some writers of Classical antiquity went so far as to claim that Homer was actually an Egyptian. In his *Aethiopica* from the middle of the third century BC, Heliodorus even credited Homer with being a son of Hermes Trismegistus. All of this was quite a feat since modern scholars doubt that a literal Homer or Lycurgus actually existed or that Lycurgus even drafted Sparta's constitution. If Solon did travel to Egypt, what he saw and heard from the Egyptian priests could not have affected the law code that he created for Athens. Any trip to Egypt would have taken place during the time he left Athens after his laws had been put into effect.

Solon's contemporary, the sage and proto-scientist Thales of Miletus (*c.* 625–547 BC), also supposedly studied in Egypt. Little is known about Thales's life but he was credited with devising a way of measuring the height of the pyramids using their shadow. Some of his scientific ideas also have probable Egyptian roots. Later, the mathematician and astronomer Eudoxus of Cnidus (*c.* 400–347 BC) went to live at Hierapolis in Egypt where he studied astronomy and wrote about the calendar. Eudoxus was a contemporary of the philosopher Plato (*c.* 427–347 BC), who it has been claimed also studied in Egypt. Ancient tradition even had the two of them sharing a house in Heliopolis and living in Egypt for thirteen years. Modern scholars tend to dismiss or at least discount the idea of Plato living in Egypt. Pythagoras (who died around 497 BC) was a mathematician and a rather mystical teacher of various religious philosophies who supposedly spent some time studying in Egypt. What he learned in Egypt was alleged to have substantially influenced his religious ideas, including the concept of the transmigration of the soul that he introduced to the Greeks.

In fact, Egyptian concepts of the afterlife were antithetical to transmigration and subsequent reincarnation. Ancient authorities such as Diodorus and Plutarch asserted this claim although Egyptian religion contained no belief that corresponded to the transmigration of the soul or any other of Pythagoras's teachings. Still, Plutarch went so far as to name the Egyptian priests who taught Eudoxus, Solon and Pythagoras. The respected classicist Mary Lefkowitz convincingly argues that most stories of early Greek scholars studying in Egypt are fictions intended to enhance the authority of their ideas by an appeal to Egyptian antiquity and secret knowledge. Erik Hornung, an eminent German Egyptologist, has reached the same conclusion. In the end, it is likely that Thales and Eudoxus were, in fact, the only notable Greek scholars to study in Egypt prior to Alexander the Great's conquest of the country.[46]

At this point it is worth reintroducing Alexander the Great, who was the first great ruler to visit Egypt. A man on a mission, Alexander came to conquer the country as part of his destruction of the Persian Empire. Ancient writers, however, make it clear that Alexander was anxious to see Egypt for more reasons than simply conquest. Alexander invaded the Persian Empire in 334 BC. He quickly inflicted a defeat on the Persian army at the Granicus River in western Asia Minor. Upon consolidating his control of Asia Minor he proceeded to plan the conquest of the entire Mediterranean coastline of the Persian Empire. His goal was to gain control of the entire Mediterranean coast of the Persian Empire in order to eliminate the threat of Persian naval forces. Entering Syria at Issus in October 333 BC, he met and delivered a crushing defeat of the Persian army commanded by their king Darius III – a force that outnumbered his own three to one. The defeat was so total that the Macedonians even captured Darius's queen. After that, Alexander resumed his conquest of the coastal cities. Tyre in Phoenicia held out from January to August of 332 BC but Alexander and his army eventually prevailed in a grinding siege. Only the Persian garrison at Gaza continued to resist but they were overcome during a brief but brutal siege from September to November. At that point Alexander was poised to enter Egypt.[47]

While Alexander the Great had sound strategic reasons for marching on Egypt, it has been suggested that his knowledge of the existing Greek literature on Egypt was the source of his fascination for the country. In other words, Alexander the Great was what we would later call an 'Egyptophile'. Entering Egypt at Pelusium, he found that the Persian governor Mazaces was ready to surrender; Alexander's conquest of Egypt was bloodless. After ordering his fleet to sail up the Nile to Memphis, Alexander and his army

Alexander the Great at the Oracle of Zeus-Amun at Siwa. In this late 19th-century American engraving the temple is overly Hellenized.

marched along the river to Heliopolis, where he crossed and made his way onwards to Memphis. There Alexander formally proclaimed his rule over Egypt. He may have even been crowned as a pharaoh, although this detail continues to be inconclusively debated by historians. Alexander also held some eclectic celebrations, which included the Greek traditions of holding athletic games and literary competitions. He made sacrifices to various gods, but paid most especial attention to the bull that represented the Egyptian god Apis. It was good politics for Alexander to do so since the Persian king Cambyses had desecrated the Apis rituals, much to the horror and loathing of the Egyptians. Alexander eventually sailed down the Nile to Canopus and visited Lake Mareotis. At the mainland by the island of Pharos he identified the location for a new port for Egypt, his great city of Alexandria. It was an unintended invitation for the surrounding birds to come and feast, which they did with alacrity. Initially, Alexander was troubled by this seemingly bad omen, but his soothsayers, particularly Aristander of Telmissus, assured him that the birds were actually a good omen. Aristander had a record for accurate prophecies and he told Alexander that the birds feeding on his barley meal survey lines signified that his new city would not only be prosperous but would help to feed the world. Alexander ordered the building of his city of Alexandria to proceed and one of the great metropolises of the ancient world was born.[48]

Alexander's next goal was to visit the famous oracle of Amun at the oasis of Siwa just as the Greek heroes Perseus and Hercules had done. Getting to Siwa was not a casual stroll. It was located more than 560 kilometres (350 miles) west of modern Cairo across a waterless desert. The Mediterranean coastline was closer but still involved a desert trek of more than 240 kilometres (150 miles). The Persian king Cambyses sent one of his armies from Thebes to conquer Siwa but a massive sandstorm engulfed the Persian soldiers and they were never seen again. Undeterred by the very real potential for danger, the ever-adventurous Alexander proceeded westwards along the coast for 320 kilometres (200 miles) to Paraetonium. From there he and his company proceeded south across the desert. Alexander experienced a remarkably easy journey; it rained a significant amount, which was most unusual, so the expedition had plenty of water to drink and the wet sand was firmer to walk on. Still, the south winds started to cause the sands to shift and obscure the trail to Siwa. When Alexander's army started to stray, however, they received some seemingly miraculous guidance. According to one account (linking Egypt with mystery), two snakes appeared in front of Alexander's company and led them to Siwa, hissing all the way. Another account credits ravens or crows with guiding the Macedonians to their destination. The latter story is more plausible, since the oasis would have attracted birds in search of water and food.

Upon his arrival at Siwa, Alexander paused to admire the temple complex of the oracle. Then he went alone to consult the oracle and when he returned he was pleased but told no one what he had learned, at least according to one version. In another version, he asked if the assassins of his father King Philip of Macedon had all been punished and if he would rule a great empire. The oracle answered yes to both questions. Having finished consulting the oracle, Alexander returned to Memphis, either by going back the way he came or travelling directly east across an even larger section of desert. But the sometimes extremely dangerous journey was uneventful for Alexander. Back in Memphis, he made Egypt a province of his empire. He appointed two Egyptians as the governors, each to half the country. As the historian Arrian put it, 'Alexander was deeply impressed by Egypt.' The final conquest of Persia beckoned though, so after spending about six months in Egypt, Alexander headed east towards the final showdown with Darius II, never to return to Egypt alive.[49] Alexander the Great established a tradition of ancient leaders visiting Egypt, sometimes as a conquering power and sometimes as a tourist. Alexander was someone to be imitated and those imitators would eventually include Napoleon.

The next great leader to visit Egypt was Julius Caesar in 48 BC. Like Alexander, he came to Egypt as a consequence of war. Caesar was pursuing his rival Pompey, who he had defeated at Pharsalus. It turned out that the luckless Pompey had more to worry about than Caesar. His ship reached the coast of Egypt, where the army of the thirteen-year-old Ptolemy XII was located. Unfortunately the young king's advisors thought their best option to curry favour with Caesar was to kill Pompey – cutting Pompey's career as an Egyptian tourist abruptly short.

Caesar arrived in Egypt with a mere 4,000 men. It was a tense time there because the Ptolemaic Dynasty was in a terminal state of decay, and a vicious struggle for control of the country was underway between the advisors of Ptolemy XII and his fabled sister, Cleopatra. Their struggle inevitably merged with Caesar's conflict with the surviving supporters of Pompey. The latter had considerable influence at Ptolemy's court and urged the ruler to attack Caesar while Cleopatra sought him out as an ally – according to Plutarch by having herself hidden in a rolled-up carpet. Heavily outnumbered, Caesar showed his usual strategic brilliance as a general and gamely protected his position in a section of Alexandria while maintaining control of the Pharos Island and the eastern harbour. He still managed to take time to admire the mountainous lighthouse, calling it 'a work of marvellous construction', and to visit the tomb of Alexander the Great, whom Caesar hoped to imitate. Unfortunately Caesar's presence in Egypt did not turn out to be beneficial for the great library of Alexandria: one of his operations to protect his position in the city resulted in a fire that burned some of its books, but it is not accurate to credit Caesar with the destruction of the entire collection. Eventually reinforcements arrived and the intrepid Caesar defeated Ptolemy XII's army in February 47 BC, which resulted in the death of the young king. Caesar quickly gained control of Egypt, at which point he placed Cleopatra and her younger brother, Ptolemy XIII, on the throne. After dallying with Cleopatra until March, he continued his victorious campaigns against the remaining Pompeian forces. Caesar never returned to Egypt; rather, Egypt came to him in the form of Cleopatra and their love-child Caesarion. His visit, however, established the vital importance of Egypt as a food supplier for Rome and a source of prodigious revenue for the empire. It also made Egypt and the tomb of Alexander the Great a fashionable destination for later emperors.[50]

After Caesar's assassination in 44 BC, the struggle for the control of Rome resumed. The culmination of those struggles came in the contest between Mark Antony and Octavian. Mark Antony was one of Caesar's most highly regarded lieutenants. Octavian was Caesar's nephew and the great general had adopted him in his will, an act of dubious legality. Mark Antony, on the other hand, had taken up with Cleopatra in 42 BC and followed her to Egypt. The problem was that Mark Antony had already made a political marriage with Octavia, the sister of Octavian. For a while he shared rule of the empire with Octavian, but their rivalry inevitably increased. Both men wanted a showdown and when Antony publicly repudiated Octavia for Cleopatra, Octavian had the excuse he needed to go to war with Antony with the support of the Roman people. Octavian's fleet decisively defeated the fleet of Antony and Cleopatra at the mammoth battle of Actium in 31 BC. The defeated lovers retreated to Egypt and the implacable Octavian invaded the country in July 30 BC. Faced with defeat, both Antony and Cleopatra, in a now-legendary act, committed suicide, leaving Octavian the master of Egypt.

Savouring his victory, the triumphant Octavian toured Alexandria. In particular he visited the tomb of Alexander the Great. Gazing on his great predecessor in world conquest, Octavian crowned the mummy of the great conqueror with a golden diadem and in the process touched Alexander's nose and a piece of it broke off. This accident was both symbolic and prophetic. Octavian was no respecter of the Ptolemaic Dynasty and when the Alexandrians proudly wanted to show him the tombs of their Macedonian kings, he refused to take a look, saying brusquely, 'I wished to see a king, not corpses.' Unlike Alexander, he declined to enter the presence of the Apis bull because, as he put it, he worshipped only gods, not cattle. At least, unlike Cambyses, Octavian did not kill the sacred bull. Clearly, Octavian was no Egyptophile when it came to Egyptian culture. He did, however, recognize the country's multifaceted strategic, political and economic importance. Accordingly he made Egypt a personal province of the Roman emperors. No senator could be its governor, in fact, no senator could even live in Egypt without written imperial permission.[51]

Other members of the imperial Julio-Claudian family were more respectful and considerate towards Egyptian customs and feelings, although not all. Among the former was Germanicus, the grandson of Mark Antony and the adopted son and heir of the emperor Tiberius, who visited Egypt in AD 19 to tour its antiquities. The trip drew the ire of Tiberius because Germanicus had neglected to get his permission for the visit. Unlike Octavian, while in Egypt Germanicus visited the Apis bull. The bull was famous for performing auguries. Visitors would ask the bull a question and offer it food. When Germanicus offered the bull food, it turned away. Shortly thereafter Germanicus died in Antioch under suspicious circumstances, which for the superstitious seemed to have been foreshadowed by the Apis bull's reaction. Emperor Caligula (r. AD 37–41), the son of Germanicus, travelled to Alexandria to see the tomb of Alexander the Great. While there he stole Alexander's breastplate and took it back to Rome, where he wore it in emulation of the great conqueror. The emperor Nero had planned a trip to Alexandria but a bad omen on the eve of the voyage caused him to cancel his journey. It probably spared Alexandria and Alexander another round of megalomaniacal looting as well.[52]

Emperor Hadrian ruled the Roman Empire from AD 117 to AD 38, during the height of its power and influence. As a man of scholarly and philosophical interests who also loved to travel, Hadrian toured his vast domain with Egypt a premier segment of his itinerary. Unfortunately the surviving sources only provide the sparsest details of his time in Egypt. It is certain that he rebuilt the burial mound of Pompey on a grander scale. Unfortunately during a pleasure cruise on the Nile, his 'favourite' Antinous died. How he died is uncertain, although some contemporary reports hinted that he committed suicide as a way to show his love for Hadrian. The loss of Antinous plunged Hadrian into intense grief. At his urging the Greeks of Egypt declared Antinous a god and attributed oracles to him, which were probably written by Hadrian. The home of the cult of Antinous was the new city of Antinoöpolis that Hadrian built in his honour across the Nile from the existing city of Hermopolis between Memphis and Thebes. Given Hadrian's wide interests in things cultural, scholarly and military, it is highly likely that he visited the pyramids, the temples and tombs of Thebes, the tomb of Alexander and the great library of Alexandria.[53]

The next emperor who is known to have visited Egypt and Alexandria was Septimius Severus (r. AD 193–211), who spent most of his reign restoring order to the empire in the aftermath of the disastrous reign of Commodus. Besides defeating various rivals for the throne, he also secured Rome's eastern frontier with the Parthians, capturing their capital of Ctesiphon during AD 197–8. Soon, Severus turned to settling Egypt, Rome's all-important breadbasket. Arriving in Alexandria in AD 199, he was appalled by the level of adherence to superstitious and potentially seditious cults that prevailed across Egypt. Severus was a devotee to the cult of Serapis, a religion created by the early Ptolemaic kings which amalgamated the gods Osiris and Apis into Serapis, who incorporated traits of a variety of Greek deities. It was a way to provide the Graeco-Egyptian kingdom with a common religion and to spread it to other parts of the Mediterranean world. To counter the superstitious practices, Severus had books of secret and magical knowledge confiscated. He also sealed up the tomb of Alexander the Great so that the body could no longer be viewed. According to some accounts, he may even have enclosed the occult books in Alexander's tomb. Severus held the memory of Alexander the Great in the highest respect, but he was worried that the Egyptian cult of Alexander and the other superstitions were developing a nationalistic aspect that threatened Roman rule. These actions were part of a general programme to provide Egypt with a more reliable local government.[54]

Severus' eldest son, Caracalla, who had accompanied his father in 199 on the visit to Egypt, succeeded him as emperor and ruled from AD 211 to 217. After he became emperor, during 213–14 he faced external threats in Germany and the Danube region. When those were successfully eliminated, news of problems on the eastern frontier caused him to travel there. In 215 Caracalla came to Egypt with a view to visiting Alexander's tomb. Caracalla was a reasonably successful military leader but unfortunately he developed some serious delusions about Alexander the Great. Arriving in Egypt, he made his way to the tomb where he laid his purple cloak and various rings mounted with jewels on the sarcophagus as gifts to the renowned Macedonian. It was a standard act of respect for a legendary general but immediately afterwards a growing pathology made its appearance. Caracalla began by imitating Alexander by ordering that people call him 'Alexander' and 'Great'. He aped Alexander's poses and even came to believe that he actually closely resembled the legendary figure. His next step was to have statues and other artworks created that depicted him as Alexander the Great, and he had them placed throughout Alexandria. The sophisticated and cynical Alexandrians mocked his pretensions. When he returned to Rome, he organized a new military unit that was equipped with obsolescent long pikes, and he paraded around the city with elephants at his heels as his hero Alexander the Great was known to have done. Finally he announced to the astonished Roman senate that he was, in fact, Alexander the Great reincarnated. All of these antics amused the Alexandrians but Caracalla was deadly earnest about these claims. Just how dangerous his delusion was became apparent when Caracalla summoned the youths of Alexandria to report to the stadium, where they would be enrolled in the anachronistic phalanxes. Instead he ordered his soldiers to massacre the young men in the stadium and afterwards allowed his troops to loot and pillage Alexandria. Soon after, Caracalla proceeded to Syria to fight the Parthians and it was there at Carrhae that one of his centurions assassinated him. Thus Caracalla's madness came to an end, but it also marked the last surviving documented mention of the tomb of Alexander. At this point the fate of the tomb of Alexander the Great becomes enveloped in a morass of speculation and guesswork about the body and tomb of the conqueror.

This episode was not the last manifestation of imperial Egyptomania: the mad Emperor Elagabalus (r. AD 218–22) was a fanatical collector of things Egyptian.[55] Still Egypt was becoming a predominantly Christian society and the lingering aspects of the venerable pharaonic civilization were fading and being replaced by the Coptic Christian civilization of the Byzantine era. The Islamic conquest four hundred years later in AD 641 completed this process and Islamic civilization superseded the native Coptic culture. Egypt, along with the rest of the Mediterranean world, had entered the Middle Ages.

Ancient people did not travel only to Egypt. Egyptian things and ideas travelled to them as well, particularly during the time of the cosmopolitan Roman Empire. As one of the wealthiest countries in the Mediterranean world, Egypt attracted a lot of trade and visitors. Egyptian grain was in high demand. As Herodotus mentioned, Greeks came to Egypt as traders, mercenaries or just to sightsee. Other later ancient travellers undoubtedly came for the same reasons. When they went home, they took other Egyptian goods with them. Artefacts with an Egyptian motif became quite popular in the Graeco-Roman world, much as they still remain popular in contemporary society.[56] Egyptian religion was an even more popular and potent export. Greeks tended to syncretize religions they encountered in other countries. Herodotus attempted to draw correspondences between the pantheon of the Olympian gods and the gods of Egypt.[57] There is evidence of temples to Egyptian gods appearing in the Greek cities of the Aegean prior to Alexander the Great's conquests. Still, it was Alexander's conquest of Egypt that opened the way for Egyptian religion to spread throughout the Mediterranean lands. The first two Macedonian kings of Egypt, Ptolemy I Soter and Ptolemy II Philadelphus, went so far as to create the new cult of the god Serapis. The Greek scholar Timotheus and the Egyptian Manetho aided the Ptolemies in this task of manoeuvring through the tricky waters of a plausible religious sycretization.

Even more popular than Serapis was the Egyptian goddess Isis, who became associated with the Greek goddess Demeter or the Roman Diana, a very popular fertility and mother-goddess. The Isis cult, along with other mystery cults and the practice of magic, gave ordinary people a sense of empowerment in the highly structured society of the Hellenistic kingdoms and the Roman Empire. It also gave them the hope of an afterlife of comfort and happiness that most people were not experiencing in their temporal lives. The great Edward Gibbon noted this hope as one of the major reasons for the success of Christianity, but as many historians have pointed out, the same observation applies to the mystery cults, including that of Isis, that were serious rivals of early Christianity. Sites of Isis's temples came to be found throughout the Roman Empire. During the era of the Five Good Emperors – Nerva, Trajan, Hadrian, Antoninus Pius and Marcus Aurelius – the Greek scholar and moralist Plutarch would attempt to explain sympathetically the cults of Osiris and Isis to his Greek and Roman readers. His essay 'Isis and Osiris' would become a major source of ancient Egyptological scholarship.[58]

The Romans and Greeks frequently adopted the cult of Isis, with its comfortable rituals of fertility, motherhood, redemption and resurrection. Unlike the Greeks, some Romans found Egyptian religion to be bizarre and off-putting rather than exotic and enticing. Egyptian cults appeared in Rome as early as the dictatorship of Sulla, 82–79 BC, and there were attempts by some Roman officials to destroy Egyptian temples prior to the triumph of Julius Caesar. Octavian, who became Emperor Augustus, did not approve of Egyptian gods as his rejection of the Apis bull clearly showed. Augustus would later ban Egyptian temples from the city of Rome's central sacred precinct, the Pomerium. The early second-century satirist Juvenal was of a like-mind with Augustus. His satire 15 mocked Egypt's animal-headed gods:

> Who has not heard, Volusius, of the monstrous deities
> Those crazy Egyptians worship? One lot adores crocodiles,
> Another worships the snake-gorged ibis; and where
> The magic chords resound from Memnon's truncated statue,
> Where old Thebes, with her hundred gates, now lies in ruins,
> There gleams
> The golden effigy of a sacred long-tailed monkey.
> You'll find whole cities devoted to cats, or to river-fish
> Or dogs – but not a soul who worships Diana. To eat
> Onions or leeks is an outrage, they're strictly taboo: how holy
> The nation that has such gods springing up in the kitchen-garden!

Despite such resistance to Egyptian gods, many citizens of the Roman Empire were drawn to them and some of those who were seduced by the Egyptian gods sat at the very head of the empire.[59]

It was Caligula, an ultimately deranged emperor, who began to harness the Egyptian cults as a powerful feature of the imperial cult of emperor worship. His successor, Claudius, was tolerant of Egyptian cults while Nero was uncharacteristically indifferent or even sceptical of them. One of Nero's short-termed successors, Otho, was a worshipper of Isis. The Flavian emperors Vespasian and his son Titus had long been stationed as generals in the Middle East. Besides suppressing the great Jewish revolt, they spent time in Egypt and participated in rites of Isis and Serapis. Vespasian, however, was not known as a man who took religion particularly seriously: as he lay dying, to earn his last laugh he quipped that he could feel himself becoming a god. The expansion of the cult of Isis continued under the sympathetic rule of the Five Good Emperors. Its high point came under the dynasty of the Severi. Although Severus was a worshipper of Serapis, his son Caracalla preferred Isis. The Egyptomania of the mad Emperor Elagabalus may have been related to his adherence to the Isis cult, although his tastes appear to have favoured more deviant Syrian or Levantine deities. Helped by its exotic and ecumenical appeal and frequent imperial patronage, the cult of Isis was one of the most popular of the mystery religions of the Roman Empire and a formidable rival to the early Christian Church. Some even argue that the veneration of the Virgin Mary is really just a Christian adaptation and syncretization of the cultic figure of Isis. If so, it is a phenomenon of a sort of hidden and forgotten Egyptomania.[60]

A fascinating portrayal of the Isis cult was provided by Apuleius' novel *The Golden Ass*, written during the mid-second century AD, which included a detailed description of the initiation ceremony of the cult of Isis. As the goddess Isis tells the novel's hero Lucius at the beginning of his initiation, 'those who are enlightened by the early rays of that divinity the sun, the Ethiopians, the Arii, and the Egyptians who excel in antique lore, all worship me with their ancestral ceremonies and call me by my true name, Queen Isis.' The exotic rituals that followed included cultic objects covered with 'the strange hieroglyphs of the Egyptians'. Clearly the mystery and the magic long associated with Egypt significantly contributed to the popular appeal of the Isis cult. Besides providing details of the secret ceremony, Apuleius' novel demonstrates just how ubiquitous the Isis cult was in imperial Roman society.[61] In its heyday, the cult of Isis towered over the religious life of the ancient world until the triumph of Christianity decisively and permanently dethroned it.

Hermeticism, in contrast to the cult of Isis, played a minor and peripheral role in the religious life of the Mediterranean world of Hellenism and Roman imperialism. That is not surprising since hermeticism viewed itself as a gathering of an initiated elite possessed of special and very secret knowledge not available or even understandable to most other human beings. Hermes Trismegistus was the supposed founder of the hermetic cult. He was a mythological ancient sage or sages and a sometime demigod who created a system of secret knowledge during a dimly known era of

Egypt's most distant past. Foreknowledge of an impending catastrophic deluge caused him to build the pyramids to preserve his secret knowledge for future generations of right-minded initiates. Various hermetic tracts circulated among small circles of adepts during the late Hellenistic era in Egypt. Others were added during the period of Roman rule in Egypt. The hermetic cult spread from Egypt to various cities of the Roman Empire. The followers of Hermes Trismegistus considered him to have been a genuine historical figure and the author of the hermetic texts. Even today, some adherents of esoteric and occult beliefs continue to consider them products of ancient Egyptian wisdom. That belief continues despite the fact that textual analysis and criticism conducted during the early years of the seventeenth century have shown it to be false. Analysis of the linguistic aspects of the Greek used in the hermetic writings and an analysis of the Neoplatonic philosophical ideas they presented dated the texts to the era of the second century BC into the third or fourth centuries AD.[62]

While hermeticism never achieved even a tiny fraction of the popularity of the cult of Isis, it proved to have greater intellectual staying power. The formidable St Augustine of Hippo forcefully rejected Hermes Trismegistus and hermeticism in his monumental *City of God,* which went on to become a classic of Christian thought while at the same time inadvertently keeping awareness of hermeticism alive – albeit in a negative light. Other Church fathers, Clement of Alexandria and Lactantius, took a more positive view and were successful in Christianizing Hermes Trismegistus. We will see that Hermeticism and the stories of the Bible kept a fascination and wonder about Egypt alive and sometimes even flourishing in the minds of scholars and in the popular culture of the West during the Middle Ages, the Renaissance and the Enlightenment.[63] Although the flame of Egyptomania flickered during the early Middle Ages it never died and vigorously returned to prominence during the Renaissance and the Enlightenment.

FOUR

MEDIEVAL EGYPTOMANIA: FROM ST AUGUSTINE TO THE RENAISSANCE

We sent Moses and Aaron with Our signs to Pharaoh and his leading
supporters, but they acted arrogantly – they were wicked people.

KORAN, 10:75

Some men say that they [the Pyramids] are the tombs of great men in
ancient times; but the common opinion is that they are the Barns of
Joseph, and they find that in their chronicles. And truly, it is not likely
that they are tombs.

SIR JOHN MANDEVILLE[1]

ST AUGUSTINE OF HIPPO (354–430) spent a lot of time in his study
during the thirteen years between AD 413 and 426. He was writing his monumental *City of God Against the Pagans*. The Roman
world had experienced a horrific shock in 410 when the Visigoths under
Alaric sacked Rome. Pagans blamed the disaster on people abandoning the
old gods in favour of Christianity – a sacrilege responsible for bringing
divine retribution down on Rome. Pagans also claimed that Christianity
was weakening the social and spiritual fabric of the once great empire.
Augustine wrote his *City of God* to refute those accusations. His masterpiece was also a compendium of the state of knowledge in late antiquity.
Augustine lived in an age of spiritual victory, of Christianity triumphing
in the Roman Empire. Some years earlier the Emperor, Theodosius I
(r. 379–95), had declared Christianity to be the official religion of the
Roman Empire and virtually outlawed paganism. Nevertheless, Augustine
also definitely lived in an age of decline both political and cultural. The
Roman Empire in the west was disintegrating, and after the Visigoths had
careened through its territories, other barbarian tribes followed. When

St Augustine of Hippo (354–430) was one of the greatest of the early Church Fathers and an opponent of hermeticism. Philippe de Champaigne, *St Augustine*, 1640s, oil painting.

Augustine died of old age, his home and diocesan seat of Hippo was under siege by the Vandals.

The state of knowledge was also decaying. Augustine was a learned man who had received an excellent education, but the number and quality of books available for him to use was far less than had been available to earlier Greek and Roman scholars. His knowledge of history was largely based on the *Chronicon* of Eusebius of Caesarea (*c.* 260–*c.* 340), which

St Jerome (*c.* 345–420) had continued. Sadly, Eusebius was no Herodotus or Thucydides. The eighteenth book of the *City of God* reflected this deficiency. In it, Augustine provided a summary of how biblical history correlated with pagan and secular history. Egypt and its history featured prominently in various sections of this book, but as a history of Egypt, it was wildly inaccurate.

Augustine related that the kings of Argos in Greece had been in contact with early Egypt. He claimed that Io was the daughter of Inachus, a river-god in the Argolid and supposedly the first king of Argos. She brought reading and writing to Egypt, among other accomplishments. After Io's death, Egyptians began calling her Isis and worshipped her as a god, although Augustine conceded that she might also have been a princess from Ethiopia who had come to Egypt as a queen. Later, when the patriarch Jacob and his son Joseph were in Egypt, the Argos king Apis sailed to Egypt with a fleet. While in that country he died, after which the Egyptians started to worship him as Serapis, the greatest of the Egyptian gods, and Augustine associated him with the Egyptian worship of the Apis bull.[2] Augustine dated the Exodus from Egypt by Moses and the Children of Israel to have taken place at the same time that the reign of Cecrops as king of Athens was coming to an end. As a believing Christian, Augustine obviously considered the gods of Egypt, Greece and Rome to be false, and that belief influenced the way he perceived and wrote about the history of Egypt. He argued that most of the pagan gods, including Egyptian deities, were originally just mere mortals who had come to be worshipped as gods because of their great deeds or the conniving work of demons.

Despite his prejudices, Augustine gave the Egyptians credit for possessing great learning and asserted that Moses gained much of his own wisdom from the education he obtained while living in Egypt. Augustine vehemently denied, however, that the Egyptians were the source and beginning of human knowledge. In fact, Abraham, Isaac, Jacob and Joseph possessed great learning that pre-dated that of Egypt. Augustine even asserted that Hebrew had been a written language from its creation – which meant Hebrew was the earliest form of writing. As Augustine put it:

> Not even Egypt, whose habit it is to plume herself, falsely and idly, on the antiquity of her learning, is found to antedate the wisdom of the patriarchs with any wisdom of her own, of any quality.

He was also none too impressed by the nature of Egyptian knowledge, exemplified by astronomy, which he opined 'generally served rather to exercise men's ingenuity than to enlighten their minds with genuine wisdom'. Augustine granted that the philosophy of Hermes Trismegistus had its origin far earlier than the philosophy of the Greeks but his venerable knowledge was not as old as that of Abraham, Joseph or even Moses.[3] The problem was that Augustine's version of Egyptian history bore almost no relation to reality. As such it was an exemplar of the state of Western European knowledge of and attitudes towards Egypt during late antiquity and the medieval era. The Byzantines, heirs of the Eastern Roman Empire, and Muslim scholars in the service of the Abbassid caliphs preserved the classical Greeks' knowledge of Egypt. In fact, scholars of medieval Islam took that knowledge and expanded it. In contrast, it was not until the Renaissance of the fourteenth, fifteenth and sixteenth centuries that classical Greek learning was recovered and extended. Europe of the Middle Ages was truly a dark age for Egyptology. But whether it was the Western Europeans, the Byzantine Greeks or the medieval Muslim scholars, Egypt continued to evoke that fascination known as Egyptomania in all of them.

The Decline and Fall of Classical Egyptomania

The popular historical imagination tends to view the fall of the Roman Empire as a relatively sudden and dramatically violent event. In fact, its decline and fall took a long time. In Edward Gibbon's view, it was a process that took about 1,000 years from the early third century AD until the fall of Constantinople to the Ottoman Turks in 1453. Obviously, the great empire's fall occurred in phases. As one of the most important and wealthy provinces of the Roman Empire, Egypt played a significant part in this whole process.

The Roman Empire experienced a serious crisis during the third century AD. One reason for this was external threats against the empire: German tribes were pressing against the imperial borders in the north at the same time as the Sassanian Persian Empire had supplanted the Parthian Empire on the eastern frontier and was proving to be a formidable enemy. Within the Roman Empire the internal economy had collapsed, causing disruption to society and government and inciting internal rebellions. Emperor Diocletian (AD 284–305) managed to stabilize the situation, although he had to suppress the dangerous rebellion of Achileus in Egypt during 293–4. His first move was the capture of Alexandria. An eight-month siege of Alexandria was followed by a savage reprisal in the form of a massacre of the inhabitants. That tragedy spurred on the brutal destruction of the ancient cities of Busiris and Copthos, which broke the Egyptians' will to resist.

Christianity was gaining adherents during these years and eventually achieved legal recognition under the emperor Constantine the Great (324–37). Later, Theodosius I (379–95) proved to be an even more enthusiastic supporter of Christianity. The growing strength of Christianity, however, was a threat to the survival of paganism, including the traditional pharaonic culture of Egypt. In 391 the fanatical patriarch Theophilus (385–412) led a Christian mob in the destruction of the temple of the Serapeum in Alexandria. This action has erroneously been considered the final destruction of the fabled Library and Museum of Alexandria. Although this was not the case, it did, however, signal the impending triumph of Christianity in Egypt, which unfortunately led to the persecution of pagans and Jews by Christians. During the patriarchate of Cyril of Alexandria (412–44), conflicts between ecclesiastical leaders and imperial officials divided Alexandrian society. Tragically, the great female philosopher Hypatia was murdered by followers of Cyril in 415 because of her support of the imperial prefect. Although Hypatia has sometimes been portrayed as a pagan martyr, she was actually a Neoplatonist with strong Christian connections.[4] By the time of Hypatia's death, Christianity was triumphant in Egypt and the ancient pharaonic religion was dead or very close to dying.

Meanwhile the Roman Empire continued to disintegrate. By AD 476 various Germanic tribes had overrun the western Roman Empire and established squabbling barbarian kingdoms in its place. In the east, of which Egypt remained a part, the rest of the Roman Empire survived and evolved into the Byzantine Empire, as its language and culture was primarily Greek rather than Latin. It faced a continuing threat from the Persian Empire of the Sassanids and war with Persia raged from AD 611 until 630. In the end the Byzantine forces triumphed, but the two great empires had fought each other to a mutual exhaustion that left them both severely weakened. A highly virulent outbreak of the bubonic plague further debilitated the Byzantines and the Persians. The Arab armies of Islam began attacking the Byzantine Empire in 634 and decisively defeated the Byzantines at the Battle of Yarmuk in 636. Palestine and Syria fell and Egypt was invaded and conquered in the years 640–42.[5] The slow Islamization of Egyptian society commenced; Egypt became a province in the great empire of the Ummayyad and Abbasid Caliphs. Meanwhile, Western Europe experienced continued decline and various raids and invasions by Vikings, Muslims and Asiatic nomads such as the Avars. Knowledge and interest in Egypt reached its nadir during these years and stayed that way until the advent of the revival of classical learning and trade during the Renaissance. But such was not the case in the world of Islam.

Islam and Egyptomania

Arabs were initially a tiny minority in early Islamic Egypt, a ratio of around one Arab for every thirty native Egyptians. It took centuries for the majority of the Egyptian population to convert to Islam. In spite of its large and devoted Christian population, however, Egypt was a firm part of the Islamic Empire.[6] Still, for the Muslim Arabs who visited or were resident in the country, they were truly strangers in a strange land. Whether Muslims considered the strangeness of Egypt to be a good or a bad thing was a subject for debate among medieval Muslims and remains a point of contention for modern scholars. What is certain is that Muslims found Egypt to be fascinating and beguiling.

When it came to having a relatively accurate view of ancient Egyptian history, the research of Michael Cook shows that the Muslim Arabs who settled in Egypt and the various Muslim visitors there had less understanding than the ancient Greeks and Romans. They were, however, more knowledgeable than the medieval Europeans, with the exception of the Greeks of the Byzantine Empire. Their Egyptian contemporaries had little to tell them. Christianity had triumphed by the fourth century, while pharaonic civilization had withered and died. Three centuries of Christianized Egypt separated the coming of Islam from the ancient, traditional culture of Egypt. Any authentic memory of pharaonic civilization was long forgotten, even though vestiges of the old ways survived in Egypt's popular culture. Otherwise, Muslims believed the largely negative view of ancient Egypt found in the Hebrew scriptures. This did not deter medieval Muslim scholars from trying to better understand ancient Egypt and reconcile its ancient past with the teachings of Islam. They possessed a traditionalist Muslim history of ancient Egypt that the early Arab conquerors had produced, which relied heavily on biblical and Koranic accounts. There was also a hermetic history of Egypt that Coptic scholars had produced which emphasized the role of magic and science in ancient Egypt's culture. Muslims also discovered a fragmentary Egyptian king list, but they did not recognize its historical significance.[7]

Muslims have always had a conflicted and contradictory attitude towards pharaonic civilization. Ancient Egypt was a pagan society and the prophet Muhammad taught that paganism was evil and faithful Muslims should eradicate it without mercy. On the other hand, it has been pointed out that the Koran in Suras 22:46, 29:20 and 40:82 also urges Muslims to study and visit other lands and cultures. Some non-Koranic Muslim traditions and sayings of Muhammad, known as Hadiths, actually praised Egypt and its culture. Still, the Koran presents a largely negative picture of Egypt that is derived from the same traditions found in the Old Testament: Egypt was a land of bondage and Pharaoh was a tyrant (which in fact refers to the pharaohs of the oppression of the Children of Israel and the Exodus, but this was extrapolated in popular thought to pharaohs in general).[8] Fundamentalist Muslims have taken this teaching to heart and the history of Muslim Egypt has been punctuated with periodic incidents of the vandalization or even the wanton destruction of Egyptian antiquities. Fortunately these episodes have been of brief duration (especially for the sake of Egyptian tourism). Recent cultural depredations by Muslim fundamentalists throughout the Middle East should be a reminder that the heritage of ancient Egypt remains threatened.

Other Islamic writers rightly credited the ancient Egyptians with important contributions to human knowledge and science. Sāid al-Andalusī (1029–1070) lived and worked in a more liberal environment when Muslim Spain was at its zenith. Al-Andalusī credited the peoples of India as the first to expand knowledge, but they were not alone. Nine nations contributed to science and learning, including the Egyptians. According to his account, the antediluvian Egyptians, although unfortunately pagans, 'cultivated various branches of science and searched into the most complex of problems'. Their successors in the pharaonic and Ptolemaic eras continued that tradition and many massive and awesome buildings and monuments in Egypt attest to that nation's commitment to expanding knowledge that enriched Islamic civilization.[9]

Other Muslims have attempted to turn Egyptian antiquities to the use of Muslim piety by arguing that they show the transitory and ultimately brief nature of worldly wealth, success and fame. They are an object lesson for demonstrating the need for humility. Medieval Arabs considered many ancient Egyptian sites to be holy places and visited them as an act of pilgrimage. The monuments of ancient Egypt were great sources for the study of history. On this basis, antiquities from the pagan Egyptian past were worth preserving for the edification of future generations of the faithful. Native Egyptians who became Muslims also continued to take pride in their land's long heritage of cultural achievement.[10] Muslim visitors, like other visitors before and after, were awestruck by Egypt's antiquities and its unique topography and environment. As the great scholar and physician Abd al-Latif al-Bagdadi (1162–1231) commented: 'Of all the countries I have visited or known by report of others, there are not any that can compare with Egypt for its antiquities.' Even more effusively he asserted that, 'In Egypt, there are wondrous and strange things by the hundreds of thousands. We have seen hundreds of them with our own eyes. Before each of them, we have been entirely beside ourselves with astonishment.'[11]

Muslims were so fascinated and impressed by the relics of ancient Egypt that they generated a whole genre of literature. This 'excellence of Egypt' or 'virtues of Egypt' literature, known as *Fadail Misr*, praised and described the knowledge and accomplishments of the Egyptians. As the historian Okasha El Daly has shown, Muslim scholars assumed that the Copts of their era were the descendents of the pharaonic Egyptians of the distant past. Uneducated people simply assumed that the ancient Egyptians were giants or had command of magic or some sort of super-science. As the scholar al-Bagdadi mused:

> The reflecting man, contemplating these vestiges of antiquity [the Egyptian ruins], feels inclined to excuse the error of the vulgar who believed that mortals in those distant ages in which they were constructed lived to a more advanced age than is usual in our days; that they were of gigantic stature, or that by striking a stone with a wand they caused it to obey their orders and to transport itself to wherever their will dictated.

But medieval Egypt never managed to create a national history or national identity using their ancient heritage within Islamic civilization, such as the Iranians had succeeded in doing. Muslim books praising Egypt saw wonders and weirdness as dominant qualities of pharaonic culture, including great accomplishments in science and mathematics. It was a land in which miracles occurred, magic was practised and lost treasures waited to be found. The popular culture of medieval Islam recognized thirty rather than seven wonders of the world and twenty of them were located in Egypt.[12]

Medieval Muslims were especially impressed by the pyramids of Giza, particularly the two larger pyramids of Khufu and Khafra. The great traveller and ecumenical historian Abū'l-Hasan 'Ali Al-Mas'ūdī (890–956) included a section on the pyramids along with other Egyptian topics in his *The Meadows of Gold and the Mines of Precious Gems*. As the poet Alī ibn Muhammad ibn Al-Sā'ātī (d. 1207) eloquently expressed: 'Among the wonders (of the world) – and there are many wonders that are too great for exaggeration and magnification – are the two Pyramids.'[13] This opinion is not surprising since in those days the pyramids were the largest manmade structures in the world. The Muslim geographer and historian Ibn Fadlallah al-'Umari (d. 1348) best captured this sentiment in his muchquoted aphorism: 'Everything fears Time, but Time fears the Pyramids.'[14]

Also during much of the Middle Ages the outer stone cover of the three pyramids was still intact, although a lightning strike had cut a breach in the fabric of the Great Pyramid early in the tenth century. Muslims speculated about the age and the purpose of the pyramids. Scholars debated whether the pyramids had been built before or after the Great Flood. When the scholar Abu Ja-far al-Idrisi (1173–1251) surveyed the debate he found that among 22 scholars, eighteen favoured an antediluvian date while four favoured a post-diluvian date. One antediluvian theory suggested that a pre-adamitic race had built the pyramids. A much more common candidate was an ancient king of Egypt named Surid ben Shaluk, who lived three hundred years before the great flood. Surid had two dreams which his astrologers interpreted as predictions of a huge catastrophe that would strike Egypt. First a great flood would sweep the land, followed by an invasion. To preserve the knowledge of ancient Egypt and the considerable treasures of the land, Surid built the pyramids to safely store these valuables. Magic spells were placed on the pyramids to prevent strangers from entering and stealing their treasure. The spells also guaranteed that while it had taken 61 years to construct the pyramids, no one would be able to destroy them even if they spent the next six centuries trying. Later versions substituted Hermes Trismegistus as the builder of the antediluvian pyramids in place of Surid. Post-diluvian builders of the pyramids included the Yemeni king Shaddad ben Ad; Baysar ben Ham, a grandson of Noah; and Aristotle, who built them as tombs for himself and Alexander the Great. Some Muslims even shared with medieval Europeans that the pyramids were actually the granaries Joseph built to store grain during the seven years of plenty. As to how the pyramids had been built, Idrisi was at a loss for a good explanation. He speculated that the Egyptians might have used winches and ropes to place the great building blocks of the pyramids or that long ramps were used to drag them up, but he also considered the possibility of magic being used in the construction. Idrisi also tried to date the pyramids more precisely by using astronomical data on the movements of the stars. He concluded that the pyramids were over 20,000 years old. His methodology was flawed so his calculations were wrong. That, however, would never stop modern-day proponents of the existence of a prehistoric super-civilization in Egypt from using Idrisi as evidence for their fringe theories.[15]

Naturally the size and the mystery of the pyramids beckoned medieval Muslims to climb on them or try to explore their interiors. Climbing the pyramids was not much of an option so long as the smooth outer casing of hard stone remained intact, which was the case for much of the medieval era. Lightning did create a breach in the casing of the Great Pyramid early

Medieval Muslims exploring the interior of the Great Pyramid, by Thomas Milton, after Luigi Mayer, c. 1802, coloured aquatint.

in the tenth century. At that point the Abbasid general Mu'nis al-Muzaffar al-Mu'tadidi (d. 933) offered a prize for anyone bold enough to climb to the top. Meanwhile, people on the ground speculated as to how big the tops of the pyramids really were. Although they looked like they came to a point, scholarly observers knew that was not the case. Debates took place as to whether there was room for one, two or even twenty camels to lie down at the top of the pyramids. In around the year 1161 a climber died from a fall while trying to reach the top of the pyramid of Khephren. Despite this, other climbers were not deterred. Eventually, successfully climbing to the top of the Great Pyramid became a commonplace activity. Over the centuries European tourists joined in the fun. Pierre Belon du Mans climbed to the top of the Great Pyramid in 1547, Filippo Pigafetta followed in 1577 and Pietro della Valle in 1615. Pyramid climbing became a staple activity of tourists in the nineteenth century. Today, the Egyptian government has prohibited the practice to save the Pyramids from wear and tear and to prevent accidents befalling clumsy, risk-taking sightseers.[16]

Medieval Muslims not only wanted to get on top of the pyramids, they wanted to get inside them, too. It was believed that magnificent treasures were hidden in their depths. Such notions undoubtedly stemmed from the conjecture that the pyramids had been built to safeguard the precious knowledge and riches of ancient Egypt.[17] Those beliefs probably had their origins in the fact that the tombs of pharaohs, whether in the pyramids or in the Valley of the Kings, had been crammed with treasures to make the afterlife pleasant for the dead monarch housed inside.

Entering a pyramid bore its own risks. Legends had it that the builders of the pyramids placed powerful curses on them to protect the hidden treasures from thieving trespassers. By late antiquity, knowledge of the location of the entrance into the Great Pyramid had been lost. Defying the ancient curses, the Caliph Al-Ma'mun (r. 813–33) had a hole punched into the Great Pyramid in an attempt to find the lost knowledge of the pharaohs and their treasure. As his workers tunnelled into the pyramid, they rediscovered its lost entrance – but no ancient books or treasure. The adventure was later retold as one of the stories in the collection *The Arabian Nights*. Al-Ma'mun claimed to have found some treasure, so his expedition, he asserted, turned out to be a break-even venture – an exactly break-even venture. It has been suggested that Al-Ma'mun may have secretly placed gold in the pyramid to save face for himself and his operation. That would explain how he neither lost nor gained treasure from his search, although for medieval Muslims, magic spells were equally persuasive explanations for Al-Ma'mun's failure. Other would-be treasure-seekers in the pyramids were not so lucky and their ventures ended in failure or fatalities. Tales abounded among the medieval Muslims of people entering the pyramids, finding secret passages, wandering about lost and finally emerging at some faraway location such as the Faiyum. One such explorer, Ridwan al-Farrash, entered a pyramid and was never seen again. That is, until his ghost began appearing to his friends to warn them not to explore the pyramids lest they suffer his fate. Abd al-Latif al-Bagdadi condemned the seeking of treasure in ancient monuments, and he was not alone. None of these happenings, however, stopped credulous medieval Muslims from continuing to believe that great treasure and hidden knowledge remained to be found in the pyramids.[18] Nor have the long list of failed searches and investigations around the pyramids dampened the enthusiasm of modern seekers of mystic secrets and riches.

Egypt's many other great monuments also attracted the awe of medieval Muslims, especially because they were in a much better state of preservation during the early Middle Ages than they are now. One monument that particularly dazzled visitors was the Sphinx. The Arabic name for the Sphinx was *Abu'l-hawl*, which means 'father of terror'. Native Egyptians considered it to be a protector of their crops.[19] Visitors, contrary to strict Islamic beliefs, would bring offerings to the Sphinx and prayed to it to grant their wishes. As late as the early fifteenth century, the historian Al-Maqrizi (1364–1440) reported that the adherents of the Sabaean sect worshipped the Sphinx. When Abd al-Latif al-Bagdadi visited Egypt in 1191 and 1192, most of the Sphinx was buried in drifting sand so that only the head was visible. Some of the red pigment that had decorated the Sphinx's face was still discernible and the face itself was undamaged. The Sphinx clearly impressed al-Bagdadi, since he told of 'a sensible man enquiring of me as to what, of all I had seen in Egypt, had most excited my admiration, I answered, "The nicety of proportion of the head of the Sphinx."'

Like other medieval visitors to Egypt, Abd al-Latif al-Bagdadi completed the usual itinerary: seeing the great obelisks and the great Lighthouse of Pharos in Alexandria. The number, size and artistry of statues of the gods of Egypt roused his admiration. Al-Bagdadi was also astonished by the extent of the ruins of ancient Memphis, which he found almost impossible to comprehend. He found them to be so vast that centuries of cannibalizing the ruins for building material had left them largely still intact. Other Muslim visitors echoed his sentiments.[20]

Despite the respect for the antiquities of ancient Egypt that many medieval Muslims exhibited, others were not above cannibalizing them for building materials or attempting to deface or destroy them for reasons of pious Muslim fundamentalism. The Umayyad Caliph Yazid II during 722–3 ordered the destruction of Egyptian antiquities, but little was done. Saladin (d. 1193) is generally and correctly depicted as a great ruler and a chivalrous warrior. As the first Ayyubid ruler of Egypt, however, he was responsible for a great deal of vandalizing of antiquities. Abd al-Latif al-Bagdadi reported that the many small mastaba tombs in the Giza area had been plundered for their stones. Saladin commanded his general Qaraqush to fortify Cairo. This order was accomplished by demolishing the mastabas and using the material to build the massive fortress known as the Citadel of Saladin along with other city walls and bridges. It was said that Saladin initially attempted to dismantle the great pyramids but the effort failed. During 1196 and 1197 Saladin's son Malik-al-Aziz (d. 1198) resumed the effort to demolish the pyramids. In his case, friends at court urged him to this action as an act of fundamentalist Islamic piety. He brought a larger number of workers to Giza and they began work on the smallest of the pyramids, the pyramid of Menkaure. Working steadily for eight months, the money allocated for the project eventually ran out. Apart from damaging the outer casing, the pyramid remained intact with little signs of damage.

Muslims' perceptions of the Sphinx may have sectarian roots. For example, the Sufi sect of Islam opposed the continuing veneration of the Sphinx. One of the Sufists struck the Sphinx with his shoe, a classic Middle Eastern insult, as a protest against people praying to the Sphinx. Later in 1378 the Sufi Sa'im al-Dahr damaged the face, nose and ears of the Sphinx. As a result, sands invaded the Giza area and were said to have buried it in retribution for the sacrilege. An outraged mob of local residents hanged the Sufi and buried him near the Sphinx to get the sands to recede. Later other Muslims who supported the preservation of Egyptian antiquities claimed that Crusader raids on Alexandria were the result of sacrilege against the Sphinx. Since the Crusader attack occurred before 1260 there was no cause and effect, natural or supernatural, as there was with the Sufi vandalism. Muhammad ben al-Halabi in the mid-thirteenth century opposed the efforts of Muslim fanatics to destroy the monuments and temples of the ancient Egyptians. He was not alone, as Abd al-Latif al-Bagdadi observed,

> The different [Muslim] rulers were careful at all times of preserving these valuable relics of antiquity, and . . . would not allow of their being damaged or destroyed at pleasure. Many advantages presented by these monuments dictated this line of conduct. In the first place, they regarded

them as a species of annals which recalled the memory of past ages. Secondly, they stood as witnesses of the truth of the books of revelation.

For medieval Muslims, Egyptomania could be a positive or a negative phenomenon.

Egyptomania in the Medieval West

The period between the years AD 500 and 1350 is generally considered to be the Middle Ages in Western Europe, if one assumes that the Renaissance starts about 1350. The first five hundred years of this era are sometimes referred to as the Dark Ages, although modern historians of that period dispute this designation. Some students of Egyptian influence and Egyptomania have characterized the western Middle Ages as a dark age. That, though, is too severe an assessment. While knowledge and awareness of Egypt declined and deteriorated, it would be more accurate to consider the Middle Ages in Western Europe as a somewhat dim age of knowledge and awareness of Egypt. Access to at least some of the relevant classical accounts of Egypt such as Herodotus' *Histories* and the *Asclepius* of Hermes Trismegistus continued, as the example of St Augustine shows. Early Christian scholars constructed chronologies based on Manetho's history and king list but bent the results to reconcile with the biblical narrative. As a result, it was claimed that Adam was the first king of Egypt, not Menes as Manetho stated – or rather, Adam was Menes. The biblical accounts of Egypt along with those of the Church Fathers also remained firmly in the consciousness of Europeans. Despite the break-up of the Roman Mediterranean, traders and pilgrims still visited Egypt. Furthermore, by AD 1000 Arabic texts that included information about Egypt were being translated into Latin. The body of information may have been spotty in coverage and of dubious accuracy in many cases but it presented an Egypt that was mysterious and fascinating. Egyptomania lived on.[21]

The Bible was the most readily available source of information about Egypt for most medieval people and would remain so until the beginning of the nineteenth century. As a result, medieval people viewed Egypt through the lens of biblical prophecy and the worldview of Christianity. Although many people were illiterate, references to Egypt in the Bible would have been mentioned in church services and have been depicted in stained glass. Clerical scholars could read the Latin Bible and read about Egypt. They interpreted these references in different ways. First, they recognized that the Bible's focus is not on the history of Egypt; the Old Testament's focus was on the Hebrews, their faith and their fate. They also interpreted biblical

Simon Bening, *The Flight into Egypt*, c. 1525, gold paint and gold leaf on parchment. The Holy Family's Flight to Egypt takes place in a landscape that is distinctly Western European. Although this painting dates to the mid-1500s, it is a good reflection of how the vast majority of medieval Europeans imagined ancient Egypt.

references to Egypt allegorically in referring to the ministry of Christ and his crucifixion. Just as the ancient Hebrews depicted the Egyptians as oppressors, idolaters and decadent, Europeans of the Middle Ages adopted these same prejudices and stereotypes. Again St Augustine provides an example of this attitude. Egypt also served as an object lesson on the punishment and humbling that God inflicted on sinful nations who practised idolatry and abominations. Medieval writers credited the Hebrews with the origins of science, the invention of writing and other firsts that ancient Greek writers had ascribed to the Egyptians. On the other hand, there was a positive view of Egypt as a place of refuge. It should not be forgotten that Jacob and his sons moved to Egypt to escape the calamity of the seven lean years. More important, Mary and Joseph fled to Egypt with the baby Jesus to escape the murderous paranoia of King Herod the Great and stayed there for either three or seven years. Traditions and legends mention miracles associated with Jesus that occurred during these years: palm trees bowed to show respect for Mary and the baby Jesus; the Church Father Origen put forth the claim that an adult Jesus studied the magical arts in Egypt, which contributed to his ability to perform miracles. Rabbinic literature of late antiquity and the early Middle Ages repeated the story. The Arabic writings about Egypt mostly added to medieval Europeans' knowledge of astrology, astronomy, magic and the teachings of Hermes Trismegistus.[22]

Still, medieval Europeans suffered from confusion and error about ancient Egypt. Medieval Europeans made no distinction between Arabs and Copts in Egypt because they had no concept of who the Copts were. They also thought the second-century AD astronomer Ptolemy was a king of Egypt. The conflation was understandable given the prodigious number of Macedonian kings of Egypt named Ptolemy up until the time of Cleopatra, but it also betrays a profound lack of knowledge about ancient history among some medieval scholars. Like Classical Greek and Roman authorities, medieval writers generally considered Egypt part of Asia, which makes sense from a cultural geography viewpoint. Africa, in this historical context, began on the western side of the Nile, while the Delta and the eastern side of the Nile were part of Asia. The so-called T-O world maps of the Middle Ages all used the Nile as a boundary between Africa and Asia. Of course, confusions among Europeans about the sources of the Nile River continued until the explorations of James Bruce for the Blue Nile and Richard Burton and John Hanning Speke for the White Nile. Very occasionally someone would place Egypt in Libya, which was another name for the continent of Africa in the medieval era.[23]

Perhaps the most outstanding confusion of medieval Europeans concerning ancient Egypt involved the pyramids. For the Greeks and Romans, a pyramid was the premier symbol of ancient Egypt. Modern culture would agree with that judgement. In the Europe of the Middle Ages, however, the situation was different. People of that era not only demoted the pyramids, they removed them from their lists of the seven wonders of the world along with other exclusively pagan structures. Lists of the seven wonders by the Gallo-Roman cleric and historian Gregory of Tours (*c.* 538–594) and the Venerable Bede (673–735) would not have been recognizable to Philo of Byzantium, the compiler of the first list of wonders. One thing that contributed to this cutting of the pyramids was that they were nowhere mentioned in the Bible. On the other hand, medieval writers added the Pharos of Alexandria to the list, which Philo did not include. He listed the walls of Babylon instead.[24]

Medieval Europeans, unlike earlier Roman writers and contemporary Muslim writers, did not use the pyramids as symbols of human ego, folly and waste. That is not to say that they did not see Egypt as a land of idolatry and excess – they did. Rather it is because they had forgotten that the original purpose of the pyramids was to serve as tombs. Instead, they thought the pyramids were the granaries of Joseph. Being granaries, the pyramids served a useful function and could not be condemned as examples of egotism and squandered resources. This error about the purpose of the pyramids originated during the era of the Roman Empire, no later than AD 333, when Egeria made her pilgrimage to the Holy Land. She also visited Egypt and saw the pyramids near Memphis. As she described it, 'There are many pyramids there which Joseph built for storing corn in.' Writing during the last quarter of the sixth century, Gregory of Tours also thought the pyramids were built by Joseph as granaries. As he described it,

> Beside the river stands the city of Babylon [originally a Roman fortress near Memphis, not the Babylon of Mesopotamia] . . . where Joseph built granaries of wonderful workmanship made of square stones and cement. They are constructed in such a way that they are very broad at the base but narrow at the top, so that corn could be poured into them through a small aperture. These granaries are still to be seen to this day.

Sometime during the eighth to the tenth centuries, a monk named Epiphanius went on a pilgrimage to the Holy Land including Egypt, where he saw the pyramids or 'the Granaries of Joseph' as he put it. The Old Testament mosaics in the narthex of the Basilica di San Marco in Venice date from around 1230 or a little after, and they include a depiction of the pyramids as granaries in the story of Joseph.[25]

Not everyone accepted that the pyramids were Joseph's granaries. Isidore of Seville (*c.* 560–636) was born into a family of nobles and high-ranking clerics in the Visigothic kingdom of Spain. Possessing one of the greatest libraries of his age, he wrote many books despite the demands of his role as archbishop of Seville. His most famous work was *Etymologies* or *Origins*, which was not quite completed at his death. In his discussion of pyramids, Isidore talked about them as both geometrical shapes and tombs. William of Boldensele visited Egypt in 1336 during his pilgrimage to the Holy Land and while there went to see the pyramids. Direct observation was enough to convince him that the massive structures were not granaries and never had been. Alas, although the author of the fictional *Travels of Sir John Mandeville* (1357) borrowed heavily from Boldensele's account of his pilgrimage, he stated, 'Some men say that they are the tombs of some great men in ancient times; but the common opinion is that they are the Barns of Joseph, and they find that in their chronicles.' Mandeville's mistaken restoration of the granaries of Joseph error did not last long; the new scholarship of the Renaissance recovered many classical sources that clearly stated that the pyramids were the tombs of pharaohs.[26]

Although the fall of the Western Roman Empire caused the volume of trade and travel to decline, it never stopped completely. Nor did diplomacy, as envoys continued to travel from the kingdoms of Western Europe to the lands of the East. Pilgrimage to the Holy Land began during the height of the Roman Empire about the time of Egeria's journey during 381–4. Holy Land pilgrimages continued throughout the Middle Ages despite the Islamic conquests of Palestine and Egypt. Merchants were the most experienced travellers since they made their journeys multiple times. They were probably the most numerous of the medieval travellers to Egypt but also the most reticent. Marco Polo was an exception. Most merchants did not write accounts of their travels, while diplomats did. Burchard of Strasbourg and Thomas of Acerra visited Egypt and the pyramids while on diplomatic missions for Frederick Barbarossa and Frederick II respectively. Crusaders visited Egypt but they were interested in conquest rather than sightseeing. Jean de Joinville (b. 1224/5) accompanied Louis IX on the Seventh Crusade but his account of the disastrous expedition to Damietta failed to mention pyramids or the Sphinx. That omission probably stems from the fact that fierce Muslim resistance prevented the crusaders from approaching Cairo. Obviously the primary destination for most pilgrims was the Holy Land but Egypt, with its numerous biblical associations, was on the itinerary for many. Besides the pyramids, pilgrims could visit St Catherine's monastery at Mount Sinai and places where Jesus, Mary and Joseph were supposed to have stayed during their time in Egypt. The Sphinx, however, was ignored. Because the lands of Upper Egypt no longer housed the capital of Egypt, had little impact on trade and had no biblical associations, very few people visited them. The great temples of Luxor, Karnak and the Valley of the Kings were unknown to medieval Europeans. The first medieval tourist, in the modern sense of the word, to visit Egypt was the Spanish noble Pero Tafur in 1436 and 1437, although many earlier pilgrims were as much tourists as they were pious travellers.[27]

Esoteric Egypt: The Origin of Hermes Trismegistus and Hermeticism

The world of Ptolemaic and Roman Egypt was the birthplace of hermeticism. It was a time when many religions flourished in the Roman Empire, most of which focused on showing their adherents how to achieve spiritual contentment and eternal salvation. Hermeticism was a religious and philosophical movement that helped its followers to achieve salvation through secret philosophical and magical knowledge gained by initiation into a selective cult through long and intense study.[28] It developed out of the writings attributed to Hermes Trismegistus and followed his supposed ideas. Other than that, hermeticism is hard to define precisely. Because the hermetic books drew heavily on other philosophical and religious concepts such as Neoplatonism, hermeticism resembles other systems of belief that never claimed any connection to Hermes Trismegistus.

Hermetic beliefs and philosophy also sometimes contradicted each other, which added further confusion. As the Egyptologist Jan Assmann observed, 'there is no "Hermeticism" in the sense of a unique and distinct movement or a single philosophical system.' At the same time, hermeticism – in the worlds of the ancient, Middle Age, Renaissance and modern civilizations – exhibited certain consistent traits that were not necessarily unique to itself. Hermeticism believed that perfect knowledge existed at the beginning of the world and the universe, but this knowledge deteriorated over time. In other words, older was better. Hermetic knowledge derived from the revelation of this ancient wisdom. Its authority was based on its age. Another trait of hermetic knowledge was that it was secret. While the biblical truths of Judaism and Christianity were open to all, the hermetic truths were only shared with a spiritual elite. That is why hermetic beliefs were written in hieroglyphs. In contrast to Gnosticism, hermeticism was optimistic, viewing the world as beautiful not evil, and humans as inherently good. To gain access to hermetic knowledge, a person had to undergo initiation and prove themselves worthy. Only a select few were allowed to be initiated and performed the rituals successfully. These were the people who were given and could handle the knowledge of the Philosopher's Stone that could change base metals into gold or provide rejuvenating elixirs. The content of the knowledge and the command of the knowledge was secondary to its age and the worthiness of the initiate. These are traits of many secret societies and give the members a sense of being special and even entitled. Thanks to Hermes Trismegistus, hermetic ideas helped create a certain type of Egyptomania that exercised a powerful and enduring attraction for people already drawn to the occult and esoteric practices. That is not to say the hermeticism in late antiquity, the Middle Ages, the Renaissance or today can be considered a mass movement or a popular cult, but it possessed and continues to exhibit a cultural influence that is not quite marginal and never quite dies out.[29]

Egypt was the homeland of hermeticism and its founder, the great sage and demigod Hermes Trismegistus. For followers of hermeticism, its origins lie in ancient Egypt, always a land of secret knowledge and mystic wisdom. It is not easy to define the nature of Hermes Trismegistus, an important but enigmatic figure. To some he was Hermes the thrice-great, an ancient and possibly divine or semi-divine sage who was a magician, astrologer and alchemist and lived in Egypt's distant past. Just how far in the past was the subject of debate among scholars, both Muslim and Christian. Most claimed he lived shortly after Moses and learned his magical skills from him. Others, however, claimed he was a contemporary of Moses or even lived before him and that he taught Moses about religion and supernatural powers. Some Jewish traditions claimed that Moses and Hermes Trismegistus were the same person. Pagan philosophers and later Renaissance scholars identified him with Thoth, the Egyptian god of wisdom and knowledge, who the Greeks equated with their god Hermes. Thoth invented writing so Renaissance scholars credited Hermes Trismegistus with inventing hieroglyphs. Other scholars suggest that Hermes Trismegistus developed out of the ancient Egyptian cult devoted to Imhotep, the legendary Egyptian wise man and inventor, who lived during the early Old Kingdom. The situation was further confused because some traditions allow for the existence of two, three or more Hermes Trismegistus. So which one of them accomplished what great act or invention was also subject to scholarly debate. Egypt has long been regarded as a land of wisdom and esoteric knowledge, so the story of Hermes Trismegistus reinforced that image and offered yet another reason for people to be fascinated by it.[30]

Although Hermes Trismegistus was an allegedly very ancient figure by the time of late Ptolemaic and Roman Egypt, his writings were actually composed by others during the Hellenistic and Roman eras. These writings partook of Platonism, Neoplatonism, Zoroastrianism, Judaism and Gnosticism with only traces of the ancient religion of the Egyptians. Hermeticism did not exist in the Egypt of the Pharaohs although aspects of it developed out of the cult of Amun. This development occurred during the era of the pharaohs named Rameses, when religious concepts similar to hermeticism appeared in the idea of a unified cosmos with a single hidden god that manifested itself in multiple divine forms. The main hermetic works were philosophical; the best-known work was *Asclepius* which had been translated into Latin. *Asclepius* was the source of St Augustine's knowledge about Hermes Trismegistus and was the only hermetic book known to medieval Western Europe. A bigger collection was the *Corpus hermeticum*, which consisted of eighteen tracts and was sometimes known as *Poimander*, after the first tract in the group. These writings did not reach Western Europe until the fifteenth century. There were other technical hermetic writings, which dealt with astrology, alchemy, magic and medicine, that became quite popular in Europe north of the Alps. Ancient writers claimed there were many more hermetic books: according to the Ptolemaic historian Manetho there were 36,525 books, while Seleucus, a first-century AD critic, claimed there were 20,000 hermetic books. Either way, if true, Hermes Trismegistus deserves a mention by the *Guinness World Records* as a most prodigiously prolific author.[31]

While Hermes Trismegistus was a pagan, that did not necessarily make him an enemy of Christianity. Lactantius (*c.* 240–320) was an early Christian scholar who viewed Hermes Trismegistus as a pagan sage whose writings such as the *Asclepius* prophesied the coming of Christianity. The source of his inspiration was divine, so that made him acceptable to Christians. St Augustine (354–430), writing some years later, took a different view of Hermes Trismegistus. Although he agreed that the hermetic writings predicted the coming of Christianity, he identified the source of that knowledge as demonic. For him, Hermes Trismegistus was a pagan danger to Christianity. Augustine's view dominated the Middle Ages but in the Renaissance, when scholars were anxious to learn from the hermetic writings, views on Hermes Trismegistus turned towards Lactantius' more congenial and tolerant assessment.[32]

Medieval Muslims had a deep respect for Hermes Trismegistus that pre-dated the Renaissance revival of hermeticism. The hermetic tradition of Muslim Egypt, however, was not unbroken. Hermeticism died out in

Egypt but not in the lands of the Sassanian Persian Empire. After the early conquests of Islam, this eastern hermeticism spread from Iran through the Islamic world from Iraq and made its way back to Egypt. Islamic scholars identified Hermes Trismegistus as the biblical patriarch Enoch, who was known as Idris by the Arabs and by the ancient Egyptians as Thoth. Medieval Muslims associated Hermes Trismegistus with alchemy. They also credited him with building the three great pyramids, one of which was his tomb. It was also said that he predicted the coming of the great flood of Noah and built the pyramids to store and to preserve the learning and science of the ancient Egyptians. Another version common among Muslims claimed there were actually three Hermes Trismegistus. The first was Enoch, who lived in Egypt before the Flood. A second Hermes lived in Babylon, another name for old Cairo, and revived science and Egyptian wisdom after the Flood. The third Hermes also lived in Egypt where he taught alchemy, mentored Asclepius and wrote the *Corpus hermeticum*. This legend of the three Hermes along with some hermetic texts and other ancient Greek books made their way to Western Europe from the Islamic lands to help fuel the Renaissance revival of hermeticism.[33]

In contrast to the worlds of late antiquity and medieval Islam, the regard for Hermes Trismegistus and hermeticism in Western Europe during the Middle Ages was at a low ebb. Various early Church Fathers such as Clement of Alexandria and Tertullian had discussed and quoted Hermes Trismegistus in some detail along with Lactantius and Augustine. These writings were well known in Western Europe. *Asclepius*, which had a great influence on medieval European views of Egypt, was available in Latin throughout the medieval period, but otherwise hermetic writings were largely unavailable. Isidore of Seville credited Hermes Trismegistus with the invention of magic. Other medieval writers thought he was a king of Egypt and that there was more than one sage named Hermes Trismegistus. By the twelfth and thirteenth centuries, Arabic hermetic texts started to appear in Latin translation. Some Christian scholars such as Peter Abelard (1079–1142) and Albertus Magnus (*c.* 1200–1280) cited Hermes Trismegistus as a fine philosopher or a great astrologer. Others valued Hermes Trismegistus for his writings on alchemy. Hermetic and Gnostic ideas also circulated in the form of the Bogomil and Cathar heresies. The somewhat opaque theologian Nicholas of Cusa used hermetic ideas to develop his concept of the coincidence of opposites as did the German mystics Meister Eckhart and Johannes Tauler. Just how much influence hermeticism had on medieval thought is difficult to gauge due to its close similarity to Neoplatonic ideas that medieval scholars also frequently cited. Medieval thought was dominated by the Catholic Church, which took a rather dim view of magic and, thanks to St Augustine, also of Hermes Trismegistus. It would take the coming of the Renaissance to revive Hermes Trismegistus' reputation.[34]

The fourteenth century witnessed the first flowerings of the Renaissance as European scholars began a sustained effort to recover the knowledge of Graeco-Roman antiquity. The revival of classical learning began in Italy and continued into the fifteenth century when it began to spread to the rest of Western Europe. Along the course of this endeavour, these scholars also recovered much of what the ancients knew about Egypt. As the next chapter shows, the dark age of limited Egyptomania in the West had ended and a new era of revitalized Egyptomania was beginning.

FIVE

EGYPTOMANIA FROM THE RENAISSANCE TO THE ENLIGHTENMENT

Pyramids, Arches, Obelisks, were but the irregularities of vain-glory, and wilde enormities of ancient magnanimity.

SIR THOMAS BROWNE[1]

The history of Egypt, as we have it, is full of the greatest contradictions. The mythical is blended with the historical, and the statements are as diverse as can be imagined.

G.W.F. HEGEL[2]

THE COMING OF the Renaissance revived Egyptomania in Western Europe. As the fifteenth century progressed, Italian scholars learned increasingly more about ancient Egypt; their new knowledge increased the scholars' desires to discover more about what they came to see as a land of mystery and magic. Ancient texts were collected and edited, and after about 1450 they began to be printed as books, which in turn reached a larger audience of readers. Medieval Europe's Bible-based view of Egypt was no longer adequate. It had to compete with the Egypt of Strabo, Plutarch and Iamblicus, all of whom presented a much more favourable image of ancient Egypt. Humanist scholars were quick to adopt the positive view of Egyptian culture and knowledge. Serious scholarly study of Egypt became possible and the discipline of Egyptology was born. Much of this early modern Egyptological scholarship, however, turned out to be wrong. Renaissance humanists could not read hieroglyphs (although some thought they could) and were bereft of the fruits of modern archaeological research. As is the pattern with the topic of ancient Egypt, revived interest often evolved into fascination, the lack of accurate knowledge about ancient Egypt led to speculation, speculation led to fantasy and thus the type of Egyptomania that still remains a part of our contemporary culture (that is, false legends and misunderstood facts) was also born during the Renaissance.[3]

Egyptomania in the Early Renaissance

More Europeans were increasingly able to travel to Egypt for trade and pilgrimage from 1400 onwards. Some of these travellers wrote accounts of what they saw and they exhibited a more discerning view than their medieval predecessors. The Italian Ciriaco de'Pizzicolli or Cyriacus of Ancona (1391–1452) visited the pyramids in 1436 and, like William of Boldensele before him, did not think they were the granaries of Joseph. Their sheer size amazed him: 'they were so huge that I would never have believed that man could raise on the earth a work of such size'. It was a reaction shared by most Renaissance visitors to the pyramids and many others throughout history.

Classical accounts describing the pyramids were more influential in forming Renaissance attitudes towards the pyramids than the accounts of contemporary travellers. By the late fifteenth century pyramids and other ancient Egyptian motifs became popular and began to possess a romantic and exotic aspect. The pyramids also regained their place among the Seven Wonders of the World when Marco Fabio Calvo (c. 1440–1527), an antiquarian, translator and friend of Raphael (1483–1520), included them in his list of the Seven Wonders. Raphael, in turn, used true pyramids in his decoration for the Chigi Chapel in Rome. Visual representations, however, generally were not realistic since they were based on the steep design of Cestius' tomb in Rome rather than the Egyptian originals. It was not until well into the sixteenth century that a fairly accurate depiction of the pyramids was produced by the architect Sebastiano Serlio. It was based on the observations and measurements taken by Cardinal Marco Grimani of Venice during his visit to Egypt in 1535. Some sixteenth-century Europeans, such as Pierre Belon du Mans (1517–1564), visited Egypt because they were interested in its archaeology. None of these visits were undertaken lightly, because Egypt during the fourteenth, fifteenth and sixteenth centuries was a dangerous place for a European to visit. Predatory locals, homicidal bandits and the fickle moods of Mameluke and Ottoman officials were an ever-present danger.[4]

Florence and Rome were the twin epicentres of the Egyptian revival in the Renaissance. The manifestations of this revival were the discovery, translation and publication of rediscovered ancient texts that referenced Egypt. These led to the renewed study of the hieroglyphs, an appreciation of

Egypt as a fount of science and magic, the collection of things Egyptian, the appearance of Egyptian motifs in art and architecture and a resurgence of hermeticism. A combination of these elements form the basis of Egyptomania. Ancient texts told of many famous Greek scholars who journeyed to Egypt to learn more about its ancient wisdom. Some of these scholarly sojourns in Egypt, such as Plato's, probably never occurred but Renaissance scholars were persuaded that the ancient Egyptians possessed secret and superior knowledge. In 1414 Poggio Bracciolini discovered the history of Ammianus Marcellinus with his translation of hieroglyphs on an obelisk. A few years later in 1419 the book hunter Cristoforo Buondelmonti found a copy of Horapollo's *Hieroglyphika*, which further increased enthusiasm for the study and decipherment of Egyptian writing. Even more exciting was the appearance of the previously unknown hermetic texts known as the *Corpus hermeticum* to join with the lonely *Asclepius* of the medieval scholars. Brother Leonard of Pistonia brought a copy to Florence in 1460 and its translation became a major project of the new Platonic Academy of Florence that had been founded just the year before. So important was the translation, in fact, that the renowned humanist Marsilio Ficino was diverted from translating Plato's works from Greek into Latin to translating the *Corpus hermeticum* instead. Thanks to the new availability of these esoteric texts, the figure of the philosopher-magician Hermes Trismegistus became a favourite among many humanists. Esotericism and occultism were given a great foundation among educated people of the Renaissance. These mystical ideas constituted a *prisca theologia* for various Renaissance scholars beginning with Ficino. They believed that a single, pure theology had existed in the primeval past. That pure theology, or *prisca theologia*, formed the foundation and united all systems of belief; it was the original religion. Unfortunately, over time, accurate knowledge of the *prisca theologia* had deteriorated and could only be imperfectly recovered. The concept itself helped to spawn all sorts of highly speculative and strange ideas and writings. Themes representative of the new Egyptomania appeared in the visual arts by the 1490s. The enigmatic *Hypnerotomachia poliphili* was published in 1499, and included a heavy dose of Egyptian symbolism.[5]

The greatest exponent of the early stage of Renaissance Egyptomania was Annius of Viterbo, an Italian originally named Giovanni Nanni (1432–1502) who became a member of the Dominican order. Proud of his Italian heritage, Annius produced historical studies claiming that the Etruscans were the most ancient people of Europe and had settled the continent by divine sanction. Etruscan culture spread directly to the Romans, making them the source of Roman civilization, not the Greeks. However, Egypt also played an important role in Annius' version of cultural diffusion. He claimed to have translated hieroglyphic documents that proved his contentions. Annius' studies were the first great example of hieroglyphic readings in the Renaissance, but his reputation has been tainted by fraudulent work. We now know that the well-meaning scholar forged documents, claimed linguistic expertise that he did not possess and presented spurious translations to bolster his claims. He even claimed to have shown that the infamous Borgia family was descended from Osiris. His archaeological dig at Viterbo in 1493 had been liberally salted with artefacts and statuary designed to prove his theories about the Etruscans and the Egyptians. Some of his contemporaries accused him of scholarly dishonesty, a charge that was later conclusively proven by the French scholar Joseph Scaliger (1540–1609). It was an inauspicious start for the new Egyptology of the Renaissance.[6]

Although Florence served as the incubator of Renaissance Egyptology and Egyptomania, Rome was the true headquarters for those interested in ancient Egypt. Renaissance Rome was the one place in the Europe of that era where a visitor could see and study a large number of Egyptian monuments and artefacts. The flow of Egyptian artefacts to Rome began with the spread of the cults of Isis and Serapis to that city during the last years of the Republic. Temples for those two gods were often decorated with genuine Egyptian artefacts. After the annexation of Egypt, Emperor Augustus had two Egyptian obelisks transported to Rome in 12 and 10 BC. Various other statues and religious objects were increasingly transported to Rome. This practice of imperial looting continued through late antiquity and even Christian emperors uprooted obelisks from Egypt and moved them to Rome and Constantinople. Since the temples of Isis and Serapis were built in the Egyptian style, they promoted an interest and a desire for Egyptian decor and interior design motifs among wealthy Romans. One of the more influential examples of this Roman Egyptomania was the pyramid-shaped tomb of Gaius Cestius Epulo erected in 12 BC. Its sides were built at a much steeper angle than the real pyramids in Egypt, but since it was the only pyramid that even well-travelled medieval Europeans were ever going to see, it became the model, albeit an inaccurate one, of what the pyramids of Egypt looked liked. Except for the pyramid of Cestius and its imitators, Egyptian architectural themes were not widely adopted in ancient Rome.[7]

Thanks to this ancient legacy, when the scholarship of the Renaissance led to a reinvigoration of interest in ancient Egypt, Rome was the one place in Europe where people could see a large amount of Egyptian artefacts without having to travel to Egypt. Popes Leo X and Clement VII, along with the banker

Agostino Chigi, utilized Egyptian motifs in the decoration of their palaces. Their example helped to popularize Egyptomania and spread it throughout Italy and into France. The selection of artefacts, however, was not very representative. There were no items from the Old Kingdom and almost none from the Middle Kingdom, while the Ramsesid era of the New Kingdom was barely represented. Instead it was artefacts from the Saite through the Ptolemaic periods that formed the most numerous of the artefacts on display in Renaissance Rome. As a result, this skewed selection of artefacts produced an image of Egypt that was more fantasy than reality. Although it provided imagery aplenty, that imagery was largely inaccurate; it resembled very little the Egypt that the research of the Egyptologists of the nineteenth and twentieth centuries would later reveal. Nevertheless, Renaissance Rome's influence helped to bring about the resurgence of Egyptomania and created the formal vocabulary used to study Egyptian artefacts and motifs until the rise of modern Egyptology in the nineteenth century.[8]

Hermes Trismegistus and the Renaissance

We tend to think of the Renaissance as an intellectual movement that presaged our modern world of rational and scientific thought; that view is correct on a certain level. It tends, however, to leave us blind to seemingly irrational and superstitious aspects within Renaissance thought. It is important to remember that Renaissance scholars put a lot of faith in the effectiveness of magic, astrology and alchemy – all the occult sciences that are today considered part of the erroneous, fringe beliefs of crackpots. In fact, Renaissance scholars appear to have given greater credence to the occult sciences than their predecessors, the clerical scholars of the Middle Ages. So when a significant body of writings ostensibly by Hermes Trismegistus were brought to Italy for translation into Latin, it is not surprising that they, and their purported author, assumed an important place in Renaissance thought.[9]

The revival of Hermes Trismegistus and hermeticism began in Florence in an Italy which was becoming increasingly fascinated with ancient Egypt. During the years 1460 to 1462 the monk Leonardo da Pistoia bought a manuscript containing fourteen dialogues in Greek that were supposedly authored by Hermes Trismegistus. He presented the manuscript to his patron Cosimo de Medici (1389–1464). Prior to receiving this gift, Cosimo had assigned the scholar Marsilio Ficino to translate the dialogues of Plato into Latin. With the arrival of Pistoia's gift, Cosimo ordered Ficino to put the translation of Plato on hold and focus his energies on translating the newly available writings of Hermes Trismegistus. Cosimo's action seems strange to a modern person. It meant that one of the pillars of the western philosophical tradition would have to await translation so that a group of writings that lay on the fringe of respectable scholarly discourses could be translated first! While that viewpoint is true today, in Cosimo's day learned people considered Hermes Trismegistus' writings to be far older than Plato (and saw him as an inspiration for Plato). In fact, in hindsight we know that the exact opposite was true. Ficino's translation was completed in 1463 and published in 1471. It became what modern scholars call the *Corpus hermeticum*.[10]

Ficino's translation of the *Corpus hermeticum* had a significant impact on Renaissance scholarship: it intensified curiosity in ancient Egypt and revived interest in hermeticism. Like his patron Cosimo, Ficino believed in the traditional view of Hermes Trismegistus. For him, Egypt was a place where wisdom originated, and Hermes Trismegistus exemplified Egyptian wisdom and was either a contemporary or a predecessor of Moses. Ficino saw strong parallels and correspondences between hermetic beliefs and the religion of Moses, hence ultimately of Christianity. There was nothing unique or new in Ficino's high regard for Hermes Trismegistus other than the fact that his translation made many more hermetic writings readily available and his reputation lent respectability to hermeticism's revival. Thanks to Ficino's translation, the *Corpus hermeticum* became the major text attributed to pharaonic Egypt in early modern Europe.[11] As will be seen later, this view was mistaken.

Along with other Renaissance scholars, Ficino believed in the existence of a *prisca theologia* – that all other religions developed out of a single true theology. Therefore, despite some degeneration, all religions still possessed some vestiges of the truth that began in the *prisca theologia*. The coming of Christianity was the fulfilment of this, so Egypt was in a sense its forerunner. In this scenario, some wise pagans served as prophets of the coming of Christ and Christianity. Of these Hermes Trismegistus was the greatest prophet and his writings *Asclepius* and the *Corpus hermeticum* contained aspects of the *prisca theologia*. For Ficino and his Renaissance colleagues, Hermes Trismegistus taught and foretold the coming of Christ in his teachings while ancient Egyptian wisdom was the best and least sullied example of the partial survival of the *prisca theologia*. Such was the reputation of Hermes Trismegistus that in 1488 he was depicted in a prominent mosaic decorating Siena Cathedral. It was a situation that could only enhance the Renaissance's fascination with Egypt.[12]

After Ficino's translation started to spread throughout Europe, other Renaissance philosophers and scholars became fascinated with Hermes

Trismegistus, hermeticism and magic. Pico della Mirandola (1463–1494) – who in the course of his studies attempted to syncretize all religions into one – worked on an assumption that Moses and the Greeks had learned their wisdom and philosophy from the Egyptians, although he also recognized the importance of Chaldean and Zoroastrian ideas. Hermetic ideas and magic appealed to all sorts of people. The maverick and dubiously orthodox Giordano Bruno and Robert Fludd asserted the importance of Hermes Trismegistus in the history of religion and philosophy. Other more respectable thinkers also used hermetic ideas. Sir Thomas More inserted hermetic concepts into the religion of the fictional society he depicted in *Utopia*. The French reformer Jacques Lefèvre d'Étaples (*c.* 1460–1536) also made significant use of hermetic ideas. Francesco Patrizi (1529–1597) was a Platonist philosopher who followed Lactantius' opinion that Hermes Trismegistus predicted the coming of Christianity in his writings. Expressing such opinions, however, attracted the unfavourable attention of the Inquisition in Patrizi's last years. Nicolaus Copernicus cited Hermes Trismegistus in his writings, advocating the heliocentric view of the universe because hermetic writings had asserted heliocentrism in late antiquity. In France, the Protestant scholar Philippe de Mornay (1549–1623) used hermetic ideas to prove the truth of Christianity by showing that pre-Christian religions contained aspects of monotheism and the Trinity in their doctrines. He also hoped to use this fundamental unity of religions to reduce the increasingly violent religious divisions that were rending French and European society.[13]

Ficino's hermeticism and his Hermes Trismegistus was not the only hermetic tradition in Renaissance Europe. Whereas Platonism, Neoplatonism and hermeticism dominated Italian philosophy, north of the Alps the dominant hermeticism was focused on alchemy and the medical ideas of Paracelsus. That identification became so closely entwined that for many northern Europeans hermeticism was alchemy. This alchemical approach towards hermeticism emphasized the quest to understand the mysteries of the universe and nature. Discovery would bring enlightenment and happiness. Such discoveries, however, were not to be shared widely. They were the prerogative of a select elite. As Florian Ebeling has succinctly noted: 'A Hermetist was someone who guarded a mystery that obliged him to secrecy.' Not surprisingly, as will be discussed in a later chapter, early Rosicrucians, who had a great interest in hermetic lore, claimed Hermes Trismegistus for their own. Otherwise, the philosophic hermeticism of Ficino did not readily penetrate into Germany or beyond.[14]

The heyday enjoyed by Hermes Trismegistus and hermeticism during the late fifteenth and sixteenth centuries was not to last. Other scholars were growing sceptical, and with good reason. Renaissance scholarship sought to recover the learning of the Greeks and Romans and restore it to purity. Greek, Latin, Hebrew and other ancient languages were studied intensely, more texts were studied and edited, and the techniques and tools of philology continued to improve. As a result, some scholars started to question the antiquity of the hermetic writings and the very existence of Hermes Trismegistus. Early on, the foremost German Hebraist Johann Reuchlin (1455–1522) asserted that Moses and Hebrew traditions, including the Kabbala, were older and superior to the wisdom of Hermes Trismegistus. His argument only served to increase the respect of Renaissance scholars for Egyptian knowledge and hermeticism. The French classical philologist Adrien Turnèbe (1512–1565), a professor of Greek at the Collège Royal in Paris, expressed doubts about the antiquity of the hermetica. His student Gilbert Genebrand (1535–1597), a professor of Hebrew, agreed and went further by re-dating Hermes Trismegistus to 303 BC during the Ptolemaic Dynasty. In 1567 he published this claim in the first edition of his *Chronographia* and based his argument on an analysis of the Platonic elements in the hermetic writings. When he brought out a revised edition of the *Chronographia* in 1580, he added more elaborate justifications by pointing out anachronistic references to the Sibyls in *Poimander* and the mention of the fifth-century BC Greek sculptor Phidias in *Asclepius*. A few years later the Italian Theodoro Angelucci (d. *c.* 1600) disputed the anti-Aristotelian ideas of Francesco Patrizi in his book *Exercitationes* (1585). He also asserted that Hermes Trismegistus was a fake and cited Genebrand's *Chronographia* as part of his evidence.[15]

The man who produced the definitive debunking of the antiquity of the hermetic books was Isaac Casaubon (1559–1614). Born in Geneva to French Protestant parents, he developed into the most gifted scholar of Greek in the Europe of his day. He taught at the Academy of Geneva and the University of Montpellier until 1599. Henry IV of France invited him to Paris and put him in charge of the royal library. While in Paris, Casaubon changed his focus from Classical Greek to the study of early Christian writings in Greek. When Henry IV was assassinated in 1610, Casaubon left France for the patronage of James I, the Protestant king of England. As a staunch Protestant, he also became embroiled in the religious controversies that raged in Europe. The Roman Catholic historian and cardinal Caesar Baronius (1538–1607) had published the twelve volumes of the *Annales ecclesiastici* between 1588 and 1607. This massive work was a refutation of the Protestant history the *Magdeburg Centuries*. Casaubon disagreed with Baronius' work and researched a detailed rebuttal, *De rebus sacris et ecclesiasticis exercitiones* (Exercises on Sacred and Ecclesiastical Matters), which was published in 1614. Death prevented Casaubon from refuting Baronius' entire twelve volumes but what he did complete contained the famous chapter which debunked the authorship and antiquity of Hermes Trismegistus' writings. For Casaubon, the chapter on hermetic writings was a small part of his evidence discrediting Baronius' scholarship. He was also aware that previous scholars had expressed similar doubts about the antiquity of Hermes Trismegistus and his writings dating to the time of Moses or earlier. His argument was based on more detailed philological and contextual evidence than Genebrand's and concluded that the hermetic books had been composed during the early Christian era. Their use of scriptural references was a common practice of the early Church Fathers, while they also utilized a style and format that was characteristic of the pagan philosophers of Imperial Rome and late antiquity. Furthermore the ideas expressed in the text were derived from Greek philosophy rather than ancient Egypt. The hermetic writings also contained anachronisms and inconsistencies that made it impossible for them to have been composed before the Hellenistic and Roman eras in Egypt. Nor could they have been written by one man.[16]

Casaubon's main purpose was to discredit Baronius, but he more effect-ively undercut Hermes Trismegistus' reputation. Catholic scholars came to the defence of Baronius but none attempted a rebuttal of Casaubon's debunking of Hermes Trismegistus. One of Baronius' defenders, Julius Caesar Bulenger, even agreed with Casaubon's conclusions about the her-metica. Hermann Conring (1606–1681), in a study published in 1648 on the relationship between ancient Egyptian medicine and Paracelsian medicine, declared that all books claiming to be written by Hermes Trismegistus were fakes. The German professor of philosophy Christoph Meiners (1747–1810) agreed with both Casaubon's dating of the hermetic writings and his contention that they presented Neoplatonic ideas rather than ancient Egyptian ones. Thanks to Casaubon's scholarship, the reputation of Hermes Trismegistus declined during the seventeenth century. Most scholars no longer saw a close connection between the hermetic writings and ancient Egypt and seldom cited them. But Hermes Trismegistus and hermeticism did not die out. Hermeticism survived by emphasizing its elite practitioners' access to primordial wisdom while de-emphasizing or even ignoring the earlier prominence of Hermes Trismegistus and ancient Egypt. Some respectable and highly learned scholars, most notably Athanasius Kircher, ignored Casaubon's scholarship and continued to treat Hermes Trismegistus as a sage from ancient Egypt who wrote the hermetic books.[17]

Esoteric Egypt: Hieroglyphs

Hieroglyphs were the other legacy of ancient Egypt that fuelled the Renaissance's concept of an esoteric Egyptian civilization possessed of magical and occult secrets – an image based on a complete misunderstanding of hieroglyphs as a writing system. Egyptian inscriptions and hieroglyphs – pictures of birds, snakes, plants and various symbols jostling with each other – have always fascinated people. It was often difficult to determine where the hieroglyphic writing ended and the pictorial reliefs began. Herodotus and other Greek visitors gazed with wonder at the hieroglyphic inscriptions that covered the walls of temples and monuments throughout Egypt. They imagined that the Egyptian priests and scribes had recorded historical, religious, philosophic and scientific knowledge in those inscriptions. And to a certain extent the Greeks were right. The problem was that hieroglyphic writing was difficult to learn and cumbersome to write. To ease the task of writing, the hieratic script evolved out of hieroglyphs but both systems were complex and therefore remained the monopoly of a priestly and scribal elite. Less than 1 per cent of the Egyptian population was literate. It was a system supported by the vast wealth accumulated by the temples of pharaonic Egypt and which persisted into the years of Ptolemaic and Roman rule.

Pharaonic civilization in Egypt succumbed to the slow processes of Hellenization, Roman imperialism and Christianization. The old temples of the Egyptian gods continued to function into the late fourth and early fifth centuries in outlying areas but they were dying institutions. The last dateable hieroglyphic inscription was composed at the temple on Philae Island far south on the Nile River in AD 490 or 494. Shortly after that the knowledge needed to write in hieroglyphs died out. No one was left who understood the true nature of hieroglyphs and various fanciful and incorrect theories developed. Even Greeks like Herodotus, who visited Egypt when there was a living and flourishing culture of hieroglyphic writing, tended to view the characters as symbolic of ideas and concepts rather than mostly representing sounds. The view of hieroglyphs as symbolic and even allegorical became solidified in late antiquity when the writings of Plutarch (*c.* 46–*c.* 121), Plotinus (205–269/70), Iamblichus (*c.* 250–325) and Ammianus Marcellinus (*c.* 330–after 378) gave hieroglyphs a Neoplatonic interpretation. The appearance of the *Hieroglyphica* of Horapollo (*c.* 450–500) codified this view in a sort of reference guide to the allegorical meaning of 189 hieroglyphs.[18]

After the fall of the Roman Empire in the West, medieval Europeans only had a very limited knowledge of hieroglyphs. They also had little opportunity to see hieroglyphs at first hand unless they visited Rome and saw the obelisks there. As noted above, Isidore of Seville was among those who studied Egypt, and he mentioned hieroglyphs in his *Etymologies*. Otherwise, medieval European scholars were limited to the classical works that had survived in the West, which did not include Horapollo's *Hieroglyphica*. They did have some knowledge of the Coptic language, which they called Egyptian. As a result, speculations about the allegorical nature of hieroglyphs and the secret, even magical, knowledge they contained were at a low ebb. In contrast, medieval Muslims had plenty of contact with hieroglyphs either because they lived in Egypt or they visited the country. Serious interest in ancient Egyptian writing began as early as the seventh century AD. Having access to the Neoplatonic writings of late antiquity, they did speculate that the hieroglyphs on the temple walls were an antediluvian attempt to preserve ancient wisdom from destruction by fire or flood. They recognized that Egyptians used three different types of scripts and even managed to determine the correct meaning and usage of some hieroglyphs; lacking a Rosetta Stone, however, they failed to make the complete breakthrough of decipherment that Champollion achieved in the early nineteenth century. Later on, some European scholars, most notably the seventeenth-century polymath Athanasius Kircher, would use medieval Muslim writings about ancient Egypt and hieroglyphs for his own research.[19]

The revival of Western European interest in hieroglyphs began about the same time as the appearance of the *Corpus hermeticum* and Ficino's translation. Cristoforo Buondelmonti, a manuscript hunter from Florence, discovered a copy of Horapollo's *Hieroglyphica* on Andros Island in 1419. Bringing it back to Italy, in 1422 he gave it to Niccolò Niccoli (1364–c. 1437), who was a prodigious collector of manuscripts and was also studying Ammianus Marcellinus's comments on hieroglyphs. Niccoli and his friend the great antiquarian Poggio Bracciolini (1380–1459) together toured and studied the many Egyptian monuments in Rome. Their investigations caused Poggio to conclude that hieroglyphs were a kind of writing and not mere decoration. Their contemporary Leon Battista Alberti (1404–1472) took enthusiasm for hieroglyphs a step further. Hieroglyphs were a symbolic form of writing that the Egyptians invented to preserve their knowledge even if Egyptian civilization collapsed and were supposedly a higher form of writing that was a universal form of communication. They stood above the various other spoken languages and alphabets and could communicate across the ages. Another thing that Alberti found attractive about hieroglyphs was that they were an elite form of writing that was not accessible to the common people. Alberti used decorative hieroglyphic emblems in some of his building designs, and he advocated that hieroglyphs should be used for

Athanasius Kircher (1602–1680) was a Jesuit polymath considered by some to be the founder of Egyptology. From Giorgio de Sepibus, Romani Collegii musaeum celeberrimum (1678).

inscriptions on buildings and monuments instead of the Roman alphabet. The problem was that scholars and artists of fifteenth-century Italy had limited familiarity with the appearance of real hieroglyphs.[20]

The Italian Renaissance's craze for hieroglyphs attracted fraud and fantasy. Annius of Viterbo, the prolific fraud of Italian antiquarianism, claimed to have translated some hieroglyphic inscriptions. It turned out that the inscriptions were neither Egyptian nor correctly translated. Fantasy came in the form of the enigmatic *Hypnerotomachia poliphili* written by Francesco Colonna and published in 1499, although scholars are still arguing about which man of the several with that name was the actual author. The book contained a number of hieroglyphs in its illustrations along with other Egyptian material, but the hieroglyphs were made-up rather than true hieroglyphs. At the time, however, Annius of Viterbo's and the *Hypnerotomachia*'s hieroglyphs were widely accepted as genuine. A fashion for creating new hieroglyphs appeared in late fifteenth-century Italy.[21]

Within a few years of the publication of the *Hypnerotomachia*, a Greek edition of Horapollo's *Hieroglyphica* was published in 1505 by the renowned publishing house of Aldus Manutius of Venice. Neither the original Greek manuscript nor this printed Greek edition contained illustrations of hieroglyphs. It was not until 1515 that the first published Latin translation included illustrations of hieroglyphic writing, in this case by Albrecht Dürer. Together the *Hypnerotomachia* and the printed versions of Horapollo heightened the passion for hieroglyphs during the Renaissance era and aided its spread outside of Italy. All the while, the idea of hieroglyphs as a symbolic and allegorical perfect language remained largely unquestioned.[22]

Some of the great names of the sixteenth century participated in the growing ardour for hieroglyphs and hieroglyphic motifs. The artist Raphael and his circle in Rome liked to use hieroglyphic motifs in the decorative designs of their buildings. Another enthusiast was Emperor Maximilian I (r. 1493–1519). A knight errant among the European rulers of his day, Maximilian I had humanistic and mystical interests which were tempered by his limited budget. He became interested in tracing his own ancestry back to Hercules Aegyptius, which was another name for the mythical all-conquering Egyptian king Sesotris. This goal fuelled his interest in hieroglyphs and all things Egyptian. One manifestation of this interest was Maximilian I ordering the German humanist Willibald Pirckheimer (1470–1530) to translate Horapollo into Latin, a task he finished in 1514. The greatest humanist scholar north of the Alps, Erasmus (*c.* 1466–1536), did not only approve of hieroglyphic studies, but held them in high esteem. His endorsement made such study both fashionable and respectable among German humanists. Interest in hieroglyphic studies and Neoplatonism had reached France by the beginning of the sixteenth century. The notorious French astrologer Nostradamus (1503–1566) became interested in hieroglyphic studies and Egyptian wisdom prior to his more famous career as a prophet. Around 1545 he wrote an unpublished paraphrase of the entire text of Horapollo's *Hieroglyphica* about two years before giving his first astrological consultation. The most influential Renaissance study of hieroglyphs was Pierio Valeriano's (1477–1558) *Hieroglyphica*, which was published in 1556. It went through many printings and editions and was translated into French and German. Valeriano had begun studying hieroglyphs as just another ancient writing system but shifted, over a lifetime of study, to regard them as a perfect, universal and timeless form of communication. His *Hieroglyphica* was the most authoritative study available from the late sixteenth to the early eighteenth centuries. A printed source for illustrations of authentic hieroglyphs finally appeared in 1610 with the publication of Johann Georg Herwarth von Hohenburg's *Thesaurus hieroglyphicorum*. It was published without explanatory text and also unfortunately included illustrations of hieroglyphs that were not genuine. Despite containing errors and lacking salient information, thanks to this underappreciated classic of early Egyptology, scholars could see hieroglyphs without having to travel to Rome or Egypt.[23]

Athanasius Kircher (1602–1680) was a Jesuit scholar whose writings mark the culmination of respectable scholarship that believed in an esoteric Egypt, the great antiquity of Hermes Trismegistus, and that hieroglyphs were a symbolic system of perfect communication. Born in Geisa in Germany, he entered the Jesuit Order in 1616. After spending four years as a novice, he continued his studies and was ordained in 1628. He wanted to be a missionary in China but Jesuit officials felt his gifts as a scholar and teacher were better used as a teacher of mathematics and Middle Eastern languages in the Jesuit colleges. The terrors of the Thirty Years War forced him to leave Germany. Taking refuge in Avignon, he developed a friendship with the great French antiquarian Nicolas-Claude Fabri de Peiresc (1580–1635). While in Speyer during 1628, Kircher read a book about the Egyptian obelisks in Rome which sparked his interest in the study of ancient Egypt. His goal was to decipher hieroglyphs by mastering the modern descendant of ancient Egyptian – the Coptic language. He asked Peiresc to help him and the French scholar used his connections to get him the position of professor of mathematics at the Society of Jesus college in Rome in 1633. His first book on ancient Egypt was *Prodromus coptus sive Aegyptiacus* (1636). It included the first published grammar of Coptic and argued correctly that old Egyptian and Coptic were closely related. Over the next twenty years he published other books on Egyptian topics; his magnum opus was the multi-volume *Oedipus Aegyptiacus* (1652–5). Kircher's books provided his readers with access to the lore and artefacts of ancient Egypt. He also helped to found the museum of the Jesuit College of Rome, which contained considerable Egyptian material. Umberto Eco called Kircher 'the father of Egyptology . . . in spite of the fact that his main hypothesis was wrong'.[24]

Kircher engaged in prodigious research on ancient Egypt but, apart from linking Egyptian and Coptic together, he was largely wrong in his conclusions. By 1636 he was claiming to be on the verge of unlocking the mysteries of the hieroglyphs. He would later publish various translations of hieroglyphic inscriptions that spouted purported hermetic wisdom. They were all woefully wrong and most of his contemporaries knew it. The root of Kircher's errors lies in his Neoplatonic assumptions, which caused him to concentrate on a symbolic system for the communication of ideas. Neoplatonism taught that ideas were the ultimate reality and Kircher believed that by unlocking the secrets of the hieroglyphs he would provide a pathway to that realm of ideas. The hermetic writings of late antiquity incorporated Neoplatonic ideas. Kircher, however, believed that these writings were the products of that great sage and teacher Hermes Trismegistus, who lived much further back in ancient Egypt. Although Kircher was not yet a teenager when Casaubon published his debunking of the antiquity of the hermetic books, later the mature Kircher would chose to reject and refute Casaubon's findings. He was not alone in his rejection of Casaubon, whose scholarship was suspect among Roman Catholics due to the author's Protestantism.[25]

Kircher's Neoplatonic worldview traced the beginning of the true and sacred knowledge of humans all the way back to Adam. God had taught Adam this great wisdom in the Garden of Eden, and the true and good knowledge was passed down through time to Noah, but it had to compete with the corrupt and evil heresies and sorceries that had their start with Cain. Unfortunately Noah's son Ham combined the two kinds of know-ledge, both good and bad. After the Flood, Ham (who was the Osiris of the Egyptians) passed this hybrid knowledge on to his son Mizraim, the founder of Egypt. Despite this tarnished pedigree, Kircher held Egyptian wisdom in the highest regard. He also dated that foremost of Egyptian sages Hermes Trismegistus to the time of Abraham rather than Moses. For Kircher, Hermes Trismegistus was not only the inventor of hieroglyphs, but a prophet of God. At the same time, Kircher believed that there were two Hermes. The first lived before the Flood and built the pyramids to preserve Egypt's wisdom from destruction; the second was the post-Flood Hermes Trismegistus. The knowledge of Hermes Trismegistus was pre-served and hidden in the hieroglyphs. Kircher's fundamental purpose in tracing all this wisdom back to Adam was to establish the equation that Adamic wisdom came directly from God, Egyptian wisdom was derived from Adamic wisdom and the Roman Catholic Church was the heir of that tradition of knowledge. Being the inheritor of all that venerable sacred knowledge justified the Roman Catholic Church's right to unify humanity under its religious teachings and its rule. Given that view of history, it is no wonder that Kircher rejected and ignored Casaubon's conclusion that the hermetica were pseudo-epigraphic writings from late antiquity.[26]

With considerable justification, Anthony Grafton has characterized Athanasius Kircher as 'that maddest of polymaths and most learned of madmen'. It is important to remember that the study of hieroglyphs was only one part of Kircher's studies and that their decipherment was a means to an end. At the same time, as Daniel Stolzenberg has made clear, Kircher very much wanted the fame of being the man who deciphered the hieroglyphs. Kircher has been called the 'last man who knew everything'. His writings sought to unify human knowledge by bringing together the truths of history, philosophy, religion and science into a universal system of Neoplatonic Christianity led by the Roman Catholic Church. He failed, but his achievements, such as they were, were not without a lasting impact. Largely thanks to his efforts, Egyptology emerged as a separate discipline in the world of academic scholarship. His contemporaries, the English scholars John Spencer (1630–1693) and Ralph Cudworth (1617–1688), helped with the emergence of Egyptology but Kircher played the greater role. At the same time, his failure to decipher hieroglyphs discouraged others from attempting the task until the discovery of the Rosetta Stone provided the essential key.[27] The image of a mystic Egypt survived Casaubon's sceptical investigations but its proponents found themselves fighting to preserve it against the assaults of the rationalism of the Enlightenment of the eighteenth century.

Esoteric Egypt and the Enlightenment

English scholars came late to an interest in Egypt and its esotericism. The accounts of English travellers to Egypt, China and other distant countries fuelled an interest in lands beyond Europe. Egypt, with its outstanding antiquities, the pyramids and the Sphinx, and its prominent place in the biblical narrative, drew more than its fair share of the enthusiasm for the mysteries of foreign lands. In 1646 John Greaves, a professor of astronomy and mathematics at Oxford, published *Pyramidographia*, which made him the first Englishman to write a book devoted to Egyptian antiquities. A second book, *Pyramidologia*, followed in 1663. Both books contributed to a growing scientific attitude towards the study of ancient Egypt; moreover they also initiated the craze for measuring the pyramids to discover deep secrets coded in their architecture and dimensions – a craze that remains active to this day. As English scholars learned more about ancient Egypt, they became troubled by the reality that Egyptian chronology appeared to be older than biblical chronology would allow. As a result, English scholars determined to support the traditional biblical chronology rejected the idea of a long Egyptian chronology. Sir Isaac Newton, although most famous for his scientific discoveries, late in life made a foray into chronology. His *The Chronology of Ancient Kingdoms Amended*, posthumously published in 1728, like the scholarship of Newton's contemporaries, tried to reconcile

Egyptian chronology to the standard biblical chronology. It was a losing battle because by the end of the eighteenth century the traditional Christian view of biblical history and the history of the ancient world faced severe challenges from continuing chronological research.[28]

The struggle over the relationship between Egyptian and biblical chronology was closely connected to hermeticism's struggle to survive the criticism of sceptical rationalism. Casaubon's dating of the hermetic writings to the centuries of late antiquity undermined their connection to ancient Egyptian wisdom and called into question the very existence of Hermes Trismegistus. Sir Francis Bacon (1561–1626) rejected the previously common belief that ancient wisdom, particularly Egyptian, was superior or even particularly valuable in comparison with modern knowledge. He was followed by John Woodward (1665–1728), a professor of geology at Cambridge, who scoffed at mummification, denied that hieroglyphs contained secret wisdom and viewed Egyptian religion as ridiculous. In Germany, Hermann Conring in 1648 attacked the validity of both ancient and modern medicine with devastating effect. The growth of scientific rationalism challenged hermetic and Neoplatonic views that the realm of ideas possessed a greater reality than the material world.[29]

Hermes Trismegistus and hermetic ideas were not dead in seventeenth-century England. The wide-ranging author Sir Thomas Browne (1605–1682) wrote his *Religio medici* in 1636 and stated that 'the severe Schooles shall never laugh me out of the Philosophy of Hermes, that this visible world is but a picture of the invisible.' Isaac Newton believed that God had revealed the true nature of existence to the hermetic philosophers in the form of the *prisca theologia*. But the outstanding exponent of hermetic or at least Neoplatonic ideas with a focus on Egypt was Ralph Cudworth. Cudworth was one of the leading Cambridge Platonists, a loose group of liberal Protestants who objected to both severe Calvinism and the atheistic tendencies of Thomas Hobbes and Baruch Spinoza's materialism. Anxious to prove that monotheism was the original religion of humanity, Cudworth wrote *The True Intellectual System of the Universe* (1678). Cudworth argued that if monotheism was the original and universal religion of ancient people, then that proved that monotheism was the true religion. It was an idea he derived from the earlier English philosopher Edward Lord Herbert of Cherbury (1583–1648), but Cudworth went on to attempt to prove it by producing a wide-ranging study of ancient religions and philosophy. Using the *Corpus hermeticum*, Horapollo and other ancient writings, he claimed that the Egyptian elite believed in an 'arcane theology' that was actually monotheistic although polytheism was the religion of the common people of Egypt. As Cudworth asserted, 'notwithstanding this multifarious poly-theism and idolatry of these Egyptians . . . they did nevertheless acknowledge one supreme and universal Numen.' Moses learned this monotheism from the Egyptian elite and taught it to the Israelites. Thus an entire people and not just a narrow elite came to practise monotheism. The problem for Cudworth was that he needed to refute Casaubon's analysis that the hermetic writings were fakes dating from late antiquity. Cudworth believed that Egypt was the original home of knowledge. According to Cudworth, Casaubon was wrong in that only three of the sixteen hermetic treatises were fakes. Furthermore, he argued that the hermetic writings marked the end of a long philosophical and religious tradition rather than its beginning. Hermetic beliefs were based on very ancient Egyptian beliefs going all the way back to that original monotheism. The phrase *hen kai pen*, meaning 'all-oneness', was for Cudworth the succinct expression of this monotheism. When this concept reached Greece it produced the Stoic and Neoplatonic philosophy that brought these Egyptian ideas to the West. In this effort, Cudworth revived the reputation of Hermes Trismegistus and hermeticism for the eighteenth century. His use of Egyptian themes and materials in his research has caused some modern scholars to consider him to be a founder of Egyptology along with Athanasius Kircher.[30]

Another early Egyptologist was John Spencer (1630–1693), the English Hebraist and the author of *De legibus hebraeorum* (1685). He argued that Egyptian customs were the source and inspiration for Hebrew ritual law. His sources were limited to the Bible and classical authors but despite the lack of access to genuine Egyptian sources, he was able to present a compelling case for Egyptian influence on early Judaism. The person who brought Egyptian religious concepts and practices to the Hebrews was, of course, Moses. Spencer professed to have a negative opinion of Egyptian religion and rituals but his book had the opposite effect on other eighteenth-century scholars. Thanks to the influence of Spencer, the eighteenth century experi-enced an outbreak of enthusiasm for Egypt comparable to Ficino's revival of hermeticism in the second half of the fifteenth century. Spencer's research also honoured him, as he was subsequently considered to be the founder of the discipline of comparative religion. Sixty years later William Warburton (1698–1779), an English clergyman who became Bishop of Gloucester in 1759, entered the debate over Egyptian influence on the ancient Hebrews with his two-volume *The Divine Legation of Moses* (1737–41). His intention was to combat deism and he used Egyptian evidence to prove his orthodox contentions about the existence of the 'arcane theology' and monotheism in Egypt. He argued that governments, including ancient Egypt's, used the fear of divine judgement and punishment to support the authority of the state. The Jews of the Old Testament did not have this concept and, for Warburton, that meant they were under the protection of God's providence. That protection, however, did not stop them from being attracted to Egyptian religion and culture. Warburton contended that 'invincibly do the Hebrew records support the Grecian evidence for the high antiquity of Egypt. And . . . in the constant attributes of antiquity and wisdom, they bestow on the Egyptian nation.' At the same time, he rejected both the idea that the Egyptian religion was a true, albeit natural, religion that decisively influenced Moses and that the Hebrews had taught the Egyptians. But Warburton's arguments did not lead to the refutation of deism, atheism or materialism. Instead, the advocates of these beliefs and philosophies were able to mine Warburton's considerable research to support their own positions that God and nature were one and the same thing. By the last decades of the eighteenth century, this view came to be called 'cosmotheism' and was essentially a coming together of deist religion, Spinozian philosophy and Egyptomania. Instead of rationalizing Egypt, the main impact of Cudworth, Spencer and Warburton's Egyptological studies was to support the image of an esoteric Egypt rather than undermine it.[31]

The eighteenth century experienced a growing scholarly interest in the practice and the results of archaeological investigation. Although the primary focus of this rise of systematic archaeology was classical antiquity, its methods and standards were also applied to the study of ancient Egypt. One of the leaders of the rise of archaeology as a true academic discipline was Bernard de Montfaucon (1655–1741), a Benedictine monk who also founded the discipline of palaeography – the study of ancient handwriting – and edited the writings of the Early Church Fathers. Although Egypt was not a primary focus of his research, he did make a substantial contribution to Egyptology with his *L'Antiquité expliquée et representée en figures* (1719–24), a critical and descriptive listing of the Egyptian monuments located in Rome and other parts of Italy. Montfaucon was a staunchly empirical scholar who rejected the esotericism and occultism that permeated the Egyptian scholarship of his predecessors from the Renaissance and the seventeenth century. He did not believe ancient Egypt possessed any special or hidden wisdom and, furthermore, he insisted that its religion and art were bizarre or even horrible. His book provided a useful guide to the terminology and concepts of early Egyptological scholarship.

William Warburton in his *Divine Legation of Moses* also tried to demystify ancient Egypt through his effort to discredit Athanasius Kircher's effort to assign deep and hidden meanings to the hieroglyphs. In 1775 Georg

Christoph Meiners, a scholar at the University of Göttingen, published a historical study of ancient religion titled *Versuch uber die Religionsgeschichte de altesten Volker besonders der Egyptier*. It was an example of the growing rejection of hermeticism by Enlightenment thinkers. Meiners praised Casaubon's debunking of the hermetic texts and he consigned Hermes Trismegistus to the realm of myth. Georg Zoëga, a Danish archaeologist and a Protestant, produced a record of Egyptian monuments in Rome in 1797 at the request of Pope Pius VI. In the course of its listing, it summarized the Egyptological knowledge of its day. Zoëga was a rationalist who rejected any suggestion that Egyptian monuments contained material of esoteric symbolism, and he was a realist about the impossibility of deciphering the hieroglyphs with the resources available to scholars at the end of the eighteenth century. It was the work of men like Montfaucon and Zoëga that largely banished views sympathetic to an occult image of Egypt from academic scholarship, although not, it would seem, from popular culture.[32]

By the middle decades of the eighteenth century, travellers' accounts with increasingly accurate illustrations of Egyptian monuments and inscriptions began to appear. Benoit de Maillet, the French consul in Cairo, published his experiences as *Description de l'Egypte* (1735), which included descriptions of the ancient monuments. The Danish naval officer Frederik Ludvig Norden (1708–1742) explored Egypt for eight months between 1737 and 1738, which resulted in the illustrated book *Drawings of Some Ruins and Colossal Statues at Thebes in Egypt* (1741). An expanded account of his travels and research appeared posthumously in 1755 as *Voyage d'Egypte et de Nubie*. Richard Pococke (1704–1765) was an Englishman who made his living as a churchman working in the Church of Ireland, eventually becoming Bishop of Ossory in 1756 and of Meath in 1765. He made his reputation as a travel writer beginning in 1743 with the first volume of his *A Description of the East and Some Other Countries*, titled *Observations on Egypt*, which contained architectural plans and illustrations of various monuments. While the contents were not particularly original, it provided the educated reading public with images of ancient Egypt that hitherto had been largely confined to scholars. Despite these additions to the literature of Egyptology, the quantity of good source material for the study of Egypt remained small.[33]

As long as hieroglyphs remained undeciphered, the written records of ancient Egypt remained inaccessible. Renaissance scholars did not make a distinction between genuine hieroglyphs and modern copies. This situation changed at the beginning of the seventeenth century with the works of Michele Mercati (1541–1593) and Lorenzo Pignoria (1571–1631).

Seventeenth-century scholars also abandoned the Neoplatonic approach of trying to interpret hieroglyphs metaphysically. They studied hieroglyphs using the techniques of philology but given the limits of their available resources little progress was made. The late seventeenth century and the eighteenth were also obsessed with the quest for a universal language that could be perfectly understood by all peoples in all periods of history. It was the language of Adam from the Garden of Eden that Hermes Trismegistus had put into written form when he invented the hieroglyphic system. This faith in the existence of a perfect Adamic language and Hermes Trismegistus faded during the eighteenth century, with opponents such as William Warburton rejecting the idea that hieroglyphs were a mystical writing system that concealed secret knowledge from all but an elite of initiates. For him, hieroglyphs were a normal writing system that was developed for the practical purpose of communication by ordinary people. After Warburton, European scholars during the second half of the eighteenth century largely gave up efforts to decipher hieroglyphs. Contributions like that of the French antiquarian Anne Claud Philippe, Comte de Caylus (1692–1765), compiled reproductions of hieroglyphs along with other ancient inscriptions. In lectures published in 1761 and 1763 Abbé Jean-Jacques Barthélemy (1716–1795) correctly guessed that the cartouches in hieroglyphic inscriptions might be royal names. Joseph de Guignes (1721–1800) agreed with Barthélemy's guess and expanded on it in 1785. For these men, hieroglyphs were a system of writing, unique but not supernatural.[34]

Johann Gottfried von Herder (1744–1803) was no Enlightenment rationalist but rather a budding Romantic with a Pietistic twist, yet he exemplified the rejection of mysterious Egyptian knowledge lying concealed in the hieroglyphs. In his *Reflections on the Philosophy of the History of Mankind* (1784–91) Herder asserted that, 'instead of inferring profound wisdom from the hieroglyphics of the Egyptians, they rather demonstrate the reverse.' He denied that hieroglyphs were a great demonstration of the superiority of ancient Egyptian civilization; rather 'the hieroglyphics of the Egyptians were rather injurious than beneficial to science. . . . Hence Egypt has always remained a child in knowledge, because it always expressed its knowledge as a child, and its infantile ideas are probably for ever lost to us.' Despite this growing rational and empirical approach that characterized eighteenth-century scholarship, a mystical and occult view survived in popular culture. It also survived in some respectable academic circles. Karl Leonhard Reinhold (1757–1823) was a professor at the University of Jena. He was also a Freemason and advocated, anonymously, the reality of Egyptian wisdom. His ideas were spread further by Friedrich Schiller (1759–1805), the poet, playwright and historian who was also a professor at Jena. In his essay of 1790, 'Die Sendung Moses' (The Legation of Moses), he elaborated on Reinhold and attempted to reconcile the deism of the Enlightenment with the sublime and hidden wisdom concealed in the hieroglyphic writings of Egypt. Esoteric Egypt continued to survive the Enlightenment's scepticism.[35]

Even if many scholars no longer accepted the idea of an esoteric Egypt possessing unimaginable and powerful ancient wisdom, they still credited Egypt with a prime or the primary role in the origins of human civilization. Eighteenth-century historians believed that Egypt was the first and therefore the oldest civilization. In turn, they assumed that civilization diffused from Egypt to other parts of the world. In 1741 eight men, all of whom had visited Egypt, founded the Egyptian Society of London. The society's president was John Montagu, the Earl of Sandwich, who believed that Egypt was the source of all arts and sciences. Among the other members were Richard Pococke, Frederik Norden and the antiquary William Stukeley. Pococke and others thought that ancient Egyptians had founded a colony in England. Stukeley claimed that the ancient druids of Britain had connections to Egypt, an assertion that William Warburton rejected, as did other thinkers of the Enlightenment including David Hume. Despite these objections other theories about the diffusion of civilization from Egypt continued to appear. Sir Isaac Newton's chronology of the ancient world had Egyptian kings engaged in wars of conquest on the Ganges River in 974 BC. Joseph de Guignes claimed that the Egyptians had colonized China and that Chinese writing was based on Egyptian hieroglyphic writing.[36] The belief that civilization had diffused from Egypt throughout the world remained popular among scholars for many years and continues to make periodic reappearances in the pseudo-historical writings.

The results of the new archaeology and the appearance of readily available travellers' accounts describing ancient Egypt combined with the biblical narrative and the classical authors to spark a fad for Egyptomania in literature, art and secret societies. Especially influential was Abbé Jean Terrasson's novel *Sethos* (1731), which depicted Egyptian religion as mysterious and magical, featuring dark rituals and initiations, some of which took place in secret chambers in the pyramids. In this view Terrasson was not alone. When the naturalist Thomas Shaw visited Cairo in 1721 he concluded that the pyramid of Cheops was a temple and speculated that hidden tunnels connected all of the pyramids. Later, in 1741, the traveller Charles Perry, probably influenced by Shaw and Terrasson, also suggested that the pyramids were used for rituals of religious initiation. Readers treated Terrasson's depiction of ancient Egypt as accurate and authoritative. *Sethos*'s popularity

John Sartain, *Johan Gottfried von Herder*, 19th-century mezzotint. The Romantic sceptic of Egyptian greatness.

inspired a host of imitators and spawned the genre of popular fiction set in ancient Egypt – the impact of Terrasson's novel on the popular image of Egypt was far greater than the truly scholarly works that were being published during the eighteenth century. Freemasons in France used *Sethos* as a handbook for creating their own Egyptianized rituals. Mozart's popular *Magic Flute* (1791) was a collaboration with a Mason, Emanuel Schikaneder, which borrowed elements of its plot and scenes from *Sethos*.[37]

Art and architecture also experienced a fad for Egyptomania during the second half of the eighteenth century. Landscape paintings increasingly featured pyramids and obelisks in their backgrounds, and made-up hieroglyphic inscriptions appeared on monuments. The landscapes seldom looked like Egypt and the pyramids, sphinxes and obelisks rarely resembled the real Egyptian ones. Most pyramids resembled the steep-sided pyramid of Cestius in Rome rather than the pyramids of Giza. Genuine Egyptian artefacts were collected for cabinets of curiosities or decor for gardens or the interiors of great homes. The supply of real Egyptian artefacts was limited so the production of copies became a flourishing business. Architects began to use Egyptian motifs as well.[38]

Academic scholars had turned away from Neoplatonism and Hermeticism during the seventeenth century along with the view of an occult Egypt. These attitudes continued and intensified during the Enlightenment of the eighteenth century but hermeticism and the idea of a mystic Egypt refused to perish. Instead they joined with the world of traditional popular culture that flourished among nobles and peasants alike. Belief in magic, ghosts, evil spirits and other supernatural phenomena were common and taken seriously. Since the magic of Egypt was old, therefore venerable, exotic and powerful, it exercised a strong fascination and attraction. Alchemical hermeticism remained popular. Translations of the *Corpus hermeticum* continued to appear in various European languages and Hermes Trismegistus recurred as a figure of note. Laurence Sterne in his novel *Tristram Shandy* (1760) has the character Uncle Toby eulogize Hermes Trismegistus as 'the greatest of all earthly beings – he was the great king – the greatest lawgiver – the greatest philosopher – and the greatest priest – and engineer.' Shandy's father wanted to name his son Trismegistus but Mrs Shandy's chambermaid Susannah could not pronounce the name, so at the baptism the curate assumes the baby is to be christened by his own name, Tristram. Secret societies often adopted Egyptian rituals and paraphernalia and attributed Egyptian origins to their beliefs and ideologies. Ancient Egypt served as a example of enlightened despotism or alternatively as a society oppressed by priestly rule. Despite some detractors, ancient Egypt tended to be viewed as a golden age of humanity.[39]

Early Freemasonry focused its origins on a descent from the Temple of Solomon and the Knights Templar. The first manifestation of Egyptian symbolism appeared in 1728 when the Perfetta Unione lodge of Naples added a pyramid and sphinx to its seal. During the second half of the eighteenth century, Egyptomania and hermeticism infiltrated Freemasonry on a larger scale. Egypt, seen as a repository of secret knowledge, was attractive to secret societies with their rites of initiation. The ritual of Crata Repoa appeared in Berlin in 1770 and became part of Masonic traditions, although no secret society adopted it during the eighteenth century. It was followed in 1778 by the establishment of the Egyptian Rite in London by the great charlatan Giuseppe Balsamo, who called himself Count Alessandro Cagliostro

(1743–1795). Cagliostro simply took existing rituals of Freemasonry and added a veneer of Egyptian symbolism. The Egyptian Rite proved very popular among Freemasons. Cagliostro's fraudulent activities, including forgery and the scandalous Affair of the Diamond Necklace, forced him to flee to Rome where in 1789 the Inquisition arrested him for heresy as a Freemason. He died in a papal dungeon in 1795. Ignaz von Born (1742–1791), a leading scientist of the Holy Roman Empire and a prominent Freemason, in 1784 promoted the view of ancient Egypt as a land of science that anticipated the Enlightenment. Egyptian religion promoted science and its priests were the original Freemasons who strove to improve the well-being of the people. Other Freemasons agreed. The somewhat obscure Rite of Misraim appeared in Milan around 1805, and this was followed by the foundation of the Rite of Memphis by the expatriate Frenchman Samuel Honis while he was living in Egypt. On his return to France in 1815 Honis founded a single lodge in France which only lasted one year. The Rite of Memphis was later revived in 1838 when it competed for members with the Rite of Misraim. Egyptomania would continue to influence Freemasonry and spread to other secret societies during the nineteenth century.[40]

As the end of the eighteenth century approached, European intellectuals maintained a fascination with ancient Egypt. As a younger Herder put it in 1774, Egypt had 'the magical power to set the best of people to dreaming'. Certainly it set the sixteen-year-old Edward Gibbon dreaming. During the summer of 1752 after his first year at Oxford, he decided to write a book, *The Age of Sesostris*, about the supposed Egyptian conqueror of Asia so beloved by overly speculative fringe historians. As Gibbon put it, he was following a 'blind and boyish taste for exotic history'. When he returned to Oxford in the autumn, he abandoned the project and twenty years later burned the masterpiece. From that point on he focused his historical interests on eras that were not 'lost in a distant cloud' of no reliable historical evidence. While Gibbon's talents were saved from a pharaonic dead end, Egyptian motifs appeared with some frequency in art, architecture and interior design in an early wave of Egyptomania that was evident throughout Europe. Lore of esoteric Egypt continued to influence secret societies and mystics. A sceptical Herder did not hold with the general high regard shown towards ancient Egypt. In his opinion, 'Egypt would not easily have attained the high reputation it enjoys for wisdom, but for its less remote situation, the ruins of its antiquities, and above all the tales of the Greeks.' Real knowledge of Egyptian history and culture was stalled. Hieroglyphs remained undeciphered. The systematic archaeological exploration of Egypt lay years in the future.[41]

By the end of the eighteenth century, the deadlock of Egyptology was about to be broken and France would play a key role in the process. Napoleon invaded Egypt in 1798 at the behest of the government of the Directory that ruled the French Republic at that time. His expedition was accompanied by over 150 French scholars whose mission was to thoroughly study Egypt and its antiquities. During the course of the expedition, French engineers working on fortifications at Rosetta on the Nile in late July 1799 found a granite stone inscribed with three ancient scripts. In 1822 the Rosetta Stone would ultimately provide the key for unlocking the secrets to deciphering hieroglyphs, a secret that had been lost for some 1,500 years. The revelations of Napoleon's scholars in Egypt would spark a surge in the existing Egyptomania of Western culture while the decipherment of hieroglyphs would revolutionize Egyptology. Georg Wilhelm Friedrich Hegel (1770–1831), the great German philosopher, wrote the lectures that were published as the *Philosophy of History* before these changes had fully manifested themselves. Hegel delivered his series of lectures five times between 1822 and his death in 1831. During these years Hegel revised his lectures but it appears he did not learn about the breakthrough of the decipherment of hieroglyphs before 1827. The effort to translate surviving Egyptian writings had barely begun when he died. So Hegel's lectures represent the state of European knowledge about ancient Egypt on the eve of modern Egyptology and modern Egyptomania. As Hegel observed, 'The history of Egypt, as we have it, is full of the greatest contradictions. The mythical is blended with the historical and the statements are as diverse as can be imagined.' Although Hegel's presentation combined the rationalism of Immanuel Kant with his own brand of Idealism, his sources for Egyptian history and religion were not significantly different from those available to Marsilio Ficino, Isaac Casaubon, Athanasius Kircher or William Warburton. Except for his late references to the hieroglyphic studies of Thomas Young and Champollion, Hegel's lectures would not have revealed any new factual information distinct from his predecessors. Egyptology stood at the beginning of almost two hundred years of continuous progress in the study of ancient Egypt. Egyptomania would also be revolutionized. All the new knowledge only increased the public's fascination with Egypt while the Industrial Revolution was transforming society so that Egyptomania was no longer a phenomenon of intellectuals and the elite. It was about to become part of the new mass culture. Hegel accurately observed that 'Egypt was always the land of marvels, and has remained so to the present day'. The same can be said for our present.[42]

SIX

NAPOLEON'S EXPEDITION TO EGYPT AND THE BIRTH OF MODERN EGYPTOMANIA

The whole army, suddenly and with one accord, stood in amazement at the sight of its scattered ruins, and clapped their hands in delight, as if the end and object of their glorious toils, and the complete conquest of Egypt, were accomplished and secured by taking possession of the splendid remains of this ancient metropolis.

ÐOMINIQUE VIVANT, BARON DE ÐENON
(describing the reaction of General Louis Charles Desaix's troops
to their first sight of the ruins of ancient Thebes, 1799)[1]

ON 19 MAY 1798 one of history's more quixotic military expeditions sailed from Toulon, France. It consisted of about 180 vessels including thirteen ships of the line, the greatest class of warships at that time.[2] The transports carried some 17,000 soldiers of the newly formed Army of the Orient but other convoys would join the fleet. In total the expedition would consist of 34,000 soldiers and another 16,000 sailors and marines. The expedition's destination was Alexandria and its objective was to wrest Egypt from the decrepit Ottoman Turkish Empire and make it a possession of the Directory, the five-man council that ruled the revolutionary French Republic.

At this time, Egypt was ruled by the Mamelukes on behalf of the Ottoman Turks. Originally around 1230 the Ayyubid Dynasty of Egypt (1169–1260) created the Mamelukes to be a professional army of slave-soldiers. The Mamelukes were purchased as young boys from Circassia and Turkmenistan and raised as Muslims. Later the Mamelukes launched a coup in 1254 that made them the rulers of Egypt. Although the Ottoman sultan Selim I conquered them in 1517, he allowed the Mamelukes to remain his surrogate rulers of Egypt with minimal interference from the few Ottoman officials sent to Egypt. Mameluke rule was violent, predatory and inefficient, so Egypt was ripe for conquest.[3]

The sorry state of Mameluke rule also allowed the directors who ruled the French Republic to portray their invasion as a liberation of the Egyptian people. Their choice of the man to command this expedition was the 29-year-old Napoleon Bonaparte, a rapidly rising star in the French military, who dreamed of emulating the achievements of Alexander the Great in Asia. The five directors who ruled France dreamed of having such an increasingly dangerous rival bogged down in an Egyptian quagmire and far away from France for some years.

The French arrived at Alexandria on 1 July and stormed the city the next day. Immediately Napoleon marched through the desert to attack Cairo. It was a gruelling and nearly disastrous experience. Nevertheless, upon reaching Cairo, the French army handily defeated the Mamelukes at the Battle of the Pyramids on 21 July. Cairo was occupied the next day and the Ottoman forces, in disarray, retreated. Egypt was now France's newest conquest. Britain, however, was determined to deprive them of it. On 1 August at the Battle of the Nile, the great admiral Horatio Nelson and his British fleet won one of the most unequal victories in naval history. The French fleet was destroyed. As a result, Britain held firm command of the seas in the Mediterranean and Napoleon's army was cut off from reinforcement and resupply from France. On land, however, the well-trained French troops continued to win victory after victory in Egypt and on 31 January 1799 Napoleon marched on Syria. He won more battles but failed to capture Acre, which he besieged from 17 March to 20 May. Britain's continued control of the seas and an outbreak of bubonic plague in Napoleon's army forced him to withdraw to Egypt. Recognizing that he was in a losing situation, Napoleon escaped to France in a fast frigate with a few close followers (deserting his troops did surprisingly little harm to his reputation). Meanwhile, back in Egypt, his abandoned generals and soldiers carried on until they were worn down and surrendered to the British on 30 August 1801.

Obviously Napoleon's expedition to Egypt was a military failure. The French conquered Egypt but could not hold on to it. On the other hand the intellectual achievements of a group of scholars who accompanied Napoleon to Egypt were quite impressive and longer lasting. They founded Egyptology as a modern empirical discipline and launched modern Egyptomania.

The Scientific Commission and Egyptology

The purpose of Napoleon's expedition was to conquer Egypt. That meant that the French needed to understand the land they were to conquer and control. To that purpose the official records state that 167 scholars and scientists were recruited or volunteered to accompany the expedition.[4] They would be known as the Scientific Commission, although the dubious soldiers of the French army dubbed them 'the mules'. The Commission's task was to gather all the information they could about Egypt, both ancient and modern. Since they were accompanying an invading army, a big part of their duties involved mapping Egypt and enumerating its natural resources. In retrospect, some people assume that Napoleon's savants were predominantly antiquaries and archaeologists. In fact, most were engineers, surveyors and cartographers, which is entirely consistent with fulfilling the military's need for information. Various natural scientists, such as biologists and chemists, accompanied the expedition. Thirty-four of the scholars were still students; only three of the scholars were actually archaeologists. This lack of archaeologists is not all that surprising when one remembers that archaeology was not yet an academic discipline in the late eighteenth century. Instead, antiquarianism and its offshoot of archaeology were for the most part the hobbies of rich amateurs.

The two leaders of the Scientific Commission were Gaspard Monge, a mathematician, and Claude-Louis Berthollet, a chemist. Both men were part of Napoleon's inner circle. They had worked for him in Italy on the crucial task of transporting looted Italian art treasures back to France. Monge and Napoleon had also developed a deep friendship as well. They recruited or selected the other members of the Scientific Commission. Among the volunteers were the artist, writer and polymath Dominique Vivant, Baron de Denon, the chemist and inventor Nicolas-Jacques Conté, the physicist Joseph Fourier and the engineer Edme-François Jomard, who would later edit and write much of the commission's massive and masterly report, *The Description of Egypt*. There were plenty of other volunteers, as Napoleon was a revered celebrity in the French Republic by 1798 due to his string of victories in Italy. So even though Monge and Berthollet only had two months to recruit the scholars, they had no trouble finding enough eager people. Although the expedition's destination was supposed to be secret, it was widely rumoured that Egypt was its target. The rumour, which turned out to be true, also helped attract scholars, because Egypt was widely regarded by many in France during the 1790s as a fantasy land from the Arabian Nights.

Napoleon was very supportive of the commission, as he considered himself to be something of a savant and claimed that if he had not followed the path of becoming a soldier, he would have been a scientist. Pre-existing Egyptomania also influenced both Napoleon and the French Republic. Even before Napoleon's expedition, the French revolutionaries had incorporated Egyptianizing iconography and motifs into artefacts and emblems of the French Revolution and the first Republic. Egypt and its mysteries were also one of Napoleon's more significant scholarly interests as well. He was an avid student of the Comte de Volney's account of his four years of residence in Egypt and used it in planning the invasion.[5]

The scholars' initial impression of Egypt was negative. Alexandria was a squalid place inhabited by a mere 6,000 people, which was a sad comedown from its glory days as the capital of Ptolemaic Egypt – the intellectual Mecca of the ancient world – with a population of half a million people. Denon called Alexandria 'this long and melancholy city'. The French scholars and soldiers were also the first large group of Westerners to experience living in a largely Islamic society since the Crusades. Napoleon had instructed his troops to be tolerant of Islam; orders that they did not always follow. The scholars, like most Europeans, educated or not, knew little about Islam as a system of belief. What they did see was a seemingly rigid religion that dominated a society full of poverty and the suppression of women. But while they abhorred those aspects of Islamic Egypt, they still thought the Muslim mosques and literature were worthy of study. Some of the scholars, particularly Nicolas Conté, managed to gain a usable command of Arabic before they returned to France.[6]

Once Napoleon's troops had occupied and secured Cairo on 22 July 1798, the scholars went to work studying Egypt. Within a month, on 22 August, the first meeting of the Institute of Egypt took place. The more prestigious of the scholars, along with intellectually minded military men (including, of course, Napoleon) were made founding members. The Institute continued to hold meetings during most of the French occupation. Their goal was threefold: to bring the Enlightenment to Egypt, to study Egypt in all its facets and to provide sound opinions and advice to the government when requested. Certainly all the French scholars were highly successful in their quest to shed light on the mystery of Egypt: cartographers proceeded to map Egypt with an accuracy never before seen in that country; naturalists studied its flora and fauna; and geologists and chemists studied the physical nature of the country. However, the longer they stayed in Egypt the more fascinated they became with the ruins of its ancient past. The ever-resourceful chemist Conté used a barometer to accurately measure the height of the Great Pyramid and thus answered that long-recurring question. It is important to keep in mind that at this time, more than two hundred years ago, the Egyptian monuments still had definite remains of their pharaonic paint. Some now-familiar buildings and statues were covered at least partially by sand; the Sphinx was buried up to its chin. But there were, simply, a lot more ruins to visit and to study at that time. Subsequent vandalism and cannibalizing for building material have caused many ancient Egyptian ruins to be lost forever.

In those days, there was no bridge across the Nile at Cairo. A visit to the pyramids involved a ferry ride. It also necessitated a military escort, as lurking bedouins would have robbed and likely killed any Frenchmen found traversing the route without sufficient protection. One of the more famous of these excursions was organized by Monge and Berthollet. It included some of the most prestigious of the scholars, and Napoleon was the guest of honour. Two students, Edouard Devilliers and Jean Dubois-Aymé, tagged along. Napoleon and Monge competed in a race to the top of the Great Pyramid, no small feat since its sides were littered with dangerous debris. The party also entered the pyramid's interior. Some accounts claim that Napoleon, when inside, experienced a disturbing vision of Alexander the Great or some other mystical vision. In reality, he never entered the pyramid, since part of the route involved crawling on all fours through a low passage. The proud Napoleon refused to engage in such a humiliating activity.[7]

Napoleon viewing a mummy during his Egyptian campaign, in an illustration from a 19th-century popular history.

Napoleon's victory at the Battle of the Pyramids broke the Mamelukes but did not destroy them. Murad Bey (1750–1801), the most prominent Mameluke commander to remain at large, retreated south to Upper Egypt to raise a new army to oust the French. To counter that threat, Napoleon assigned one of his best generals, Louis-Charles Desaix (1768–1800), to pursue Murad Bey into Upper Egypt and destroy Mameluke resistance. Desaix set out on the evening of 25 August 1798 with an army numbering just under 3,000 soldiers equipped with two cannons. Murad Bey's forces varied in size from a few hundred to many thousands over the nine months that Desaix chased him, but the core of his troops were always mounted. Therefore Murad Bey's forces had a definite advantage in mobility over Desaix's infantrymen. Although the Mamelukes generally could evade Desaix's forces, they were eventually worn down by their dogged pursuers. The chase lasted eleven months, ranging down the Nile past Aswan and over to the Red Sea and finally back to Cairo in July 1799. All along the way Desaix was pacifying Upper Egypt. The local population referred to him as the 'Just Sultan'. Accompanying Desaix as an artist and chronicler of the expedition was the oldest of the scholars, Vivant Denon.

The irrepressible Vivant Denon experienced the greatest adventure of all the scholars who accompanied Napoleon to Egypt. Born into a noble family, he developed an enduring interest in art and literature. After moving to Paris as a young man, he quickly became a welcome personality in the city's social circuit thanks to his congeniality and entertaining conversational skills. He attracted the friendship of the influential Madame de Pompadour and served as a diplomat under Louis xv and Louis xvi. When the French Revolution broke out, Denon was living in Venice. The revolutionary government condemned him and confiscated his property. Undaunted, Denon returned to Paris in an effort to salvage his situation. Thanks to his friendship with the painter Jacques-Louis David, he was not executed or imprisoned. David even put him to work designing a republican style of clothing. Once again active in Paris society, he entered the circle of Madame Joséphine de Beauharnais, the mistress and later wife of Napoleon Bonaparte. After an unpromising start, Denon and Napoleon, through Joséphine, became friends and associates – a relationship that led to his invitation to join the Egyptian expedition.[8]

For his part, Denon's fascination with Egypt was a long-time interest: 'I had from my infancy wished to make a voyage to Egypt.' Once he arrived, he was captivated by everything he saw. Impressed by Egypt's many ancient ruins, including the pyramids and the Sphinx, he wrote: 'It would appear to be the lot of Egyptian monuments of every description to resist alike the ravages of time and man.' As a good Frenchman, he noted that young Egyptian women bore a noticeable resemblance to statues of the goddess Isis. But as a man of the Enlightenment and a convert to Republicanism, he mused on the construction of the pyramids that 'one hardly knows which is the most astonishing, the madness of tyrannical oppression, which dared to order the undertaking, or the stupid servility of obedience in the people who submitted to the labour.' By travelling with Desaix he was able to visit ruins in Upper Egypt that almost no Westerner had seen since the collapse of the Roman Empire. Throughout the pursuit of Murad Bey, he took notes and made sketches of what he saw. On several occasions he even made his drawings while under fire from Murad Bey's troops. Ever versatile, Denon had no complaints. He and Desaix's army had the marvellous experience of visiting the site of Egyptian Thebes. They were so amazed by what they saw there 'that the whole army, suddenly and with one accord, stood in amazement at the sight of its scattered ruins, and clapped their hands in delight'. Although Denon had no real understanding of most of the monuments, he made some intelligent speculations. Furthermore, as some of the monuments that he visited have since been demolished, his descriptions and sketches are the only information that now survive.[9]

Once Napoleon returned from his failed invasion of Syria on 14 June 1799, the French faced a counter-attack by the Ottoman Turks. Turkish forces landed at Aboukir on 15 July, but were handily defeated by Napoleon on 25 July at the Battle of Aboukir. Despite his victory, Napoleon had decided that staying in Egypt was doing neither his career nor his ambitions any good. On 23 August he boarded a fast frigate and returned to France. Among those he asked to accompany him were Monge, Berthollet and Denon. The abrupt departure by the leadership of the Scientific Commission was met by some rather droll and mordant Gallic jeers from their colleagues. Napoleon left the tough, capable Jean-Baptiste Kléber in command of the French in Egypt, much to Kléber's disgust. Thousands of French soldiers and sailors, along with about 150 scholars, were abandoned to their fate.

Arriving back in France, both Napoleon and Denon quickly went on to great accomplishments. For Napoleon, it was becoming First Consul and then Emperor. As for Denon, he turned his notes and sketches into a book: *Voyage dans la basse et la haute Egypte* (Travels in Upper and Lower Egypt). Writing may have helped assuage his longing to return to Egypt. His book appeared in France in 1802 and went through forty printings. An English translation appeared in 1803 along with German and Italian translations. It was written for a popular readership anxious for more information

The Rosetta Stone, currently in the collection of the British Museum.

about Egypt. Not simply fulfilling that curiosity, Denon's book sparked and fuelled a new surge of Egyptomania and became the first popular travel account of the nineteenth century. His colleagues on the Scientific Commission were critical of the book and resented its anticipation of their own great report of their findings about Egypt, although Denon tried to be conciliatory. Napoleon continued his support of Denon and appointed him as the director of the Imperial Museums, including the newly created Musée Napoléon (the Louvre). Denon held that position until 1815 when the restored Louis XVIII asked for his resignation. In the meantime, the enthusiastic and tenacious Denon followed Napoleon's armies and looted the art treasures of Europe for the museums of France. After his forced retirement, he worked on a history of ancient and modern art that remained unfinished at his death in 1825.[10]

In fact, the most important discovery made by the French expedition occurred a few weeks before Napoleon's departure – the finding of the Rosetta Stone. Threatened with a Turkish invasion, the French proceeded to strengthen Egypt's defence against a landing by enemy forces. The strategic port of Rosetta at the mouth of the Rosetta branch of the Nile River was a prime entryway into Egypt, so the French began to strengthen its defences at Fort Julien. One of its outer walls, built by the Mameluke Sultan Qait Bey (r. 1468–96), was deemed to need demolition and replacement. The man put in charge of this project was Lieutenant Pierre Bouchard (1771–1822), who had come to Egypt as one of the students attached to the Scientific Commission. He finished his engineering studies and received a lieutenant's commission with Napoleon's engineers. During July 1799 in the course of dismantling the wall, his workers discovered a large black stone. Bouchard saw that it had writing incised on its surface and that one section of the writing was Greek while the other two parts were undecipherable hieroglyphs and demotic characters. The French general Jacques-François Menou had the scholars at Rosetta translate the Greek. Their translation confirmed that the three sets of writing were three versions of the same official document. Recognizing the significance of the find for deciphering hieroglyphs, news of Bouchard's discovery was reported to the scholars at the Egyptian Institute at their meeting on 29 July 1799. It was announced to the audience that the Greek inscription was dated to 196 BC, during the reign of Ptolemy Epiphanes (r. 205–180 BC). Menou then had Bouchard transport the Rosetta Stone down to the Egyptian Institute in Cairo. It arrived on 19 August. Menou would later claim the Rosetta Stone for his personal property, but the British forced him to turn it over to them when the French in Egypt finally surrendered. The Rosetta Stone then became the property of George III, who gave it to the British Museum where it has remained ever since – becoming a centrepiece of the British Museum's collections – despite the best efforts of the Egyptian archaeologist Zahi Hawass to recover it while he was Egypt's Minister of Antiquities. The Rosetta Stone made the decipherment of hieroglyphs possible, thus making it the greatest single discovery and advance in the history of Egyptology – ensuring its continuing fame as one of the icons of this field of study and in popular Egyptomania.[11]

Although Napoleon, Monge, Berthollet and Denon may have abandoned them, the French scholars continued their studies of all things Egyptian for another two years. Jacques Fourier, a physicist who would later make important studies of heat, became the new leader of the Scientific Commission.

The antiquities of Egypt increasingly attracted the attention of the scholars, whose initial studies were not very well organized. Eventually they developed a systematic approach, but, living in the infancy of academic archaeology, they did not engage in excavation. Nor did they have the time, the resources or the need to excavate. There were more than enough ruins and monuments above the ground to keep them busy. Other scholars collected or took notes on the animals, plants and minerals of Egypt. The hope of the scholars was that they would illuminate the mysteries of Egypt to the world. But the French in Egypt were facing defeat.

On 14 June 1800 an Egyptian assassinated the French commander General Kléber. Leadership passed to the significantly less competent Menou, who finally surrendered to the British on 30 August 1801. The initial British demand was that the scholars had to surrender all their notes and specimens. In response, the scholars refused and threatened to destroy them rather than give up all their precious research. Fortunately, the biologist Geoffroy Saint-Hilaire (1772–1844) led the French scholars in a resistance that caused the British to relent and allowed them to keep their personal research. Snatching that intellectual victory out of a military failure, the French scholars made their way back to France. Of the scientists and savants who followed Napoleon to Egypt, 31 died there or died shortly after their return to France. Most of the survivors had spent over three years in Egypt. The camaraderie, hardships, discoveries and wonders they experienced there bonded them for life. They called themselves 'the Egyptians' and had yearly reunions to remember their adventures.[12]

The Description of Egypt

Returning to France did not end the work of the Scientific Commission. The scholars had amassed a huge amount of research that they were anxious to share with the intellectual world. Geoffroy Saint-Hilaire, along with a few of the scholars, hoped that the publication of their research would give some meaning to the deaths of over 20,000 Frenchmen during the Egyptian expedition. Fourteen of the scholars even formed a company for the publication of their book while they were still in Cairo. Napoleon did not approve and had the company disbanded. He placed the project to publish the Scientific Commission's report under the authority of the Ministry of the Interior, which paid the scholars for their work on the great book. Readying the work for publication began in 1803. The first volume of *Description de l'Egypte* (The Description of Egypt) appeared in 1809 and was followed by several more volumes that included copious praise of

Napoleon. The scholars used the great *Encyclopedia* of Denis Diderot as the model for their work. Joseph Fourier was assigned to write the preface – this would also be a history of Egypt, but Fourier complained continually that he could not finish his assignment until the other contributors turned in their sections. When the first two men assigned to edit the *Description* died, the cartographer Edme-François Jomard took the reins and spent eighteen years working as its editor. During the length of time it took to publish the complete *Description*, Napoleon was defeated and the old Bourbon dynasty of French kings was restored. Louis XVIII's restoration to the throne in 1814 put the plan to complete the publication of the *Description* into jeopardy. It had been a Napoleonic project, but Fourier and others were suitably obsequious to the Bourbon regime and excised the references to Napoleon. As a result, the project was spared and continued to completion.[13]

The *Description of Egypt* was published in two editions. The first was the Imperial Edition published by the Napoleonic regime and then the Bourbon government between 1809 and 1828. It consisted of nine volumes of text, one volume describing the plates – of which there were ten volumes – two further elephant or Mammut folio volumes of plates, and an atlas. The total number of volumes was 23, but variant editions with additional volumes exist. A second edition was called the Panckoucke Edition and was published by Charles-Louis-Fleury Panckoucke. It was a cheaper and smaller format edition published in 37 volumes between 1821 and 1830, and the plates were produced in black and white.

Physically and visually, *The Description of Egypt* was an impressive work. The French government sent copies to various other countries so the appreciation of its discoveries could be shared and admiration for French scholarship increased. The problem for the authors of the *Description* was that Egyptological scholarship was advancing rapidly during the years when their volumes made their appearance. The decipherment of hieroglyphs rendered many of the *Description*'s conclusions about ancient Egypt obsolete. On the other hand, its text and its beautiful plates radiated the enthusiasm of its authors for Egypt. In this way the *Description* inspired Egyptomania and Egyptophilia among many of those who read it and viewed its plates. Thanks to the *Description*, Denon's *Travels* and the news associated with the French expedition to Egypt, that ancient land was on people's minds. Architects, artists and interior designers were all inspired to produce Egyptianized motifs. Some have suggested that the Egyptomania produced by the French expedition also prompted the looting frenzy that Egyptian antiquities experienced during most of the nineteenth century. Others, however, would disagree.[14]

Jean-François Champollion
(1790–1832), decipherer of
hieroglyphs and founder
of modern Egyptology.

The Rosetta Stone and the Decipherment of Hieroglyphs

As noted above, the Rosetta Stone found by Napoleon's expedition provided
at long last the key needed to decipher hieroglyphs, a task that had been the
seemingly unattainable goal of scholars for centuries. William Warburton had
developed a few promising approaches in the late seventeenth century, but the
lingering belief that hieroglyphs were a symbolic script encoding profound
secret knowledge kept scholars distracted. The Abbé Barthélemy in 1761 had
correctly surmised that the cartouches in the inscriptions were the names of
gods or royalty. Unfortunately Joseph de Guignes a few years later noted that
Chinese hieroglyphs also used cartouches and he erroneously concluded from
that coincidence that China was an Egyptian colony. This spurious reasoning
prompted Guignes to argue that the path to deciphering Egyptian hieroglyphs
existed in Chinese script. It was a false path, but Egyptology (like many other
studies) was no stranger to bizarre theories. Later, in 1797, a Danish scholar,
Georg Zoëga, correctly concluded that hieroglyphs might have a phonetic
component. It was the Rosetta Stone, however, that provided the necessary
key to open the door leading from speculation to true decipherment.[15]

Jean-François Champollion is generally credited with the decipherment of hieroglyphs, despite the cavils of some who assert that the Englishman Thomas Young was the true decipherer. The fact is, as is the case with many of the most important discoveries, a number of people contributed to the result. In the case of hieroglyphs, Champollion deserves recognition as the most important contributor although he was not alone in his efforts. The discovery of the Rosetta Stone had sparked a race to decipher hieroglyphs. Accurate copies had been made by the French scholars in Egypt and quickly circulated through Europe, so the British did not have a monopoly on the text. In 1802 Silvestre de Sacy (who had taught Champollion) and his student Johan David Åkerblad, another Dane like Zoëga, attempted to decipher the demotic text but failed. Count Nils Gustaf Palin attempted to unravel the hieroglyphic text, but also to no avail.[16]

The first person to make significant progress in deciphering hieroglyphs was Thomas Young. Born into a Quaker family living in Milverton, Somerset, in England, he received an extensive education in languages – classical, modern and biblical. He went on to study medicine in London and Edinburgh before moving to the University of Göttingen in Germany, where he earned a doctorate in physics. His scholarly interests were wide-ranging. During the first decade of the nineteenth century he made significant contributions to a number of fields including optics, physiology and general linguistics. The arrival of the Rosetta Stone captured Young's attention during the second decade of the nineteenth century. He did extensive work on the demotic and the hieroglyphic scripts. By 1819 he had published a study of hieroglyphs in the *Encyclopaedia Britannica* that identified phonetic values for a number of hieroglyphs, of which forty turned out to be correct. However, he also misidentified some hieroglyphs, and he lacked an understanding of hieroglyphic grammar. Not being familiar with the earlier hieroglyphic scholarship of Barthélemy and Zoëga, he mistakenly thought that he was the first person to identify the cartouches as royal names. Champollion read Young's analyses of hieroglyphs, made corrections and built on Young's findings until he was able to recreate Egyptian grammar and achieve consistent results. At the time many people credited Young with the fundamental breakthrough in the decipherment of hieroglyphs, but that support largely broke down along national lines, with British scholars supporting Young's priority of discovery. That is no longer the case. Egyptologists now recognize that Young made fundamental discoveries that allowed the demotic script of ancient Egypt to be deciphered. Nevertheless, Young's achievement has been overshadowed by the more romantic and dramatic decipherment of hieroglyphs and the controversies over that discovery.[17]

Jean-François Champollion was the scholar who ultimately and success-fully broke down the mysteries of the hieroglyphs. Born into a family of modest means and republican sympathies, he was educated by his brother Jacques-Joseph Champollion-Figeac (1778–1867). Jacques-Joseph was a classical scholar with an interest in ancient Egypt who had volunteered for Napoleon's expedition but was not accepted into the Scientific Commission. The two brothers were close and Jacques-Joseph was an active partner in much of his brother's hieroglyphic research and a huge support both financially and emotionally.[18]

Jacques-Joseph was an instructor at the Grenoble Academy and there the young Jean-François revealed an almost preternatural talent for learning and mastering languages. At sixteen years old he possessed a command of twelve languages including Latin, Greek and Hebrew, along with African and Asian languages such as Sanskrit, Pahlavi, Syriac and Coptic. Jean-François developed a passionate interest in ancient Egypt very early on as well. This obsession brought him into contact with Joseph Fourier, the veteran of Napoleon's expedition and the scholar assigned to write the preface or introduction to the *Description of Egypt*. In 1802 Napoleon rewarded Fourier with the appointment to be prefect for the area that included Grenoble. When Fourier visited the school at Grenoble, Jean-François's enthusiastic interest in ancient Egypt came to his attention. He invited the eleven-year-old to see his collection of Egyptian antiquities. Initially the meeting with Fourier left the youth speechless, astounded by seeing the antiquities and hieroglyphic scripts. The experience set him on the course of his life's work. He would study and decipher those mysterious hieroglyphs. Both Jean-François and Jacques-Joseph would assist Fourier in his research for the *Description of Egypt*. In turn, until his death in 1830, Fourier became a supporter of Champollion's scholarship.[19]

Jean-François was not always so fortunate in the professional contacts that he made. In the course of working with Fourier, he met Edme-François Jomard, who was serving as the editor of the *Description of Egypt*. Unfortunately for the younger Champollion, Jomard took an instant and permanent dislike to him. When Jean-François moved to Paris in 1807 to study languages at the Collège de France, his teacher, Silvestre de Sacy, came to see him as an upstart and a serious competitor in the academic world. As a result, Jean-François suffered from faint praise and covert backstabbing from Sacy for years. Jomard and Sacy were not alone either, as other scholars were sceptical about Champollion's discovery.[20]

Jean-François Champollion began his effort to decipher the hieroglyphs of the Rosetta Stone in 1808. Even with the Rosetta Stone, it was not an easy task: a significant portion of the hieroglyphic text had broken off at some point before its discovery and was never found. Eventually, the younger Champollion had to seek out other hieroglyphic texts. Like Athanasius Kircher, Jean-François believed that Coptic was the descendant of the ancient Egyptian language. Unfortunately he also adhered to an incorrect assumption held by Kircher and other Renaissance- and Baroque-era scholars that hieroglyphs were a form of symbolic writing connected to esoteric and occult knowledge. Even as late as 1821, on the eve of his breakthrough in decipherment, he worked on the erroneous assumption that hieroglyphs were ideographic and not phonetic. When he brought out his book *Egypt of the Pharaohs* in 1814, he sent a copy to the Society of Antiquaries in London but he mistakenly sent his cover letter to the Royal Society, whose foreign secretary was Thomas Young. The letter made Young aware that he had a serious rival in the race to decipher the hieroglyphs. Problems with the new Bourbon government of France prevented the republican Champollion from working on the decipherment of hieroglyphs between 1816 and 1817, and this meant that his being the winner in the race to decipher hieroglyphs was no foregone conclusion.[21]

Slowly but surely Champollion achieved a greater and more accurate understanding of Egyptian writing. By late 1821 he had come to the correct conclusion that the hieratic script of the Egyptians was a simplified version of hieroglyphs and that the demotic script was a simplified version of hieratic. He compiled a chart of correspondences between the three scripts that allowed him to successfully transcribe from one to another. Also, he counted that there were 486 Greeks words in the Rosetta Stone's inscription but there were 1,419 hieroglyphs. This discovery meant that hieroglyphs were not simply ideographs, where one symbol represented one word or idea. Some of the hieroglyphs had to be phonetic. Champollion's eureka moment came on 14 September 1822. He was working on newly arrived copies of hieroglyphic texts from the temples at Abu Simbel. When he looked at the cartouches, he realized that he was able to read the names phonetically. Euphoric over his discovery, he rushed from his home to his brother Jacques-Joseph's office in the Institute of France in Paris. Upon entering his brother's office, he exclaimed, '*Je tiens l'affaire!*' (I have found it) and promptly fainted. The shocked Jacques-Joseph thought his brother had died.[22]

Champollion recovered and managed to incorporate his findings into the paper he presented at the Academy of Inscriptions on 27 September 1822. Thomas Young attended the meeting and Champollion unknowingly sat next to him as neither of them had ever met in person before. A revised version of Champollion's paper was published as 'Letter to M. Dacier' at the end of October. The breakthrough, however, did not bring Champollion automatic recognition and adulation. Some scholars refused to believe that his system worked, and because no previous system of decipherment had proven to be accurate and effective, they had good grounds to be sceptical. Jomard was critical and Young indicated that he should be given credit for the discovery since Champollion had only added to Young's breakthrough in decipherment. Champollion rejected Young's contention and so, too, did some of Young's friends. Meanwhile, between August 1823 and the end of 1824, Champollion published a series of booklets on the gods and goddesses of Egypt entitled *Panthéon Égyptien* which was partially based on his hieroglyphic discoveries. Young damned the book with faint praise but, ever the polymath, he was losing interest in hieroglyphic research and looking at new problems to solve in other fields. He did not, however, lose interest in being credited with the hieroglyphic breakthrough. At the same time in April 1824 Champollion brought out a book-length description of his system of decipherment titled *Précis du système hiéroglyphique des anciens Égyptiens* (Summary of the Hieroglyphic System of the Ancient Egyptians). It was received with great enthusiasm in France. In 1826 Champollion was named the curator of the Egyptian collection in the Louvre. Five years later, a chair of Egyptian history and archaeology was created in 1831 at the College of France especially for Champollion.[23]

Nevertheless, controversy over the hieroglyphic breakthrough dogged Champollion for the rest of his life and for some years after his death. Late in his life, further studies of Egyptian inscriptions by him and others consistently bore out that his system of decipherment worked. These studies included Champollion's first and only trip to Egypt during 1828 and 1829 with the Italian Egyptologist Ippolito Rosellini. His research in Egypt also indicated that human history covered a much longer span than the 6,000-year chronology asserted by the Christian Church. Such findings did not endear him to conservatives similar to how his earlier debunking of the supposed great age of the Dendara zodiac (1st century BC–1st century AD) in early 1822 did not make him friends with Jomard or secularists and radicals intent on attacking the soundness of the teachings of the Church.[24]

Never a particularly healthy man and seriously overweight, Champollion's journey to Egypt left him drained and vulnerable to ailments. He suffered a stroke and died on 4 March 1832. On 6 March he was buried at the famous Père Lachaise Cemetery in Paris near the grave of Joseph Fourier. Jacques-Joseph Champollion took on the herculean labour of literary executor for his younger brother and saw to the publication of Jean-François's Egyptian grammar from 1836 to 1841 and his Egyptian dictionary, 1841 to 1843.

Champollion's grave at Père Lachaise Cemetery in Paris, with a predictable obelisk marking the grave site.

He also defended his brother's reputation and scholarly legacy from various detractors such as Jomard and the German scholar Heinrich Klaproth. Fortunately, other scholars, notably the great German Egyptologist Karl Lepsius, used Champollion's methods, found them accurate and defended them vigorously. Incredibly, as late as 1873 and 1874, the great Victorian traveller and popular author Amelia Edwards could report that a seemingly intelligent English gentleman still rejected out of hand that hieroglyphs were being deciphered correctly. This scepticism prevailed in some circles despite the many Egyptian documents and inscriptions that has been translated based on Champollion's system.[25]

As Jean-François Champollion recognized, the decipherment of hieroglyphs would allow scholars to reconstruct Egyptian chronology in a generally accurate manner. In turn, the very antiquity of Egyptian chronology would allow scholars to compile a useable chronology for the rest of the ancient world. Champollion also persuaded Mohammad Ali Pasha, the Egyptian ruler, to create a government office charged with protecting Egyptian antiquities and to establish a museum for Egyptian archaeology and history in Cairo.[26] All of this thrill of discovery and scholarly controversy from Napoleon to Champollion helped to keep ancient Egypt in the public's consciousness, from Europe to North America. The result was a new surge of Egyptomania and Egyptophilia. Since the West was developing into a mass, industrial society during the nineteenth century, this surge of Egyptomania penetrated to all levels of society and despite ups and downs has remained endemic ever since.

The Looting of Egypt

Napoleon's expedition to Egypt, Vivant Denon's book, the publication of *The Description of Egypt* and the decipherment of the Rosetta Stone all combined to intensify Western society's interest in the ancient land of the Pharaohs. Thousands of French and British troops had experienced something few others had – they had set foot on Egyptian soil. What they and other European visitors saw was a land full of ancient buildings, monuments and other antiquities which were lying around for the taking and largely unappreciated by the Egyptian people at that time. Some of them brought Egyptian artefacts home with them, the Rosetta Stone only being the most famous example. Back in Europe, demand rose for Egyptian relics by both museums and private collectors, particularly when the Napoleonic Wars ended in 1815. Knowledge and interest in Egypt that went beyond the Bible was no longer the special preserve of rarefied scholars or the highest level of the social elite; middle- and working-class citizens could now indulge in a fascination with Egypt. A rush to acquire Egyptian antiquities and bring them back to Europe developed; this urgent activity has since been dubbed the Rape of the Nile.[27]

The three great entrepreneurs engaged in the looting of Egypt's antiquities were Bernardino Drovetti (1776–1852), Henry Salt (1780–1827) and Giovanni Battista Belzoni (1778–1823). Drovetti was born in the kingdom of Piedmont-Sardinia and made his career in the Piedmontese army, which was incorporated into the army of Revolutionary France. In 1803 Napoleon sent Drovetti to Egypt to represent France as proconsul. He dealt with the Ottoman viceroy of Egypt, Mohammad Ali Pasha, who ruled the country from 1805 to 1848 – to all intents independent of Ottoman control. Mohammad Ali wanted to convert Egypt into a modern and powerful country. To curry favour and support from the European powers, Mohammad Ali was willing to give away Egyptian antiquities. As a result of his consular duties, Drovetti became friends with the Pasha. When Napoleon was finally defeated and the Bourbons were restored, Drovetti left his diplomatic post but remained in Egypt. He travelled the country, explored its ruins and looted them relentlessly, supposedly in the service of France. Thanks to his friendship with Mohammad Ali, he was

Giovanni Belzoni, 'Mode in Which the Young Memnon's Head (Now in the British Museum) was Removed', from *Six New Plates Illustrative of the Researches and Operations of G. Belzoni in Egypt and Nubia* (1820).

given choice concessions to excavate Egyptian ruins and engaged in a very lucrative trade in artefacts and relics. His agents combed the country for saleable antiquities and he was not above destroying duplicate antiquities to raise the prices of those he kept. Drovetti also accumulated a fine personal collection of Egyptian objects.[28]

Drovetti's rival was Henry Salt, the British consul-general in Cairo who had been appointed in 1815. Like Drovetti, Salt began to collect Egyptian artefacts, but in his case for the British Museum, and engaged in excavations in the area around the pyramids of Giza. He also employed agents to find choice artefacts from various parts of Egypt. His most famous agent was Giovanni Belzoni from Padua in Italy. Belzoni was a giant of a man at six foot and seven inches. His father was a barber but the young Belzoni chose not to follow in these footsteps and attempted to enter the priesthood, but during the turmoil of the wars of revolutionary France, he finally took up his father's trade of barbering. For a while he also made a living as a circus strongman and engaged in carnival tricks, performing in various parts of the Mediterranean. On Malta he met an emissary of Mohammad Ali Pasha who was investigating methods of irrigation. Belzoni had an idea for a water pump to draw the waters of the Nile into Egyptian fields and travelled to Egypt to sell the Pasha on his idea. When that endeavour proved to be a dead-end, he became an agent of Henry Salt's quest for Egyptian antiquities thanks to an introduction by the Swiss orientalist and explorer Ludwig Johann Burckhardt.[29]

Belzoni worked for Salt from 1817 to 1819 although he considered himself a free agent rather than an employee. During that time he made three journeys around Egypt collecting antiquities. In the course of these explorations he not only travelled up and down the Nile, but made side-trips to locate the ancient Red Sea port of Berenice and to the oasis of Bahariya in the Sahara. As it turned out, Belzoni possessed the type of instincts and the luck needed to locate important ruins and significant artefacts. One of his great achievements was to drag the great head of Rameses II, known as the 'Young Memnon', to the Nile. There it was transported down to a warehouse in Alexandria where Salt took possession of it after paying Belzoni a mere £100 (the equivalent of between £6,000 and £7,000 today) for his efforts. From Alexandria, Salt shipped the head to the British Museum. Seeing it on display, Percy Bysshe Shelley was inspired to write his poem 'Ozymandias'. Belzoni went on to excavate the sand that had buried the great temple at Abu Simbel and to thus enter its interior. He also was the first person to enter the pyramid of Khefren. Among his other discoveries were the tombs of the Pharaohs Ay and Seti I, although because hieroglyphs had not been deciphered at that time, he really did not know what exactly he had discovered. Recovering the sarcophagus of Rameses I, Belzoni would see the lid go to the Fitzwilliam Museum in Cambridge and the base to the Louvre in a compromise between Drovetti and Salt.[30]

Belzoni was not as ruthless a plunderer as Drovetti and his agents, but he was a plunderer none the less and not a true archaeologist. Belzoni's relationship with Salt was always an uneasy one, so in 1819 he decided to leave Egypt. Visiting his native Padua, he received a hero's welcome. Proceeding on to England, he delivered the manuscript of his *Narrative of the Operations and Recent Discoveries within the Pyramids, Temples, Tombs, and Excavations in Egypt and Nubia*, which appeared in October 1820. His collection of artefacts, casts and sketches were exhibited in the new Egyptian Hall in Piccadilly in London. Huge crowds visited the exhibit, and Belzoni became a popular celebrity. Ultimately he found his fame to be oppressive and his wanderlust drew him back to Africa. This time his goal was to find the source of the Niger River. Instead he found his own grave; after contracting dysentery, he died at Gato near Benin.[31]

Fate was not kind to Salt or Drovetti either. Salt died from an intestinal infection at Alexandria in 1827, never having achieved the fame or the wealth he had hoped for. Drovetti lived until 1852 but he ended his life miserably in an insane asylum. Mohammad Ali Pasha also developed mental illness towards the end of his life. To the superstitious, it might appear that looting resulted in this pattern of serious bad fortune. Salt never managed to get a good price for his collections from the parsimonious British Museum, accordingly much of what he had accumulated ended up in the more generous Louvre. Britain, however, did benefit as Belzoni's collection ended up in the British Museum. Despite being an agent of France, Drovetti's artefacts became the nucleus of the fine Egyptological collection of his native Turin in Piedmont-Sardinia.[32]

Other pilfered Egyptian antiquities poured into the museums and private collections of Europe and North America. One of the most famous and most horrific acquisitions was the Dendara zodiac. Vivant Denon and Desaix had discovered the Temple of Hathon at Dendara, which included the amazing zodiac in its ceiling. The zodiac became famous back in France, so much so that Sébastien Louis Saulnier, a former police commissioner of Lyon for the Napoleonic government, and his agent Jean-Baptiste Lelorrain decided to cut it out of the temple's roof. They secured the permission of the ever-agreeable Mohammad Ali to take the zodiac to France. Making their way to Dendara, they spent 22 days trying to hack it out of the ceiling to no avail. At that point, Saulnier resorted to explosives. Miraculously, the

The obelisk at the Place de la Concorde in Paris.

zodiac survived the blast although a lovely statue of Isis in the temple was destroyed. It was then dragged down to the Nile River, where it became stuck in the mud. Saulnier and Lelorrain were again able to extract it without breaking it. Louis XVIII bought the zodiac for 150,000 francs and displayed it in the Bibliothèque Nationale, where it remained until 1919 when it was moved to the Louvre. Upon its arrival in France, the zodiac became the focus of a bitter controversy between religion and science over whether the zodiac was far older than the 6,000-year chronology of the Bible.[33]

Other famous antiquities that made their way west were the Cleopatra's Needles of Paris, London and New York. Mohammad Ali presented the London needle, actually an obelisk of Thutmosis III, as a gift to Britain in 1819; however, the British government declined to pay for moving it. Ever generous with his country's antiquities, Mohammad Ali gave France an obelisk in 1826. King Louis-Philippe had it erected at the Place de la Concorde in 1833. It was the first of the obelisks to be dubbed 'Cleopatra's Needle', although it was really an obelisk of Rameses II. The British finally got around to transporting their obelisk to London more than half a century later in 1877. It was a trying journey. The barge carrying it almost sank in a storm and, though the obelisk was saved, the ship had to be abandoned; eventually it was recovered for salvage. After the obelisk arrived in London, it was erected on the Thames Embankment and was flanked by two sphinxes where it became the best known of the Cleopatra's Needles. Meanwhile the saga of the London needle aroused the interest of New York City, which was bolstered by a false rumour that the Khedive Mehmet Ali had already agreed to give the United States an obelisk. Fortunately for Americans, who shared Europe's enthusiasm for things Egyptian, the U.S. Consul in Cairo, Elbert Eli Farman, managed to persuade the Khedive to make the gift of an obelisk to the United States. It was transported to New York in 1880, where it was erected in Central Park near the Metropolitan Museum of Art.[34]

While this indiscriminate removal of antiquities robbed Egypt of some of its cultural heritage, Mohammad Ali was not alone in his lack of concern for the preservation of the ancient Egyptian monuments. Egyptians have been robbing tombs since the Pyramid Age. For centuries, Egyptians had also viewed the ancient monuments as convenient quarries of building materials. As a result Egyptian monuments suffered severe damage and in some cases disappeared completely. It should be remembered that the Rosetta Stone was found as part of a fortification built by the early Mameluke sultans several centuries before Napoleon. Nevertheless, the looting of antiquities created a situation that concerned Champollion – enough so that he pointed out to Mohammad Ali that Egypt's antiquities would attract tourists, and that tourism would bring money. This advice prompted the Pasha to set up a museum for antiquities in Cairo and to create a government service to protect them. Both Champollion and his nemesis Jomard agreed that the acquisition of the Dendara zodiac was an egregious abuse of an ancient monument. Not that Champollion was above doing a little pillaging of antiquities himself. The American diplomat George Robins Gliddon, who had served as vice-consul in Alexandria, protested against the looting in his 1841 book *An Appeal to the Antiquaries of Europe on the Destruction of the Monuments of Egypt*. Still, the pilfering of antiquities continued and prompted another American diplomat sixty years later in 1908 to write a book about the corruption of the Khedives and British subversion of good government, *Egypt and its Betrayal: An Account of the Country During the Periods of Ismail and Tewfik Pashas, and of How England Acquired a New Empire*. The author was Elbert Eli Farman, the man who had secured New York's Cleopatra's Needle thirty years previously. Although the unregulated pillaging of Egyptian monuments has ended, the demand for antiquities by Egyptophiles anxious to own something from ancient Egypt ensures that illegal looting still continues.[35] Thanks to Napoleon and his scholars, the nineteenth century was the era when Egyptomania became a component of popular culture, as Chapter Seven shows.

SEVEN

NINETEENTH-CENTURY EGYPTOMANIA TO THE DISCOVERY OF TUT

If I were to have the choice of a fairy gift, it should be like none of the many things that I fixed upon in my childhood, in readiness for such an occasion. It should be for a great winnowing fan, such as would, without injury to human eyes and lungs, blow away the sand which buries the monuments of Egypt. What a scene would be laid open then!

HARRIET MARTINEAU (1848)[1]

Egypt is one big undertakers' emporium.

RUDYARD KIPLING (1913)[2]

NAPOLEON S EXPEDITION opened Egypt up to the outside world in a way that had not existed since the time of Herodotus through the height of the Roman Empire. The discovery of the Rosetta Stone and the decipherment of its hieroglyphs by Jean-François Champollion and Thomas Young made possible the rescue of Egypt's history from wild speculations and fantasies. An unfortunate side-effect of the opening of Egypt was the looting of its antiquities for a European and North American populace hungry for artefacts to display in their museums, parks and homes. The nineteenth century saw the expansion of Egyptomania from acquisitive nobles and arcane scholars to middle-class citizens. Egyptomania manifested itself in tourism, architecture, literature and popular fads.

Mummymania

An Egyptian antiquity that has held particular fascination for the West is the mummy. The idea of a dead body supposedly perfectly preserved by mystic embalming procedures seemed exotic and enigmatic to people living in wetter

181

Egyptians digging up mummies for the mummy trade, from Amelia Edwards,
A Thousand Miles Up the Nile (1891).

climates where the bodies of the dead mouldered away in their graves until they
had rejoined the soil. During the medieval and early modern eras, mummy
parts were used as medicine, and were found on apothecaries' shelves until
the early twentieth century. This peculiar and rather distasteful practice had
its origin in a linguistic misunderstanding. Bitumen had been used in healing
wounds, mending broken bones and counteracting poisons. Particularly valued
was the Persian bitumen, a dark-brown hydrocarbon known as *mumiya*. Roman
physicians recognized the medicinal value of bitumen, but their access to the
Persian *mumiya* was extremely limited. Instead, they made do with bituminous
substances available within the Roman Empire from Albania and the Dead
Sea. Arabic civilization also considered bitumen to be valuable for healing. It
was the great Islamic physician Rhazes (d. 923) who first applied the name
mumia to these drugs. Later Arabic doctors began to use the bitumen–like
substance that had oozed from the embalmed bodies found in Egyptian tombs
as a substitute for natural bitumen. Eventually, medieval medical practitioners
extended the definition of *mumia* to include the resins and later asphalt used
to embalm bodies in Egypt. The final step in the process was to consider the
entire embalmed corpse of an ancient Egyptian to be medicinal. At that point,
an embalmed Egyptian corpse became known as a 'mummy'.[3]

The idea that mummies had medicinal value as *mumia* created a demand
for mummies in the West and in the Islamic world during the late medieval

period. By the sixteenth century, demand for *mumia* had become so great that the Egyptians began making fake mummies to sell. As the century progressed, however, an increasing scepticism about the efficacy of *mumia* began to grow among medical scholars, such as Leonhart Fuchs (d. 1566) and Ambrose Paré (d. 1590). The French naturalist Pierre Belon and the English herbalist John Gerard (*c.* 1545–1612) both pointed out that *mumia* was an asphalt substance and not the same as a mummy – but to no avail. Despite such scepticism, the practice survived through the seventeenth century and as the physician and philosopher Sir Thomas Browne put it, 'The Ægyptian Mummies, which Cambyses or time hath spared, avarice now consumeth. Mummie is become Merchandise, Mizraim cures wounds, and Pharaoh is sold for balsams.' By the beginning of the eighteenth century, however, use of *mumia* had declined significantly. Although *mumia* remained in limited use after Napoleon's expedition to Egypt, the decline continued through the nineteenth century and into the early twentieth, when the practice finally ended.[4]

The French invasion brought Europeans into direct contact with Egypt which served to increase popular interest in its mummies. Initially mummies were no longer considered a particularly valuable commodity. Belzoni, like other antiquity hunters, ransacked mummies for the papyrus scrolls that had been deposited in their wrappings. He told of entering the tombs at Gournou which were so cluttered with mummies that it was impossible to walk through them without stepping on one. Belzoni was not concerned by the destruction except in so far as it produced choking dust in the stuffy tombs while he recovered any papyri. During the first decades of the nineteenth century such cavalier attitudes towards mummies were common because they were not considered valuable commodities. That opinion would change in a few years.[5]

At the beginning of the nineteenth century, scholarly interest in mummies increased. Academics wanted to know who the ancient Egyptians were as a culture and a people. One way to do that was to study Egyptian funerary practices. In 1779 Johann Friedrich Blumenbach, a German natural scientist, classified humans into five races. Scholars wanted to know how this diversity from the primordial humans that had been created by God had come about. Blumenbach classified humans by studying the shape of their skulls and facial characteristics. He began to examine the preserved bodies of ancient Egyptians to determine the race to which they belonged. To that end the British Museum allowed him to unwrap three of the mummies in its collection. As a result Blumenbach determined that the Caucasian or white race was either the oldest or the second oldest of the five human races. Other scholars followed Blumenbach's example and began unwrapping mummies in public showings that imitated the very popular public dissections of medical schools. People were willing to pay to view both dissections and unwrappings. This circumstance caused mummy unveilings to evolve from a scholarly investigation that attracted popular attention to events staged purely for entertainment.[6] Egyptomania had now inspired something akin to a theatrical event.

In 1837 Giovanni D'Athanasi, a dealer in Egyptian antiquities, decided to stage the unwrapping of a mummy at Exeter Hall in London. He hoped it would help to advertise his forthcoming sale of Egyptian antiquities. To add credibility, he got Thomas Pettigrew, an expert on mummies, to conduct the event. The cost of the tickets for seats varied according to their view of the operating table. Almost five hundred people paid to attend. Unfortunately for Pettigrew and the audience, the unrolling of the mummy's casing did not go smoothly. Once Pettigrew removed the bandages, he revealed a body that was completely covered by a thick layer of the resins with which it had been embalmed. This shell of resin proved impenetrable to Pettigrew's instruments (including a hammer and chisel). Despite this setback, mummy unwrappings experienced a burst of popularity that spread through Britain, Europe and North America, from exhibition halls to the private homes of the rich, although their popularity declined during the 1850s. One of the great American promoters of these events was the British-born George Robins Gliddon, who moved to the United States to become an archaeologist and a race theorist. He was an adherent of the American anthropologist Thomas Morton's theory of polygenesis – that is, where God had made multiple creations of humans – as well as an advocate of the theory that Caucasians were descendents of Adam and the most perfect versions of all humans. Gliddon's unwrappings were particularly popular in the antebellum South, since they supported the theory of the innate inferiority of the negro and provided a justification for the institution of slavery.[7]

Gliddon's activities naturally attracted the attention of the morbidly inclined Edgar Allan Poe, who in 1845 wrote the short story 'Some Words with a Mummy' to satirize the unrollings. In the story, a group that includes George Robins Gliddon conducted an unwrapping of a mummy in the home of a Dr Ponnonner. What they reveal is a well-preserved body – a testament to the skill of the ancient Egyptians. This particular dissection was especially dramatic: since it was late, the group decided to postpone the dissection until the following night. At that point, someone suggested that they apply an electrical charge to the mummy. This little experiment, in the manner of *Frankenstein*, brings the mummy back to life. It turns out that the mummy's name is Allamistakeo, which is a pretty good indication that Poe was poking fun at the public's mummy obsession. A dialogue between Allamistakeo and the group of Americans ensues. Allamistakeo is none too impressed by what Gliddon and the others think they know about ancient Egypt. He goes on to inform them that ancient Egypt was actually scientifically and technologically more advanced than America in the 1840s. In fact, Poe was using Allamistakeo to engage in criticisms of American exceptionalism and Jacksonian democracy.[8]

As the fad for unwrapping mummies in public settings came to an end, both museums and individual collectors desired to add a mummy or even mummies to their collections of antiquities. Joseph Smith, Jr, the founder of the Church of Jesus Christ of Latter-day Saints, purchased two mummies in 1835. He extracted the papyrus enclosed in the wrappings of one of the mummies. Then he proceeded to translate it using his own techniques – not those of Champollion. His translation turned out to be colossally wrong when Champollion's system was used later to translate the same papyrus. To Smith it was the book of Abraham but later study revealed that it was a woman's funerary document. Other stories about real and fanciful uses of mummies circulated among Westerners. Long before the nineteenth century, painters used material from mummies in the pigments of their paints. Some of them did not even realize that they were using mummy for certain pigments. In 1881 the Dutch-born painter Lawrence Alma-Tadema discovered that the man mixing his pigments was using ground-up mummy. He quickly passed this news on to his friend, the Pre-Raphaelite painter Edward Burne-Jones. Shocked by the news about mummy pigments, Burne-Jones buried his tube of paint in his back garden. Mark Twain jokingly reported in 1867 that trains in Egypt used mummies to fuel their locomotives. His joke, however, may have been playing off reliable reports that Egyptian peasants did use mummies as fuel for their fires. In matters of mummies, truth and fiction could be equally strange.[9]

The Egyptian Revival

One of the most visible and intense manifestations of Egyptomania occurred during the early to mid-nineteenth century and is known as the Egyptian Revival in architecture and art. This revival was not the first or the last of the Egyptian revivals. Instead it was part of a long tradition of fascination with things Egyptian stretching back to the Hellenistic era. The impact of the Egyptian Revival was masked because it was part of the Neoclassical Revival of the Romantic Era which combined simplicity, grandeur and massiveness in its buildings and monuments. Many of its architectural creations were eclectic and combined Greek elements, especially Doric, with Egyptian motifs. The Greek elements often overshadowed the Egyptian elements. The second half of the eighteenth century had experienced a growing appreciation of the Classical motif of the Doric style along with ancient Egyptian motifs. The promoters of Egyptian Revival architecture, in their works, sought to portray the sublime, a sensation that Edmund Burke had first promoted in 1756. Sublime buildings and monuments would provoke feelings of terror, awe, amazement, passion and gloom, which were essentially the same powerful emotions that ancient Egyptian buildings engendered.[10]

The moving force behind the Egyptian Revival of the eighteenth century was the Italian artist Giovanni Battista Piranesi (1720–1778), who produced books of drawings that included illustrations of Egyptian or Egyptianized buildings or artefacts. These provided models that other artists, architects and interior designers could use in their work. The influential philosopher and historian Johann Gottfried Herder (1744–1803) promoted Egyptian motifs and pointed out that Egypt had produced the world's first great monuments. These men and their followers laid the foundation for the more widespread and popular Egyptian Revival that occurred after Napoleon's invasion of Egypt. Due to its size and starkness, Egyptian architecture was particularly associated with funerary architecture well before Napoleon's expedition. When Frederick the Great, King of Prussia, died in 1786, some members of his court suggested constructing his tomb as a pyramid based on the ancient pyramid tomb of Cestius in Rome.[11]

Napoleon's invasion of Egypt raised popular awareness of ancient Egypt in both France and Britain as well as other parts of Europe. The fighting in Egypt resulted in medals, monuments and satirical prints using Egyptian motifs. Vivant Denon's *Travels* was very popular among readers and was translated into several languages. *The Description of Egypt* contained many beautiful plates of illustrations that would provide inspiration and models for artists and architects using the Egyptian Revival style. Champollion's decipherment of hieroglyphs also contributed to an intensification of Egyptomania. The English designer Thomas Hope (1769–1831) used the newly available architectural knowledge for models and motifs when designing furniture and interiors. Initially, however, the primary source of Egyptian motifs remained Piranesi. Even as more and more accurate modern sources became available, architects and designers tended to prefer using the outdated and inaccurate works of Piranesi, Montfaucon and Kircher for inspiration. Artistic imagination rather than the actual Egyptian artefacts served as prototypes.[12]

As hinted at earlier, Freemasonry also played a part in the Egyptian Revival. According to Masonic lore, the Egyptians taught the Israelites the craft of architecture, which after the Exodus was in turn carried into ancient Israel when the Hebrews conquered and occupied that land. Further Egyptianization of Masonic rites and symbols occurred during the late eighteenth century due to the influence of the persuasive confidence man Count Alessandro Cagliostro (1743–1795), who introduced Egyptian rites into the lodge in Paris when he became its Grand Master. From there the Egyptianized rituals and symbols spread to some of the other lodges in France and Central Europe. Pyramids, Egyptian temples, the Sphinx and other Egyptian motifs proliferated in Masonic literature. By the early nineteenth century, Egyptian motifs and styles began to appear in newly constructed Masonic buildings.[13]

The Egyptian Revival in architecture got its start in the United States with Benjamin Latrobe (1764–1820), who used Egyptian motifs in his design of 1808 for the Library of Congress. England saw the first appearance of the style of Egyptian Revival known as 'Commercial Picturesque' with the construction in 1812 of the Egyptian Hall on Piccadilly in London. P. F. Robinson (1776–1858) designed the building and used Vivant Denon's book for design motifs. William Bullock, the owner of the Egyptian Hall, exhibited Belzoni's collection of antiquities in the Egyptian Hall for a number of years. Unfortunately the Egyptian Hall was torn down in 1905. Egyptianized architecture proved to be a popular style for commercial buildings in England and even more so in the United States despite the buildings being inauthentic and generally cheaply built.[14]

Egyptian architecture had close associations with death and its designs were simple in form but imposing in size while presenting an aspect of strength, solidity and timelessness. These traits made Egyptian motifs a perfect expression of the sublime – of mystery, terror and awe. The use of Egyptian motifs in the design of cemeteries, particularly the gates of their entrances, was very popular in many parts of England, North America and Europe. Fifteen cemetery entrances built in the United States between 1830 and 1850 used Egyptian motifs even though traditionalists criticized the use of pagan designs for the essentially Christian grave sites. The most successful practitioner of Egyptian Revival designs in cemetery architecture was A. J. Davis (1803–1892). The style was also used in the design of courthouses and prisons. It was thought to be very appropriate for these buildings to project the sublime by evoking a sense of the awe and majesty of the law. Particularly famous was New York's Halls of Justice and the House of Detention, popularly known as the 'Tombs', designed by John Haviland (1792–1852) and constructed between 1835 and 1838. Even though the Egyptian Revival building was demolished at the end of the nineteenth century, the name 'Tombs' continues to be used for both of the buildings that successively took its place as the House of Detention – as contemporary viewers of police dramas set in New York City are well aware. Egyptian Revival motifs were also used for several synagogues and churches. The Downtown Presbyterian Church in Nashville was constructed with Egyptian motifs between 1848 and 1851. Its interior is even more elaborately Egyptianized. The architectural historian Richard G. Carrott has pointed out that the Egyptian Revival was only used by Calvinistic churches. He speculated that the Egyptian style evoked an antiquity that meshed very well with the Calvinist goal of reviving the purity of the ancient Church.[15] The United States experienced the most enthusiastic use of the Egyptian Revival although, as Carrott further noted, it was still not a major revival. Instead, it was a subset of the Romantic Classical Revival.

The Egyptian Revival also had its critics. Augustus Pugin (1812–1852) was both an advocate of the Gothic Revival in church architecture and a harsh and carping critic of the Classical and Egyptian Revivals. His opinions carried weight in Great Britain but were little heeded in the United States. By 1858 the spurt of Egyptianizing architecture had declined significantly in the United States after the construction of the Dubuque City Jail in Iowa. The Egyptian Revival failed to become a popular style for homes or churches. Most people evidently did not want to live in something that resembled a tomb. But the Egyptian Revival in architecture has

Interior of the Downtown Presbyterian Church in Nashville, Tennessee. Note the winged sun disc over the altar.

never truly ended and many prominent buildings bear witness to this craze: the Egyptian Halls in Glasgow were built between 1871 and 1872; Frank Lloyd Wright's Unity Temple in Oak Park, Illinois, was constructed in 1905 to 1906; the W. C. Reebie & Brother Storage Warehouse in Chicago was erected in 1921–2; the Louvre Pyramid in Paris in 1989; and the Luxor Hotel and Casino, Las Vegas, was built in 1993.[16]

The Rise of Tourism in Egypt

The Egyptomania that followed Napoleon's expedition sparked a growing interest among Europeans and Americans to visit Egypt and experience its wonders for themselves. Prior to 1798, travel to Egypt was confined to merchants and diplomats. The Ottoman rulers did not welcome Western travellers and the predominantly Muslim population tended to be hostile. During the six hundred years between the end of the Crusades and 1798, fewer than twenty-five European visitors ventured more than 160 kilometres (100 miles) inland from the coast of Egypt. Travel in Egypt was expensive, uncomfortable and dangerous.[17]

After Napoleon's expedition, travel to Egypt became easier. As noted above, the government of Mohammad Ali Pasha brought stability to Egypt and the Pasha welcomed Westerners because he wanted to westernize Egyptian society. True tourists, rather than just merchants and diplomats, began to appear in Egypt. Among the earliest of these travellers was François René de Chateaubriand (1768–1848), who journeyed to Palestine, Egypt and North Africa in 1806. His time in Egypt caused him to ponder how the downtrodden and seemingly debased modern population could be the descendants of the builders of the pyramids. During his stay in Egypt he only viewed the pyramids from afar, but still became one of the first Western visitors to have his name inscribed on the Great Pyramid – he arranged for someone else to go to the pyramid and carve his name on it for him. Soon after Chateaubriand, Lady Hester Stanhope (1776–1839) followed with her own visit. She was the niece of William Pitt the Younger and had run his household. Upon his death, she received a very generous pension and in 1810 decided to travel. In 1812 she visited Egypt, becoming the first Englishwoman to do so. Her stay was comfortable and relatively brief; she travelled to Cairo where she was received as an honoured guest by the Mohammad Ali Pasha. The Turkish officials were not sure who she was but they knew she was somebody important and rumour had it that she was royalty. Although Hester Stanhope had a wonderful time in Egypt, it was the mountains of Lebanon that she fell in love with. Taking up residence among the Druze, she had a meeting with the explorer Johann Ludwig Burckhardt, who inspired her to do some exploring of her own. She became a local potentate and lived in a villa on Mount Lebanon until she died.[18]

A particularly intrepid traveller and explorer, Burckhardt was born in Switzerland but came to work for the African Association of Great Britain in 1808. Burckhardt studied Arabic at Cambridge to prepare for the explorations that the African Association expected him to undertake. They sent him to the Middle East in 1809. Landing at Aleppo in Syria, he disguised himself as a Muslim and continued to study Arabic and the Koran. Such was his dedication to roaming the lands of Islam that part of his disguise consisted of having himself circumcised. Burckhardt was so adept in his studies that Muslims came to consider him a great scholar of the Koran and he assumed the name Ibrahim ibn Abdullah. Travelling south, he discovered the desert city of Petra and then moved on to Cairo by 3 September 1812. His goal was to visit Mecca, but since no caravan was travelling there he made his way down the Nile into Upper Egypt and beyond into Nubia. During his travels Burckhardt discovered the great temple at Abu Simbel in March 1813. Continuing to voyage along the Nile and into Nubia, he eventually found a caravan headed towards the Red Sea coast where he could pick up a boat to Jeddah, Arabia. Encountering Mohammad Ali Pasha he was declared a devout Muslim, which allowed him to visit Mecca where he lived for three months. By 24 June 1815 Burckhardt had returned to Cairo. Further explorations of Egypt followed while he waited for a caravan to take him to West Africa. Sadly he contracted dysentery and died on 15 October 1817. Fortuitously, he had already sent his travel journals to England where they were published posthumously. Burckhardt was a great scholar, fearless and a generous soul who had proved to be very helpful to Giovanni Battista Belzoni.[19] Few early nineteenth-century Western travellers to Egypt went native and none went as native as Burckhardt, although Belzoni followed some of his methods. During his travels in Egypt between 1817 and 1819, Belzoni ventured into areas that Burckhardt had recently pioneered. The memoirs of his travels in Egypt are liberally peppered with stories of harrowing encounters with armed and initially hostile desert tribesmen along with descriptions of his archaeological discoveries.

The two men who truly brought Egypt and the great discoveries arising from Napoleon's expedition and Champollion's decipherment of hieroglyphs to the attention of the English-speaking reading public were John Gardner Wilkinson (1797–1875) and Edward William Lane (1801–1876).[20] Wilkinson was the only surviving child of a clerical family in Buckinghamshire. Both his parents were interested in the classics and antiquities and they imparted that interest to their son. Wilkinson was schooled at Harrow and attended Oxford but left after three years and did not graduate. His plan was to go on a grand tour and then join the army. Instead, while in Italy, he met the prominent classicist Sir William Gell, who persuaded him to go to Egypt to study its history. Wilkinson arrived in Egypt on 22 November 1821 and fell in love with it. He gave up all thought of a career in the army and remained in Egypt for twelve years. It was a time of phenomenal accomplishments for Wilkinson. He managed to travel throughout Egypt, made his way up the Nile to Nubia twice and ventured into both the eastern and western deserts. He also managed to do fieldwork at the great majority of the significant Egyptian archaeological sites discovered up to that time. His main focus was ancient Thebes. After learning Coptic, he took up the study of hieroglyphics and managed to improve on aspects of Champollion's breakthrough decipherment.

Returning to England in 1833 Wilkinson proceeded to publish several books that brought Egypt to life for the reading public. The greatest and most influential of these was his *Manners and Customs of the Ancient Egyptians,* which came out in 1837 and appeared in many editions over the years. His work earned him a knighthood in 1839 and the praise of both actual and armchair travellers to Egypt. As Harriet Martineau noted regarding her visit to Egypt in 1846, 'he [Wilkinson] was, by his books, a daily benefactor to us in Egypt. It is really cheering to find that any one can be so accurate, and on so large a scale, as his works prove him to be.' Amelia Edwards, the great benefactor of Egyptological studies in England, credited Wilkinson with inspiring her lifelong passion for ancient Egypt: 'As a child *The Manners and Customs of the Ancient Egyptians* had shared my affections with *The Arabian Nights.*'[21] Other books and travels followed, including Wilkinson's *Handbook for Travellers in Egypt,* which John Murray published in 1847 as part of its series of travel guides. While Wilkinson's *Handbook* was quite popular, it was not the first tourist guide to focus on Egypt. That was published over a decade earlier in 1835. Wilkinson made further trips to Egypt in 1842, 1844, 1848–9 and 1855–6. After suffering sunstroke on his last trip he returned to England, married Caroline Catherine Lucas, a botanical author some twenty-five years his junior, in 1856, and took up residence in Wales. There he continued to study his voluminous notebooks of Egyptian research while also developing an interest in British antiquities. By the time of his death, Wilkinson had laid the foundations of Egyptology as a formal academic discipline in Britain and also provided the general public with an accurate and updated image of ancient Egypt based on the revolutionary discoveries of Napoleon's savants and Champollion.[22]

Working in tandem with Wilkinson was Edward William Lane, who was born in Hereford in 1801, also into a clerical family. Lane's family had hoped he would enter the clergy, but instead he followed his brother into an apprenticeship in engraving. By the early 1820s he succumbed to the seduction of the popular Egyptomania that had become prevalent in the West. Lane attended one of Belzoni's lectures and it has been suggested that it was this event that triggered his enthusiasm for Egypt. Deciding to make the study of Egypt his life's work Lane journeyed there in 1825. Like Burckhardt before him, Lane went native. Taking up residence in an Arab neighbourhood, he quickly learned to speak Arabic to a good standard. He also adopted traditional Middle Eastern dress and went by the name Mansur Efendi. Despite this Lane did not eschew Westerners, and met with Wilkinson and other British scholars in Egypt. He worked extensively at the archaeological sites around Cairo and made two trips up the Nile to Nubia, although he was also quite interested in modern Egypt as well. When he returned to London in 1828 he composed a manuscript titled 'Description of Egypt', which largely focused on ancient Egypt. Lane approached the publisher John Murray about publishing his manuscript, but Murray delayed bringing out the book. Murray had already agreed to publish John Wilkinson's books and he did not want to have competing titles on his publication list. Instead he persuaded Lane to write an expansion of the modern section of his 'Description'. Lane heeded Murray's advice, and his two-volume work was published in 1836, titled *An Account of the Manners and Customs of the Modern Egyptians*. It served as a companion piece to Wilkinson's book on ancient Egypt and was immediately popular; Lane's work remains in use by students and researchers to this day and generations of people interested in Egypt had their curiosity satisfied or further stimulated.[23]

In retrospect, Murray's intervention diverted Lane from a career as an Egyptologist to a career as an Arabist. Lane went on to compose the first English translation of the *Thousand and One Nights*, which appeared heavily annotated in three volumes between 1839 and 1841. He began working on the massive *Arabic–English Lexicon* in 1863 but had not completed it when he died in 1876. The main body of the *Lexicon* was completed in 1893 but the entire project as Lane envisioned it remains incomplete. His first love, the 'Description of Egypt', remained unpublished until 2000. Lane remains regarded as an important figure in Egyptology and Egyptomania.

By the 1830s the standard itinerary for Western tourists in Egypt had become established. The first stop was Alexandria, but no one lingered there for long because the fabled capital of the Ptolemies was long gone. In its place was a somewhat squalid Western-style port – a disappointment

Dahabeah, from C. W. Wilson, *Picturesque Palestine, Sinai, and Egypt* (1881–4), engraving.

for those hoping for the romance of walking in the footsteps of Cleopatra and the scholars of the greatest library of the ancient world. With little to keep them in Alexandria, most visitors hurried on to Cairo, initially by sailboat but later by steamboat. After arriving in Cairo, they took in the pyramids, the Sphinx, the sites associated with the biblical sojourns of the Hebrews and the Holy Family in Egypt, and the great medieval mosques. Then it was up the Nile to various ancient ruins including Karnak and Luxor, the Isle of Philae, Abu Simbel and the Second Cataract. Initially such a journey was taken on a traditional Nile sailboat called a *dahabeah* that the traveller hired for several months with the help of a guide known as a dragoman. Normally the crew of the *dahabeah* would sail or row it to the second cataract as quickly as possible. At that point the traveller would begin a leisurely cruise down the Nile investigating all the many sites along the way. In a pre-air-conditioning age the travel season for Egypt was the winter, from October to March at the latest.

During the nineteenth century, the technology and the infrastructure of travel steadily improved and expanded worldwide; progress that was especially true for travel to Egypt. After 1830 visitors to Egypt could arrive by steamship. As time went on, sailings became more frequent, the voyages became shorter and more comfortable, and there was increasing competition between tour operators. The Peninsular and Oriental Steam Navigation Company (P&O), a British firm, pioneered steamship travel in the Mediterranean, but even English travellers came to consider that the foreign steamships – of the Austrian Lloyd Company and the French Messageries Impériales – offered a greater level of comfort. From the 1840s to the 1890s, the time needed to travel from Southampton to Alexandria fell from seventeen days to six days.[24]

Steamboats appeared on the Nile early on and became an established feature of river traffic during the 1830s. By the late 1850s they were taking travellers up the Nile to Aswan, although the more hardy, leisured and connoisseur-types among the Nile voyagers, like Amelia Edwards, preferred the traditional *dahabeah*. As she observed in 1873, 'Such is the *esprit du Nil*. The people in dahabeeyahs despise Cook's tourists.' Western hotels also began to appear in Cairo, such as the Hotel des Anglais in the 1840s. It was renamed Shepheard's Hotel in 1861 after its owner Samuel Shepheard (1816–1866) and maintained a somewhat mixed reputation among its patrons. Lucie Duff Gordon considered it 'horrid' in 1862, while in 1867 Mark Twain called it 'the worst on earth except for the one I stopped at once in a small town in the United States'. Other Western hotels followed in both Cairo and Luxor. The railroad also came to Egypt. Pasha Abbas signed a contract for the building of a railroad between Alexandria and Cairo in 1851. Built with British expertise, it was completed in 1856 and soon was joined by a railroad between the cities of Cairo and Suez. Egypt continued to add steadily to its railroad system throughout the nineteenth century. Thomas Cook's Tours revolutionized tourism in Egypt in 1869 when it began offering package tours along the Nile in its own fleet of steamboats in the aftermath of the Prince of Wales's trip to Egypt. By the early 1870s, the Egyptian segment of the company's business had become the most important and in 1878 Cook's began operating its own line of steamboats.[25] In more recent years, air conditioning, cruise ships and air travel have further altered the nature of Egyptian tourism – as have periodic political upheavals – but the fundamental features of tour routes and sightseeing attractions were established during the middle decades of the nineteenth century.

Among American travellers to Egypt, the world-walking John Ledyard (1751–1789) led the way. Ledyard arrived at Alexandria on 5 August 1788. His plan was to find a caravan travelling west and trace the route of the Niger River for the African Association in London. Ledyard was not impressed by Alexandria and Cairo, or for that matter the Nile and the monuments of ancient Egypt. After locating a caravan, he set out for West Africa, but died from an overdose of emetic. The full account of his Egyptian and African travels was left unwritten except for a few letters to Thomas Jefferson and other friends.[26]

The first American to visit Egypt and write a popular and successful book about the experience was John Lloyd Stephens (1805–1852). He had developed an interest in New York politics during his youth but had contracted a throat infection from giving frequent speeches, so his doctor advised him to take a European tour. In 1834 he embarked on a grand tour. Like many well-to-do travellers of the Victorian era, he also planned to write a book about his experiences. Travel narratives to exotic locales were a popular genre of nineteenth-century literature. After crossing the Atlantic, he learned that Egypt was a good place to visit and in December 1835 landed at Alexandria. Like many travellers in the modern era, he found Alexandria to be a disappointingly shabby place. He attributed Alexandria's vanished greatness to the fact that 'like everything else which falls into the hands of the Mussulman, it has been going to ruin.' Learning that Muslims considered the Nile's water to possess a marvellous taste, he partook of it, only to suffer badly from the malady of the traveller – diarrhoea – during his time in Cairo. Upon arriving at Cairo, he also discovered that it did not measure up to the Cairo of the Caliphs and the *Arabian Nights*. Like a number of Western visitors to Egypt, Stephens got to meet Mohammad Ali Pasha. He assured the Pasha that more tourists would be visiting Egypt now that transportation facilities were improving and safety from crime was as good as that of European cities such as London. Although Egypt had acquired a reputation as a dangerous place for Westerners, by the mid-1830s Stephens found it to be quite safe – he would travel by himself in a traditional *dahabeah* with a native crew. Nor was he alone in this opinion; Harriet Martineau in 1846 stated adamantly that she found Egypt to be quite secure. It was not until Stephens travelled into the Arabian Desert to visit Petra that he began journeying incognito as Abdel (Abdulah) Hasis (the slave of God).[27]

During his time in Egypt, Stephens followed an itinerary that had already become standard. Although he had sighted the pyramids off in the distance from Cairo every day, he did not manage to get out to see them until his tenth day in Cairo thanks to his bowel-loosening misadventure with Nile water. In those days tourists could climb to the top of the Great Pyramid with the sometimes unwelcome assistance of Arab guides. Stephens himself made his way to the pyramid's top and once there, he found the view to be marvellous. On the other hand, he considered his guides to be a great distraction from the enjoyment and contemplation of the moment.[28]

On 1 January 1836 Stephens began his voyage up the Nile in his hired *dahabeah* with his Maltese servant, Paul, and the native crew. Travelling along the river, he found the Nile valley green and verdant, the antiquities impressive but the people living on the ancient sites were poor, ignorant and degraded by Turkish oppression. Although he readily granted that the Pasha was bringing progress and modernization to Egypt, he lamented how the ruins were ruthlessly mined for materials for the government's building projects. He also discovered that the fleas of Egypt were extremely irksome. The cataracts, furthermore, did not impress him when compared to the majesty of Niagara Falls. At Philae he engaged in a common practice of nineteenth-century tourists and carved his initials on the propylon of the temple right under the initials of Napoleon's general Desaix. On his way back down the Nile, he found Thebes and the temple of Karnak to be particularly impressive. It was clear to him that Egyptian civilization had reached an advanced stage much earlier than the ancient Greeks. As for the tombs of the Valley of the Kings, Stephens stated: 'The world can show nothing like them; and he who has not seen them can hardly believe in their existence.' Although the ruins of Thebes were the most impressive in Egypt, the locals were the 'most miserable'. In common with other European travellers, Stephens did not find the Coptic Christians to be any better than the Muslim Arabs, although he did manage to worship with some of them before he arrived back in Cairo.[29]

Stephens's journey up and down the Nile was very typical and he would be followed by tens of thousands of tourists over the years. At first they travelled on the *dahabeahs* but many switched to the steamboats of the line belonging to Cook's Travel. Although Stephens roughed it to a significant degree on his *dahabeah*, he luxuriated in not shaving for two months. Still, he considered the *dahabeah* a mode of travel that would be most comfortable and enjoyable if the traveller was accompanied by a good friend, good books and a good cook. For him, thanks to its ruins, 'Egypt [was] perhaps the most interesting country in the world.' Furthermore, although his account of his travels is peppered with critical comments about native Egyptians and Muslims, he developed a genuine friendship and respect for the crew of his *dahabeah*. Reviewers gave Stephens's account of his travels in Egypt and the Holy Land an enthusiastic reception. As Edgar Allan Poe put it in his review for the *New York Review*: 'We take leave of Mr Stephens with sentiments of hearty respect. We hope it is not the last time we shall hear from him. He is a traveller with whom we shall like to take other journeys.' Readers agreed. Copies of *Incidents of Travel in Egypt* sold extremely well in an era when American authors had a difficult time competing with English writers. As Richard Francaviglia has pointed out, Stephens has written the ideal Victorian travel book: 'it combined adventure and education'. Although Stephens is also known for his 1842 accounts of his discoveries of the cities of the ancient Maya, it was the profits from his book on Egypt and the Holy Land that supplied him with the money to explore Central America. *Incidents of Travel in Egypt* was his most popular and successful book and as such it contributed to the continuation of Egyptomania in the English-speaking world.[30]

Visual support for Egyptomania received a big boost from the pictorial fruits of the travels of the artist David Roberts (1796–1864). Prior to Roberts, Westerners had had access to many accurate images of Egyptian antiquities. Frederick Norden's posthumously published *Travels in Egypt* (1751) was heavily illustrated, as was Vivant Denon's *Travels in Upper and Lower Egypt* (1802). Of course, the cornucopia of plates depicting Egyptian ruins and monuments in the French *Description of Egypt* (1809–28) was a visual feast. Roberts's art, however, was different. Born in Stockbridge near Edinburgh, Roberts's father was a cobbler. At a young age, he showed remarkable talent for drawing, but his family was too poor to send him to school. Instead he was apprenticed to a house painter. From there he moved on to become a scene painter for theatrical productions and soon began to produce paintings as well. He moved to London in 1822 where he did scene painting for Drury Lane. Within a few years his paintings began to be exhibited in London galleries and his fame grew along with demand for his work. After making two trips to Europe for artistic inspiration, he travelled to Egypt in 1838. Arriving at Alexandria on 24 September 1838 he began sailing up the Nile from Cairo to Abu Simbel on 8 October. He returned to Cairo on 21 December and worked there until his departure for the Holy Land on 6 February 1839. Once he returned to London, he sought a publisher for his drawings, which were reproduced as 247 lithographs appearing in the six volumes of *Egypt and Nubia* (1846–9) and *The Holy Land, Syria, Idumea, Arabia, Egypt and Nubia* (1842–9). It was this work that secured his permanent reputation as an artist. Roberts's drawings were done in the Romantic style, which contrasted favourably with the somewhat antiseptic realism of the plates of the *Description of Egypt*. Equally important, Roberts's work was more readily accessible to the public than the rare and bulky *Description of Egypt*. Once more Egyptomania was provided with a further boost – this time a visual one. Even today Roberts's lithographs remain veritable icons of Egyptian antiquity and postcards of his lithographs are readily available for sale in Cairo.[31]

Egypt attracted the attention of many people, and some who would go on to become famous. Just at the time he was starting to earn fame as a writer, William Makepeace Thackeray (1811–1863) travelled with a friend to Egypt on a P&O steamer. After departing Southampton on 22 August 1844, the ship stopped in Spain and Portugal and visited various ports in the eastern Mediterranean, including Athens, Constantinople, Rhodes and Jaffa, along with an additional stop in Jerusalem. The steamer finally reached Alexandria on 12 October and Thackeray was 'ready to gaze on it with pyramidal wonder and hieroglyphic awe'. Predictably, Alexandria disappointed Thackeray's high expectations. As he put it: 'You might be as well impressed with Wapping as with your first step on Egyptian soil.' Making his way by boat up the Nile to Cairo, he was stirred by the view of the pyramids and the panoramic view from the Citadel of Saladin. Close up, the pyramids were a different story. During the obligatory excursion to the pyramids with a party from his hotel, Thackeray found his enjoyment of the visit diminished by the incessant badgering of the locals, who made their living guiding visitors around the precinct of the pyramids or assisting them with the climb to the top of Great Pyramid. For Thackeray, 'There is nothing sublime in it . . . the cursed shrieking of the Arabs prevents all thought or leisure.' Although he did not fall in love with Egypt, Thackeray still managed to enjoy his few weeks there. Cairo marked the farthest that he travelled into the country. The itinerary for his visit was extremely truncated, but the cruise around the Mediterranean provided him with the materials for a book, *From Cornhill to Cairo*, which he initially published in 1846 under the pseudonym Michael Angelo Titmarsh.[32]

Gustave Flaubert (1821–1880) journeyed to Egypt when he was not quite 28 years old. At that age, he was hoping to have a career as a writer. He and his friend Maxime du Camp travelled to Egypt on a mission for the French government, although Flaubert noted several times in his travel journal and letters home that the pair grievously neglected their diplomatic duties. Arriving at Alexandria on 17 November 1849, Flaubert suffered the usual disappointment when he discovered that the famed city was 'almost a European city, there are so many Europeans here'. He reached Cairo on 25 November and took up residence in the Hôtel d'Orient, although later he moved to the Hôtel du Nil. Flaubert and Du Camp set out for the pyramids on 7 December. They camped out near the pyramids that night and then climbed the Great Pyramid early the next morning so they could take in the view from the top at sunrise. After spending several days exploring the Giza Plateau, the pair also managed to visit the smaller pyramids at Saqqara.[33]

Flaubert took the standard journey up the Nile from Cairo to Nubia in a hired *dahabeah* with a lengthy stop at Thebes. The great temples at Luxor and Karnak impressed Flaubert deeply, unlike the other Egyptian monuments he had already visited. As a young aspiring literati, Flaubert assumed a blasé attitude to most things – except for prostitutes. (His letters – besides those to his mother, of course – and travel journals contained many accounts of encounters with prostitutes.) On the other hand, because Flaubert had read Edward William Lane's *Manners and Morals of the Modern Egyptians*, the knowledge he gained aided his appreciation of what he saw in Egypt. Flaubert's time in Egypt ended on 19 July when he sailed from Alexandria. When he departed he took with him the foot of a mummy, which he gave a place of honour on his desk for the rest of his life. Despite the apparent super-ficiality of Flaubert's reaction to his time in Egypt, scholars widely credit his journey there with causing him to shift his writing style from Romanticism to Realism. While he never wrote a book about his travels in Egypt, various segments from his travel journals made their way into his later novels.[34]

By contrast, the trip undertaken by Herman Melville (1819–1891) from 28 December 1856 to 4 January 1857 was too brief to significantly impact his work. Only a few references in poems reflected what he had seen in Egypt. He was also older than Thackeray or Flaubert when he made the trip and had just about given up on novels and had turned to poetry instead. Visiting Egypt was only a small part of his grand tour that lasted seven months and included Scotland, much of the Mediterranean including Palestine, Turkey, Greece and Italy, followed by Switzerland and the Netherlands. After arriving in Alexandria, he took the newly completed railway line to Cairo and checked into Shepheard's Hotel on 30 December. He spent the next day at the pyramids but had to return to Alexandria on 1 January to catch his ship. The ship's sailing was delayed, which rather irritated Melville as he would have much preferred to stay in Cairo. The delay, however, gave him time to work on his journal entries concerning Egypt – the forced leisure allowed Melville to expand on his observations at the pyramids while they were still fresh.[35]

Melville was clearly fairly well read on the subject of ancient Egypt. He supported the theory that the monotheism associated with Judaism had its birth in Egypt and that Moses had studied the wisdom of the Egyptians. On the other hand, he rejected a theory that the pyramids had been built as bar-riers to the encroaching sands of the desert. Along with other Westerners, he climbed the Great Pyramid and entered the King's Chamber. It was a difficult climb and a claustrophobic entry for Melville. The pyramids left a definite impression on him as he characterized them as 'something vast, undefiled, incomprehensible, and awful'.[36]

Female visitors to Egypt during this period seem to have had more specific reasons for visiting that enigmatic land, or at least experienced more visceral reactions to it than male tourists. Along with Harriet Martineau, Florence Nightingale (1820–1910) and Lucie, Lady Duff Gordon (1821–1869) are good examples of this approach. None of these three women travelled to Egypt in the company of a husband. Martineau and Nightingale, however, did travel in company with another married couple. In Martineau's case, it was her friends Mr and Mrs Richard Reeves, while for Nightingale it was an older couple who were friends of her parents and surrogate parents in their own right – Charles and Selina Bracebridge. Lucie Duff Gordon, although married, journeyed to Egypt and took up residence there with only her maid, Sally Naldrett, for a companion. The three women were also connected by family or socially. Martineau and Duff Gordon were cousins, while Martineau was friends with Julie Smith, Nightingale's maternal aunt.

Harriet Martineau was an intellectual and very independent-minded, traits not encouraged in women by Victorian society. Raised a Unitarian, she took a devout and spiritual approach to religion when she was younger. Her early books were devotional literature but she became interested in social reform and is widely considered the first female sociologist. Possessed of great curiosity, she also liked to travel. During the years 1834 to 1836 she visited the United States where she took up the cause of abolitionism, generating great controversy with Southerners. Her belief in Unitarianism faded and eventually died as she grew older; by the time of her trip to Egypt she was an atheist.

Martineau first sighted Egypt from the deck of a steamer on 20 November 1844. Her sojourn there lasted until 23 February 1845 when her party left Cairo for the Sinai and then Palestine and Syria. While she was in Egypt, Martineau followed the standard itinerary – Alexandria to Cairo, take in the sights of Cairo, up the Nile to the second cataract and back down the river stopping at all the fabled ruins on the way back to Cairo. When Martineau returned to England, she wrote *Eastern Life: Past and Present*, which appeared in 1848. At first the book appears to be simply a travel narrative written in a lively style. But as the book progresses, Martineau expounds on her theory that religion evolves into a more and more abstract concept of God bolstered by observations of what she saw in Egypt, the Sinai, Palestine and Syria. The ultimate result would be a philosophical atheism. While that conclusion was not made explicit by Martineau, it was implicit enough for the publisher John Murray to decline to publish such an infidel book.

Florence Nightingale's sojourn in Egypt began on 19 November 1849 and lasted until 7 April 1850. She and the Bracebridges followed the standard tourist itinerary during their time in Egypt and travelled up and down the Nile on a *dahabeah*, which they named *The Parthenope* after Florence's sister. Their journey was filled with wonderful sights and experiences, although nothing that other tourists were not experiencing as well. Nightingale came prepared with an extensive library of books on Egypt, including Gardner Wilkinson's guide to Thebes along with the massive six-volume *Egypt's Place in Universal History* written by her friend, the

German Egyptologist Christian von Bunsen. She was also quite familiar with Martineau's recently published *Eastern Life*. Nightingale recorded her adventures through letters to her family back in England and in her diary entries. Prior to going on the tour of Egypt and Greece, the 29-year-old Nightingale was struggling to find a way to give her life a worthwhile purpose. While her letters to her parents reveal a young women joyfully relating her fascinating experiences, her diary reveals a woman who was groping towards a purpose in life and who believed God was speaking directly to her on numerous occasions during her travels. The sense of the sublime engendered by visiting the massive and exotic ruins of Egypt could only have encouraged such thoughts. These spiritual struggles would eventually lead Nightingale to her destiny – the convalescent hospital at Scutari during the Crimean War and the ensuing fame that resulted.[37]

Lucie Duff Gordon (1821–1869) was about the only nineteenth-century visitor whose time in Egypt turned her into a celebrity of the Victorian era even though she made no geographical or archaeological discoveries.[38] Born Lucie Austin, she was the daughter of the Victorian intellectuals John and Sarah Austin and her mother provided her with a fine education. Lucie grew up to be beautiful and vivacious, her pleasing qualities attracting Sir Alexander Duff Gordon, an impecunious baronet and then a minor Treasury clerk. The couple married in 1840 and had a happy marriage with many friends. But during the 1850s Lucie developed escalating symptoms of tuberculosis. Her condition deteriorated in the cool, damp weather of England and she began coughing up blood. The standard Victorian medical advice for people in her condition was to seek a warm, dry climate, if they could afford it. Initially, from 1860 to 1862, Lucie tried living in South Africa but her sojourn there did not bring the necessary relief. So in 1862 she travelled to Egypt. Except for some brief visits back to England, Lucie Duff Gordon lived in Egypt until her death in 1869.

Lucie was a charming person and began making friends, both Western and Egyptian, as soon as she arrived in Egypt. One of these was the American consul in Cairo, William Thayer. Even more significant was Lucie's hiring of Omar Abu Halaweh as her man-servant. Omar turned out to be a faithful guide, a protective guardian, a skilled cook and eventually a loving nurse until the day Lucie died. The Egyptian climate also proved kind to her respiratory ailments, which explains why she decided to take up permanent residence there. During her first months in Egypt, she did the standard itinerary: landing in Egypt, visiting Cairo, and making her way up the Nile to the second cataract and back on a *dahabeah*. Incredibly she found Cairo in the winter too cool for her good health, so she decided she would need to find a place to live in the Luxor area about 640 kilometres (400 miles) to the south. After making some inquiries, she was able to rent the Maison de France in December 1863, which belonged to the French government but had originally been built on top of the roof of an ancient temple by the energetic treasure-hunter and English consul Henry Salt. Taking up residence at the Maison de France also made Lucie a resident of the Arab village that occupied that area of the ruins and included a simple mosque at one end and a brothel at the other. Lucie refrained from mentioning the latter.[39]

The typically hospitable Egyptians welcomed Lucie and unlike most of her fellow Westerners, she was not stand-offish. Although she had no medical training, Lucie shared her medical supplies and what knowledge she possessed. Her skills helped the villagers with their simpler maladies and she became known as *Sitt Hakima*, the lady doctor. Even more significantly, her neighbours dubbed her *Noor ala Noor*, which meant 'light from the light'. Lucie dressed in Egyptian clothing, ate their food and lived under the same conditions that they did. While remaining an English lady, she managed to assimilate to a great degree. She loved Egypt and its people, and they loved her back in return.

All the while she lived in South Africa and Egypt, Lucie wrote long letters full of evocative observations to her husband, mother, daughter and friends in England. Initially it was suggested that her South African letters were worth gathering together and publishing. As these were in preparation, she decided to also work on publishing her Egyptian letters. Her *Letters from*

The French House where Lucie Duff Gordon made her home near Luxor, Egypt; from Amelia Edwards, *A Thousand Miles Up the Nile* (1891).

the Cape appeared in 1864 and this collection was followed by the first set of her Egyptian letters in 1865. An acute observer, Lucie famously remarked that Egypt 'is a palimpsest, in which the Bible is written over Herodotus, and the Koran over that'. Lucie was very sympathetic to the Muslim Egyptians of Upper Egypt and criticized her cousin and predecessor Harriet Martineau for lacking empathy for the natives. Lucie found them to be generous and kind and in most ways morally superior to her fellow Westerners. Coming from a Unitarian/agnostic background, Lucie also found Islam more congenial philosophically and theologically than most typical Victorians.[40] The Egyptian letters turned Lucie into a celebrity. Tourists began stopping at Luxor to visit her, although in most cases this was not especially welcome. It is probably the case that most of her visitors simply wanted to meet the author of the letters because of the fame of her eccentric lifestyle rather than that they agreed with her opinions. A second set of *Last Letters from Egypt* appeared posthumously in 1875. Family members had gathered them together in several different compilations. The letters are a monument to one of the most astute and empathetic Westerners ever to visit Egypt. Her writings helped to nurture a unique strain of Egyptomania that treated the modern Egyptians as worthwhile human beings rather than as the degraded descendants or epigones of ancient Egypt's lost grandeur.

During Lucie's sojourn in Egypt, Mark Twain visited the country for a few days, but he never mentioned her or made it to Luxor. Twain's Egyptian expedition was but one of many stops made from 10 June to 19 November 1867 during the course of the excursion of the ship *Quaker City* to the Holy Land. Twain would immortalize his travel there in his experiences in *The Innocents Abroad*. After leaving the port of Jaffa in Palestine, *Quaker City* arrived at Alexandria on the evening of 2 October. Twain and some friends immediately went on shore to explore but like most Western visitors found Alexandria to be a disappointment. As he put it: 'Alexandria was too much like a European city to be novel, and we soon tired of it.' On 4 October, passengers from *Quaker City* took the train to Cairo and checked into Shepheard's Hotel – a facility that did not find favour with Twain. Then on 5 October they travelled from Cairo to Giza by donkey. Once at the pyramids, Twain and his companions made the standard climb to the top of the Great Pyramid and entered it. He experienced the usual manhandling from Arab guides while climbing the pyramid, along with the usual demands from them and other Arabs for payment and tips for dubiously rendered services. This custom very much detracted from his enjoyment of the visit. But unlike many visitors, he did not complain about the heat inside the Great Pyramid. Twain found his inspection of the Sphinx to be a very moving experience:

The Sphinx is grand in its loneliness; it is imposing in its magnitude; it is impressive in the mystery that hangs over its story. And there is that in the overshadowing majesty of this eternal figure of stone, with its accusing memory of the deeds of all ages, which reveals to one something of what he shall feel when he shall stand at last in the awful presence of God.

Alas, that train of thought was also ruined by the unedifying spectacle of a fellow passenger trying to chisel off a piece of the Sphinx's chin! Despite these incidents, the often cynical Twain departed Egypt with a deep respect for the achievements of ancient Egyptian civilization, as recorded in *The Innocents Abroad*, which sold 70,000 copies in its first year of publication.[41]

One of the great celebrities of the Victorian era to tour Egypt was the Prince of Wales, the future Edward VII. His visit in 1869 definitely shows that tourism in Egypt was becoming more organized and routine rather than rough and ready. The Prince was never much of a trendsetter so his visit to Egypt shows how conventional travelling to that exotic land had become. One of the most influential tourists to visit Egypt came a few years after the Prince of Wales. The English writer Amelia Edwards toured Egypt for about five months from the end of November 1873 to late April 1874. Edwards travelled with another Englishwoman whom she simply refers to as 'L'. In some ways, Edwards followed the standard itinerary; that is, Alexandria and quickly on to Cairo, arranging a cruise up to the second cataract and then a visit to the ancient monuments of Egypt as the boat floated back down the Nile. Edwards, however, recognized that the oldest Egyptian monuments were in the Cairo region, those of Middle Egyptian and Thebes were the next oldest and represented the highpoint of Egyptian culture, and finally the monuments farther up the Nile into Nubia were the youngest and also represented a decline in the quality of Egyptian civilization. Thus, to hurry south to the second cataract and then proceed slowly back to Cairo was to do Egyptian history backwards. Accordingly, Edwards and her party made a number of stops to do preliminary explorations on their way to the second cataract. Few nineteenth-century travellers on the Nile, however, were as well versed in the latest developments of Egyptology as Edwards.[42]

It is surprising to learn that Edwards visited Egypt on a whim. She and 'L' had travelled to the Continent to get away from dreary English weather but found that miserable weather had followed them as they travelled south. Giving up on southern France and Italy, the pair headed for Egypt. Once Edwards arrived in Cairo, she made a quick trip to see the pyramids but otherwise spent ten days shopping for a *dahabeah* to hire. Edwards, 'L' and several others settled on a boat called the *Philae*. Despite their lack of prior planning, Edwards managed to take some useful Egyptological books, including works by Champollion and Gardner Wilkinson, on her Nile cruise.[43]

Although Edwards visited places that had been visited many times before, her reactions to what she saw did not agree with the consensus of her fellow travellers. Like others before and after her, she readily agreed that the pyramids became more impressive the closer the observer was to them. Despite universal complaints about the bothersome and importunate Arab guides who lurked around the pyramids pestering with offers of unwanted services or pleas for baksheesh, Edwards found them to be reasonably well-behaved aides. This situation, however, may say more about the force of Edwards's personality than the normal behaviour of the Arab guides. Describing her visit to Saqqara, she commented on how she and other tourists abhorred the pilfering of the tombs of the ancient Egyptians; however, at the same time she confessed to being almost irresistibly drawn into acquiring relics and antiquities herself. Edwards was a fairly conventional late Victorian Anglican so she put some thought into harmonizing the facts of ancient Egyptian history with the biblical narrative. For probably much the same reason, she took a generally favourable view of the Coptic Christians of Egypt. On the other hand, she considered camels to be hateful and despicable creatures, a sentiment voiced by many Arabs. Unlike John Lloyd Stephens, Edwards's party did not encounter any crocodiles until they were travelling on the section of the Nile between the first and second cataracts. All along the river, Edwards luxuriated in the many ruins she visited. The ruins of Abu Simbel in particular fascinated her. At Luxor she stopped to see the house where Lucie Duff Gordon had lived, along with the great temples and tombs of that region.[44]

Back in Cairo, Edwards visited the Egyptian Museum in its original home in the Boulak neighbourhood. For her, that museum was, on its own merits, worth the journey from Europe. Returning to the Great Pyramid, she and 'L' made the climb to the top but declined to enter the hot and filthy interior chambers. Edwards found the view from the top of the Great Pyramid to be outstanding. It also confirmed for her, 'how clearly the place is a great cemetery, one marvels at the ingenious theories which turn the pyramids into astronomical observatories and abstruse standards of measure. They are the grandest graves in the world – and they are nothing more.'[45] As she put it: 'It is impossible to get tired of the Pyramids.'

After Edwards returned to England she spent two years writing an account of her travels. *A Thousand Miles Up the Nile* was published in 1877 and sold extremely well, greatly increasing Edwards's fortune. In contrast to some people who developed an obsession with the weird speculations about Egypt, Edwards always maintained a scholarly and realistic view of Egypt. The charm of her book was that it combined a love of things Egyptian with highly readable and witty prose, and a grasp of the latest advances in Egyptological studies. Her passion for Egypt continued throughout the rest of her life. She helped found the Egypt Exploration Society, was a generous patron of the great Egyptologist Flinders Petrie and founded the chair of Egyptology at the University of London, of which Petrie was the first occupant. Her continuing fascination with Egypt helped to establish Egyptology as an academic discipline in England and contributed to popular culture's continuing attraction to ancient Egypt.[46]

One visitor to Egypt who was little remarked upon was the former U.S. president Ulysses S. Grant, who began a world tour with his wife on 17 May 1877 shortly after leaving office. During the entire trip the couple was accompanied by John Russell Young, a reporter for the *New York Herald*. Grant's travels and Young's reporting of them were commemorated in the beautifully illustrated two-volume *Around the World with General Grant* that appeared in 1879 and graced the homes of many proud Americans. The Grants arrived at Alexandria on 5 January 1878 on the American warship *Vandalia*. At that time Egypt was under the rule of Pasha Ismail, who gave the former president a warm welcome and let him stay in one of the khedival palaces. In Egypt, Grant's escort was Elbert Eli Farman, the American consul general who would later describe the experience in 1904 in his *Along the Nile with General Grant*. Over the course of a month on the Nile, Farman took them to all the usual spots on the Egyptian tourist itinerary, although the Grants only made it as far south as the first cataract and so missed Abu Simbel and the second cataract. All along the way they were enthusiastically cheered by Egyptian villagers who were under the mistaken impression that the king of America was visiting. Both the Egyptian people and the Egyptian antiquities fascinated Grant, particularly the Sphinx. He told his son Fred: 'I have seen more to interest me in Egypt than in any of my other travels.' Thanks to newspaper reports and the books of Young and Farman, many stay-at-home Americans got to enjoy exotic Egypt vicariously through their former president.[47]

By the beginning of the twentieth century, touring Egypt had become more prosaic despite the country's exotic mystique. Between plentiful railway, steamboats and modern hotels, Westerners could experience the aura of ancient Egypt and the orientalism of contemporary Arabic Egypt with all the comforts of home. Rudyard Kipling's account of his travels in Egypt exemplifies the change. We generally associate Kipling with India but in

Ulysses S. Grant and his tour party in Egypt in 1877.

early 1913 he spent several weeks touring Egypt. That should not be a surprise. For most of the nineteenth century, at least half of the English visitors in Egypt stopped there on their way to or from India. Even before the opening of the Suez Canal in 1869 Egypt was the bridge between the Mediterranean and the Red Sea, which is the route most people took to get to India rather than sailing around Africa. Kipling published an account of his time in Egypt under the intriguing title of *Egypt of the Magicians* (1914), which derives from Exodus 7:22. Sadly, there was nothing magical about Kipling's Egypt. Arriving in Egypt on a P&O ship, he complained about the line's poor service, which seems to have been the common practice of most of the line's customers. Kipling did not think too much of the train from Alexandria to Cairo either. Cairo was dirty and failed to charm him. He found the municipal administration to be ineffectual. Later securing a place on a steamer going up the Nile, he found most of its passengers more or less tedious and mostly American, two things that apparently went hand in hand in Kipling's mind. Hypocritically, he complained that travel on the steamer kept him and his fellow passengers isolated from the real, traditional Egypt, but he made little effort to escape the confines of the boat. Arriving at Aswan, he got to see the impact of the first modern dam built on the Nile and the great reservoir lake that it had created.[48] By the time of Kipling's visit, the romantic age of Western travel in Egypt was over, although the desire of many to see Egypt for themselves remained strong and has continued to remain strong. Whether the traveller is riding a tour bus to Cairo, a camel at Giza, a cruise ship on the Nile or is simply an armchair traveller reading about the wonders of Egypt or watching a documentary on the television, the desire to experience Egypt in person or vicariously remains strong among many Westerners.

Egyptomania in Fiction

The nineteenth century saw the appearance of a new literary genre – Egyptian-themed fiction. Given that the phenomenon of Egyptomania can be traced back to the Greeks and the Hebrews, it might initially seem surprising that works of fiction using ancient Egypt as the setting were uncommon prior to the 1820s.[49] It should be remembered, however, that a reasonably accurate understanding of pharaonic Egypt's history was not available until several decades after the decipherment of hieroglyphs occurred. Furthermore, a mass market for fiction really did not develop until the early and middle decades of the nineteenth century, as new techniques of printing and binding made books cheaper and mass literacy created demand. So Egyptological advances, technological innovations and greater opportunity for education all helped to make the Egyptian-themed genre possible.

Literary works using Egypt for a setting have an ancient pedigree. Egypt gets numerous mentions in Greek mythology and the Homeric epics. Aeschylus' play *The Suppliants* was partially set in Egypt. Some of the action in *An Ethiopian Story* or *Aithiopika* by Heliodorus takes place in Egypt, although the setting of the novel ranges from Delphi to Ethiopia. Although its chronological setting is never identified, the action in the novel took place many centuries back in the BC era. Heliodorus wrote *An Ethiopian Story* sometime during the third or fourth centuries AD and it is the longest of the surviving ancient Greek novel and has the most intricate plot. It contained no hermetic elements, which were quite popular in late antiquity and during the Byzantine era. Some Greek scholars fallaciously argued that it was even a covert Christian work.[50] After *An Ethiopian Story*, what little fiction was written during the Middle Ages and the Renaissance did not use Egyptian settings.

The eighteenth century welcomed works of fiction set in a hermetic or mystic version of ancient Egypt. Abbé Jean Terrasson, a priest and a professor of classical languages at the Collège de France, began this literary trend. In 1731 he brought out a long novel in three volumes titled *Sethos: A History or Biography, based on Unpublished Memoirs of Ancient Egypt.* The novel uses the literary device of claiming to be a translation of an old manuscript by a nameless Greek from the second century AD. Terrasson, however, assures his readers that *Sethos* is fiction but he also claims it was based on authentic ancient sources. As a result, many people took the novel to be a reliably accurate historical account – in a similar way to how Dan Brown's *The Da Vinci Code* (2003) has been received by some of his readers. In reality, though, it was nothing of the sort. All Terrasson had for sources was the often inaccurate accounts of ancient Graeco-Roman visitors such as Strabo and Diodorus or the Renaissance and Baroque hermetic speculations about ancient Egypt. Sethos, the eponymous hero of the novel, was a prince of Egypt in the thirteenth century BC and an avid seeker of knowledge and truth. After going through much study, many esoteric initiations and long travels through Africa in the course of the novel, Sethos decides to forego his royal inheritance and his intended bride. Instead he devotes himself to his priestly duties and studies. As Mary Lefkowitz has pointed out, Terrasson's ancient Egypt is simply an idealized version of eighteenth-century Europe with a hermetic emphasis. Such an Egypt met the needs of Terrasson's plot in a way that a true depiction of ancient Egypt could never have done, even if such knowledge had been available in 1731. Despite being a very long and sometimes tedious novel, *Sethos* was very popular in the eighteenth century and was translated from French into English and German. It influenced Masonic thinking and rituals at the time and in the mid-twentieth century would be used for Afrocentric purposes by George G. M. James.[51]

Similar fictional works quickly followed. In 1739 Alexandre Tanevot composed *Sethos, Tragedie Nouvelle*, a verse tragedy based on *Sethos*. Jean-Philippe Rameau was inspired by Terrasson's novel to compose the ballet *The Birth of Osiris* in 1751, as was Johann Gottlieb Naumann when he created his opera *Osiris* in 1781. Mozart belonged to a Masonic lodge in Vienna. Masonic lore based on *Sethos* along with his own reading of Terrasson's novel inspired Mozart to compose incidental music for the play *Thamos, King of Egypt* in 1773–80 and *The Magic Flute* in 1791. There is even a character named Sethos in *Thamos*. It was *The Magic Flute*, however, that was the big success. Opera-goers loved it from its first performance and it went through a hundred performances in a little over a year. Sadly, Mozart died a little over two months after *The Magic Flute*'s debut. The opera had staying power, as it remains one of Mozart's best-loved works and is the fourth most-performed opera in the world. Similar hermetic or Masonic works of fiction having a hermetic or Masonic depiction of ancient Egypt would become obsolete thirty years later, when Champollion finally deciphered hieroglyphs. The consequence would be the appearance of a new genre of fiction based in ancient Egypt.[52]

Napoleon's expedition to Egypt generated an intense and growing interest in the ancient land. The discoveries and publications that followed, especially Champollion's deciphering of hieroglyphs, only fuelled that interest further. The mummymania of unwrapping mummies quickly led to the appearance of fiction involving mummies. Mummy fiction usually is set in a Western locale with a mummy or mummies being brought there from Egypt. Once the mummy is settled in its new home in a foreign country, some sort of adventure occurs (which generally involves the ancient Egyptian coming back to life). The results of such encounters between modern Westerners and reanimated ancient Egyptian mummies ranged from tragic to romantic to comic. It is important to keep in mind, however, that early mummy stories seldom involved a vengeful mummy. The mummies in the earliest stories tended to be benign or even were portrayed as victims of thoughtless grave robbery. Some mummies could be evil, but they were not evil because they sought revenge; their being evil was, rather, simply that those particular ancient mummies had been evil when they were alive. The idea of a vengeful mummy arose out of the myth of the mummy's curse. Sources for the creation of the mummy's curse originated from the rumours and misinformation associated with the 'Unlucky Mummy' of Thomas Douglas Murray, the supposed curse connected to the coffin of Nesmin and the tragic death of Walter Henry Ingram, and finally the curse of Tutankhamun that came to prominence after Howard Carter's discovery of King Tut and the untimely death of his patron Lord Carnarvon soon after.[53]

Several different motivations have been suggested for the writing of mummymania fiction. All of them probably played a role in the creation of this genre, in particular, and historical fiction set in ancient Egypt in general. One approach suggests that the influx of mummies and other ancient Egyptian artefacts, mostly grave goods, created a new type of commodity. Ownership of mummies had both a prestige and an aura of danger that became a reality in mummymania fiction. Possessing a mummy or some grave goods could result in misfortune and even death. If the owner of the mummy managed to survive, such a frightening fantasy could actually be reassuring to Victorian readers living in a rapidly changing economy with a deluge of new commodities. Possession of mummies and other plundered Egyptian artefacts also aroused feelings of guilt among Victorians. Archaeologists, especially those working in Egypt with its many tombs, could be regarded as grave robbers. Initially mummy stories depicted the sufferings people experienced due to owning a mummy or grave goods as a form of justified retribution. In this scenario, archaeologists were more villains than heroes. After the discovery of Tutankhamum's tomb, thanks to the film industry, archaeologists were portrayed as heroic scholarly adventurers while angry mummies were not avengers but the revived corporeal forms of a mindless, ancient evil. This shift is, in effect, an affirmation or vindication of imperialism and colonialism. A less overtly political interpretation, however, is offered by the literary historian Roger Luckhurst, who suggests that the curse of the mummy was a spin-off of an existing genre of stories related to cursed possessions and misfortunes of the rich and famous. The Koh-i-Noor and the Hope diamonds supposedly had curses that afflicted those who owned them, so why not Egyptian mummies? Cursed possessions added drama, mystery and thrills to a story. Sir Arthur Conan Doyle's *The Hound of the Baskervilles* drew its inspiration from the curse of the 'Unlucky Mummy'. So rumour, myth, fiction and fact all interacted to create a rich body of lore regarding mummies' curses well before the discovery of Tutankhamun's tomb.[54]

Beyond mummymania fiction, historical fiction set in ancient Egypt appeared in the mid-nineteenth century. This development is not surprising given the popular fascination with ancient Egypt – a fascination that has lasted to this day among readers. Historical fiction and thrillers have continued to use ancient Egyptian settings or themes to a far greater degree than many other historical or geographical settings. The evolution of Egyptian-themed and mummymania fiction from the 1820s to the 1920s is a fascinating aspect of Egyptomaniac popular culture.

Jane Webb Loudon (1807–1858) was an early pioneer of science fiction writing. Her book *The Mummy! A Tale of the Twenty-second Century* appeared in 1827 and reflected the Egyptomania that was sweeping Western societies in the aftermath of Napoleon's expedition to Egypt. As one of the characters says, hyperbolically: 'Egypt is rich in monuments of antiquity, and all historians unite in declaring her ancient inhabitants to have possessed knowledge and science far beyond even the boasted improvements of modern times.' Originally published in three volumes, it was the first lengthy story to feature a mummy and it also introduced the mummy that walked. In this futuristic tale, the mummy of the old pharaoh Cheops (Khufu) is awakened by electricity in 2126. From Egypt he travels to England, and finds the degenerate society that he encounters there disagreeable. Loudon's Cheops is the cruel tyrant depicted by Herodotus, but he has learned the error of his ways. He is not the stereotypical vengeful mummy that has come to increasingly dominate modern fiction and films. Rather, in his newly resurrected state, Cheops is more like a philosopher–king who seeks to banish corruption from English society by helping a benevolent monarch to gain the throne. Despite the novel's title, Cheops is merely a deus ex machina. Loudon's depiction of Cheops and ancient Egypt appeared too early to benefit from the flood of knowledge resulting from the decipherment of hieroglyphs. The new knowledge that eventually emerged, however, was inconsequential to the novel's plot, since Loudon only used her Cheops to criticize the society of her own Regency England.[55]

During the 1840s the French writer Théophile Gautier (1811–1872) wrote several works of mummy fiction. The first, a short story, appeared in 1840, titled 'The Mummy's Foot'. The narrator wanders into a Parisian bric-a-brac shop looking for something unique to decorate his desk. He decides to buy the mummified foot of an Egyptian princess to use as a paperweight. Taking it home, he congratulates himself on his acquisition. After an evening out with friends that includes a lot of wine, the narrator returns home and goes to bed. Although he falls into a deep sleep, he awakens to a strange visitor, the Egyptian princess Hermonthis looking for her foot. The narrator gallantly agrees to give her the foot back. In return, the princess gives him a small green statue of an idol. Then they whisk off on a mystical night flight to Egypt to meet her father. Arriving at a red mountain, they enter its subterranean passages and proceed to a great hall filled with the ancient kings of Egypt, including Hermonthis' father, antediluvian kings and 72 pre-Adamite kings. The old pharaoh asks the narrator what he would like as a reward for returning his daughter's foot. Boldly, the narrator asks for her hand in marriage, but he is refused because of the age difference: Hermonthis is 3,000 years old while the narrator is only 27! More importantly, the narrator has no access to good procedures of mummification. The old pharaoh begins to shake his hand at which point the narrator awakens. The mystical journey to Egypt was a dream, but on the narrator's desk is the little green statue rather than the mummified foot. Gautier's story demonstrates not only insecurities about the relative recency of European culture, but also a sense of guilt and uncertainty about the unchecked despoiling of Egyptian mummies. There is no deadly mummy and no curse to terrorize the narrator, just a sense that the ancient Egyptian dead deserve respect – a sentiment no doubt further emphasized by Hermonthis' beauty. Gautier continued the theme of respect for ancient Egypt in his novel *The Romance of the Mummy* (1858).

Not everyone took mummy fiction seriously. An example of a comic or satirical mummy story is Edgar Allan Poe's 'Some Words with a Mummy', which appeared in the *Broadway Journal* in November 1845. Poe does not appear to have succumbed to Egyptomania despite his interests in the macabre and esoteric. His story instead pokes fun at mummy unwrapping and the purveyors of Egyptomania and even seems to be parodying Loudon's *The Mummy!* Poe's story tells of an unwrapping of a mummy that does not quite go as planned. Instead of going on a rampage like most cinematic mummies, Poe's mummy is resurrected by electricity and proceeds to engage the attendees of the unwrapping in a conversation approaching a debate. The mummy's name is Allamistakeo, signalling Poe's satirical intent. Allamistakeo proceeds to question the superiority of contemporary American science and culture and goes on to show a degree of contempt for the Egyptologist George R. Gliddon, who appears in the story along with several other real people.[56]

Louisa May Alcott, by contrast, did show respect for mummy fiction. Her short story 'Lost in a Pyramid or, the Mummy's Curse' appeared in 1869. The protagonist, Paul Forsyth, has been to Egypt to study its ancient ruins with the teacher Professor Niles. While exploring in the labyrinthine passageways of the pyramid of Cheops, they get lost. During their wanderings, they discover a mummy and its coffin, which they burn to attract help. In the process of burning the mummy – a powerful sorceress protected by the usual curses against disturbers – they take the jewellery and other items buried with the body. Among those possessions is a golden box with some strange seeds in it. Returning to America, Forsyth shows the seeds to his fiancée, Evelyn. She asks to plant the seeds but he refuses. Unbeknown to Forsyth, when he drops the box, he loses one seed while picking up the rest. Evelyn finds that lone seed and plants it. An unfamiliar plant with lovely white flowers grows from the seed. But it is an evil plant. Evelyn ends up wearing one of its flowers, which drains her energy and turns her into an aged, invalid husk of her former self. The 3,000-year-old curse of the ancient sorceress prevails against her desecrators. The lesson is obvious. Robbing mummies is dangerous and their grave goods can be deadly; metaphorically this story also contrasts the age of ancient Egypt with the headstrong youth of America. As Dominic Montserrat has pointed out, Alcott's story brings together all the elements of the mummy's curse into a work of fiction. A mummy is pillaged and destroyed notwithstanding its being protected by a curse. Its grave goods are taken out of Egypt to the West, in this case the United States. There they bring misfortune on the desecrators.[57] Similar vengeful mummy tales followed and continue to be published.

Not to be left out of the growing pack of writers cashing in on Egypt, the prolific Sir Arthur Conan Doyle also wrote a couple of mummy tales. One story, which appeared in *The Strand* in 1890, was a convoluted tale of thwarted love and romance titled 'The Ring of Thoth'. John Vansittart

Smith is an aspiring Egyptologist who travels to the Louvre for research. While working in its collections, he falls asleep and is locked inside the museum for the night. There he encounters Sosra, a museum attendant. Sosra turns out to be an ancient Egyptian scientist who developed an elixir of immortality. He fell in love with a woman, Atma, and wanted to make her both his wife and immortal, but she died before he could do either. Since Sosra was already immortal, he could not join her in the afterlife. For thousands of years he has been trying to reverse the elixir of immortality. Atma's mummy is housed in the Louvre and has a ring of Thoth that can reverse the effects of the elixir. Upon obtaining the ring, Sosra does just that and dies happy with a somewhat perplexed Smith witnessing the entire drama. Along the way Sosra also criticizes Egyptologists for ignoring 'our hermetic philosophy and mystic knowledge of which you say little or nothing'.[58] Once again, this type of story plays on the theme of the youthful West's struggle to comprehend the far more ancient existence of Egypt.

Doyle's second story, which appeared in 1892, is titled 'Lot No. 429'. In this story the mummy personifies evil. Set in Oxford University during the spring of 1884, a medical student named Abercrombie Smith shares a staircase with two other students – Edward Bellingham and William Monkhouse Lee. Although he is a somewhat strange fellow, Bellingham is also a gifted student of Middle Eastern languages and is engaged to Lee's sister. One night Smith is called down to Bellingham's rooms by Lee. Bellingham has been badly frightened and Lee wants Smith's help to bring him out of his terrified state. While in Bellingham's rooms, he cannot help but notice that they are full of Egyptian artefacts – including a mummy case. Smith also gets the distinct impression that someone else is staying in Bellingham's rooms. Immediately afterwards Smith and Bellingham become more friendly, but later, Lee and Bellingham have a falling out. Soon after that, Lee almost drowns under mysterious circumstances. Smith's suspicions are aroused when he learns that another Oxford student who quarrelled with Bellingham earlier also had been attacked. Smith concludes that Bellingham and his mummy might have something to do with the attacks. On another night Smith himself is chased by a mummy as he is going to visit a friend. Now thoroughly convinced that Bellingham and the mummy are up to no good, Smith gets a gun and forces Bellingham to destroy his mummy and a mystical papyrus containing the incantations used to reanimate and control the mummy. This he does by burning them in his fireplace. Bellingham remonstrates to the relentless Smith: 'Why, man, you don't know what you do. It [the papyrus] is unique; it contains wisdom which is nowhere else to be found.'[59] Doyle never makes clear the nature of the relationship between Bellingham and the mummy. Were they master and servant, were they equals or was the mummy leading Bellingham into an evil life? The mummy appears to be a sort of thuggish protector, but he is only vengeful as a surrogate for Bellingham. 'Lot No. 429' shows that Egyptomania and the obsessive collecting of things Egyptian can lead to trouble. On another level, it suggests that modernity should not molest ancient Egypt's many historical artefacts and legends.

A similar lesson can be drawn from *The Jewel of Seven Stars* (1903), a novel by Bram Stoker (1847–1912). In this tale, a young barrister named Malcolm Ross is called to the house of Abel Trelawny, who has been found in a coma. Trelawny is an Egyptologist and his home, particularly his study room, is full of Egyptian artefacts, including mummies. Trelawny has left instructions that none of the artefacts are to be removed from the study. His condition baffles medical experts, while a police investigation determines that his coma was caused by something from inside his house. His daughter Margaret Trelawny follows her father's instructions and refuses to let any artefacts be removed, including the mummy of Queen Tera. Various eerie incidents occur in the Trelawny house that involve the artefacts. Medical and police personnel leave the case perplexed. Finally Abel Trelawny awakens and, together with the newly arrived explorer Eugene Corbeck, relates the story of how Trelawny had acquired the mummy of Queen Tera in Egypt. It seems that Queen Tera is coming back to life and her resurrection is linked to Margaret Trelawny.

The action moves from London to Cornwall where the protagonists gather to conduct an unwrapping ceremony. The unwrapping of Tera is depicted as a rather voyeuristic exercise by the men that titillates them and degrades Tera. But Queen Tera gets her revenge in an explosion of magic power that leaves everyone dead except Malcolm Ross, and Queen Tera disappears. Readers and critics complained so much about the ghastly ending that Stoker gave the novel's second edition of 1912 a happy one: Queen Tera dies and Ross and Margaret marry. The novel's original ending shows that ownership of and obsession with Egyptian artefacts, particularly mummies, can be a deadly hobby. Stoker also hints that Margaret Trelawny is somehow a reincarnation of Queen Tera, which makes her a conduit for the dead queen to magically resurrect herself. This suggests that regal ancestry, in this case from ancient Egypt, can be inherited, albeit by mystical means. On another level, the novel also can be seen as a criticism of the looting of Egyptian antiquities. Stoker's Egypt is depicted as a land of mystery possessing scientific knowledge that may have even surpassed that of Western civilization at the dawn of the twentieth century. It has also been pointed out that Stoker shows a respect for Egypt's mysteries not often found in Egyptomania fiction. Stoker, in this early horror novel, was also responsible for creating the deadliest mummy of those in the fiction of the time.[60]

Other Egyptian-themed fiction also appeared in the late nineteenth century. The prominent German Egyptologist Georg Moritz Ebers (1837–1898) sought to popularize Egyptology and the new and growing knowledge of ancient Egyptian history by writing historical novels set in ancient Egypt. Ebers, however, did not go back to the classic era of ancient Egypt during the Old, Middle or New Kingdoms. Instead, his novels were set in the era of the Persian conquest and then through to the time when Egypt was a province of the Roman Empire. Besides providing his readers with an entertaining story, Ebers tried to be extremely authentic in his description of the material culture of ancient Egypt as revealed by archaeological discoveries. His first novel was titled *An Egyptian Princess* and appeared in 1864. It was a great success, particularly among female readers, and other similar novels followed.[61] Ebers's works established the genre of authentic historical novels set in ancient Egypt that has flourished ever since. In a sense, Egyptomania helped female readers find a place in a modern fad, in part because Egyptian history itself offered examples of women in powerful roles.

Another influential depiction of ancient Egypt that involved strong female characters was in the Italian composer Giuseppe Verdi's opera *Aida*, first performed in Cairo in 1871 and commissioned by the Egyptian khedive Ismail Pasha. There is a common misconception that Ismail Pasha commissioned *Aida* to celebrate the completion of the Suez Canal or the opening of the Khedivial Opera House, but neither is true. The Khedive wanted to westernize Egypt, and promoting opera was one of many ways to achieve this. *Aida* is set in the Old Kingdom era of ancient Egypt but otherwise the historical content of the opera is generic and non-specific. Its elaborate sets are a feast of Egyptomaniac images. The plot involves a love-triangle between the Ethiopian slave girl Aïda, who is also a princess in her homeland; Amneris, the daughter of the unnamed King of Egypt; and Radamès, the captain of the royal guard. Amonasro, the king of Ethiopia and the father of Aïda, wants his daughter to return to Ethiopia and marches on Egypt with his army. Radamès commands the Egyptian army that defeats and captures Amonasro. Although he is engaged to marry Amneris and has been named the Egyptian king's successor, Radamès falls in love with Aïda. He gets her father spared from execution and the couple plot their own escape to Ethiopia, but their plan is discovered. Radamès is captured, tried and condemned to death. In the opera's final act, Aïda is reunited with Radamès in a vault beneath the temple, having concealed herself within it so that she and Radamès can die together.

When it first appeared, *Aïda* was an immediate success and has remained so ever since – it is the thirteenth most performed opera in the world today. Part of its enduring appeal can be credited to its Egyptian setting, despite its not relying on ancient Egyptian mysteries to advance its plot. It is, however, an enduring artefact of Egyptomania.[62]

In 1913 H. Rider Haggard (1856–1925) made a contribution to the genre of mummymania fiction with his 'Smith and the Pharaohs'. It is the story of James Ebenezer Smith, a young Englishman of good education and good family who has fallen on hard times just as he was about to graduate. Smith manages to secure a minor clerkship in a bank through the good offices of a rich uncle. Later, this same uncle leaves him a very small bequest in his will. By prudent management and astute speculation Smith transforms this little nest egg into a small fortune to provide him with a second income to supplement his bank salary. One day rain forces Smith into the British Museum, where he explores the Egyptian collection and falls in love with a woman depicted on a small statue. Soon after that he travels to Egypt where he visits the Cairo Museum. There he sees the original of the statue he fell in love with in England and discovers her name was Ma–Mee. Smith starts to take winter holidays to Egypt, supposedly for chronic bronchitis, and engages in archaeological fieldwork. Eventually getting his own permit to dig, he discovers a tomb that has been robbed, but it still contains some artefacts, which includes a mummified hand with two rings on it. Taking the finds to the Cairo Museum for inspection, the director allows him to keep one of the rings. Afterwards Smith researches in the collections of the museum but falls asleep and gets locked in overnight, during which he witnesses an annual supernatural gathering of the royalty of ancient Egypt. Their biggest complaint is the looting of their tombs by archaeologists; they dislike being on display in museums, too. Unfortunately for Smith, they discover him and some of the angry pharaohs want to punish him. But an advocate appears: Ma–Mee is in the room along with her pharaoh husband. As things unfold, it turns out that Ma–Mee is unhappily married. Their household had employed a sculptor named Horu who created the beautiful statue of Ma–Mee. The two fell in love and the pharaoh became jealous. He had Horu poisoned and Ma–Mee died soon after. Smith, it turns out, is the reincarnation of Horu, hence his strong attraction to Ma–Mee's statuette. When Smith's alter-ego identity is revealed, the gathering of pharaohs spare his life and then depart. Ma–Mee lingers and promises Smith that they will be reunited when he dies. He returns to England and gives up further excavating in Egypt. He found the treasure he was unconsciously looking for all along.[63]

In 'Smith and the Pharaohs', H. Rider Haggard used one of his familiar plot devices, the reuniting of ancient lovers through reincarnation (Haggard, personally, believed reincarnation was possible). Here again we find a sincere person from the present privileged to interact with the ancient Egyptian past. To this theme he adds another more potently moralistic message about the ethics of appropriating Egypt's past. Although there are the ghostly pharaohs gathering in the Cairo Museum, there are no vengeful or reanimated mummies. Instead Haggard used 'Smith and the Pharaohs' as a vehicle to promote his own criticisms of the continued desecration of Egyptian tombs by archaeologists and illegal traffickers in antiquities. In 1904 Haggard had already written an essay condemning the shameful treatment of Egyptian mummies and tombs. 'The Trade in the Dead' appeared in the 4 June issue of the *Daily Mail*, and later in his posthumously published autobiography of 1926, and in it Haggard called for the return and secure reburial of all mummies and their grave goods to their tombs. These tombs should then, he advised, be sealed up in concrete so that they could never be disturbed again. Such a sentiment would have been true to character for Haggard, who throughout his life and writings demonstrated an admirable but rare respect and sympathy for the native peoples of Africa. So it is not surprising that he eventually became an advocate for the vandalized and dishonoured dead of ancient Egypt.[64]

Although Haggard wrote the mummy story 'Smith and the Pharaohs', he is best known as the author of adventure romances and for popularizing the 'lost race' novel, even though he did not invent the genre. Haggard sometimes used themes of Egyptomania in his fiction long before he wrote 'Smith and the Pharaohs' and after it as well. His Egyptian-themed novels tended to be inspired by his visits to Egypt, which took place four times during his life: in 1887, 1904, 1912 and 1924. Although he used Egyptian settings and themes, he did not depict individual ambulatory mummies in his other novels and short stories. Instead, he presented groups of mummies, such as the scene in *King Solomon's Mines* where Allan Quatermain and his companions encounter the mummified kings of the Kukuana.[65]

After writing two very mediocre novels of contemporary melodrama, the young Haggard wrote his two greatest and most successful novels in quick succession: *King Solomon's Mines* (1885) and *She* (1887). The fictional Africa depicted in these novels was dotted with lost cities and/or lost races. In the case of *King Solomon's Mines*, it was the great mines of Ophir. *She* is largely set in the lost city of Kor, inhabited by a degenerate race ruled by She-Who-Must-Be-Obeyed, who possesses great beauty and fearsome mystical powers. Her real name was Ayesha and she was an Arabian princess who had become

Cleopatra on the Nile from H. Rider Haggard's *Cleopatra* (1889), engraving by Richard Caton Woodville for the *Illustrated London News*.

a priestess of Isis. The ancestors of the inhabitants of Kor had been a brilliant civilization that had civilized the Egyptians. Haggard was also fond of using spiritualist themes in his novels. One of the English visitors to Kor in the novel, Leo Vincey, is the reincarnation of She's long-dead lover, a Greek mercenary in Egypt named Kallikrates. Neither *King Solomon's Mines* nor *She* has ever been out of print.

Haggard's follow-up novels to *She* and *King Solomon's Mines* were sequels or prequels to *She*, and others were stories featuring Allan Quatermain, the protagonist of *King Solomon's Mines*. In one novel – *She and Allan* (1921) – Haggard even brings Quatermain and Ayesha together. Most of Haggard's novels exhibited spiritualist themes of reincarnation, metempsychosis and even telepathy. Many of these novels also used the 'lost race' theme as well. Some of Haggard's novels were historical romances, although these contained spiritualist themes, too.

One of his other early novels, *Cleopatra* (1889), was set in Egypt during the reign of that most famous of queens. The protagonist is Harmachis, a descendant of Egypt's last pharaoh Nekt-nebf (Nectanebo II), who was defeated by the Persians. Egypt and its priesthood have formed an underground that plots to throw out the foreign conquerors and restore the rule of native pharaohs in the person of Harmachis. Instead of overthrowing Cleopatra, Harmachis falls in love with her. She promises that they will rule Egypt together, but Cleopatra needs money. So Harmachis leads her to the priests' great hoard of treasure, which is to be used to free Egypt. Cleopatra takes the treasure for herself and Mark Antony instead and repudiates Harmachis. Years later Harmachis, posing as a soothsayer, lures Antony and Cleopatra into fighting the fateful battle of Actium and gets his revenge when they are defeated. Harmachis then goes to the Temple of Isis. Confessing his sins, he is condemned to death by the priests. *Cleopatra* is a typical Egyptomania historical novel and appeared soon after Haggard's first journey to Egypt in 1887. During that visit, he followed the usual Egyptian traveller's itinerary. Making his way to Cairo, he visited the Cairo Museum, an archaeological dig, and the Pyramids of Giza. Then he proceeded up the Nile as far as Aswan and stopped at Luxor all the while soaking up details for his novel.

After *Cleopatra*, Haggard stayed away from Egyptian themes in his novels until his second journey to Egypt in 1904. Returning after an absence of almost twenty years, Haggard found Egypt had become a tawdry tourist warren. This disappointing experience inspired him to write *The Way of the Spirit* in 1906, which includes an isolated lost race community trying to preserve some semblance of ancient Egypt's former greatness. Later novels – *Queen Sheba's Ring* and *Morning Star* – both appeared in 1910 and were set in ancient Egypt.

In 1912 Haggard made his third trip to Egypt, after which he wrote *The Ivory Child* (1916), about a lost city in Africa that contains an Osiris–Isis cult. It also includes elements of spiritualism in the form of reincarnation and clairvoyance. *Moon of Israel: A Tale of the Exodus* is a historical novel that appeared in 1918 and is set during the Exodus, which of necessity includes some Egyptian elements in the story. The plot may have been inspired by Haggard's visit to see the newly discovered mummy of Merenptah, the supposed pharaoh of the Exodus. *The Ancient Allan* (1920) is a sequel to *The Ivory Child* and tells of one of Allan Quatermain's earlier incarnations in Egypt and Babylon during the era of the Persian Empire. In 1923 Haggard brought out the ultimate *She* prequel in *Wisdom's Daughter: The Life and Love Story of She-Who-Must-Be-Obeyed*. It tells the story of how Ayesha, an Arabian princess, comes to live in Egypt and serve as a priestess in the Isis cult. She meets and falls in love with Kallikrates the mercenary. Events force her to flee Egypt and a faithful retainer leads her to Kor where she uses the sacred fire to make herself impossibly beautiful, immortal and possess deadly magical powers. In a fit of jealous rage she uses her powers to kill Kallikrates when he stumbles into Kor accompanied by another lover and refuses to return to Ayesha. After his murder, Ayesha alone rules Kor with megalomaniacal zeal for 2,000 years until Leo Vincey arrives. It was a long, boring wait for Ayesha, but then for most readers, *Wisdom's Daughter* is a long, boring read.

In 1925 Haggard made his fourth and final visit to Egypt. He was 68 years old and as a conservative elitist was deeply depressed by the Labour Party's victory in the recent Parliamentary elections. While in Egypt he stayed in Cairo to shop for antiquities. After that he visited Abydos and Tell-el Amarna. Then he paid a return visit to Luxor where he had an outing to the Valley of the Kings and Howard Carter gave him a tour of Tutankhamun's tomb. Otherwise, Haggard was distressed to find that Egypt contained so many American and German tourists and the streets were overrun with their motor cars. He also viewed Egypt's newly independent national government with grave misgivings. His *Queen of the Dawn: A Love Tale of Old Egypt* (1925) came out as a result of this last trip just as Haggard was dying. It is a historical romance about the overthrow of the Hyksos invaders and the restoration of native Egyptian control of Egypt. Spiritualist elements play a big part in the plot. The posthumous novel *Belshazzar*, a historical romance set in Babylon, Egypt and Cyprus, was published in 1930.

Haggard wrote 56 novels and romances. Of these, only eight were set in Egypt or incorporated Egyptian motifs or themes to a minor degree or more. Nevertheless, akin to many popular authors, Haggard was drawn to the mysteries of Egypt and their popularity with readers. Ultimately, however, southern Africa was Haggard's true focus, and after that, spiritualism. His last few novels were written when the discovery of King Tut's tomb by Howard Carter had prompted a renewed wave of Egyptomania in the West. As will be shown, this new outbreak of Egyptomania was much more a mass-culture, mass-market phenomenon than its nineteenth-century counterpart.

EIGHT

THE RISE OF MASS EGYPTOMANIA: TUTANKHAMUN, TUTMANIA AND THE CURSE OF THE MUMMY

I have heard the most absurd nonsense talked in Egypt by those who believe in the malevolence of the ancient dead; but at the same time, I try to keep an open mind on the subject.

ARTHUR WEIGALL[1]

NOVEMBER 1922 witnessed the most famous discovery in the history of Egyptology and archaeology: the tomb of King Tutankhamun. The man in charge of the excavation was the Englishman Howard Carter (1874–1939), an experienced and tenacious field archaeologist, but the man paying for the excavation and the possessor of the concession to dig in the Valley of the Kings was George Herbert (1866–1923), the fifth Earl of Carnarvon. Carter and Lord Carnarvon had been digging in the Valley of the Kings since 1917 and had little to show for their hard work and the fortune that the Earl had spent. Discouraged, the Earl had decided not even to continue excavating in the Valley of the Kings in 1922, but a determined Carter travelled to England to see Carnarvon and personally managed to convince him to pay for one more season of digging.[2]

Most Egyptologists at that time had long believed that all the tombs of pharaohs had been discovered. That was the view of Theodore Davis, the flamboyant American millionaire, who had held the concession to excavate in the Valley of Kings for many years.[3] In 1914 he gave up the concession, which was then awarded to the Earl of Carnarvon, who had been employing Carter on other archaeological projects. The outbreak of the First World War, however, prevented Carnarvon and Carter from getting started on their quest for the tomb for several years.

When excavations in the Valley of the Kings resumed in 1917, Carter had a methodical plan – which is not surprising since archaeology had for some time been transformed into a systematic discipline thanks to Flinders Petrie, the great British Egyptologist. Although the general consensus among Egyptologists was that all the tombs of the pharaohs in the Valley of the Kings had been discovered, Carter disagreed. In his opinion, the tomb already identified as Tutankhamun's was not a tomb at all. It was a storage chamber. So the tomb of Tutankhamun was still somewhere in the Valley of the Kings waiting to be discovered. And not just anywhere in the Valley, there was a specific area where artefacts associated with Tutankhamun had been discovered. Carter was also aware that the Valley of the Kings was subject to periodic flash floods of enormous size. These floods altered the terrain of the floor of the Valley and caused some areas to silt up and cover over entrances to ancient tombs. Carter took every bit of surviving evidence into consideration when he planned his exploratory digs. Despite all his planning, from 1917 to 1921, Carter and Carnarvon failed to find anything of even moderate archaeological significance. Not surprisingly, over time Carnarvon had become increasingly pessimistic about the possibility of success, particularly since the cost of the excavation was putting a painful dent in his family fortune.

The excavation season of 1922 was Carter's last chance. He arrived at Luxor on 28 October while Carnarvon remained home in England. By 1 November Carter had assembled his crew of diggers and began work the next day. Their first task was to clear off some ancient workers' huts. On the morning of 4 November, Carter's workers had uncovered a stone step and by the end of the next day they had cleared the steps of debris. At the bottom was a door with seals bearing the name 'Tutankhamun'. On the morning of 6 November, Carter cabled Lord Carnarvon that a discovery had been made and the Earl needed to come immediately to the Valley of the Kings. (Carter did not want to open the tomb unless Carnarvon was present, since the Earl was paying for all of the excavation.) After sending the cable, Carter refilled the stairway with debris as if it had never been found in order to protect the tomb from robbers. Carnarvon arrived at Luxor on 23 November. Several days earlier Carter had asked Arthur Robert Callender (1875–1936), a retired railway manager and personal friend, to join him at the dig. On the day of Carnarvon's arrival, Carter asked Callender to supervise the clearing of the steps. By the afternoon of 24 November, the door at the bottom of the steps had been fully revealed. After carefully recording and photographing the seals, the first door was removed on 25 November revealing a passage with another door at the end. Both doors showed signs of entry by robbers and resealing by ancient officials. The question for Carter and Carnarvon was what was to be found on the other side of that door – a looted, empty tomb or one with its treasures left largely intact?

The day of reckoning, 26 November, was one of high drama. As Carter put it, it was 'the day of days, the most wonderful that I have ever lived through, and certainly one whose like I can never hope to see again'. After clearing the passage of debris, Carter had formed the opinion that the next room might be a cache of grave goods rather than an actual tomb, but only opening the door would provide a definite answer. Carter made a small breach in the door. The idea was to put a lit candle through the opening to test for nasty and dangerous gases. As Carter prepared to peer in the hole, Carnarvon, his daughter Lady Evelyn Herbert and Callender hovered next to him in anxious anticipation. As Carter peered into the dimly lighted room and his eyes accustomed themselves to the partial darkness, images of animals, statues and the glitter of gold appeared. Carter would later state: 'I was struck dumb with amazement.' Meanwhile, Carnarvon nervously asked, 'Can you see anything?' In reply, Carter choked out his famous and pithy phrase: 'Yes, wonderful things.' Or at least, that is how he told it in print when the first volume of *The Discovery of the Tomb of Tutankhamun* appeared in 1923.[4]

Other less formal records indicate that Carter's response may have been somewhat less stirring and evocative. In his contemporaneous notes from the discovery, Carter recorded that his reply to Carnarvon's 'Can you see anything?' was 'Yes, it is wonderful.' Lord Carnarvon told two different versions of their exchange at the tomb. In an article for *The Times*, he asked, 'Well, what is it?' to which Carter replied, 'There are some marvellous objects here.' In a later version, Carnarvon asked 'Can you see anything?' To which Carter answered with, 'Yes, yes. It is wonderful.' Carnarvon's second version is almost identical to Carter's initial version but it was 'Yes, wonderful things' that made it into print between two hard covers. Although the first volume of *The Discovery of the Tomb of Tutankhamun* listed Carter as an author, it was really largely written by Arthur Mace of the Metropolitan Museum in New York City with assistance from Carter's friend Percy White, a professor and author of almost thirty novels. There are some scholars who dispute the book's accuracy. (Thomas Hoving has controversially suggested that Carter, Carnarvon, Carnarvon's daughter Evelyn and A. R. Callender secretly opened the door into the tomb's chambers during the night of 26 November and removed some small artefacts.) Still, Carter's *Discovery* became a best-seller and for good reason – Tutmania had erupted in the West.[5]

The official opening of the antechamber of Tutankhamun's tomb took place on 29 November, with the first press report appearing the next day

Howard Carter (1874–1939), discoverer of the tomb of Tutankhamun, in 1924.

in *The Times*. What became clear to all was that the pharaoh's tomb was packed with a vast amount of extremely valuable artefacts. Two break-ins by robbers had been limited in their thievery to small items, such as some of the jewellery and the unguents which would have soon spoiled anyway. Emptying the tomb would be a slow and meticulous process. Each item would have to be recorded in its exact location and context within the tomb, then labelled, numbered and catalogued. The task would prove to be a life sentence for Carter. He never managed to write a full report of his discovery, even as his greatest achievement consumed much of the rest of his life.

The discovery of Tutankhamun's tomb was the first time that a largely intact tomb and its grave goods had been discovered. Its massive hoard of artefacts provided archaeologists with hundreds of examples of the finest

Egyptian furniture, pottery, jewellery and art. One of the outstanding items was the golden mask of Tutankhamun, which instantly became an iconic image of ancient Egypt and has graced the jackets and title pages of many books of history, art and fiction. It was this feature of the tomb's contents that helped to make it the most famous archaeological discovery of the time. Its actual scholarly significance turned out to be far less. The treasures of the tomb belonged to a very minor pharaoh – little was known about Tutankhamun before the discovery of his tomb, and its contents added little to the existing knowledge about ancient Egypt in general and Tutankhamun in particular. It had been hoped that Tutankhamun's tomb would contain a substantial library of informative papyrus documents that would shed light on the poorly documented and confused era of the heretical Pharaoh Akhenaten and his obscure successors. That hope, disappointingly, did not prove to be the case. Despite this, rumours and speculations about secret papyri remained rife, including conspiracies to suppress the papyri's explosive contents about the true events connected to the Exodus of the Children of Israel from Egypt. Carter used this secret papyri story, even though he knew it was not true, during his dispute with the Egyptian government in the first half of 1924 over his rights regarding the discovery of Tutankhamun's tomb. He threatened to reveal the secret papyri in order to intimidate the British vice-consul into coming to his assistance against the Egyptians. At that time, political relationships in the Middle East were particularly tense because of the issue of establishing a Jewish homeland in Palestine. The appearance or even the rumour of such secret papyri would have further destabilized the situation.[6]

The discovery of Tutankhamun's tomb created tremendous excitement among the general public. It bolstered the existing Egyptomania in the West and created the new phenomenon of Tutmania, a subset of Egyptomania. For several months after the discovery of the tomb, the public was enthralled by the prospect of seeing the treasures of the pharaoh. Buried treasure is always fascinating and Tutankhamun's treasure had the added enchantment of being Egyptian. Newspaper reporters rushed to Luxor to provide the public with the latest stories about the discovery. Once the team of excavators started to remove artefacts from the tomb on 27 December, curious tourists gathered to catch a glimpse of the latest Egyptian treasure emerging multiple times each day from the tomb.[7] On 10 January 1924 Lord Carnarvon made a bombshell of an announcement. He had signed an agreement granting *The Times* of London exclusive rights to news about the excavation and archaeological work at the tomb. It was a decision that universally enraged other newspapers and their reporters. Among the Egyptian newspapers,

The Times's monopoly over Tutankhamun stories stirred their nationalist passions and anti-colonialist grievances. Egypt had recently gained its
independence, but it still chaffed under the residual weight of the delayed
outgoing British protectorate. As for the Western reporters, they had come
to Egypt in search of scoops about the Tut discovery that would make their
reputation and their fortune. Cut off from genuine news about the tomb,
they resorted to fabrication and sensationalism. The greatest fountainhead
of speculation involved the alleged curse of the pharaohs.[8]

Sometime around 6 March, a mosquito bit Lord Carnarvon on the
cheek. Soon after, Carnarvon cut the bite area while shaving and caused
the wound to become infected. Not a particularly robust man, the hapless
Earl became ill from the infection, but he also refused to rest and to take
proper care of himself. His condition experienced ups and downs during
the following weeks, but the trend was tragically downwards. Finally, on 5
April, Lord Carnarvon died at the age of 57. A curse on any desecrators of
the pharaoh's tomb was widely blamed, but putting Carnarvon's death in
context creates a different picture. In 1923 the average life expectancy of a
male in the United Kingdom was just under 57, so it was not the case that
Carnarvon had died particularly young.[9] In 1934 Herbert E. Winlock, the
director of the Metropolitan Museum in New York, looked into the fates
of the 26 people present at the opening of the tomb. Twenty of them were
still alive more than ten years later. Obviously the curse was not operating
comprehensively against supposed desecrators of Tutankhamun's tomb.
Of the six who were deceased, including Carnarvon, most had died of old
age. Arthur Mace (1874–1928) died in his mid-fifties but he suffered from a
fragile constitution that did not thrive under the rigours of an archaeological
dig in the Valley of the Kings. Those facts did not stop people seeing something sinister in the death of Carnarvon and the others. Was it the curse
of the pharaohs? That was the question on everyone's lips. In fact, public
interest in the death of Carnarvon was so high that an appreciation of the
Earl eclipsed news of the death of Vladimir Lenin in the Soviet Union on
the front page of the 30 April issue of *The Times*.[10]

The Origin of the Mummy's Curse

By the time of the discovery of Tutankhamun's tomb, Westerners were
already well programmed to resort to the curse of a mummy, particularly
a royal mummy, to explain death and misfortune among excavators. Bram
Stoker's *The Jewel of the Seven Stars* very clearly associates Egypt with evil
magic and disturbing an Egyptian tomb was a sure way to trigger curses

by exciting the wrath of a vengeful mummy. But tales of nasty mummies and deadly curses were not confined to works of fiction. Two tales of cursed mummies circulated prominently in the rumour mills of Victorian and Edwardian urban legend. One story involved the so-called 'Unlucky Mummy' of Thomas Douglas Murray, who was later prominent in spiritualist and psychical circles in England. Murray had bought an ancient coffin lid as a memento during one of his trips to Egypt during 1868. It depicted a rather malevolent-looking Egyptian woman, thought to be a priestess of Amun-Ra. The coffin lid made its way to England in the possession of an Arthur Wheeler, one of Murray's travelling companions. Possession of the lid, however, brought misfortune: one of Wheeler's travelling companions was wounded when his gun blew up (in some versions, the victim of the exploding gun was Thomas Douglas Murray), and another travelling companion fell into poverty within a year of returning home to England. Even Wheeler lost most of his fortune and had to give the coffin lid to his sister, Mrs Warwick Hunt, who displayed it in her house. When the flamboyant Madame Blavatsky, the founder of the Theosophical Society, who is discussed in Chapter Nine, visited the Hunt house during the 1880s, she declared that the coffin lid had an evil aura. Later a photographer attempted to photograph it; he died shortly thereafter and his photograph contained a ghostly image of a woman. While it is not clear that the coffin lid did any harm to Mrs Hunt or her house, friends persuaded her to give the coffin lid to the British Museum for safety's sake.[11]

One version of the transfer of the artefact claims that the curse was deactivated when the coffin lid reached the British Museum. Other versions, however, claim that the curse continued. Officials of the museum were said to have fallen victim to misfortunes. Another story told of a woman mocking the coffin lid and then suffering a bad fall down one of the museum's sets of marble steps. Another photographer attempting to take pictures of the coffin lid died within a year of his sacrilege. When Bertram Fletcher Robinson, the intrepid reporter and editor of the *Daily Express*, wrote a newspaper story about the coffin lid in 1904, he also died (although not until 1907). Robinson was a friend of Sir Arthur Conan Doyle and provided him with substantial help in the writing of *The Hound of the Baskervilles*. In 1923 Doyle would claim that angry Egyptian 'elementals' brought about Robinson's demise.

H. Rider Haggard in his autobiography related another version of the cursed coffin lid story that the Egyptologist Ernest Wallis Budge had told him in 1912. Thomas Douglas Murray was a friend and fellow psychical researcher with W. T. Stead, who had visited the British Museum Egyptian collection and was allowed by Budge to spend a night there. Some claimed that the curse of the coffin lid must have rubbed off on him; he went down with the *Titanic* in 1912. This story inevitably got tangled up with another about a Lord Canterville, who was transporting a mummy with him on the *Titanic* – this act awakening a curse that caused the ship's sinking. But the mummy, unlike most passengers and Leonardo di Caprio's Jack Dawson, managed to survive the *Titanic* disaster. According to a story told by the Egyptologist Margaret Murray, after causing a second disastrous sinking and helping to bring on the First World War it was decided that such a potently maleficent mummy should be returned to Egypt before it could do any further damage. Not to be placated, the vicious and ungrateful mummy's curse brought about the sinking of the hapless *Lusitania* in 1915. Margaret Murray also claimed, however, that she spread the rumour to test the credulity of a gullible public, including a professor at University College, London.

Roger Luckhurst has done some first-class research into the somewhat obscure life of Thomas Douglas Murray. He found that Murray's account of the curse of the mummy's coffin lid grew with the telling. Murray had an interest in ghosts and spiritual phenomenon and in 1894 he attended the Ghost Club of London for the first time. The Ghost Club was a gathering of respectable Victorians interested in spiritualism and ghosts. Over time, Murray gave them what they wanted and regaled them with stories of the carnage created by the unlucky mummy's cursed coffin lid. He even managed to persuade Ernest Wallis Budge to attend one of the club's dinner meetings. The social-climbing Budge was happy for an opportunity to associate with well-to-do members of London's upper middle-class elite. The story of the unlucky mummy circulated through the channels of London's middle-class gossip network until Robinson's newspaper story gave it an even wider circulation that stretched to North America. The story continued to circulate after the discovery of Tutankhamun's tomb. Its existence made it easier to put the spin of an occult curse on the death of Carnarvon.

The second prominent story of a mummy's curse involved Walter Herbert Ingram's ultimately fatal encounter with the cursed coffin of Nesmin.[12] Ingram joined the efforts in 1885 to relieve General Gordon, who was besieged at Khartoum by Mahdist rebels. The rescue attempt failed, but Ingram had shown great bravery during the fighting. During a stop at Luxor he decided to buy a souvenir of his time on the Nile River. For the rather extravagant sum of £50 he bought a mummy from the English consul and sent it back to England. The mummy contained an inscription which was translated in London. It turned out to be bad news for Ingram.

The mummy was the cadaver of a priest and its inscription put a curse on anyone who disturbed the priest's grave or body. Any desecrator would die a violent death and would be denied a decent burial as flowing waters would carry the cursed remains down to the sea and oblivion.

Back in Africa, the adventurous Ingram travelled to Somaliland to hunt elephants in 1889. While on a hunt with Sir Henry Meux, Ingram picked a gigantic female elephant for his prey. His method was to shoot the elephant from horseback. Fleeing the enraged elephant, his plan was to zigzag his horse through the forest until he got a chance for another shot and continue this manoeuvring until the elephant died. Unfortunately for Ingram, while galloping through the trees, he was unhorsed when he struck a low hanging branch. While lying stunned on the ground, the angry elephant caught up with him and proceeded to trample Ingram to death. As Rudyard Kipling would colourfully describe it, the elephant turned Ingram into 'blackcurrant jam'. For days the vengeful elephant would not allow anyone to approach Ingram's mangled remains. When the elephant finally went away, Ingram's hunting companions buried him in a ravine. Later, a party travelled to the ravine to bring back the remains for a proper burial but all they could find was a piece of bone and a sock. Heavy rains had caused flash flooding which carried the shattered corpse down to the sea. The mummy's curse was fulfilled in a rather brutal manner. As might be expected, the curse stories of Ingram's demise left out some crucial details. Ingram was recklessly hunting on dangerous terrain while riding a horse. Furthermore, he had loaned his powerful hunting rifle to a friend and was using an ineffectual small-calibre gun that was incapable of inflicting a mortal wound on a large elephant. So unless the mummy had cursed Ingram with stupidity, he was largely responsible for his own death.

Ingram's story provided such a fine example of the curse of the mummies that various newspapers published versions of it. It became widely known and was a mummy story that Wallis Budge liked to tell when he visited with the Ghost Club. The mummy, known to be that of a priest named Nesmin, had become the property of the Meux family. Lady Meux attempted to give it to the British Museum but she insisted that her Egyptian collection be displayed together. As a result, the British Museum refused the gift and the collection was auctioned off. The mummy had come with a coffin and a cartonnage mask. These items became separated and the coffin was purchased by William Randolph Hearst. When Hearst went bankrupt, his collection of antiquities was sold off and the coffin went to the Rhode Island School of Design. Whether Ingram's mummy brought misfortune to Hearst is debatable. That it did not bring ill luck to the Rhode

Island School of Design is obvious. Believers said that the curse's impact was abating while sceptics denied the curse had ever had any impact. As Luckhurst has pointed out, the true effect of curse stories like Murray's and Ingram's was to bring on 'the wholesale transformation during the course of the nineteenth century of feelings of awe, sublimity and wonder at the surviving traces of Ancient Egypt to a sense of threat and menace.'[13] Popular fiction had aided this process and continued to do so on the eve of the discovery of Tutankhamun's tomb.

Sax Rohmer, the Mummy's Curse and Egyptomania Fiction

Sax Rohmer (1883–1959), real name Arthur Henry Sarsfield Ward, is best known as the creator of the iconic villain Dr Fu Manchu, and that reputation has meant that his contributions to Egyptomania fiction have been little noted. However, Egypt played a big role in Rohmer's early fiction as a land of mystery, menace and evil magic.

In 1918 he brought out one of his better novels, *Brood of the Witch-Queen*. The story follows Robert Cairn who, while a student at Oxford, encounters a rather eerie fellow student named Antony Ferrara who has an excessive fascination with ancient Egypt. Ferrara is also up to no good, and soon people close to him – including his father, the eminent Egyptologist Sir Michael Ferrara – start to die. Robert's father, Dr Bruce Cairn, a medical doctor and a fellow Egyptologist, becomes involved in the case. Both men are determined to protect Myra Duquesne, a ward of Sir Michael, the love object of Robert Cairn and the target of nefarious designs by the evil Antony Ferrara. Then Ferrara disappears. His nerves shattered, Robert Cairn journeys to Egypt for a relaxing break. Instead, he and his father encounter Ferrara, who is increasing his command of black magic at the Pyramid of Méydûm. Dangerous encounters with Ferrara occur at the site of ancient Bubastis and the Pyramid of Méydûm but Ferrara again escapes. So the Cairns return to England, only to discover that Ferrara has also returned to London to once more menace the unsuspecting Myra. At last Dr Cairn reveals to Robert that Antony Ferrara is actually the reanimated mummy of an infant that he and Sir Michael revived. Sir Michael decided to adopt the baby who he named Antony. In reality, Antony is the love-child of the ancient and infamous Witch-Queen and the high priest of Egypt, Hortotef. Antony is also a vessel for the Witch-Queen's wandering spirit. He has acquired the magical Book of Thoth, which allows him to control an elemental spirit that he directs against the Cairns and Myra. Fortunately Dr Cairn possesses substantial knowledge of Egyptian magic and is able to fend off the elemental's attacks.

The Cairns go on the offensive and destroy Ferrara's Book of Thoth. In turn, the elemental attacks the weakened Ferrara and incinerates him. Clearly Egyptian magic is evil and bringing it to England can have deadly results.

In the same year, 1918, Rohmer published a collection of twelve short stories titled *Tales of Secret Egypt*, which is also a good indication where Rohmer is going with these stories. The first six stories are set in Cairo and are narrated by Neville Kernaby, the agent of an English firm importing antiquities to England. In his dealings he continually encounters the mysterious imam Abû Tabâh, a force of justice in Cairo, who helps him out of various tight spots but also deprives him of the profits of Kernaby's better shady deals. In 'The Death-Ring of Sneferu' Kernaby becomes involved in a quest for the signet ring of the early pharaoh Sneferu. Sneferu's tomb is located at the sinister pyramid of Méydûm, but Abû Tabâh delays Kernaby from reaching it. When Kernaby finally does reach the tomb, he finds the dead body of an English acquaintance, Theo Bishop, killed by the bite of a viper guarding the tomb. Kernaby's life is saved from the viper while Bishop is buried with the cursed ring. Another short story, 'In the Valley of the Sorceress', concerns the attempt by an archaeologist, Edward Neville, to excavate the tomb of the sorceress-queen Hatasu (Hatshepsut). Another archaeologist named Condor has already died while trying to open the

A late 19th–early 20th-century photograph of the step pyramid at Meidum, Sax Rohmer's favourite location for sinister sorceries and dark deeds in his short stories and novels.

tomb, and Neville experiences similar danger. Uncanny cats seem to be guarding the tomb and though the entranceway to the tomb is each day cleared, during the night it is mysteriously filled again with rubble. After three attempts to excavate it, a thoroughly frightened Neville abandons the dig. Hatasu's tomb is definitely protected by some powerful and potentially deadly magic that arises if an intruder dares to trespass too far.

Not all of Rohmer's stories in this volume are concerned with ancient Egypt. One frequent plot device used by Rohmer is that of a westerner, usually British, becoming fascinated with the exoticism of a young Egyptian woman. In most ways Rohmer's fiction bears the stamp of Eastern imagery. After all, Egypt has its secrets and they are not Western secrets. On the other hand, there are intimations that life for a westerner in Egypt could be quite mundane once the superficial exoticism wore off. As the narrator of the story 'Lure of Souls' comments: 'We all come out with the idea of the mystic East strong upon us, but it is an idea that rarely survives one summer in Cairo.'[14] Of course, the content of Rohmer's stories tend to belie that assertion.

In *The Green Eyes of Bast* (1920), Rohmer returns to the theme of mayhem caused by Egyptian magic brought to England. The protagonist is Jack Addison, a well-to-do young Englishman who engages in personal scholarship and freelance newspaper reporting. On his way home one evening, he becomes involved in the investigation of the murder of Sir Marcus Coverly. Suspicion falls on Eric Coverly, the last surviving male in the family. From the beginning of the case, however, Addison notices a mysterious cat-like presence prowling around. Later in the investigation, he encounters a mysterious Middle Eastern doctor named Damar Greefe and his companion Nahemah, a woman of feline appearance. In fact, she is the daughter of Sir Burnham Coverly, the former Coverly patriarch, and his wife. Years ago, while travelling in Egypt, the Coverlys were forced to spend the night in the town of Zagazig, located on the former site of Bubastis, an ancient Egyptian city dedicated to the worship of Bast, the cat goddess. Lady Coverly was pregnant and on that night an abnormally large feral cat entered her room. The female baby that is born later turns out to be a hybrid creature, both cat and human. The Coverlys believed their daughter was stillborn, but actually the infant was taken and raised by Dr Greefe as Nahemah. Nahemah grows up harbouring a deep, though unexplained, resentment against the Coverly family. She is determined to destroy them and with the growing body count of male Coverlys, she is doing a good job of it. The final confrontation occurs when Nahemah attempts to kill Isobel Merlin, the fiancée of Eric Coverly and a former girlfriend of Addison, who is still in love with her. Addison and the police ultimately foil Nahemah's murderous plot but she manages to escape, leaving Addison and Isobel deeply disturbed by their adventure. Again, Egyptian magic has created a monster which makes its way to England with fatal results.

Egyptian settings even managed to make their way into the Fu Manchu novels. The first novel in the series, *The Mystery of Fu Manchu* (1913), introduced the scholar Sir Lionel Barton, an expert on Egypt, Tibet and China. At the end of the novel, the protagonists Dr Petrie and Nayland Smith are planning an excursion to the Nile. In the series' second novel, *The Return of Fu Manchu* (1916), it is revealed that Smith and Petrie spent their time in Egypt searching for Petrie's love interest Kâramanèh, a reluctant slave of Fu Manchu. Reunited but once again separated from Kâramanèh at the end of the second novel, Dr Petrie again returns to Egypt with Smith but they are called back to England to combat a new plot in *The Hand of Fu Manchu* (1917). This time, Smith faces the Si-fan, a secret cult associated with Fu Manchu and the 'Yellow Peril' plot against the West. Both the second and third Fu Manchu books reveal that although she is a slave of Fu Manchu, the beautiful Kâramanèh grew up in a noble Egyptian family. In addition, the stories contain many references to Egypt. The best examples of Egyptian elements in the Fu Manchu series, however, are found in *Daughter of Fu Manchu* (1931) and *The Mask of Fu Manchu* (1932). Much of the action in *Daughter of Fu Manchu* takes place in Egypt and involves the excavation of the mysterious Tomb of the Black Ape. Nayland Smith and Dr Petrie assume that the nefarious interest shown towards the tomb by Fu Manchu's minions is motivated by the search for some diabolical ancient Egyptian secret or sorcery that will be used to secure world domination and the subjugation of the white race. In fact, Fu has simply stored some of his own nefarious equipment in the forbidden tomb. *Mask of Fu Manchu* includes a hostage exchange in the interior of the Great Pyramid which is connected to the possession of diabolical artefacts of great power. Fu Manchu's escape from the Great Pyramid is predicated on his knowledge of secret entrances and passages unknown to archaeologists. The plots of both novels are based on the assumption that powerful but lost Egyptian magic or technology exists and can be recovered. For Rohmer and popular culture, Egypt was a land of the supernatural, the enigmatic and the sinister.

The Curse of Tutankhamun in the Media

Given this popular ambience of an occult and dangerous Egypt immersed in sinister magic and populated by vengeful mummies and spirits, it is not surprising that the sudden death of Lord Carnarvon, coming so soon after the discovery of Tutankhamun's tomb, would attract rampant speculation over the existence of a curse that protected the pharaoh's earthly remains from disturbers. This belief combined with the widespread unease that many people felt over the excavation and opening of the ancient tombs. Many people felt it was wrong to defile the graves of Egyptians, so the mayhem caused by the curse of the pharaohs was considered righteous retribution. The monopoly of *The Times* over official news concerning the unfolding discoveries coming out of Tutankhamun's tomb aggravated the situation. It virtually forced the other reporters to look for gossip and to make unwarranted speculations in order to supply the newspapers' insatiable appetite for copy.

The novelist Evelyn Waugh (1903–1966) was particularly critical of the press coverage of the discovery. In his informed opinion, the newspapers and their reporters had 'vulgarized' the discovery so that all focus was on the event as a fanciful adventure while the wonders of ancient Egyptian art were ignored. Popular culture already assumed that Egyptian tombs were protected by curses and more tangible things like poisons and booby traps. So when the news of Lord Carnarvon's death came out, as Waugh described it, 'the public imagination wallowed in superstitious depths'. One rumour told of a cursed tablet that protected Tutankhamun's tomb. No such tablet existed. The *Daily Mail* mused that a mosquito might have come into contact with poison in Tutankhamun's embalming fluid, which it transmitted to Lord Carnarvon in the fatal bite that would kill him. Ever a purveyor of dubious news, the *Daily Mail* also reported that the lights of Cairo went dim or went out completely at the time of Carnarvon's death.[15]

To keep things interesting for their readers, the newspapers sought commentary on the discovery of Tutankhamun from popular authors, such as the horror writer Algernon Blackwood. Egyptologists were apparently too boring. In particular, they sought the opinion of Sir Arthur Conan Doyle. Despite being the creator of that ultimate rationalist Sherlock Holmes, Doyle was also an ardent believer in spiritualism. As a believer in unseen but supernatural and dangerous forces, he attributed the death of Lord Carnarvon to the ire of spiritual beings called 'elementals'. It was a suggestion that H. Rider Haggard condemned as encouraging superstition. Haggard was ploughing the sea. Superstition was the order of the day for popular culture when it came to ancient Egypt.[16]

Arthur Weigall (1880–1934) was a British archaeologist who served as Inspector General of Antiquities for the Egyptian government from 1905 to 1914, and he carried out his duties with great efficiency. After he left that position, he became a writer and a journalist of considerable wit and verve. Standing above the entrance to Tutankhamun's tomb on the day of its opening, Weigall watched the ebullient Lord Carnarvon enter. Turning to another reporter, he jokingly remarked, 'If he goes down in that spirit, I give him six weeks to live.' His flippant reference to a curse turned out coincidentally to be true, although Carnarvon lasted longer than six weeks. As a journalist who did not work for *The Times* of London, Weigall was one of the many on the outside of the Tutankhamun story looking in. That Howard Carter disliked him did not help Weigall's situation either. To compensate, he related various tales of supernatural goings-on in Egyptian tombs and then damned them with very, very faint scepticism. In 1924 Weigall published the essay 'The Malevolence of Ancient Egyptian Spirits'. He began by telling the story of how a cobra had eaten Howard Carter's pet canary at the time of the discovery of Tutankhamun's tomb. In some quarters it was taken as vengeance for Carter's violation of the tomb. Weigall quickly proceeded to emphatically state that Carnarvon did not die as the result of a curse. Acting as a proper Egyptologist, he pointed out that curses were rare in ancient Egypt. In addition, he pointed out that any curse would not have been directed at archaeologists since their goal was to preserve the name of the dead person along with the body, which is also what Egyptian mummification and entombment was all about. Then he continues his catalogue of eerie happenings involving mummies, including a mummified cat coming back to life, cursed artefacts, the unlucky mummy of Thomas Douglas Murray and the ill-fated attempt of Weigall and his friends to stage a play about Pharaoh Akhenaten. His essay concluded on an ambiguous note: 'I have heard the most absurd nonsense talked in Egypt by those who believe in the malevolence of the ancient dead; but at the same time, I try to keep an open mind on the subject.'[17] It was hardly a tough-minded refutation.

At the same time, H. P. Lovecraft (1890–1937) ghostwrote a short story titled 'Under the Pyramids' that first appeared as 'Imprisoned with the Pharaohs' in the May–July 1924 issue of *Weird Tales*. Ostensibly the story's author was the famed magician Harry Houdini. The story was supposed to be an account of how Houdini had been kidnapped by a group of sinister Arabs and lowered into the shaft of a pyramid. Lovecraft concluded that Houdini's adventure was a complete fabrication but, undaunted by that potentially embarrassing fact, he sought the permission of J. C. Henneberger, the owner and publisher of *Weird Tales*, to embellish Houdini's story even further. Lovecraft's Egypt positively oozed with uncanny magic and, as Lovecraft might have to put it, eldritch horrors from untold ages in the distant past. In the story, Houdini manages to escape his imprisonment in the tomb shaft of the pyramid, but not before witnessing some rather nasty and unearthly creatures. As he laments while wandering lost in corridors of the pyramid, 'God! . . . If only I had not read so much Egyptology before coming to this land which is the fountain of all darkness and terror!' The ending of the story is pure Lovecraft: Houdini encounters a lumbering and grotesque monstrosity being worshipped in some obscene ceremony in the depths of the pyramid. It causes him to ponder about what unearthly beast served as the model for the Sphinx. As for Egypt, 'truly this dark cradle of civilization was ever the well-spring of horrors and marvels unspeakable.' Compared to that view, any curse connected to Tutankhamun was relatively mundane. It was, of course, definitely an occult Egypt that a readership of popular fiction would love.[18]

Carnarvon's death brought self-proclaimed seers and soothsayers out of the woodwork to comment on his death. The first was Marie Corelli, a novelist. On 24 March 1923 she claimed to have warned Lord Carnarvon against violating Tutankhamun's tomb but he participated in the opening anyway. Corelli also suggested that the ancient Egyptians had placed poisons in their tombs to ward off tomb robbers. Following Corelli, the palmist Velma claimed in 1927 to have read Lord Carnarvon's palm twice prior to the discovery of Tutankhamun's tomb. Her first reading was very inauspicious but the second reading was even worse. Velma advised Carnarvon to abandon his excavations in the Valley of the Kings but he refused. When he died, Velma blamed his death on the curse of the pharaohs. Later in 1934, the psychic Cheiro, again well after the fact, claimed to have warned Lord Carnarvon of impending doom. During an archaeological dig prior to the First World War, Cheiro came to possess a perfectly preserved hand of a mummified princess. The princess began to communicate with Cheiro by means of automatic writing. At the time of the discovery of Tutankhamun's tomb, she told Cheiro to warn Carnarvon against entering the tomb or removing any of its treasure. Of course, Carnarvon ignored the warning and the curse protecting the tomb killed him. Or at least that was Velma and Cheiro's story, and they were sticking to it. An occult Egypt was good for business for fortune-tellers and psychics.[19]

Tutmania

The discovery of Tutankhamun's tomb created the phenomenon of Tutmania, which soon became an industry in itself that was very good for all sorts of business. Tutmania appeared rapidly and intensely after *The Times* reported the discovery of Tutankhamun's tomb. Egyptian-themed music, architecture, interior design, jewellery and fashions appeared. In many cases, the items had little or no real connection to Egypt.

Egyptian-sounding names were merely slapped on them. At the Winter Palace Hotel of Luxor the orchestra played the 'Tutankhamun Rag' in the ballroom, although not all the bright young things dancing had the slightest idea who Tutankhamun was. Vaguely Egyptian-esque footwear was dubbed 'Pharaoh's Sandals', while evening gowns came with 'Mummy Wraps'. It was a practice that led some people to try and trademark 'Tut' and 'Tutankhamun'. Art historians widely and correctly credit the art deco style with using Egyptian themes. The problem is that art deco was an eclectic style that incorporated aspects of many different traditions but in a very abstract manner. Egyptian motifs in art deco were often barely recognizable to the uninitiated layperson. In other cases, the use of Egyptian references was more direct, such as cosmetics sold in kohl pots. All of this constituted a new Egyptian revival. But it was also a different revival from previous times. The revival of the 1920s was a phenomenon of mass culture spurred by the relatively new mass media of newspapers, photography and motion pictures and sustained by the mass production of Egyptian bric-a-brac. Previous revivals had revolved around much more elite phenomena, such as Renaissance scholars studying rare manuscripts or the huge price paid for a set of the *Description of Egypt*.[20]

Movie theatres of the 1920s often incorporated various exotic motifs into their designs, such as an arabesque or a Chinese pagoda. Thanks to the discovery of Tutankhamun's tomb, theatres decorated their exterior facades as Egyptian temples with accompanying Egyptian elements in the interior design. Between 1926 and 1930, four cinemas in the greater London area were built with Egyptian temple facades – the Kensington, the Carlton, the Luxor and the Astoria. It was the era of silent films and the young Cecil B. DeMille wanted to make a film about Moses and the Exodus, to be titled *The Ten Commandments*. Initially Adolph Zukor of Paramount Pictures was sceptical of the project, but the popularity of Tutmania helped to change his mind. He gave DeMille the chance to make his dream film, but such was the strength of Tutmania that Paramount even contemplated changing the name of the pharaoh of the Exodus from Rameses II to Tutankhamun. The film debuted in December 1923. Before its release, people had already been speculating that there was a connection between Akhenaten's monotheism and Moses. The ever-brazen Arthur Weigall muddied the waters further on 13 October 1923 when he hypothesized that Tutankhamun was the pharaoh of the Exodus. Meanwhile rumours were circulating that a papyrus had been found in Tutankhamun's tomb that proved the Bible's account of Moses and the Exodus was historically accurate. Life was supposedly imitating art; or rather, dubious history was imitating Hollywood hype.[21]

Robert Graves (1895–1985) – the poet, novelist, scholar and survivor of the First World War – lived through Tutmania as a young man. In 1926 he went to Egypt to work briefly as a professor of literature. In 1941 he published with Alan Hodge *The Long Week-end: A Social History of Great Britain, 1918–1939*, which contained many personal observations from those years. He recalled that the discovery of Tutankhamun created a vogue for ancient Egypt. Fashions and jewellery copied the newly discovered Egyptian artefacts. Even the latest model of the Singer sewing machine adopted an Egyptian motif in its design. Wordplays on Tutankhamun's name abounded – it was even seriously suggested that the extension of the London Underground Northern Line from Morden to Edgware be named the Tootancamden Line since it passed through Tooting and Camden. Rambunctious students at the University of Cambridge staged the resurrection of Phineas, the stolen and deceased mascot of University College. Using the public lavatory at the Market Square as Phineas's tomb and dressing up as Egyptians, the students commanded Phineas to rise with the words 'Tut-and-Kum-in'. The artist Wyndham Lewis named his dog 'Tut'; it is no wonder people tried to trademark the name. Graves also reported that the public widely believed that Lord Carnarvon had died because of the curse associated with the defilement of the pharaoh's tomb. During the British Empire Exhibition of 1924, a replica of Tutankhamun's tomb with facsimiles of many of the artefacts was set up outside the official exhibition grounds. Arthur Weigall served as a consultant for the exhibit. It proved very popular, but it also aroused the ire of Howard Carter. He attempted to have the exhibit closed by bringing a lawsuit alleging that its displays were based on proprietary information from the Tutankhamun excavation. When it was proven that the replica of the tomb and the facsimiles were modelled on readily available public photographs, the courts ruled against Carter. The legal controversy did provide the tomb exhibit with some marvellous free publicity, while doing Carter's ailing reputation in England absolutely no good. Over in the United States, Carter went on a successful lecture tour about the Tutankhamun discoveries that even attracted the attention of Calvin Coolidge, not normally one of the more intellectually curious of American presidents. Academic archaeologists expressed surprise at the appearance of Tutmania because, while the contents of the tomb were vast and rich, they added virtually nothing new to knowledge of ancient Egypt. By contrast, Sir Leonard Woolley's discoveries at Ur, with their evidence of a great, although local, flood in ancient times confirming the biblical legend of Noah's Flood, did not attract much attention from the public.[22]

Fads, vogues and crazes all have their beginnings and their ends. Tutmania was no exception. The press had moved on to other sensations by the 1930s, even though the archaeologists employing their slow and methodical methods continued to reveal new artefacts.[23] What had caused Tutmania? Obviously the endemic Egyptomania that pervaded in popular culture provided a foundation for it. After all, Tutmania was really just a subset of the greater phenomenon of Egyptomania. At the same time, other circumstances contributed to make Tutmania a particularly intense form of Egyptomania. Howard Carter gave a predictably mundane explanation for Tutmania: he attributed the public's extraordinary interest in the discovery to 'a state of profound boredom with news of reparations, conferences, and mandates'.

Other explanations are more satisfying. First of all, the discovery of a largely intact tomb of a pharaoh was unique; all other pharaonic tombs had been thoroughly looted. Second, not only was the tomb largely intact, its grave goods were extremely rich as well as being exquisite works of art. It is no wonder that Lady Winifred Herbert (Baroness Burghclere), the daughter of Lord Carnarvon, described the discovery as 'a story that opens like Aladdin's Cave'. Arthur Mace, writing for the December 1923 issue of the Metropolitan Museum's *Bulletin*, agreed with Lady Burghclere that it was human nature for people to 'thrill deliciously at the very idea of buried treasure'. The fact that Tutankhamun had died young added an element of pathos to the event; it was particularly poignant given that only a few short years earlier millions of young men had died tragically during the First World War. Later quarrels between Howard Carter and Egyptian authorities, which in early 1924 culminated in Carter locking up the tomb, added further to the drama of the discovery.[24] Finally, the unexpected death of Lord Carnarvon simply added fuel to the fire of the growing frenzy of Tutmania.

The contents of Tutankhamun's tomb greatly increased the size of the Egyptian Museum of Cairo's collection. In 2003 a guidebook to the museum showed that the museum contained 75 rooms with permanent collections. Thirteen of those rooms are devoted to Tutankhamun; the rest of the entire New Kingdom collection is covered in another thirteen rooms. The Middle Kingdom only occupies a mere six rooms, while the Old Kingdom takes up nine rooms. Tutankhamun's artefacts form over one-sixth of the museum's public exhibits. Despite providing this boost to the Egyptian Museum, Egyptians did not warm to Tutankhamun. The discovery of Tutankhamun's tomb occurred during the waning days of British control over Egypt. In the eyes of the Egyptians, Tutankhamun's tomb was spoiled by associations with imperialism and colonialism. These feelings have persisted among some Egyptians ever since.[25]

Tutankhamun's tomb contained a vast cache of beautiful and priceless artefacts. It took nine years to clear the tomb and move its treasures to the Egyptian Museum of Cairo. Cataloguing and studying the finds was an immense task that took years and years and has never been fully completed, though in their new home in the Egyptian Museum the displays have attracted millions of tourists since the late 1920s. For several decades the artefacts never left the museum. That changed in 1961. An exhibition of 34 small pieces under the title *Tutankhamun Treasures* toured eighteen cities in the United States and six cities in Canada with stops in Japan and France from 1961 to 1967. The goal of the tour was to garner support for UNESCO's efforts to save the temple at Abu Simbel and other Nubian monuments from inundation by the great lake that would be created by the Aswan Dam project. Millions of people viewed the exhibition, almost three million in Japan alone, and Abu Simbel was saved.

The greatest travelling exhibit of Tutankhamun artefacts was called *The Treasures of Tutankhamun* and travelled in the West from 1972 to 1981. This tour became the first of the 'blockbuster' exhibitions favoured by museums for their popularity and their profitability. The exhibit consisted of 53 pieces from the Tutankhamun collection, including the iconic burial mask that has graced the jackets of so many books. Its itinerary began at the British Museum, where it was displayed from 30 March to 30 September 1972. When the tour began, Egypt was allied with the Soviet Union and took a jaundiced view towards the United States due to its support of Israel. Egyptian authorities proved reluctant to schedule venues for the exhibit in American cities. Their attitude changed as a result of the Yom Kippur War of 1973. After initial successes the Egyptian Third Army was surrounded by Israeli forces and its destruction was imminent. The United States under the leadership of Richard Nixon and Henry Kissinger put tremendous pressure on Israel not to overrun the trapped Egyptians. Their hope was to wean Egypt from its pro-Soviet alliance and open the way for better relations with the United States. The ploy worked. One of the results was that Egyptian opposition to United States participation in the Tutankhamun tour disappeared. Ultimately the United States hosted a somewhat larger exhibit than the one that toured the Soviet Union and the exhibit toured more American cities. The Tutankhamun artefacts visited seven American cities including Washington, DC, Chicago, Los Angeles and New York. More than eight million people visited the seven American museums – the blockbuster status of the Tutankhamun exhibition was affirmed. From the United States the tour visited Canada and West Germany through 1981. The enthusiasm for Tutankhamun reached such heights in the West that a new wave of Tutmania ensued, rivalling the Tutmania of the 1920s. Also revived was talk of the curse of the pharaoh. Police Lieutenant George LaBrash volunteered to guard the Tutankhamun exhibit during its time in San Francisco. While on duty, LaBrash suffered a minor stroke that prevented him from working for eight months, but because he was not on the city payroll when the stroke occurred, the city refused to pay him full disability compensation. Undaunted, LaBrash turned to the reoccurrence of the curse of the pharaoh to explain his misfortune and as a means to receive full disability benefits. The judge rejected LaBrash's claim about the curse: according to the judge, as a guard, LaBrash was protecting the pharaoh's body from desecration rather than disturbing it.[26]

The great tour was not the end of Tutankhamun's travels. A second major exhibit toured from 2004 to 2011. Initially the exhibit travelled under the title *Tutankhamun: The Golden Hereafter* while it toured Switzerland and Germany in 2004. The exhibit's name was changed to *Tutankhamun and the Golden Age of the Pharaohs* when it visited Los Angeles, Fort Lauderdale, Chicago and Philadelphia during 2005–7. Of fifty artefacts from Tutankhamun's tomb only ten items had been part of the first tour. Unfortunately the iconic golden burial mask was not part of this exhibit.[27] Despite that absence, the exhibit attracted three million visitors during its first United States visit. In late 2007 the exhibit travelled to London for almost ten months and then returned to the United States for venues in Dallas, San Francisco and New York. The tour concluded with a nine-month stop in Melbourne, where it attracted the largest box-office sales for a touring exhibition in Australian history. Another exhibition toured from 2008 to 2013 under the title *Tutankhamun: The Golden King and the Great Pharaohs*. Despite featuring the name Tutankhamun, the exhibit consisted of 140 artefacts from various royal tombs from the Valley of the Kings, including Tutankhamun's tomb. It did not attract the media attention of the two previous exhibits.

The Tutankhamun exhibit of 1972 started the trend of major museums hosting blockbuster exhibits of famous artefacts. Museums owning the popular artefacts and museums exhibiting them have found the massive revenues generated by blockbuster exhibits to be very handy in paying for needed improvements and desired acquisitions for the museum's collections. (The Cairo Museum used its share of the profits of the exhibits to pay for much-needed improvements.) For these reasons, it is highly likely that Tutankhamun's grave goods will travel again sooner or later, unless thieves loot them or some mullah destroys them as unwanted reminders of a pagan past, however glorious that past might have been.

PART TWO

VARIETIES OF MODERN EGYPTOMANIA

NINE

OCCULT EGYPTOMANIA

Truly the land of Egypt is another abode of mystery.

H. P. BLAVATSKY[1]

The Great Pyramid, in this writer's opinion, is probably by far the oldest structure on earth. Its main purpose was to serve as a temple of initiation for those who were admitted to the fellowship of the Atlantean Adepts, established in Egypt more than a hundred thousand years ago!

SAX ROHMER[2]

ANCIENT GYPT has always been thought of as a land of magic and secrets. Ancient Egyptian religion contained many magical elements in the form of spells, incantations and mystic rituals. According to the Talmud, the world contains ten measures of magic; nine of them were located in Egypt. Magic formed part of Egypt's reputation with the Hebrews, Greeks, Romans and their successors in the Middle Ages, Renaissance, Baroque and Enlightenment eras.[3] Egypt was strongly associated with the occult – magic, alchemy, astrology and other mystic arts. All sorts of theories, speculations and just plain wild tales about the super or supernatural knowledge possessed by the ancient Egyptians has arisen in recent history and these continue to proliferate into the present.

Just as Egypt and the occult are closely tied, secret societies and the occult are also commonly paired together. When a secret society adopted occult rituals and symbols they often turned to Egypt for inspiration as a source for the legendary origins of the society. Claiming an association with ancient Egyptian practices confirmed the credibility of any occult practices and rites. The fact that the adoptive occult rituals and symbols were not authentically Egyptian did not matter as long as their appearance had a stereotypical Egyptianized motif. Secret societies and their members are natural Egyptophiles. The three main secret societies that incorporated Egyptian magic, rituals, lore and motifs were the Rosicrucians, the Freemasons and the Theosophists. These societies were not alone; other unrelated occult and secret societies have also blended Egyptian lore and symbols into their traditions. Historically, none of these groups had or have a genuine Egyptian origin, but that did not stop any of them from claiming one.[4]

Rosicrucians

The oldest of the three secret societies is probably the Rosicrucians. That is hard to say for certain due to the fuzziness that surrounds the origins of both the Rosicrucians and the Freemasons. What is known for sure is that the so-called Rosicrucian Manifestos appeared in 1614 and 1615. They were followed in 1616 by the publication of *The Alchemical Wedding of Christian Rosenkreutz*, which later turned out to have been written by the Lutheran pastor Johannes Andreae (1586–1654). These works outline the beliefs and philosophy of the Rosicrucians and tell of the life of the German monk Christian Rosenkreutz (1378–1484). By his account, Rosenkreutz went on a pilgrimage to the Holy Land. Afterwards he lived in Yemen for three years where he studied the wisdom of the Arabs. From Yemen he travelled to Fez in Morocco for two more years of studying the Jewish mystical writings known as the Kabala, as well as magic. Along the way he visited Egypt, although the manifestos have little to say about his brief time there. He then returned to Germany where the authorities dismissed his newfound esoteric knowledge. Undeterred, Rosenkreutz returned to his monastery and founded Rosicrucianism. Mainstream scholars believe that Rosenkreutz was not a real person but was instead an allegory. They also credit the English polymath John Dee (1527–1608) as the source for the occult philosophy that forms the basis of Rosicrucianism.[5]

The confusing aspect of Rosicrucianism is that no one knew who wrote the first two Rosicrucian manifestos even though it has been suggested that Andreae wrote them as well as *The Alchemical Wedding*. The manifestos seemed to be evidence for the existence of a Rosicrucian secret society at the cutting edge of the occult sciences. It is important to remember that even in the seventeenth century there was not a clear divide between science on the one hand and magic and superstition on the other. The so-called occult sciences were perfectly respectable at that time; some great scientific minds studied astrology and attributed supernatural powers to alchemy.[6]

Johannes Andreae (1586–1654): founder of Rosicrucianism or practical joker?

Rosicrucian ideology also seemed to provide a potentially effective counterbalance to the threat of resurgent Counter-Reformation Catholicism. Therefore Rosicrucianism came under attack, mostly from Catholic critics. As a result, Rosicrucianism attracted Protestant defenders such as the German Michael Maier (1569–1622) and the Englishman Robert Fludd (1574–1637), a rather eccentric physician and astrologer. Neither Maier nor Fludd claimed to be a Rosicrucian; nor, for that matter, did the Rosicrucians' other defenders. No Rosicrucians came out of the shadows of their secret society to communicate with or thank their defenders because there was no Rosicrucian society – it did not exist. Many scholars have even suggested that Andreae's *Alchemical Wedding* was a prank. Nevetheless people believed in the existence of the Rosicrucians and sought their wisdom. Eventually some of the enthusiasts founded their own Rosicrucian society and new Rosicrucian societies have continued to be founded ever since.

One early Rosicrucian society was the Order of the Golden and Rosy Cross. It was founded in the 1750s by the German Freemason Hermann Fichtuld, who used the ideas of the earlier occultist Sincerus Renatus. To join the Order, the potential member had to be a Master Mason, one of the many instances of overlap between Freemasonry and Rosicrucianism. Unlike most Rosicrucian orders, the Order of the Golden and Rosy Cross traced its origins back to the Egypt of AD 98. Supposedly, an Egyptian priest and convert to Christianity named Ormus founded the Order under the name of the Society of Ormus. His objective was to Christianize the occult knowledge of the ancient Egyptians. Soon after its foundation the Society of Ormus joined with a secret Gnostic society of the Essenes to form the Order of the Rose Cross. Much later, in 1118, members of the Order initiated the first Templars into the society. Eventually the Templars carried the Order of the Rose Cross to Scotland where they founded an early form of Freemasonry – at least, this was the story told by Fichtuld when he established the Order of the Gold and Rosy Cross in Germany. During the reign of Frederick William II of Prussia (1786–97) the Order of the Golden and Rosy Cross dominated the highest levels of the Prussian government. During the Napoleonic wars, however, the Order quickly collapsed.[7]

Most of the Rosicrucian societies that followed merely claimed to have their medieval origin described in the Rosicrucian manifestos. In the case of the prominent Hermetic Order of the Golden Dawn (HOGD), founded in 1887, however, it claimed a medieval origin while still incorporating Egyptianized rituals and accoutrements. In fact, any society incorporating Hermetic in its name is ultimately harkening back to the wisdom of the Egyptians. There is a famous picture from around 1895 of the HOGD member Samuel Liddell MacGregor Mathers dressed in a ceremonial headdress of Egyptian design. Apparently an occult ritual works better when one is dressed like an ancient Egyptian. Despite the testimony of the Rosicrucian manifestos asserting a medieval origin for the Rosicrucians, several later important Rosicrucian societies traced their origins back to ancient Egypt.

One of the first of the Egyptianized Rosicrucian societies was the Hermetic Order of Egypt. Its founder was the English scholar Kenneth MacKenzie (1833–1886). Born into a well-to-do family, MacKenzie pursued a career as a gentleman–scholar. He translated German works, contributed to *Notes & Queries* and other scholarly periodicals, and was elected a Fellow of the Royal Society of Antiquaries in 1854. He began to study magic about 1858 and went to Paris to study the occult in 1861. In 1866 he helped Robert Wentworth Little to create rituals for the Societas Rosicruciana in Anglia (SRIA) but did not join the SRIA until 1872 and resigned a few years later in 1875. He was also initiated into the Freemasons in March 1870 but resigned soon after in January 1871. Around 1874 MacKenzie founded the Hermetic Order of Egypt. Its organization was at least partially based on the secret Rosicrucian fraternity described by Edward Bulwer-Lytton in his novel *Zanoni* (1842). MacKenzie went on to claim that he possessed the philosopher's stone – the elixir of life – the ability to be invisible and the power to communicate with spiritual beings. Despite this impressive occult arsenal and its Egyptianizing name, the Hermetic Order of Egypt was not successful. William Wynn Westcott would use MacKenzie's papers later on to help create rituals for the Hermetic Order of the Golden Dawn.

Another Egyptianized Rosicrucian society was the Hermetic Brotherhood of Luxor (H. B. of L.) It was founded in London during 1884 by Peter Davidson and Thomas Burgoyne with guidance from the shadowy European mystic Max Theon. The H. B. of L. claimed to be part of an unbroken succession of practitioners going all the way back to Egyptian priest-initiates. Advertisements in magazines and on book covers were used to recruit new members who were enrolled in correspondence courses. These courses taught the new members about the beliefs and ideas of the society. H. B. of L. quickly became a serious rival of the Theosophical Society but just as quickly it collapsed when it was discovered that Thomas Burgoyne had been convicted and spent time in prison during 1883 for mail fraud. Once the attention garnered by his legal problems had faded, revivals of the H. B. of L. occurred as Burgoyne strived to rehabilitate his career as a leader of occult societies. Burgoyne moved to the United States in 1886 and there he wrote a summary of the teachings of the H. B. of L. entitled *The Light of Egypt* (1889). Eventually his activities resulted in the formation of the Hermetic Brotherhood of Light in Boston during 1895. It continued to recruit and initiate new members through correspondence. The Hermetic Brotherhood of Light operated as a very secret society to insulate itself against the Theosophical Society's campaign of vilification, which was targeting the various Rosicrucian societies that had succeeded the defunct H. B. of L. In 1914 one of the society's members, Elbert Benjamine, became its sole leader. He began transforming the group into an occult correspondence school. In 1915 he moved the society to Los Angeles where it became the Brotherhood of Light. Benjamine created a very elaborate system of fifty degrees of initiation to be completed by a massive array of

The Egyptian Museum of the Rosicrucians in San Jose, California.

correspondence courses. In 1932 he transformed the Brotherhood of Light into the Church of Life, which continued to claim its unbroken descent from Egyptian priests. After straying somewhat from its Egyptian roots, the Church of Light revived the Order of the Sphinx, which engaged in the magical practices of the H. B. of L. The Church of Light managed to survive the social changes that threatened the survival of older occult societies and has today established itself on the internet.

The foremost Rosicrucian society to employ Egyptian themes was the Ancient Mystical Order Rosae Crucis (AMORC). It was also, perhaps not coincidentally, the most successful Rosicrucian organization in America. Harvey Spencer Lewis (1889–1939), an American advertising man, was its founder. Lewis developed a strong interest in the occult early on in life and founded the New York Institute of Psychical Research in 1904. Despite the name, there was nothing scientific about the Institute. It was an occult study group with a special focus on Rosicrucian beliefs. In 1915 Lewis founded a chapter of the controversial Ordo Templi Orientis, widely viewed as a sex cult that practised black magic.

Lewis, like many leaders of occult societies, had problems with the law. He was arrested for fraud, though not convicted, but this episode prompted Lewis to make an immediate move to San Francisco. In 1925 he relocated from San Fransisco to Tampa, Florida, where he set up a new headquarters for AMORC. Lewis claimed that AMORC's origins could be traced back to ancient Egyptian mystery schools founded by Pharaoh Thutmoses III and Queen Hatshepsut. Another prominent later member of the ancient order was the failed religious revolutionary Pharaoh Akhenaten, the heretic. To promote this strong Egyptian connection, AMORC began collecting Egyptian artefacts. To increase AMORC's membership, Lewis created the most successful of all the occult societies' correspondence courses to recruit and to educate new members. In 1927 he relocated AMORC's headquarters to San Jose when it became apparent that California was the primary market for AMORC's correspondence courses. Its buildings were designed using an Egyptian temple motif and an Egyptian museum was created in the grounds to house and display AMORC's growing collection of artefacts – the museum remains open to the public today. The collection is authentic and extensive enough to be regarded as having scholarly merit, but as the historian Richard Francaviglia has pointed out, it also serves the spiritual purposes of the Rosicrucians and is designed to allow visitors to experience the various themes of Rosicrucianism. As such it is an impressive combination of Egyptomania and Orientalism.[8] Surviving the late twentieth-century drift away from traditional occult societies, AMORC is today an international Rosicrucian organization and has moved its headquarters to France, although San Jose remains the North American headquarters. AMORC amply demonstrates the appeal of Egypt for occult secret societies.

Rosicrucianism developed side by side during the course of the seventeenth and eighteenth centuries with another significant society: the Freemasons. There was considerable interaction and overlap between the two groups (The Order of the Golden and Rosy Cross was a Rosicrucian society that only admitted Master Masons as members), but Freemasonry developed its own distinctive history.

Freemasonry

Freemasonry has various claims to ancient origins but it really was for the most part a creation of the early Enlightenment. The murky historical origins of the Freemasons purport to lie in the associations created by medieval stonemasons, hence the masonry garb and tools that are used in the rituals and symbols by the Order. The intellectuals who founded modern Freemasonry used the existing craft organizations of stonemasons as their model. Freemasonry developed in Europe in the seventeenth century during a time when royal absolutism was growing in power in much of the continent and the Roman Catholic Church was resurgent. In response,

Freemasonry developed to promote individual liberty and human equality as opposed to privilege for a few and unrestrained power for the state and the Church. Freemasons were also very critical of what they saw as superstition. In this category they included folk magic, lore about fairies and trolls, and belief in luck. They also included among the superstitions many aspects of Christian beliefs, especially some that were dear to the Roman Catholic Church, which resulted in the Church's hostile opinion of Freemasonry. Given their aversion to superstition, there was nothing occult about Freemasonry. Mainstream Freemasonry had no need for the recovery of lost ancient wisdom or the discovery of venerable antecedents that went all the way back to ancient Egypt.[9]

Freemasonry did, however, have its origin myths. The predominant origin myth traced the beginning of Freemasonry to the building of King Solomon's temple in Jerusalem about 1000 BC. This myth is deeply embedded in the rituals of the basic Masonic degrees. There are other origin myths that are not part of mainstream Masonry. One credits the Knights Templar with creating Freemasonry. The Knights Templar comprised a crusading religious order that was headquartered in Jerusalem at the site of the Temple of Solomon, hence the name Templar. Another origin myth claims that the Freemasons developed out of the medieval Rosicrucians (who did not truly exist but inconvenient facts seldom deter true believers). Others suggest that the Freemasons had their origin in the Greek mystery cults such as the Eleusinian or Dionysian mysteries. Finally, the most ancient origin myth traced the Freemasons back to Egypt and the time of the pyramids. The Egyptians were the first master builders. In turn, they taught their building skills along with other esoteric knowledge to Moses and the Hebrews. A variant of the Egyptian origin myth credited Joseph and his Hebrew brethren with bringing the knowledge of building to the Egyptians. Freemasonry might have officially rejected superstition but that did not mean all of its members spurned the quest for ancient wisdom which Egypt represented. Freemasons believed in the quest for individual self-improvement and the acquisition of ancient wisdom was seen, by some, as a good shortcut to self-improvement. It is human nature for people to seek an ancient origin – the Egyptian myth of origin gave the Freemasons the most venerable pedigree possible, at least by the state of seventeenth-, eighteenth- and nineteenth-century knowledge about ancient history.[10]

Despite their professed rationalism, Freemasons could also engage in both the occult and Egyptomania. Andrew Michael Ramsay (1686–1743) was the first Mason to extend the society's origins back to the Templars and so provided support for the new Scottish degrees of Freemasonry that were becoming popular in France. Ramsay's background – the son of a Scottish baker – was modest. After attending university, he became a disciple of the French Archbishop François Fénelon. Moving to the Continent in 1709, he entered Fénelon's service. He would also become an associate of the Regent, the Duke of Orleans, and a tutor to the children of James Stuart, the Old Pretender, and the exiled son of the deposed James II. Around 1728 he was admitted into a Masonic lodge in London. Historians strongly suspect that Ramsay might have been a double-agent who had contact with the Jacobites supporting the restoration of the Stuart dynasty while also working for the Hanoverian kings of England. Ramsay first presented his Templar theory of the origins of the Freemasons in his famous oration of 1736. However, what he was actually suggesting was that the Templar origin of Freemasonry was actually a refoundation. He asserted that Freemasonry originated in knowledge that had been preserved from destruction by Noah during the Great Flood. This knowledge was passed on from patriarch to patriarch until Joseph carried that knowledge to Egypt. The ancient Egyptians later lost these secrets, which were rediscovered by the Templars.[11]

The lure of ancient Egypt with its antiquity and its supposed secret wisdom appealed to other early Freemasons as well. The rite known as Crata Repoa appeared in Germany before 1770. German Freemasons claimed it was the highest form of the Egyptian mystery cults. Of course, in 1770 no one could read ancient Egyptian documents and inscriptions so their claim for the authenticity of Crata Repoa was superficially credible or at least not subject to refutation. In fact, the ritual of Crata Repoa was based on an established Masonic degree system. Claiming an Egyptian origin simply gave Crata Repoa added respectability and authority. It appears that the Crata Repoa was simply an anonymously produced Masonic document that circulated among German Freemasons but was not adopted by any secret society. Later nineteenth-century French occult groups did adopt the Crata Repoa, however. In 1970 the American magician Carroll Runyon used the Egyptianized Crata Repoa to help create a set of rituals for his new society, the Ordo Templi Astarte, based in Silverado, California. It was an eclectic system of rituals and degrees which also incorporated material from the Hermetic Order of the Golden Dawn and Phoenician mythology.[12]

Alessandro Cagliostro (1743–1795) was a conman and an adventurer who contributed significantly to Egyptomania in Freemasonry. Born Giuseppe Balsamo, he initially tried to make a career in the Catholic Church by joining the monastic order the Brothers of Mercy. He was not suited for a religious life. After being expelled from the order, he made his living through confidence schemes, forgery and selling fraudulent patent medicines and elixirs. He married a pretty young girl with few scruples and they worked together as a team. In 1777 he sought admission into a Masonic Lodge in London that followed the Rite of Strict Observance. After completing the first four degrees, he claimed to have discovered an old document that consisted of the rituals for an ancient Egyptian rite of Masonry. These rites were supposedly as old as the pyramids and the document contained other occult and alchemical secrets. Cagliostro dubbed the ancient rituals the Egyptian Rite and in 1778 introduced it to the community of Freemasons in London. He also allowed women to be admitted into the Egyptian Rite, which was contrary to traditional Freemasonry's men-only policy. The seduction of ancient Egypt made the new rite very popular almost immediately and Cagliostro was the Rite's leader. As leader, he controlled the initiation fees paid by new members, and there were many. He proceeded to travel around Europe recruiting more and more Freemasons to the Egyptian Rite. Arriving in Paris in 1785 he soon became involved in the scandal known as the Affair of the Diamond Necklace. As a result he ended up in the Bastille prison for almost a year. The notoriety of his arrest and imprisonment attracted the attention of the scandal-hungry popular press of France, which mocked him as a fraud and a fake. By the end of 1786, one of the newspapers discovered his humble origins as Giuseppe Balsamo. Fleeing France and England, Cagliostro went to Rome at the urging of his wife, who wanted to visit her family. There the Roman Inquisition arrested him as a Freemason, which the Roman Catholic Church considered a heresy. Cagliostro was sentenced to death, but the pope reduced the sentence to

The Egyptian Room of the Masonic Hall in Fort Wayne, Indiana.

life imprisonment. He died in a papal prison in 1795. Although reviled in Roman Catholic circles in Protestant Europe he continued to be considered a mysterious but respectable master of Masonic lore. In the late nineteenth century, the occult society Fratres Lucis claimed it received its teaching from Cagliostro through a crystal ball. Moreover, the prominent but controversial Theosophist Charles W. Leadbeater (1854–1934) was fond of the Egyptianizing aspects of Cagliostro's rituals and identified the conman as one of the ascended masters of Theosophy.[13]

Other Egyptian-based Masonic rites appeared during the course of the nineteenth century. The first was the Rite of Mizraim, which probably began in Italy in 1805, and became popular in France. It claimed to be descended from the rituals of the mystery temples of ancient Egypt. The Rite of Mizraim consisted of ninety degrees of initiation. In 1814 Frenchmen living in Cairo founded another Egyptian-style Masonic rite which they called the Rite of Memphis. The founders again maintained that the Rite of Memphis had its origins in the mystery rites of the temples of ancient Egypt. In fact, one legend of the Rite of Memphis would have deprived them of the status of being the rite's founders. It claimed that during August 1798 an old man who was a descendant of the sages of Egypt initiated both Napoleon and General Jean-Baptiste Kléber into Freemasonry using the Rite of Memphis. This initiation ceremony even took place inside the Pyramid of Cheops.[14]

The Rite of Memphis was even more complicated than the rival Rite of Mizraim since the Rite of Memphis consisted of 95 degrees of initiation. One of the founders, Samuel Honis, brought the rite back to France in 1815 where he set up a Lodge which quickly came to nothing. The Rite of Memphis was refounded in 1838 and proved attractive to political radicals. Given the questionable reputation that Freemasonry held with conservative and reactionary forces in Europe, a Masonic rite that attracted radicals was doubly suspect. The French police suppressed it in 1841. The Rite was refounded again in 1848 and came to attract people who opposed Napoleon III's rule in France. Traditionalist Masons, however, did not approve of the Rite of Memphis and it faded away during the 1860s. The residues of the Rite of Memphis's membership were simply taken in by traditionalist Masonic Lodges. In 1872 John Yarker (1833–1913), an Englishman who had a fascination for off-beat, non-traditional Masonic rites, combined the Rite of Mizraim and the largely defunct Rite of Memphis into the Rite of Memphis and Mizraim. Yarker took what he considered were the best degrees of the Rites of Mizraim and of Memphis and created an immense 96-degree path of initiation. When Yarker died in 1913, a struggle for control of the Rite of Memphis and Mizraim erupted between the Theosophists Annie Besant and Charles Leadbeater, widely suspected of pederasty, on the one side and the followers of Yarker led by the rather sexually deviant occultist Aleister Crowley. Yarker's supporters won the struggle but the Rite of Memphis and Mizraim had lost momentum and became dormant and has stayed that way despite a number of attempts to revive it.[15] Despite the fundamentally rationalist nature of Masonry, fringe Masonic rites have appeared periodically. Those rites that claim to possess roots in ancient Egypt were and are common and popular. The mystique and antiquity of Egypt lent respectability and credibility to almost any endeavour or organization, which is why mainstream Masons during the nineteenth and twentieth centuries have frequently adopted Egyptian motifs in the architecture or interior designs of their buildings.[16]

The Theosophical Society

Compared to Rosicrucianism and Freemasonry, the Theosophical Society was a newcomer in the world of occult secret societies. The story of the foundation of the Theosophical Society is convoluted, including much globetrotting and some episodes that stretch credulity.[17] Helena Petrovna Blavatsky (1831–1891) is the person most closely identified with Theosophy but she had many like-minded colleagues and partners in the enterprise. Born in Russia, her family, the von Hahns, were of German origin but had become part of the affluent Russian nobility. Some of the female members of the family were quite accomplished, and the young Helena von Hahn grew up to be a free spirit. When she was seventeen years old, she married Nikifor V. Blavatsky, who was twenty years her senior. Supposedly she married simply to spite her governess. The marriage was not a love-match and was never consummated; within a few months of marrying, Helena Blavatsky went on her travels, never to return to her hapless husband, although she would use her husband's surname for the rest of her life.

Blavatsky's life is poorly documented for the years 1848 to 1858. Most of what is recorded is based on information provided by Blavatsky and there is considerable reason not to give much of it credence. She apparently travelled extensively in Europe and the Middle East but just how extensively is not clear. She claimed to have met the Tibetan Master Morya at an exhibition in London in 1851. According to the teachings of Theosophy, the Masters were people who had gone through many reincarnations accompanied by spiritual growth. Eventually these people obtained the enlightenment needed to transcend the physical world. In this state the Masters served as teachers to others seeking

Madame Helena Blavatsky (1831–1891), founder of the Theosophical Society.

the path of enlightened knowledge. As a result of this meeting, Blavatsky made her way to Tibet where she studied for seven years with Morya and another Master named Koot Hoomi, both of whom would serve as spiritual guides to Blavatsky for the rest of her life, or so she claimed. If Blavatsky had actually travelled to Tibet in 1851, it would have made her an intrepid female traveller of the ilk of Freya Stark or Gertrude Bell.

In 1858 Blavatsky returned to Russia to visit her family. There she met the opera singer Asgardi Metrovich and they became a couple. The two remained together until Metrovich's death, caused by an explosion on a ship bound for Egypt. Blavatsky proceeded on to Cairo and entered into a séance business with Emma Cutting in 1872. Their enterprise crumbled when their clients began accusing them of fraud. Blavatsky made her way to Paris where, in 1873, Master Morya told her to move on to New York City. About a year later Blavatsky met the American spiritualist Henry Steel Olcott. The two became friends and with the help of Master Tuitit Bey of Luxor and other Masters they formed the Theosophical Society on 17 November 1875. Besides the Masters, Blavatsky also claimed to have been assisted in organizing the Theosophical Society by the Brotherhood of Luxor, an American secret society. Some Theosophists have suggested that the Brotherhood of Luxor was an offshoot of the British occult society known as Fratres Lucis. Mainstream scholars, however, believe that the Brotherhood of Luxor never existed. Blavatsky had simply made it up and after she settled in India, she eliminated the Brotherhood of Luxor from her narrative of Theosophical origins.[18]

In 1877 Blavatsky published her two-volume work *Isis Unveiled*. The title refers to Isis, the god who brought civilization to Egypt both material and spiritual. A statue of Isis in the temple on Philae Island in the Nile River bore an inscription that partly read, 'My veil no one has lifted.' Therefore, Madame Blavatsky's book would lift the veil of Isis and would reveal a great mystery. In her book, Madame Blavatsky sought to reveal ancient wisdom for modern readers. Ancient wisdom, however, had been veiled for centuries by the retrograde forces of Christianity and scientific materialism. *Isis Unveiled* claimed to be an exposition of the rise and suppression of the ancient wisdom. Blavatsky claimed to have written the book with the assis-tance of the Masters. They often communicated with Blavatsky in the form of precipitated letters, that is, letters appearing out of thin air. In the case of *Isis Unveiled*, the Masters provided precipitated pages of text. The prob-lem was that many of the precipitated pages had been copied from works by other writers without attribution. Someone had plagiarized and that person was either Blavatsky or one of those Masters. Since an ascended Master would never stoop to plagiarism, that leaves Madame Blavatsky.

Obviously with a title like *Isis Unveiled*, Blavatsky's book had a lot to say about Egyptian wisdom and its relation to Theosophy. Blavatsky argued that Christianity and scientific materialism had corrupted and suppressed the original hermetic philosophy and religion that permeated the various religions of the ancient world. Humanity would be threatened with the loss of its spiritual nature if this process was allowed to continue. According to Blavatsky, the ancients were not primitives. They, particularly the Egyptians, possessed knowledge that was equal or superior to that of the Victorian world of 1877. The impressive achievements of the Egyptians are cata-logued in various parts of *Isis Unveiled*. Unlike many of her contemporaries, Blavatsky did not believe that the Egyptians were the world's first high civilization. Instead, she identified the Aryans of India as the original and oldest civilization. Egyptian civilization was the product of diffusion from India. The Egyptians, in fact, were the descendants of Aryan migrants from India. According to Blavatsky, Egyptian pyramids were not only tombs, they were meeting-places for the performance of the rituals of the Egyptian mysteries and astrological observatories. Blavatsky also argued that the pyramids were far older than the archaeologists and historians of her day were willing to concede. The ancient Aryans discovered how to make iron far earlier than was thought by most scholars and some of them brought that knowledge to Egypt. Blavatsky also extolled the wonders of Egyptian mummification techniques while failing to mention how the dryness of Egypt's climate contributed to the preservation of the mummies. Then again, Blavatsky also believed in Atlantis and that Atlanteans had settled and civilized much of the world. Just how the Atlanteans and the Aryans of India were related to each other in terms of culture and ethnicity, however, is not made clear.[19] In late 1878 Blavatsky and some of her Theosophical associates moved to India on the instruction of Masters Morya and Koot Hoomi. They set up their headquarters at Aydar in 1882. After she arrived in India, Blavatsky shifted her emphasis from Western to Eastern esotericism which meant that Egypt would play a lesser role in her Theosophical thinking. Many American and European Theosophists did not agree with this shift, hence her colleague Charles Leadbeater's continued interest in the Egyptian origins of occult wisdom. Despite Blavatsky's change in emphasis the Egyptophile elements have remained significant in Theosophy ever since.

Other Egyptophile Occult Societies

Some occult societies were or are combinations of Freemasonry and Rosicrucianism with some Theosophy thrown into the mix. Other occult societies, however, had or have little or nothing to do with Freemasonry, Rosicrucianism or Theosophy. The common denominator among them was their adoption of supposed Egyptian beliefs, rituals and motifs. As such, these groups were further manifestations of Egyptomania in popular culture. The most influential of these groups was the Hermetic Order of the Golden Dawn, founded in London in 1887 by William Wynn Westcott (1848–1925), Samuel Liddell MacGregor Mathers (1854–1918), and William Robert Woodman (1828–1891). All three men were Freemasons.[20]

Supposedly Westcott unearthed an old manuscript in a London bookshop. It was in cipher and attached was an address for contacting a German occultist. Westcott got in touch with the German who provided him with the charter for founding the Hermetic Order of the Golden Dawn. In reality, the manuscript came from the collection of Kenneth Mackenzie, whose papers had come into Westcott's possession. The manuscript was a draft of the rituals for the failed Hermetic Brotherhood of Egypt that Mackenzie had tried to start. These rituals, in turn, took their inspiration from rituals of the Societas Rosicruciana in Anglia.

The Hermetic Order of the Golden Dawn was obviously a hybrid Rosicrucian and Masonic organization. Some of its members were Masons who sought a society that was more secret and more occult than mainstream Freemasonry. It traced its origins back to medieval Rosicrucians, not ancient Egyptian priests. That origin, however, did not prevent the Hermetic Order from adopting all sorts of Egyptian elements in its rituals, costumes and decor: its London temple and headquarters, for example, was named Isis-Urania, a combination of Isis – one of the chief gods of Egypt, associated with wisdom and mystery – and Urania, one of the muses in Greek mythology who was the patron of astrology and the sister of wisdom. Pictures of Mathers show him dressed in various faux-Egyptian regalia in preparation to preside over rituals using Egyptian motifs. Not everyone in the leadership of the later Golden Dawn organization was enthusiastic about the adoption of Egyptomaniac rituals, customs or ideas.[21] Still, such accoutrements gave the society the semblance of the ancient wisdom and mystery that ancient Egypt evoked.

The Hermetic Order of the Golden Dawn quickly rose to the position of being the most prominent secret society in Great Britain. Unlike most of its contemporary secret societies, the Hermetic Order allowed women to be members. The new order quickly spread to Paris and several American cities. It also attracted some very prominent members. The Swedish playwright August Strindberg, the Irish poet William Butler Yeats and the Norwegian painter Edvard Munch were all members. Most significantly, the writers H. Rider Haggard and Bram Stoker, who shared a penchant for Egyptomania, reputedly joined the Hermetic Order. Another prominent member was Arthur Edward Waite, a prolific scholar of occultism. Despite its popularity among important cultural figures, the Hermetic Order only lasted for fifteen years. Infighting – which had its roots in the megalomania of Mathers and his rivalry with Aleister Crowley – led to the schism that shattered the society. Some of the offshoots of the Hermetic Order survived until well into the twentieth century. Despite its relatively brief existence, the Hermetic Order and its organization and rituals were widely used as models by other occult societies and continue to be used to this day.

Another occult society with strong Egyptian associations was the Brotherhood of Heliopolis, founded in Paris by Frenchmen with an interest in alchemy, sometime before 1914. It was named after the ancient Egyptian city of Heliopolis, which was known for its leadership in alchemical study. Its founders went so far as to claim descent from the ancient priests of Heliopolis. Otherwise, the society left few records concerning its origins and activities. It appears to have gone out of existence before the outbreak of the Second World War.

Back in the United States, another occultist appeared to follow in the footsteps of Madame Blavatsky and her supernatural communications with the Masters or some other spiritual entity. Edgar Cayce (1877–1945) was born in Hopkinsville, Kentucky. His grandfather Thomas Cayce had been a comfortably well-off landowner, albeit a drinking man. Edgar's father Leslie Cayce continued the family's drinking tradition but as a second son financial success eluded him. Life for Leslie's wife and children was meagre as a consequence of his repeated failures. As a child, Edgar Cayce claimed to demonstrate psychic and clairvoyant abilities. He was a loner who purported to converse with 'little people' and his deceased grandfather Thomas. Others would have considered his claims a bit delusional, except for the fact that, to the local population, his grandfather Thomas was also considered to possess clairvoyant abilities. When he was ten years old, Cayce suffered an injury that left him temporarily bedridden. During his convalescence, he read the Bible to pass the time and improve himself. He showed most interest in the Old Testament and especially the story of Moses in Egypt and the supernatural competition with the Egyptian sorcerers. It was the beginning of his Egyptomania. Edgar's interest in the Bible continued and he contemplated studying to become a minister, but a disappointing romance caused him to abandon that plan.[22]

In 1898 the 21-year-old Cayce suffered from a chronic sore throat that interfered with his speech and ended up costing him his job. Linking up with a hypnotist, Cayce obtained some relief when he was put into a trance. Another hypnotist named Al Layne went further. While Cayce was under a trance, Layne proceeded to ask him about his symptoms, the cause of his illness and treatments. Cayce gave him answers that led to a cure. From that point onwards, Layne suggested that Cayce use his talent for psychic healing to help others. All that Cayce needed to perform a psychic reading for a person suffering from an illness was the patient's name and address. They did not have to be present for him to do a reading. From his trance, Cayce would suggest a cure and often his cure worked. Cayce claimed that he derived his knowledge from 'the Source', which he later identified as the Akashic Records, and which he could only access during a trance. Akashic Records were supposed to be a repository of every event, act or thought that ever occurred or will occur. Some students of the paranormal have suggested that the Akashic Records represent another dimension that humans are usually unaware exists. Cayce was not alone in his ability to access the Akashic Records – Madame Blavatsky and other Theosophists and Anthrosophists also claimed that they could access them. In the case of Cayce, when he awoke from trances, he could remember nothing. After 1911 Cayce expanded into so-called life readings in which he told patients about their previous lives or reincarnations. He believed that problems from earlier lives could make people sick in their present incarnation. His explorations of the past lives of people took him back to ancient civilizations and even to the lost land of Atlantis. Ancient Egypt was a particularly frequent destination for Cayce's life readings.

Awake, Edgar Cayce was a staunchly conservative Christian; in a trance, he was a New Age forerunner of the first order. His readings described a primordial history in which Atlantis was the first great civilization. He himself even had a previous life in Atlantis. When Atlantis suffered its final destruction, its survivors dispersed and spread its civilization most successfully to ancient Egypt. Cayce also had an Egyptian incarnation as the high priest Ra-Ta. Cayce's ancient Egypt was a bit more ancient than mainstream Egyptologists would concede: he dated both Ra-Ta and the pyramids to 10,500 BC.[23]

Cayce did life readings for members of his own family. It was revealed that his son Hugh Lynn Cayce was currently in his sixth life. Previously he had lived in primordial times, presumably on Atlantis. Most recently he had been a noble during the Crusades, a monk living during the reign of King Alfred and also Andrew, the disciple of Jesus. While having been one of the twelve disciples was quite an impressive pedigree, Hugh Lynn's second life was an Egyptophile's dream. He was a pharaoh of Egypt, although it is not clear which pharaoh. Initially reluctant to do life readings on himself, when he did Cayce discovered he was living his eighth life. In his earlier lives, Edgar was a British soldier serving in North America, a resident of Jamestown, a member of the French court during the time of Cardinal Richelieu, a defender of Troy, a Persian healer and utopian, and a person living at the time when humans had first appeared on earth. Like Hugh Lynn, Edgar's second life was lived in ancient Egypt. There he was the high priest Ra-Ta at the time his son Hugh Lynn was pharaoh. Father and son were not alone either. It turned out that Cayce's wife Gertrude was a dancer at the court of the pharaoh. But in this era of history, Edgar and Hugh Lynn were rivals for the affections of Gertrude, the palace dancing girl. Edgar won and the couple gave birth to a daughter, who turned out to be Cayce's secretary and soulmate Gladys Davis in one of her earlier lives! Another result was that the enraged pharaoh (Hugh Lynn) banished Ra-Ta (his father Edgar). Filial and paternal roles were getting very confused by these revelations. In yet another life reading Cayce discovered that Hugh Lynn's fiancée, Olive Koop, had also been present during the time of Ra-Ta and followed him into exile. Hugh Lynn as pharaoh had a rather tumultuous love-life. The life readings revealed that Edgar's friend Fred Batterson had been the brother of the pharaoh. Both princes fell in love with the reincarnation of Olive and their quarrel plunged Egypt into a civil war. On several occasions, 'the Source' informed Cayce that there was something special about the Egyptian incarnations of Cayce and his family and friends. Certainly their intertwined stories made for a convoluted ancient Egyptian soap opera.[24]

Life readings from ancient Egypt formed a significant portion of the life readings that Cayce conducted during his lifetime, and they have been collected and summarized in several books. Interest in ancient Egypt did not die with Edgar Cayce either. In 1931 at Virginia Beach, Virginia, he and some of his associates formed the non-profit foundation Association for Research and Enlightenment (ARE), also known as the Edgar Cayce Foundation. While the primary focus of ARE's efforts are the promotion of Cayce's ideas about holistic medicine and psychic healing, it has also maintained a significant interest in the archaeology of ancient Egypt. In one of his readings, Cayce revealed that when Atlanteans fled the destruction of their homeland in 10,700 BC, they brought the records of their vast knowledge with them to Egypt. There, in 10,500 BC, the records were deposited in an underground pyramid known as the 'Hall of Records' or the 'Pyramid of Records'. The Hall of Records lies buried somewhere between the front of the Sphinx and the Nile River with a secret passage connecting the underground cavern to the Sphinx.

Edgar Cayce, though, was hardly the first person to suggest the existence of a cache of ancient Egyptian super-knowledge. Such beliefs go back at least as far as the Muslim legends that the pyramids had been built as repositories to preserve the knowledge of Egypt from destruction by flood or other catastrophes. In the years after Cayce's death, however, the ARE had become the beneficiary of some very wealthy donors, meaning it had the financial resources to fund searches for the Hall of Records. Cayce's son Hugh Lynn was very interested in finding those lost records. The ARE also funded the education of the Egyptologists Mark Lehner and Zahi Hawass, the celebrity archaeologist. Cayce's prophecy about the Hall of Records helped to publicize the supposed existence of the undiscovered Hall of Records, prompting others to search for it on the Giza Plateau. These beliefs have the potential to stir all sorts of intrusive digging and drilling, which worries and annoys the Egyptian officials responsible for preserving the complex of monuments in Giza.[25] In this way Egyptomania is once again fuelled by a fantasy that is almost certainly without any basis in historical fact.

The attraction for ancient Egypt among secret societies has continued unabated into the twenty-first century, as the saga of the Nuwaubian Nation clearly demonstrates. Dwight York (b. 1935 or 1945), also known as Malachi Z. York, is a professional cult organizer. He got his start in New York by founding several Black Muslim groups, beginning in 1967. During the late 1980s, York largely abandoned the Islamic aspects of his cult work to teach the ancient Egyptian origins of his cult and its association with ancient aliens, Freemasons, Native American religions and Rastafarianism. The one constant in York's proselytizing was a bedrock belief in Black Supremacy. He named his new group the Nuwaubian Nation. According to York, 'Nuwaubu' was a term referring to the way of life of supreme beings. Since York concocted the beliefs of the Nuwaubians himself, little genuine ancient Egyptian theology or cosmology can be found in Nuwaubu. In 1993 York relocated his group from Brooklyn to Eatonton, Georgia. There he began the construction of a compound for his African American followers that he named Tama-Re. Despite the eclectic group of religious doctrines, ancient history and fringe scholarship that constituted Nuwaubian beliefs, Egyptian motifs dominated Tama-Re's buildings and decor. The compound even had its own pyramid. By 2000 the Nuwaubian Nation had five hundred members along with about 5,000 visitors a year. Dwight York was also starting to make various claims about being divine, or that he was actually of extraterrestrial origin, as was the Pharaoh Rameses II. He took the title of pharaoh as well. Unfortunately for the Nuwaubians, York slipped down the path frequently followed by cult leaders and engaged in sexual excess. He was accused of transporting children across state lines and sexually abusing them. These accusations led to his arrest by Federal authorities in May 2002 for some one hundred counts of child molestation. During his trial York appeared in the courtroom attired in full Egyptian regalia, much to the wonderment of observers. In the end the court sentenced him to prison for 135 to 175 years. The Nuwaubian Nation collapsed as a result and the Federal government seized Tama-Re under forfeiture laws. The compound was sold and its buildings were demolished, thus seemingly ending yet another bizarre episode in the history of occult Egyptomania. However, a remnant of Nuwaubian loyalists remain active, so perhaps their story is not over.[26] The fact remains that occult Egyptomania endures. It is continually reincarnated in the morass of misinformation that constitutes the cultic milieu of alternative religions and fringe scholarship.

TEN

EGYPTOMANIA ON THE FRINGE OF HISTORY

Nothing succeeds like Egypt. Although its fabled magic and mystery have by now become something of a well-worn cliché, it is, largely, only academic historians who lament the fact. Something about the land of Tutankhamun, the Sphinx and the Great Pyramid instantly dwarfs all other cultures in our imaginations.

LYNN PICKETT AND CLIVE PRINCE, *The Stargate Conspiracy*[1]

I could be talking complete rubbish. That's the thing about working with the ancient past. You can put forward any crackpot theory you like – no one's ever going to prove you wrong. It is all interpretation.

PAUL SUSSMAN, *The Lost Army of Cambyses*[2]

EGYPT IS A LAND OF MYTH AND MYSTERIES. It is the abode of hidden wisdom and esoteric lore. The many monuments of Egypt inspire awe and wonder. They speak to an immense antiquity and seemingly preternatural abilities. Egypt is a land like no other. We know much about ancient Egypt, but there is a lot we do not know and will never know. All of these traits make Egypt attractive to the purveyors of fringe history. Because Egypt is both comfortably familiar and at the same time exotic, it makes a great land of refuge for Atlantean refugees or a colony of extraterrestrial visitors, or as a treasure-house of lost or forgotten super-knowledge. This chapter will look at some of the more significant subjects of Egyptomaniac fringe history – pyramids, hyper-diffusion of culture, extreme antiquity and ancient aliens.

Pyramids, Pyramidology and Pyramidiots

Along with the Sphinx, mummies and King Tutankhamun, the pyramids are the most iconic images of ancient Egypt. The pyramids are cited as one of the Seven Wonders of the Ancient World – the only one of those wonders that still survives. Their sheer size impresses anyone who has visited them, even in the modern world of skyscrapers, massive hydroelectric dams and leviathan cruise ships. For over 4,000 years the pyramids were the tallest man-made structure. Only the Lighthouse or Pharos of Alexandria rivalled them in terms of height. It was not until the late nineteenth century, in 1884, that the Great Pyramid lost the title of being the world's tallest building when the Washington Monument – an obelisk of all things – was constructed. This, in turn, was swiftly supplanted by the Eiffel Tower in 1889.

What was the ancient Egyptians' reason for building the towering edifices? What are their purpose? The ancient Greeks and Romans were in no doubt about that – they were the tombs of pharaohs who had ruled Egypt in the distant past. The ancient Egyptians had built them, however apparently incredible that might have seemed. In his famous history, Herodotus is quite clear about these things and he got his information from the Egyptians themselves. Other ancient authorities agreed. In fact, the ever-practical Romans, such as Pliny the Elder, considered building such elaborate tombs to be the height of vainglory. During the medieval period, some alternative ideas about the purpose of the pyramids appeared. Muslim scholars of the Middle Ages thought the pyramids had been built to store and to protect the treasure and secret knowledge of the Egyptian sages in the event of a catastrophe such as Noah's flood. Medieval Europeans developed the misconception that the pyramids were the granaries where the biblical patriarch Joseph stored grain in preparation for the seven lean years of universal famine.[3] Otherwise, the pyramids remained tombs in the minds of most people.

Today, things are different. All sorts of strange and preposterous theories about the pyramids abound: they were built by extraterrestrial visitors or Atlanteans; they were a repository of ancient measurements (that is, the ancient Egyptian version of a bureau of standards); they show that the Egyptians understood the mathematical concept of Pi; secrets are supposed to be embedded in the architecture of the Great Pyramid of Khufu, including prophecies about the future; and that they are an earthly map of the stars – at least, Orion's belt – and, furthermore, the Great Pyramid is an observatory of the stars. It is also claimed that the Great Pyramid functioned as a power plant for the ancient Egyptians. Where did all these fringe theories come from?

It started in the seventeenth century with an English scholar named John Greaves (1602–1652). Greaves was a man of many interests – ancient Asian languages, astronomy, mathematics and the history of ancient weights and measures. He was appointed the professor of geometry for Gresham College, London, in 1630 and met William Laud, the Archbishop of Canterbury. Laud was promoting the translation and publication of Greek and Arabic works and Greaves started to collect manuscripts for Laud on his travels. Greaves made several lengthy trips abroad starting in 1633. His trip to the eastern Mediterranean in 1637 made him an expert on pyramids. His manuscript-hunting in Istanbul and Greece was unsuccessful, so in 1638 he decided to visit Egypt. His goal was to use measurements at the Great Pyramid to help him establish a more accurate circumference for the earth. Arriving in Alexandria, Greaves proceeded to Cairo and then went on to Giza where he began measuring the Great Pyramid. He entered the interior and explored it extensively. His diagram of the passages and chambers inside the Great Pyramid was quite accurate. Climbing to the top of the pyramid he made further measurements. Working for several months, Greaves produced the first accurate survey of the Great Pyramid. In 1640 he returned to England and was named the Savilian Professor of Astronomy at Oxford. Besides working on a plan to reform the calendar, Greaves also wrote a book about his experience in Egypt and his measurements of the Great Pyramid. It appeared in 1646 with the title *Pyramidographia; or a Discourse of the Pyramids of Aegypt*. Greaves recognized that the Great Pyramid was a tomb. Using his measurements, Greaves tried to determine what standard of measure the ancient Egyptians used in their building work. He identified the Egyptian or Memphis cubit as just short of 56 centimetres (22 inches) in length. Sir Isaac Newton would later use Greaves's work to determine the length of the Hebrew cubit so that the true size of Solomon's Temple and Noah's Ark could be determined. Since he was a Royalist, which put him on the losing side of the English Civil War, Greaves was ejected from his Savilian professorship and from Oxford in 1648. He moved to London, where he died in 1652.[4]

Greaves's survey of the Great Pyramid, despite some inaccuracies, was a big improvement over the surveys of earlier travellers. It made an accurate study of ancient Egyptian measures possible, as the work of Newton demonstrated. Ancient metrology, the system of weights and measures, was considered very important since it would help to reveal some of the secret and lost scientific knowledge of the Egyptians. One of Napoleon's scientists in Egypt, Edme-François Jomard, theorized that accurate scientific measurements were embedded in the architecture of the Great Pyramid. Ancient authors stated that the apothem (the straight line from the pinnacle of the pyramid down the centre of one of its sides to the base) of the Great Pyramid was one stadia long or 183 metres (600 feet). The stadia was the basic unit of length in the Hellenistic and Roman world. A stadia was also supposed to be one-six-hundredth of a degree. With that measure, the accuracy of other ancient measures could be determined. Jomard argued that the Egyptians possessed an accurate knowledge of the size of the earth, which pre-dated Eratosthenes' measurement of the earth. They also used a cubit that was 0.46 metres in length (less than 20 inches). Jomard also suggested that the Great Pyramid might not have been a tomb, but rather a bureau of standards in stone. His theory about the Egyptian system of measurements being preserved in the Great Pyramid was rejected by his fellow French scientists, but Jomard was undeterred and continued to argue for his cubit and stadia for the rest of his life. Thus Jomard introduced the idea that the architecture of the pyramids was embedded with ancient scientific knowledge.[5]

After Jomard, the next step was to suggest that the Great Pyramid's architecture was full of embedded supernatural and prophetic information – the very definition of pyramidology. John Taylor (1781–1864), an English writer and publisher, made that suggestion in 1859. His book *The Great Pyramid: Why was it Built? And Who Built it?* was published by Taylor's own company. He suggested that the dimensions of the Great Pyramid reflected the golden ratio (when the sum of two quantities has the same ratio to the larger of the two quantities as it has to the sum of the two quantities, that is, A + B is to A, as A is to B). He also claimed that the value of Pi was embedded in the dimensions of the exterior of the pyramid, a fact that appears to be true, although whether it was the result of art or chance is still debated. More crucially, he claimed that the Great Pyramid had been built using a measure he called the 'pyramid inch', which was 1/25 of Newton's sacred cubit. According to Taylor, the building of the Great Pyramid was divinely inspired and its builders were the ancient Hebrews. In fact, he speculated that Noah, the builder of the Ark, was the architect of the Great Pyramid as well. Divine inspiration also meant that the structure of the Great Pyramid, within and without, was embedded with various prophecies. To bolster his claims, Taylor cited various passages from the Bible, especially Job 38:5–7 and Isaiah 19:19–20. This, as the great debunker of pseudo-history and pseudoscience Martin Gardner has put it, was how Christian pyramidology was born.[6]

Taylor was a perfectly respectable member of the Victorian world of letters, although he was a bit eccentric. He published the works of John Keats, Charles Lamb and Samuel Taylor Coleridge, among others. He became associated with the respected *Blackwood's Magazine.* The University of London made him its bookseller and publisher and he was a pioneer in the publication of academic textbooks, but he was not a recognized scientist or mathematician, so his theories about the Great Pyramid would normally have disappeared into obscurity. Instead, Charles Piazzi Smyth (1819–1900), the Astronomer-Royal of Scotland and professor of astronomy at the University of Edinburgh from 1845 and Fellow of the Royal Society in 1857, discovered Taylor's book and found his ideas compelling and inspirational. The two men became friends and at his death in 1864, Taylor passed the baton of pyramidological studies on to Smyth. That same year, Smyth brought out the first edition of his *Our Inheritance in the Great Pyramid.* In it, he attempted to provide further proof for Taylor's theories and greatly expanded them with his own ideas. Smyth realized that he would need to make his own accurate measurements of the Great Pyramid if he was to prove pyramidology was a scientific revelation of divine prophecy. Following in the footsteps of John Greaves, Smyth travelled to Egypt in 1865 and took the needed detailed measurements of the Great Pyramid. When he returned to Great Britain, he published the three-volume *Life and Work at the Great Pyramid* (1867). Taylor was not the only pyramidologist that Smyth learned from. Robert Menzies, a fellow Scotsman and seeker of pyramidical prophecies, had suggested in 1865 that markings along the wall of the Grand Gallery were a chronology of prophetic events. Smyth adopted Menzies's ideas and expanded them. Events such as the Great Flood, events in the life of Christ, the fall of Rome and various wars were seen in these markings as well as a future apocalypse that would occur between 1882 and 1911. The problem for Smyth was that, while scholars respected his survey of the Great Pyramid, they regarded his theories and those of Taylor and Menzies as a great edifice of misguided religious imaginings with no scientific basis. Devastating criticisms by experts, however, did not blunt the popularity of Smyth's theories. Other editions of *Our Inheritance in the Great Pyramid* appeared in 1874, 1880 and 1890 and continued to appear after Smyth's death. The 1880 edition was a greatly expanded work with 675 pages, compared to the four hundred pages of the original edition.[7]

Smyth's critics were too numerous to mention and many of them wrote for a scholarly audience. Two of his more influential critics were James Bonwick (1817–1906) and William Flinders Petrie. Bonwick was a writer of popular educational books for students and the general public. In 1877 he brought out *Pyramid Facts and Fancies*, a handy compendium of what was known about the pyramids at that time along with a summary of the various theories about why the pyramids were built, whether plausible or fantastic.

Bonwick was a conservative Baptist with a tendency towards mysticism, so he was sympathetic to Smyth's idea that the Great Pyramid was a record in stone of prophecies: 'To Prof Piazzi Smyth belongs the honour of popularizing the pyramid. Although failing to receive his theories, I respect his learning, reverence his motives, and am grateful for his labours.' But he was also a critical enough scholar to reject Smyth's mathematical calculations and interpretations as forced and invalid and produced evidence from competent authorities to show it. A more authoritative debunker of Smyth's theories was Petrie. Reading Smyth was what first aroused the thirteen-year-old Petrie's interest in Egypt. Before he became a mainstream Egyptologist, he visited Egypt from 1880 to 1882 intending to make a survey of the pyramids to support Smyth's theories. Instead, Petrie's calculations refuted them.[8]

Others, however, found the ideas of Taylor and Smyth to be quite congenial and believable. Charles Taze Russell (1852–1916), the founder of the religious body that became known as the Jehovah's Witnesses, had become an advocate of pyramidology by 1891. He predicted that the Millennium (the thousand-year reign of Christ prior to the end of the world) would arrive in 1914. When the Millennium did not arrive in 1914, and the First World War began instead, a certain disappointment and disillusionment set in among Russell's followers. By 1928 the Jehovah's Witnesses had formally rejected pyramidology as a means for determining the end of the world.

The followers of British Israelism were another fringe religious body that enthusiastically adopted pyramidology. British Israelism believes that the peoples of Britain are descendants of the Ten Lost Tribes of Israel. Besides believing in all sorts of biblical prophecies, the British Israelists would have found pyramidology's contention that ancient Hebrews (who would have been their ancestors) had built that great generator of prophecy, the Great Pyramid, to be very congenial. The Scottish engineer David Davidson (1884–1956) produced the greatest of the British Israelite texts advocating pyramidology, *The Great Pyramid: Its Divine Message* (1924). Davidson started out with the purpose of following in the footsteps of Petrie and further refuting Smyth. Instead, he became fascinated by the ideas of pyramidology and found a way to reconcile Petrie's calculations to the conclusions of Smyth. British Israelists are not a large religious body but the members are wealthy, educated and they like to write books. Many British Israelite books on pyramidology appeared before and after Davidson's great tome, although they all say essentially the same thing. Between 1957 and 1972 another British Israelist, Adam Rutherford, published his massive four-volume *Pyramidology*. British Israelist books continue to appear despite the fact that numerous contemporary prophecies have failed to come to pass. In 1971 Peter Tompkins (1919–2007) published his *Secrets of the Great Pyramid*, which provided a modern defence of pyramidology. The book is useful for summarizing the ideas of the pyramidologists although the reader should be aware that the author is a supporter of pyramidological ideas, which makes his conclusions unreliable.[9]

Readers of Smyth's books or of books like that of Peter Tompkins, which summarized pyramidological ideas, are confronted by a deluge of numbers and calculations. On the one hand, the massive volume of mathematical evidence seems overwhelming. A bewildered reader could easily conclude that surely it must be true. On the other hand, the evidence presented, while vast, is also incoherent. One might ask, does this make sense? Why would anyone do what Smyth and other pyramidologists claim was done? Martin Gardner considered Smyth as a popularizer of pyramidology in the same manner that Ignatius Donnelly popularized modern theories about Atlantis. Both men used enough scientific information for their theories to appear plausible to many ordinary people in the reading public. Gardner goes on to demonstrate that a set of calculations similar to Smyth's can easily be done using the dimensions of the Washington Monument. All it takes is a little imagination and some playing with numbers. The same could be done for other buildings including the golden arches of the nearest McDonald's. The fact is that the type of numbers and calculations used by Taylor, Smyth and other pyramidologists are highly malleable. These theorists committed the great sin against scientific method, because they form their conclusion first and then find or construct the evidence that seems to prove it. Pyramidology works well in retrospect. All that needs to be done is to pick a section of the Great Gallery, match its dimensions to a series of historical events, and then claim it prophesied these events from the time the Great Pyramid was built. But as the great philosopher and mathematician Bertrand Russell observed: 'It is a singular fact that the Great Pyramid always predicts the history of the world accurately up to the date of the publication of the book in question, but after that date it becomes less reliable.'[10]

In 1877 James Bonwick listed 47 theories for why the pyramids were built. A goodly number of them are rather silly, such as the Great Pyramid being a filter to purify the muddy waters of the Nile or that they were a barrier to the encroaching sands of the desert, or are obvious – that the pyramids were tombs. Besides a lengthy discussion of the theory of John Greaves and others that the Great Pyramid provided a standard for measurements, Bonwick also summarized other ideas that were dear to the pyramidologists, such as the Great Pyramid being an astronomical observatory; a marker for latitude; a measurement of the circumference of the earth, the distance from the sun and the planets or the days of the year; a demonstration of the unity of God, that is, primordial monotheism; a prophecy of the Messiah, or a prophecy of the Second Coming. Occultist ideas that the Great Pyramid was a place for conducting Egyptian religious rites or that it was a Masonic Hall are also touched upon but rejected, because as Bonwick points out, the Great Pyramid had been sealed up and so could not have been used for ceremonies. Most of these ideas have continued to circulate almost 150 years later with fluctuations in their popularity.[11]

One topic that Bonwick referred to was the 'Great Pyramidal System'. The idea is that three pyramids of the Giza complex are laid out in some sort of pattern. Bonwick's source for this theory is H. C. Agnew's *A letter from Alexandria on the evidence of the practical application of the quadrature of the circle, in the configuration of the great pyramids of Gizeh* (1838), which speculated about such an arrangement. Various angles and distances between three pyramids are described, with Agnew concluding that they were planned out as a group – for purposes unknown. The modern Orion Correlation theory is simply an extension of Agnew's concept which claims that the three pyramids were arranged in imitation of the belt of the constellation of Orion, which ancient Egyptians associated with the god Osiris. The Sphinx was part of the pattern and represented the constellation of Leo in its relation to the Orion constellation, while the Nile River was said to be the Milky Way. Why would the Egyptians have built the pyramids according to such a plan? Supposedly it was to help deceased pharaohs make their journey up to the heavens in order to join the gods. This theory was proposed by Robert Bauval in an article in *Discussions in Egyptology* in 1989 and was the subject of his book *The Orion Mystery: Unlocking the Secrets of the Pyramids* (1994). Bauval was joined in promoting the Orion Correlation theory by Graham Hancock in their co-authored book *Keeper of Genesis: A Quest for the Hidden Legacy of Mankind* (1996). Their theory went beyond pointing out the superficial resemblance between the positions of the three pyramids and the stars in Orion's belt. Bauval and Hancock asserted that the positions of the stars in Orion represented by the pyramids were actually the positions of those stars in 10,000 BC. Their claim meant that the Sphinx and possibly the pyramids were far older than the dates assigned by mainstream archaeologists and Egyptologists. Apart from the fact that archaeological evidence does not support the existence of a higher civilization in 10,000 BC, there was also a problem with the astronomy. The claim that the Giza complex of the pyramids and the Sphinx is a terrestrial map or image of the constellation was not convincing when examined closely. While the layout was superficially similar, at best it was an upside down mirror image of the Orion constellation. Mainstream scholars argue that the Orion Correlation is an illusion and any similarity to Orion is a matter of coincidence or chance.[12]

Pyramid power is another aspect of the mysteries of the pyramids that includes but is not limited to the Egyptian pyramids. The idea is that the shapes of the pyramids wield mystical powers. According to the various proponents of pyramid power, storing food under a pyramid shape helped to keep it fresh and storing razors under a pyramid shape helped to keep them sharp. Sleeping under a pyramid shape could help with healing, improve thinking or enhance sexual performance. Therefore it was argued that it was no coincidence that the ancient Egyptians used pyramids as tombs since they were so concerned to preserve the bodies of their rulers. The idea of pyramid power was first suggested during the 1930s in France by Antoine Bovis, a shopkeeper. Pyramid power, however, did not become popular until the 1970s as part of the New Age movement. Pyramidological mythology claims that Bovis discovered the phenomenon of pyramid power while visiting the interior of the Great Pyramid and noticed that dead animals deposited as waste inside the Great Pyramid were not decomposing. In truth, Bovis never visited Egypt and actually attributed his insight on pyramids to extrapolating from the phenomenon of dowsing. Various books were published in the mid-1970s on the matter – Patrick Flanagan's *Pyramid Power: the Millennium Science* (1973), Max Toth and Greg Nielsen's *Pyramid Power* (1974) and Warren Smith's *Secret Forces of the Pyramids* (1975) – and cover stories on pyramid power appeared in the magazines *Time* and *Newsweek*. The concept's credibility ultimately suffered, however, because it promised concrete results. When the results did not materialize, popular support and belief declined rapidly, which tends to be the fate of pseudosciences that fail to deliver. The phenomenon of pyramid power had a boom and then a bust and has not yet shown any indication of heading into another boom phase. In the world of pseudoscience, however, it is rare for bad ideas to die permanently. So it would be premature to stop hoping for or dreading the reappearance of this particular theory.[13]

Related to pyramid power are claims that the Great Pyramid is in fact a power plant. According to this theory, the ancient Egyptians possessed advanced technologies: the Great Pyramid is not a tomb (or a repository for prophecies), but was a power generator fuelled by harmonic resonance, which converts the vibrations of the earth into microwave radiation. Supposedly the great Nikola Tesla had proposed a similar apparatus. Christopher Dunn, born in England and trained as a machinist before being recruited to work in aerospace manufacturing in the United States (where he worked with lasers and robotic technologies), presented this idea in *The Giza Power Plant: Technologies of Ancient Egypt* (1998). He followed this with *Lost Technologies of Ancient Egypt: Advanced Engineering in the Temples of the Pharaohs* (2010), which argues that the Egyptians used advanced engineering techniques and power tools to build their temples. Alternative historians and scientists are enthusiastic about his Giza Power Plant theory, because it supports the existence of an advanced civilization in ancient Egypt. Mainstream Egyptologists and scientists are unconvinced – with good reason, since no archaeological evidence bears out Dunn's ideas, which also require the rejection of the pyramids as tombs.[14] The pyramids are not the only target for Egyptomania in fringe history. Another is the idea that Egypt was the original site of human civilization.

Egyptomania and the Hyper-diffusion of Civilization

Egypt produced one of the world's oldest civilizations. In fact, up until the middle of the twentieth century and the invention of radiocarbon dating, Egypt was widely thought to be *the* oldest civilization. This belief merged with the human desire to determine the origin, preferably the single origin, of civilization and how it spread across the world.

The Bible encouraged the idea of a single origin for human civilization, which in a first instance began with Adam and Eve being expelled from the Garden of Eden and humans then spreading across other lands. But God destroyed humanity in a universal flood – except for the families of Noah and his three sons. Their children then gathered and attempted to build the Tower of Babel to reach heaven, but God, making their shared language indecipherable to each other and thus preventing such plans, caused them to scatter throughout the earth. Based on the biblical account, all civilizations spread along with Noah's descendants from Babel. But not all the people who spread out from Babel created great civilizations. The Egyptians, however, did. Thanks to their unique culture of massive tombs and temples of obviously immense age, enigmatic hieroglyphs and weird hybrid human–animal gods, the Egyptians have perennially attracted scholarly attention as well as the fascination of the general public. It was assumed that Egypt was a fount for the civilizations of other countries. Certainly the Greeks credited Egypt as their teacher. They also told tales of the great conqueror pharaoh Sesostris who supposedly overran much of the eastern Mediterranean and the Middle East and spread Egyptian culture wherever he went. The Greeks speculated that the people of Colchis were descendants of Egyptian colonists.

During the fifteenth, sixteenth and seventeenth centuries, scholars debated whether the Egyptians taught the Hebrews their civilization or if the Hebrews taught the Egyptians. Meanwhile the great explorations of Christopher Columbus, John Cabot and others revealed to Europe the existence of the Americas along with the Native Americans. Further expeditions encountered the great civilizations of the Native Americans, first the Maya and the Aztecs of Mexico and Central America followed by the Incas of Peru. When Francisco Hernández de Córdoba and his men reached the Yucatán in 1517, they encountered a large town with temple pyramids that the Spaniards promptly dubbed Great Cairo. Initially no one drew the conclusion that pyramids of the Native Americans were inspired by the ancient Egyptian visitors or descendants of Egyptian colonists. They were just noting the similar shape of the two sets of buildings. It was not until 1589 that the historian Juan Suárez de Peralta (b. 1537) published *Tratado del descubrimiento de las Indias*, which suggested that ancient Egyptians might have colonized the Americas. Egyptians, however, were not Peralta's primary focus. He was more interested in proving that the Ten Lost Tribes of Israel had settled in the Americas along with Canaanites and Carthaginians. The Egyptians, therefore, were only one group among several who had reached the Americas in ancient times and were the ancestors of the Native Americans. Other Spanish historians in the seventeenth and eighteenth centuries compiled lists of pre-Columbian settlers of the Americas that included Egyptians, but did not give them pride of place.[15]

The quest to decipher the hieroglyphic writing of the Egyptians inspired other speculations about Egyptian colonies and cultural influences. Abbé Jean-Jacques Barthélemy suggested that there were connections between the Phoenicians, Greek and Egyptian languages as well as correctly guessing that the cartouches on hieroglyphic inscriptions enclosed royal names. He was followed by Joseph de Guignes, who further asserted that China was an Egyptian colony that owed its entire culture to Egyptian civilization and that Chinese ideographic writing was closely related to Egyptian hieroglyphs.[16]

Just as Napoleon's expedition to Egypt had intensified mainstream Egyptomania in Europe, it also increased the wilder speculations about Egypt's influence on world history and culture. The nineteenth century not only saw the rise of a broadly popular Egyptomania, but its later decades were the time when the disciplines of archaeology, anthropology, ethnology and ethnography emerged as formal subjects of study at universities. All of these disciplines were concerned with the origin and development of civilization and culture. One approach to explain this was evolution. Various cultures responded to the challenges of their environment by innovation and invention. All around the world, human societies developed their unique cultures. Often different cultures would create similar innovations, such as the domestication of plants for agriculture or the invention of systems of writing. These instances were called independent invention or parallel evolution. Another approach attributed cultural change to the movement of ideas from one society to another via diffusion or migration. The diffusion of artefacts and ideas generally took place through exchanges that occurred in the course of trade or travel. The migration of a people, often due to invasion or conquest, from one place to settle among another culture also resulted in transplanted cultures. Dominant cultures would be imposed upon the conquered cultures. Obviously theories of cultural development that emphasized independent invention or parallel evolution attributed a degree of innovativeness and creativity to humans. Diffusionist theories tended to place less emphasis on human inventiveness. During much of the nineteenth century, most scholars had attributed cultural change to a combination of independent invention and diffusion. After the 1880s and through to the 1950s, diffusionism – at least, a moderate form of it that allowed for the role of independent invention in cultural change – became the dominant explanation of cultural change. From the 1910s to the 1930s, however, an extreme form of diffusionism arose that strongly denied humans were all that inventive. It claimed that ancient culture began in Egypt and spread from that unique environment throughout the world. There was an assumption that complex inventions and techniques could only have been invented once. This extreme form of diffusionism is known as hyper-diffusionism and it is closely associated with the anatomist and anthropologist Grafton Elliot Smith.[17] This approach provided a simple explanation for the origin of civilization that also incorporated mystic Egypt and so appealed to popular Egyptomania.

Theories that claimed Egyptian culture had diffused far beyond the eastern Mediterranean and Nubia pre-dated Elliot Smith. Well over one hundred years before, Charles Vallancey (1721–1812) asserted that the ancient Egyptians had exercised a great influence on the development of Irish language and culture. Vallancey was a British military engineer who was stationed in Ireland about 1750 and remained there for the rest of his life. His parents were Huguenots and he was born in Flanders but the family moved to England, where he was educated. Once he arrived in Ireland, his job as a military surveyor brought him into frequent contact with the monuments, ruins and antiquities of ancient Ireland. Vallancey developed a fascination and love for ancient Ireland and engaged in detailed research that resulted in a number of books which began to appear in 1772. Some of his research made claims for connections between the Irish language and that of the Algonquin Indians, Phoenicians, Persians, Hindustanis and Egyptians. Other books argued that Irish civilization had its origins in the Middle East including Persian, Phoenician and Egyptian influences. While he was not laser-focused on Egypt as the sole source of cultural diffusion, Vallancey did place a significant emphasis on the Egyptian contribution to Irish civilization. The great philologist William Jones corresponded with and advised Vallancey on his scholarship but ultimately considered his ideas to be 'very stupid'. In fact, Vallancey's scholarship was a mixture of overly speculative theorizing based on diffusionism and extreme diffusionism, and reasonably accurate archaeological interpretation. Based on his focus on both Egypt and Ireland, Vallancey apparently engaged in both Egyptomania and a Hibernomania.[18]

Another proto-hyper-diffusionist was the anthropologist Anne Walbank Buckland, who was active during the later part of the nineteenth century in England and was a member of the Anthropological Institute of Great Britain and Ireland. She published a series of essays in the *Westminster Review* and the *Journal of the Anthropological Institute*, which she later revised, updated and collected in 1891 as *Anthropological Studies*. The book was intended to popularize anthropology among Great Britain's educated reading public. Like Vallancey, Buckland's hyper-diffusionism did not concentrate exclusively on Egypt although she cited numerous examples of cultural diffusion involving the Egyptians. In her essay 'Primitive Agriculture', she suggested that the Egyptians were growing maize thousands of years before Columbus, but their process of cultivation of maize was lost. According to Buckland, other sources for the diffusion of culture included a hypothetical Turanian race in Central Asia and the inhabitants of Atlantis, as her essay 'The Serpent in Connection with Metallurgy' argues. Such a kaleidoscope of diffusion amounted to hyper-diffusionism and helped to pave the way for the Egyptocentric diffusionism of Elliot Smith.[19]

Gerald Massey (1828–1907) was a contemporary of Anne Walbank Buckland who combined both hyper-diffusionism and Egyptomania in his ideas about ancient cultures. Massey's father was a canal boatman from Hertfordshire and the family lived in poverty. As a child Massey received little formal education but his mother provided him with reading material in the form of the Bible, *The Pilgrim's Progress* and other religious books. He moved to London when he was fifteen for work and there he took up poetry and radical politics. By the 1850s his poetry was well regarded in radical circles as it focused on freedom and the common people. He also worked as a contributor and a critic for various Victorian periodicals. Massey's

Grafton Elliot
Smith (1871–1937),
respected anatomist
and controversial
hyper-diffusionist.

attention turned to spiritualism in 1871 and he went on several lecture
tours through the English-speaking world into the 1880s. At the same time,
Massey developed an interest in ancient Egypt which he combined with his
spiritualism. His research on Egypt sought to find the roots of spiritualism
in the culture of ancient Egypt. He began with the two-volume *A Book of
the Beginnings* (1881). Its subtitle is a concise summary of Massey's views
on ancient Egypt: 'Containing an attempt to recover and reconstitute the
lost origins of the myths and mysteries, types and symbols, religion and
language, with Egypt for the mouthpiece and Africa as the birthplace.'
Massey also asserted that Egyptians had settled in ancient Britain, which
resulted in the English language, place-names and customs exhibiting many
Egyptian influences. According to Massey, Egypt was an African culture
rather than an Asian culture and the ancient Egyptians were black. As he
put it, 'The type of the great sphinx, the age of which is unknown, but it
must be of enormous antiquity, is African, not Aryan or Caucasian.' These
ideas have endeared him to Afrocentrists from the last decades of the

twentieth century to the present.[20] Massey continued to write about Egyptian mysticism and the spread of its ideas in his next book, *The Natural Genesis* (1883). His final book, *Ancient Egypt: The Light of the World: A Work of Reclamation and Restitution in Twelve Books*, was published in 1907, the year of his death. It was nearly 1,000 pages long and according to his preface, the book that 'made my life worth living'. He drew parallels between Christ and the Egyptian god Horus as well as pointing out Egyptian influences on the Jewish religion. Both *Natural Genesis* and *Ancient Egypt: The Light of the World* espoused ideas that had great appeal to adherents of New Age religions and philosophy. They also continued Massey's approach of Egyptocentric hyper-diffusionism, and he would soon be joined in his beliefs by the very respectable scholar Grafton Elliot Smith.

Elliot Smith was born in Grafton, New South Wales, in Australia. His father was a teacher and Elliot Smith attended the University of Sydney where he studied to be a doctor of medicine and showed a particular talent for neurology. In 1896 he received a scholarship to study at the University of Cambridge, where he also gained a research fellowship in 1899. By that time he had earned a reputation as one of the foremost neurologists in the world as well as being an expert in craniology. He also attracted the favour of Alexander Macalister, the professor of anatomy at Cambridge and someone with a great interest in anthropology and ancient Egypt. Macalister offered Elliot Smith the position of being the first chair of anatomy at the Government Medical School of Cairo. The years before the First World War were an exciting time for a Westerner to live in Egypt, particularly Cairo. As Elliot Smith described it, Cairo was 'the gayest and most cosmopolitan city on the face of the earth and intensely fascinating'. Although a man of science, he fell under the spell of Egypt's antiquities. In 1901 he confessed, 'I have not quite resisted the temptation to dabble in Egyptology.' Egypt was a cornucopia of mummies for Elliot Smith to study. Many excavations were underway in the region of Aswan to preserve the region's antiquities from being lost under the impending waters of the great dam being built there. In 1907 Elliot Smith and his associates proceeded to autopsy 8,000 of the refugee mummies with great enthusiasm. He was notably interested in the process of mummification. In fact, he developed a fascination with mummies, particularly specific parts of them. After his death, it was discovered that Elliot Smith had been collecting the penises of mummies and took copious notes of these appendages. Embarrassed relatives attempted to destroy the collection but failed to eliminate all traces in his notebooks, which were discovered by later researchers. Although an avid publisher of research, Elliot Smith never published on the topic of mummy genitalia. It would appear that his collection was a private and rather quirky form of Egyptomania. Meanwhile, in Elliot Smith's judgement, the process of Egyptian mummification was so complex that it could have only been invented once. Based on that contention, Elliot Smith argued that all other occurrences of mummification in the rest of the world were due to diffusion of the Egyptians' original idea and all techniques could be traceable back to ancient Egypt.[21]

Elliot Smith returned to England in 1909 to serve as Professor of Anatomy at the University of Manchester. He would move to London in 1919 to become head of the department of anatomy at University College London, a position he held until his retirement in 1936. He died the following year. At Manchester he published *The Ancient Egyptians and their Influence upon the Civilization of Europe* in 1911. It would appear in a second edition in 1923 with a new title: *The Ancient Egyptians and the Origin of Civilization*. Elliot Smith believed along with most Egyptologists at that time that Egypt was the first and oldest complex civilization. From that assumption he contended that the culture of the Egyptians in the form of mummification and megaliths had spread through the Mediterranean and into Europe. Egypt was inhabited by a brown-skinned people of slight build who were identified as the 'Mediterranean Race'. At the same time a people that Elliot Smith called 'Armenoid' moved into, or rather invaded, Egypt about 3000 BC. So Elliot Smith was arguing for both diffusion of culture and migrations of people being significant in the development and spread of Egyptian culture. It was a thesis that was very much at variance with the rival evolutionary theories of cultural change and independent invention. H. G. Wells in his immensely popular *The Outline of History* (1920) gave credence to Elliot Smith's theories of diffusionism.[22]

Other works on ancient Egypt and cultural diffusion followed over the years. *Migrations of Early Culture* appeared in 1915, then *The Evolution of the Dragon* (1919), *Elephants and Ethnologists* (1924), *In the Beginning: The Origin of Civilization* (1930) and *The Diffusion of Culture* (1933). These books expanded the diffusion of Egyptian culture to the entire world including, very controversially, the Americas, in *Elephants and Ethnologists*. While at Manchester, Elliot Smith came into contact with another hyper-diffusionist named W. J. Perry and the two men became friends and partners in scholarship.

W. J. Perry (1888–1949) was born in England and attended the University of Cambridge. He studied mathematics but while at the university he attended lectures by the anthropologist W.H.R. Rivers which fascinated him. In 1913 Rivers persuaded Perry to do research in Indonesia.

Rivers believed that the Melanesian cultures that he was studying had been heavily influenced by diffusion from cultures to the west. He hoped that Perry would find the same thing in Indonesia. Perry investigated megaliths and tombs and reached the conclusion that their forms were the result of diffusion from much further west, where Egypt was located, although initially Perry was not ready to attribute Indonesian culture to diffusion all the way from there. Perry, however, added the detail that the migrants from the west had come in search of gold and other valuables. Elliot Smith and Perry became aware of the similarities between their ideas about diffusion and soon became collaborators. The results of Perry's Indonesian research were published as *The Megalithic Culture of Indonesia* in 1918 with the help of Elliot Smith. Soon after, in 1919, Elliot Smith secured for Perry the position of Reader in Comparative Religion at the University of Manchester. When Elliot Smith went to University College London, to become head of the department of anatomy, Perry followed and took up the position of Reader in Cultural Anthropology within the same department. Both men placed great emphasis on mummification and megaliths as the proof of diffusion from ancient Egypt. Elliot Smith continued to firmly believe that the practice of mummification was so complex that it could have only been invented once. He made the same assumptions about the Egyptian invention of agriculture, pyramids, religious beliefs and other basic aspects of civilization. Such inventiveness was attributed to the unique environment of the Nile valley and delta that presented challenges and stimuli to creativity that were not present elsewhere. Variations from the Egyptian cultural practices or artefacts were explained as degeneration due to a later weakening of Egyptian influences.[23]

Perry quickly became a convert to Elliot Smith's ideas that civilization had originated in Egypt and diffused from there throughout the world. He had already travelled far down the road of hyper-diffusionism thanks to his work for Rivers. Both men believed that the ancient Egyptians travelled to distant lands in search of gold and materials to be used in their magical rites, the so-called 'Givers of Life'. In the course of their travels, these treasure-hunting Egyptians also spread their culture to other people. Perry elaborated on this concept in his *The Children of the Sun: A Study in the Early History of Civilization* (1923). Elliot Smith and Perry dubbed the civilization that diffused from ancient Egypt as 'heliolithic' or the 'archaic civilization'. The next year, in 1924, Perry started to focus on the decline and demise of this archaic civilization, which he attributed to the rise of an aggressive warrior culture. Meanwhile Elliot Smith and Perry had gathered a group of like-minded people around them, first at Manchester and then at University

College. Their school of extreme diffusionism never completely dominated archaeological and anthropological scholarship but it did provide an important stimulus for more moderate diffusionists such as V. Gordon Childe.[24]

The hyper-diffusionism of Elliot Smith and Perry faced a wide array of critics who had solid reasons for rejecting their ideas about the spread of culture from a single Egyptian origin. During the 1920s the growing archaeological record did not bear out the theories of Elliot Smith and Perry and caused other archaeologists to reject them. When carbon-14 dating became a reliable tool for determining the absolute age of ancient artefacts in the 1960s, it was discovered that many European megaliths were far older than the pyramids which hyper-diffusionists claimed had been their inspiration and model. Elliot Smith's foray into pre-Columbian civilizations and diffusion in *Elephants and Ethnologists* aroused the wrath of American anthropologists and archaeologists, as the trenchant criticisms of R. H. Lowie in 1937 clearly demonstrate. He accused Elliot Smith and Perry of not providing sufficient evidence to support their theories. Instead their tactic of presentation was repetition. He found the claims for the lack of inventiveness by humans to be ridiculous. He also faulted their ethnographic knowledge saying of Elliot Smith that 'in ethnography his crass ignorance darkens counsel'. The English archaeologist Glyn Daniel in 1962 was just as critical. He accused Elliot Smith and Perry of abandoning scientific method. Instead, 'Elliot Smith had been swept away by Egypt.' Due to this form of Egyptomania, Elliot Smith simply forced all evidence into the pigeonholes of his Egyptocentric diffusionism. When they compared artefacts as evidence for diffusion, they concentrated on form, for example the pyramid of Egypt and Mesoamerica, but ignored function – the idea that Egyptian pyramids were tombs and Mesoamerican pyramids were platforms for temples.[25]

Fellow Australian A. P. Elkin rallied to support Elliot Smith's theories of diffusionism in 1974, long after hyper-diffusionism's influence had declined. Elkin had been a student of Elliot Smith's and was anxious to preserve his teacher's scholarly reputation. Furthermore, it is clear that Elliot Smith was a fine teacher and mentor to his students as well as being a warm and generous man who was also good company. But Elkin's defence of Elliot Smith was not simply based on friendship. He also defended the validity of Elliot Smith's hyper-diffusionism. He argued that Elliot Smith's ideas had been over-simplified and caricatured by his critics. At that time hyper-diffusionism seemed to be making a comeback. In 1968 a symposium at the national meeting of the Society for American Archaeology was devoted to a large number of papers presenting diverse evidence for pre-Columbian contacts between the Eastern Hemisphere and the Americas.

The papers were later published in 1971 as *Man Across the Sea: Problems of Pre-Columbian Contacts*. Meanwhile in 1969 and 1970 the daring Thor Heyerdahl led two expeditions whose goals were to cross the Atlantic from Morocco to the West Indies in reed rafts based on Egyptian models. His first attempt failed but the second succeeded. The problem was the evidence supporting hyper-diffusionism and pre-Columbian contacts did not continue to accumulate, whereas evidence for independent invention did. During the 1980s archaeologists working on the prehistory of the north coast of Chile and the Atacama Desert discovered that the ancient people of those lands had been mummifying their dead some 2,500 years before the Egyptians.[26]

Grafton Elliot Smith's ideas had their heyday but eventually succumbed to the harsh reality of archaeological discoveries that contradicted them. But it is important to understand that pseudo-historical ideas never die, they just ebb and flow with the fads of popular culture as new generations of alternative scholars discover them anew. In 2000 Lorraine Evans published *Kingdom of the Ark: The Startling Story of How the Ancient British Race is Descended from the Pharaohs*. The title is a concise description of the book's contents. Evans contends that Meritaten, the daughter of the heretic Pharaoh Akhenaten and his beautiful wife Nefertiti, had fled Egypt with her husband Abi-Milku, prince of Tyre, and a group of fugitive followers of the despised Aten cult. They made their way to the land of Numidia (now Algeria) in North Africa. From there they crossed over to Europe, stopping at Cadiz and then the lower Ebro Valley, where they subdued the locals. Eventually, they reached the British Isles where they attempted to establish a colony in Scotland but were forced to move on to Tara in Ireland. There, the Meritaten died in battle, and the surviving Egyptians were absorbed into the existing population.[27]

Evans based her theory of ancient Egyptians travelling to the British Isles on Book One of Walter Bower's (c. 1385–1449) *Scotichronicon*, a nationalistic myth-history of early Scotland. The actual author of Book One was an earlier historian, John of Fordun (c. 1320–1384), and the text includes extensive quotations and citations from other medieval scholars such as St Brendan and Robert Grosseteste. In John of Fordun's telling of the early history of Scotland, he includes the tale of Gaythelos and Scota. Scota was the daughter of Chencres, the pharaoh of the Exodus, and the wife of Gaythelos, a Greek prince. After Chencres and his army were destroyed trying to prevent the escape of Moses and the Children of Israel, the Egyptian people refused to accept Gaythelos as their king. So he, Scota and the loyal Greek and Egyptian nobles left Egypt and wandered for forty years. There was a stop at Numidia in North Africa but they moved on to Cadiz and later the Ebro Valley in Spain where they created a settlement called Brigantia. Relentless hostility from the Spanish tribes caused Gaythelos to seek a safer home for his people. Scouts reported finding a pleasant island, fertile and uninhabited, in the Atlantic Ocean. But before the Egyptians could depart Brigantia, Gaythelos died suddenly. The death of Gaythelos left his son Hiber in charge, and he and his people sailed for the newly discovered island. The new land was, in fact, Ireland and the Egyptian settlers named it Hibernia after Hiber. They settled at Tara, which became the capital of the high kings of Ireland. From this legend, the Irish and the Scots are able to claim very ancient descent from the Egyptians. It was a claim that trumped the English claim to seniority among the British peoples by asserting their descent from Trojan refugees.[28]

Evans has taken the tale of Gaythelos and Scota and connected it to the turmoil of the reign of Akhenaten. In addition, she uses various archaeological finds of artefacts in the British Isles that could possibly be of Egyptian origin to bolster her theory. The Egyptian material in *Kingdom of the Ark* provides a good overview of current scholarship on the reign of Akhenaten along with considerable information on Egyptian culture and religion. Evans has studied Egyptology and started but apparently has not yet finished her PhD. Once she goes beyond mainstream Egyptological topics, things proceed rapidly to the fringe. According to Evans, the ancient Egyptians were accomplished seafarers in the manner of the Phoenicians and their 'Great Green' sea was actually the Atlantic Ocean, not the Mediterranean Sea. She also claims that the Tuaregs of the Sahara were descendants of wandering Egyptians who were apparently diffusing their culture into the African interior. She also asserts that the colonizing efforts of the Phoenicians throughout the Mediterranean were done at the behest of their Egyptian masters. The Guanches of the Canary Island are also identified as the descendants of Egyptian settlers as their use of mummification and building of pyramids supposedly demonstrates. Evans also suggests that Scota and her people were the Beaker People who appeared about 1300 BC and left their cultural imprint on the British Isles. Despite her unorthodox ideas, Evans was published by Simon & Schuster UK, a mainstream, commercial publishing house with a respectable reputation. *Kingdom of the Ark* might be sensationalistic, but sensationalism sells.[29]

Evans claims to be a revisionist Egyptologist. In the course of defending her thesis against the scepticism of mainstream archaeologists and Egyptologists, she falls back on the standard lament of the fringe scholar that mainstream scholars are close-minded and collude to suppress anomalies in the evidence and innovative ideas about the past. The centrepiece of Evans's argument for Egyptians in ancient Britain is the account of Gaythelos and Scota in the *Scotichronicon*. Supposed medieval fabulism is really historical fact. But if that were the case would not the legends of the prophet Jeremiah and the Hebrew princess Tamar settling in Ireland be equally plausible. This event occurred within a few years after the fall of Jerusalem to the Babylonians in 586 BC. The biblical account tells of Jeremiah, his secretary Baruch, and the daughters of King Zedekiah of Judah fleeing to Egypt. According to the Irish legend, their journey did not end there. They travelled on to Ireland where the princess Tamar married an Irish king and Jeremiah was recognized at a great prophet. They also set up the Stone of Scone, which was moved to Scotland. Ultimately, the royal houses of Ireland, Scotland and England all had the blood of Tamar flowing in their veins. It just so happens that a lot of the archaeological evidence cited by Evans to bolster her Egyptian theory has been used by adherents of the Ireland legend of Jeremiah as well.[30] Which begs the question – who is right? Neither?

Obviously the hyper-diffusion of Grafton Elliot Smith has joined the ranks of the fringe scholars of ancient Egypt as another popular manifestation of Egyptomania. Hyper-diffusionism is only one of many varieties of fringe scholarship about ancient Egypt. Egypt and Atlantis, an ancient Egyptian super-civilization, ancient aliens in Egypt and pyramidology are other aspects of the voluminous fringe scholarship on ancient Egypt.

Extreme Antiquity, Atlantis and Ancient Aliens

It is probably safe to say that everyone agrees that Pharaonic Egypt was a very ancient civilization. Just how old ancient Egyptian civilization was, however, is more debatable. Mainstream Egyptologists and ancient historians date the beginning of the Old Kingdom of Dynastic Egypt to approximately 3000 BC, while the zenith of the Pyramid Age of the Fourth Dynasty occurred around 2500 BC. Prior to the Old Kingdom, there was the Archaic Age (5000–3000 BC), which was a cluster of late Neolithic societies scattered along the Nile Valley and in the Nile Delta. In contrast, alternative historians claim that Egyptian civilization was much older – spanning from 5000 BC, 7000 BC, 10,000 BC or even earlier. Various people assert the pyramids of Giza, in addition to the Sphinx, are much older than the mainstream scholars claim. These alternate theories of Egyptian history propose several different scenarios for the origin of civilization in Egypt. One group of theories suggests that there was an advanced civilization in Egypt thousands of years before the Old Kingdom. It was, or was a part of, what some alternative historians call Civilization X or the Ice Age Super-civilization. A closely related group of theories claim that Egypt was a colony of the great primordial civilization of Atlantis or was one of the places that survivors of the destruction of Atlantis fled to and settled. Another cluster assert that Egyptian and other ancient civilizations sprang up quite rapidly because extraterrestrial visitors settled among them and taught them the foundations of civilization, including much advanced knowledge that has now been lost. Other variations suggest that the aliens altered the DNA of primitive humans to make them more intelligent, or even interbred with our ancient ancestors, resulting in humans becoming smarter and more civilized. The outpouring and accumulation of the many theories that alternative historians advanced about ancient Egypt could be considered a cornucopia, but since so many of the theories clash with and contradict each other a better description might be a cacophony. How did this babel of baloney get started?

The ancient Egyptians and their neighbours believed that the origins of Egypt and its civilization stretched back in time for thousands and thousands of years. Plato in his *Timaeus* wrote that Egyptian priests had told the Greek sage Solon that Egyptian history went back at least 9,000 years to when Atlantis was thriving as an aggressive imperial power. Thus began the career of the lost continent of Atlantis. Most scholars feel that Plato was simply inventing another myth to illustrate his political philosophy, but his crediting Egypt with being at least 9,000 years old probably reflected what his contemporaries in Greece believed. Other ancient historians also credited Egypt with great antiquity. Manetho (early third century BC), the Egyptian historian of the Hellenistic era, presented a history of the rule of the gods, demigods and spirits of the dead ruling over Egypt for almost 25,000 years before the time of the pharaohs. The Christian historian Eusebius (c. 260–390) cited Manetho in his *Chronicle* but he claimed that Manetho was using lunar years not solar years. Lunar years were only thirty days long and corresponded to a month, which reduced the era of the gods, demigods and spirits of the dead to about 2,250 years. His authority for the claim that Manetho was using thirty-day lunar years is not stated and scholars have found no evidence of the Egyptians using such a lunar-year dating system. Later, the Byzantine historian George Syncellus (fl. 801) wrote a chronicle that began with Creation and continued to the reign of the emperor Diocletian. He cited a so-called *Old Chronicle* from the late second century AD that claimed the length of Egyptian history spanned some 35,500 years – with much of that time being under the rule of gods and demigods.[31]

Egypt was not the only ancient society to claim extreme antiquity. Babylonian scholars credited the early kings of Mesopotamia with long reigns running into the thousands of years. So did the ancient Chinese, while the Hindus of India laid claim to a history that was a million years or more in length. Such claims of extreme antiquity conflicted with the approximately 6,000-year chronology followed by Jews, Christians and Muslims. Thus from late antiquity until the nineteenth century, claims that Egypt possessed a history that was tens of thousands of years in duration went into abeyance. Meanwhile discussions about Atlantis also entered a dormant state until they were revived during the Age of Discovery in the sixteenth century. When Europeans unexpectedly encountered the Americas, they found the land there teeming with other human beings. All sorts of speculation arose about who these people were and how they had reached the Americas. Out of this situation, long-dormant thinking about Atlantis re-entered the consciousness of Western scholars. It was suggested that at least some of the Native Americans were the descendants of Atlantean colonizers or refugees, or that the Americas were together the lost land of Atlantis. Of course, Egyptians were also credited with settling the Americas along with a host of other ancient peoples. At that point, however, Atlantis was just an ancient society destroyed in a cataclysm.[32] It was not yet the great primeval empire possessed of a fantastic, super technology.

Modern concepts of Atlantis did not arise until the later decades of the nineteenth century. In 1882 the American politician Ignatius Donnelly brought out his *Atlantis: The Antediluvian World*. The book was a tremendous success and has remained in print ever since. Donnelly's book enshrined the foundations of what Atlantis was supposed to have been. Following Plato, he placed Atlantis in the Atlantic near the Straits of Gibraltar and asserted

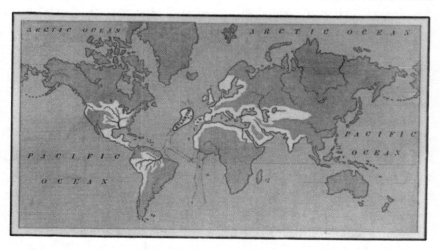

Ignatius Donnelly's concept of the worldwide empire of Atlantis, including its most important colony: Egypt.

that it was a historical place rather than a myth. It was also the location of the first civilization and from it civilization spread to the Americas, Europe, the Mediterranean basin and the Middle East. Atlantean rulers and nobles were the basis for the gods and goddesses of the Greeks, the Phoenicians, the Hindus and the Scandinavians. Egypt was the oldest colony of Atlantis and its civilization was the most similar to that of the Atlanteans. They were also the first culture to discover how to produce iron, but he did not credit them with any super technology.[33] That said, Donnelly clearly identified Atlantis as the source for Egyptian civilization. This contrasts with Plato, whose Atlantis was an aggressive empire bent on conquering the Mediterranean world of the primordial Athenians and the already civilized Egyptians. Thus a new thread of pseudo-history and Egyptomania was born.

Donnelly's concept of Atlantis as an ancient super-civilization that spread throughout the world quickly made its way into fiction. The prolific English writer C. J. Cutcliffe Hyne (1866–1944) brought out his novel *The Lost Continent: The Story of Atlantis* (1900), which was clearly modelled on Donnelly's Atlantis. Robert E. Howard delved into Atlantis fiction with his first Kull story set in the primordial past: 'The Shadow Kingdom' appeared in 1929 and began the 'sword and sorcery' genre. Kull stories, however, did not find favour with pulp fiction editors. Howard moved on and in 1932 created his famous character Conan the Barbarian. Conan lived in the world of Hyboria that existed between the age of primordial Atlantis and the current historical era. Hyborian lands and cultures paralleled lands of the current age. His Turan was a sort of Persia while the country of Shem was modelled on Babylon or Assyria. Most importantly from the perspective of Egyptomania, Howard created a proto-Egypt in the mysterious and sinister land of Stygia. Other imitators of Cutcliffe Hyne and Howard would follow. The point is that this genre of Atlantis fiction created a milieu in which ideas about Atlantis and ancient super-civilizations with an Egyptian connection could move from the realm of obvious fiction into the fuzzy world of highly speculative alternative history.[34]

The idea that Atlantis possessed super-technology had its origins in the psychic readings of Edgar Cayce (discussed in Chapter Nine). During the 1920s and 1930s, Cayce conducted life readings for various individuals that revealed they had led past lives. Many of these people had lived one of their earlier existences on the lost continent of Atlantis tens of thousands of years earlier. Cayce's readings of past lives purported to show that Atlantis was not just the birthplace of civilization, it was the birthplace of humanity. They contained references to the scientific and ultimately deadly creations of the Atlanteans. First came great, carnivorous animals that got out of control and ended up harassing the Atlanteans and came close to rendering their land uninhabitable. Next came the mysterious 'firestones' that served the Atlanteans as sources of power and as weapons against the gigantic beasts. Misuse of the 'firestones' resulted in an accident that devastated and nearly destroyed Atlantis and the earth about 28,000 BC. Finally they developed additional weapons, one of which sounded like nuclear weapons, and lasers generated by power crystals. The Atlanteans proceeded to use these terrible weapons in wars against each other. These wars resulted in the final and complete destruction of Atlantis in 10,500 BC. The survivors fled to Egypt, which was Atlantis's oldest colony. With them they brought many books containing the knowledge of the Atlanteans, which they secretly placed in a hidden chamber under or near the Sphinx or the Great Pyramid.[35] In this way began the idea that the Atlanteans possessed super-technology that they passed on to the Egyptians. The revelation about the existence of the hidden chamber containing the Atlantean archive also ignited a quest to find the room and its secrets. Cayce's ideas about Atlanteans colonizing Egypt were adopted by Peter Lemesurier in his *The Great Pyramid Decoded* (1977). Although the book is largely a work of pyramidology, Lemesurier did not take the standard approach that the Great Pyramid was a Judaeo-Christian prophecy in stone. Thus several new threads were added to pseudo-historical Egyptomania.

An alternative to the Atlantean origin of Egyptian civilization was the less specific concept of a prehistoric super-civilization that existed during a former ice age and was the source of high culture. Whether that super-civilization was indigenous to Egypt and simply preceded pharaonic Egypt, or flourished in a once-verdant Sahara desert, or was located in what is now Antarctica or some other place varies with the author. In France, the occult philosopher Joseph Alexandre Saint-Yves d'Alveydre (1843–1909) created the political movement he named Synarchy. He claimed that society consisted of three segments – religion, politics and economics – that were in conflict with each other. This conflict caused the degradation of society and created anarchy, but things did not have to be that way. Synarchy sought to create a secret elite who would direct and harmonize the worlds of religion, politics and the economy. Such a situation existed in the distant past when Rama founded the Universal Empire, an ancient super-civilization, in 6729 BC. Unfortunately, the Universal Empire fell apart and great spiritual leaders such as Moses have been driven to regain Synarchy ever since. Another Frenchman, the enigmatic occultist René A. Schwaller de Lubicz (1887–1961), took up the idea of an ancient super-civilization practising Synarchy but moved the focus from the India of Saint-Yves d'Alveydre to

Egypt. Besides seeing all sorts of symbolism in ancient Egyptian monuments, Schwaller de Lubicz contended that Egyptian civilization was much
older than the mainstream chronology of the Egyptologists allowed. With
its pharaohs and priestly establishments, Egypt was an outstanding example
of Synarchy in action. Both Saint-Yves d'Alveydre and Schwaller de Lubicz
were extremely conservative and have been classified as proto-fascists.

The idea of a primordial super-civilization was further bolstered in
1966 with the appearance of Charles H. Hapgood's *Maps of the Ancient Sea
Kings: Evidence of Advanced Civilization in the Ice Age*. Hapgood (1904–1982),
a professor at Keene State College, suggested that the Piri Reis maps from
the early sixteenth century reflected geographical knowledge passed down
from a very ancient civilization that flourished during the most recent ice
age. While Hapgood's book had little to say about ancient Egypt, it promoted
belief in primordial civilizations that existed long before pharaonic Egypt,
as did Saint-Yves d'Alveydre and Schwaller de Lubicz. Later, in the waning
days of the first fad for Von Däniken's ancient astronauts, John Anthony
West (b. 1932) brought out his *Serpent in the Sky: The High Wisdom of Ancient
Egypt* (1979). Inspired by Schwaller de Lubicz, West contended that hieroglyphs contained hermetic messages; the level of Egyptian scientific knowledge and technology was far greater than Egyptologists admit, and this had
its origins in an ancient civilization thousands of years older than pharaonic
Egypt – that civilization, he claimed, was Atlantis. West would later become
embroiled in the ongoing controversy concerning the age of the Sphinx.[36]

The final component of pseudo-historical Egyptomania is the supposed
role played by extraterrestrial visitors in ancient Egypt, the so-called Ancient
Aliens. The Ancient Astronaut/Ancient Alien phenomenon superficially
would seem to have begun with the publication of Erich von Däniken's
Chariots of the Gods in 1968. In fact, the origins of ancient alien theories go
back a good bit further. People have been speculating about the existence
of extraterrestrial life for over 2,000 years and some of that speculation
included contemplating the possibility that intelligent life might exist on
other worlds. In 1898 H. G. Wells imagined Martians invading the earth in
his classic *War of the Worlds*, but the scholar Jason Colavito has traced the
origin of the ancient astronaut phenomenon of Erich von Däniken to the
horror writer H. P. Lovecraft. Lovecraft's stories and novelettes frequently
feature alien and usually monstrous races that have visited and inhabited
the earth since far into the distant past, sometimes millions of years. *At the
Mountains of Madness* (1936) is a good example, with its monstrous aliens
lurking in a seemingly abandoned ancient city in the frozen wasteland of
an Antarctic mountain range. Lovecraft's fiction sparked the interest and

imagination of other writers, some of whom seemed to think they were writing non-fiction. Lovecraft's writings had become fashionable in French intellectual circles by the late 1950s. His tales influenced the writings of Louis Pauwels and Jacques Bergier, whose *The Morning of the Magicians* (1960) speculated about ancient super-civilizations and extraterrestrial visitors in the distant past. They were joined by Robert Charroux and his *One Hundred Thousand Years of Man's Unknown History*, which presented similar speculations about humanity's distant past.[37] Another writer who very much anticipated Von Däniken and his ancient astronauts was W. Raymond Drake, a retired British customs official. In 1957 he began writing about extraterrestrial visitors in ancient times including the earth of millions of years ago when the continent of Lemuria existed. He published *Gods or Spacemen?* in 1964 and by 1985 had published eight additional books on the same topic. According to Drake, extraterrestrials had ruled the earth in primordial times. In the eyes of early humans, they were considered to be gods and Osiris was an alien who brought civilization to Egypt. The pharaohs of Egypt were the human successors of the alien rulers and had arrived in Egypt as refugees from the destruction of Atlantis. Winged discs appearing on the walls of Egyptian temples were really flying saucers.[38] Much of the evidence used by these authors would be presented again by Von Däniken to prove the contentions of his *Chariots of the Gods*.

Before *Chariots of the Gods* the initial ancient astronaut theorists did not show any special interest in ancient Egypt. The reading public also showed only limited interest in the ancient astronaut theorists. The book itself contained only a few mentions of ancient Egypt. As Von Däniken described it, the ancient astronauts visited many prehistoric or ancient sites on the earth from the Nascas of the Andes Mountains to Easter Island to the ancient Middle East. Egypt was just one of many places that they visited. Von Däniken points out that sophisticated crystal lenses from ancient Egypt and Iraq could only be made today with high-tech equipment and techniques. The same observation is made about the pyramids. Solar boats of the Egyptian gods and the winged suns on their temples are spaceships and flying saucers. Mummification was a technique to preserve human bodies for future resurrections when the aliens return to earth.[39] Other ancient civilizations are given the same attention or more by Von Däniken. But while *Chariots of the Gods* was worldwide in its geographical coverage, it did not get too detailed or too technical in its presentation of the evidence. It was a simple read. Von Däniken's other early books on ancient astronauts would take the same approach. It is likely, however, that the very simplicity of Von Däniken's books contributed to their popularity. The ancient astronaut theories that preceded his own, or appeared at the same time as his, were more detailed and technical.

Von Däniken and his ancient astronaut theory became a popular cultural phenomenon of the 1970s. His books were best-sellers. A theatrical movie based on *Chariots of the Gods* appeared in cinemas and documentaries appeared on television. Von Däniken's success inspired imitators, as well as enhancing the fortunes of previously less successful writers like W. Raymond Drake and Peter Kolosimo (1922–1984). Zecharia Sitchin (1920–2010) was Von Däniken's only serious competition. Sitchin, a Russian-born American, brought out *The 12th Planet*, which proposed that aliens called Annunaki from the planet Nibaru began visiting the earth about 500,000 years ago seeking gold. About 250,000 years ago, they started to do some genetic engineering on *homo erectus* to create *homo sapiens* to work as their slaves. Over time the Annunaki gave the humans more privileges and shared their civilization and technology with them sometime during the fourth millennium BC. But the first humans that the Annunaki began civilizing were the Sumerians of lower Mesopotamia, not the Egyptians. Civilization was diffused out from Sumeria by the Annunaki to Egypt and other places. Needless to say, the Annunaki built the pyramids and all the other monumental structures from around the world that ancient astronaut theorists consider so impossible to build without highly advanced technologies. In all Sitchin wrote seven more books in his Earth Chronicles series. He also published another eight related titles. Sitchin's books had the appearance of being more scholarly and presented a more clear-cut ancient astronaut theory. Working in Von Däniken's shadow, Sitchin also managed to avoid much of the attention that debunkers focused on *Chariots of the Gods* and Von Däniken's subsequent books.

There was an exception to the global approach of ancient astronaut theories. In 1976 the American Robert Temple (b. 1945) entered the fray with *The Sirius Mystery: New Scientific Evidence of Alien Contact 5,000 Years Ago*. An expanded edition of *The Sirius Mystery* presenting new evidence appeared in 1998. The basic thesis, however, remained unchanged. In brief, Temple claims that extraterrestrials from the solar system of the star Sirius came to earth in ancient times and civilized humans. These extraterrestrials were amphibians and so were the inspiration for god-like aquatic beings depicted on the walls of many ancient temples. They also travelled around the ancient world, visiting the Dogon tribe of modern Mali in Africa and journeying all the way to ancient China as well. Egyptians, however, were particular favourites of the Sirian visitors and the star Sirius played an important role in Egyptian religion. Temple's book marked the beginning of a narrowing of the focus of many ancient astronaut theorists to crediting extraterrestrials with the origin of Egyptian civilization. Once more the lure of Egypt attracted the imagination of a new breed of alternative historian. At the time, Temple did not attract the success or the imitators that Von Däniken did. That would change by the early 1990s with the revival of ancient astronaut and ancient super-civilization theories.

The 1990s witnessed the penetration of highly speculative theories about ancient Egypt into mainstream popular culture in a way that challenged conventional academic Egyptology's version of ancient Egypt. This phenomenon has been dubbed Alternative Egyptology. It has been pointed out that these speculative theories about ancient Egypt's history have been around since ancient times; it was academic Egyptology with its beginnings in the early nineteenth century that was the newcomer. Modern Alternative Egyptology, however, has some specific, defining traits. Alternative Egyptologists are invariably amateurs with no academic training in Egyptology although they may be highly educated in fields such as engineering. They focus on the very early history of Egypt, which also tends to be the least documented. Alternative Egyptologists dissent from the mainstream chronology of Egyptian history, claiming that Egyptian civilization was far older than what the history books say. Not only was Egyptian civilization far older, it was far more advanced scientifically and technologically, even to the extent of being more advanced than our modern society. To these aspects of the Egyptian past, the Alternative Egyptologists added the idea that an ancient super-civilization had existed prior to pharaonic Egypt and had given the Egyptians their knowledge and civilization. Some Alternative Egyptologists even went so far as to claim that extraterrestrial visitors had taught the Egyptians their science and culture, in agreement with Erich von Däniken and other ancient astronaut theorists.[40] How these ideas of Alternative Egyptology came together is a fascinating story.

Two conditions helped Alternative Egyptology enter the mainstream of popular culture during the 1990s. First, the Millennium was approaching, which prompted all sorts of anxieties and speculations about what that supposedly important date might bring. Would the world end or would a new age begin? The idea that a new age would begin was advocated by many groups, some fundamentalist Christians and some esoteric and occult in nature. One group particularly interested in the potential events that might happen during the year 2000 was the Association for Research and Enlightenment (ARE), the institution founded by the seer and psychic healer Edgar Cayce, which had become very well funded thanks to wealthy converts. The 1990s also saw many new archaeological discoveries or alleged discoveries at the Giza complex of the pyramids, temples and the Great

Sphinx. These discoveries received considerable coverage in the media, which kept ancient Egypt very much in the public mind. Many of these discoveries were funded openly or covertly by the ARE.[41]

John Anthony West started the upsurge of public interest in Alternative Egyptology when he persuaded an academic geologist at Boston University, Robert Schoch, to study weathering and erosion of the Great Sphinx. As a follower of the ideas of Schwaller de Lubicz, West hoped to prove that the Great Sphinx was older than the 4,500 years assigned to it by Egyptologists. Based on his investigations of the Sphinx and some seismic measures, Schoch concluded that the erosion experienced by the Great Sphinx was due to water erosion rather than erosion caused by wind and sand. That conclusion caused Schoch to re-date the Great Sphinx to the era of 7000–5000 BC, which was a rainy period in prehistoric Egypt. Schoch reported his findings in an article in *Kmt*, a popular magazine of Egyptology, in 1992. West's recruitment and partnership with Schoch was a major coup for Alternative Egyptology. For the first time, an academic from a reputable university was giving credence to a speculative theory about ancient Egypt. That gave the appearance of respectability and opened doors. The very next year, the NBC television network provided West and Schoch with a huge amount of free publicity when it aired a documentary titled *Mystery of the Sphinx* based on West and Schoch's research and hosted by Charlton Heston (one of his several forays into dubious causes). This success opened the door for Alternative Egyptology to go mainstream.[42]

Schoch's hypothesis about the age of the Sphinx did not find favour with Egyptologists. It did not find particular favour with his fellow geologists either. A debate over Schoch's article developed in *Kmt* in 1994. The first person to rebut Schoch was a geologist, James A. Harrell, who suggested alternative explanations for the erosion of the Sphinx and its chronology. Of course, Schoch was unmoved. Mark Lehner, an Egyptologist specializing in the Giza complex, followed with a rebuttal of Schoch based on a preponderance of the archaeological evidence. Criticisms have continued ever since. Of course, Schoch has continued to push his theories in a series of books detailing his ideas about the ancient past (with a focus on Egypt that includes yet another revival of hyper-diffusionism).[43]

The 1990s were a time of florescence for Alternative Egyptology along with Ufology and other forms of pseudoscience and pseudo-history. It was the decade of *The X-Files* with its story arc of alien abduction and conspiracies about extraterrestrials, genetic manipulation of the human species and helped revive ancient astronaut theories. These theories were further super-heated in popular culture as the Millennium drew nearer.

In the background, adherents of the ARE sought to bring to pass Edgar Cayce's prediction that a hidden Hall of Records on the Giza plateau containing records of lost Atlantis knowledge would be found in 1998. The quest for the Hall of Records became seemingly more plausible when Rudolf Gantenbrink's miniature robot explored a shaft in the Great Pyramid in 1993 and discovered what appeared to be a small door. All sorts of speculations about hidden burial chambers, caches of treasure and the Hall of Records appeared. As a result Schoch and West were joined and quickly eclipsed in the public mind by a new set of Alternative Egyptologists.

Robert Bauval and Adrian Gilbert's *The Orion Mystery: Unlocking the Secrets of the Pyramids* led the way in 1994. The authors suggested that the arrangement of the three large pyramids at Giza mimicked the arrangement of the stars in the belt of the constellation Orion. This hypothesis has been dubbed the Orion Correlation and the idea was extended to include the entire complex of ruins on and around the Giza Plateau conforming to stars in the constellation Leo. Compared to later Alternative Egyptological hypotheses, the ideas present in *The Orion Mystery* were relatively tame. The authors suggested that the Great Pyramid was not simply a tomb but over the centuries was used as the location for various rituals related to ancient Egyptian religion. Using astronomical data, the authors also dated the Great Pyramid to 10,500 BC, which conformed with Edgar Cayce's ideas about the chronology of ancient Egyptian history. Otherwise there was no mention of Atlantis, other ancient super-civilizations or extraterrestrials. Egyptologists and astronomers, however, have correctly pointed out that the astronomical evidence used to prove the date of 10,500 BC is highly selective. The celestial patterns and events cited were not unique to 10,500 BC. They were reoccurring phenomena that had taken place numerous times before and after this time. Despite the criticisms, *The Orion Mystery* became a best-seller and paved the way for publishers to embrace similar types of books.[44]

The next year Graham Hancock's *Fingerprints of the Gods* (1995) appeared and was even more successful than *The Orion Mystery*. It claimed that a lost advanced civilization had existed prior to 10,500 BC. That civilization was the teacher of ancient Egypt along with other ancient cultures throughout the world. Hancock cited Bauval, West and Schoch's findings as supporting his assertions. Although he rejects, somewhat regretfully, the idea that Plato's Atlantis could have existed in the Atlantic Ocean or any other ocean, he managed to find a solution. Hancock suggests that Plato's story of Atlantis is simply a fuzzy memory of the long-gone ice age super-civilization. The real location of the super-civilization lies under the massive Antarctic ice cap, which was created by the pole shift postulated by Charles Hapgood as evidenced by the Piri Reis Map.[45]

Graham Hancock studied sociology at the University of Durham. He started his career as a journalist and came to specialize in East Africa and the Horn of Africa. After writing several books on issues of poverty, disease and underdevelopment in East Africa, he became interested in the Ark of the Covenant and its associations with Ethiopia. He wrote *The Sign and the Seal: A Quest for the Lost Ark of the Covenant* in 1992, which proved to be quite popular with the general reading public, although much less so with knowledgeable scholars. That success led Hancock to venture further down the path of speculative history, which inspired his even more popular *Fingerprints of the Gods*.[46]

Since they were working along the same lines and in broad agreement about their vision of the most ancient Egyptian past – and the market for their brand of speculative history was highly favourable – Hancock and Bauval joined forces. The result was *Keeper of Genesis: A Quest for the Hidden Legacy of Mankind*, which was published in the UK in 1996. Its title in the U.S. was *The Message of the Sphinx*. The co-authored book was an elaboration of the contentions presented in the authors' previous books regarding ancient Egypt, such as the 10,500 BC dating for the Sphinx. But *Keeper of Genesis* added a new component: claims about potential messianic events that would accompany the arrival of the Millennium. A new age would begin and Edgar Cayce's predictions would be fulfilled. In fact, a minor new age did take place. The ever vigilant Erich von Däniken saw a chance to revive his fortunes by joining the surge of Alternative Egyptology. He brought out his *The Eyes of the Sphinx: The Newest Evidence of Extraterrestrial Contact in Ancient Egypt*. Written in Von Däniken's classic jaunty style, he suggested that the animal-headed gods of Egypt were actually experimental human/animal hybrids created by alien visitors. He also argued that the Great Pyramid might have been built by aliens, is much older than Egyptologists admit and that it contains a hidden chamber. In addition, he claimed that mummification was an attempt by humans to imitate the process of suspended animation used by aliens travelling through interstellar space. Not surprisingly, in 1998 Bauval, Hancock and his research assistant John Grigsby added their own version of an extraterrestrial connection to the rise of Egyptian civilization in their *The Mars Mystery: The Secret Connection Between Earth and the Red Planet*. It is based on the assumption that the alleged Face on Mars is some sort of gigantic sphinx and that pyramidal ruins are in evidence in the Cydonia region of Mars. The thriving civilization that built these ruins was wiped out by the explosive impact of a huge comet over Mars that turned the red planet into a desert. The authors also coyly hint at contact between the Martians and the humans on prehistoric earth which inspired the civilizations of Egypt and Teotihuacan. Meanwhile Bauval added more fuel to the millennial fire with his *Secret Chamber: The Quest for the Hall of Records.* It tells the story of the idea of a hidden chamber storing Atlantean knowledge and the search to find it. He also asserted that the discovery was imminent and would bring about a new age of enlightenment.[47]

The late 1990s were a time when an orthodoxy espoused by Hancock, Bauval, West and their supporters came to dominate and even to monopolize Alternative Egyptology. It focused on the 10,500 BC dating of the ruined monuments of the Giza plateau and their supposed prophetic and millennial message with a nod to ancient astronauts. Alternative Egyptologists with differing hypotheses began to complain of the close-minded attitude of Hancock, Bauval and West to the consideration of other possibilities. They found themselves marginalized and shut out. Their complaints were virtually identical to the usual objections that speculative and alternative writers have made against mainstream academics, complaints that Hancock, Bauval and West have also raised. As a result, a rare phenomenon occurred. Some of the marginalized speculative writers started to go public with their criticisms. Normally, before the general public and mainstream academics, alternative writers and pseudo-historians close ranks and refrain from criticizing each other no matter how incompatible their various pet hypotheses are. Two books appeared in 1999 as millennial fever was approaching its zenith. One was Lynn Picknett and Clive Prince's *The Stargate Conspiracy: Revealing the Truth Behind Extraterrestrial Contact, Military Intelligence and the Mysteries of Ancient Egypt.* Picknett and Prince, both English, are known for their speculative writings about religion. In particular they published *The Templar Revelation* (1997), which claimed that Christianity, instead of originating within Jewish traditions, was really an offshoot of the ancient Egyptian religion, which was fundamentally monotheistic. They happily consider themselves to be alternative scholars or historians.

They do not, however, like the rise and dominance of the orthodox clique within Alternative Egyptology. But there is more to their opposition than an intellectual disagreement or professional rivalry. They believe that a conspiracy exists. All Hancock, Bauval and West's (Picknett and Prince include Robert Temple in this group) talk of messianic prophecies, the role of alien gods in human history and their imminent return, and the impending dawn of a new age, have assumed a religious mantle – a religion being promoted to the broader public in Western nations for murky and possibly nefarious purposes. Who is behind this conspiracy? Picknett and

Prince are not sure but they claim there is evidence that various intelligence agencies including the CIA and MI6 are involved. The whole thing might be an experiment in psychological manipulation. Other members of the conspiracy are wealthy people associated with the ARE and the Freemasons who are pursuing their own occult goals. The cosy relationship between the orthodox Alternative Egyptologists and Zahi Hawass, the flamboyant Egyptian scholar who served as chief inspector and then director of the Giza plateau during most of the 1990s, and Mark Lehner, a mainstream Egyptologist, are revealed. In addition the connections between all of these people and the ARE are also discussed. Lurking behind all of these shady activities are possibly the aliens themselves who are seeking to enslave humanity. It is all very *X-Files*. Or it might be a gigantic hoax. But if the reader glosses over their multifaceted conspiracy theory, what is left is a very useful historiography and critique of the Alternative Egyptological scholarship leading up to and including Hancock, Bauval, West and Temple. Basically, Picknett and Prince judge the hypotheses of the new orthodoxy in Alternative Egyptology to be unconvincing and wrong.[48]

The other critique of the orthodox Alternative Egyptologists came from Ian Lawton and Chris Ogilvie-Herald in their *Giza: The Truth – The People, Politics, and History Behind the World's Most Famous Archaeological Site* (1999). Like Picknett and Prince, Lawton and Ogilvie-Herald are English and have an interest in Alternative Egyptology and other speculative history, although Lawton has a greater interest in debunking the orthodox Alternative Egyptologist's hypotheses. In contrast to *The Stargate Conspiracy*, this book does not engage in conspiracy theories about Masons, extraterrestrials, the CIA or ARE. Instead it tells a story of misguided alternative researchers and nasty literary rivalries and politics. Although Lawton and Ogilvie-Herald believe there is a strong possibility that an advanced lost civilization existed in prehistory during the last ice age, they reject the various theories that Egypt was the heir of that civilization. Based on their assessment of the evidence, they find the chronology of academic Egyptologists to be fundamentally correct. They also agree with the mainstream idea that the pyramids were tombs, the Egyptians built them (although possibly with the aid of some lost technologies) and that Khufu was the pharaoh who built the first Great Pyramid. Alternative Egyptologists' accusations of fraud and forgery against Richard Howard Vyse's discovery of quarry marks in the Great Pyramid bearing the name of Khufu are thoroughly debunked. Robert Schoch's hypothesis that the erosion of the Great Sphinx dates the creation of the monument to around 7000–5000 BC is shown to be based on shaky and contested geological evidence. Nor is his claim borne out by any of the plentiful archaeological evidence that has long been available. Also they reject the belief, largely deriving from Edgar Cayce's prophecies, that there is a hidden hall of records somewhere on the Giza Plateau, particularly near or under the Great Sphinx. Their assessment of Robert Bauval and Graham Hancock is negative in terms of both their scholarship and their ethics. On the other hand, they approve of James Anthony West's character and some aspects of his hypothesis. Zahi Hawass is presented in a generally favourable light despite his restless striving for celebrity. Overall, *Giza: The Truth* provides a non-sensationalized history of the archaeology of the Giza Plateau and the associated Alternative Egyptologists, particularly those who published during the over-heated run up to the Millennium.[49]

Academics generally avoid dealing with alternative scholars. This attitude is justified by the excuse that debating alternative or fringe scholarship only gives it a false credibility. Some consider debating speculative scholars as a dialogue of the deaf, since the speculative ideas tend to be treated by their adherents in the manner of religious faith rather than scientific inquiry, while some academics just hold speculative ideas in contempt. Ignoring the Alternative Egyptologists did not, however, serve the academic Egyptologists well during the 1990s. They found themselves marginalized in the popular mind and put on the defensive. It was not until 1999 that an effective academic rebuttal of the orthodox Alternative Egyptological hypotheses appeared. It came in the form of a two-part documentary produced by the BBC's *Horizon* series. The episodes, titled *Atlantis Uncovered* and *Atlantis Reborn*, provided a devastating debunking of Alternative Egyptology, especially the ideas of Graham Hancock. Alternative Egyptology's credibility with the public was severely undermined. Of course, the fact that the Millennium passed without incident also called the messianic and prophetic aspects of Alternative Egyptology into disrepute. The fortunes of the orthodox Alternative Egyptologists ebbed as ancient aliens and the Maya apocalypse took pride of place in satisfying popular culture's appetite for the simple answers of fringe scholarship, pseudoscience and pseudo-history. Hancock and Bauval continue to write books, although Hancock's interests have shifted away from Egypt. Robert Temple even rejoined the fray in 2010 and published a new book, *Egyptian Dawn*. Interest in Alternative Egyptology faded but did not die.[50] The perennial fascination with Egypt – Egyptomania in its many forms – will ensure that never happens.

ELEVEN

AFRICAN AMERICAN EGYPTOMANIA

Ethiopia, land of the blacks, was thus the cradle of Egyptian civilization.

W.E.B. DU BOIS[1]

Every period of history has had an Egypt of its own, onto which it has projected its fears and its hopes, down to the black Egyptians of contemporary African-Americans.

ERIC HORNUNG[2]

IF THERE IS ONE GROUP of people in the United States who have a special interest in ancient Egypt it is African Americans. They have been claiming ancient Egypt for their own for at least two centuries. That claim has its emotional roots in the traumatic era of the Atlantic slave trade, which gave life to a black nationalist Egyptomania that eventually saw the rise of Afrocentric Egyptomania during the last four decades of the twentieth century.

What is Afrocentrism and its unique form of Egyptomania?[3] That is actually a somewhat complex and rather contentious question to answer. Afrocentrists claim that Africa played a major role in cultural development that has since been erased by a white culture seeking to dominate blacks. At one level, Afrocentrism is an effort to recognize the legitimate place of Africa and Africans in world history and to gain equality with the European heritage. This quest includes the achievements of people of African descent living in the Americas. Therefore Afrocentrism is simply redressing the balance with the previous dominance of Eurocentric scholarship. It is placing a needed focus on a neglected ethnic and geographical area of history. Unfortunately, at another level, some Afrocentric scholarship is highly questionable, such as the Nile Valley School's form of Afrocentric Egyptomania.

The Nile Valley School of Afrocentrism is based on a series of ideas about the past that centre on ancient Egypt.[4] Afrocentrists assert that humanity originated in Africa. This claim in itself is not contentious, since the findings of evolutionary anthropology have determined that humans first appeared in Africa. However, some Afrocentrists go on to claim that Africa is the original source of civilization, a claim that archaeological evidence does not necessarily support. The Nile Valley School, of course, asserts that ancient Egypt was the original civilization. Once again, the scholarly consensus on the archaeological evidence does not necessarily support the priority of Egyptian civilization – although consensus on this matter is tentative and subject to change. Many Afrocentrists assert that ancient Egypt was also a black civilization and that its inhabitants had arrived from the south, originating somewhere in the African interior such as the Great Lakes region. It is even claimed that the foundations of civilization, including agriculture and writing, first developed in the African interior. Once more, the archaeological evidence is mixed. Most evidence suggests that the original Egyptian population moved into the Nile Valley from the savannah lands of the Sahara and the lands east of the Nile by the Red Sea in what is now Sudan. The archaeological evidence does not indicate that the ancestors of the Egyptians came from much further south or west in the African interior. The archaeological evidence for agriculture first developing in the African interior is also highly speculative and problematic. Evidence for writing originating in that region is even more unconvincing, particularly since that theory also involves the original art of writing later being lost. When it comes to the knowledge and science of ancient Egypt, Afrocentrists insist that it was the greatest of all the ancient civilizations. This, too, is questionable. Moreover, some Afrocentrists, much like white occultists and fringe historians, maintain that the ancient Egyptians had developed now-lost magical or super-scientific knowledge not even equalled by today's science and technology.

Alternatively, the more narrowly focused Nile Valley School considers Egyptian civilization to be the inspiration for all African culture and philosophy rather than the Great Lakes region centred on Lake Victoria. It asserts that Egypt established colonies in various parts of Africa and had trading relations with other regions. These colonies and trading posts provided the mechanism for spreading Egyptian civilization throughout Africa and formed the basis for the essential cultural unity of the continent. Egyptian civilization and the literature, philosophy and religious values that it espoused are the common heritage of all black people. The Nile Valley Afrocentrists also claim that black Egyptians colonized Greece, India and the Americas. Egyptian civilization formed the basis for the culture of the ancient Greeks and for subsequent European culture. In the case of Africa and the spread of Egyptian civilization, the adoption of Egyptian culture occurred through normal processes of cultural diffusion. In contrast, when the Greeks acquired Egyptian culture, the process was one of theft and slavish imitation on the part of the Greeks.

Needless to say, the Nile Valley School of Afrocentrism is controversial. The findings and interpretation of mainstream Egyptology contradict and repudiate all or large parts of all of its major concepts and contentions. It has been pointed out that there is nothing new under the sun of Afrocentric scholarship. All of its ideas are based on existing fringe historical ideas about ancient history. The only difference is that the older fringe ideas worked on an assumption that ancient Egyptians were white, whereas Afrocentrism contends that the ancient Egyptians were black. It has even been said that Afrocentrism is merely Eurocentrism in 'black face'. That analogy can be extended to suggest that Afrocentric Egyptomania is simply a version of the older occult or pseudo-historical Egyptomanias of the Europeans.[5] In the world of Egyptomania, where many different people tend to imagine and to make the ancient Egyptians in their own image, the Afrocentrists are hardly unique.

The Roots of African American Egyptomania

Starting in the sixteenth century, the overwhelming majority of black Africans who arrived in the Americas came as slaves. At the same time, from the sixteenth century to the nineteenth century, in lands controlled by Europeans, slavery increasingly was confined to black Africans. By the eighteenth century European scholars, such as Charles White (1728–1813) and Christoph Meiners (1747–1810), repeatedly claimed that black people were inferior to whites and as such opined that enslavement was their natural state. Ironically, the argument for black inferiority was particularly popular among many of the intellectuals of the Enlightenment of the eighteenth century, such as Voltaire and Immanuel Kant. Black slaves were said to be childlike, in need of control for their own good. They were viewed as primitive and incapable of creating, achieving and maintaining an advanced civilization on their own.[6]

From the eighteenth century to well past the middle of the twentieth, it was commonly asserted that, prior to European colonialism, sub-Saharan Africa was a land without history. The venerable *Encyclopaedia Britannica*'s famed eleventh edition of 1910–11 enshrined this view for its readers when it stated,

Africa, with the exception of the lower Nile valley and what is known as Roman Africa is, so far as its native inhabitants are concerned, a continent practically without a history, and possessing no records from which such a history might be reconstructed . . . The negro is essentially the child of the moment; and his memory, both tribal and individual, is very short.

Some well-known historians of the twentieth century, such as Arnold Toynbee, held this opinion. Hugh Trevor-Roper, Regius Professor of History at the University of Oxford, was still presenting this canard in widely read publications as late as 1963 and 1965. This history-less state was supposedly due to the primitive nature of black African cultures. In truth, sub-Saharan Africa has plenty of history; it was home to complex societies such as Ghana and Great Zimbabwe. It is just that very few scholars were researching and writing about these black cultures and their stories were not being taught in the classrooms of schools and universities.[7]

Slaves laboured under this burden of distain but they did not necessarily accept it as true. Some slaves gained freedom over the years, but they and their descendants still continued to suffer from the same stigma that racial prejudice and the ideology justifying slavery had placed on all black people of African descent. Whether slave or free, many of these black Africans in the Americas did not accept the subhuman and second-class status that white society assigned to them. They argued vigorously against the prevailing racial prejudice, and some began to write their own histories of Africa.

The masters also saw to it that their slaves were converted to Christianity. Some African Americans, both free and slave, learned to read and write and even acquired some education. One of the books that would have been widely read by or to African Americans, both slave and free, was the Bible. From the Bible they would have learned about the Children of Israel and their enslavement in an oppressive Egypt. Many slaves transported from Africa were Muslims and so would already know the story of the Exodus from Egyptian slavery. Those early African Americans who were able to read more widely would have discovered more about ancient Egypt – one thing being that some scholars claimed that the ancient Egyptians, or at least some of them, were black. A black Egyptian civilization was proof that black people were capable of achieving a higher civilization. In fact, they had created the first great civilization of the ancient world. It was considered wonderful proof that the black people were not inferior. In the first decades of the nineteenth century, a tradition began of African Americans claiming ancient Egypt as their ancestral home. Their logic was straightforward: Egyptians were black and Egypt was part of Africa. Since African Americans were originally from Africa and since Egypt was part of Africa, they could lay claim to the glories of Egypt. Afrocentrists have been claiming this unique form of Egyptomania ever since.

The Rise of Black Nationalism and Egyptomania

The Afrocentric approach to ancient Egyptological studies is also a manifestation of the rise of nationalism among the African American population during the nineteenth century and the early decades of the twentieth century. The man who got African Americans interested in ancient Egypt as a black civilization was actually a white man: Abbé Henri-Baptiste Grégoire (1750–1830), a prominent French abolitionist, an advocate of various social reforms and supporter of the ideals of the French Revolution. Racial prejudice was abhorrent to Grégoire and he was an unwavering supporter of the newly free and independent people of Haiti. To combat the prevailing view that blacks were innately inferior, he published *De la littérature des Nègres, ou, Recherches sur leurs facultés intellectuelles* in France during 1808. It appeared in an English translation as *An Enquiry Concerning the Intellectual and Moral Faculties, and Literature of Negroes* in 1810. What Grégoire presented was an argument for the equality of black Africans. He also considered the ancient Egyptians to be black since he classified their descendants, the Copts, as black. He repudiated the mass of Enlightenment scholars including Thomas Jefferson who asserted the inferiority of black people. Grégoire's ideas were music to the ears of free African Americans. Previously they could only rely upon the moral and religious arguments that slavery was against God's will and racial prejudice was contrary to divine laws. Following Grégoire's example, African American writers produced increasingly sophisticated arguments against slavery and white supremacy.[8]

Grégoire was read by a large number of people. His book would have been readily available to African American readers, if they were literate or had someone to read it to them. His book would also have provided English-speakers with a second-hand introduction to the ideas of Count Constantin de Volney about Egypt as a black civilization. In 1827 Grégoire was joined by the American diplomat Alexander Hill Everett (1790–1847), who wrote *America: Or a General Survey of the Political Situation of the Several Powers of the Western Continent.* In the sixth chapter of *America*, Everett asserted that the ancient Egyptians were black, Ethiopia was the source of Egyptian civilization, that the Egyptians had colonized Greece and a great black civilization had flourished in the lands between the Nile and the Ganges rivers. He also argued that blacks were not inferior to whites.[9] Like Grégoire, Everett was a white man defending the humanity of black people through a historical argument that would have been most welcome to African Americans suffering from the racial prejudices that prevailed in the western world in the early nineteenth century. Aspiring African American historians read Grégoire and Everett and started to produce their own writings on ancient Egypt. In 1827 *Freedom's Journal*, the first black newspaper in the United States, published articles claiming that the ancient Egyptians were black.[10]

A particularly influential African American publication, David Walker's *An Appeal in Four Articles; Together with a Preamble, To the Coloured Citizens of the World, But in Particular and Very Expressly, to Those of the United States of America*, appeared in 1829. Walker (1796–1830) was born in North Carolina, the child of a slave father and a free black mother, which meant he was born free. In 1825 he moved to Boston. Once he settled in the city, he joined the anti-slavery movement. His big contribution was his *Appeal*, which was popular with anti-slavery advocates and the free blacks of Boston but, unsurprisingly to Walker, was very unpopular with most white citizens of Boston and the slaveholders of the South. Despite the criticism, his book went into a third edition by 1830, the year that Walker died. Walker was so unpopular that it was widely rumoured that he was in fact poisoned. It is far more likely that he died of tuberculosis, which was sweeping through Boston at that time. Walker's *Appeal* was an argument for the equality of African Americans and the abolition of slavery in the United States. He also discussed the ancient past of Africa and described the ancient Egyptians as 'Africans or coloured people'. Other fundamental ideas of this view of ancient history made a brief appearance in Walker's *Appeal*: Egypt was the first civilization and the origin of learning, from where it was later passed to Greece 'where it was improved upon and refined', and from the Greeks it was passed to the Romans and other later enlightened peoples and has continued to influence civilization to Walker's day. He also claimed Hannibal as an African. Walker's *Appeal* provided the central themes of black historical writing from the 1830s onwards.[11]

Other African American abolitionists supported and promoted Walker's ideas about the contributions of blacks in ancient history. Free blacks living in Michigan held a convention on 26–7 October 1843 in which they declared that ancient history showed that blacks were neither intellectually nor morally inferior. Egyptians were black and they had created the greatest civilization of the ancient world, and people from all over the ancient world travelled to Egypt to learn from them. These students of

Egyptian culture included Solon, Pythagoras, Plato, Herodotus, Homer and Lycurgus among others. The black nationalist Henry Garnet (1815–1882) in an address at Troy, New York, in February 1848 made similar claims. Egyptians were black and along with the Ethiopians had been the first people to develop science and other learning. They were civilized when the inhabitants of Europe were ignorant savages. The great black abolitionist Frederick Douglass (1818–1892) in 1854 added his voice to the claim that Egyptians were black while giving the polygenesist American School of Ethnology a well-deserved drubbing. In his book *The Black Man: His Antecedents, His Genius, and His Achievements*, William Wells Brown (1814–1884), the novelist and historian, advanced the claim that Ethiopians had originated civilization and the ancient Egyptians learned from their knowledge. But the black nationalists were not alone. John Stuart Mill, a very white Englishman, in his *The Negro Question* (1850), rebutted Thomas Carlyle's racist comments asserting black inferiority by stating that the Egyptians were black and had taught their civilization to the Greeks.[12]

Many black nationalist writings appeared in the United States during the nineteenth century. They were often the works of clergymen, who tended to be the most educated people in the African American community. There were many references in their pages to Egypt which argued for black equality in American society. One prominent example was Martin R. Delany (1812–1885). Delany, born in Virginia to a slave father and a free mother, was a free American. As a child he moved to Chambersburg, Pennsylvania, and from there sympathetic white abolitionists helped him to get an education. At various times in his life he practised medicine and sold real estate but his avocation was the promotion of equal rights for African Americans. In contrast with most of his contemporaries, Delany was a supporter of freed blacks immigrating back to Africa. Part of his enthusiasm for African immigration stemmed from his high regard for the civilizations of Egypt and Ethiopia and his adherence to the tenets of Freemasonry. In 1853 Delany wrote and delivered a treatise, *The Origin and Objects of Ancient Freemasonry: Introduction into the United States, and Legitimacy among Colored Men*. It argued that Freemasonry had originated among the Egyptians and Ethiopians early in their history. They sought to discover how men could become like God but kept their knowledge among the elite. Later, King Solomon's contribution would be to share Masonic knowledge more widely. Delany also claimed that Moses had been a slave in Egypt but was also a Mason. Since the blacks of Ethiopia and Egypt had originated Masonry, it was appropriate that blacks should be allowed to join Masonic Lodges in the United States. Travelling to England, Delany lectured at a Presbyterian church in Newcastle during September 1860 and made claims that in central Africa there were Egyptian artefacts that depicted various pharaohs, such as Rameses, Osiris and Sesostris, who were portrayed as black. Central Africans also worshipped gods that were really Jupiter Ammon and used Egyptian burial customs. Egyptian influence had spread widely into Africa, which meant that the blacks of those lands were civilized and not savage.[13]

When Delany returned to the United States, he joined the Union army as a recruiter after the Civil War broke out. He eventually rose to the rank of major and was the highest-ranking African American in the northern armies. He was sent to South Carolina where he was the first African American to be given a field command. After the war he worked for the Freedmen's Bureau and was active in South Carolina politics. But the return of white Democrats to power brought about Delany's removal from the political realm. He returned to his back-to-Africa activities and black nationalist writings. In 1879 he brought out his magnum opus, *Principia of Ethnology: The Origin of Races and Color, with an Archaeological Compendium of Ethiopian and Egyptian Civilization, from Years of Careful Examination and Enquiry*. It presented Delany's view of ancient history and the place of black people in it. Delany claimed that from Adam to Noah there was one race – a red one – but after the Flood, Noah and Shem were still red but Ham was black and Japheth was white. Why this colour difference occurred is unclear, but Delany argues that the three races were 'pure races', which meant that although the races could interbreed and create mixed descendants, over time the descendants would revert to the pure type of red, black or white. After the Flood and the confusion of tongues at Babel, Ham and his children moved to the land of Midian. From there, Ham and Cush travelled to Africa. Ham settled in Egypt while Cush moved further into the African interior. Later Mizraim, another of Ham's sons, joined him in Egypt. Meanwhile Cush had reached and settled the land of Ethiopia. Back in Egypt, Ham was given the royal title of Rameses I and after his death was deified as Jupiter Ammon. Mizraim followed him as the ruler of Egypt and took the royal title of Rameses II or Sesostris. Cush in Ethiopia took the royal title of Rameses III and became identified as Osiris. The two brothers jointly ruled Egypt and Ethiopia together. Delany believed that during these years hieroglyphic writing was invented, probably by the Ethiopians who also invented alphabetic writing. Egyptians under Ham's sons built the pyramids in imitation of the Tower of Babel. The Pyramid of Cheops was built for Ham and the other two pyramids were for Mizraim and Cush. Delany also claimed that Egyptian and Ethiopian religion was basically monotheistic, with a concept of a trinity of the one God's personality traits. Ham, Mizraim and Cush as the first three kings of Egypt and Ethiopia served as a metaphor for this divine trinity.

Needless to say, the ancient Egyptians of Delany's theory were black, but the Copts and Berbers of his day were nothing like them in colour and ethnicity. They are a mixed race, not a pure black race like the ancient Egyptians. In all of these early developments of civilization, Delany considered the Ethiopians, not the Egyptians, to be the senior partners of this cooperative effort. He was not afraid to disagree with the conclusions of someone of the Egyptological stature of Jean-François Champollion, the famed decipherer of hieroglyphs. Quirkier ideas about ancient Egypt did not attract him. He firmly rejected the fantasies of pyramidology. Apart from basing his conception of ancient history on the biblical narrative in Genesis, Delany appears to be presenting as historical fact his personal opinions and speculation based on little or no evidence. In espousing these ideas, Delany was more of a proto-Afrocentrist than most of his contemporary black nationalist colleagues. His writings influenced W.E.B. Du Bois and are now part of the foundation of Afrocentric Egyptomania.[14]

Edward Wilmot Blyden (1832–1912) was an author and an advocate of Pan-Africanism, the idea that all Africans and all people of African descent have common interests and a common destiny. He was born on the island of St Thomas in the Virgin Islands and was a generation younger than Delany. His family were free blacks and part of the middle class. When he was twelve his father apprenticed him to a tailor. About that time, he came to the attention of John Knox, a white minister serving a Dutch Reformed church on St Thomas. Knox recognized Blyden's intellectual potential and took him back to the United States in 1850 to be educated as a minister, although racial prejudice prevented him from attending school there. That circumstance prompted the American Colonization Society to offer him passage to Liberia, where he enrolled in the Alexander High School of Monrovia in 1851. By 1858 he had risen to the position of principal of the school and had also been ordained as a Presbyterian minister. He became an advocate of Pan-Africanism and the uplift of all black people in both Africa and the Americas. During 1866 he visited Egypt as part of a pilgrimage to the Holy Land, which greatly increased his appreciation of ancient Egypt's accomplishments. To boost the self-esteem of downtrodden blacks he stressed the glories of ancient Egypt, although he did not have the same level of respect for the cultures and societies of sub-Saharan Africa.[15]

In January 1869 Blyden published an essay titled 'The Negro in Ancient History' in the *Methodist Quarterly Review*. It has been claimed that this

Edward Blyden (1832–1912), founder of Pan-Africanism.

piece was the first essay ever published by a black man in a scholarly journal. Blyden pointed out that according to the Bible, the descendants of Ham were depicted as very accomplished while nothing is said of the accomplishments of Shem and Japheth's descendants. They 'erected the pyramids in imitation of the celebrated tower [of Babel].' He rejected the claim that people had only developed black skins later as a response to the hot and sunny environment of the tropics and therefore the Egyptians of the pyramid age were not black. Instead, he drew attention to biblical evidence that Ham and his descendants had dark complexions and curly hair. Citing Homer, he also pointed out that the dark-skinned Ethiopians were regarded highly in the ancient world. But while Blyden rejected the idea that the tropical climate had created people with black skins, he did believe that it brought about an 'intellectual and physical degradation' of the people living in it. The Ethiopians, however, were able to resist environmental degradation and adverse circumstance. Even more degrading than the stultifying heat of the tropics, however, was the pernicious effects of slavery on black people.[16]

In 1878 Blyden published *From West Africa to Palestine*, an account of his pilgrimage to Palestine in 1866 which included a three-day tour of Alexandria and the region of Cairo. Blyden's ship arrived at Alexandria on

10 July. In contrast to many Victorian tourists, he did not exhibit a sense of entitlement or a disdain for the natives of the countries he visited. Nor did he comment on Alexandria being too modern, too dirty or too un-Egyptian. After clearing customs and checking in with the United States consul, he took a train to Cairo. During his rail journey, he observed that the landscape and vegetation was verdant and diverse. He also mused on Egypt's relation to the biblical narrative. His one complaint about Egypt was the cigar smoking of his fellow passengers on the train: it seemed that everyone in Egypt was a smoker.[17]

The next day Blyden visited the pyramids. He and his guide started out at 4.30 am because it was summer and extremely hot. Unfortunately they were unable to find a boat to ferry them across the Nile until 11 am. By then the heat of the day was in full force. Initially disappointed by the vista of the pyramids from a distance, like many visitors he became more impressed the closer he came. Arab guides appeared offering to provide Blyden with a climb up the Great Pyramid or an excursion inside. First he tried the climb but only got about one-third of the way before his fear of heights brought his progress to a halt. His guides made a condition that, if they helped him back down, he would have to visit the interior of the pyramid – an experience that he found quite strenuous. In addition, his guides demanded more money to show him the way out again. When Blyden's visit ended, they asked for even more money. Blyden, however, maintained fortitude and forbearance in the face of the guides' chicanery.[18]

Blyden was impressed by the pyramids. His training as a minister showed when his musings on the pyramids took a biblical turn. He speculated that 'Perhaps Abraham . . . Jacob, Joseph, and his brethren, Moses and Aaron, stood and wondered at these structures.' When it came to the Greeks, he had no doubts and asserted: 'It is certain that Homer, Thales, Solon, Pythagoras, Herodotus, Plato, and many other distinguished Greeks, who visited Egypt for purposes of study and travel, saw them.' Blyden was also familiar with the various pseudoscientific theories and dubious historical claims made about the pyramids, including those of John Taylor and Piazzi Smith. But for Blyden, the pyramidological fantasies were 'far-fetched'. As for the Sphinx, Blyden saw its face as 'decidedly of the African or Negro type'. It was the face of a king and, as he rhetorically asked his readers, 'is not the inference clear as to the peculiar type or race to which that king belonged'. But after an all-too-brief visit to Cairo, back in Alexandria Blyden boarded a Russian steamer bound for Palestine on 13 July. In 1890 he would tell the American Colonization Society that 'Nothing has come down from Egypt so grand and impressive as the Sphinxes . . .

They are a symbol of Africa.' Later in 1900 he told an audience at Liberia College that 'Greece sat at the feet of Egypt – Socrates, Plato, Aristotle, all drank at the Egyptian fountain – and Egypt is in Africa. Rome got it [civilization] from Greece, and the rest of Europe from Greece and Rome.'

Blyden was a popular and influential Pan-Africanist writer and his ideas about a black Egypt as the teacher of Greece have had a long-lasting influence among African Americans to this day.[19]

W.E.B. Du Bois

The most prolific and influential African American scholar to advocate for a black and African Egypt was W.E.B. Du Bois (1868–1963). Born in Great Barrington, Massachusetts, Du Bois attended Fisk University but transferred to Harvard, where he earned his bachelor's degree in 1890. He immediately began graduate studies in history under the tutelage of Albert Bushnell Hart. Philosophy, however, was the his great love, and his professors William James, Josiah Royce and George Santayana deeply influenced him. Between 1892 and 1894 he studied at the University of Berlin. He successfully completed his PhD in 1895 with the dissertation 'The Suppression of the African Slave-Trade to the United States of America, 1638–1870'.[20]

Du Bois dedicated his life to promoting equality for the black people of the world and in particular the African Americans of the United States. Unfortunately, the last decades of the nineteenth century in the United States witnessed the establishment of the Jim Crow laws in the South as well as a general stagnation in the improvement of the legal and social status afforded to African Americans. Undeterred by these adverse conditions, Du Bois early on rejected the accommodationism of Booker T. Washington. Throughout his lifetime he grew more militant as well as more sympathetic to socialism and even communism. In the years before the beginning of the Civil Rights movement in the 1950s, Du Bois was the premier black public intellectual. He helped found the National Association for the Advancement of Colored People in 1909, edited the *Crisis* magazine from 1910 to 1934 and wrote many books. Three of his books were intended to provide a survey of the place of black people in world history based on mainstream scholarship. These were *The Negro* (1915), *Black Folk Then and Now* (1939) and *The World and Africa* (1947). The second and third books were extensive revisions and updates of their predecessor. All three books presented a Black Nationalist and Pan-Africanist interpretation of ancient Egypt.

W.E.B. Du Bois
(1868–1963),
historian and
advocate of
Africa's place
in world history,
c. 1919.

In *The Negro*, Du Bois initially stated that Negroes from the African interior moved down the Nile Valley and settled that region. There they mingled with Semitic people and the resulting ethnically mixed people formed the culture of Ethiopia and Egypt. That culture was 'probably the first of higher human cultures'. Twenty years later he continued to claim that Negro tribes had migrated down the Nile to settle in Egypt where they mixed with Semitic people from the east and whites from the north to form a people based on 'the three primitive stocks of mankind'. Thirty years later he still claimed that pre-dynastic Egypt was settled by 'Negroid people' moving north from Nubia, but additionally he claimed that they mingled with 'Mongoloid' people entering Egypt from Asia. For Du Bois, one way or the other the Egyptians were a 'mulatto' people – using the racial idiom of the United States, he suggested that ancient Egyptians 'would be described in America as a light mulatto stock of octoroons or quadroons'. Ancient Egyptian society was a racially and ethnically mixed one. But despite those assertions, he also concluded that 'the Egyptians were Negroids, and not only that, but by tradition they believed themselves descended not from the whites or the yellow, but from the black peoples of the south'. Du Bois's Egyptians were racially black and culturally African.[21]

Du Bois was a Pan-Africanist and more specifically supported Ethiopianism in its secular sense. Ethiopianists promoted the idea that Ethiopia was the home of one of the world's first great civilizations. Some even claimed that Ethiopia was the first great civilization and that the Ethiopians had taught it to the Egyptians. Initially, in *The Negro*, Du Bois raised the possibility that Nubia and Ethiopia were where the ancient Egyptians learned their culture. Quickly he came to treat that claim as a proven fact. As he put it, 'From this centre [Ethiopia] the black originators of African culture, and to a large degree of world culture, wandered not simply down the Nile, but also westward.' In *Black People Then and Now*, he declared that the Egyptians believed that the mysterious land of Punt was 'the cradle of their race'. He located Punt in the Great Lakes region of East Africa, rather than the more commonly accepted location in Somalia. Citing Flinders Petrie for his authority, he asserted that the pharaohs of the First Dynasty in Egypt had migrated from Punt. It was a claim he would repeat in *The World and Africa*. He also insisted that the Greeks writing about Egypt considered 'Kush and Egypt as forming essentially one people.' For Du Bois, Ethiopians were 'more purely Negroid' than the ancient Egyptians. Their civilization and culture pre-dated the Egyptians: 'Ethiopia, land of the blacks, was thus the cradle of Egyptian civilization.'[22]

For most of his adult life, Du Bois lived in a scholarly world where the Hamitic Hypothesis dominated thinking about pre-colonial African history. Most scholars thought that sub-Saharan Africa was a region without history, of black people who were not capable of creating and sustaining a high civilization on their own. That is if the scholars even thought about Africa at all. As Du Bois described it, 'One must remember that Egyptology, starting in 1821, grew up during the African slave trade, the Sugar Empire, and the Cotton Kingdom. Few scientists during that period dared to associate the Negro race with humanity much less with civilization.' For scholars of Africa working during the unabashedly racist second half of the nineteenth and the first half of the twentieth century, that imperative was even greater. As a result, any time evidence of a high civilization was discovered in Africa dating from ancient or medieval times, it was credited to some segment of the Hamites. They were a people who, though dark-skinned due to the heat and sun of Africa, were otherwise white or Caucasian in their physiognomy. Egyptians were Hamites who also mixed with other light-skinned races on occasion. Ethiopians and other tribes, including the Masai, were also Hamites, as were the founders of the empire of Ghana and Great Zimbabwe. Du Bois considered the Hamitic Hypothesis to be a racist piece of legerdemain. Regarding sub-Saharan Africa, he was on firm ground. By the time of Du Bois's death in 1963, the Hamitic Hypothesis was thoroughly discredited. Regarding his claims that Egypt was a black society, the ground is much less stable.[23]

Du Bois saw Africa as an interconnected group of cultures that were inspired by Ethiopia and Egypt. He vehemently rejected Arnold Toynbee's classification of Egypt as an Asian civilization. Ethiopian and Egyptian cultures formed the basis for other African cultures. Even though these cultures evolved individually over time, their Ethiopian/Egyptian roots were still discernible. Du Bois claimed that agriculture began in the Nile Valley. Furthermore Egyptian religion provided the basis for the indigenous religions of sub-Saharan Africa. He proudly asserted that 'When persons wished to study science, art, government, or religion, they went to Egypt. The Greeks, inspired by Asia, turned towards Africa for learning, and the Romans in turn learned of Greece and Egypt.' In 1947 he even declared, over-exuberantly, that Egypt under the Eighteenth Dynasty was the first example of state socialism (not a politically correct thing to do in an America on the verge of the Red Scare). Du Bois also raised the possibility that the act of melting down iron began in Africa. In addition, he claimed that Egyptian pharaohs sent expeditions into western Sudan.[24]

Du Bois did not stop with simply declaring Africa as the land of black people and Egypt as a black society. He raised the possibility that the Hyksos were also a black people. He suggested that the king and queen of Punt who received the expedition of Hatshepsut were Bushmen or Hottentots. 'Negro peoples' founded the civilizations on the Ganges, the Euphrates river and the Nile. Babylon was founded by a 'Negroid race' while the Assyrians exhibited a 'distinct Negroid strain'. He also asserted that black people were living in the Aegean basin during pre-Homeric times. Egyptian invaders brought their burial customs to Europe during the Bronze Age. He also claimed that Alexander the Great's companion Black Clitus, along with Hercules, Hannibal and Cleopatra, were all black.[25]

Du Bois was a man of many achievements and was intensely proud of being African American. He was also acutely aware of the unremitting prejudice and discrimination that black people throughout the West faced on a daily basis. Like other black nationalists and Pan-Africanists, Du Bois sought to refute racist assertions of black inferiority and lift black self-esteem by asserting the basic unity of all black people and connecting them to the achievements of ancient Egypt. As the leading black public intellectual in the United States, he had ample opportunity to do that through his books.

These books also formed a significant link in the chain of scholarly works that led to the rise of Afrocentrism and its peculiar form of Egyptomania. Of course, he was not alone in his efforts to write black people back into their proper place in world history. There were other black scholars such as Carter Woodson and William Leo Hansberry. In fact, it was not an African American who lit the fire of Afrocentrism and Afrocentric Egyptomania: it was a Senegalese historian named Cheikh Anta Diop, although he had considerable help from an obscure Guyanese immigrant scholar living in the United States.

The Stolen Legacy

Another future classic of Afrocentric history and Egyptomania appeared in English in 1954, the year before Diop published his Afrocentric classic *Nations nègres et culture*. It was George G. M. James's *Stolen Legacy: The Greeks were not the Authors of Greek Philosophy, but the Peoples of North Africa commonly called the Egyptians.* James's title is a concise summary of the argument of his book. Previously, African Americans and like-minded white writers had argued that Greek civilization had been deeply influenced by ancient Egyptian learning and that the Egyptians were, of course, black. James went much further. Instead of the Greeks being influenced by the diffusion of Egyptian culture which they adopted, adapted and improved, James accused them of intellectual plagiarism (or just plain theft of intellectual property).[26] James's Greeks are completely uncreative, slavish imitators; they are thieves of the discoveries and ideas that should be credited to black Egyptians.

George G. M. James (1892–1954) was born in Georgetown, British Guiana, now Guyana. His father was the Reverend Linch B. James. Travelling to England, he entered Durham University in January 1909 and graduated in December 1911 with a bachelor's degree in ancient languages with a theological specialization, and in 1918 with a master's degree. On 11 June 1920 he arrived in the United States, where he probably worked in New York City as a high school teacher for a few years. Moving to North Carolina in 1923, he joined the faculty of Livingston College teaching logic and Greek. It was the beginning of an on-again and off-again career as a professor in various historically black colleges and universities. He moved to Johnson C. Smith College in 1925 where he taught classics and philosophy at least through to 1932 and possibly until the 1935 academic year. Whether James was a victim of the Great Depression or had a falling out with the Johnson C. Smith administration is unclear. He may have taught

George G. M. James (1892–1954) and his book *Stolen Legacy* deeply influenced the rise of Afrocentrist scholarship.

at a high school in North Carolina, but by no later than 1941 he was back in New York City and living in the Harlem YMCA while writing, tutoring and teaching. In 1944 and 1945 he worked at Georgia State College, a technical college in Savannah. There he taught mathematics and may have served as dean of men. His next stop was Alabama A&M College in Normal, Alabama, where he served as a professor of social sciences and mathematics during the 1946 academic year. After that there is a two-year gap in James's career as a college professor. He reappears as a professor of social sciences at the University of Arkansas at Pine Bluff in the academic year of 1949. He taught there for five years and in 1954 his *Stolen Legacy* was published. On 14 May 1954 he attended a banquet hosted by the president of the Pine Bluff campus – however, he was not teaching in the autumn semester of that year. Some accounts say that he died during a trip to Nashville to visit family and friends. Others imply that he died in Nashville. And as is often the case, some people hint darkly that the restorer of the stolen reputation of 'black' Egypt might have been the victim of conspiracy and foul play. African Americans in Jim Crow's South were frequently victims of racially motivated intimidation, brutalization and murder. Still, it is hard to believe that an obscure book published by a small press written by an unrecognized African American professor teaching at a minor university could have come to the attention of semi-literate members of the Ku Klux Klan.

James died but his book lives on. Though the original is now hard to find, it has been reprinted many times by several publishers, in some cases with a different subtitle. What did James have to say about ancient Egypt and Greece? Obviously he claims Egypt was a black civilization and an African civilization, much like Blyden, Du Bois and others before him, and Chiekh Diop, his contemporary. James, however, made several unique contributions to the debate over black Egypt's contribution to Western civilization. According to James, Egyptian scholars did not write down their knowledge. Instead, they passed it on orally to their students – the initiates of the Egyptian mystery system that was religious, philosophical and scientific knowledge rolled into one. The Greeks, for James, were thieves of this Egyptian knowledge: 'We can at once see how easy it was for an ambitious and even envious nation to claim a body of unwritten knowledge which would make them great in the eyes of the primitive world.' This theft meant that the profound contributions of Africans to civilization were credited to someone else and paved the way for the racial prejudice that portrayed black people as inferior. The purpose of James's book was to restore the reputation of black Egyptians and black people in general and re-instil pride in the achievements of their race. He asserted, however, somewhat contradictorily, that the Egyptians did have books and libraries. After Alexander the Great's conquest, the Greeks, led by Aristotle, looted the Egyptian libraries to 'usurp Egyptian philosophy'. James proceeded to look at individual concepts of Greek philosophy and then drew the conclusion that they were completely plagiarized from the unwritten Egyptian mystery lore. As he bluntly put it: 'The Greek philosophers practiced plagiarism and did not teach anything new.' How he purported to know that this heinous action took place, since a description was not written down by any ancient writer, is unclear based on the authorities that he cites. The bottom line is that James asserted that the ancient Greeks did not have an original thought in their heads and that they had set out with malicious forethought to steal Egypt's glory.[27]

Reading *Stolen Legacy* tends to raise serious concerns for those expecting a standard historical argument based on reliable sources. James cites numerous histories of philosophy, but the conclusions he draws do not seem to follow from the texts. References to the works of ancient Greek authors are sometimes very vague, making it hard to determine just what is being used for evidence. James asserts that his Egyptian Mystery System was the original Masonic organization. Its first Grand Lodge was located in Thebes on the Nile and had been built some 5,000 years ago. Other Egyptian mystery lodges were scattered all over the ancient world, including in Greece.

James himself was a Mason and for his evidence of Egyptian masonry he frequently cited Charles H. Vail's *Ancient Myths and Modern Freemasonry* (1909) but, as Mary Lefkowitz has pointed out in her book *Not Out of Africa* (1996), not very accurately. She has also thoroughly demolished James's views about ancient Egyptian mysteries and his equating them with Freemasonry.[28]

There are also various problems with the chronology presented in *Stolen Legacy*. James asserts that the existence of Alexandria pre-dated Alexander the Great's conquest of Egypt, and that it contained a royal library apparently belonging to the pharaohs. The problem is that Alexander the Great founded Alexandria when he was in Egypt during 332–331 BC. But all he did was lay out a street plan on a promising bit of coastline with a humble fishing village nearby. After that he marched off to complete the conquest of the Persian Empire. Once he accomplished that, he sought new conquests in Central Asia and India before being forced to turn back by his mutinous soldiers in 326 BC. By 324 BC he was back in Babylon where he died in 323 BC. Serious work on building Alexandria did not begin until the reigns of Alexander's successors Ptolemy I Soter (r. 305–282 BC) and Ptolemy II Philadelphus (r. 282–246 BC). Ptolemy I is generally credited with founding Alexandria's Museum while Ptolemy II is credited with founding the fabled Library of Alexandria. James claimed that the looting of Egyptian libraries began with the Persian king Cambyses. Aristotle, however, was the greatest thief. Besides looting the pre-existing royal library in pre-Alexander Alexandria (which only James claims existed), he also pillaged other Egyptian libraries. The problem is that Aristotle died in 322 BC – some forty years *before* the earliest date that Ptolemy II could have begun building the great Library. Moreover, despite being Alexander the Great's tutor, Aristotle never travelled with the conqueror to Egypt or anywhere else. Alexander did send back books and specimens to Aristotle's school, the Lyceum in Athens, that he picked up along the route of his march through Asia. These gifts, however, could hardly compare to the rich holdings of the later Library of Alexandria. The problem is that James's contentions do not match what is known from the ancient writers. There is a well-documented scholarly consensus about the origins of Alexandria and its library along with the life of Aristotle, but it does not match what James asserted.[29]

Like many black nationalist and Afrocentric writers, James asserts that a large number of Greeks travelled to Egypt seeking its mystery knowledge. But, in James's case, he viewed these visits more as scouting expeditions in preparation for the grand theft of wisdom by Aristotle and his pupils. He goes on to credit Socrates with being a Master Mason and Eratosthenes of

Cyrene, a later chief librarian of Alexandria, with being black. Presumably James's assertion was based on Cyrene being in North Africa, west of Egypt. Cyrene, however, was a Greek colony founded by Thera about 400 BC, not a Libyan city. James further claims that the Greeks did not use chariots. At the very least, this statement indicates a lack of familiarity with the *Iliad* – remember the vengeful Achilles dragging Hector's body with his chariot around the walls of Troy. He also credits the ancient Egyptians with knowledge of the nine planets centuries before the formally recognized discoveries of Uranus (1781), Neptune (1846) and Pluto (1930, although demoted from planet status in 2006). James attempted to establish a slavishly derivative Egyptian lineage for Greek philosophy. Unfortunately many of his assertions about ancient history are unconvincing.[30] Nevertheless, James has become a revered icon of Afrocentric Egyptomania and his book popularized the concept of a 'stolen legacy' of Egyptian culture – for better or for worse.

The Pharaoh

As noted above, Cheikh Anta Diop (1923–1986) was born in the French colony of Senegal. His family was part of the Muslim elite in the Wolof tribe. After earning a bachelor's degree from a Senegalese college, he moved to Paris for graduate studies in 1946 at the Sorbonne. He began studying mathematics but switched to philosophy. After earning the licenciate in philosophy in 1948, he went on to complete two diplomas in chemistry in 1950. Prior to finishing these qualifications, he began work on a Doctor of Letters in 1949, first studying African philosophy before switching to the topic of 'Who were the pre-dynastic Egyptians?'. He completed his thesis in 1954. During this time, there is an unfounded story that the young graduate student Diop met the American scholar George G. M. James in Paris and the older man encouraged him in his Egyptian scholarship. But in 1976 Diop stated that during the 1950s he was unfamiliar with James's *Stolen Legacy*.[31]

In Paris, after completing his thesis in 1954, Diop could not get a jury of examiners to read his thesis on the pre-dynastic Egyptians for a degree. Undeterred, he later used that material in his *Nations nègres et culture* (1955), which would be partially translated into English as *The African Origin of Civilization: Myth or Reality* (1974). He began another doctoral thesis in 1956 while he taught physics and chemistry in lycées. In 1957 he switched to yet another thesis topic, on the 'Comparative Study of Political and Social Systems in Europe and Africa, from Antiquity to the Formation of Modern States and How they Evolved.' He finally earned his Doctor of

Letters in 1960. During those years, he also studied history and Egyptology. All of these varied studies contributed to the interdisciplinary nature of Diop's scholarship.

Diop arrived in Paris as the *négritude* movement was gaining prominence in France and the rest of Europe. Founded in 1932 by African students studying in Paris, *négritude* asserted the value of traditional African culture and opposed the French imperial policy of assimilating the native peoples of the colonies. The journal *Présence Africaine* was founded in 1947 to promote the values of *négritude* and it published Diop's important text *Nations nègres et culture.*

Besides being influenced by the ideas of *négritude,* Diop was influenced, along with many people, by the work of Leo Frobenius (1873–1938), the maverick scholar of Africa. Frobenius, while an important influence on

Leo Frobenius (1873–1938), maverick archaeologist of Africa.

African studies, promoted some dubious theories about African history and ethnology. He relied heavily on the concept of diffusion to explain cultural changes – too heavily for the anthropological establishment, then and now. He also located mythical Atlantis in West Africa and suggested that the Yoruba people were the descendants of Atlanteans. Despite those flawed ideas, Frobenius has been rightly credited with his defence of ethnology as a historical science and his advocacy of Africa's importance in world history. His work constituted a strong and telling critique of the Eurocentric scholarship that dominated the writing of history in the nineteenth and into the twentieth centuries. Du Bois referred to Frobenius as 'this greatest student of Africa' and incorporated his ideas about Africa into his later studies. In turn, Diop's work was deeply influenced by Frobenius, as were other followers of the *négritude* movement and later adherents of Afrocentrism.[32]

Diop has been called the 'philosophical godfather of Afrocentrism', although the black nationalists of the nineteenth-century United States, as well as Du Bois and Frobenius, are all equally deserving of that title. Certainly they are all significant contributors to the rise of Afrocentrism and Afrocentric Egyptomania. The difference with Diop is that he was far more focused on what would become the tenets and interests of Afrocentrism and Afrocentric Egyptomania. As Stephen Howe has noted, Diop stayed focused for his entire life on a compact set of ideas. Diop placed the origin of human beings in Africa, which was a contention later borne out by the discoveries of ancestral human remains by Mary and Louis Leakey at Olduvai Gorge in East Africa. He also maintained that civilization first arose in Africa, specifically in Egypt. Diop also claimed that Egyptians were black, at least until the time of the Arab conquest. Egyptian civilization was also the most advanced manifestation of a broad culture that existed across all of Africa. This African culture was the origin of all important aspects of human culture. Furthermore, this general cultural complex that characterized Africa was matriarchal, and was kinder and gentler than the patriarchal, violent and greedy culture that characterized Eurasian societies. Greece and later all European cultures took most of what was worthwhile in their civilization from this African culture, particularly the civilization of Egypt. Diop called his work 'historical sociology' and his writings followed the methodologies of the Annales School of French historical writing that was increasingly popular from the 1950s onwards. His research made use of historical sources, social theory, Marxian concepts and the natural sciences. Ultimately Diop was a proto-Afrocentrist.[33]

When Diop published *Nations nègres et culture* in 1955, he was known among the African students who were members of the *négritude* movement but otherwise unknown within mainstream society. Then, in the late 1960s, the Afrocentric movement appeared in the United States, and Diop and his writings were discovered. *The African Origin of Civilization* appeared in 1974: it was a translation of ten chapters from *Nations nègres et culture* and three chapters from Diop's *Antériorité des civilisations nègres: mythe or vérité historique?* (1967). *African Origin* quickly became one of the central texts of the Afrocentric movement and by extension a work that enhanced the pre-existing Egyptomania in the African American community.

A preface to the book written in 1973 by Diop insisted that African and Egyptian history were inextricably linked even if European historians worked hard to separate them. As he unequivocally put it, 'The African historian who evades the problem of Egypt is neither modest nor objective, nor unruffled; he is ignorant, cowardly, and neurotic.' His first chapter asked, 'What were the Egyptians?' and Diop answered emphatically that they were black while he criticized the racist assumptions of the Hamitic Hypothesis. Following that assertion, in his second chapter he discussed the 'Birth of the Negro Myth' in which he accuses European scholars of creating a myth of negro inferiority to justify slavery and imperialism. In his next chapter, Diop condemned the discipline of Egyptology with the blunt statement that 'The birth of Egyptology was thus marked by the need to destroy the memory of a Negro Egypt at any cost and in all minds.' Diop's Egyptians, Ethiopians and other Africans were fundamentally the same people. Migrants from Nubia and Ethiopia populated the rest of Africa. Meanwhile, the Coptic peoples of medieval and modern Egypt were the result of interbreeding after the Arab conquest. Diop also claimed that blacks were the original race and that the other races only appeared after the beginning of the fourth glaciation during the last 100,000 years. Predictably Diop translated *kemet*, the ancient Egyptian name for Egypt, as 'land of the blacks' although mainstream Egyptologists translate it as 'black land' in reference to the colour of the soil, not the people. In later chapters Diop rejected the Nile Delta as the birthplace of Egyptian civilization or that it had an Asian rather than an African origin. He mocked what he saw as the efforts by anthropologists to depict the ancient Egyptians as white. He then proceeded to list arguments supporting a Negro origin of Egyptian civilization which consisted of comparisons to African cultures with regard to totemism, kingship, matriarchy and language among other things. Arguments against a Negro origin of Egyptian civilization are also presented but swiftly dismissed. He traced the supposed Egyptian roots of various African peoples such as the Wolof and the Yoruba. Diop also included a summary of the history of ancient Egypt that stressed its Negro population was untouched by cross-breeding with whites. Egypt was under periodic assault by white invaders from the north and the east during ancient times until it succumbed to the Persians and the Macedonian Ptolemies. *African Origin* swiftly became a classic of Afrocentric historical writing as well as a foundation for Afrocentric Egyptomania. Diop followed up with his contribution to UNESCO's *General History of Africa,* volume II: *Ancient Civilizations of Africa* in 1981. His chapter was titled 'Origin of the Ancient Egyptians'. It was based on a paper he had prepared for the Cairo symposium on the people of ancient Egypt in 1974. Diop presented arguments for a black Egypt based on physical anthropology, linguistics, melanin testing and the testimony of ancient authors. But as the appendix to Diop's chapter shows, other European and Egyptian Egyptologists disagreed with his conclusions. Diop remained undaunted, as did his Afrocentrist supporters. His stature rose so high that among American Afrocentrists, Diop was given the title of 'The Pharaoh'.[34]

Diop's other important book was *Civilization or Barbarism: An Authentic Anthropology,* first published in French in 1981 but not translated into English until 1991. In *Civilization or Barbarism,* Diop reiterated many of the assertions that he had made in *The African Origin of Civilization*: Africa was the original home of humanity, a contention firmly established at this point; blacks are the original race, other races evolved due to the adaption of black people moving into cooler and less sunny climates; civilization began in the Great Lakes region of East Africa. During prehistory members of this culture made their way northwards along the Nile Valley to found a civilization in Upper Egypt. The stress on the Nubian/Ethiopian origins of Egyptian culture is much stronger in *Civilization or Barbarism.* Its third chapter connects the massive volcanic explosion of the island of Thera with the myth of Atlantis. That theory is hardly unique to Diop. However, he added to the story the contention that the cataclysm on Thera was connected to the rise of the vast overseas empire of the Egyptian Eighteenth Dynasty. Diop dated the Thera eruption to 1420 BC, which is right after the reign of the conquering pharaoh Thutmose III (1479–1425 BC) and shortly after the beginning of the reign of Amenhotep II (1427–1400 BC). According to Diop, it was a time when Egypt ventured out and created a great empire that sprawled across the eastern Mediterranean from the Adriatic Sea to the eastern shores of the Black Sea and back.[35]

There are two big problems with Diop's thesis. First, even when Diop published *Civilization or Barbarism* in French in 1981, the existing scholarly consensus placed the Thera eruption at around 1520–1500 BC – about one hundred years *earlier* than Diop. From 2006 onwards, discoveries of wood samples buried by the eruption of Thera have been radiocarbon dated to

1627–1600 BC with high reliability. That is around a full two hundred years earlier than Diop has suggested. The eruption can no longer can be correlated to the Eighteenth Dynasty but instead to the middle of the Second Inter-mediate Period (1650–1550 BC). This timing thus disconnects the volcanic eruption from Egypt's massive imperial expansion during the Eighteenth Dynasty. Diop is not alone in claiming the existence of a huge and highly centralized Egyptian empire during much of the New Kingdom. The prob-lem is that the archaeological evidence so far discovered in the eastern Mediterranean does not support the existence of that empire or of an Egyptian colonization of Greece.[36]

There were other problems with Diop's *Civilization or Barbarism*. He adopted Marx's concept of the Asiatic Mode of Production, which he applied to ancient Egypt and suggested it might better be called the African Mode of Production since Egypt was the first example. Such an approach meant that he treated Egypt as a static culture. He has also been criticized of 'presentism' for treating all history as contemporary. His ideas about the diffusion of Egyptian culture and language throughout the rest of Africa are not supported by the evidence of archaeology or linguistics. Finally, Diop used dated sources, particularly Frobenius, from the beginning of his career as a historian and continued to use them throughout the rest of his career. This has rendered his scholarship increasingly unreliable for serious scholars.[37]

Diop concluded *Civilization or Barbarism* with two lengthy chapters, together accounting for 40 per cent of the book, that purport to prove how advanced Egypt was in terms of science and philosophy. He contended that many scientific discoveries and philosophical concepts attributed to Greeks were actually first developed by the Egyptians. Apparently most of Archimedes' discoveries were pre-existing knowledge that he picked up while visiting Egypt. Diop does not call it a stolen legacy but he does seem to consider the Greeks to be mere copycats and imitators.[38] The historian Stephen Howe has aptly assessed Diop's contribution to historical writing in the following way:

> If *Civilization or Barbarism* had been Diop's first or only book, instead of coming near the end of a long, stormy progress, he might have been noted as an idiosyncratic but extremely interesting metahistorian on the lines of Toynbee or Spengler, rather than dismissed as a crank. And he might have escaped the attentions of his American Afrocentric friends, who have proved to be the worst enemies of his wider repute.

But Diop's writings were enthusiastically adopted by Afrocentrist writers and have greatly contributed to Afrocentric Egyptomania. Now it is time to turn to Diop's American Afrocentrist colleagues.[39]

Afrocentrism and Ancient Egypt

Afrocentrism represents a culmination of the scholarly efforts of the black nationalists W.E.B. Du Bois, Marcus Garvey and George G. M. James, along with many African American intellectuals of the early twentieth century. It is a worldview that combines many concepts related to Africa in general but at the centre is a focus on ancient Egypt in particular.[40] To lay claim to Egypt was a way to assert equality with and even priority over the European and American societies who traced their cultural roots to Greece and Rome. It was a strategy pioneered by the black nationalist writers of the nineteenth century and their modern-day Afrocentrist successors have continued the strategy.

The Afrocentric movement had its origin in the late 1960s at a tumultuous meeting of the African Studies Association when militant African American scholars seceded from the association to form their own African Heritage Studies Association. As we have seen, many have been credited with the paternity of Afrocentrism, including Leo Frobenius, W.E.B. Du Bois, George G. M. James and Carter Woodson. Once Diop's writings were translated into English, they formed the basis for the Afrocentric view of culture and history. One of the leading exponents of Afrocentrism remains Molefi Kete Asante of Temple University in Philadelphia, although most of his ideas on Egypt and Africa are a rehash of Diop's claims.[41]

The problem is that Afrocentrist scholars often espouse some highly dubious ideas about ancient Egypt and its history. Moreover, these ideas are not even new, but discredited hyper-diffusionist theories: that Egypt was the first great sedentary civilization (now disproved by modern archaeology and radiocarbon dating) and fantasies about the extent of the wisdom of the Egyptians. As Stephen Howe has put it, 'All that remained to be added by the Afrocentrists was an insistence that the Egyptians themselves were black.' Or as Clarence Walker states it even more succinctly, if somewhat caustically: 'Afrocentrism is Eurocentrism in blackface.'[42] In 1963 Constance Irwin suggested that ancient Egyptians had visited Mesoamerica accompanied by some Nubian mercenaries, hence the Olmec heads with black African features. A bit over a decade later, Ivan van Sertima in 1975 put the Nubians in charge of the transatlantic expeditions rather than the Egyptians, thus making these voyages a black initiative. He reiterated this contention in 1992 and 1998.

As has been discussed in more detail in Chapter Nine, the Scottish cleric Walter Bower, in around 1441–7, wrote his massive *Scotichronicon*. It told of how the Egyptian princess Scota and her followers, in the years after the Exodus, migrated to Scotland and Ireland. The descendants of Scota became the Scots. In 1740 the English antiquarian William Stukeley suggested that ancient Egyptian priests had sought refuge in England and then had influenced the building of Stonehenge and other ancient monuments. It was an intriguing form of diffusionism and gave the Scots an alleged ancient pedigree. So intriguing, in fact, that the Englishman Gerald Massey, a poet and spiritualist, revived the tale in greater detail. Massey has been called an Egyptologist, although this title was not bestowed by professional Egyptologists. In 1881 he published his two-volume *A Book of the Beginnings*. The first volume, subtitled *Egyptian Origines in the British Isles*, posited a significant Egyptian colonization of the British Isles. Others had made claims about Egyptians in ancient Britain before Massey. Atypically for a Victorian Englishman, however, he asserted that the ancient Egyptians were dark complected although their features were not particularly characteristic of sub-Saharan Africans. Such a contention has made Massey's books a staple of Afrocentric bookstores and a classic of Afrocentric scholarship.[43] These are just two examples of Afrocentric adaptations of European and Anglo-American pseudo-scholarship about ancient Egypt.

Another Afrocentric fallacy concerns Egypt's place in the geographical concepts of the ancient world. The concept of Africa as a continent did not come into being until late antiquity. Originally there were only three known continents: Asia, Europe and Libya. Libya consisted of all the North African lands west of the Nile River. There was no awareness of sub-Saharan Africa. Instead, the ancients generally placed both Egypt and Ethiopia in Asia. Herodotus was vague about whether Egypt was located in Africa or Asia, but he did refer to an Arabian side of the Nile and a Libyan side of the Nile. Plato and others viewed the lands surrounding the Mediterranean Sea as a unified geographical unit. As the great philosopher poetically described it: 'We who dwell in the region extending from the river Phasis to the Pillars of Heracles inhabit a small portion only about the sea, like ants or frogs about a marsh.' The Christian apologist Orosius would later state: 'Africa begins at the borders of Egypt and those of the city of Alexandria.' On medieval maps, the Nile was a boundary between Africa and Asia.[44] If there was a close cultural and geographical unity between Egypt and the rest of Africa, the Greek and European scholars of antiquity and the medieval era failed to notice. The notorious difficulties and perilous journeys facing explorers travelling south on the Nile belied the contention that it was a busy highway of contact and cultural diffusion between Egypt and the rest of Africa.

A further bone of contention between Afrocentrists and mainstream Egyptologists is the meaning of the word *kemet*, 'Egypt'. The ancient Egyptians had several names for their country. One was 'the two lands', which was phonetically rendered 'T3.wy.' Another was *timuri*, which meant 'beloved land'. Afrocentrists insist that *kemet* should be translated as 'land of the blacks', that is, black people. It is a claim that was popularized by Cheikh Diop. This translation supports the Afrocentrist claim that Egyptians were black Africans. Mainstream Egyptologists disagree. They translate *kemet* as 'black land', a reference to the fertile dark soil of the Nile Delta and along the banks of the Nile that was constantly replenished by the annual floods of the river. In contrast, the Egyptians referred to the desert land that bordered the fertile Nile Valley as *deshret*, meaning 'red land', which refers to the red sand and rocks of the desert. In many places it is possible to stand with one foot in the black land and the other foot in the red land. But for the Afrocentrist, it is crucial that *kemet* be translated as 'land of the blacks' to strengthen their claim to Egypt as a black African civilization.[45]

Were the ancient Egyptians black or white? That is a very vexed and badly posed question based on anachronistic modern concerns. So how would the ancient Egyptians have answered the question? They certainly would not have answered it using nineteenth-century racial concepts. For ancient Egyptians, the world consisted of them – Egyptians – and various other people. Most immediately those various people consisted of Asiatics, Libyans and Nubians. Considerable pictorial evidence has survived from pharaonic Egypt. In the great majority of cases, Egyptian males are depicted with a red hue although females are depicted in a somewhat lighter colour. On the other hand, Libyans and Asiatics are a portrayed as lighter coloured with beards and different styles of dress. Nubians are portrayed as darker and also dressed in a distinctly different way than the Egyptians. What is important to understand, however, is that ancient Egyptians discriminated on the basis of culture rather than skin colour. Egyptians were completely self-assured that they were the superior people due to their superior culture. If a Nubian, Libyan or Asiatic assimilated into Egyptian culture, they became an Egyptian as far as native Egyptians were concerned. Mainstream Egyptologists are in agreement that this description depicts how Egyptians viewed themselves and other peoples in the world of the Eastern Mediterranean and Nile Valley. On the other hand, Cheikh Anta Diop and his Afrocentrist followers disagree and insist that Egyptians and

Nubians were both black, shared a basically common culture and were for the most part indistinguishable from each other. Neither the preponderance of the pictorial evidence from ancient Egypt or the archaeology from ancient Nubia supports this conclusion, but that has had no impact on people continuing to repeat Diop's claims.[46]

What do the modern Egyptians think? Generally they consider themselves to be white. It has been reported that Egyptians were dismayed when the African American actor Louis Gossett Jr. was cast to portray Anwar Sadat in a TV miniseries made in 1983. An observer travelling in a tour bus down the streets of Cairo and looking out the window at the population of the city would predominantly see people who share the same general appearance as those from Algeria, Tunis, Libya, Jordan, Iraq, Saudi Arabia and Yemen. Arguments are made that the racial and ethnic make-up of the Egyptian population has changed over time as various groups of foreigners invaded or moved into the country, meaning that Egyptians became lighter skinned. Part of this argument asserts that the Copts of Egypt are not descendants of the aboriginal inhabitants but instead are 'mongrelized' Arabs from after the Islamic conquest. Mainstream Egyptologists are sceptical about these contentions. For one thing, the distinguishing feature of the Copts from the rest of the Egyptian population is that they are Christians who never converted to Islam. That circumstance hardly supports the idea that they are the product of assimilation into the conquering Arabs, let alone the more pejorative assertion of 'mongrelization'. Furthermore, Egyptologists maintain that the numbers of foreign invaders and settlers were simply never large enough at any point to alter the basic ethnicity of the Egyptian population. This circumstance means that ancient and modern Egyptians have remained very similar in appearance over the course of recorded history.[47]

Afrocentrists hotly dispute this view of Egyptians, ancient or modern. Egypt is the jewel in the crown of Afrocentric ideology. A black Egypt directly connects African Americans to one of the greatest and most fascinating civilizations of the ancient world. That contention is a source of immense pride. To go a step further and claim that the ancient Egyptians were, at best, the teachers of the Greeks or, at worst, the Greeks stole their civilization from the ancient Egyptians, is to make African Americans the biological descendants of the originators of civilization, particularly Western civilization. It allows them to rightly claim equality on the stage of history. Some overly exuberant Afrocentrists, such as Leonard Jeffries with his theory of blacks as 'sun-people', go even further and claim racial superiority. Unfortunately, to make this claim, they have taken the discredited ideas of white supremacy and scientific racism and simply turned them upside down. Modern racial categories may not have mattered to the ancient Egyptians but they matter quite a bit to Afrocentrists. Egyptologists are largely content to let Egyptians simply be Egyptians. For Afrocentrists, Egyptians must be black. It was not always that way. On the eve of Afrocentrism's appearance, the African American popular historian Lerone Bennett described the ancient Egyptians as 'a black-, brown-, and yellow-skinned people who sprang from a mixture of Negro, Semitic, and Caucasian stocks.' The Afrocentrist writers who came after Bennett have been spilling a lot of ink to prove Egyptians were black.[48]

Afrocentric writings about ancient Egypt tend to be rather repetitive. Cheikh Diop's and George G. M. James's writings provided the foundation but their Afrocentric followers have done little to expand, enhance and advance their scholarship. Yosef Ben-Jochannan in his *Black Man of the Nile and his Family* (1970) and Chancellor Williams in his *The Destruction of Black Civilization* (1987) have provided new classics of Afrocentrism, but if someone has already read Diop and James, they will not find much that is new. More recently, Robin Walker's massive *When We Ruled: The Ancient and Medieval History of Black Civilizations* (2006) covers a vast span of time and geography. Walker presents a synthesis or summary of Afrocentric views of ancient history. His tone is combative and even rather strident. He makes the assertion that not only was all of Africa populated by black people but so was the Middle East, as well as other countries such as India. Needless to say, Walker's Egyptians were black, but then apparently so was everyone else at that time except for a small group shivering in a cave near the glaciers of Europe – these primitives were apparently the ancestors of the Vikings and the Swedish Bikini Team. The ancient Hebrews, Phoenicians and Assyrians, among others, were also black. If one accepts Walker's claims, none of this is surprising since he claims the ancient Egyptians thoroughly colonized the Middle East and the Aegean regions. His claim about black Egyptians builds on Diop's work and it also stems from the theory dear to Afrocentrists that white people evolved from the African blacks who had migrated to glacial Europe. The various 'Mongoloid' peoples in turn evolved out of the newly white Europeans. As for Egypt, Walker adds an extra couple of thousand years to Egyptian history, although the archaeological evidence to support his claim is lacking. A refreshing change of pace is that, unlike most chronological revisionists, Walker is at least adding centuries rather than subtracting them. Inspired by the work of George G. M. James and Martin Bernal's *Black Athena* (1987 and 1991), Richard Poe's more moderate *Black Spark, White Fire: Did African Explorers Civilize Ancient Europe?* (1997) argues that the Egyptians colonized Greece. Contact with Egyptian culture provided the prehistoric Greeks with the foundations for their later renowned classical civilization.

I would like to re-introduce Ivan van Sertima (1935–2009) at this point. Van Sertima was a professor at Rutgers University and the editor of the *Journal of African Civilizations*. He is best known as an advocate of the idea that various Africans made voyages to pre-Columbian America, particularly in his *They Came Before Columbus* (1976), where he chronicled various supposed African voyages to pre-Columbian America. He claimed that Egyptian voyages to the Americas took place from around 750–654 BC. These expeditions occurred during the era of the Twenty-fifth Dynasty of the Nubian kings who had conquered Egypt. Nubians led the fleets that sailed to the Americas, but it was Egyptians and Phoenicians who manned the vessels. Once they arrived on the shores of the Americas at the coast of the state of Tabasco in Mexico, the Nubians managed to displace the local elite as the rulers of the Olmec civilization. Their presence, according to this theory, was commemorated by the gigantic Olmec heads.

Oddly, the Nubians, Egyptians and Phoenicians left few other traces of their encounter with the Olmec. The suggestion that these voyages occurred is not an original idea of Van Sertima's; Constance Irwin in her *Fair Gods and Stone Faces* (1963) and James Bailey in his *The God-Kings and the Titans* (1973) made similar claims, but they described the Phoenicians or the Egyptians as the leaders of the voyages while the Nubians were merely slaves or mercenary soldiers. Van Sertima simply stood their theories on their heads. Unfortunately, no archaeologist studying the Olmecs has found evidence to support Van Sertima or the theories of Irwin and Bailey.

Van Sertima also edited three volumes in his *Journal of African Civilizations* that deal with ancient Egypt – *Nile Valley Civilization* (1985), *Egypt Revisited* (1989) and *Egypt: Child of Africa* (1994). Each of these volumes consists of essays written by various Afrocentrist writers and deal with typical Afrocentric concerns about Egypt: the ancient Egyptians were black; Egyptian and African cultures are really one culture; pharaohs were black; and criticisms of the Hamitic Hypothesis. Some of the essays are reprints of previously published work such as Cheikh Anta Diop's controversial essay 'Origin of the Ancient Egyptians', which first appeared in the second volume of the UNESCO *General History of Africa*, and Basil Davidson's 'The Ancient World and Africa: Whose Roots?' from the respected journal *Race & Class*. Van Sertima followed standard scholarly conventions in terms of writing, footnoting and bibliography, which is not always the case with many Afrocentric writers. The same observation applies to St Clair Drake's two-volume *Black People Here and There* (1987 and 1990), which plays off

Du Bois's *Black People Then and Now*. Ultimately, neither Van Sertima nor Drake's ideas about ancient Egypt have found acceptance from mainstream Egyptologists. Their evidence is not particularly convincing. The case is even worse when a book like Robin Walker's *When We Ruled* is considered. It is neither good scholarship nor a felicitious read.

Writings on Afrocentric Egypt, however, have a following among enthusiastic but uncritical readers. As a result, a popular culture of Afrocentric Egyptomania has developed. Tours of Egypt promoting an Afrocentric viewpoint are thriving. The tours of the Afrocentrist writer Anthony T. Browder are a good example.[49] Obviously these tours appeal primarily to African American tourists. It is a return to Mother Egypt. In emotional terms, it is the equivalent of an American of Irish or German ancestry visiting Ireland or Germany and tracking down the village their immigrant ancestor came from. In cultural terms, however, it is the equivalent of a European American travelling to Greece as the fountainhead of Western civilization and claiming Greece as their homeland. That said, the average historically literate European American and African American both realize that when Classical Greece and Pharaonic Egypt were flourishing, their respective ancestors were either living in simple villages, painting themselves blue and worshipping oak trees, or beating drums and worshipping their local animistic river-god.

As is the case with Egyptomania in general, Afrocentric Egyptomania has produced its own paraphernalia and iconic images. One fascinating combination of popular history and Afrocentric propaganda was the Budweiser Brewing Company's poster series 'The Great Kings and Queens of Africa'. From 1975 to 2000 Budweiser commissioned a series of posters that depicted thirty individuals – great African rulers – ranging chronologically from 1500 BC to the early twentieth century. The Afrocentric scholar John Henrik Clark was the consultant who made the selections. Most of the posters are very good contributions to the popular history of Africa. Thanks to these posters, viewers are educated about important figures in African history such as Mansa Musa, Sunni Ali, Shaka Zulu and Menelik II. Seven of the posters depicted the ancient Egyptian rulers Hatshepsut, Tiye, Akhenaten, Thutmose III, Taharqa, Nefertari and Cleopatra VII. Four of the Egyptian group were queens. Hatshepsut and Cleopatra ruled in their own right while Tiye and Nefertari were wives respectively of Amenhotep III and Rameses II (great pharaohs, neither of whom made Clark's or Budweiser's cut for the great ruler list). All seven are portrayed as black, often with rather heavy and clichéd 'negroid' features. That depiction would be quite accurate in the case of Taharqa, who was one of the kings of the Nubian Twenty-fifth Dynasty of pharaohs. The man depicted on the Thutmose III poster has a very dark complection and in good enough shape that he could have gone ten rounds with a young Mike Tyson. But alas, he looks nothing like any of the surviving depictions of Thutmose III from his lifetime. While the poster's text is relatively accurate, the Budweiser website entry changes Thutmose III's vital dates from around 1479–1425 BC to 753–712 BC and provides him with a biographical sketch that is verbiage without facts. The caption on the posters of Tiye and Nefertari refer to each of them as a 'Nubian Queen of Egypt'. Neither of these women were Nubian princesses who came to Egypt as the brides of diplomatic marriages, which the appellation 'Nubian Queen' implies. The documentary on the Budweiser website makes the claim that they were Nubian princesses explicitly, but in reality the 'Nubian Queen' reference is inaccurate and gratuitous. Tiye was the daughter of the courtier Yuya and his wife Tuya. Oddly neither Hatshepsut nor Nefertari are portrayed as obviously black on their posters. In contrast, Cleopatra is very much depicted as a classically beautiful African American woman. But since she was a member of the Ptolemaic dynasty of Macedonians that married almost exclusively their brothers and sisters in the biological rather than the ethnic sense, it is difficult to understand how Cleopatra could have looked anything other than Greek.[50]

Budweiser's advertisements exist to sell beer. 'The Great Kings and Queens of Africa' poster series engages African American pride and fulfils a desire for self-esteem. It also appeals to customers. The posters were sent out to liquor stores all over the United States and later were sent to schools. An exhibition of the poster series toured various historically black colleges. Eventually Budweiser gave the collection to the United Negro College Fund. What educational impact such a conflicted collection of well-founded historical fact and highly speculative fantasy might have is hard to gauge.

Another manifestation of Afrocentric Egyptomania in popular culture is the comic book *Heru, Son of Ausar* by Roger Barnes. In it, Heru is an ancient Egyptian superhero, who, instead of Superman's Metropolis, is the protector of Egypt. Unlike Superman, Heru is not entirely fictional. Heru is simply the Egyptian name for Horus and Ausar is the Egyptian name for Osiris. Ausar's wife Auset is also better known as Isis. Besides being a very big, very muscular and very strong man, Heru also possesses a type of X-ray vision. Heru's Egypt is the black civilization of Afrocentric Egyptomania. Such a compelling hero combined with an Afrocentric Egypt for a setting has a powerful and lasting impact on how young African American readers will view ancient history. But Barnes's presentation of history is defective. The historical setting for Heru is the Eighteenth Dynasty and the reign of Akhenaten, but Akhenaten's Egypt is still plagued by the Hyksos, who occupy the Delta region. Akhenaten's premature monotheism is portrayed as a long-standing aspect of Egyptian religion. Akhenaten and his advisors fret about ever being able to educate non-Egyptians into the subtle truths of Egyptian theology. Meanwhile a rather nasty god, Seth, plots to make life difficult for Heru and Egypt. Unfortunately Barnes should either have set his story and his hero into the neverland of the mythological past or have got his history right.[51]

The Problems with Afrocentric Egypt

Afrocentric Egyptology is not well accepted by other Egyptologists and ancient historians. What makes Afrocentric Egyptomania a flawed phenomenon is that it fails to provide sufficient evidence to back up its claims. Afrocentrists assert that Egypt was both the first civilization of humanity and a black civilization. The foundations of Egyptian civilization may have begun further south in the region of the Great Lakes of East Africa depending on which Afrocentrist is being read. But Egypt became the first true civilization. All other civilizations were the result of the diffusion of Egyptian culture and all African cultures are derived from Egypt and thus share a deep unity. The promotion of such ideas by Afrocentric scholars is intended to provide black people of African descent throughout the world with an indisputable source of pride and self-esteem. These ideas, however, are disputable.[52]

Mainstream Egyptologists and other scholars strongly object to Afrocentric Egyptology. It is viewed as a 'therapeutic mythology' that is not based on convincing evidence or persuasive interpretations. Afrocentrists have adopted the long-discredited hyper-diffusionism of earlier European scholars from the nineteenth and early twentieth centuries. Accumulating archaeological evidence and radiocarbon dating have disproved the hyper-diffusion of the Hamitic hypothesis and other similar ideas about the spread of culture. Changing the skin colour of the people doing the diffusing from white to black does not negate the evidence against the diffusionist explanation of how civilization evolved and spread. The idea that all of Africa was a black continent, including the Egyptians, and that Egyptians and Ethiopians were one and the same people also does not bear up when the evidence is examined. The Greeks and Romans distinguished clearly between Egyptians and Ethiopians in terms of physical appearance and skin colour. The biblical narrative also depicts the Egyptians and the people of Cush or Nubia as separate and distinct peoples. It never refers to the Egyptians as black. As for the unity of all Africans, the medieval Arabs did not refer to Egyptians or Christian Ethiopians as black. Those peoples were not considered part of the *Bilad-al-Sudan*, or land of the blacks, that in modern times is now referred to as sub-Saharan Africa. Furthermore, despite Diop's and other Afrocentrist claims, the Egyptian language along with the languages of the Sudan and Ethiopia are not related to the languages of the rest of sub-Saharan Africa. Modern Egypt is a multiracial and mixed society and has been that way for thousands of years.[53]

Afrocentrists are also guilty of careless scholarship and a lack of self-critique. As noted previously, after having composed his early writings, Diop did not keep up with current scholarship from the 1950s onwards and he remained especially fond of citing the very obsolete work of Leo Frobenius. Diop was not alone among Afrocentrists in failing to keep up with new scholarship. They also tend to cite each other uncritically with no concern about the reliability of their fellow Afrocentrists' work. There is a lack of attention to chronology and logic that is reminiscent of claiming Aristotle looted the Alexandrian library, even though he had died before the great library was built, let alone before Alexandria was a fully settled city. The Afrocentrist Clinton Crawford has claimed that Champollion used the Papyrus Ebers to demonstrate that the ancient Egyptian religion was fundamentally monotheistic despite its polytheistic veneer. The problem with this argument is that Champollion died *before* the Papyrus Ebers had been discovered.[54]

Afrocentrists dismiss criticism of their ideas as white racism, particularly of the North American or British variety although other Western Europeans are implicated as needed. Unfortunately for Afrocentrists, their critics are not just white scholars in the United States and Europe. The African American historian Clarence Walker is particularly critical of Afrocentrism and by extension Afrocentric Egyptomania. Walker is sympathetic to the human reality that people all over the world and throughout history have needed myths to sustain them but the effect must be empowering and uplifting and it must be grounded in reality. He views Afrocentrism as a jumble of 'simplistic fantasies', a 'racist, reactionary' mythology. Regarding Afrocentrism's Egyptomania, he has commented that it 'places an emphasis on Egypt that is, to put it bluntly, absurd'. The Israeli historian Yaacov Shavit would heartily agree with Walker. African scholars generally do not accept Afrocentric ideas about Egypt or Africa – Cheikh Anta Diop being the most notable exception.[55]

Even modern Egyptians reject Diopian and Afrocentric views of a black Egypt. During the course of the planning and composition of the UNESCO *General History of Africa*, a conference on 'The Peopling of Ancient Egypt and the Deciphering of the Meroitic Script' was held at Cairo in 1974. Heated discussion between Cheikh Anta Diop and various European and Egyptian scholars ensued. The Egyptians forcefully rejected Diop's ideas.

That did not end the debate. The discussion continued in the pages of the second volume, *Ancient Civilizations of Africa*, in the UNESCO *General History of Africa*. Most scholars consider the UNESCO *General History of Africa* to be a flawed work of scholarship of very uneven quality that contains contradictory presentations about various aspects of African history. The debate over ethnicity of the ancient Egyptians is a case in point. Mainstream Egyptologists generally feel that the Egyptian scholars presented the best arguments. But in the *Rashomon* world of Afrocentric debates, Diop has been acclaimed the winner. Let the objective and astute reader decide.[56]

Meanwhile the debate over Afrocentric Egyptomania continues. In 1989 the Dallas Museum of Natural History brought an exhibition about Egypt in the age of Rameses II to the Texas State Fair Grounds, which prompted the Blacology Speaking Committee to threaten a boycott if Rameses II were not depicted as black. Abou-Ela, the director of cultural affairs at the Egyptian Embassy, weighed into the debate by accusing the Blacology Speaking Committee of distorting the point of the exhibition with racial politics. He bluntly stated that 'Rameses II was neither black nor white but Egyptian.' In a further jab at Afrocentric ideology, he went on to say 'Egypt of course is a country in Africa, but that doesn't mean that it belongs to Africa at large.' Then to reiterate his position, he commented, 'We [Egyptians] cannot say by any means we are black or white. We are Egyptians.' But in the dialogue of the deaf that is the debate over the colour of the ancient Egyptians, his comments were hardly persuasive. Looking back from the early years of the twenty-first century, the Afrocentrist writer Robin Walker would comment: 'This is all irrelevant. Quoting an Arab or Turk as if he was descended from the ancient Egyptians is as inappropriate as quoting a European-American as if he was descended from the Aztecs.' It is noteworthy that Robin Walker feels free to deny a citizen of Egypt of his identity as an Egyptian while claiming that identity for himself and other Afrocentrists. In other words, he is an appropriator.

The Afrocentric approach to history exemplified by Walker has also been entering the curriculum of various urban school districts since the 1970s. In 2014 the Chicago Public Schools decided to introduce an entire Afrocentric curriculum; this was met by a barrage of criticism about the subject matter's reliance on fringe scholarship. Needless to say, conservative groups were highly critical, but it is doubtful that African American scholars like Clarence Walker and John H. McWorter would welcome this news either. They rightly deplore the crippling of young African Americans when they are taught a false view of the human past. That is the sorrow – and the pity – of Afrocentric Egyptomania.[57]

TWELVE
EGYPTOMANIA AND FICTION

God . . . If only I had not read so much Egyptology before coming to this land which is the fountain of all darkness and terror.

H. P. LOVECRAFT[1]

You know, I'm not much of a fellow for temples and sight-seeing and all that, but a place like this [Abu Simbel] sort of gets you, if you know what I mean. Those old Pharaohs must have been wonderful fellows.

AGATHA CHRISTIE[2]

Egypt isn't just a foreign country; it is special.

EDWARD SAID[3]

AWESOME PYRAMIDS, mysterious sphinxes, vainglorious pharaohs, sinister bald priests, massive ruined temples, malevolent magic, cursed tombs, seductive Cleopatras, lost knowledge, dangerous secrets, dumbfounded tourists, intrepid archaeologists, Atlantean refugees and ancient alien visitors are all features of Egyptian-themed novels and films. These motifs and themes are just the sort of things that make that genre of Egyptomania fiction so popular. It is important to remember, however, that because contemporary popular culture is inundated with new novels and films, Egyptian settings and themes appear in only a tiny minority of all these works of fiction. At the same time, Egypt is over-represented compared to most ancient cultures. Film is a wonderful medium for presenting the myths and archetypes that are the foundation of Egyptomania. Only novels and films about ancient Greece and Rome or those with biblical settings have a similar or greater popularity. Otherwise, who has read or seen a novel or a film with a Sumerian, Assyrian, Hittite, Persian, Lydian, Carthaginian or

Etruscan setting?[4] Egypt, like ancient Greece and Rome, holds a privileged place in fiction. Like Egypt itself, it is both familiar and exotic.[5]

Egyptian-themed fiction assumed its current form during the nineteenth century. Prior to the upsurge of Egyptomania after Napoleon's expedition to Egypt, the country only made very sporadic appearances in plays, novels and operas – fiction was largely confined to plays before the rise of opera in the late seventeenth century and the rise of the novel in the eighteenth century. Cleopatra provided a popular subject for plays during the sixteenth century, of which William Shakespeare's *Antony and Cleopatra* is the best-known example. During the eighteenth century, the few Egyptian-themed works of fiction that existed were related to Freemasonry and its connection to the secret knowledge of ancient Egypt, for example Abbé Jean Terrasson's novel *The Life of Sethos* (1732) and Wolfgang Amadeus Mozart's opera *The Magic Flute* (1791).[6]

After Napoleon's expedition and Champollion's decipherment of hiero-glyphs, accurate knowledge of ancient Egypt began to grow rapidly. This development coincided with the rise of a mass market for popular fiction and the increase in variety of new genres such as short stories, mysteries, historical novels, occult fiction and science fiction. In this environment, Egyptian-themed fiction bloomed. One of the earliest writers to use Egyptianizing elements in one of his novels was Edward Bulwer-Lytton in *The Last Days of Pompeii* (1834). Although the novel was set in Italy in AD 70, a significant element of its plot involved the machinations of an evil Egyptian priest, Abraces, living in Pompeii. Like many of Bulwer-Lytton's novels, *The Last Days of Pompeii* exhibited occult elements. Later Egyptomaniac fiction would often include occult aspects as well. H. Rider Haggard, the prolific writer of romances set in various exotic places, but mostly Africa, produced several Egyptian-themed novels, starting with *She* (1886), but most specifically with *Cleopatra* (1889). The prolific French writer Anatole France joined the realm of Egyptomania in 1890 when he published *Thaïs*, a novel of religious conflict in the Egypt of late antiquity. In an effort to popularize Egyptology, the German archaeologist Georg Ebers wrote several historical novels set in the ancient Egypt of the late period of the Saite, Persian and Ptolemaic dynasties. He also ventured a novel about Cleopatra in 1894.[7]

Other writers returned to the occult Egypt setting that Bulwer-Lytton had pioneered. Sir Arthur Conan Doyle wrote the short stories 'The Ring of Thoth' (1890) and 'Lot No. 249' (1892), which introduced the ideas of an Egyptian love affair spanning millennia and a resurrected mummy that commits mayhem. In 1897 Richard Marsh published his thriller *The Beetle*, in which an English diplomat travelling in Egypt becomes embroiled with the clandestine cult of Isis. Although he escapes to England, a vengeful priestess with supernatural powers, including the ability to transform into a scarab beetle, follows him with a view to vengeance. Guy Boothby followed with *Pharos the Egyptian* (1898), which involves an evil Egyptian priest who has been resurrected in modern times and seeks to destroy humanity with a deadly plague. Five years later Bram Stoker, of *Dracula* fame, published *The Jewel of the Seven Stars* (1903). This tale involves archaeologists despoiling the tomb of a wicked queen whose mummy contrives to resurrect itself and wreak havoc on the desecrators. The extremely prolific author E. F. Benson produced the novel *The Image in the Sand* in which an English gentleman attempts to contact his dead wife through an evil medium, who instead summons a dead Egyptian king who takes possession of the wife's body. All of the plot elements of these novels would become standard features in many thrillers and films with Egyptian settings from the late nineteenth century onwards. Sax Rohmer, best known for his Fu Manchu novels, is an excellent example. Those unfamiliar with the Fu Manchu stories naturally assume they are set in China since the main villain is Chinese. In fact, most of the early Fu Manchu stories, which first appeared in 1913, had Egyptian settings. Furthermore, Rohmer produced other works with Egyptian settings: *Brood of the Witch Queen* (1918), *Tales of Secret Egypt* (1918) and *Green Eyes of Bast* (1920). All of these featured supernatural resurrection, reincarnation and revenge.[8]

The early film industry was quick to begin producing movies with Egyptianizing or Egyptomaniac themes or settings. Georges Méliès, the pioneering French film-maker, produced several films involving trick photography and featuring Egyptian sarcophagi. Films portrayed Egypt, particularly ancient Egypt, as a mystical and sinister land: for example, *An Egyptian Mystery* appeared in 1909 and involved a magical pendant of invisibility.

Mummy films began to proliferate during cinema's early era. In 1911 a film titled *The Mummy* appeared and told the story of an Egyptian princess's mummy being accidentally reanimated by electricity. The mummy's owner, an American scientist, falls in love with her. In this case, the mummy is an object of romance not terror. It was followed by another with the same title in 1914. Two films both titled *The Egyptian Mummy* appeared in 1913 and 1914. But mummies were not just scary or romantic, they could be the subject of farce too, as the films *The Mummy and the Cowpunchers* (1912) and *The Mummy and the Hummingbird* (1915) showed. The thrillers *The Vengence of Egypt* (1913) and *The Avenging Hand* (1915), unfortunately now

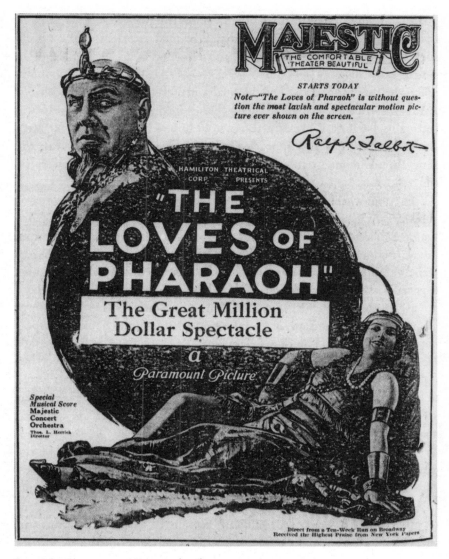

Poster for *The Loves of Pharaoh* (1922), directed by Ernst Lubitsch.

lost, presented a sinister Egypt of supernatural skullduggery and violence. Melodrama was well represented, too, by *An Egyptian Princess* (1914) and *The Dust of Egypt* (1915). In the latter film an ancient Egyptian princess falls asleep and wakes up amid the modern bustle of New York City. The great German director Ernst Lubitsch (1892–1947) followed these films with his *The Eyes of the Mummy* (1918). Mummies have little to do with the plot of this film, which focuses on an English painter in Egypt wresting a young woman from an evil guardian and taking her home to England. The guardian follows them to England and stalks the couple, which results in the death of the fragile young woman. The mad guardian then commits suicide – not a happy ending. Lubitsch returned to an ancient Egyptian setting with his epic *The Loves of Pharaoh* (1922), a tale of diplomatic marriages, unrequited love and doomed romance. As was the case with *The Eyes of the Mummy*, most of the main characters die. Its supposed historical setting is also false. Cleopatra also proved to be a popular character, with five films titled *Cleopatra* appearing in 1908, 1909, 1913 and 1918.[9] By the time Tutankhamun's tomb was discovered and before Tutmania took hold, the basic themes of Egyptian fiction had been established.

Egyptian-themed fiction can be classified into a number of categories or subgenres. There are plays, novels and films of historical fiction (Cleopatra fiction is a significant subdivision of this category). There is the subgenre of biblical fiction related to ancient Egypt. Occult and hermetic themes characterize another subgenre. Finally there is mummy fiction. Egyptian settings especially attract the attentions of writers of mysteries and thrillers: there are archaeological thrillers involving mysterious and sinister happenings around Egyptian ruins and artefacts; others that include occult and supernatural elements; and tourism-related mysteries such as Agatha Christie's *Death on the Nile*. Other mysteries and thrillers are set in ancient Egypt, but not all periods of Egyptian history attract the attention of authors. The era of Akhenaten and Tutankhamun and the reign of Hatshepsut are popular settings, otherwise Egyptian-themed mysteries and thrillers are scattered sparsely across the span of that ancient land's history.

Egyptian-themed fiction has provided the settings for some of the greatest epic films ever made, although such productions are tremendously expensive. Most Egyptian fiction, including mysteries and thrillers, tends to be in the form of novels. Historical settings, whether for ancient Egypt or other lands and ages, are generally expensive to portray in film and therefore are risky projects for production companies. Mummy movies are an exception. They tend to use modern locations and use intimate and even claustrophobic, and thus inexpensive, settings. Some films and novels with Egyptian themes can also be hybrids of more than one subgenre, for example, one novel that portrays Cleopatra as a vampire is both historical (at least a little bit) and a thrilling horror tale. A novel from the reign of Tutankhamun can be historical and a mystery. The one certain thing is that Egyptomaniac fiction is a perennial aspect of popular novels and films.

Historical Fiction

Georg Ebers and his contemporaries were the pioneers of historical fiction set in ancient Egypt. It was a popular genre of fiction, which continued its popular appeal after the discovery of King Tut's tomb. Cecil B. DeMille's biblical epic *The Ten Commandments* appeared in 1923. It had been preceded by four earlier silent films depicting the same story. DeMille set a new standard, however, with his opulent sets that portrayed a magnificent Egypt. They were modelled on surviving monuments and temples as well as research in the scholarship of Egyptology to ensure historical accuracy. A pylon gate was erected that was 228 metres (750 feet) wide and 33 metres (109 feet) high, along with an avenue of sphinxes. It was one of the largest film sets constructed up to that point. DeMille would reuse the idea in his 1956 remake. He also had three hundred chariots constructed for the army of Pharaoh, a figure he upped to six hundred in the 1956 film. *The Ten Commandments* of 1923 cost $1.5 million compared to the $2.5 million spent on D. W. Griffith's *Intolerance* (1916) – for many decades considered the most expensive movie ever made. The biblical story only took up one-third of the film's running time although it consumed the lion's share of the budget. Its remaining two-thirds consisted of a morality tale of two brothers, one good and one bad, set in modern times. DeMille conceived of this *Ten Commandments* as the first part of a trilogy of biblical epics that included his *The King of Kings* (1927) and *The Sign of the Cross* (1932). He enjoyed making biblical epics and it did not hurt that they were profitable ventures. He also recognized that audience interest was greater when you placed the holy people in a wicked land rather than the Holy Land. Egypt, like ancient Rome, could be a wonderfully wicked land.[10]

During the 1950s heyday of epic films, DeMille would remake *The Ten Commandments* in 1956 as a three-and-a-half hour film. Its budget of $13.2 million allowed for even more lavish sets and special effects, which prompted jokes that the film cost over a million dollars per commandment. These features, and the redoubtable Charlton Heston who played Moses very effectively, made *The Ten Commandments* a wildly popular film, and although expensive to make, it earned $43 million at the box office. Even more than in 1923, DeMille and his staff engaged in research into ancient Egypt and the Hebrew captivity there. At the beginning of the film, DeMille even appears to address the audience about freedom and dictatorship, which marked the film's roots in the Cold War between Western democracy and communist totalitarianism. He also emphasized the authenticity, particularly the biblical authenticity, of the film. DeMille proceeded to present a very detailed and, nevertheless, highly speculative story of Moses' life, little of which appears in the biblical account. Moses does not even discover he is a Hebrew until a third of the way through the film. According to DeMille's script, Moses grows up thinking he is the son of Bithiah, the sister of Pharaoh Sethi (Seti I). Sethi holds Moses in such high regard that he is contemplating making Moses heir to the throne of Egypt rather than Rameses, his natural son. At the same time Sethi's daughter, Nefretiri, has also fallen in love with Moses, even though the normal practice would have been for her to marry her brother Rameses. As a result, Moses is faced with some serious temptation from the delectable and high-spirited Nefretiri, as played by Anne Baxter. Later, Moses returns from his exile in Midin to free the Hebrews. Rameses does not capitulate and let the Hebrew slaves go free until three hours into the film and it is another fifteen minutes before they cross the Red Sea and witness the destruction of the pursuing Egyptian army, including DeMille's six hundred chariots. As a result, the great majority of the film takes place in Egypt and the film drips with shots of pyramids, sphinxes, temples and the Nile River. Sumptuous Egyptian costumes abound. The film is a feast of Egyptianized sets and props – an Egyptophile's delight.[11]

The combination of ancient Egypt and the Bible make the story of Moses and the Ten Commandments powerfully attractive for film-makers. DeMille's 1956 production of *The Ten Commandments* set such a high standard that no one was willing to make a new version of the Moses in Egypt story lest they suffer from the comparison. It was not until 1975 that *Moses the Lawgiver* appeared with Burt Lancaster in the title role. It originally aired as a series on television but was recut as a theatrical release. In comparison to DeMille's lavish film, *Moses the Lawgiver* was quite modest. Another twenty years passed before DreamWorks Studios created an animated Moses in its *The Prince of Egypt* (1998), which was also done in a musical format. Thanks to the wonders of computer-generated animation, DreamWorks was able to create an ancient Egypt that was more impressive than DeMille's. Like *The Ten Commandments*, *The Prince of Egypt* has the foundling Moses raised as part of Pharaoh Seti's family. The difference is that instead of being rivals, Moses and Rameses are playmates and good friends. They even manage to destroy a temple in the course of racing their chariots, much to the distress of Pharaoh Seti. It is only when Moses wants the Hebrews freed that Rameses turns against him and the ten plagues fall upon Egypt. Otherwise, the story follows the biblical account of Mount Sinai and the issuing of the Ten Commandments. A more traditionally Christian version appeared as the made-for-TV film *The Ten Commandments* in 2006. Another animated version appeared in 2007 with the American actor Christian Slater as the voice of Moses. This film followed the biblical account more closely than the others although its animation was not quite as high quality as the DreamWorks tale. The year 2014 saw the appearance of the most recent film to feature Moses in Egypt – film director Ridley Scott's *Exodus: Gods and Kings*. It set a new standard for not following the biblical account and for its inaccurate Egyptian elements. Christian Bale played Moses, a dubious casting choice. While the film presented impressive special effects, little of it was impressively Egyptianized. Accusations of racist casting, or Hollywood whitewashing, also emerged as Egyptians were played by white actors. A similar problem arose with the film *Gods of Egypt* (2016), and in this case the producers and the director tackled the criticism by publicly apologizing for the controversial casting. Audiences can only hope that the next remake of the Moses and the Ten Commandments story, or any story concerning ancient Egypt, is better. Good or bad, movies about the Ten Commandments are a perennial favourite of Hollywood film-makers.[12]

The story of Cleopatra is another popular theme in historical fiction with an Egyptian setting. How could it not be? Beyond the exotic allure of Egypt, Cleopatra's biography is ripe with storytelling potential: a powerful queen, supposedly extremely beautiful, who is the lover of two of the most powerful men of her time, and whose life ends with a tragic double suicide. All these elements combine to make Cleopatra one of the most compelling figures of all time. Lucy Hughes-Hallett has written a wonderful history of how Cleopatra has been depicted by her contemporaries over the centuries to 1990. Cleopatra has had many personas: temptress, goddess, childish kitten, *femme fatale*, nationalist leader and martyr, among others. The poet Dante placed her in Hell and called her 'wanton Cleopatra'. William Shakespeare would later depict her and Mark Antony as lovers doomed by their blind devotion to each other, their reason blunted by love. For Shakespeare and his audiences they were a foolish couple rather than tragically romantic. But Shakespeare's Cleopatra was a woman of great beauty and character. As the play's Enobarbus famously put it, 'Age cannot wither her, nor custom stale / Her infinite variety' (Act II.2).

Other pre-Tutankhamun depictions of Cleopatra include H. Rider Haggard's novel *Cleopatra* (1889) in which she is a ruthless woman, though not Egyptian, seeking power and capable of great cruelty. Georg Ebers's novel *Cleopatra* (1894) portrayed her as a mistress of the magic that was rife in ancient Egypt from highest to the lowest in the land. A few years later, when George Bernard Shaw wrote his play *Caesar and Cleopatra* in

1898, he infantilized her as a flighty, naive, selfish and immature teenager badly in need of Julius Caesar's mentoring. All traces of any intimate relations between Caesar and Cleopatra were eliminated by Shaw. The point of Shaw's play was to criticize British imperialism in the Sudan. All of the works mentioned were popular in their day and had a significant influence on how Cleopatra would appear in future novels and films.[13]

Cleopatra attracted the pioneers of the silent film industry. In 1912 *Cleopatra*, with Helen Gardner in the title role, appeared as the first feature-length film to depict the Egyptian queen. It focused on her various love affairs, both historical and fictional. The early sex symbol Theda Bara portrayed her in the film *Cleopatra* that came out in 1917 and was based on H. Rider Haggard's novel. After the strict rules of the Hays Code came to dominate Hollywood's output, this *Cleopatra* was declared unsuitable for viewing due to its risqué presentation. Only fragments of the film now survive. After that era of film-making, the character of Cleopatra was given a rest for almost two decades until Cecil B. DeMille asked Claudette Colbert, 'How would you like to be the wickedest woman in history?' She, of course, said yes. The result was the classic film of 1934, *Cleopatra*, with its elaborate art deco sets. Twelve years later the Hungarian director Gabriel Pascal brought Shaw's play *Caesar and Cleopatra* (1945) to the silver screen. It is a faithful adaptation of the play, with Claude Rains as Caesar

Claudette Colbert as Cleopatra in Cecil B. DeMille's *Cleopatra*.

and Vivien Leigh as Cleopatra. The film's sets were elaborate, impressive and very much Egyptianized. Sphinxes abound and the Lighthouse of Alexandria is depicted with reasonable accuracy. The film was an attempt by the British film industry to compete with Hollywood spectacles, but faithfully following Shaw's play did not make for an exciting film. Another Cleopatra film came out in 1956 titled *Serpent of the Nile*, which starred the American actress Rhonda Fleming and inexplicably ignored the affair between Cleopatra and Mark Antony. Apparently the moral of the film is, as one reviewer quipped, 'indiscriminate necking doesn't pay.' It is hardly a conclusion that does justice to the legendary Cleopatra.[14]

When it comes to the legendary Cleopatra, the quintessential work of fiction has to be the Joseph L. Mankiewicz film of 1963. Starring Richard Burton, Elizabeth Taylor and Rex Harrison, this *Cleopatra* took two and a half years to film and ended up being one of the most expensive films ever made, eventually costing $44 million, around $320 million in today's money. The studio, Twentieth Century Fox, was saddled with massive short-term losses. The film also generated titillating tales of antics on or around the set of the film. Burton and Taylor met and fell in love on the set while each being married to someone else. Such behaviour was not all that well tolerated in the early 1960s and the stars' affair became known as *Le scandale*. In fact, the Burton/Taylor off-screen romance strangely paralleled the way the film portrayed the relationship of Mark Antony and Cleopatra.[15]

Cleopatra did not simply take a long time to make, it ended up being a long film. By the time shooting had ended, the studio had over 96 hours of film that needed to be edited into a coherent motion picture. The film's editors faced a daunting task and did a mediocre job. Burton's best scenes were cut out, which reduced him to the rather pathetic Mark Antony of the final version. After meeting Cleopatra, Antony is seldom without a wine cup in his hand. In other cases, significant background information was cut and many transitions ended up being too abrupt. Suggestions to split the film into two, each running over two hours, were rejected by the Fox executives. The runtime of the initial release was four hours and 24 minutes. Within two weeks that had been cut to four hours and three minutes and some months later that had been reduced to just over three hours. The standard DVD runs to 248 minutes. Besides the length and editing of the film, it was widely acknowledged that Elizabeth Taylor's voice was too weak in many scenes to be convincing as a ruler such as Cleopatra.

Nonetheless, as a work of historical fiction and Egyptomania, the film is quite good. It presents the romance between Julius Caesar and Cleopatra as a combination of hardheaded political alliance and mutual love. Cleopatra's romance with Mark Antony is a more passionate and tempestuous romance, ultimately self-destructive as any good tragedy should be. (Shakespeare would have approved.) Cleopatra shows the expected concern for Caesarion, son of Julius Caesar, but the film omits all mention of Antony and Cleopatra's two children. The sets reflect the massive amounts of money expended on the making of the film. Scenes depicting Alexandria show a city where Hellenistic and Egyptian architecture jostle with each other for prominence and the great Lighthouse is shown in the background. Elaborate costumes proliferate, particularly those of Cleopatra. Egyptian magic appears in scenes of fortune-telling and is taken seriously. Sphinxes are lined up in avenues or scattered about as decoration inside and outside buildings. In fact, Cleopatra rides into the Roman forum on a massive, rolling Sphinx to join Julius Caesar as crowds of Romans go wild with excitement. Interior decor is Egyptianized as are the dark and mysterious temples. And, of course, Elizabeth Taylor makes an iconic Cleopatra, combining great beauty and an irrepressible force of personality. Although the film is over sixty years old, no subsequent telling of Cleopatra's story has surpassed the standard set by the *Cleopatra* of 1963 and Elizabeth Taylor's performance.

Other films and novels about Cleopatra have followed. The excesses of Fox's *Cleopatra* were parodied merely one year later in the British comedy *Carry on Cleo* (1964). It mangled the history quite entertainingly, transforming Cleopatra into an ancient airhead. The year 1970 saw the appearance of an early Japanese anime film titled *Cleopatra* that was borderline pornographic. Charlton Heston tried to raise the tone in 1972. He had played Antony in a theatrical version of Shakespeare's *Antony and Cleopatra* and he decided to produce the play as a film, but the end result suffers from the same problem that the film of Shaw's *Caesar and Cleopatra* experienced. A literal filming of a play does not an enjoyable film make. Poor reviews resulted in very limited distribution and the film ultimately failed to perform well, despite featuring exotic Egyptian costumes and sets.[16]

Cleopatra also remains a perennial subject for historical novels. Some recent examples are Margaret George's *The Memoirs of Cleopatra*, published in 1997. The novel was quickly adapted into a three-hour TV miniseries in 1999. Leonor Varela stars as Cleopatra with Timothy Dalton as Julius Caesar and Billy Zane as Mark Antony. The novel and television series both cover the usual ground of Cleopatra's relationships with Caesar and Antony. Colleen McCullough's *Masters of Rome* series consists of impressively thick novels about the era of the fall of the Roman Republic beginning with the rise of Marius and Sulla. In the sixth and seventh novels in the series,

The October Horse (2002) and the final novel *Antony and Cleopatra* (2007), McCullough covers the encounter of Caesar and Cleopatra. Cleopatra was also a recurring character in the HBO/BBC series *Rome* (2005–7), set in the period of the fall of the Roman Republic and portraying the accompanying civil wars. In this depiction, Cleopatra is a ruthless schemer looking for the best deal for her and Egypt in the labyrinthine world of Roman politics. She is also a prodigious smoker of opium and a nymphomaniac who thoroughly corrupts Mark Antony. Beyond this, it was of course inevitable that the current fad of vampire-mania would connect with Egyptomania too, as Maria Dahvana Headley's *Queen of Kings: A Novel of Cleopatra, the Vampire* (2011) demonstrates. Meanwhile a new Cleopatra movie starring Angelina Jolie as the Egyptian queen is tentatively in development. Predictably, Brad Pitt is rumoured to play Antony. Clearly, Shakespeare's Enobarbus was right when he credited Cleopatra with 'infinite variety'.[17]

Another popular subject for historical fiction about ancient Egypt has been the reign of the heretic pharaoh Akhenaten. Because he challenged the Egyptian religious establishment and lost, Akhenaten's name had been suppressed and he remained an unknown pharaoh for centuries. Then, in the middle of the nineteenth century, archaeological discoveries began to reveal his existence and the highly controversial and dramatic events of his reign. His entry into the popular consciousness of the West was speeded along by the publication of the Egyptologist Arthur Weigall's *The Life and Times of Akhenaten, Pharaoh of Egypt* in 1910. It made the pharaoh a mythic figure. Akhenaten was credited with being a proto-monotheist and an inspiration for Judaism and by extension Christianity. Many writers would explore this connection, including most famously Sigmund Freud in his *Moses and Monotheism* (1939). A tragic fall from power and close connections with two of the world's great religions make Akhenaten an attractive figure for novelists. Being viewed, rightly or wrongly, as a pacifist and a humanitarian in most accounts also helped. Dominic Montserrat has pointed out that more works of fiction have been written about Akhenaten than any figure from ancient history except Alexander the Great and Cleopatra. There are more than fifty Akhenaten/Amara novels. They started to appear during the First World War and have continued to be written ever since. Generally novelists use the story of Akhenaten to reflect on their own contemporary world and its problems: novels of the 1920s and 1930s tended to focus on the theme of a powerful dynasty falling into ruin, which was particularly poignant given the falls of the Romanov, Habsburg and Hohenzollern dynasties in the debacle of the Great War. Even the crime novelist Agatha Christie wrote the play *Akhnaton* in 1937, which presented the pharaoh as a pacifist brought down by evil priests and military men. It had little impact at the time, however, since it was not published until 1973.[18]

Three novels of the Akhenaten genre particularly stand out. The first is Thomas Mann's monumental *Joseph and His Brothers*, which appeared in four volumes between 1933 and 1943. The novel's primary focus is on the biblical story of the patriarch Joseph and its place in the history of the Jewish people, but in the fourth volume Akhenaten appears as a religious reformer. Mann was writing during the rise of Nazism and he considered ancient Egypt to be a humane culture that contrasted with the barbarism Mann was living through. A few years later the Finnish historical novelist Mika Waltari brought out *The Egyptian* (1945, English translation 1949). The protagonist is the disillusioned physician Sinuhe, and the setting is the reign of Akhenaten and its accompanying turmoil, inhumanity and oppression. It was a fitting topic for the post–Second World War era and reflected Waltari's Christian beliefs. The novel proved popular and made Waltari an internationally known literary figure. Later, in 1985, the Egyptian writer Naguib Mahfouz would write *Akhenaten, Dweller in Truth*. The novel is set during the reign of Tutankhamun, where the young scholar/nobleman Meriamun has decided to investigate the murky events of Akhenaten's reign. The novel is a series of accounts that Meriamun collected from people close to Akhenaten, both friends and foes. Essentially it is a *Rashomon*-style narrative. Mahfouz was ultimately awarded the Nobel Prize in Literature in 1988.[19]

Waltari's novel proved popular enough to be made into a film, also titled *The Egyptian* (1954). The film's intriguing plot and sumptuous sets brought images of ancient Egypt to a large audience. Michael Curtiz directed the film and it had a budget of $5 million, which was fairly generous in 1954. The set for the throne room of the pharaoh alone cost $85,000. Some of *The Egyptian*'s sets would be reused in DeMille's *Ten Commandments*. Some critics interpret the film as a Cold War allegory but since the film follows the main plot points of Waltari's novel, that assertion seems unlikely. The film skips quickly over Sinuhe's travels outside of Egypt. It also gives the Hittite discovery of iron weaponry greater significance than the novel. Finally, the depiction of the conflict between the followers of Akhenaten and those of the god Amun is depicted in far more Good versus Evil terms. *The Egyptian* was joined the next year by the film *Land of the Pharaohs* directed by Howard Hawks and starring the young and very sultry Joan Collins. *Land of the Pharaohs* is set during the reign of Khufu and concerns his conquests and the building of his Great Pyramid. He wants his tomb to be forever safe from violation. Captured Nubian slaves are ordered to build it. These Nubians, however, are white, not black, and their situation in Egypt appears to be more akin to that of the Hebrew slaves of the Bible and *The Ten Commandments*.[20]

The Egyptian and *Land of the Pharaohs* were fairly successful non-epic films. (Technically neither *The Egyptian* nor *Land of the Pharaohs* were biblical epics although both films contained significant biblical and Christian references.) Public interest in Egypt had spiked around the time the two films were released due to the accidental discovery of the solar boat of Khufu on the Giza plateau during the spring of 1954. As a consequence, ticket sales at the theatres for the two Egyptian-themed films received a boost. In *The Egyptian*, Sinuhe is a foundling set adrift in a reed boat in the same manner as Moses. Akhenaten's religion is a proto-monotheism and so a precursor of Judaism and Christianity. The followers of Akhenaten's god Aten are persecuted as the later early Christians would be persecuted. As was mentioned earlier, the Nubians of *Land of the Pharaohs* are sort of surrogate Hebrews, except the pharaoh lets them go home as a reward for building the Great Pyramid. The Nubians are also good people who are kind and show respect to others, unlike the way most of their Egyptian masters behave. In the 1950s such religious references would have attracted audiences, especially when contrasted with the likes of a scantily clad Joan Collins and other ancient decadence. However, high production costs and uncertainty about potential box-office revenues, for historical epics in general and Egyptian epics in particular, tend to discourage film-makers from a lot of films with Egyptian settings.[21]

Ancient Egypt has a history that stretches over almost 3,000 years, and other periods of that vast history besides the Exodus and Cleopatra have attracted the attention of various novelists. Three of Naguib Mahfouz's early novels dealt with ancient Egypt. *Khufu's Wisdom* appeared in 1939 and is set during the Old Kingdom era. It is a tale of succession disputes generated by Khufu's longevity but had surprisingly little to say about the building of the Great Pyramid. Mahfouz used the idea of Egyptian magic in the plot, which concerns a prophecy that Khufu will be succeeded by an unwelcome successor. The sixth dynasty of the Old Kingdom is the setting for *Rhadopis of Nubia* (1943). The protagonist of the title is the courtesan Rhadopis, who has attracted the amorous attentions of the Pharaoh Merenra (2287–2278 BC). Their love affair brings them into conflict with the Egyptian establishment in a way that anticipates that of Antony and Cleopatra by 2,000 years. Mahfouz's third ancient Egyptian novel, *Thebes at War* (1944), is a fictional account of the struggles by the Theban princes Kamose and Ahmose to overthrow the foreign Hyksos conquerors of Egypt.[22]

Two of the best-known and most popular writers of historical fiction about ancient Egypt are currently Wilbur Smith and Christian Jacq. Wilbur Smith is a prolific South African author with an international following. He has written many novels including an Egyptian series. The first novel in this currently five-book series is *River God* (1994). It is set during the Second Intermediate Period when the invasions of the Hyksos threatened Egypt's survival. In it, resistance to the Hyksos crumbles and many Egyptians flee to Nubia for refuge. Among them are the eunuch-slave Taita and his companions. Although the rulers of Egypt are irresolute in the face of the Hyksos threat, Taita and his friends are not. The second novel, *The Seventh Scroll* (1995), is a modern archaeological novel that deals with records left by the characters of *River God*. The direct sequel to *River God* is *Warlock* (2001) in which Taita has become a powerful sorcerer – Smith's plots presuppose the reality of magic. In *The Quest* (2007), Taita travels up the Nile to determine why the river is drying up and threatening Egypt with complete devastation. In the latest book, *Desert God*, Taita is in the service of Pharaoh Tamose in the fight against the Hyksos. Smith's novels are only loosely historical but they are enjoyable reads.[23]

The French writer Christian Jacq, in contrast to Smith, has a doctorate in Egyptology from the Sorbonne and has completely focused on Egypt in his fiction. He has produced seven series of novels about ancient Egypt or Egyptian themes in addition to a number of stand-alone novels and non-fiction books. His most popular series consists of five novels (1995–7) with Ramses II the Great as the protagonist. Jacq is a great admirer of Ramses. Another series is 'The Stone of Light', which appeared in English translation during 2000–2001, and is comprised of four novels focusing on the villagers of ancient Deir al-Madinah (or Medina) near the Valley of the Kings. These novels are heavily based on archaeological research into the lives of the inhabitants who decorated the royal tombs and fashioned some of the grave goods during the era of the Eighteenth, Nineteenth and Twentieth dynasties. Magical elements form part of the plots in this series. Interestingly, the cover art for these novels features the pyramids in the background even though Giza was hundreds of miles north of ancient Thebes and the royal tombs. But such are the expectations of the pyramids in popular culture. Jacq then turned to a third series, 'The Queen of Freedom'. It consists of a trilogy (English translation 2002–3) providing a fictionalized account of Queen Ahhotep, who was part of the Egyptian war of liberation against the Hyksos. She is thought to be the mother of the future pharaoh Ahmose. A fourth series appeared in 2004 called 'The Judge of Egypt'. It was another trilogy set during the reign of Ramses II.

Pazair, a young novice judge, and his friends discover a plot to overthrow the great pharaoh and thus work tirelessly to thwart the traitors. Moving back in time, Jacq's next series, 'The Mysteries at Osiris', is set during the reign of Senusret III (Sesostris) in the Twelfth Dynasty. Iker, an apprentice scribe, discovers that someone is trying to kill the sacred acacia tree at Abydos to disrupt the Osirian rituals that maintain pharaonic government in peace and prosperity. Once more, mystical aspects of Egyptian religion drive the plot. Four novels which appeared in English in 2005 detail Iker's efforts to save Egypt from ruin. Jacq's sixth series, 'The Vengeance of the Gods' (which consists of two books that appeared in English during 2007 and 2008), is set in 528 BC at the end of the Saite era and includes, again, a plot against the Egyptian government of the usurper Ahmose, but there is considerable authentic period detail. There is also danger of invasion by Cambyses, the ruler of the expanding Persian Empire. The protagonist is a young scribe named Kel. He and his friends, including a preternaturally intelligent donkey named North Wind, along with some supernatural interventions, try to stave off disaster over the course of two novels. Alas the Persians invade and Kel and friends flee to Nubia to mount a resistance. The composer Mozart is the protagonist of Jacq's seventh series. In this case, the eternal knowledge of Egypt has been preserved in secret by Egyptian priests. The keeper of the secrets in the last decades of the eighteenth century is Count Thamos of Thebes. Encountering the young Mozart, Thamos concludes that Mozart is the long-awaited Great Magician who will bring enlightenment to the world through Masonic rites and the power of music. Of course, dark forces oppose such enlightenment. The struggle between the forces of light and darkness proceeds through four novels culminating in the production of Mozart's *Magic Flute*. Meanwhile, Jacq has published a new series, *Les Enquêtes de Setna* (The Investigations of Setna), in France. Setna is a junior son of Ramses II who is conducting detective work for his father. In addition to these series, Jacq has also written a number of stand-alone novels set in ancient Egypt. Smith and Jacq are hardly alone in writing novels set in ancient Egypt, they are just among the more prolific and successful authors working in the genre. Among the others are Stephanie Thornton, whose *Daughter of the Gods* is a novel about the female pharaoh Hatshepsut, and Stephanie Dray, who has written three novels about Cleopatra's and Mark Antony's daughter Selene – *Lily of the Nile*, *Song of the Nile* and *Daughters of the Nile*. Clearly there is a continuing interest in the historical fiction set in ancient Egypt.[24]

Another popular variety of Egyptian-themed fiction is archaeological/occult thrillers. An early example of this genre in cinema is the film *Valley of the Kings* starring Robert Taylor. The film appeared in 1954, about the same time as *The Egyptian,* and benefited from the spike in popular interest in ancient Egypt resulting from the discovery of the solar boat of Khufu. The story of *Valley of the Kings* concerns Americans seeking archaeological proof for the biblical story of Joseph in Egypt. Their quest, however, threatens the ongoing plundering of secrets in the undiscovered tomb of Pharaoh Ra-Hotep (a fictional pharaoh) by grave robbers. It all turns out well, however, as Taylor's character finds Ra-Hotep's tombs, uncovers definitive proof for the Joseph story and gets the girl as well. In later versions of the plot, in which an archaeological discovery would prove or disprove the biblical account, it would more often be dark forces seeking to suppress the truth and threaten the archaeologists rather than greedy grave robbers.

The film *Sphinx* (1981) was adapted from a Robin Cook novel and had a very similar plot to *Valley of the Kings*. An archaeologist named Erica Baron (played by Lesley-Anne Down) comes across some intriguing antiquities in Egypt's black market. After much suspense, some mayhem and a few apparently supernatural happenings, it is revealed that the undiscovered tomb of Seti I is the source for the antiquities. An Egyptian family of tomb robbers discovered the tomb and had been plundering it little by little. No momentous religious or occult secret drives the plot of *Sphinx,* nor does a sphinx appear. The only secret is the wealth of the tomb of Seti I, which remained hidden under the tomb of Tutankhamun and was a far richer trove of grave goods. In fact, both *Valley of the Kings* and *Sphinx* are loosely based on a true story. During the late 1870s a series of royal artefacts had appeared on the illegal antiquities market. By 1881 Gaston Maspero (1846–1916), the new director of the Cairo Museum, realized something needed to be done. He assigned a recently arrived staff member to investigate undercover. Posing as a rich tourist, the museum staffer discovered that the culprits were the El-Rasul family and the village of Kurna. The village was a hive of tomb robbers who had been operating clandestinely for centuries. The El-Rasul family had discovered a cache of royal mummies and had been looting it for about six years. Under the supervision of Brugsch, what remained of the royal mummies were taken to the Cairo Museum and became part of its collection.[25]

The greatest of the archaeological thrillers with an Egyptian setting is, undoubtedly, *Raiders of the Lost Ark* (1981). Written by George Lucas, the story was directed by Steven Spielberg. It is set in 1936 and follows the intrepid archaeologist and university professor Indiana Jones, who is assigned by the United States government to locate and acquire the Ark of the Covenant before a Nazi expedition can find it. Hitler believes that possession of the Ark will make his armies invincible. The bulk of the film takes place in Egypt as one of the premises of the story is that the Ark was taken to Egypt by the Pharaoh Shishak. There it was placed in a chamber known as the Well of Souls located in the ancient city of Tanis. The Staff of Ra, with its special headpiece, is the key to locating the Well of Souls. The film features a lot of scenes in the streets of exotic Cairo and in an archaeological dig at the buried and mysterious city of Tanis. Of course, the Nazis lose in the end, but it takes some significant, divine intervention to achieve that result. Interestingly, *Raiders of the Lost Ark*'s premise that the Nazis were seeking to get possession of various sacred and magical artefacts is true. That Shishak captured the Ark during his invasion of the Kingdom of Judah, however, is only one of several theories concerning the fate of the lost Ark of the Covenant. Lucas made a good choice in setting his film in Egypt though, because the film would not have been as successful without this iconic location.

Other movies have employed elements of Egyptian-themed plots very effectively. One particularly entertaining film is *Young Sherlock Holmes* (1985), which imagines the childhood origins of the partnership between the expert sleuth Sherlock Holmes and John Watson, while its plot is based on themes inspired by Egyptomania. Holmes and Watson meet in a London boarding school where a series of deaths occur. Holmes suspects, correctly, that the victims have been murdered. The men who were killed were all involved in building a luxury hotel in Cairo. During the course of the hotel's construction, the men discover a buried pyramid and some tombs – the sanctuary of the heretical Rame-Tep sect of the worshippers of Osiris. Local adherents attempt to forcefully stop construction but British troops brutally suppress them. The son and daughter of villagers killed in the uprising swear revenge and create a Rame-Tep cult in London. They meet at a wooden pyramid, a temple, concealed in a Wapping warehouse and engage in rituals involving human sacrifice. This also explains the growing number of missing young women in the area. It's a case of a sinister cult being desecrated in Egypt and seeking revenge in London.

Stargate (1994) is a film based on premises from alternative Egyptomania, which is not surprising since the director Roland Emmerich has made a career of making films based on theories from fringe history and pseudo-science. In this film's history, in 1928 archaeologists discovered a gigantic metallic ring engraved with mysterious symbols. The extended cut of the film includes a glimpse of a petrified jackal-headed figure buried with the ring. In 1994 the ring has been dated to 10,000 BC and is thought to be some sort of advanced technology. The United States government has brought together some Egyptologists to translate the figures on the mysterious ring and figure out how to use it. The ring, it turns out, is a stargate that creates wormholes, which allow instantaneous travel to other worlds. The researchers also discover that technologically advanced extraterrestrials had visited the earth in prehistoric times and enslaved humankind. The humans considered the extraterrestrials to be gods but eventually they rose up in revolt, drove out the aliens, threw down the stargate and buried it. These alien overlords were the gods worshipped by the ancient Egyptians. The animal heads on the gods of Egypt were protective helmets used by the alien soldiers. An exploring party goes through the stargate to discover another world where the alien oppressors have not been overthrown. An alien ruler, Ra, returns periodically to collect the materials mined by the enslaved people and visit other abuses on them. The Americans also find out that the pyramids were actually a landing platform for a pyramid-shaped alien spacecraft. The aliens also possess a resurrection machine that looks like a sarcophagus and the implication is that such a machine was the model for the Egyptian sarcophagi. It is an imaginative use of the theories of Erich von Däniken, which helped him make one of his comebacks in popular culture. The film also spawned a television series, *Stargate SG1*, which had a ten-season run from 1997 to 2007. *Stargate SG1* inspired two more live-action series – *Stargate Atlantis* and *Stargate Universe* – along with the animated series *Stargate Infinity*.

Combining Egyptomania with fringe history and science fiction has proven successful, but this is not always the case. Despite the popularity of the *Stargate* concept, two planned sequels to the original film have never been made. *Prisoners of the Sun*, another attempt to exploit the premise of ancient aliens oppressing the ancient Egyptians, was produced in 2006 but was not released until 2013 and went straight to DVD. According to *Prisoners of the Sun*, aliens known as the Osiris civilized the Egyptians but also enslaved them. The humans rebelled, defeated the Osiris and imprisoned them beneath a great underground pyramid. Archaeologists are excavating the site when clandestine cultists arrive who want to resurrect the Osiris. After various deadly adventures and close-calls, the archaeologists save the world.

Luc Besson's film *The Fifth Element* (1997) took a somewhat different approach. Every 5,000 years, a great evil appears in the universe and threatens to bring existence to an end. It can only be defeated by a combination of elements: the four classic elements – earth, air, fire and water – and a fifth element in the form of a human being. The fifth element was stored in an ancient Egyptian temple for safe keeping by an alien race called the

Mondoshawans. They come to Earth in 1914 to collect the fifth element just as archaeologists are investigating the temple. It is a great shock to the archaeologists, although one of their workers is a priest of a secret cult that has remained in communication with the Mondoshawans. Once again, Egyptian monuments are used by ancient aliens as storehouses for secret knowledge with potentially universe-shattering implications.

When archaeological thrillers take the form of novels, they generally involve occult knowledge that some want to find and others want to remain hidden, or else there is a discovery of some religious truth that would help one group but would damage the interests of another. The plots can take a variety of forms. Anthony O'Neill's *The Empire of Eternity* (2006) posits that a Chamber of Eternity exists within the pyramid complex at Giza. It contains a hieroglyphic code that reveals secrets that can foretell the future, explain the meaning of life and confer immortality. This, apparently, is what Napoleon was really after when he invaded Egypt. Queen Victoria would become interested in the legend of the Chamber, too. Tom Martin's *Pyramid* (2007) brings in a lot of ideas from alternative history, such as the quest for ancient super-knowledge located in Egypt. The super-knowledge, however, originated with an ice-age super-civilization located in Antarctica that was devastated by the shift of the Earth's crusts (which Charles Hapgood theorized about in the 1950s and 1960s). The novel also brings in the idea of the Giza power plant. Trying to get their hands on the super-knowledge is a shadowy elite seeking to rule the world, an apocalyptic sect seeking the end the world, and a crazy Russian. James Rollin's thriller *Map of Bones* is the story of a conflict over the control of ancient super-knowledge with connections to Alexander the Great. It utilizes several plot elements common to the fiction of Egyptomania: the myth that Alexander was actually the son of the wizard/pharaoh Nectanebo and that he supposedly spent ten years collecting ancient Egyptian knowledge, a fact unknown to ancient writers; and that the Library of Alexandria was supposed to be a great repository of ancient super-knowledge. The emperor Septimius Severus closed the tomb of Alexander to the public and sealed up the body with books from the great library in a vault located under the Lighthouse of Alexandria.

The Buried Pyramid by Jane Lindskold (2004) is set during the 1870s or 1880s. The gentleman-archaeologist Neville Hawthorne has been seeking the lost tomb of the Pharaoh Neferankhotep, which is located in a buried pyramid in the desert. He is travelling with his tomboy American niece along with some friends and a rival treasure-hunter. There is also trouble from an ancient sect dedicated to protecting the buried pyramid. They find the pyramid but they also find the old Egyptian gods incarnate. It is a far-fetched scenario, reminiscent of H. Rider Haggard's short story 'Smith and the Pharaohs', that reinforces the mythic Egypt of Egyptomania. Valerio Massimo Manfredi's *Pharaoh* was published in Italy in 1998 and appeared in English translation in 2008. In the story, amid all the religious and nationalistic animosity that keeps the Middle East in turmoil, the tomb of Moses is discovered in the Sinai desert. It initially appears that Moses' burial shows that he remained faithful to the gods of Egypt at his death. Such a finding would badly undermine the foundations of Judaism, Christianity and Islam with incalculable results. A lot of powerful people do not want this information getting out to the public. In the end, however, it turns out that Moses died faithful to the God of his ancestor Abraham. Just as there was no sphinx in *Sphinx*, there was no pharaoh in *Pharaoh*, although that did not prevent the publisher from using the iconic image of Tutankhamun's golden mask on the cover of the paperback.

Grappling with the biblical account of the origins of Judaism, and by extension Christianity and Islam, is a perennial subject for archaeological thrillers. Matt Bondurant's *The Third Translation* (2005) is set in London during 1997. Walter Rothschild is a contract researcher on a term appointment with the British Museum to translate the enigmatic Stela of Paser. His work gets him involved with some rather bizarre people seeking to revive Akhenaten's Atenist religion. In *The Exodus Quest* by Will Adams (2008) an archaeologist working with a fundamentalist preacher comes across intriguing information in a Dead Sea Scroll about an ancient Jewish sect. The trail leads to the heretic Pharaoh Akhenaten and his capital Amarna and connects to the Hebrew Exodus from Egypt. Adam Palmer covers the same ground in his *The Moses Legacy* (2011). On the other hand, Scott Mariani's *The Heretic's Treasure* (2009) shifts the goal from priceless knowledge to a priceless treasure belonging to Akhenaten that has been hidden in the desert. Egyptologists and greedy treasure-hunters battle for possession of the much sought-after treasure. The Egyptian desert is full of lost treasure, it seems, as Paul Sussman's *The Lost Army of Cambyses* (2002) also shows.

Egyptomania meets Steampunk in George Mann's *The Osiris Ritual* (2010). Once again Egyptian magic and advanced technology drive the plot. Various people are seeking the heretical Osiris Ritual which is supposed to prolong life. Perhaps the best of these Egyptomania novels are those of William Dietrich, who has created a series of thrillers featuring Ethan Gage, a ne'er-do-well American former student of Benjamin Franklin. In the first two novels, *Napoleon's Pyramids* (2007) and *The Rosetta Key* (2008), Gage joins Napoleon's invasion of Egypt as one of the savants. Gage has to flee France because he won a mysterious medallion in a card game and some sinister people want it back. Once he arrives in Egypt, the mysteries mount up and adventures ensue in secret chambers under the pyramids, explorations beneath the Temple Mount in Jerusalem and an encounter with the Rosetta Stone. Templar secrets, Egyptian magic and Masonic machinations abound as Dietrich weaves real history and the theories of alternate history into some highly entertaining novels. Dietrich's Egypt is a land of mystery, exoticism and adventure. These novels have plots that are a cross-section of legendary and mythical themes present in the archaeological thrillers that form part of the fiction of Egyptomania.

Mummymania fiction could be considered part of the archaeological/ occult thriller genre of fiction with Egyptian settings, but in fact it is really quite distinct. The focus of mummy fiction is the mummy, or at least the revived or resurrected corpse, whether it is in the form of a mummy or an unwrapped cadaver. Scholars of mummy fiction from its nineteenth-century origins onwards have determined that these stories are frequently about conflicts between the East and the West. Either British or American citizens encounter evil in the form of ancient Egyptian dead, in Egypt itself or in England or the United States. The evil dead seek vengeance on the desecrators of their tombs but in most cases they ultimately suffer defeat at the hands of the intrepid British or American protagonists. Mummy films are said to reflect a fear of the Other, whether that fear stems from religious, cultural or racial differences. From the middle of the nineteenth century, mummy fiction also reflected the desire and anxieties of imperialism, at least for British writers. Imperialist mummy fiction reflected both the desire to dominate and to acquire the exotic, and the guilt that such desires created in the would-be colonialists. It is also permeated by an atmosphere of threat or menace.[26]

Unlike other genres of the fiction of Egyptomania, mummy fiction tends to appear more in the medium of film rather than the novel. Mummy films became a part of the genre of horror films that arose at the beginning of the 1930s, when iconic monsters such as Frankenstein and Dracula became the leading creatures of classic Hollywood horror. A lumbering but relentless ambulatory mummy seeking vengeance became another such iconic monster. Interestingly, the mummy of the first classic film, *The Mummy* of 1932, was not that sort of monster at all. It is erroneously thought that mummy fiction arose out of the discovery of the tomb of Tutankhamun and the resulting sensationalism of the supposed mummy's curse. But as has been discussed in earlier chapters, mummy fiction had its origins in the early years of the nineteenth century. Initially resurrected mummies were portrayed as relatively benign, by writers such as Jane Webb Loudon and

Edgar Allan Poe, although Bram Stoker's evil Tara in his novel *Jewel of the Seven Stars* along with the ambulatory mummy of Arthur Conan Doyle's story 'Lot No. 49' were exceptions. Starting with *The Mummy* of 1932, screen mummies became much more sinister and threatening.[27]

The Mummy did not even start out featuring a mummy. Universal Studio's *Frankenstein* and *Dracula* films had been very successful the previous year. The studio hoped to continue the momentum with another popular horror film and they also wanted a film that would properly showcase the actor Boris Karloff. One suggestion was to make a film about the enigmatic Masonic charlatan Cagliostro (the eighteenth-century occultist Giuseppe Balsamo). The writer Nina Wilcox Putnam produced a screenplay titled 'Cagliostro' in February 1932. The title character was an ancient Egyptian priest who used an elixir to keep himself alive for 3,000 years, all the while slaughtering any woman who reminded him of the lover who had left him heartbroken in his original life. In effect, it was a rather morbid story about eternal vengeance misplaced against innocent victims. Another screenwriter did some minor revisions to the script to add a slightly more Egyptian flavour. Thus far, still, there was no mummy in the story. Then John Balderston, a veteran writer, was brought in to revise the script. As a newspaper journalist he had reported on the discovery of Tutankhamun's tomb and was quite knowledgeable about ancient Egypt and archaeology. The title of the script was changed to 'Im-Ho-Tep' and a lot more Egyptian elements were added, including a mummy. Instead of being the story of a vengeful spurned lover, Balderston's story is about the quest to be reunited with a lost love through reincarnation. Balderston was working on a script for *She* at the same time, which was also a story about eternal love over the centuries and reincarnation. Balderston's screenplay drew on the themes and motifs of nineteenth-century mummy literature, including the short stories of Arthur Conan Doyle, while the curse associated with Tutankhamun provided some indirect influences. *The Mummy*, unlike the films *Dracula* and *Frankenstein*, did not have its origin in one readily identifiable literary work. What it added was the idea of the mummy's curse falling with grim and implacable consequences on anyone who desecrated the mummy's tomb.[28]

Although *The Mummy* of 1932 is considered to be the archetypal mummy movie, it is rather different from its sequels. In the prologue, the film talks of a Scroll of Thoth that contained the magic spell which allowed Isis to raise Osiris from the dead. The story begins in 1921 with an archaeological expedition of scholars from the British Museum finding a mummy which had not had its viscera removed. The mummy was that of Imhotep, a priest of the sun at Karnak, who was buried alive for the sacrilege of attempting to bring the Egyptian princess he loves back from the dead. Accompanying the mummy was a mysterious sealed box that had terrible curses on it to protect against anyone opening it. An occult scholar, Dr Muller, urges the archaeologists not to open the box. Unfortunately a young archaeologist named Ralph Norton does not heed this advice. Upon opening it, he begins to read the scroll inside. He recites one of the spells, awakening the mummy. The mummy takes the scroll and drives Norton to madness.

Years later, in 1932, a second expedition comes to Egypt. It fails to discover anything significant when the revived mummy Imhotep, calling himself Ardif Bey, approaches the archaeologists and reveals to them the location of the tomb of the princess Ankhsenamun, which has lain undisturbed for 3,700 years. The contents of the tomb are taken to the Cairo Museum where Imhotep plans to use them to raise the mummy of his long-lost love from the dead. It turns out that a young woman named Helen Grosvenor, who is half British and half Egyptian, is the reincarnation of Ankhsenamun. Imhotep wants to use the Scroll of Thoth to allow Ankhsenamun's soul to enter Helen's body. The archaeologists try to stop him but what really saves Helen is when she appeals to the goddess Isis for help. Isis destroys the Scroll and Imhotep crumbles to dust. The fact is that Imhotep was cursed and anyone who disturbed his grave was also cursed. The curse, however, is not what kills people in *The Mummy*. They die because they get in the way of Imhotep's plan to revive Ankhsenamun. *The Mummy* is a story of love persisting across the centuries, made possible by magic and reincarnation. Imhotep was not evil so much as obsessed – an obsession that caused him to look for love in all the wrong places.

The Mummy was not a historically and archaeologically authentic film. It did contain plenty of Egyptianized sets and content, and that was sufficient to satisfy the desires of Egyptomania. The advertising for the film included the note: 'This picture is highly recommended and endorsed by the Rosicrucian Order (AMORC) which recommends that all members in this community attend this unusual picture.' The purpose of the film was to tell a good story rather than be historically accurate or proselytizing. The film was a success in the theatres, and it also had a great impact on popular culture in the form of sequels and remakes, all of which have promoted the myths of Egyptomania.[29]

Universal Studios made four other low-budget Mummy films: *The Mummy's Hand* (1940), *The Mummy's Tomb* (1942), *The Mummy's Ghost* (1944) and *The Mummy's Curse* (1945). These films are not sequels to *The*

Mummy. Instead, they present a new story. These mummy films featured a wrapped and mute mummy that shambled around choking anyone who had the misfortune to be too slow to avoid his grasp – a significant contrast to the sinister but tragic Imhotep of the original film. American archaeologists prior to the First World War discover and excavate the tomb of the Princess Ananka. This arouses the wrath of her lover Kharis, who was mummified with her, and the cult that protects her tomb. The Americans foil Kharis and the cult and take Ananka's sarcophagus to the United States. *The Mummy's Tomb* takes place thirty years later in Mapleton, a town in New England where Ananka's mummy is in the possession of the local museum. A cultist and Kharis arrive and proceed to kill the people who desecrated Ananka's tomb. Kharis is caught in a burning house and is supposedly consumed by the fire. In *The Mummy's Ghost*, a new cultist revives Kharis and they attempt to steal Ananka's body. They also discover a young Egyptian woman who turns out to be a reincarnation of Ananka. Kharis kidnaps her and an angry posse of townspeople pursue him into a swamp where he and the Egyptian girl are swallowed up by quicksand. That is still not the end of Kharis, who reappears in *The Mummy's Curse*. The swamp is drained and yet another cultist revives Kharis and Ananka. This time Kharis and the cultist plan to return Ananka to Egypt. They use an abandoned monastery for their base of operations. In a final confrontation, however, the cultist and Kharis are buried as part of the monastery collapses. Ananka returns to a mummified state and everyone else lives happily ever after. Of course, the way is open for Kharis to make a comeback from under all that rubble in the ruined monastery, but another sequel was never made. The film critic Leslie Halliwell has pointed out that mummy films were not a major cycle of theatrical films. Most female viewers disliked mummy movies but they were great favourites of young boys. They also became great fodder for late-night horror movie shows and Halloween horror film marathons.[30]

After a gap of about fifteen years, the British studio Hammer Films revived the subgenre in 1959. The first to appear was *The Mummy* (1959) starring Peter Cushing and Christopher Lee. It is a remake of *The Mummy's Hand* and *The Mummy's Tomb* rather than the original film. The Hammer film uses the characters and plots of the two Universal films but shifts the timeframe to 1895–8 and the location to Britain from the United States. Kharis the priest supervises the burial of Ananka and then tries to revive her, but is caught red-handed and buried alive. It has an informative ancient Egyptian segment with lots of detail on religious rituals and magic. Hammer's next two mummy films were *The Curse of the Mummy's Tomb* (1964) and *The Mummy's Shroud* (1967). They are, respectively, set in 1900 and 1920. In both films archaeologists discover a tomb, remove the burial artefacts to England and then face the relentless wrath of the guardian mummy. Like the four earlier Universal films, the first three Hammer films were full of mummy mayhem but otherwise were very pedestrian horror films. They exuberantly projected the message that the consequence of desecrating a tomb was the wrath of a vengeful mummy. As Peter Cushing's character John Banning described his feelings about the recently excavated tomb of Ananka: 'I have never worked in a place with such an aura of menace. There's something evil in there.'[31]

Hammer's fourth mummy film, *Blood from the Mummy's Tomb* (1971), was in a class by itself. The movie was an adaptation of Bram Stoker's novel *Jewel of the Seven Stars*. The previous wrapped mummy villains were replaced by a beautiful but bloodthirsty and malevolent Egyptian princess. The setting of the story is updated from the late Victorian era to the present of 1971. *Blood from the Mummy's Tomb* broadly follows the plot of Stoker's novel. An archaeologist named Julian Fuchs has the sarcophagus of an evil Egyptian princess named Tera, in the basement of his house along with a lot of other Egyptian paraphernalia. He also has a beautiful daughter Margaret, who it turns out is Tera reincarnated. Corbeck, one of his archaeologist colleagues, wants to use a resurrection spell on Tera, while Fuchs does not. All the archaeologists who excavated Tera's tomb are fearful of the curse that resides on it, but in fact, what – or rather, who – they need to fear is Tera herself. The film culminates in a struggle over the resurrection of Tera in which everyone dies except Margaret, who wakes up in the hospital bandaged like a mummy. But is the survivor Margaret or Tera? The problem for Hammer was that gothic horror films including mummy movies went out of fashion soon after the release of *Blood from the Mummy's Tomb*, so a sequel was never made and audiences were never given answers.

Remakes of *Jewel of the Seven Stars* did not go out of fashion. Another film adaptation titled *The Awakening* appeared in 1980. Charleton Heston starred as the archaeologist Matthew Corbeck, who discovers the tomb of Queen Kara. His daughter Margaret is born at the same time as the discovery of Kara's tomb and is a reincarnation of the queen. Most of the film's action is set in Egypt. Again the spirit of Kara is attempting to resurrect herself through Margaret. A struggle occurs between Kara and Matthew Corbeck, which ends with Kara fully resurrected in Margaret's body. Stoker's novel was adapted for film for a third time as *Bram Stoker's Legend of the Mummy* (1997), set in modern America. Unfortunately a low budget blunted the film's quality. Low budgets have generally been the fate of mummy films, but the scholar David Huckvale has suggested that financial constraints often have benefited mummy films since it compels them to focus on generating anxiety and fear in more imaginatively eerie ways rather than awing the audience with spectacle. Fred Olen Ray's *The Tomb* (1986) tells an entertaining story that is scary and campy at the same time. An archaeologist has robbed a tomb and taken the artefacts back to the United States to sell them. But he has also awoken the mummy of an Egyptian princess named Nefratis. She pursues the archaeologist to recover her possessions and to inflict gruesome punishments on the thief and the purchasers of her property.[32]

It was during the time after the demise of the gothic horror film that Anne Rice, who had achieved great success in the realm of vampire fiction, wrote one of the few modern novels featuring a mummy: *The Mummy or Ramses the Damned* (1989). Pharaoh Ramses II, during his conquests, comes across an elixir that confers immortality. At various intervals of his long life, he is interred in a tomb. Deprived of sunlight, he lapses into a state of suspended animation and becomes cadaver-like. In ancient times, he was periodically revived to advise various Egyptian monarchs, most recently and notably Cleopatra. Returning to his tomb, Ramses remains undisturbed until the Edwardian era when an archaeologist disinters him. Ramses the mummy is handsome and highly intelligent. He is not a mere bandaged and shambling killing machine. Instead, he views the modern world in the detached and critical manner of someone from an ancient civilization. Various social commentaries ensue. While Ramses is not a bloodthirsty mummy, he revives the deceased Cleopatra, who turns out to be a serial killer without a conscience. Ramses then faces the dilemma of possessing eternal life in a world of mortal humans with a homicidal Cleopatra. The novel leaves open the possibility of a sequel (which has never been written). Rice's Ramses is very much in the tradition of Jane Webb Loudon's mummy Khufu and Edgar Allan Poe's Allamistakeo. Unlike her vampires, Rice's *The Mummy* did not become a cultural phenomenon despite its connection to Egyptomania.[33]

The mummy film finally got its chance with a budget fit for an epic with the remake of *The Mummy* in 1999. The film was initially planned to be a low-budget thriller but Universal was eventually persuaded to increase their spending to $80 million. The story also changed as the budget increased. The original concept was for the film to be a dark and brooding horror, but it ended up an Indiana Jones-style adventure with thrilling and comedic elements intertwined. Thanks to a very healthy budget, the film's sets and the Egyptian elements are sumptuous. It is a great feast of the iconography of Egyptomania. Although the film contains authentic elements from

Egyptology, ultimately the film is a morass of historical and geographical errors. Viewers looking for a history lesson will be disappointed (anyone looking for a history lesson in this type of movie has to be a little delusional). It is meant to be fun and light entertainment. On that level it is successful. The heroic characters are very likeable and Brendan Fraser and Rachel Weisz possess great chemistry as a couple. The film turned out to be a great financial success and grossed over $400 million worldwide. Its success spawned two sequels, a prequel and an animated series, and even a roller coaster ride at Universal Studios in Orlando, Florida.

The plot of the film is very loosely based on *The Mummy* of 1932. Once again the mummy of the title is Imhotep, a priest. His love interest is Anck-Su-Namun but she is also the wife of Pharaoh Seti I. Caught committing adultery by Seti, the ruthless lovers murder him, but the pharaoh's guards discover the crime. Imhotep flees and Anck-Su-Namun commits suicide in the hope that Imhotep will resurrect her. Imhotep and his loyal priests spirit her body to the desert Necropolis of Hamunaptra for the resurrection ceremony, but the Pharaoh's guards, the Medjay, arrive and stop the sacrilege. Imhotep's loyal priests are buried alive along with Imhotep, who has terrible curses placed upon him. The Medjay then set an eternal vigil on Hamunaptra, because if Imhotep is ever brought back from the dead, he will possess terrible world-destroying powers. That, however, is what a motley crew of American and English adventurers inadvertently do during the early 1920s, resurrecting the supernaturally powerful Imhotep to dire results, although the villainous mummy is defeated in the end. But not defeated so as to preclude a sequel, *The Mummy Returns* (2001). Critics were generally lukewarm or even hostile towards the film's artistic merit but they often conceded that it was fun to watch. Certainly it had an impact on popular culture for a time. As the scholar Carter Lupton has sensibly observed, mummy films actually serve to promote a positive awareness of Egyptology among the public.[34]

Mummymania, like Egyptomania, has its ups and downs in terms of popularity. New mummy films continue to appear in the low-budget, independent world of film-making. One recent example is *Isis Rising: Curse of the Lady Mummy* (2012). Based on the Osiris/Isis legend, the film portrays the pair not as gods but mortals living in ancient Egypt and practising magic. The couple come into conflict with the evil Set, and Osiris is killed. Isis wants to resurrect him but Set kills her too. Thousands of years later, Egyptian artefacts go on display in a museum somewhere in urban America. College students are working on the project as well as smoking marijuana and fooling around. Unwittingly they resurrect Isis and one by one she slaughters people trapped in the museum with her. Isis is played by Priya Rai, an adult performer apparently seeking to become a mainstream actress. It is doubtful that *Isis Rising* will be her big break.

Writing before the success of *The Mummy* of 1999, Leslie Halliwell had observed that mummy films were not a hugely influential film genre. But mummies over the decades have appeared in the most out-of-the-way places and manners: the comedians Abbott and Costello made a movie with a mummy in 1955; the Three Stooges had two Egyptian adventures; the time-travelling alien of *Doctor Who*, in his Tom Baker persona, battled the evil Sutekh (Set), who was entombed in a prison on Mars in the excellent *Pyramids of Mars* episode of 1975. On a lower note, the film *Bubba Ho-Tep* (2002) imagines a mummy as a sort of Elvis impersonator, but despite the clever concept is a dire movie. Truly, *Evil Dead* star Bruce Campbell is a terrible performer to waste. Only time will tell if another blockbuster mummy film will ever be made again. What is certain is that Egyptomania is embedded enough in Western popular culture that new mummy films or television shows will continue to appear, big budget or not.[35]

Mysteries and Egyptomania

Mystery novelists often set their books in exotic locations and Egypt is, of course, a prime location for exoticism. Since Egypt is a land of mystery, that makes it a great place to set a mystery novel. Some Egyptian mysteries dwell on the magic or occult aspects of ancient Egypt; its lost treasures, hidden knowledge and secrets form important elements of the story. They may be the motive, or the weapon of murder or the means of solving the mystery. The chronological settings of Egyptian mysteries can be ancient Egypt or the modern era from the nineteenth century onwards.[36]

Mysteries with Egyptian settings generally fall into just a few categories: there are tourist mysteries, which almost invariably have modern settings; tales where somebody gets murdered in Egypt and the protagonist needs to find the killer, as in Agatha Christie's *Death on the Nile*; archaeological mysteries that are also set in the modern era, often in the nineteenth century when pioneering discoveries were being made and rules concerning antiquities were very lax – these novels will also sometimes bring in aspects of the occult or secret knowledge – and finally there are mysteries set in Egypt of the ancient world. Ancient Egypt was a land with some 3,000 years of history, so there are myriad potential events and characters to use as source material for fiction. The problem is that intimate details about the lives of many pharaohs are scarce. As a result, ancient Egyptian mysteries frequently cluster around the era of Akhenaten and Tutankhamun or the reign of the female pharaoh Hatshepsut. The intrigue, deaths and disappearances among the royals of these eras readily lend themselves to speculative plots for mystery novels. Only a few mysteries have settings that are scattered across the rest of Egypt's long history.

Agatha Christie wrote *Death on the Nile* in 1937. The central mystery involves a young woman murdered on a Nile cruise that includes Hercule Poirot among its passengers. The indefatigable detective manages to ferret out the killers before the end of the cruise. It has been commented that *Death on the Nile*'s Egyptian setting was merely incidental, as the plot of the novel would have worked in any setting which kept a small group of people in close and enforced proximity. This is not a particularly fair judgement because Christie's characters make authentic observations about touring Egypt and express awe at the monuments of the pharaohs. One scene takes place among the ruins of Abu Simbel while the passengers are on an excursion. Christie set many of her novels in places she had visited during her travels and she often used the device of an enclosed and isolated group setting in many of her plots, including her most famous novels *And Then There Were None* (1939) and *Murder on the Orient Express* (1934). Christie married her second husband, Sir Max Mallowan, in 1930. He was an archaeologist but not an Egyptologist, specializing instead in the history of the Middle East. Christie accompanied him on some of his digs and wrote other novels with archaeological settings – *Murder in Mesopotamia* (1936), *Appointment with Death* (1938) and *They Came to Baghdad* (1951). She even set one of her mysteries, *Death Comes as the End* (1944), in 2000 BC, right before the beginning of the Middle Kingdom period of ancient Egypt. It has good historical detail and its plot involves a family dispute over inheritance. The same plot, however, would have worked just as well in a wealthy family's country house.[37]

Other mystery writers have followed Christie's lead and written novels with a tour of Egypt as the setting. Joan Hess's *Mummy Dearest* (2008) is part of her Claire Malloy series, which are normally set in fictional Farberville, Arkansas, which in reality is Fayetteville. Malloy owns a bookshop in Farberville and solves mysteries on the side. She has just married the police detective Peter Rosen and they choose to honeymoon in Luxor, Egypt. Of course, they encounter murder, antiquities, thieves, terrorists and academic envy. The novel is a pleasant read but despite the title no mummies are encountered. In fact, the protagonists do not get near the pyramids since their travels are limited to Luxor and Abu Simbel and points in-between. Another mystery about tourists in modern Egypt is *Death on*

Tour by Janice Hamrick (2011), which involves a series of murders on a package tour in Egypt prior to the fall of the country's former president Hosni Mubarak. The heroine is Jocelyn Shore, a recently divorced high school teacher from Texas, who has splurged on a dream holiday to Egypt with her cousin Kyla. Instead of a peaceful holiday, Jocelyn gets involved in discovering who committed the murders. Once again antiquities smuggling is involved and forms part of the motive for the murders. Like Hess's book, *Death on Tour* does a good job of describing the experience of visiting Egypt on a guided tour. It also earned Hamrick a first crime novel award from the Mystery Writers of America.

Other mystery series with historical settings have also included stops in Egypt on their protagonist's itineraries. Three of these series are set in ancient Rome. The first series to appear was the creation of the British writer Lindsey Davis, featuring the detective Marcus Didius Falco. He works in Rome, sometimes as an informer for Emperor Vespasian. The first novel in the series was *The Silver Pigs* (1989). Falco's adventures have taken him all over the Roman Empire but it was not until *Alexandria* (2009), the nineteenth book in the series, that Falco makes it to Egypt. Once he gets there, he has a full Alexandrian experience with adventures in both the legendary Library and the Pharos, the great Lighthouse, as well as a near fatal encounter with a Nile crocodile. The American writer John Maddox Roberts began his Roman series the year after Davis with the appearance of *SPQR* (1990). Decius Caecilius Metellus the younger is a patrician and a sometime detective living during the era of the Roman civil wars leading up to the triumphs of Caesar and then Augustus. There are thirteen novels in the series and Decius makes it to Egypt in the fourth, *The Temple of the Muses* (1999), where he investigates the death of a scholar working at the Alexandrian Library. Later, in the ninth novel *The Princess and the Pirates* (2005), Decius encounters a young Cleopatra, but in Cyprus not Egypt. Steven Saylor, also an American writer, created a series known as *Roma Sub Rosa*. Its hero is Gordianus the Finder, a detective living and working in Rome. He is a contemporary of Decius but Gordianus is a mere plebeian who lives by his wits. In the first novel *Roman Blood* (1991) Gordianus works as an investigator for Cicero during the Roscius trial. *The Judgment of Caesar* (2004), the ninth novel in the series, is the first with an Egyptian setting. Gordianus and his family visit Egypt in 48 BC and become involved in the intrigues involving Caesar and Cleopatra. There is, in fact, an Egyptian connection present in the series from the very beginning because Bethesda, Gordianus's slave/mistress and later wife, is a Jewish Alexandrian. Gordianus met her in his youth while visiting Alexandria.

Saylor's most recent Gordianus novels are actually prequels to *Roman Blood*. *The Seven Wonders* (2007) and *Raiders of the Nile* (2009) are set in 90 BC and tell how Gordianus met Bethesda and of his other adventures in Egypt. All these authors of Roman mysteries carefully research the historical settings of their novels and those with Egyptian settings are no exception.[38]

Other historical novels about touring in Egypt are set in the modern era. Jane Jakeman's aristocratic amateur detective Lord Ambrose Malfine travels to Egypt in 1830 to rescue Lilian Westmorland in *The Egyptian Coffin* (1997). Lilian had travelled to Egypt for her health as so many people did during the nineteenth and early twentieth centuries, but in her case she encountered danger instead. *The Serpent and the Scorpion* (2008) by Clare Langley-Hawthorne includes a business trip to Egypt in March 1912 whereupon a murder occurs. The heroine, Ursula Marlow, returns to England and the nefarious happenings follow her there. Langley-Hawthorne provides an accurate depiction of Egyptian tourism on the eve of the First World War. Another interesting example of a mystery using a traveller in Egypt is *The Illusion of Murder* (2011) by Carol McCleary, the second of a series of novels in which the protagonist is the female journalist Nellie Bly during her famous journey around the world from 1889 to 1890. What these Egyptian tourism mysteries demonstrate is the attraction of ancient Egypt for novelists. Whether it is an ancient Roman sleuth or a modern amateur detective, many of them will visit Egypt during the course of their adventures. An Egyptian setting always enhances the plot of any mystery.

The mistress of mysteries using a setting in Egyptian archaeology is Elizabeth Peters, the pen name of Barbara Mertz (1927–2013). Mertz earned a PhD in Egyptology from the Oriental Institute of the University of Chicago in 1952. She then had a successful career as a novelist writing mostly mysteries. One of her earliest books was *The Jackal's Head* (1968), which was a thriller novel set in contemporary Egypt involving the theft of antiquities. She published another seven novels before returning to an Egyptian setting, which is about the same time that she began writing a couple of mystery series. *Crocodile on the Sandbank* (1975) marked the beginning of Mertz's successful Amelia Peabody series. Amelia is an independent-minded Englishwoman who has unexpectedly inherited a considerable fortune from her father. In 1884, besieged by suitors and relatives needing money, Amelia decided to travel. In Rome she meets and becomes friends with a young woman, Evelyn Barton Forbes. They decide to visit Egypt, where they encounter crime, experience adventure and fall in love with the Emerson brothers, Radcliffe and Walter – an Egyptologist and a philologist, respectively. Amelia also falls in love with Egyptology.

To a degree, Amelia Peabody's fictional life is very similar to the real life of the English novelist and Egyptologist Amelia Edwards. Evelyn Forbes ends up marrying Walter Emerson and Amelia later marries Radcliffe Emerson. Amelia and Radcliffe go on to have adventures and solve crimes for a total of nineteen novels (1975–2010). Their adventures span the years from 1884 to 1923 and they are involved in the discovery of Tutankhamun's tomb. The novels are full of accurate Egyptological lore and depictions of various people from the golden age of Egyptology. There is a continuous procession of witty dialogue and humorous situations while the characters are endearing. The real-life E. A. Wallis Budge is often the target of disparaging remarks by Radcliffe. Radcliffe is a sort of Professor Challenger figure while the relationship between him and Amelia is one of egalitarian give and take. It is very similar to the feisty relationship between Rick O'Connell (Brendan Fraser) and Evelyn Carnahan (Rachel Weisz) in the 1999 film *The Mummy*. Mertz in 1973 created another series with the heroine Vicky Bliss, a professor of art history. Bliss does not get involved with Egypt until the fifth and sixth novels in the series, *Night Train to Memphis* (1994) and *The Laughter of Dead Kings* (2008). Barbara Mertz writing as Elizabeth Peters has set a high standard for anyone daring to attempt an archaeological mystery set in the golden age of Egyptology.[39]

As stated earlier, historical mysteries set in ancient Egypt have tended to focus on either the reign of the female pharaoh Hatshepsut (1478–1458 BC) or the reigns of Akhenaten and Tutankhamun. The reign of Hatshepsut is full of fodder for mystery writers. As the great wife of Thutmose II and also his sister, she was aunt and a quasi-stepmother to his successor, the infant Thutmose III. She served as regent for her nephew but some scholars suggest that she tried to keep the throne for herself and a serious rivalry developed as Thutmose III grew older. Hatshepsut died relatively young, especially by modern standards, and the cause of her death was unstated in Egyptian records. That has led to speculation about foul play, although the discovery of what is likely her mummy indicates that she died from a combination of diabetes and bone cancer. Adding to the intrigue, Hatshepsut had a favourite minister, Senemut, who many suggested was also her paramour. Senemut also disappears sometime during the last few years of her reign. Whether he retired or died is not known but he was not buried in either of the tombs he prepared.

Akhenaten and Tutankhamun's reigns present similar murky happenings. Thutmose, Akhenaten's older brother and the crown prince, died before his father Amenhotep III. Akhenaten died in the seventeenth year of his reign but whether his death was due to natural causes is debated among scholars. The fate of his famously beautiful wife Nefertiti is unclear, as are the fates of another wife, Kiya, and his daughters Meritaten and Akhnesenamun. All sorts of speculations surround the death of the young king Tutanknamun. Each one of these provides a compelling basis for a murder mystery and writers have had no hesitation about exploiting these cloudy events for the sake of a good plot.

Anton Gill, a British writer of wide interests, brought out the first series of mystery novels dealing with events from the era of Akhenaten and his successors. His protagonist is Huy the Scribe, who had worked for Akhenaten's government and as a result of the defeat of the Aten cult is now in a very precarious position. No longer able to practise his trade as a scribe, he has become a proto-private detective in order to earn a living. *City of the Horizon* (1991) is the first novel and it concerns Huy's efforts to bring a group of tomb-robbers to justice in a case that includes shadowy involvement by the priests of Amun. In *City of Dreams* (1993), Huy takes on a serial killer of young women in Thebes. Finally he is asked to investigate the death of Tutankhamun in *City of the Dead* (1993). All three novels are good reads as well as being dark, atmospheric and characterized with accurate historical detail. One wishes that Gill would have continued his interest in ancient Egypt and written more Huy mysteries.[40]

Lauren Haney, whose real name is Betty Winkelman, set her mystery series in the reign of Hatshepsut. The first novel is *The Right Hand of Amon* (1997) and Haney's detective is Lieutenant Bak, an Egyptian stationed at the fortress of Buhen, which guards the second cataract of the Nile. Bak is an officer in the Medjay, the Nubian troops in the service of Egypt. He has to solve the murder of another Egyptian officer in the garrison. In all Haney wrote eight Bak mysteries between 1997 and 2003. The early novels concern crime and intrigue in or around Buhen. Later novels have Bak return to Thebes and other parts of Egypt where his investigations become entangled in court politics and plots. Haney is a fine writer and has a gift for describing landscapes and scenes. Her attention to historical detail is accurate and meticulous while her characters are well drawn. Sadly she has not written a new Bak novel since 2003.[41]

Another writer to use the Akhenaten and Tutankhamun era in mysteries is Lynda S. Robinson. She originally planned for an academic career, and earned a PhD in anthropology and archaeology. After tiring of the pursuit of an academic post, she took up writing under the name Suzanne Robinson. Her first published novel was a historical romance set in the reign of Tutankhamun named *Heart of the Falcon* (1990). In 1994 she began a series of mysteries set in ancient Egypt with the publication of *Murder in the Place of Anubis.* Lord Meren, the chief investigator for Tutankhamun, is the protagonist. Robinson ultimately wrote six novels in that series between 1994 and 2001 before returning to romance novels. They were well researched and written with likeable characters. Again, it is too bad that she abandoned Lord Meren (or too bad that her publisher did).[42]

Paul C. Doherty, a British writer, is also a history teacher and head-master. When he began writing historical mysteries set in ancient Egypt in 1998, he had already written over thirty mysteries, most which were set in medieval Britain. In his Egyptian mysteries he also has the distinction of setting his mysteries in both the reign of Hatshepsut and the era of Akhenaten and Tutankhamun. Doherty's first Egyptian mystery, *The Mask of Ra* (1998), is set during the reign of Hatshepsut, who Doherty calls Hatusu. His protagonist is Amerokte, the chief judge of the temple of Ma'at. Unlike in Haney's mysteries, Hatshepsut and the schemes and conspiracies of her court are the focus of Amerokte's investigations. Like the great majority of Doherty's novels, the mood of his Egyptian novels is dark and most of the characters are unpleasant and self-serving. Doherty also brings in fringe historical elements such as a nod to ancient aliens in Egypt. So far seven Amerokte mysteries have appeared, the last in 2008. It is unclear whether there will be more. Doherty has also written an Akhenaten trilogy – *An Evil Spirit Out of the West* (2003), *The Season of the Hyaena* (2005) and *The Year of the Cobra* (2006). The novels are told from the point of view of Mahu, a boyhood friend of Akhenaten's who later becomes chief of police for Amarna under the heretic pharaoh. The trilogy covers the years from the reigns of Amenhotep III through Akhenaten, Tutankhamun and Ay to the accession of Horemheb. There is an almost bewildering amount of conspiracies and betrayals. Doherty makes numerous allusions to the murky origins of Akhenaten's monotheism stemming from the family of Ay and Tiya, who are supposed to be descendants of Apiru nomads from the desert and Canaan. Other references predict a Moses-like messiah who will lead people to Canaan. The trilogy is detailed and accurate in its history although much is highly speculative. It is a tribute to the attraction of Egyptomania that of Doherty's occasional forays away from his medieval British settings, ancient Egypt is the time and place to have received the most attention.[43]

The latest person to write mysteries about ancient Egypt is Nick Drake, a British poet and novelist. He has written a trilogy set in ancient Egypt during the time of Akhenaten and Tutankhamun. In the first novel *Nefertiti: The Book of the Dead* (2006), it is year twelve of the reign of Akhenaten. His queen Nefertiti has disappeared. Rahotep, the youngest chief detective of the Thebes division of the Medjay, has been called in to find her. It is an almost impossible task since he is confronted by myriad hidden agendas, plots and conspiracies that the troubled reign of the heretic pharaoh Akhenaten has produced. And the kindly Akhenaten has given Rahotep a mere ten days to find Nefertiti or else he and his wife and three daughters will be executed for his failure. *Tutankhamun: The Book of Shadows* (2008) is the second book featuring Rahotep. Tutankhamun is about to become an adult but he faces opposition from his regent Ay and Horemheb, the chief general of the Egyptian armies. Threats and intrigue surround the young king. To make matters worse, a serial killer is operating in Thebes. Once again, Rahotep is called in to solve the problem. The third volume is *Egypt: The Book of Chaos* (2011). Ankhesenamun, the widowed queen of Tutankhamun, is surrounded by enemies. Her only hope is to secure a Hittite prince for her next husband and Rahotep is the envoy sent to broker the marriage alliance. Events in Thebes are further complicated by a ruthless and bloodthirsty opium-dealing gang stirring up unrest. Drake's trilogy covers a lot of the same ground as Doherty's but with less negativity. Rahotep is a likeable character and the novels are excellently researched and enjoyable reads.[44]

Leaving the familiar territories of Hatshepsut's reign and the Akhenaten era, Brad Geagley, an American writer and former entertainment industry executive, has chosen the setting of the reign of Rameses III for his mystery novels. Ancient documents show that Rameses III faced an assassination plot by members of his court and harem and that incident forms the plot of *The Year of the Hyenas* (2005). Authorities in Thebes assign the hard-drinking, maverick investigator Semerket to investigate the murder of an elderly priestess. They neither expect nor desire him to succeed. But the deeper he digs the wider the plot becomes. It is an entertaining mystery that Geagley has followed up with *Day of the False King* (2006), which takes Semerket on a mission to Babylon – a place suffering from its own intrigues.

This overview of films and novels with Egyptian settings is not exhaustive although it is fairly comprehensive. It is certain that some films, novels and authors have been overlooked. What this overview documents is the continuing fascination that Egypt exercises over popular culture in the West. It forms a part of Egyptomania that has been with us since the nineteenth century and it shows no signs of fading away.

POSTSCRIPT

I S EGYPTOMANIA ALIVE and well? That is a question that any author will frequently ask themselves when working on a subject such as this. As I finished the manuscript for this book during the summer and autumn of 2015, that question entered my mind on a regular basis. In fact, an examination of some events that took place during those months would indicate that the question itself can be answered with an assured yes.

May and June 2015 saw American Pharoah win the Triple Crown of horse racing. Although his name was unfortunately but permanently misspelled, the name harkened to the Egyptian descent of American Pharoah's owner Ahmed Zayat. As a further nod to Egyptomania, American Pharoah's sire was named Pioneerof the Nile (with 'pioneer of' written as one word). So, Egyptomania has arrived at the horse races.[1]

The summer of that same year was also marked by the debut broadcast of the three-episode miniseries *Tut*, which began airing on 19 July. It was a Canadian production that was filmed in Morocco and aired on the Spike Network. Ben Kingsley played the role of the priest Ay, otherwise the cast consisted of relative unknowns. Unlike other recent television or film adaptions with settings in ancient Egypt, *Tut* did not engender controversy over whether the ancient Egyptians were black or white. Its cast was quite multi-racial, with the black British actor Nonso Anozie appearing as the general and future pharaoh Horemheb. On the other hand, Tushratta, the king of Mitanni, is played by Steve Toussaint, another black British actor of Barbadian descent. Since the kingdom of Mitanni, located in what is now northwestern Iraq and northeastern Syria, was created and ruled by an Indo-Aryan people, that particular bit of casting was more politically correct than historically accurate. The same observation applies to Kylie Bunbury, an African American/Canadian actress, who plays the fictional character who is half Mitannian and half Egyptian and becomes the lover of Tut.

Of course, all this contact with Mitanni during the reign of Tutankhamun ignores the fact that the kingdom of Mitanni collapsed under the onslaughts of the Hittites and the Assyrians during the reign of Akhenaten. The mini-series garnered mostly negative reviews as a rather poor drama, whose history was either often wrong or mostly a fictionalized telling of Egypt's ancient past.[2]

Meanwhile the cable network HBO is getting ready to air another Egyptian series, *Pharaoh*, although the 'if' and 'when' remain uncertain. Ridley Scott is the director, but further details on the series are a bit vague; the basic premise is that aliens visited Earth during ancient times, and they were integral to the rise of the ancient civilizations such as Egypt. One presumes the series is set at the beginning of the pyramid age since the aliens show humans how to build pyramids. Otherwise, we don't know if the ancient aliens are benevolent or malevolent, cute or ghastly, friendly or hostile, but what little has been shown would indicate that malevolent, ghastly and hostile will be the approach taken. Another American show, the Fox Network series *Hieroglyph*, was supposed to air in 2015, but was cancelled prematurely in June 2014 with only one episode completed. It was set in a fictional Egypt and involved a non-historical pharaoh hiring a pardoned thief to acquire supernatural knowledge and sorcerers' equipment to help maintain his faltering rule over Egypt. Earlier than this attempt, in 2010, HBO had contemplated another series set in ancient Egypt, also titled *Pharaoh*. This series, to be directed by John Milius and based on the career of the conquering pharaoh Thutmose III, was intended to be a follow-up to the HBO series *Rome*. Instead Ridley Scott's *Pharaoh* will be a follow-up to *Stargate* with the hope that it will emulate the success of HBO's fantasy series *Game of Thrones*. It is unlikely that modern Egyptians will approve of the new *Pharaoh* since they find the suggestion that the pyramids were built by ancient Hebrews, ancient aliens or anyone else except the ancient Egyptians an offensive claim. Still, Egypt remains a perennial setting for costume dramas, particularly those with an emphasis on magic, mystery and otherworldliness.[3]

Ancient Egypt remains a popular topic for magazines devoted to history and archaeology as a survey of any well-stocked magazine rack will show. Hardly an issue of the venerable *Archaeology* magazine published by the Archaeological Institute of America appears without at least one article dealing with ancient Egypt. Besides the popular magazine *Kmt*'s focus on it, there is the British magazine *Ancient Egypt*, which is occasionally available in the magazine racks of American chain bookshops. *Biblical Archaeology Review* frequently publishes articles dealing with ancient Egypt: the July/

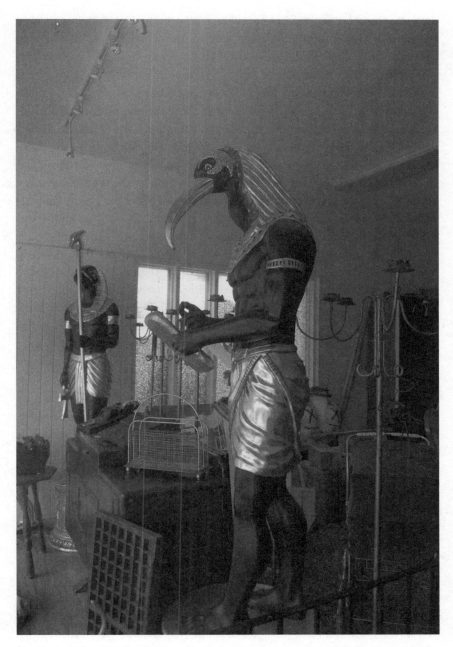

The Gods of Egypt in New Orleans: Thoth and Horus in an antique shop's window display.

August issue of 2015 featured a cover with a picture of Akhenaten with the caption 'The First Monotheist, Did he Influence Moses?' The actual title of the article is 'Did Akhenaten's Monotheism Influence Moses?', by the archaeologist Brian Fagan, who reviews current scholarship. In the realm of fringe scholarship, *Ancient American: Archaeology of the Americas Before Columbus* is a cornucopia of theories about the myriad ancient peoples who supposedly visited or settled in the pre-Columbian Americas. Of course, ancient Egyptians played a role in these alleged visitations. So volume XVIII, issue no. 106 raises the question on its cover, 'Egyptians in the Grand Canyon?', which is a teaser for a short article written by the *Ancient American* staff. As a bonus, another article – 'Evidence of Phoenicians in Ancient America' – stresses that many of the artefacts that the authors identify as Phoenician also have definite Egyptian stylistic elements and motifs.

Ancient Egypt also remains a constant topic of archaeological news headlines. Most recently, during August and September 2015 claims were made that the hitherto lost tomb of Nefertiti had been found. On 11 August *The Times* of London even featured the story 'Is Nefertiti in King Tut's Tomb too? A British Expert Claims to have Found Signs of a Secret Room behind a Hidden Door.' Claims to have discovered Nefertiti's tomb have been made a number of times before. What was unique about this supposed discovery was that the archaeological speculation places it by or under the tomb of Tutankhamun in previously undiscovered chambers. The Egyptologist Nicholas Reeves claims to have found evidence of two hidden chambers. Other archaeologists are sceptical but the Egyptian authorities are taking Reeves seriously enough that they have allowed radar scans to detect if the secret chambers actually exist. Preliminary results from the radar scans conducted in November were promising. A full report on the radar scans was announced by Egypt's minister of antiquities Mamdouh El Damaty in a press conference held on 11 March 2016. The report stated that radar had not only detected the existence of the chambers that Reeves predicted were there, but indicated that the rooms contained something within them. The readings from the scans are consistent with metal objects and organic material. Beyond that, it is impossible to say what is in those hidden chambers until they are opened. Meanwhile Reeves continues to assert that the chambers are a hidden tomb of Nefertiti. Given the history of Egyptological discovery, it is not all that outlandish that Reeves could be right. After all, Howard Carter was about the only person who believed that Tutankhamun's tomb was still waiting to be found. Perhaps Reeves will become the next Carter? If Nefertiti's tomb actually is found, it would also be a case of life imitating art: the film *Sphinx* of 1981 was based on the premise that the incredibly rich tomb of Pharaoh Seti I had been hidden under the tomb of Tutankhamun all along.[4]

Egyptomania even made an appearance in American politics when it was revealed that Ben Carson, a retired neurosurgeon and candidate for the Republican Party's 2016 presidential nomination, believes that the pyramids had been built by the biblical figure Joseph to store grain. During a speech made in 1998 at Andrews University, which is affiliated with the Seventh-day Adventist Church, Carson stated his belief that the pyramids were the granaries of Joseph. Asked by CBS News on 4 November 2015 if he still held that belief, he answered, categorically, 'Yes.' Carson cited the Bible as one of the foundations for his belief that the pyramids were used to store grain, although the Bible is silent on the topic of the pyramids. Furthermore, no chronology attempting to harmonize the biblical narrative with the accepted chronology of ancient Egypt places the time of Joseph in Egypt as earlier than the late Middle Kingdom period, some 600 to 900 years after the Pyramid Age during the Old Kingdom. An official of the Egyptian Antiquities Service, Mahmoud Affi, on 9 November 2015 scoffed at Carson's claims that the pyramids were granaries. He suggested that Carson was simply making sensationalistic statements to attract publicity. Who could think such a thing of an American political candidate![5]

I had a personal encounter with Egyptomania myself. On a trip to New Orleans with some friends from Great Britain on 27 May 2015 we were passing the shop Thibodeaux's on Carrollton Street in the Garden District. The shop's front window was an unexpected treasure trove of Egyptianized artefacts. There stood man-sized statues of both Horus and Thoth along with ottoman-sized sphinxes. I took some pictures while the owner politely inquired if I was interested in buying the statues. We had driven down in a rental car with no room for Egyptian gods, so I had to decline. There was also the dilemma of just where a person would put two six-foot tall statues of Egyptian gods in their house. Furthermore, what if some arcane Egyptian magical spell brought them back to life? But like the Houdini of H. P. Lovecraft, maybe I had been reading too much about the wild side of ancient Egypt.

The point of all this is that Egyptomania continues to be very much alive. It is an ongoing process that entertains and enlightens us, gets used commercially and occasionally politically, fascinates us and generates a profusion of cultural icons that never fail to grab our attention. Why Egypt is so attractive in popular culture remains something of a mystery, but its existence is undeniable.

REFERENCES

Introduction

1 Kurt Vonnegut, *Breakfast of Champions*, in *Novels and Stories, 1963–1973*, ed. Sidney Offit (New York, 2011), p. 587.
2 Jean-Marcel Humbert, Michael Pantazzi and Christine Ziegler, *Egyptomania: Egypt in Western Art, 1730–1930* (Ottawa, 1994); Richard G. Carrott, *The Egyptian Revival: Its Sources, Monuments, and Meaning, 1808–1858* (Berkeley, CA, 1978); and James Stevens Curl, *The Egyptian Revival: Ancient Egypt as the Inspiration for Design Motifs in the West* (London, 2005).
3 Clifford Price and Jean-Marcel Humbert, 'Introduction: An Architecture Between Dream and Meaning', in *Imhotep Today: Egyptianizing Architecture*, ed. Jean-Marcel Humbert and Clifford Price (London, 2003), p. 1.
4 Michael Rice and Sally MacDonald, 'Introduction – Tea with a Mummy: The Consumer's View of Egypt's Immemorial Appeal', in *Consuming Ancient Egypt*, ed. Sally MacDonald and Michael Rice (London, 2003), p. 11; Jean Marcel Humbert, 'Egyptomania: A Current Concept from the Renaissance to Postmodernism', in *Egyptomania: Egypt in Western Art, 1730–1930* (Ottawa, 1994), p. 21; Dominic Montserrat, *Akhenaten: History, Fantasy and Ancient Egypt* (London, 2000), p. 8; Donald Malcolm Reid, *Whose Pharaohs? Archaeology, Museums, and Egyptian National Identify from Napoleon to World War I* (Berkeley, CA, 2002); Elliott Colla, *Conflicted Antiquities: Egyptology, Egyptomania, Egyptian Modernity* (Durham, NC, 2007); and Eric Hornung, *The Secret Lore of Egypt: Its Impact on the West* (Ithaca, NY, 2001), pp. 1–4.
5 Joyce Tyldesley, *Egypt: How a Lost Civilization was Rediscovered* (Berkeley, CA, 2005), p. 7; and Tim Schadla-Hall and Genny Morris, 'Ancient Egypt on the Small Screen: From Fact to Faction in the UK', in *Consuming Ancient Egypt*, p. 195.

6 See Brian A. Curran et al., *Obelisk: A History* (Cambridge, MA, 2009).

7 John Ray, *The Rosetta Stone and the Rebirth of Ancient Egypt* (Cambridge, MA, 2007), pp. 4–5.

8 'Tombs', in *The Encyclopedia of New York City*, ed. Kenneth T. Jackson (New Haven, CT, 1995), p. 1190; and Carrott, *The Egyptian Revival*, pp. 146–78.

9 Charlotte Booth, *The Myth of Ancient Egypt* (Stroud, Gloucestershire, 2011), p. 188; Humbert, 'Egyptomania', p. 25, and Hornung, *The Secret Lore of Egypt*, p. 169.

10 Alex Werner, 'Egypt in London: Public and Private Displays in the 19th Century Metropolis', in *Imhotep Today: Egyptianizing Architecture*, ed. Jean-Marcel Humbert and Clifford Price (London, 2003), pp. 95–100; Marie-Stephanie Delamaire, 'Searching for Egypt: Egypt in 19th Century American World Exhibitions', in *Imhotep Today*, pp. 123–34; Rice and MacDonald, 'Introduction – Tea with a Mummy', in *Consuming Ancient Egypt*, p. 7; Curl, *The Egyptian Revival*, p. 345; 'Crystal Palace' and 'Great Exhibition' in *The London Encyclopedia*, ed. Ben Weinreb and Christopher Hibbert, 2nd revd edn (London, 1995); E. L. Branchard, *Bradshaw's Guide Through London and its Environs* (London, 1861, facsimile repr., 2012), pp. 220–21; Jill Jonnes, *Eiffel's Tower: The Thrilling Story Behind Paris's Beloved Monument and the Extraordinary World's Fair that Introduced it* (New York, 2009), p. 156; *The Complete Letters of Vincent Van Gogh*, 3 vols (Greenwich, CT, 1958), vol. III, pp. 179–80; and Robert Muccigrosso, *Celebrating the New World: Chicago's Columbian Exposition of 1893* (Chicago, IL, 1993), pp. 165–8.

11 Timothy Champion, 'Beyond Egyptology: Egypt in 19th and 20th Century Archaeology and Anthropology', in *The Wisdom of Egypt: Changing Visions Through the Ages*, ed. Peter Ucko and Timothy Champion (London, 2003), pp. 167–8; Carrott, *Egyptian Revival*, pp. 47–50; Hornung, *Secret Lore of Egypt*, pp. 177–8; and Fawn M. Brodie, *No Man Knows My History: The Life of Joseph Smith the Mormon Prophet*, 2nd edn (New York, 1989), pp. 170–75 and 421–5. Paul C. Gutjahr, *The Book of Mormon: A Biography* (Princeton, NJ, 2012), pp. 62–3, 72, 81, and 203 discusses *The Pearl of Great Price* but fails to mention its origin and the controversy over mistranslation. For an excellent detailed study of nineteenth-century American Egyptomania, see Scott Trafton, *Egypt Land: Race and Nineteenth-century American Egyptomania* (Durham, NC, 2004). Although Trafton's study has a focus on race, he does not touch on the episode of Joseph Smith mistranslating the papyri.

12 Harper Lee, *To Kill a Mockingbird* (1960; repr. London, 1996), p. 66. This moment occurs in Chapter 7.

13 See 'Walk Like An Egyptian', www.wikipedia.com, for background on the song. For the lyrics, see www.lyricsfreak.com.

14 'Katy Perry Angers Muslims by Burning Allah Pendant in "Dark Horse" Video', *Daily News*, 26 February 2014, www.nydailynews.com.

15 Fekri A. Hassan, 'Selling Egypt: Encounters at the Khan el-Khalili', in *Consuming Egypt*, p. 111; Fayza Haikal, 'Egypt's Past Regenerated by its Own People', in *Consuming Egypt*, pp. 123 and 137–8; and Okasha El Daly, 'What do Tourists Learn of Egypt?', in *Consuming Egypt*, pp. 143 and 149.

16 Agatha Christie, *Death on the Nile* (1937; repr. London, 2001), p. 108.

17 Booth, *Myth of Ancient Egypt*, p. 202; Tyldesley, *Egypt Rediscovered*, p. 7; and Brian M. Fagan, *The Rape of the Nile: Tomb Robbers, Tourists, and Archaeologists in Egypt* (Wakefield, RI, 1992), p. 370.

18 Montserrat, *Akhenaten*, pp. 2–3.

19 Rice and MacDonald, 'Introduction', pp. 2 and 15–16.

20 Ibid., pp. 3, 5, and 11; and Booth, *Myth of Egypt*, pp. 14, 185 and 202. For concise and clear introductions to Jung's ideas see the entries 'Archetype', 'collective unconscious', 'myth', 'myth criticism' and 'mythopoeia' in Chris Baldick, *The Concise Oxford Dictionary of Literary Terms* (Oxford, 1990) and 'archetype', 'collective unconscious' and 'Jung, Carl Gustav' in David Macey, *The Penguin Dictionary of Critical Theory* (London, 2000).

21 Fagan, *Rape of the Nile*, p. 370; and Rice and MacDonald, 'Introduction', p. 1.

One: The Real Egypt

1 Diodorus, *Library of History*, trans. C. H. Oldfather (Cambridge, MA, 1933), vol. I, p. 159 (Book 1.44).

2 James Henry Breasted, *A History of Egypt: From the Earliest Times to the Persian Conquest* (1909; repr. New York, 1948), p. 11.

3 Herodotus, *The Landmark Herodotus: The Histories*, ed. Robert B. Strassler (New York, 2007), book 2, section 5, p. 118. All citations and quotations from Herodotus will be from the Landmark edition and will be hereafter cited as Herodotus, *Histories*.

4 Diodorus, *Library of History*, vol. I, p. 103 (Book 1.31.6).

5 *Manetho*, trans. W. G. Waddell (Cambridge, MA, 1980), pp. vii–xx; and Gerald P. Verbrugghe and John M. Wickersham, *Berossos and Manetho, Introduced and Translated: Native Traditions in Ancient Mesopotamia and Egypt* (Ann Arbor, MI, 1996), pp. 95–120.

6 For a good, jaunty but authoritative read about the history of ancient Egypt, Barbara Mertz, *Temples, Tombs, and Hieroglyphs: A Popular History of Ancient Egypt*, 2nd edn (New York, 2007) is a great choice. For in-depth scholarly books see *The Oxford History of Ancient Egypt*, ed. Ian Shaw (Oxford, 2000), hereafter referred to as OHAE, Toby Wilkinson, *The Rise and Fall of Ancient Egypt* (New York, 2010) and George Hart, *The Pharaohs* (London, 2010).

7 The dates used here and throughout this book are those found in OHAE.

8 Stan Hendrick and Pierre Vermeersch, 'Prehistory: From the Palaeolithic to the Badarian Culture (*c.* 700,000–4000 BC)', in OHAE, pp. 17–36.

9 Ibid., pp. 36–9; and Toby Wilkinson, *Genesis of the Pharaohs: Dramatic New Discoveries Rewrite the Origins of Ancient Egypt* (London, 2003).

10 Béatrix Midant-Reynes, 'The Naqada Period (*c.* 4000–3200 BC)', in OHAE, pp. 44–60.

11 Wilkinson, *Rise and Fall of Ancient Egypt*, pp. 40–41.

12 Kathryn A. Bard, 'The Emergence of the Egyptian State (*c.* 3200–2686 BC)', in OHAE, pp. 61–7; and Wilkinson, *Rise and Fall of Ancient Egypt*, Chapter 1.

13 Herodotus, *Histories*, book 2, sections 4 and 99; *Manetho*, trans. W. G. Waddell, pp. 27, 29, 31 and 33; and George Hart, *Pharaohs*, Chapter 1, 'The Beginning of Dynastic Egypt', pp. 3–9.

14 Bard, 'Emergence', pp. 67–88; and Hart, *Pharaohs*, Chapter 2, 'Successor Pharaohs of the First Dynasty', pp. 11–20 and Chapter 3, 'A Dark Age', pp. 21–6.

15 Jaromir Malek, 'The Old Kingdom (2686–2160 BC)', in OHAE, pp. 89–117; and Hart, *Pharaohs*, Chapter 4, 'The First Rulers of the Old Kingdom', pp. 27–36; Chapter 5, 'Khufu and the Great Pyramid', pp. 37–52; Chapter 6, 'Khafra's Great Sphinx', pp. 53–62; Chapter 7, 'The Advent of the Sun-Kings', pp. 63–80; Chapter 8, 'The End of the Old Kingdom', pp. 81–91; and Wilkinson, *Rise and Fall of Ancient Egypt*, chapters 2–4.

16 Herodotus, *Histories*, p. 175 (book 2.126).

17 Stephan Seidlmayer, 'The First Intermediate Period (*c.* 2160–2055 BC)', in OHAE, pp. 118–47; Wilkinson, *Rise and Fall of Ancient Egypt*, Chapter 5; and Hart, *Pharaohs*, Chapter 9, 'A Fragmented Egypt', pp. 93–8.

18 Gae Callender, 'The Middle Kingdom Renaissance (*c.* 2055–1650 BC)', in OHAE, pp. 148–83; Wilkinson, *Rise and Fall of Ancient Egypt*, chapters 7–8; and Hart, *Pharaohs*, Chapter 10, 'The Dawn of the Middle Kingdom', pp. 99–106; Chapter 11, 'An Era of Dynamic Pharaohs', pp. 107–20; Chapter 12, 'Splendour Lost', pp. 121–32.

19 OHAE, pp. 169 and 180–83.

20 Towards the end of the Sixth Dynasty a woman named Nitokris or Nitiqret is listed as a king by both the Turin king list, which dates from the Ramesside era of the New Kingdom, and by Manetho. But no Old Kingdom documents mention her.

21 Janine Bourriau, 'The Second Intermediate Period (*c.* 1650–1550 BC)', in OHAE, pp. 184–217; Wilkinson, *Rise and Fall of Ancient Egypt*, Chapter 9; Hart, *Pharaohs*, Chapter 13, 'Foreign Rule and the War of Liberation', pp. 133–51; and Donald B. Redford, *Egypt, Canaan, and Israel in Ancient Times* (Princeton, NJ, 1992), Chapter 5, 'The Hyksos in Egypt', pp. 98–122.

22 Betsy M. Bryan, 'The Eighteenth Dynasty before the Amarna Period (*c.* 1550–1352 BC)', in OHAE, pp. 218–71; Wilkinson, *Rise and Fall of Ancient Egypt*,

chapters 10–13; and Hart, *Pharaohs*, Chapter 14, 'The First Pharaohs of the New Kingdom', pp. 153–65; Chapter 15, 'The Rise of Hatshepsut', pp. 167–87; Chapter 16, 'Thutmoses III, the Empire Builder', pp. 189–206; Chapter 17, 'Confrontation and Diplomacy', pp 207–21; Chapter 18, 'Amenhotep, the "Dazzling Sun-disk"', pp. 223–36.

23 Jacobus van Dijk, 'The Amarna Period and the Later New Kingdom (*c.* 1352–1069 BC)', in OHAE, pp. 272–313; Wilkinson, *Rise and Fall of Ancient Egypt*, chapters 14–18; and Hart, *Pharaohs*, Chapter 19, 'The Revolutionary Akhenaten', pp. 237–64; and Chapter 20, 'Tutankhamun and the End of the New Kingdom', pp. 265–81; Chapter 21, 'A Return to Tradition', pp. 283–90; Chapter 22, 'A New Beginning', pp. 291–301; Chapter 23, 'Ramesses II', 'Wealthy in Years, Great of Victories' pp. 303–25; Chapter 24, 'Upholding the Kingdom', pp. 327–30; Chapter 25, 'The Path to Turmoil', pp. 331–6; Chapter 26, 'Ramesses III, Egypt's Last Warrior Pharaoh', pp. 337–49; Chapter 27, 'The Last Rulers of the New Kingdom', pp. 351–68; and Redford, *Egypt*, Chapter 9, 'The Coming of the Sea Peoples', pp. 241–56.

24 OHAE, pp. 292–302.

25 Redford, *Egypt*, pp. 245–50.

26 Ibid., pp. 250–56; and Wilkinson, *Rise and Fall of Ancient Egypt*, pp. 327–32.

27 Robert Drews, *The End of the Bronze Age: Changes in Warfare and the Catastrophe ca. 1200 BC* (Princton, NJ, 1993) and Eric H. Cline, *1171 BC: The Year Civilization Collapsed* (Princeton, NJ, 2014).

28 John Taylor, 'The Third Intermediate Period (1069–664 BC)', in OHAE, pp. 330–68; Wilkinson, *Rise and Fall of Ancient Egypt*, chapters 19–21; and Hart, *Pharaohs*, Chapter 28, 'Egypt Divided', pp. 369–87 and Chapter 29, 'The Black Pharaohs', pp. 389–401.

29 Alan B. Lloyd, 'The Late Period (664–332 BC)', in OHAE, pp. 369–94; Wilkinson, *Rise and Fall of Ancient Egypt*, Chapter 22; and Hart, *Pharaohs*, Chapter 30, 'The Saite Renaissance', pp. 403–17; Chapter 31, 'The Persian Domination', pp. 419–29; and Chapter 32, 'The Last Egyptian Pharaohs', pp. 431–43.

30 Alan B. Lloyd, 'The Ptolemaic Period (332–30 BC)', in OHAE, pp. 395–421; Wilkinson, *Rise and Fall of Ancient Egypt*, chapters 23 and 24; and Hart, *Pharaohs*, Chapter 33, 'Alexander the Great', pp. 445–62; Chapter 34, 'Egypt's Greek Kings', pp. 463–79; Chapter 35, 'The Later Ptolemies and Cleopatra VII', pp. 481–508.

31 James Romm, *The Ghost on the Throne: The Death of Alexander the Great and the War for Crown and Empire* (New York, 2011); and Robin Waterfield, *Dividing the Spoils: The War for Alexander's Empire* (Oxford, 2011).

32 Wilkinson, *Rise and Fall of Ancient Egypt*, pp. 444–64.

33 Ibid., pp. 465–82. A classic popular biography of Cleopatra is Ernle Bradford, *Cleopatra* (1971; repr. London, 2000). For an excellent recent biography see Stacy Schiff, *Cleopatra: A Life* (New York, 2010).

Two: Ancient Egyptomania: Hebrews, Pharaohs and Plagues

1 Strabo, *Geography*, trans. Duane W. Roller (Cambridge, 2014), p. 709 (book. 16.2.34).

2 Lionel Casson, *Travel in the Ancient World* (1974; repr. Baltimore, MD, 1994), p. 32, and Herodotus, *Histories*, book 3.139, in *The Landmark Herodotus: The Histories*, ed. Robert B. Strassler (New York, 2007), p. 271. Also see François Hartog, 'The Greeks as Egyptologists', in *Greeks and Barbarians*, ed. Thomas Harrison (New York, 2002), pp. 211–27.

3 Phiroze Vasunia, *The Gift of the Nile: Hellenizing Egypt from Aeschylus to Alexander* (Berkeley, CA, 2001), pp. 2–3 and 126.

4 William A. Ward, 'Egyptian Relations with Canaan', in *The Anchor Bible Dictionary*, ed. David Noel Freedman, 6 vols (New York, 1992), vol. II, pp. 399–408; and James K. Hoffmeier, 'Israel', in *The Oxford Encyclopedia of Ancient Egypt*, ed. Donald B. Redford, 3 vols (Oxford, 2001), vol. II, pp. 194–6.

5 Josephus, *The Antiquities of the Jews*, in *The Complete Works of Flavius Josephus*, trans. William Whiston (1850) (Green Forest, AR, 2008), Book 1, Chapter 8.

6 See James K. Hoffmeier, *Israel in Egypt: Evidence for the Authenticity of the Exodus Tradition* (New York, 1996), especially Chapter 3, 'Semites in Egypt: The First and Second Intermediate Periods', pp. 52–72.

7 Ian Shaw, *Ancient Egypt: A Very Short Introduction* (New York, 2004), pp. 16–19 and 35; Eric Cline, *Biblical Archaeology: A Very Brief Introduction* (New York, 2009), pp. 23 and 76; Eric Cline, *From Eden to Exile: Unraveling Mysteries of the Bible* (Washington, DC, 2007), Chapter 4, 'Moses and the Exodus'; Israel Finkelstein and Neil Asher Silberman, *The Bible Unearthed: Archaeology's New Vision of Ancient Israel and the Origins of its Sacred Texts* (New York, 2001), Chapter 2, 'Did the Exodus Happen?'; Manfred Görg, 'Exodus', in *The Oxford Encyclopedia of Ancient Egypt*, vol. I, pp. 489–90; K. A. Kitchen, 'The Exodus', in *The Anchor Bible Dictionary*, vol. II, pp. 701–3; Thomas B. Dozeman, *Commentary on Exodus* (Grand Rapids, MI, 2009), pp. 26–31; and Carol Meyers, *Exodus* (Cambridge, 2005), pp. 2–12.

8 Josephus, *Antiquities*, Book 2, Chapter 9.

9 Ibid and Exodus 1. Josephus claims that the midwives were Egyptians while the biblical account says that they were Hebrew women.

10 It has been pointed out that the narrative of the Ten Plagues of Egypt demonstrates a detailed knowledge of the Egyptian religion and its many gods. Scholars making this point go on to argue that such knowledge is good indirect evidence that the Exodus story has a basis in history and is not mere fabrication, along with much of the rest of the Old Testament, as the biblical Minimalists assert. See John D. Currid, *Ancient Egypt and the Old Testament* (Grand Rapids, MI, 1997), Chapter 6, 'An Exegetical and Historical Consideration of the Ten Plagues of Egypt', pp. 104–20; and Hoffmeier, *Israel in Egypt*, pp. 149–53.

11 Shaw, *Ancient Egypt*, p. 14; and Strabo, *Geography*, trans. Horace Leonard Jones and J. R. Sitlington Sterret, 8 vols (London, 1917–32), vol. VII, pp. 281 and 283, book 16.2.34 and 35 and vol. VIII, p. 153, book 17.2.5.

12 Jan Assmann, *Moses the Egyptian: The Memory of Egypt in Western Monotheism* (Cambridge, MA, 1997); and Bruce Feiler, *America's Prophet: Moses and the American Story* (New York, 2009).

13 The sources used to locate references to Egypt in the Bible are James Strong, *Strong's Exhaustive Concordance of the Bible* (Nashville, TN, 1986) and Centre Informatique et Bible, *A Concordance to the Apocrypha/Deuterrocanonical Books of the Revised Standard Version* (Grand Rapids, MI, 1983).

14 Cline, *Biblical Archaeology*, pp. 59–61.

15 Finkelstein and Silberman, *The Bible Unearthed* (New York, 2001); and Donald B. Redford, *Egypt, Canaan, and Israel in Ancient Times* (Princeton, NJ, 1992) are good examples of a moderate minimalism based on archaeological evidence.

16 Exodus 20:2; Leviticus 26:13; Deuteronomy 5:6 and 15, 6:12 and 21, 7:8, 8:14, 13:5 and 10; 15:15; 16:12; 24:18 and 22, and 26:6; Judges 6:8–13; Jeremiah 34:13; and Micah 6:4.

17 Norman C. Habel, *Jeremiah: Lamentations* (St Louis, MS, 1968), pp. 14–16.

18 Isaiah 19 and 20, 30:2–3, 31:1, 36:6 and 9; Jeremiah 36; Ezekiel 17:15 and 29–32.

19 Exodus 23:9; Leviticus 19:34; and Deuteronomy 10:19.

20 1 Kings 10:28–9; 2 Chronicles 1:16–17; and Tomoo Ishida, 'Solomon', in *The Anchor Bible Dictionary*, vol. VI, pp. 105–13.

21 Josephus, *Against Apion*, trans. William Whiston (1737), Book 1, sections 14 and 15.

Three: Classical Egyptomania: The Greeks and Romans

1 Heliodorus, *An Ethiopian Story*, in *Collected Ancient Greek Novels*, ed. B. P. Reardon (Berkeley, CA, 1989), p. 401.

2 Johann Gottfried von Herder, *Reflections on the Philosophy of the History of Mankind* (Chicago, IL, 1968), p. 158.

3 Ian Shaw, *Ancient Egypt: A Very Short Introduction* (Oxford, 2004), p. 12; Diodorus Siculus, *Library of History*, trans. C. H. Oldfather (Cambridge, MA, 1933), vol. I, pp. viii and xiii; and Plutarch, 'Isis and Osiris', in *Moralia*, trans. Frank Cole Babbitt (London, 1927 2004), vol. V, pp. 3 and 5.

4 Shaw, *Ancient Egypt*, p. 11; Gae Callender, 'The Middle Kingdom Renaissance', in *Oxford History of Ancient Egypt*, ed. Ian Shaw (Oxford, 2000) [OHAE], pp. 178 and 183; Janine Bourriau, 'The Second Intermediate Period', in OHAE, pp. 216–17; Betsy M. Bryan, 'The Eighteenth Dynasty before the Amarna Period', in OHAE, pp. 219–20, 242–3 and 268; and Homer, *The Odyssey*, trans. Samuel Butler (Chicago, IL, 1952), p. 204, book 4.483.

5 See Jenny March, *The Penguin Book of Classical Myths* (London, 2008); Robert Graves, *The Greek Myths* (London, 1955); and Edith Hamilton, *Mythology* (Boston, MA, 1940).

6 Eleanor Guralnick, 'The Egyptian–Greek Connection in the 8th to 6th Centuries BC: An Overview', in *Greeks and Barbarians: Essays on the Interactions of Greeks and Non-Greeks in Antiquity and the Consequences for Eurocentricism*, ed. John E. Coleman and Clark A. Walz (Bethesda, MD, 1997), pp. 127–54.

7 Stanley M. Burstein, 'Hecataeus, Herodotus, and the Birth of Greek Egyptology', in Stanley M. Burstein, *Graeco-Africana: Studies in the History of Greek Relations with Egypt and Nubia* (New Rochelle, NY, 1995), pp. 3–17; James Redfield, 'Herodotus the Tourist', in *Greeks and Barbarians*, ed. Thomas Harrison (New York, 2002), pp. 24–49; and Lionel Casson, *Travel in the Ancient World* (Baltimore, MD, 1994), pp. 95–111. Also see James Romm, *Herodotus* (New Haven, CT, 1998).

8 Stanley M. Burstein, 'Hecataeus of Abdera's History of Egypt', in *Graeco-Africana*, pp. 19–27, and 'Images of Egypt in Greek Historiography', in *Ancient Egyptian Literature: History and Forms*, ed. Antonio Loprieno (Leiden, 1996), pp. 591–604; Erik Hornung, *The Secret Lore of Egypt: Its Impact on the West* (Ithaca, NY, 2001), pp. 19–20. Also see John Ball, *Egypt in the Classical Geographers* (Cairo, 1942); Graham Shipley, *Pseudo-Skylax's Periplous: The Circumnavigation of the Inhabited World: Text, Translation and Commentary* (Exeter, 2011); and Frank E. Romer, *Pomponius Mela's Description of the World* (Ann Arbor, MI, 1998).

9 Diodorus, *Library of History*, vol. I, p. 97 (book 1.29).

10 Strabo, *Geography*, trans. Horace Leonard Jones and J. R. Sitlington Sterret, 8 vols (London, 1917–32), vol. VIII, pp. 15 (book 17, 1.4), 71 (book 17, 1.21), and 135 (book 17, 1.53). Pliny the Elder in his *Natural History*, trans. Harris Rackham, 10 vols (Cambridge, MA, 1939–63), vol. II, pp. 253 and 255 repeats some of the same observations.

11 Strabo, *Geography*, vol. VIII, pp. 9 and 11 (book 17, 1.3); Herodotus, *Histories*, in *The Landmark Herodotus: The Histories*, ed. Robert B. Strassler (New York, 2007), p. 123 (book 2.14) hereafter referred to as Herodotus, *Histories*; and Diodorus, *Library of History*, vol. I, pp. 103 (book 1.31) and 215 (book 1.63).

12 Herodotus, *Histories*, p. 118 (book 2.5); Strabo, *Geography*, vol. I, pp. 111 (book 1.2.23) and 131 (book 1.2.29); and Diodorus, *Library of History*, vol. I, p. 121 (book 1.36); and Seneca, *Natural Questions*, trans. Harry M. Hine (Chicago, IL, 2010), pp. 59–60.

13 Herodotus, *Histories*, pp. 121 (book 2.10) and 303 (book 4.40); and Diodorus, *Library of History*, vol. I, pp. 107 (book 1.32) and 123 (book 1.36).

14 Herodotus, *Histories*, p. 125 (book 2.19).

15 Diodorus, *Library of History*, vol. I, pp. 133–49 (book 1, 38–41); Strabo, *Geography*, vol. VIII, p. 17 (book 17.5); and Seneca, *Natural Questions*, pp. 57–64 (p. 64).

16 The classic accounts of the explorations of the Nile and its sources are Alan Moorehead's *The White Nile* (New York, 1960) and *The Blue Nile* (New York, 1962).

17 Herodotus, *Histories*, pp. 128–9 and 133 (books 2.28 and 34).

18 Stanley M. Burstein, 'Alexander, Callisthenes and the Sources of the Nile', in *Graeco-Africana*, pp. 63–76; Lucan, *Pharsalia: Dramatic Episodes of the Civil Wars* (Baltimore, MD, 1957), p. 230; Ammianus Marcellinus, *Roman History*, ed. J. C. Rolfe, 3 vols (Cambridge, MA, 1935–40), vol. II, p. 281 (book 15.3); and Pliny the Elder, *Natural History*, vol. II, pp. 257 and 259.

19 M. Cary and E. H. Warmington, *The Ancient Explorers* (Baltimore, MD, 1963), pp. 211–15; Derek A. Welsby and David W. Phillipson, *Empires of the Nile* (London, 2008), pp. 63–6; and Pliny the Elder, *Natural History*, vol. II, p. 473.

20 Herodotus, *Histories*, p. 153 (book 2.91); Strabo, *Geography*, vol. VIII, pp. 27 and 29 (book 17.1.6) and 69 (book 17.1.19); Diodorus, *Library of History*, vol. I, p. 235 (book 1.67); and Isocrates, 'Busiris', in *Works*, trans. George Norlin and LaRue Van Hook, 3 vols (London, 1928–9), vol. III, pp. 100–131. Also see Phiroze Vasunia, *The Gift of the Nile: Hellenizing Egypt from Aeschylus to Alexander* (Berkeley, CA, 2001), pp. 14 and 183.

21 Herodotus, *Histories*, pp. 117 (book 2.2) and 123 (book 2.15) and Ammianus Marcellinus, *Roman History*, vol. II, p. 279 (book 15.2).

22 Herodotus, *Histories*, pp. 118 (book 2.4), 159 (book 2.99–100), 172 and 174 (book 2.124) and 184 (book 2.142); Diodorus, *Library of History*, vol. I, pp. 33 and 35 (book 1.9), 73 (book 1.23), 157 (book 1.44), 159 (book 1.45), and 179, note 1; and Plutarch, 'Isis and Osiris', in *Moralia*, vol. V, p. 23.

23 Herodotus, *Histories*, pp. 133 (book 2.35), 146 (book 2.66) and 148 (book 2.69); Strabo, *Geography*, vol. VIII, p. 109 (book 17.1.40); Diodorus, *Library of History*, vol. I, pp. 285 and 287 (book 1.83); Ammianus Marcellinus, *Roman History*, vol. II, pp. 287 and 289 (book 15.15–24); and Seneca, *Natural Questions*, p. 60.

24 Herodotus, *Histories*, pp. 152–3 (book 2.82–90); Diodorus, *Library of History*, vol. I, pp. 309–19 (book 1.91–3); Geraldine Pinch, *Egyptian Myth: A Very Short Introduction* (Oxford, 2004), p. 116; and Ian Shaw, *Ancient Egypt: A Very Short Introduction* (Oxford, 2004), pp. 119 and 121–2. For a good account of modern obsessions with mummies see Heather Pringle, *The Mummy Congress: Science, Obsession, and the Everlasting Dead* (New York, 2001).

25 Herodotus, *Histories*, pp. 118 (book 2.4) and 141 (book 2.50); Diodorus, *Library of History*, vol. I, pp. 37 (book 1.11) and 55 (book 1.17); Plutarch, 'Isis and Osiris', in *Moralia*, vol. V, pp. 3, 11, 21, 25 and 35. For more on the cult of Isis among the Greeks and Romans see R. E. Witt, *Isis in the Ancient World* (London, 1971, repr. Baltimore, MD, 1997). Good introductions to Egyptian religion can be found in Rosalie David, *Religion and Magic in Ancient Egypt* (London, 2002) and Claude Traunecker, *The Gods of Egypt* (Ithaca, NY, 2001).

26 Herodotus, *Histories*, pp. 137 (book 2.37), 150 (book 2.77); Diodorus, *Library of History*, vol. I, pp. 241–7 (book 1.70–71) and 277 (book 1.80); and Strabo, *Geography*, vol. VIII, p. 135 (book 17.1.53).

27 Herodotus, *Histories*, pp. 118 (book 2.4) and 163 (book 2.109); Diodorus, *Library of History*, vol. I, pp. 175 and 177 (book 1.50), 239 and 242 (book 1.69) and 279 (book 1.81); Strabo, *Geography*, vol. VIII, p. 11 (book 17.1.3); and Vasunia, *Gift of the Nile*, p. 14 and Chapter 4, 'Writing Egyptian Writing', especially pp. 138 and 148.

28 Herodotus, *Histories*, p. 144 (book 2.58), 150 (book 2.77) and 172 (book 2.123); Diodorus, *Library of History*, vol. I, pp. 53 (book 1.15), 81 (book 1.25) and 239–42 (book 1.69); Strabo, *Geography*, vol. VIII, p. 11 (book 17.1.3); and Pliny the Elder, *Natural History*, vol. II, p. 271.

29 Herodotus, *Histories*, p. 133 (book 2.35).

30 Ibid., pp. 172 and 174 (book 2.124–5).

31 Ibid., pp. 174–8 (book 2.125–34).

32 Diodorus, *Library of History*, vol. I, pp. 215, 217, 219, 221 and 223 (book 1.63–4); and Strabo, *Geography*, vol. VIII, pp. 89, 91 and 93 (book 17.1.33).

33 Pliny the Elder, *Natural History*, vol. X, pp. 63 and 65; Pliny the Elder, *Natural History: A Selection*, trans. and intro John F. Healy (London, 1991), p. 352; Ammianus Marcellinus, *Roman History*, vol. II, pp. 293 and 295 (book 15.28 and 30); *Frontinus, The Stratagems and the Aqueducts of Rome*, trans. Charles E. Bennett and ed. Mary B. McElwain (London, 1925), pp. 357 and 359 (book 1.16); and *Frontinus, De Aquaeductu Urbis Romae*, ed. R. H. Rodgers (Cambridge, 2004), pp. 188–9.

34 Pliny the Elder, *Natural History: A Selection*, p. 352; and Paul Jordan, *Riddles of the Sphinx* (New York, 1998), pp. 14 and 22.

35 Herodotus, *Histories*, pp. 186–7 (book 2.148); Diodorus, *Library of History*, vol. I, pp. 221, 227 and 229 (book 1.60 and 66); Strabo, *Geography*, vol. VIII, pp. 103 and 105 (book 17.1.37); and Pliny the Elder, *Natural History*, vol. X, p. 67.

36 Herodotus, *Histories*, pp. 187–8 (book 2.149 and 150); Diodorus, *Library of History*, vol. I, pp. 181 and 183 (book 1.51); and Strabo, *Geography*, vol. VIII, p. 103 (book 17.1.37).

37 Homer, *The Iliad*, trans. Samuel Butler (1898), book 9, line 383.

38 Diodorus, *Library of History*, vol. I, pp. 49 and 51 (book 1.14); Strabo, *Geography*, vol. VIII, pp. 121, 123 and 125 (book 17.1.46); Pliny the Elder, *Natural History*, vol. X, p. 75; Ammianus Marcellinus, *The Later Roman Empire (AD 354–378)*, pp. 121–2 (book 3.4).

39 Pinch, *Egyptian Myth*, pp. 3 and 5–6; Brian A. Curran et al., *Obelisk: A History* (Cambridge, MA, 2009), pp. 13–33, passim for a good introduction to the religious, political and physical aspects of obelisks in ancient Egypt and pp. 35–59 on the Romans moving obelisks to Alexandria, Rome and Constantinople; Pliny the Elder, *Natural History*, vol. X, pp. 51, 55, 57 and 59; and Ammianus Marcellinus, *Roman History*, p. 122 (book 3.4).

40 Herodotus, *Histories*, pp. 192–3 (book 2.158); Diodorus, *Library of History*, vol. I, pp. 111 and 113 (book 1.33); Strabo, *Geography*, vol. VIII, p. 77 (book 17.1.25); and Pliny the Elder, *Natural History*, vol. II, pp. 461 and 463. For an excellent up-to-date account of what is known about the ancient and medieval canals connecting the Nile to the Red Sea, see John P. Cooper, *The Medieval Nile: Route, Navigation, and Landscape in Islamic Egypt* (Cairo, 2014), pp. 94–9 and 230–31.

41 James Romm, ed., *The Landmark Arrian: The Campaigns of Alexander* (New York, 2010), pp. 101–8; Pringle, *Mummy Congress*, pp. 134–5; Strabo, *Geography*, vol. VIII, pp. 35 and 37 (book 17.1.8); and Vasunia, *Gift of the Nile*, pp. 268–70. For an accessible and authoritative overview of the history and significance of Alexandria, see Justin Pollard and Howard Reid, *The Rise and Fall of Alexandria: Birthplace of the Modern Mind* (New York, 2006) and for a detailed and highly scholarly history see P. M. Fraser, *Ptolemaic Alexandria*, 3 vols (Oxford, 1972). For contemporary archaeological thriller novels involving Alexander the Great's tomb see James Rollins, *Map of Bones* (New York, 2005) and Will Adams, *The Alexander Cipher* (London, 2009).

42 Peter Clayton and Martin Price, eds, *The Seven Wonders of the Ancient World* (London, 1988), pp. 138–57; John and Elizabeth Romer, *The Seven Wonders of the World: A History of Modern Imagination* (New York, 1995), pp. 48–76; Strabo, *Geography*, vol. VIII, p. 25, 27, 31 and 35 (book 17.1.6–8); and Pliny the Elder, *Natural History: A Selection*, p. 353 (book 36.83); Ammianus Marcellinus, *Roman History*, vol. II, pp. 299, 303, 305 and 307 (book 16.7–10, 13, and 16–18); and Luciano Canfora, *The Vanished Library: A Wonder of the Ancient World* (Berkeley, CA, 1990).

43 Arrian, *Campaigns of Alexander*, pp. 104–6; Strabo, *Geography*, vol. VIII, pp. 63, 65, 87, and 113 (book 17.1.17, 31, and 43); Herodotus, *Histories*, p. 219 (book 3.26).

44 Shaw, *Ancient Egypt*, p. 34.

45 Pinch, *Egyptian Myth*, pp. 7–8; Plato, *Timaeus and Critias*, trans. Desmond Lee (London, 1971), p. 35; and Vasunia, *Gift of the Nile*, Chapter 6, 'Plato's Egyptian Story', pp. 216–47.

46 Diodorus, *Library of History*, vol. I, pp. 239, 327, 335 and 337 (book 1.69, 96 and 98); Strabo, *Geography*, vol. VIII, pp. 83 and 85 (book 17.1.29); Ammianus Marcellinus, *Roman History*, vol. II, pp. 307 and 309 (book 16.19–22); Pliny the Elder, *Natural History*, vol. VII, p. 145; Plutarch, 'Isis and Osiris', in *Moralia*, vol. V, pp. 25 and 27; and Mary R. Lefkowitz, 'Some Ancient Advocates of Greek Cultural Dependency', in *Greeks and Barbarians*, ed. John E. Coleman and Clark A. Walz (Bethesda, MD, 1997), pp. 237–53. For more details on Pythagoras in Egypt see Kitty Ferguson, *Pythagoras: His Lives and the Legacy of a Rational Universe* (London, 2010), pp. 18–24. On Homer as an Egyptian and son of Hermes Trismegistus see Hornung, *Secret Lore of Egypt*, pp. 22–3; and Heliodorus, 'An Ethiopian Story', in *Collected Ancient Greek Novels*, ed. B. P. Reardon (Berkeley, CA, 1989), p. 420, Book 3, section 14.

47 Vasunia, *Gift of the Nile*, Chapter 7, 'Alexander's Conquest and the Force of Tradition', pp. 248–88, especially p. 265.

48 Arrian, *Campaigns of Alexander*, pp. 101–2; Plutarch, 'Alexander', in *The Age of Alexander: Nine Greek Lives*, trans. Ian Scott-Kilvert (Harmondsworth, 1973), pp. 281–2; and Pollard and Reid, *The Rise and Fall of Alexandria*, pp. 1–4; and Stanley M. Burstein, 'Alexander in Egypt: Continuity or Change' and 'Pharaoh Alexander: A Scholarly Myth', in *Graeco-Africana*, pp. 43–52 and 53–61; and Vasunia, *Gift of the Nile*, p. 265.

49 Arrian, *Campaigns of Alexander*, pp. 104–6; and Plutarch, 'Alexander', in *The Age of Alexander*, pp. 282–4.

50 Julius Caesar, *The Civil War*, trans. Jane F. Gardner (Harmondsworth, 1985), pp. 160–64 and pp. 289–91; Lucan, *Phasalia*, p. 225; and Nicholas J. Saunders, *Alexander's Tomb: The Two Thousand Year Obsession to Find the Lost Conqueror* (New York, 2006), pp. 81–90.

51 Cassius Dio, *The Roman History: The Reign of Augustus*, trans. Ian Scott-Kilvert (London, 1987), pp. 67–78; and Suetonius, *The Twelve Caesars*, trans. Robert Graves (Harmondsworth, 1979), p. 63.

52 Pliny the Elder, *Natural History*, vol. III, pp. 129 and 131; and Suetonius, *The Twelve Caesars*, pp. 139–40, 153, 180, 222 and 268.

53 *Lives of the Later Caesars: The First Part of the 'Augustan History', with Newly Compiled Lives of Nerva and Trajan*, trans. Anthony Birley (London, 1976), p. 72; Saunders, *Alexander's Tomb*, pp. 83–5; and Elizabeth Speller, *Following Hadrian: A Second-century Journey Through the Roman Empire* (Oxford, 2003), which at various points provides details and speculations about Hadrian in Egypt.

54 Saunders, *Alexander's Tomb*, pp. 85–7; Anthony Birley, *Septimius Severus: The African Emperor* (London, 1971), pp. 201–21; and Hornung, *Secret Lore of Egypt*, pp. 59–60 .

55 Saunders, *Alexander's Tomb*, pp. 88–90; Herodian, *History of the Empire*, trans. C. R. Whittaker (Cambridge, MA, 1969), vol. I at chapters 8.7–8 and 9.1–8; Cassius Dio, *Dio's Roman History*, ed. G. P. Gould (London, 1982), vol. IX, book 79.7.1–4; and *Lives of the Later Caesars*, p. 310.

56 Sally-Ann Ashton, *Roman Egyptomania* (London, 2004); and James Stevens Curl, *The Egyptian Revival: Ancient Egypt as the Inspiration for Design Motifs in the West* (London, 2005), pp. xx–xxvi and chapters 1 and 2.

57 See Cul, *Egyptian Revival*, pp. 16–17 on Herodotus and Egyptian religion.

58 Witt, *Isis in the Ancient World*, pp. 11–58; Plutarch, 'Isis and Osiris', in *Moralia*, vol. V, pp. 3–191; Hornung, *Secret Lore of Egypt*, pp. 64–5; Edward Gibbon, *The History of the Decline and Fall of the Roman Empire* (London, 1995), vol. I, pp. 463–71 (Book 1, Chapter 15); Curl, *Egyptian Revival*, pp. 12–22 and 30–39; and Peter Green, *Alexander to Actium: The Historical Evolution of the Hellenistic Age* (Berkeley, CA, 1990), Chapter 33, 'Foreign and Mystery Cults, Oracles, Astrology, Magic', pp. 586–601.

59 Witt, *Isis in the Ancient World*, pp. 222–4; Cassius Dio, *Roman History*, p. 77; Juvenal, *The Sixteen Satires* (London, 1974), p. 281; Hornung, *Secret Lore of Egypt*, p. 25; and Christine Ziegler, 'From One Egyptomania to Another: The Legacy of Roman Antiquity', in *Egyptomania: Egypt in Western Art, 1730–1930* (Ottawa, 1994), pp. 15–16.

60 Witt, *Isis in the Ancient World*, pp. 224–42; Francesco Tiradritti, Sanaya Shaarrauy Lanfranchi and Mathaf al-Misri, *Isis: The Egyptian Goddess Who Conquered Rome* (Cairo, 1998); Curl, *Egyptian Revival*, pp. 44–73; and Ziegler, 'From One Egyptomania to Another', pp. 16–17.

61 Apuleius, *The Golden Ass* (Bloomington, IN, 1962), 'Book the Eleventh' with quotes at pp. 238 and 242; Hornung, *Secret Lore of Egypt*, p. 14.

62 Garth Fowden, *The Egyptian Hermes: A Historical Approach to the Late Pagan Mind* (1986; repr. Princeton, NJ, 1993) is the definitive study of Hermes Trismegistus and Hermetism in the ancient world. See Anthony Grafton, 'Protestant versus Prophet: Isaac Casaubon on Hermes Trismegistus', *Journal of the Warburg and Courtauld Institutes*, XLVI (1983), pp. 78–93 for the discrediting of the idea that the Hermetic texts originated in ancient Egypt.

63 St Augustine, *Concerning the City of God Against the Pagans*, trans. Henry Bettenson (London, 2003), pp. 330–37, Book 8, chapters 23 and 24; Florian Ebeling, *The Secret History of Hermes Trismegistus: Hermeticism from Ancient to Modern Times* (Ithaca, NY, 2007), pp. 38–44.

Four: Medieval Egyptomania: From St Augustine to the Renaissance

1 C.W.R.D. Moseley, ed. and trans., *The Travels of Sir John Mandeville* (London, 1983), p. 67.

2 St Augustine, *Concerning the City of God against the Pagans*, trans. Henry Bottenson (London, 2003), Book XVIII, chapters 3–5.

3 Ibid., chapters 37–40.

4 For good, brief discussions see Christopher Haas, 'Alexandria', and Maria Dzielska, 'Hypatia', in *Late Antiquity: A Guide to the Postclassical World*, ed. G. W. Bowersock, Peter Brown and Oleg Grabar (Cambridge, MA, 1999). For more detailed information see Christopher Haas, *Alexandria in Late Antiquity: Topography and Social Conflict* (Baltimore, MD, 1996) and Maria Dzielska, *Hypatia of Alexandria* (Cambridge, MA, 1995).

5 Hugh Kennedy, *The Prophet and the Age of the Caliphates: The Islamic Near East from the Sixth to the Eleventh Century* (London, 1986), pp. 64–6 for a brief overview of the Muslim conquest of Egypt. For the environmental background to the rise of Islam see David Keys, *Catastrophe: An Investigation into the Origins of the Modern World* (New York, 1999). William Rosen, *Justinian's Flea: Plague, Empire and the Birth of Europe* (New York, 2007) provides a synthesis of

environmental, political and military reasons for the problems of the Byzantine and Persian empires and the successes of Islam.

6   Hugh Kennedy, *The Great Arab Conquests: How the Spread of Islam Changed the World We Live In* (Philadelphia, PA, 2007), pp. 165–7.

7   Michael Cook, 'Pharaonic History in Medieval Egypt', *Studia Islamica*, LVII (1983), pp. 69–72 and 99–101; Ulrich Haarmann, 'Medieval Muslim Perceptions of Pharaonic Egypt', in *Ancient Egyptian Literature: History and Forms*, ed. Antonio Loprieno (Leiden, 1996), pp. 606–7; and Ulrich Haarmann, 'Islam and Ancient Egypt', in *The Oxford Encyclopedia of Ancient Egypt*, ed. Donald P. Redford, 3 vols (Oxford, 2001), vol. II, p. 191.

8   Haarmann, 'Medieval Muslim Perceptions of Pharaonic Egypt', p. 606; and Okasha El Daly, 'Ancient Egypt in Medieval Arabic Writings', in *The Wisdom of Egypt: Changing Visions Through the Ages*, ed. Peter Ucko and Timothy Champion (London, 2003), pp. 41–3.

9   Sāid al-Andalusī, *Science in the Medieval World: 'Book of the Categories of Nations'*, trans. and ed. Semaan L. Salem and Alok Kumar (Austin, TX, 1991), pp. 4, 10, and 35–7.

10 Ulrich Haarmann, 'In Quest of the Spectacular: Noble and Learned Visitors to the Pyramids around 1200 AD', in *Islamic Studies Presented to Charles J. Adams*, ed. Wael B. Hallaq and Donald P. Little (Leiden, 1991), p. 58; Haarmann, 'Medieval Muslim Perceptions of Pharaonic Egypt', pp. 623–4; Ulrich Haarmann, 'Regional Sentiment in Medieval Islamic Egypt', *Bulletin of the School of Oriental and African Studies*, XLIII (1980), pp. 56–7 and 66; Abd al-Latif al Baghdadi, *The Eastern Key: Kitab al-Ifadah Wa'l-I'Tibar of 'Abd al-Latif al-Baghdadi*, trans. Kamal Hafuth Zand, John A. and Ivy E. Videan (London, 1965), p. 159; and El Daly, 'Ancient Egypt in Medieval Arabic Writings', pp. 54–6.

11 *The Eastern Key*, pp. 107, 147 and 149; and the Ottoman traveller Evliya Celebi, quoted in Erik Hornung, *The Secret Lore of Egypt: Its Impact on the West* (Ithaca, NY, 2001), p. 189.

12 Haarmann, 'Medieval Muslim Perceptions of Pharaonic Egypt', p. 607; Haarmann, 'Regional Sentiments in Medieval Islamic Egypt', pp. 58–9; Cook, 'Pharaonic History in Medieval Egypt', p. 102; El Daly, 'Ancient Egypt in Medieval Arabic Writings', pp. 42–3; and quote from *The Eastern Key*, pp. 147–9.

13 Mas'ūdī, *From The Meadows of Gold*, trans. Paul Lunde and Caroline Stone (London, 2007), pp. 1–2 and 48, Mas'ūdī is sometimes referred to as the 'Arab Herodotus' and Jalāl Al-Dīn Al-S'ūyutī, 'The Treatise on the Egyptian Pyramids', ed. Leon Nemoy, *Isis*, XXX/1 (1939), pp. 2–37, quote at pp. 34–5.

14 Jalāl Al-Dīn Al-S'ūyutī, 'The Treatise on the Egyptian Pyramids', pp. 27, 32–4 and 36. The historian Al-S'ūyutī (1445–1505) includes extracts from several medieval Muslim scholars saying that time fears the pyramids in more or less the same words. It was clearly a popular proverb in the world of medieval Islam.

15 Al-S'ūyutī, 'Treatise on the Pyramids', in which Al-S'ūyutī compiles and summarizes earlier Arabic scholarship about the pyramids; A. Fodor, 'The Origins of the Arabic Legends of the Pyramids', *Acta orientalia academiae scientiarum*, XXIII/3 (1970), pp. 335–63, provides a comprehensive modern overview; Haarmann, 'Medieval Muslim Perceptions of Pharaonic Egypt', pp. 608–11; Cook, 'Pharaonic History in Medieval Egypt', pp. 86–7; Haarmann, 'In Quest of the Spectacular', pp. 62–3 and 65; John and Elizabeth Romer, *The Seven Wonders of the World: A History of the Modern Imagination* (New York, 1995), pp. 173–4; Hornung, *Secret Lore of Egypt*, p. 157; David Pingree, *The Thousands of Abu Ma'Shar* (London, 1968), pp. 5–6.

16 Haarman, 'In Quest of the Spectacular', p. 59; Haarmann, 'Medieval Muslim Perceptions of Pharaonic Egypt', p. 614; and Anne Wolfe, *How Many Miles to Babylon? Travels and Adventures to Egypt and Beyond, 1300 to 1640* (Liverpool, 2003), pp. 168, 178 and 181.

17 Al-S'ūyutī, 'Treatise on the Egyptian Pyramids', pp. 22–3, provides a good example of this belief.

18 Haarmann, 'Medieval Muslim Perceptions of Pharaonic Egypt', pp. 615 and 622; Haarmann, 'In Quest of the Spectacular', p. 66; Okasha El Daly, *Egyptology: The Missing Millennium: Ancient Egypt in Medieval Arabic Writings* (London, 2005), Chapter 3, 'Treasure Hunting', pp. 31–44; and *The Eastern Key*, pp. 115, 117, 161 and 163.

19 Al-S'ūyutī, 'Treatise on the Egyptian Pyramids', p. 29.

20 Haarmann, 'Medieval Muslim Perceptions of Pharaonic Egypt', p. 612; *The Eastern Key*, pp. 123, 125, 129, 133, 137, 141, 143 and 155; El Daly, 'Ancient Egypt in Medieval Arabic Writings', pp. 54–6 and 62; and El Daly, *Egyptology*, pp. 173–6.

21 Charles Burnett, 'Images of Ancient Egypt in the Latin Middle Ages', in *The Wisdom of Egypt*, pp. 65, 72–4 and 83; Hornung, *Secret Lore of Egypt*, p. 78; and Erik Iversen, *The Myth of Egypt and its Hieroglyphs in European Tradition* (Princeton, NJ, 1993), pp. 58–9.

22 Burnett, 'Images of Ancient Egypt in the Latin Middle Ages', pp. 70–72, 75–6, 78–9 and 84–9; Harry Bober, 'The Eclipse of the Pyramids in the Middle Ages', in *Pyramidal Influence in Art* (Dayton, OH, 1980), pp. 13–16; and Hornung, *Secret Lore of Egypt*, p. 76.

23 Burnett, 'Images of Ancient Egypt in the Latin Middle Ages', pp. 65–6, 68, and 84–9, and O.G.S. Crawford, 'Some Medieval Theories about the Nile', *Geographical Journal*, CXIV (July–September 1949), pp. 6–23. For accurate and readable accounts of the explorations of the Blue and White Niles see Christopher Hibbert, *Africa Explored: Europeans in the Dark Continent, 1769–1889* (New York, 1982), chapters 1 and 8; Alan Moorehead, *The White Nile* (New York, 1960), chapters 1–7; and Alan Moorehead, *The Blue Nile* (New York, 1962), chapters 2 and 3.

24 Richard Brilliant, 'Pyramids in the Classical World of Greece', in *Pyramidal Influence in Art*, p. 2; Bober, 'The Eclipse of the Pyramids in the Middle Ages', pp. 6 and 12; and Romer, *Seven Wonders*, pp. 183, 189 and 191.

25 Bober, 'The Eclipse of the Pyramids in the Middle Ages', pp. 8–11; Gregory of Tours, *The History of the Franks*, trans. Lewis Thorpe (Harmondsworth, 1974), pp. 74–5, book I, section 10; Iverson, *Myth of Egypt*, p. 59; and Romer, *Seven Wonders*, pp. 184–6 and 188.

26 Bober, 'Eclipse of the Pyramids in the Middle Ages', p. 6; Burnett, 'Images of Ancient Egypt in the Latin Middle Ages', p. 69; Hornung, *Secret Lore of Egypt*, pp. 155–6; and Sir John Mandeville, *The Travels of Sir John Mandeville*, pp. 66–7.

27 Burnett, 'Images of Ancient Egypt in the Latin Middle Ages', pp. 68–70; Haarmann, 'In Search of the Spectacular', p. 57; Hornung, *Secret Lore of Egypt*, pp. 92–3; Jean de Joinville and Geffroy de Villehardouin, *Chronicles of the Crusades*, trans. M.R.B. Shaw (Harmondsworth 1963); and Romer, *Seven Wonders*, p. 186.

28 Brian B. Copenhaver, 'Hermeticism', in *Encyclopedia of the Renaissance*, ed. Paul F. Grendler (New York, 1999), vol. III, pp. 142–5; Brian P. Copenhaver, 'Hermes Trismegistus and Hermeticism', in *The Classical Tradition*, ed. Anthony Grafton, Glenn W. Most and Salvatore Settis (Cambridge, MA, 2010), pp. 430–32; and Brian P. Copenhaver, 'Introduction', in *Hermetica*, trans. and ed. Brian P. Copenhaver (Cambridge, 1992), pp. xiii–xl.

29 Jan Assmann, 'Introduction', pp. ix–xii, 35–6, 105 and 107; and Iverson, *Myth of Egypt*, p. 46.

30 Assmann, 'Introduction', p. ix and pp. 3–7, 21–5, and 27–9, and Hornung, *Secret Lore of Egypt*, pp. 17–18, 48–53 and 80–81.

31 Ebeling, *Secret History*, pp. 7–12 and 30–31.

32 Frances A. Yates, *Giordano Bruno and the Hermetic Tradition (*1964; repr. Chicago, IL, 1991), pp. 6–12; Ebeling, *Secret History*, pp. 38–44; and Hornung, *Secret Lore of Egypt*, pp. 53 and 78. Also see St Augustine, *The City of God*, Book VIII, chapter 23.

33 Cook, 'Pharaonic History', pp. 78–9, 93 and 95–6; El Daly, 'Ancient Egypt in Medieval Arabic Writings', pp. 52–3; A. Fodor, 'The Origins of the Arabic Legends of the Pyramids', *Acta orientalia academiae scientiarum hungaricae*, XXXIII/3 (1970), p. 345; Hornung, *Secret Lore of Egypt*, p. 82; Ebeling, *Secret History*, pp. 45–51; and Charles S. F. Burnett, 'The Legend of the Three Hermes and Abu Ma'shar's Kitab Al-Uluf in the Latin Middle Ages,', *Journal of the Warburg and Courtauld Institutes*, XXXIX (1976), pp. 231–2. For a more detailed study see Kevin van Bladel, *The Arabic Hermes: From Pagan Sage to Prophet of Science* (Oxford, 2009).

34 Burnett, 'Images of Ancient Egypt in the Latin Middle Ages', pp. 81 and 89–91; Ebeling, *Secret History*, pp. vii, 37–8 and 52–8; and Hornung, *Secret Lore of Egypt*, pp. 73 and 78–9.

Five: Egyptomania from the Renaissance to the Enlightenment

1 Sir Thomas Browne, *Hydriotaphia Urne Buria: or, A Brief Discourse of the Sepulchrall Urnes Lately Found in Norfok* [1658], in *The Voyce of the World: Selected Writings of Sir Thomas Browne*, ed. Geoffrey Keynes (London, 2007), p. 158.

2 Georg Wilhelm Friedrich Hegel, *The Philosophy of History*, trans. T. O. Churchill (Chicago, IL, 1952), p. 248B.

3 Brian A. Curran, 'The Renaissance Afterlife of Ancient Egypt (1400–1650)', in *The Wisdom of Egypt*, ed. Peter Ucko and Timothy Champion (London, 2003), pp. 101 and 106; Florian Ebeling, *The Secret History of Hermes Trismegistus: Hermeticism from Ancient to Modern Times* (Ithaca, NY, 2007), p. 89; and Erik Iverson, *The Myth of Egypt and its Hieroglyphs in European Tradition* (Princeton, NJ, 1993), pp. 59–60.

4 Curran, 'The Renaissance Afterlife of Ancient Egpt', p. 103; Erik Hornung, *The Secret Lore of Egypt: Its Impact on the West* (Ithaca, NY, 2001), p. 94; John Paoletti, 'Renaissance', in *Pyramidal Influence in Art* (Dayton, OH, 1980), pp. 27, 29 and 31–3; John and Elizabeth Romer, *The Seven Wonders of the World: A History of Modern Imagination* (New York, 1995), pp. 196 and 200–201; and Anne Wolff, *How Many Miles to Babylon? Travels and Adventures to Egypt and Beyond from 1300–1640* (Liverpool, 2003), which is a useful study of European travellers in Egypt during the later Middle Ages and the early modern eras.

5 Curran, 'The Renaissance Afterlife of Ancient Egypt', pp. 106 and 111; David Boyd Haydock, 'Ancient Egypt in 17th and 18th Century England', in *The Wisdom of Egypt*, p. 133; Hornung, *Secret Lore of Egypt*, pp. 83–4; and Iverson, *Myth of Egypt*, p. 60.

6 Curran, 'The Renaissance Afterlife of Ancient Egypt', pp. 101–2; Iverson, *Myth of Egypt*, pp. 62–3; and James Steven Curl, *The Egyptian Revival: Ancient Egypt as the Inspiration for Design Motifs in the West* (London, 2005), pp. 86–8.

7 Curran, 'The Renaissance Afterlife of Ancient Egypt', p. 105; Hornung, *Secret Lore of Egypt*, pp. 68 and 72; and Christine Ziegler, 'From One Egyptomania to Another: The Legacy of Roman Antiquity', in *Egyptomania: Egypt in Western Art, 1730–1930*, ed. Jean-Marcel Humbert et al. (Ottawa, 1994), pp. 15 and 19.

8 Curran, 'The Renaissance Afterlife of Ancient Egypt', p. 119; and Ziegler, 'From One Egyptomania to Another', pp. 15 and 17–19.

9 Frances A. Yates in her classic 1964 study *Giordano Bruno and the Hermetic Tradition* (repr. Chicago, IL, 1991) actually placed Hermes Trismegistus and hermeticism at the core of the philosophy of Renaissance Florence. It is a view that later scholars have moderated somewhat, although Hermes Trismegistus remains an important element of Renaissance thought: see Ebeling, *Secret History*, pp. 68–70.

10 Yates, *Giordano Bruno*, pp. 12–17; Curran, 'The Renaissance Afterlife of Ancient Egypt', p. 109; and Hornung, *Secret Lore of Egypt*, p. 84.

11 Ebeling, *Secret History*, pp. 60–63; Iverson, *Myth of Egypt*, p. 60; and Haydock, 'Ancient Egypt in 17th and 18th Century England', p. 134.

12 Yates, *Giordano Bruno*, pp. 14, 17–18, 56, 58, and 151–5; Assmann, 'Foreword', in Ebeling, *Secret History*, p. viii; and Curran, 'The Renaissance Afterlife of Ancient Egypt', p. 109.

13 Yates, *Giordano Bruno*, pp. 205–359; and for Fludd see pp. 403–7 and 432–55; Ebeling, *Secret History*, pp. 65–70 and 84–5; Hornung, *Secret Lore of Egypt*, pp. 84, 88 and 90–91; Curl, *Egyptian Revival*, pp. 128–32.

14 Ebeling, *Secret History*, pp. 35–6, 59–60, 70 and 90; and Hornung, *Secret Lore of Egypt*, pp. 90 and 106–10.

15 Anthony Grafton, 'Protestant versus Prophet: Isaac Casaubon on Hermes Trismegistus', *Journal of the Warburg and Courtauld Institutes*, XLVI (1983), pp. 86–7; Anthony Grafton, 'Rhetoric, Philology and Egyptomania in the 1570s: J. J. Scaliger's Invective Against M. Guilandinus's *Papyrus*', *Journal of the Warburg and Courtauld Institutes*, XLII (1979), p. 183; Iversen, *Myth of Egypt*, pp. 76–7; and Frederick Purnell, Jr., 'Francesco Patrizi and the Critics of Hermes Trismegistus', *Journal of Medieval and Renaissance Studies*, VI (1976), pp. 158–64.

16 Grafton, 'Casaubon on Hermes Trismegistus', pp. 78 and 82–5; Purnell, 'Francesco Patrizi', pp. 155–6; Hornung, *Secret Lore of Egypt*, pp. 98–9; and Yates, *Giordano Bruno*, pp. 398–403.

17 Curran, 'The Renaissance Afterlife of Ancient Egypt', p. 124; Assmann, 'Foreword', in Ebeling, *Secret History*, pp. xii–xiii; Ebeling, *Secret History*, p. 92 and 123–4; Grafton, 'Casaubon on Hermes Trismegistus', pp. 87–8; and Hornung, *Secret Lore of Egypt*, pp. 98–9.

18 Timothy Champion and Peter Ucko, 'Introduction: Egypt Ancient and Modern', in *The Wisdom of Egypt* (London, 2003), p. 12; Ebeling, *Secret History*, pp. 19–21; Umberto Eco, *The Search for the Perfect Language* (Oxford, 1995), pp. 149–54; Hornung, *Secret Lore of Egypt*, p. 13; *The Hieroglyphics of Horapollo*, trans. and intro. George Boas with a new foreword by Anthony Grafton (1950; repr. Princeton, NJ, 1993); Iverson, *Myth of Egypt*, pp. 38, 41–6, 49, and 64–5; Ammianus Marcellinus, *The Later Roman Empire (AD 354–378)* (Harmondsworth, 1986), book 17.4, pp. 122–3; and Plotinus, *The Six Enneads*, trans. Stephen MacKenna and B. S. Page, in *Great Books of the Western World*, vol. XVII, ed. Robert Maynard Hutchins (Chicago, IL, 1952), Fifth Ennead, eight tractate, section 6, p. 242.

19 Burnett, 'Images of Ancient Egypt in the Latin Middle Ages', pp. 77–8; Okasha El Daly, 'Ancient Egypt in Medieval Arabic Writings', in *The Wisdom of Egypt: Changing Visions Through the Ages*, ed. Peter Ucko and Timothy Champion (London, 2003), pp. 56 and 59–60; Okasha El Daly, *Egyptology: The Missing Millennium: Ancient Egypt in Medieval Arabic Writings* (London, 2005), Chapter 3, 'Medieval Arab Attempts to Decipher Ancient Egyptian

Scripts', pp. 58–73; Haarman, 'Medieval Muslim Perceptions of Pharaonic Egypt', p. 613; and Iverson, *Myth of Egypt*, p. 59.

20 Curran, 'The Renaissance Afterlife of Ancient Egypt', pp. 101 and 108; Brian Curran, *The Egyptian Renaissance: The Afterlife of Ancient Egypt in Early Modern Italy* (Chicago, IL, 2007), pp. 72–4; Eco, *Perfect Language*, p. 145; and Iverson, *Myth of Egypt*, pp. 65–6.

21 Curran, *Egyptian Renaissance*, pp. 121–31 and 133–58; and Iverson, *Myth of Egypt*, pp. 67–9.

22 Curran, *Egyptian Renaissance*, p. 89; Eco, *Perfect Language*, p. 145; Hornung, *Secret Lore of Egypt*, p. 86 (Hornung refers to the 1505 publication of Aldus Manutius as a Latin translation but this appears to be a typo); Iverson, *Myth of Egypt*, pp. 65 and 70.

23 Curran, *Egyptian Renaissance*, pp. 147 and 283; Curran, 'Renaissance Afterlife of Ancient Egypt', pp. 118–19 and 121; Hornung, *Secret Lore of Egypt*, pp. 88 and 90; and Iversen, *Myth of Egypt*, pp. 70–73, 75–7, 80–84 and 86–7.

24 Curran, 'The Renaissance Afterlife of Ancient Egypt', pp. 124 and 127; Eco, *Perfect Language*, pp. 154–5; Paula Findlen, 'Athanasius Kircher', in *Europe 1450 to 1789: Encyclopedia of the Early Modern World*, ed. Jonathan Dewald, 6 vols (New York, 2004); Iversen, *Myth of Egypt*, pp. 89–93 and 98; Daniel Stolzenberg, 'Kircher's Egypt', in *The Great Art of Knowing: The Baroque Encyclopedia of Athanasius Kircher*, ed. Daniel Stolzenberg (Stanford, CA, 2001), pp. 115–25; and Daniel Stolzenberg, *Egyptian Oedipus: Athanasius Kircher and the Secrets of Antiquity* (Chicago, IL, 2013), pp. 11–16 and 71–94.

25 Curran, 'The Renaissance Afterlife of Ancient Egypt', p. 101; Grafton, 'Casaubon on Hermes Trismegistus', p. 90; Iversen, *Myth of Egypt*, pp. 95–7; and Stolzenberg, *Egyptian Oedipus*, pp. 215–19 and 225.

26 Champion, 'Introduction: Egypt', p. 14; Curran, 'The Renaissance Afterlife of Ancient Egypt', p. 102, 124 and 128; Grafton, 'Casaubon on Hermes Trismegistus', p. 90; Hornung, *Secret Lore of Egypt*, , pp. 99–103; and Daniel Stolzenberg, 'Kircher among the Ruins: Esoteric Knowledge and University History', in *The Great Art of Knowing*, pp. 127–39; and Stolzenberg, *Egyptian Oedipus*, pp. 129–79.

27 Curran, 'The Renaissance Afterlife of Ancient Egypt', p. 101; Grafton, 'Casaubon on Hermes Trismegistus', p. 90; Paula Findlen, ed., *Athanasius Kircher: The Last Man Who Knew Everything* (New York, 2004); Hornung, *Secret Lore of Egypt*, p. 103; Iversen, *Myth of Egypt*, pp. 82–94 and 99; and Stolzenberg, *Egyptian Oedipus*, p. 225.

28 Haydock, 'Ancient Egypt in 17th and 18th Century England', pp. 134, 136 and 144; and Hornung, *Secret Lore of Ancient Egypt*, p. 158.

29 Ebeling, *Secret History*, pp. 97–103 and 113–15; and Haydock, 'Ancient Egypt in 17th and 18th Century England', pp. 142–4.

30 Sir Thomas Browne, *Religio Medici* [1643], pt. 1, section 12; Haydock, 'Ancient Egypt in 17th and 18th Century England', p. 137; Stuart Piggott, *Ancient Britons*

and the Antiquarian Imagination: Ideas from the Renaissance to the Regency (London, 1989), p. 41; Jan Assmann, 'Jehova-Isis: The Mysteries of Egypt and the Quest for Natural Religion in the Age of Enlightenment', in *Egypt and the Fabrication of European Identity*, ed. Irene A. Bierman (Los Angeles, CA, 1995), pp. 46–9; Jan Assmann, *Moses the Egyptian: The Memory of Egypt in Western Monotheism* (Cambridge, MA, 1997), pp. 80–90; Ebeling, *Secret History*, pp. 93–6; Hornung, *Secret Lore of Egypt*, p. 103; and Ralph Cudworth, *The True Intellectual System of the Universe: Wherein All the Reason and Philosophy of Atheism is Confuted and its Impossibility Demonstrated*, 3 vols (London, 1845), vol. I, p. 523.

31 Assmann, 'Jehova-Isis', pp. 38–46, 49, 52–3, 55 and 70–71; Assmann, *Moses the Egyptian*, pp. 55–79 and 96–114; and Hornung, *Myth of Egypt*, p. 103. William Warburton, *The Divine Legation of Moses Demonstrated in Nine Books*, 4th edn in 5 vols (London, 1765) with much of the material on Egypt appearing in vol. III, book 4. The quote comes from vol. III, p. 32.

32 Hornung, *Secret Lore of Egypt*, pp. 131–2; and Iverson, *Myth of Egypt*, pp. 100–101 and 118–20.

33 Hornung, *Secret Lore of Egypt*, p. 137; and Iverson, *Myth of Egypt*, pp. 108–10.

34 Haydock, 'Ancient Egypt in 17th and 18th Century England', p. 137; Hornung, *Secret Lore of Egypt*, p. 131; and Iverson, *Myth of Egypt*, pp. 84–6, 88, 104–7; and 112–14. For the universal and perfect language see Eco, *Perfect Language*.

35 Assmann, 'Jehova-Isis', pp. 63–6; and Johann Gottfried von Herder, *Reflections on the Philosophy of the History of Mankind*, intro. Frank E. Manuel (Chicago, IL, 1968), pp. 155 and 157. For other comments critical of hieroglyphs see pp. 155–7.

36 Haydock, 'Ancient Egypt in 17th and 18th Century England', pp. 148–9, 152–5, 159–60; Hornung, *Secret Lore of Egypt*, p. 131; and Iverson, *Myth of Egypt*, p. 107.

37 Hornung, *Secret Lore of Egypt*, pp. 118, 125 and 158; and Mary Lefkowitz, *Not Out of Africa: How Afrocentrism Became an Excuse to Teach Myth as History* (New York, 1996), pp. 111–20, 122–3 and 126–9.

38 Hornung, *Secret Lore of Egypt*, pp. 125 and 158–61; Iverson, *Myth of Egypt*, pp. 111–14, 116 and 121–2; and Curl, *Egyptian Revival*, chapters 4 and 5.

39 Ebeling, *Secret History*, pp. 116–18; Hornung, *Secret Lore of Egypt*, pp. 111, 160–61 and 192; Iverson, *Myth of Egypt*, p. 121; and Laurence Sterne, *Tristram Shandy* (Chicago, IL, 1952), book IV, chapters 8 and 14.

40 Ebeling, *Secret History*, pp. 121–2 and 129; Haydock, 'Ancient Egypt in the 17th and 18th Century England', p. 148; Hornung, *Secret History of Egypt*, pp. 118, 121–5 and 192; Iverson, *Myth of Egypt*, pp. 122–3; and Jasper Ridley, *The Freemasons: A History of the World's Most Powerful Secret Society* (New York, 2001).

41 Herder, *History of Mankind*, p. 158; Hornung, *Secret Lore of Egypt*, pp. 189–90 quoting the young Herder; and Edward Gibbon, *Autobiography of Edward Gibbon as Originally Edited by Lord Sheffield*, ed. J. B. Bury (Oxford, 1907), pp. 43–4; and Roy Porter, *Edward Gibbon: Making History* (London, 1988), p. 45.

42 Stuart Harten, 'Archaeology and the Unconcious: Hegel, Egyptomania, and the Legitimation of Orientalism', in *Egypt and the Fabrication of European Identity*, pp. 6–13, 28 n.2, and 30 n.8; and Georg Wilhelm Friedrich Hegel, *The Philosophy of History*, in *Great Books of the Western World*, ed. Robert Maynard Hutchins (Chicago, IL, 1952), pp. 247–8. For his comment on Thomas Young also see p. 248 and for the decipherment of hieroglyphs' impact on Hegel's scholarship see Harten, pp. 3–5.

Six: Napoleon's Expedition to Egypt and the Birth of Modern Egyptomania

1 Vivant Denon, *Travels in Upper and Lower Egypt*, 3 vols (1803; repr. New York, 1973), vol. II, pp. 83–4.

2 J. Christopher Herold, *Napoleon in Egypt* (1963; repr. Barnsley, 2005); and Paul Strathern, *Napoleon in Egypt* (New York, 2008) are both excellent accounts of the French invasion of Egypt. Alan Moorehead, *The Blue Nile* (New York, 1962), chapters 4–7, provides a shorter account of the French invasion. For a good brief overview of Napoleon's military career that places the expedition to Egypt in context, see Gunther E. Rothenberg, *The Napoleonic Wars* (New York, 2006), but for a more detailed study see Philip Dwyer, *Napoleon: The Path to Power* (New Haven, CT, 2008), especially chapters 14–19.

3 For more detailed assessments of the Mamelukes see Herold, *Napoleon in Egypt*, pp. 6–9; Strathern, *Napoleon in Egypt*, pp. 10–13; and Moorehead, *Blue Nile*, pp. 72–5.

4 Most sources say that the number of scholars was 167, for example, Herold, p. 30, and Strathern, p. 38, but two of those were left behind when the fleet stopped at Malta. Other general histories repeat this number, such as Joyce Tyldesley, *Egypt: How a Lost Civilization was Rediscovered* (Berkeley, CA, 2005), p. 47; and Brian M. Fagan, *The Rape of the Nile: Tomb Robbers, Tourists, and Archaeologists in Egypt* (Wakefield, RI, 1993), pp. 66–7. Nina Burleigh, *Mirage: Napoleon's Scientists and the Unveiling of Egypt* (New York, 2007), pp. 2–3, gives 151 scholars; while Lesley and Roy Adkins in *The Keys of Egypt: The Obsession to Decipher Egyptian Hieroglyphs* (New York, 2000), p. 10, cautiously suggest there were 'over 150' scholars who accompanied Napoleon, before mentioning the official number of 167.

5 Burleigh, *Mirage*, pp. 13 and 241–2; and Fagan, *Rape of the Nile*, p. 63.

6 Denon, *Travels in Upper and Lower Egypt*, vol. I, pp. 87–8; and Burleigh, *Mirage*, pp. 41–2 and 47.

7 Burleigh, *Mirage*, pp. 56, 59–60, 70–71, 98, 167 and 169–70.

8 Tyldesley, *Egypt Rediscovered*, pp. 47–8.

9 Denon, *Travels*, vol. I, pp. 23, 193, 220, 256, 263–4, 268–70; vol. II, pp. 83–5, 94–5, 120–21, 313 and vol. III, pp. 105–6; and Burleigh, *Mirage*, p. 175. For

a study of Denon's travels with Desaix's army see Terrence M. Russell, *The Discovery of Egypt: Vivant Denon's Travels with Napoleon's Army* (Stroud, 2005).

10 Tyldesley, *Egypt Rediscovered*, pp. 48–9; Peter A. Clayton, *The Rediscovery of Ancient Egypt: Artists and Travellers in the 19th Century* (1982; New York, 1990), pp. 18–19; and Burleigh, *Mirage*, pp. 144, 184 and 233.

11 John Downs, *Discovery at Rosetta* (New York, 2008), pp. xviii, 69 and 74–81, provides a detailed description of the discovery of the Rosetta Stone. Downs also includes a discussion of the date of the discovery, which is not stated in any documents. He shows that the discovery could have taken place any time in July on or before the 25th. John Ray, *The Rosetta Stone and the Rebirth of Ancient Egypt* (Cambridge, MA, 2007), pp. 1–5, discusses the popularity and the iconic status of the Rosetta Stone. He also provides a translation of the demotic inscription on the Rosetta Stone. E. A. Wallis Budge, *The Rosetta Stone* (1929; repr. New York, 1989), though a more technically detailed look at the Rosetta Stone, is also dated and provides a somewhat muddled account of its discovery.

12 Burleigh, *Mirage*, pp. xiv, 168–9 and 212–14.

13 Ibid., pp. 221–4 and 226.

14 Ibid., pp. 241 and 248; Fagan, *Rape of the Nile*, p. 78; and Tyldesley, *Egypt Rediscovered*, p. 49.

15 Adkins, *Keys of Egypt*, p. 61, and Tyldesley, *Egypt Rediscovered*, p. 54.

16 Adkins, *Keys of Egypt*, pp. 63–4; Tyldesley, *Egypt Rediscovered*, p. 59; and Fredrik Thomasson, *The Life of J. D. Akerblad: Egyptian Decipherment and Orientalism in Revolutionary Times* (Leiden, 2013).

17 Tyldesley, *Egypt Rediscovered*, pp. 61–2; and Adkins, *Keys of Egypt*, pp. 114–22, 149, 151 and 277. The Adkins throughout their book describe the relationship between Young and Jean-François Champollion as mercurial with periods of scholarly cooperation and professional jealousy. Ray, *The Rosetta Stone*, pp. 66–71, tends to be a bit more sympathetic to Young's behaviour towards Champollion but he also agrees that Champollion really deciphered hieroglyphs while Young's major contribution was to decipher demotic script: see pp. 45–6 and 47–9. Andrew Robinson, *The Last Man Who Knew Everything: Thomas Young, The Anonymous Polymath Who Proved Newton Wrong, Explained How We See, Cured the Sick, and Deciphered the Rosetta Stone, Among Other Feats of Genius* (New York, 2006), Chapter 10, 'Reading the Rosetta Stone', and Chapter 15, 'Dueling with Champollion' is quite sympathetic to Young.

18 Robert Steven Bianchi, 'Champollion, Jean-François', in *The Oxford Encyclopedia of Ancient Egypt*, ed. Donald B. Redford, 3 vols (Oxford, 2001) is a useful and concise biographical account. For a recent full-scale biography see Andrew Robinson, *Cracking the Code: The Revolutionary Life of Jean-François Champollion* (Oxford, 2012) – for Champollion's early life see chapters 2 and 3.

19 Burleigh, *Mirage*, p. 231; Adkins, *Keys of Egypt*, pp. 42, 51–2 and 66; Tyldesley, *Egypt Rediscovered*, p. 58; and Robinson, *Cracking the Code*, Chapter 4.

20 Adkins, *Keys of Egypt*, pp. 78, 92, 98, 111, 120–21, 128–9, 139, 146, 164, 198–9, 246 and 294. Ray, *Rosetta Stone*, pp. 56 and 59–64 again tends towards a more sympathetic explanation of Sacy, Jomard and Young's animosities towards Champollion. Robinson, *Cracking the Code*, Chapter 5.

21 Tyldesley, *Egypt Rediscovered*, pp. 59–60; Adkins, *Keys of Egypt*, pp. 59–60, 85–6, 104, 113, 139–45 and 159; Robinson, *Cracking the Code*, chapters 6–9.

22 Tyldesley, *Egypt Rediscovered*, pp. 54 and 64–5; Adkins, *Keys of Egypt*, pp. 1, 171–5 and 180–81; and Robinson, *Cracking the Code*, Chapter 10.

23 Adkins, *Keys of Egypt*, pp. 182, 198–200 and 203–4; and Robinson, *Cracking the Code*, Chapter 12.

24 Adkins, *Keys of Egypt*, pp. 166–7, 176–7 and 241–2; Ray, *Rosetta Stone*, pp. 64–5; and Robinson, *Cracking the Code*, chapters 13 and 14. For the controversy over the Dendara Zodiac see Jed Z. Buchwald and Diane Greco Josefowicz, *The Zodiac of Paris: How an Improbable Controversy over an Ancient Egyptian Artefact Provoked a Modern Debate between Religion and Science* (Princeton, NJ, 2010), in particular see Chapter 2, 'Champollion's Cartouche'.

25 Amelia B. Edwards, *A Thousand Miles up the Nile*, 2nd edn (1891; repr. Los Angeles, CA, 1983), p. xiv. The first edition appeared in 1877.

26 Adkins, *Keys of Egypt*, pp. 287, 292–5 and 305–6; Tyldesley, *Egypt Rediscovered*, p. 67; Fagan, *Rape of the Nile*, pp. 261–2; and Robinson, *Cracking the Code*, Chapter 15.

27 Fagan, *The Rape of the Nile* is a very good overview.

28 Tyldesley, *Egypt Rediscovered*, chapters 4 and 5; Fagan, *Rape of the Nile*, pp. 81–93; and Ronald T. Ridley, *Napoleon's Proconsul in Egypt: The Life and Times of Bernardino Drovetti* (London, 1998).

29 Fagan, *Rape of the Nile*, chapters 6–15 and the biographies of Belzoni: Ivor Noel Hume, *Belzoni: The Giant Archaeologists Love to Hate* (Charlotte, VA, 2011); and Stanley Mayes, *The Great Belzoni: The Circus Strongman Who Discovered Egypt's Ancient Treasures*, 2nd edn (London, 2006). Belzoni's memoirs are available in a convenient modern edition: Giovanni Battista Belzoni, *Travels in Egypt and Nubia* (Vercelli, 2007).

30 For Belzoni's activities see the sources listed in note 29. For Shelley see Tyldesley, *Egypt Rediscovered*, pp. 86–7. Belzoni's own account of his discovery of the entry for the pyramid of Khephren can be found in his *Travels in Egypt and Nubia*, pp. 290–311.

31 Clayton, *Rediscovery of Ancient Egypt*, pp. 42–3; Fagan, *Rape of the Nile*, pp. 245–6; and Tyldesley, *Egypt Rediscovered*, pp. 100–102.

32 Fagan, *Rape of the Nile*, pp. 247–8; and Tyldesley, *Egypt Rediscovered*, pp. 102–4.

33 Sharon Waxman, *Loot: The Battle Over the Stolen Treasures of the Ancient World* (New York, 2008), pp. 74–5; and Buchwald and Josefowicz, *The Zodiac of Paris*.

34 Waxman, *Loot*, pp. 103–6.

35 Fagan, *Rape of the Nile*, pp. 261–2 and 267; Burleigh, *Mirage*, p. 246; George Robins Gliddon, *An Appeal to the Antiquaries of Europe on the Destruction of*

the *Monuments of Egypt* (London, 1841); and Elbert Eli Farman, *Egypt and its Betrayal: An Account of the Country During the Periods of Ismail and Tewfik Pashas, and of How England Acquired a New Empire* (New York, 1908). Both Fagan and Burleigh say that Gliddon published his *Appeal* in 1849 but the publication date on the book is 1841. It is likely that Burleigh was relying on Fagan for her information and that Fagan's date is probably a typographical error.

Seven: Nineteenth-century Egyptomania to the Discovery of Tut

1 Harriet Martineau, *Eastern Life, Present and Past* (Philadelphia, PA, 1848), p. 45.
2 Rudyard Kipling, 'Egypt of the Magicians', in *Letters of Travel, 1892–1913* (Garden City, NJ, 1920), p. 269, first published as 'Interviewing Pharaoh', *Nash's Magazine* (October 1914).
3 Karl H. Dannenfeldt, 'Egyptian Mumia: The Sixteenth Century Experience and Debate', *Sixteenth Century Journal*, XVI (1985), pp. 163–73; and Jasmine Day, *The Mummy's Curse: Mummymania in the English-speaking World* (London, 2006), p. 24.
4 Dannenfeldt, 'Egyptian Mumia', pp. 170 and 174–80; Sir Thomas Browne, *Hydriotaphia Urne Burial*, in *The Voyce of the World: Selected Writings of Sir Thomas Browne*, ed. Geoffrey Keynes (London, 2007), p. 156; Heather Pringle, *The Mummy Congress: Science, Obsession, and the Everlasting Dead* (2001; New York, 2005), pp. 192–200; and Eric Hornung, *The Secret Lore of Egypt: Its Impact on the West* (Ithaca, NY, 1999), p. 94.
5 Belzoni, *Travels in Egypt and Nubia*, pp. 180–84.
6 Pringle, *Mummy Congress*, pp. 171–5.
7 Ibid., pp. 175–85; Warren R. Dawson, 'Pettigrew's Demonstrations upon Mummies: A Chapter in the History of Egyptology', *Journal of Egyptian Archaeology*, XX (1934), pp. 170–82; and Day, *Mummy's Curse*, pp. 27–30.
8 Edgar Allan Poe, *Poetry and Tales*, ed. Patrick F. Quinn (New York, 1984), pp. 805–21.
9 Pringle, *Mummy Congress*, pp. 194 and 200–204; Mark Twain, *The Innocents Abroad: Roughing It* (New York, 2004), p. 505; Day, *Mummy's Curse*, pp. 24–5; and Richard G. Carrott, *The Egyptian Revival: Its Sources, Monuments, and Meaning, 1808–1858* (Berkeley, CA, 1978), pp. 48–9.
10 James Stephen Curl, *The Egyptian Revival: Ancient Egypt as the Inspiration for Design Motifs in the West* (London, 2005), pp. xx–xxi, xxvii–xxviii, 154 and 244.
11 Ibid., pp. 155, 165, 167, 170, 172–93.
12 Ibid., pp. 204–18, 220, 226, 246–7 and 312; Carrott, *The Egyptian Revival*, pp. 22–4; and John Hamill and Pierre Mollier, 'Rebuilding the Sanctuaries of Memphis: Egypt in Masonic Iconography and Architecture', in *Imhotep*

Today: Egyptianizing Architecture, ed. Jean-Marcel Humbert and Clifford Price (London, 2003), pp. 207–20.

13 Curl, *Egyptian Revival*, pp. xxix, 230–31 and 366.

14 Carrott, *Egyptian Revival*, pp. 2–3, 34, and 132; and Curl, *Egyptian Revival*, pp. 260–80.

15 Carrott, *Egyptian Revival*, pp. 53, 66–7, 83, 95–6, 103, 109, 112, 116 and 120–21; Curl, *Egyptian Revival*, p. 286; and Joseph P. Viteretti, 'Tombs', in *The Encyclopedia of New York City*, ed. Kenneth T. Jackson (New Haven, CT, 1991), p. 1191.

16 Carrott, *Egyptian Revival*, pp. 2–4 and 136–7; and Curl, *Egyptian Revival*, pp. 304–6, 340 and 346.

17 Lynne Withey, *Grand Tours and Cook's Tours: A History of Leisure Travel, 1750 to 1915* (New York, 1997), p. 224.

18 Ibid., pp. 228 and 230–31; Edward W. Said, *Orientalism* (1979; repr. New York, 1994), pp. 174–5; Raymond John Howego, *Encyclopedia of Exploration, 1800–1850* (London, 2004), entries for Chateaubriand and Stanhope on pp. 190 and 194; *Memoirs of the Lady Hester Stanhope*, 3 vols (London, 1845); and Virginia Childs, *Lady Hester Stanhope: Queen of the Desert* (London, 1990), pp. 90–94.

19 Howego, *Encyclopedia of Exploration*, entry for Burckhardt at pp. 81–3; Withey, *Grand Tour*, pp. 227–8; Moorehead, *Blue Nile*, chapters 10 and 11; and John Lloyd Stephens, *Incidents of Travel in Egypt, Arabia Petraea, and the Holy Land*, ed. Victor Wolfgang von Hagen (Norman, OK, 1970), p. xxxi.

20 For good brief biographical overviews of Wilkinson and Lane see 'John Gardner Wilkinson' and 'Edward William Lane' in *Who Was Who in Egyptology*, ed. Morris L. Bierbrier, 4th edn (London, 2012); 'John Gardner Wilkinson' and 'Edward William Lane', in the *Oxford Dictionary of National Biography*, ed. H.C.G. Matthew and Brian Harrison (Oxford, 2004); and Brian Fagan, *The Rape of the Nile: Tomb Robbers, Tourists, and Archaeologists in Egypt* (Wakefield, RI, 1993), pp. 263–4. For full-scale biographies see Jason Thompson, *Sir Gardner Wilkinson and His Circle* (Austin, TX, 1992) and *Edward William Lane: The Life of the Pioneering Egyptologist and Orientalist* (Cairo, 2010).

21 Harriet Martineau, *Eastern Life*, p. iv; and Amelia B. Edwards, *A Thousand Miles up the Nile* (1891; repr. Los Angeles, CA, 1983), p. 415.

22 Thompson, *Sir Gardner Wilkinson and His Circle* is a good biography.

23 Robert Irwin, *Dangerous Knowledge: Orientalism and Its Discontents* (Woodstock, 2008), pp. 163–4. For a good brief biographical overview of Lane see 'Edward William Lane', in *Who Was Who in Egyptology*, ed. Morris L. Bierbrier, 4th edn (London, 2012); 'Edward William Lane', in *The Oxford Dictionary of National Biography*; and Fagan, *Rape of the Nile*, pp. 263–4. For a full-scale biography see Thompson, *Edward William Lane*.

24 John Pemble, *The Mediterranean Passion: Victorians and Edwardians in the South* (Oxford, 1988), pp. 23 and 25.

25 Withey, *Grand Tours and Cook's Tours*, pp. 224, 241–2 and 258–61; Edwards, *A Thousand Miles up the Nile*, p. 36; Jason Thompson, *A History of Egypt from Earliest Times to the Present* (New York, 2009), p. 236; Lucie Duff Gordon, *Letters from Egypt* (1902; repr. London, 1986), p. 19; Mark Twain, *The Innocents Abroad*, p. 491; and Piers Brendon, *Thomas Cook: 150 Years of Popular Tourism* (London, 1991), Chapter 7, 'Egypt and Beyond', pp. 120–40.

26 James Zug, *American Traveller: The Life and Adventures of John Ledyard: The Man Who Dreamed of Walking the World* (New York, 2005), pp. 212–17 and Chapter 14, 'I Go Alone: Grand Cairo'.

27 John Lloyd Stephens, *Incidents of Travel in Egypt*, pp. xxxi, 4, 8, 12, 16–17, 20 and 66; and Martineau, *Eastern Life*, p. 160. Von Hagen provides biographical information about Stephens in his introduction. There is also concise biographical sketches of Stephens's travels in both the Middle East and Central America in Howego, *Encyclopedia of Exploration*, pp. 565–6. Richard V. Francaviglia, *Go East, Young Man: Imagining the American West as the Orient* (Logan, UT, 2011), pp. 69–71, has insightful discussion that places Stephens in the world of Victorian travel writing.

28 Stephens, *Egypt*, pp. 31–8.

29 Ibid., pp. 39, 50, 52–3, 68–9, 72, 83, 87, 101, 105, 110, 113 and 120. Regarding the depredations of Mohammad Ali's government against the Egyptian ruins for building materials, Stephens related a story about how the French scholar Maurice-Adolphe Linant in the Pasha's employ managed to talk him out of dismantling one of the great pyramids for building materials, see pp. 145–6.

30 Ibid., pp. xxxvii–xl and 134–7; Edgar Allan Poe, 'John L. Stephens', in *Essays and Reviews*, ed. G. R. Thompson (New York, 1984), p. 941; and Francaviglia, *Go East, Young Man*, p. 70. Sir Richard Burton's *Personal Narrative of a Pilgrimage to Al-Madinan and Meccah* (1855–6; repr. New York, 1964), vol. I, Chapter 3, 'The Little Asthmatic', provides a good description of Nile steamboats. I would like to thank Richard Francaviglia for alerting me to the Burton reference.

31 David Roberts, *Egypt Yesterday and Today: Lithographs and Diaries by David Roberts R. A.* (Vercelli, 2004). For brief biographical sketches of Roberts see Howego, *Encyclopedia of Exploration*, p. 193 and 'David Roberts' in *Who Was Who in Egyptology*. For a visually impressive overview of depictions of Egypt from the first half of the nineteenth century, see Franco Serino and Catharine H. Roehrig, *Ancient Egypt: Artists and Explorers in the Land of the Pharaohs* (Vercelli, 2003).

32 William Makepeace Thackeray, *The Paris Sketch Book of Mr M. A. Titmarsh and Eastern Sketches: A Journey from Cornhill to Cairo* (New York, 1887), pp. 466 and 498–9; and Howego, *Encyclopedia of Exploration*, p. 194.

33 Francis Steegmuller, ed. and trans., *Flaubert in Egypt: A Sensibility on Tour* (Boston, MA, 1972), pp. 29 and 49–59.

34 Ibid., pp. 163–77 for Thebes, p. 78 for Lane and pp. 9, 43–5, 63, 67–8, 83–7, 110–22, 126–30, 153–9, 161, 192 and 200 for various sexual encounters. For

the mummy's foot, see Jasmine Day, *The Mummy's Curse: Mummymania in the English-speaking World* (London, 2006), p. 22.

35 Herman Melville, *Journal of a Visit to Europe and the Levant, October 11, 1856–May 6, 1857*, ed. Howard C. Horsford (Princeton, NJ, 1955), pp. vii–ix, 3–29 and 113–14.

36 Melville, *Journal*, pp. 117–24.

37 Florence Nightingale, *Letters from Egypt: A Journey on the Nile, 1849–1850*, ed. Anthony Sattin (New York, 1987); and Michael D. Calabria, *Florence Nightingale in Egypt and Greece: Her Diary and 'Visions'* (Albany, NY, 1997).

38 There is a brief but useful biographical sketch for Lucie Duff Gordon in the *Oxford Dictionary of National Biography*. For an excellent full biography see Katherine Frank, *Lucie Duff Gordon: A Passage to Egypt* (1994; repr. London, 2007). A readily available edition of Lucie's letters is Lucie Duff Gordon, *Letters from Egypt with a Memoir by Her Daughter Janet Ross and a New Introduction by Sarah Searight* (1902; repr. London, 1993).

39 Lucie Duff Gordon, *Letters*, p. 86, letter to Alexander Duff Gordon, 17 December 1863. Also see pp. 101 and 108.

40 Ibid., pp. 67–8, letter to Sarah Austin, 21 May 1863; pp. 111–12, letter to Sarah Austin, 7 February 1864, and pp. 123 and 127.

41 Mark Twain, *The Innocents Abroad* (New York, 1984), pp. 487–506 with quotes at pp. 490–91 and 503.

42 Edwards, *Thousand Miles up the Nile*, pp. 69–79 and 136. *Who Was Who in Egyptology* contains a good overview of Edwards's life and career.

43 Edwards, *Thousand Miles Up the Nile*, pp. 2, 12, 35 and 90.

44 Ibid., pp. 13, 17, 51, 52, 80, 186–7, 290, 304, 315 and 454.

45 Ibid., pp. 487 and 489–90.

46 J. Rees, *Amelia Edwards: Traveller, Novelist, and Egyptologist* (London, 1998) and Brenda Moon, *More Usefully Employed: Amelia B. Edwards, Writer, Traveller and Campaigner for Ancient Egypt* (London, 2006) are good biographies of Edwards.

47 William S. McFeely, *Grant: A Biography* (New York, 1981), pp. 450–53 and 466–7; Geoffrey Perret, *Ulysses S. Grant: Soldier and President* (New York, 1997), pp. 453–4; Elbert Eli Farman, *Along the Nile with General Grant* (New York, 1904); and John Russell Young, *Around the World with General Grant*, ed. and intro. Michael Fellman (Baltimore, MD, 2002), pp. 95–115.

48 Rudyard Kipling, 'Egypt of the Magicians', pp. 224, 233, 238–9, 246 and 255–67; and Rudyard Kipling, *Kipling Abroad: Traffics and Discoveries from Burma to Brazil*, ed. Andrew Lycett (London, 2010), pp. 198–9.

49 Day, *Mummy's Curse*, pp. 33 and 38–63.

50 Heliodorus, *An Ethiopian Story*, in B. P. Reardon, ed., *Collected Ancient Greek Novels* (Berkeley, CA, 1989), pp. 5 and 349–52. The text of the novel is on pp. 353–588. 'Heliodorus' in *The Oxford Classical Dictionary*, ed. Simon

Hornblower and Antony Spawforth, 3rd edn (Oxford, 1996) provides a concise synopsis of the plot.

51 Mary Lefkowitz, *Not Out of Africa: How Afrocentrism Became an Excuse to Teach Myth as History* (New York, 1996), pp. 110–17, and the English translation of *Sethos* is Jean Terrasson, *The Life of Sethos taken from Private Memoirs of the Ancient Egyptians*, trans. Thomas Lediard (London, 1732).

52 Lefkowitz, *Not Out of Africa*, pp. 117–21; the entry for *Magic Flute* in Arthur Jacobs, *The Wordsworth Book of Opera* (London, 1996), p. 91 and liner notes from the Telarc CD *Highlights from Die Zauberflöte*; and 'Opera Statistics 2012–2013' at www.operabase.com.

53 Roger Luckhurst, *The Mummy's Curse: The True History of a Dark Fantasy* (Oxford, 2012), chapters 1–3, provides great descriptions and analyses of the mummy curses associated with Tutankhamum, the 'Unlucky Mummy' of Thomas Douglas Murray, and the curse on Walter Henry Ingram. In each case, the existence of any sort of curse does not stand up under close examination.

54 Nicholas Daly, 'That Obscure Object of Desire: Victorian Commodity Culture and Fictions of the Mummy', *Novel: A Forum in Fiction*, XXVIII (Autumn 1994), pp. 24–51; Day, *Mummy's Curse*, chapters 2 and 3; and Luckhurst, *Mummy's Curse*, pp. 17–23 , 82–4 and chapters 4–6.

55 Jane Webb Loudon, *The Mummy! A Tale of the Twenty-second Century*, abridged A. Rauch (1827; Ann Arbor, MI, 1994). The quote is from p. 42.

56 Edgar Allan Poe, 'Some Words with a Mummy', in *Poetry and Tales*, pp. 805–21 and 1396.

57 Louisa May Alcott, 'Lost in a Pyramid or, the Mummy's Curse', in *Into the Mummy's Tomb: Mysterious Tales of Mummies and Ancient Egypt*, ed. John Richard Stephens (1999; repr., New York, 2006), pp. 16–25; and Dominic Montserrat, 'Louisa May Alcott and the Mummy's Curse', *Kmt: A Modern Journal of Ancient Egypt*, IX/2 (1998), pp. 70–75, esp. p. 75.

58 Arthur Conan Doyle, 'The Ring of Thoth', in *The Wordsworth Book of Horror Stories* (Ware, 2004), pp. 133–45.

59 Arthur Conan Doyle, 'Lot No. 429', in *The Wordsworth Book of Horror Stories*, pp. 251–75.

60 Bram Stoker, *The Jewel of Seven Stars*, ed. and intro. Kate Hebblethwaite (London, 2008), pp. xii, xxi, xxiii–xxiv, xxvi and xxxv. My account uses Stoker's original ending of 1903, not the happy ending of 1912. Jasmine Day, *Mummy's Curse*, pp. 43–4 and 62 asserts that Stoker explicitly depicts the unwrapping of Queen Tera as a rape. Furthermore, her interpretation is that God intervenes as a storm and defeats Tera's attempt at reincarnation, destroying her and killing everyone but Ross. Not a happy ending, but the evil mummy is defeated. As I read the novel, the unwrapping is voyeuristic as it reveals a beautiful, well-preserved body that uncannily resembles Margaret Trelawny. The fatal storm is a product of Tera's magical powers and destroys everyone in the party who stands too close.

When Ross awakens, Tera has disappeared to who-knows-where to do who-knows-what.

61 'Georg Moritz Ebers', in *Who Was Who in Egyptology*, pp. 169–70; and Fagan, *Rape of the Nile*, p. 328.

62 David Huckvale, *Ancient Egypt in the Popular Imagination: Building a Fantasy in Film, Literature, Music and Art* (Jefferson, NC, 2012), pp. 196–8; and Jean-Marcel Humbert, 'How to Stage *Aida* ', in *Consuming Ancient Egypt*, ed. Sally MacDonald and Michael Rice (London, 2003), pp. 47–62.

63 H. Rider Haggard, 'Smith and the Pharaohs', in *The Best Short Stories of Rider Haggard*, ed. and intro. Peter Haining (London, 1981), pp. 148–91.

64 H. Rider Haggard, 'The Trade in the Dead', in *The Best Short Stories of Rider Haggard*, pp. 141–7; and *The Days of My Life: An Autobiography*, 2 vols (London, 1926).

65 Luckhurst, *Mummy's Curse*, pp. 193–9.

Eight: The Rise of Mass Egyptomania: Tutankhamun, Tutmania and the Curse of the Mummy

1 Arthur Weigall, 'The Malevolence of Ancient Egyptian Spirits', in *Into the Mummy's Tomb: Mysterious Tales of Mummies and Ancient Egypt*, ed. John Richard Stephens (1999; New York, 2006), p. 15.

2 Joyce Tyldesley, *Tutankhamen: The Search for an Egyptian King* (New York, 2012) is a first-class telling of the discovery, aftermath and significance of the discovery of Tutankhamun's tomb. Daniel Meyerson, *In the Valley of the Kings: Howard Carter and the Mystery of Tutankhamun's Tomb* (New York, 2009), focuses on Howard Carter and the discovery. The classic first-hand account is Howard Carter and A. C. Mace, *The Discovery of the Tomb of Tutankhamen* (1923, repr. New York, 1977). There is a brief overview of the discovery in Chapter 4, 'King Tut's Tomb: The Key to Egypt's God-kings' of Patrick Hunt, *Ten Discoveries that Rewrote History* (New York, 2007). In fact, the discovery of Tutankhamun's tomb did not rewrite history. Christopher Frayling, *The Face of Tutankhamun* (London, 1992) is a wonderful cultural history of the discovery and also is an anthology of a wide variety of writings connected to Tutankhamun, Egyptology and Egyptomania. For the dirt on the discovery see Thomas Hoving, *Tutankhamun: The Untold Story* (New York, 1978), which stirred up controversy. The best biography of Howard Carter is T.G.H. James, *Howard Carter: The Path to Tutankhamun* (Cairo, 1992). The literature on Tutankhamun is vast.

3 John M. Adams, *The Millionaire and the Mummies: Theodore Davis's Gilded Age in the Valley of the Kings* (New York, 2013) is a well-researched and entertaining biography of Davis.

4 Carter and Mace, *Discovery of Tutankhamen*, pp. 94 and 96.

5 Frayling, *Face of Tutankhamun*, pp. 3–5, and Hoving, *Tutankhamun: The Untold Story*, pp. 15–16 and 89–107. Hoving's book is critical of the behaviour of Carter, Carnarvon and the New York Metropolitan Museum of Art during the opening and the emptying of the tomb. His opinion of Carter is not favourable either. His account is not generally accepted by professional archaeologists although it is well written and makes use of some previously unused sources.

6 Frayling, *Face of Tutankhamun*, pp. 62–3 and 124; and Hoving, *Tutankhamun*, pp. 172 and 311.

7 Carter and Mace, *Discovery of Tutankhamen*, pp. 142–8; and Frayling, *Face of Tutankhamun*, pp. 27–8.

8 Roger Luckhurst, *The Mummy's Curse: The True History of a Dark Fantasy* (Oxford, 2012) and Jasmine Day, *The Mummy's Curse: Mummymania in the English-speaking World* (London, 2006), pp. 48–64.

9 Tyldesley, *Tutankhamen*, p. 225.

10 Frayling, *Face of Tutankhamun*, pp. 39 and 52–3.

11 Luckhurst, *Mummy's Curse*. This paragraph and the following concerning the Unlucky Mummy of Thomas Douglas Murray are based on Chapter 2 of Luckhurst's book.

12 The following paragraphs are based on Chapter 3 of Luckhurst, *Mummy's Curse*.

13 Ibid., p. 83.

14 Sax Rohmer, *Tales of Secret Egypt* (New York, 1920), p. 194.

15 Frayling, *Face of Tutankhamun*, pp. 39, 44–6 and 50–51; and Carter and Mace, *Discovery of Tutankhamen*, pp. 142–3.

16 Frayling, *Face of Tutankhamun*, pp. 46–8; and Evelyn Waugh, *Labels: A Mediterranean Journal* (1930; Harmondsworth, 1985), p. 88.

17 'Arthur Weigall', in *Who Was Who in Egyptology*; Julie Hankey, *A Passion for Egypt: Arthur Weigall, Tutankhamun and the 'Curse of the Pharaohs'* (London, 2001); Hoving, *Tutankhamun*, p. 194; Arthur Weigall, 'The Malevolence of Ancient Egyptian Spirits', in *Into the Mummy's Tomb: Mysterious Tales of Mummies and Ancient Egypt*, ed. John Richard Stephens (1999; New York, 2006), pp. 1–15; and Frayling, *Face of Tutankhamun*, p. 53. The story of the cobra eating Carter's canary has been viewed with scepticism due to supposedly being physically impossible (the snake could not have squeezed into the cage). Christopher Frayling reported that he and his film crew tested the story by placing a caged canary near a cobra. The cobra performed some amazing contortions that got it into the cage. The hapless canary was rescued but just barely. Frayling, *Face of Tutankhamun*, p. 56.

18 H. P. Lovecraft, 'Under the Pyramids', in *The Thing on the Doorstep and Other Weird Stories*, ed. S. T. Joshi (New York, 2001), pp. 53–77, quotes from pp. 68 and 71. For background on the story and Houdini see the notes on pp. 378–83.

19 Frayling, *Face of Tutankhamun*, pp. 43–4 and 243–54.

20 Hoving, *Tutankhamun*, pp. 200 and 212; Frayling, *Face of Tutankhamun*, pp. 10–19; Curl, *Egyptian Revival*, pp. xxx and 373–89.

21 Frayling, *Face of Tutankhamun*, pp. 20, 24–6 and 51–2; and Chris Elliott, Katherine Griffis-Greenberg and Richard Lunn, 'Egypt in London: Entertainment and Commerce in the 20th Century Metropolis', in *Imhotep Today: Egyptianizing Architecture*, ed. Jean-Marcel Humbert and Clifford Price (London, 2003), pp. 111–14.

22 Robert Graves and Alan Hodge, *The Long Week-end: A Social History of Great Britain, 1918–1939* (1941; New York, 1963), pp. 125–7; Frayling, *Face of Tutankhamun*, pp. 21 and 32–7; and Hoving, *Tutankhamun*, pp. 326 and 329.

23 Frayling, *Face of Tutankhamun*, p. 60.

24 Lady Burghclere, 'Introduction: Biographical Sketch of the Late Lord Carnarvon', in Carter and Mace, *Discovery of Tutankhamen*, p. 1; Frayling, *Face of Tutankhamun*, p. 123; Carter and Mace, *Discovery of Tutankhamen*, p. 141; and Tyldesley, *Tutankhamen*, pp. 90–92; and Hoving, *Tutankhamun*, pp. 271–317 for a more unfavourable view of Carter's behaviour.

25 Alessandro Bongiovanni and Maria Sole Croce, eds, *The Illustrated Guide to the Egyptian Museum in Cairo* (Vercelli, 2003); and Frayling, *Face of Tutankhamun*, p. 32.

26 For a good overview of the several Tutankhamun exhibits see the Wikipedia article, 'Exhibitions of Artefacts from the Tomb of Tutankhamun', accessed 8 March 2016; Frayling, *Face of Tutankhamun*, pp. 260–61; 'Chatter', in *People*, XVII/4 (1 February 1982), at www.people.com; and 'Tut, Tut', *Futility Closet* (21 January 2012), at www.futilitycloset.com.

27 When I visited the Tutankhamun exhibit at the Field Museum in Chicago, I was disappointed when I discovered the burial mask was not in the exhibit. But I made up for it by buying a tie with a pattern of the burial mask. Egyptomania makes one resourceful and resilient!

Nine: Occult Egyptomania

1 H. P. Blavatsky, *Isis Unveiled: A Master-key to the Mysteries of Ancient and Modern Science and Theology*, Centenary Anniversary Edition, Two Volumes in One (Los Angeles, CA, 1931), vol. I, Chapter 14, especially, p. 551.

2 Sax Rohmer, *The Romance of Sorcery: The Famous Exploration of the World of the Supernatural* (1914; New York, 2014), p. 8.

3 For a good introduction to Egyptian religion and magic see Rosalie David, *Religion and Magic in Ancient Egypt* (London, 2002); and Geraldine Pinch, *Magic in Ancient Egypt* (Austin, TX, 2010). For the longer historical context see Erik Hornung, *The Secret Lore of Egypt: Its Impact on the West* (Ithaca, NY, 1999), pp. 55 and 61.

4 In this chapter basic information about Rosicrucian, Freemasonry and related secret societies comes from David V. Barrett, *A Brief History of Secret Societies* (London, 2007); John Michael Greer, *The Element Encyclopedia of*

Secret Societies and Hidden History: The Ultimate A–Z *of Ancient Mysteries, Lost Civilizations and Forgotten Wisdom* (New York, 2006); and Joel Levy, *The Secret Societies Bible: The Definitive Guide to Mysterious Organizations* (Buffalo, NY, 2010).

5 This paragraph and the following one are based on Frances A. Yates, *The Rosicrucian Enlightenment* (1972; repr. New York, 1996). For the history of Rosicrucianism after the early seventeenth century, see Arthur Edward Waite, *The Brotherhood of the Rosy Cross* (1924; repr. New York, 1993).

6 Allen G. Debus, *Man and Nature in the Renaissance* (Cambridge, 1978), pp. 11–12.

7 Hornung, *Secret Lore of Egypt*, p. 111.

8 Ibid., pp. 112–14; and Richard V. Francaviglia, *Go East, Young Man: Imagining the American West as the Orient* (Logan, UT, 2011), pp. 238–40.

9 Jay Kinney, *The Masonic Myth: Unlocking the Truth About the Symbols, the Secret Rites, and the History of Freemasonry* (New York, 2009). Other good resources are Jasper Ridley, *The Freemasons: A History of the World's Most Powerful Secret Society* (New York, 2001); and J. M. Roberts, *The Mythology of the Secret Societies* (1972; repr. London, 2008).

10 Albert Gallatin Mackey, *The History of Freemasonry: Its Legendary Origins* (1898; repr. Mineola, NY, 2008) is an overview of most of the origin legends of the Freemason. For a more modern account of Freemasonry's legendary origins see Laurence Gardner, *The Shadow of Solomon: The Lost Secret of the Freemasons Revealed* (San Francisco, CA, 2007).

11 Kinney, *The Masonic Myth*, pp. 66–7 provides an excellent overview of Masonry. Another good resource is Ridley, *The Freemasons*. Also see Cyril N. Batham, 'Ramsay's Oration: The Epernat and Grand Lodge Versions', *Heredom*, I (1992), pp. 49–59; and Lisa Kahler, 'Andrew Michael Ramsay and his Masonic Oration', *Heredom*, I (1992), pp. 19–47.

12 'Crata Repoa', in Greer, *The Element Encyclopedia of Secret Societies and Hidden History*. For an occultist's view of Crata Repoa see Manly P. Hall, *Freemasonry of the Ancient Egyptians* (1937); repr. in Manly P. Hall, *The Lost Keys of Freemasonry* (New York, 2006), pp. 99–238.

13 Iain McCalman, *The Last Alchemist: Count Cagliostro, Master of Magic in the Age of Reason* (New York, 2003) is a good recent biography of Cagliostro. Also see 'Fratres Lucis', in Greer, *The Element Encyclopedia of Secret Societies and Hidden History*.

14 Hornung, *Secret Lore of Egypt*, p. 137.

15 Albert Pike and William L. Cummings, 'The Spurious Rites of Memphis and Misriam', *Heredom*, IX (2001), pp. 147–97; Ellic Howe, 'Fringe Masonry in England, 1870–85', *Ars quatuor coronatorum*, LXXXV (1975), pp. 242–95; Ellic Howe, 'The Rite of Memphis in France and England, 1838–70', *Ars quatuor coronatorum*, XCII (1979), pp. 1–14; and Ellic Howe and Helmut Moller, 'Theodor Reuss: Irregular Freemasonry in Germany, 1900–23', *Ars quatuor coronatorum*, XCII (1978), pp. 28–46.

16 John Hamill and Pierre Molier, 'Rebuilding the Sanctuaries of Memphis: Egypt in Masonic Iconography and Architecture', in *Imhotep Today: Egyptianizing Architecture*, ed. Jean-Marcel Humbert and Clifford Price (London, 2003), pp. 207–20. The wave of Egyptomania probably had a lot to do with the inclusion of Egyptian rooms in the great Masonic Halls built in the United States during the 1920s. Example of this Egyptomania would be the Masonic Halls built in Detroit, Michigan (1926); Guthrie, Oklahoma (1923); and Fort Wayne, Indiana (1926).

17 Bruce F. Campbell, *Ancient Wisdom Revived: A History of the Theosophical Society* (Berkeley, CA, 1980) and Peter Washington, *Madame Blavatsky's Baboon: A History of the Mystics, Mediums, and Misfits who Brought Spiritualism to America* (New York, 1995) are excellent overviews. Washington is a sceptic while Campbell is more sympathetic. Alex Owen, *The Place of Enchantment: British Occultism and the Culture of the Modern* (Chicago, IL, 2004) places the Theosophical Society in the context of other late nineteenth-century occult movements in Great Britain. Greer, *The Element Encyclopedia of Secret Societies and Hidden History* includes many articles related to Theosophy. Biographies of most major figures in Theosophy are available; in some cases, like Madame Blavatsky, there are several biographies.

18 Blavatsky, *Isis Unveiled*, vol. II, pp. 307–9.

19 Ibid., vol. I, Chapter 14, especially, pp. 515–16, 519–23, 539, 542, 545, 557–8, 589 and 595; and vol. II, p. 434.

20 'Hermetic Order of the Golden Dawn', in Greer, *The Element Encyclopedia of Secret Societies and Hidden History*; Joel Levy, *The Secret Societies Bible*, pp. 184–9; Alex Owen, *The Place of Enchantment*; and David V. Barrett, *A Brief History of Secret Societies* provide useful accounts of the Hermetic Order of the Golden Dawn.

21 Alex Owen, *The Place of Enchantment*, pp. 129–30.

22 Sidney D. Kirkpatrick, *Edgar Cayce: An American Prophet* (New York, 2000) is a good recent biography. A useful, concise account of Cayce's life and influence can be found in the 'Edgar Cayce' entry in Rosemary Ellen Guiley, *Harper's Encyclopedia of Mystical & Paranormal Experience* (1991; Edison, NJ, n.d.).

23 Edgar Evans Cayce, *Edgar Cayce on Atlantis* (New York, 1968); and Edgar Cayce, *Edgar Cayce's Egypt: Psychic Revelations on the Most Fascinating Civilization Ever Known* (Virginia Beach, VA, 2004).

24 Kirkpatrick, *Edgar Cayce*, pp. 284–5, 300–302, 308, 323, 332–3 and 359 summarizes the relevant life readings. The original readings can be found in *Edgar Cayce's Egypt*.

25 Lyn Picknett and Clive Prince, *The Stargate Conspiracy: Revealing the Truth Behind Extraterrestrial Contact, Military Intelligence and the Mysteries of Ancient Egypt* (1999; New York, 2001), pp. 57–63. Picknett and Prince's book is somewhat unique in that they are very open to alternative or fringe history but are very critical of some writers of fringe history such as Graham Hancock,

Robert Bauval and Robert Temple. For more on the connection between the successors of Edgar Cayce, the Association for Research and Enlightenment, Egyptology and Zahi Hawass, see Robert Bauval and Ahmed Osman, *Breaking the Mirror of Heaven: The Conspiracy to Suppress the Voice of Ancient Egypt* (Rochester, VT, 2012), pp. 18–34.

26 Susan Palmer, *The Nuwaubian Nation* (Burlington, VT, 2010).

Ten: Egyptomania on the Fringe of History

1 Lynn Pickett and Clive Prince, *The Stargate Conspiracy: Revealing the Truth Behind Extraterrestrial Contact, Military Intelligence and the Mysteries of Ancient Egypt* (1999; New York, 2001), p. 12.

2 Paul Sussman, *The Lost Army of Cambyses* (New York, 2002), p. 276. The character of Professor Mohammed al-Habibi to his former student Inspector Yusuf Khalifa of the Egyptian police.

3 See Chapters 3 and 4.

4 John Greaves, *Pyramidographia* (1646) is in *Miscellaneous Works of Mr John Greaves*, compiled by Dr Thomas Birch, 2 vols (London, 1737); available at https://archive.org, accessed 29 March 2016; the first volume contains a life of Greaves, pp. i–lxxii; 'John Greaves', in Morris L. Bierbrier, *Who Was Who in Egyptology*, 4th rev edn (London, 2012); Daniel J. Boorstin, 'Afterlives of the Great Pyramid', *Wilson Quarterly*, XVI/3 (1992), pp. 130–38; Peter Tompkins, *Secrets of the Great Pyramid* (1971; repr. New York, 1997), pp. 21–31.

5 'Edme François Jomard', in *Who Was Who in Egyptology*; Boorstin, 'Afterlives'; and Tompkins, *Secrets of the Great Pyramid*, pp. 44–9.

6 Martin Gardner, *Fads and Fallacies in the Name of Science* (New York, 1957; originally published in 1952 under the title *In the Name of Science*), pp. 174–6; and Tompkins, *Secrets of the Great Pyramid*, pp. 70–76. Tompkins takes Taylor seriously while Gardner considers him to be wrong-headed.

7 Charles Piazzi Smyth, *The Great Pyramid: Its Secrets and Mysteries Revealed* (New York, 1978) is a reprint of the expanded 1880 fourth edition of *Our Inheritance in the Great Pyramid*. It contains some autobiographical information from Smyth. Also see 'Charles Piazzi Smyth', in *Who Was Who in Egyptology*; Gardner, *Fads and Fallacies*, pp. 176–80; and Tompkins, *Secrets of the Great Pyramid*, pp. 77–94.

8 James Bonwick, *The Great Pyramid of Giza: History and Speculation* (1877; repr. Mineola, NY, 2002), pp. v and 134–9; 'William Matthew Flinder Petrie', in *Who Was Who in Egyptology*; and Tompkins, *Secrets of the Great Pyramid*, pp. 96–107.

9 Gardner, *Fads and Fallacies*, pp. 181–3; and Tompkins, *Secrets of the Great Pyramid*, pp. 108–16.

10 Gardner, *Fads and Fallacies*, pp. 179–80.

11 Bonwick, *Great Pyramid*, pp. 110–224.

12 Ibid., pp. 202–9; H. C. Agnew, *A Letter from Alexandria on the evidence of the practical application of the quadrature of the circle, in the configuration of the great pyramids of Gizeh* (London, 1838), at www.babel.hathitrust.org, accessed 1 April 2016; Robert Bauval and Adrian Gilbert, *The Orion Mystery: Unlocking the Secrets of the Pyramids* (New York, 1994); Robert Bauval and Graham Hancock, *Keeper of Genesis: A Quest for the Hidden Legacy of Mankind* (London, 1996), also published under the alternative title of *Message of the Sphinx* (New York, 1997); Ian Lawton, 'The Fundamental Flaws in the Orion-Giza Correlation Theory', www.ianlawton.com, accessed 15 July 2015; and E. C. Krupp, 'Pyramid Marketing Schemes', www.antiquityofman.com, originally published in *Sky & Telescope* (February 1997).

13 Patrick Flanagan, *Pyramid Power: The Millennium Science* (Glendale, CA, 1973); Max Toth and Greg Nielsen, *Pyramid Power* (New York, 1974); and Warren Smith, *Secret Forces of the Pyramids* (New York, 1975). For the debunking of the story of Bovis in Egypt see Daniel Loxton, 'Pyramid Power', *Junior Sceptic*, no. 23, in *Sceptic Magazine*, XII/2 (2006). The Loxton material is online at www.sceptic.com. Besides debunking pyramid power, the online material includes the original pamphlet of Bovis in which he states he never visited Egypt. The complete French pamphlet is posted along with an English translation of the relevant section. Peter Tompkins repeats the Bovis in Egypt story in *Secrets of the Great Pyramid*, pp. 275–7.

14 Christopher Dunn, *The Giza Power Plant: Technologies of Ancient Egypt* (Rochester, VT, 1998); and Christopher Dunn, *Lost Technologies of Ancient Egypt: Advanced Engineering in the Temples of the Pharaohs* (Rochester, VT, 2010). For a refutation of Dunn's ideas by another alternative historian, see the works of Margaret Morris.

15 Bernal Díaz del Castillo, *The History of the Conquest of New Spain*, ed. David Carrasco (Albuquerque, NM, 2008), p. 3; and Lee Eldridge Huddleston, *Origins of the American Indians: European Concepts, 1492–1729* (Austin, TX, 1967), pp. 36–7, 85 and 107.

16 Erik Iverson, *The Myth of Egypt and its Hieroglyphs in European Tradition* (1961; repr. Princeton, NJ, 1993), p. 107.

17 'Diffusion', in *The Oxford Companion to Archaeology*, ed. Neil Asher Silberman, 2nd edn, 3 vols (Oxford, 2012), vol. I, pp. 402–5; and Bruce G. Trigger, *A History of Archaeological Thought*, 2nd edn (Cambridge, 2006), pp. 217–18.

18 'Charles Vallancey', in *Oxford Dictionary of National Biography*; and Glyn Daniel, *The Idea of Prehistory* (Harmondsworth, 1964), pp. 23–4.

19 Daniel, *Idea of Prehistory*, p. 91; and A. W. Buckland, *Anthropological Studies* (London, 1891).

20 '(Thomas) Gerald Massey', in *Oxford Dictionary of National Biography*; Gerald Massey, *A Book of the Beginnings* (London, 1881), p. 18; and Stephen Howe, *Afrocentrism: Mythical Pasts and Imagined Homes* (London, 1998), pp. 252–5;

Glyn Daniel, *A Hundred and Fifty Years of Archaeology* (London, 1975), p. 226.

21 Daniel, *Idea of Prehistory*, pp. 88–93; Timothy Champion, 'Egypt and the Diffusion of Culture', in *Views of Ancient Egypt since Napoleon Bonaparte: Imperialism, Colonialism and Modern Appropriations*, ed. David Jeffreys (Walnut Creek, CA, 2011), pp. 127–9; and Paul Crook, *Grafton Elliot Smith, Egyptology & the Diffusion of Culture* (Brighton, 2012), pp. 1–12; Heather Pringle, *The Mummy Congress: Science, Obsession, and the Everlasting Dead* (2001; repr. New York, 2005), pp. 27 and 49–50.

22 Crook, *Grafton Elliot Smith*, pp. 13–18.

23 Daniel, *Idea of Prehistory*, pp. 93–4; Champion, 'Egypt and the Diffusion of Culture', p. 132; Trigger, *Archaeological Thought*, p. 220; and Daniel, *A Hundred and Fifty Years of Archaeology*, p. 297.

24 Daniel, *Idea of Prehistory*, pp. 94–5; Champion, 'Egypt and the Diffusion of Culture', pp. 133–9; and Trigger, *Archaeological Thought*, pp. 220–21, 324 and 345; and Pringle, *Mummy Congress*, p. 298.

25 Trigger, *Archaeological Thought*, p. 221; Robert H. Lowie, *The History of Ethnological Theory* (New York, 1937), pp. 160–69; Daniel, *Idea of Prehistory*, pp. 95 and 99.

26 A. P. Elkin, 'Elliot Smith and the Diffusion of Culture', in *Grafton Elliot Smith: The Man and His Work*, ed. A. P. Elkin and N.W.G. MacIntosh (Sydney, 1974), pp. 139–59; Carroll L. Riley et al., eds, *Man Across the Sea: Problems of Pre-Columbian Contacts* (Austin, TX, 1971); Thor Heyerdahl, *The Ra Expeditions* (Garden City, NY, 1971); and Pringle, *Mummy Congress*, p. 298.

27 Lorraine Evans, *Kingdom of the Ark: The Startling Story of How the Ancient British Race is Descended from the Pharaohs* (2000; London, 2001).

28 Walter Bower, *Scotichronicon*, ed. John and Winifred MacQueen (Edinburgh, 1993), vol. I: Books I and II. The story of Scota and Gaythelos is in Book I. Also see Colin Kidd, 'Scottish Historiography', in *A Global Encyclopedia of Historical Writing*, ed. D. R. Woolf, 2 vols (New York, 1998), vol. II, pp. 819–20.

29 Evans, *Kingdom of the Ark*, pp. 148–50, 186–9, 200–203 and 219; and Lorraine Evans's website at www.lorraineevans.com, accessed 27 June 2015.

30 See John E. Wall, *Jeremiah in Ireland: Proof From the Bible and the Irish Annals*; and John Dunham-Massey, *Tamar Tephi: or The Maid of Destiny. The Great Romance of the Royal House of Britain*, available at www.originofnations.org, accessed 5 May 2015. The website is devoted to the study of the origins of the various nations as described in the Bible. Besides the two books listed, the website provides access to various other books on similar topics including many by British Israelist writers.

31 Plato, *Timaeus and Critias*, trans. and intro. Desmond Lee (London, 1971), pp. 33–40; and *Manetho*, ed. W. G. Waddell (Cambridge, MA, 1940), pp. 3–35 and 227–9.

32 Lee Eldridge Huddleston, *Origins of the American Indians: European Concepts, 1492–1729* (Austin, TX, 1967), pp. 25, 28, 30, 37, 85, 107 and 141; and Ronald H. Fritze, *Legend and Lore of the Americas before 1492: An Encyclopedia of Visitors, Explorers, and Immigrants* (Santa Barbara, CA, 1993), pp. 18–21 and 76–8.

33 Martin Ridge, *Ignatius Donnelly: Portrait of a Politician* (Chicago, IL, 1962); Ignatius Donnelly, *Atlantis: The Antediluvian World* (New York, 1976), pp. 1–2; and Ronald H. Fritze, *Invented Knowledge: False History, Fake Science and Pseudo-religions* (London, 2009), pp. 34–9.

34 C. J. Cutcliffe Hyne, *The Lost Continent: The Story of Atlantis* (Lincoln, NB, 2002); and Mark Finn, *Blood & Thunder: The Life & Art of Robert E. Howard* (Austin, TX, 2006), pp. 107–13 and 165–70.

35 Sidney D. Kirkpatrick, *Edgar Cayce: An American Prophet* (New York, 2000), pp. 374–83 and 464; Edgar Evans Cayce, *Edgar Cayce on Atlantis* (New York, 1968); Edgar Evans Cayce, Gail Cayce Schwartzer and Douglas G. Richards, *Mysteries of Atlantis Revisited* (New York, 1988 and 1997); and Editors of the A.R.E. Press, *Edgar Cayce's Egypt: Psychic Revelations on the Most Fascinating Civilization Ever Known* (Virginia Beach, VA, 1989 and 2004).

36 Lynn Picknett and Clive Prince, 'Alternative Egypt', in *Consuming Ancient Egypt*, ed. Sally MacDonald and Michael Rice (London, 2003), pp. 179–81; and 'René A. Schwaller de Lubicz' and 'Synarchy', in John Michael Greer, *The Element Encyclopedia of Secret Societies and Hidden History* (New York, 2006). André VandenBroeck, *Al-Kemi: Hermetic, Occult, Political, and Private Aspects of R. A. Schwaller de Lubicz* (New York, 1987) is a biographical study. Charles H. Hapgood, *Maps of the Ancient Sea Kings: Evidence of Advanced Civilization in the Ice Age* (Philadelphia, PA, 1966); Fritze, *Invented Knowledge*, pp. 197–201; and John Anthony West, *Serpent in the Sky: The High Wisdom of Ancient Egypt* (1979; repr. New York, 1987).

37 Michael J. Crowe, ed., *The Extraterrestrial Life Debate, Antiquity to 1915: A Source Book* (Notre Dame, IN, 2008); Jason Colavito, *The Cult of the Alien Gods: H. P. Lovecraft and Extraterrestrial Pop Culture* (Amherst, NY, 2005), pp. 11–161; Fritze, *Invented Knowledge*, pp. 201–10; H. P. Lovecraft, *At the Mountains of Madness*, in H. P. Lovecraft, *The Thing on the Doorstep and Other Weird Stories*, ed. S.T. Joshi (New York, 2001), pp. 246–340 and 420–37.

38 W. R. Drake, *Gods or Spacemen?* (1964; New York, 1976); and 'W. Raymond Drake', in *The Encyclopedia of Extraterrestrial Encounters: A Definitive Illustrated A–Z Guide to All Things Alien*, ed. Ronald D. Story (New York, 2001).

39 Erich von Däniken, *Chariots of the Gods: Unsolved Mysteries of the Past* (1969; New York, 1999), pp. 34, 78–80 and 98–9. For recent critical evaluations of Von Däniken, see 'Erich von Däniken', in Kenneth L. Feder, *Encyclopedia of Dubious Archaeology: From Atlantis to the Walam Olum* (Santa Barbara, CA, 2010); and Fritze, *Invented Knowledge*, pp. 201–10.

40 Picknett and Prince, 'Alternative Egyptology', pp. 175–8.

41 Ibid., p. 181. References to the Association for Research and Enlightenment's role in funding archaeological expeditions in Egypt appear frequently in Picknett and Prince's 'Alternative Egyptology' as well as their *The Stargate Conspiracy*; and Ian Lawton and Chris Ogilvie-Herald, *Giza: The Truth: The People, Politics and History Behind the World's Most Famous Archaeological Site* (London, 1999).

42 Picknett and Prince, 'Alternative Egyptology', pp. 181–2; Robert M. Schoch, 'Redating the Great Sphinx of Giza', *Kmt: A Modern Journal of Ancient Egypt*, III/2 (1992), pp. 52–9 and 66–70; *The Mystery of the Sphinx* produced by the Sphinx Project, aired 10 November 1993 on National Broadcasting Company's network; and Paul Jordan, *Riddles of the Sphinx* (New York, 1998), pp. 127–61.

43 James A. Harrell, 'The Sphinx Controversy: Another Look at the Geological Evidence', *Kmt*, V/2 (1994), pp. 70–74; Mark Lehner, 'And Yet More Sphinx Age Considerations: Notes and Photographs on the West–Schoch Hypothesis', *Kmt*, V/3 (1994), pp. 40–48. Jordan, *Riddles of the Sphinx*, pp. 145–63 is an accurate summary of the *Kmt* debate that is scrupulously fair to Schoch. Also see the website of civil engineer and independent scholar David P. Billington that brings together a tremendous amount of material critical of Schoch's hypothesis at www.davidpbillington.net. Schoch's subsequent publications were all co-authored with Robert Aquinas McNally: *Voices of the Rocks: A Scientist Looks at Catastrophes and Ancient Civilizations* (New York, 1999); *Voyages of the Pyramid Builders: The True Origins of the Pyramids from Lost Egypt to Ancient America* (New York, 2003); *Pyramid Quest: Secrets of the Great Pyramid and the Dawn of Civilization* (New York, 2005); and *Forgotten Civilization: The Role of Solar Outbursts in Our Past and Future* (Rochester, VT, 2012).

44 Robert Bauval and Adrian Gilbert, *The Orion Mystery: Unlocking the Secrets of the Pyramids* (1994; Toronto, 1996); Picknett and Prince, 'Alternative Egyptology', pp. 183–4; and Jordan, *Riddles of the Sphinx*, pp. 127–43.

45 Graham Hancock, *Fingerprints of the Gods* (New York, 1995). For Hancock's use of West, Schoch and Bauval, see pp. 275–458. For his use of Hancock see pp. 461–70. Picknett and Prince, 'Alternative Egyptology', pp. 184–5.

46 Tudor Parfitt, *The Lost Ark of the Covenant: Solving the 2,500 Year Old Mystery of the Fabled Biblical Ark* (New York, 2008), pp. 152–3, 156–7, 167, 183 and 188.

47 Bauval and Hancock, *Keeper of Genesis*; Erich von Däniken, *The Eyes of the Sphinx: The Newest Evidence of Extraterrestrial Contact in Ancient Egypt* (New York, 1996); Graham Hancock, *The Mars Mystery: The Secret Connection between Earth and the Red Planet* (New York, 1998), pp. 261–4 (the British version lists Robert Bauval and John Grigsby as co-authors); Robert Bauval, *Secret Chamber: The Quest for the Hall of Records* (London, 1999); and Picknett and Prince, 'Alternative Egyptology', pp. 185–6.

48 Picknett and Prince, 'Alternative Egyptology', pp. 186–9; and Picknett and Prince, *The Stargate Conspiracy*, pp. xiv–xv, 25–35, 152–3, 189–254, 300–301, 305–7, 314–16, 319 and 330–31.
49 Lawton and Ogilvie-Herald, *Giza: The Truth*.
50 Picknett and Prince, 'Alternative Egyptology', pp. 190–92.

Eleven: African American Egyptomania

1 W.E.B. Du Bois, *The World and Africa: An Inquiry into the Part which Africa has Played in World History* (1946; repr. New York, 1965), p. 117.
2 Erik Hornung, *The Secret Lore of Egypt: Its Impact on the West* (Ithaca, NY, 2001), p. 191.
3 For concise definitions and descriptions of Afrocentrism see Robert Fay, 'Afrocentrism', in *Africana: The Encyclopedia of the African and African American Experience*, ed. Kwane Anthony Appiah and Henry Louis Gates, Jr. (New York, 1999); 'Afrocentricity', in David Macey, *The Penguin Dictionary of Critical Theory* (London, 2000); Ann Macy Roth, 'Afrocentrism', in *The Oxford Encyclopedia of Ancient Egypt*, ed. Donald B. Redford, 3 vols (Oxford, 2001).
4 Stephen Howe, *Afrocentrism: Mythical Pasts and Imagined Homes* (London, 1998), pp. 231–2; and Yaacov Shavit, *History in Black: African-Americans in Search of an Ancient Past* (London, 2001), pp. ix–x, both provide extensive lists of extreme Afrocentric concepts and beliefs. I have only highlighted those that are related to ancient Egypt.
5 Clarence E. Walker, *We Can't Go Home Again: An Argument about Afrocentrism* (Oxford, 2001), pp. 4–6.
6 Winthrop D. Jordan, *White Over Black: American Attitudes Towards the Negro, 1550–1812* (Chapel Hill, NC, 1968); and Andrew S. Curran, *The Anatomy of Blackness: Science and Slavery in an Age of Enlightenment* (Baltimore, MD, 2011).
7 *The Encyclopaedia Britannica: A Dictionary of Arts, Sciences, Literature and General Information*, 11th edn (New York, 1910), vol. I, p. 325. This quote from the entry on 'Africa, Ethnology' was written by T. Athol Joyce, assistant in the Department of Ethnography of the British Museum; Maghan Keita, *Race and the Writing of History: Riddling the Sphinx* (Oxford, 2000), p. 68; Andrew Reid, 'Ancient Egypt and the Source of the Nile', in *Ancient Egypt in Africa*, ed. David O'Connor and Andrew Reid (Walnut Creek, CA, 2003), p. 73; and Walker, *We Can't Go Home Again*, pp. 10–11.
8 Henri Grégoire, *An Enquiry Concerning the Intellectual and Moral Faculties, and Literature of Negroes* (Armonk, NY, 1997), pp. xix–xx and 3–5.
9 Alexander H. Everett, *America or A General Survey of the Political Situation of the Several Powers of the Western Continent with Conjectures on their Future Prospects* (1827; repr. New York, 1970), pp. 213–23.

10 Shavit, *History in Black*, pp. 6–7; and Walker, *We Can't Go Home Again*, p. 16.

11 *David Walker's Appeal in Four Articles; Together with a Preamble, To the Coloured Citizens of the World, But in Particular and Very Expressly, to Those of the United States of America*, intro. Sean Wilentz, revd edn (New York, 1995), pp. viii–xix, 2, 8 and 19–20; Walker, *We Can't Go Home Again*, pp. 16–17; and Howe, *Afrocentrism*, p. 36.

12 Philip S. Foner and George E. Walker, *Proceedings of the Black State Conventions, 1840–1865* (Philadelphia, PA, 1980), vol. I, pp. 193–4; Frederick Douglass, *The Claims of the Negro Ethnologically Considered: An Address Before the Literary Societies Western Reserve College at Commencement, July 12, 1854* (Rochester, NY, 1854), pp. 21–6; Tunde Adeleke, *The Case Against Afrocentrism* (Jackson, MS, 2009), p. 81; and Walker, *You Can't Go Home Again*, pp. 13 and 18–19.

13 Howe, Afrocentrism, p. 35; Walker, *We Can't Go Home Again*, pp. 8–9; Martin R. Delany, *The Origin and Objects of Ancient Freemasonry: Its Introduction into the United States, and Legitimacy among Colored Men*, in *Martin R. Delany: A Documentary Reader*, ed. Robert S. Levine (Chapel Hill, NC, 2003), pp. 53–5, 64–5 and 67; and Martin R. Delany, 'Africa and the African Race', in *Martin R. Delany: A Documentary Reader*, pp. 362–4.

14 Martin R. Delany, *Principia of Ethnology: The Origin of Races and Color, with an Archaeological Compendium of Ethiopian and Egyptian Civilization, from Years of Careful Examination and Enquiry* (1879; repr. Baltimore, MD, n.d.), pp. 7, 9, 11, 20–27, 41–4, 46–7, 49, 54, 56–9, 63–4, 69, 72–3 and 91–2; and Adeleke, *Afrocentrism*, pp. 70 and 82.

15 Walker, *We Can't Go Home Again*, p. 20; and Adeleke, *Afrocentrism*, pp. 56–7.

16 Edward W. Blyden, 'The Negro in Ancient History', in *The People of Africa: A Series of Papers on Their Character, Condition, and Future Prospects* (New York, 1871), pp. 4, 7–10, 16–17, 19–21 and 29.

17 Edward Wilmot Blyden, *From West Africa to Palestine* (Freetown, Sierra Leone, 1878), pp. 89–92.

18 Ibid., pp. 95–102, 111 and 115.

19 Ibid., pp. 102–3, 114, 118–20 and 130; Edward Wilmot Blyden, 'The African Problem and the Method of its Solution', in *Black Spokesman: Selected Published Writings of Edward Wilmot Blyden*, ed. Hollis R. Lynch (London, 1971), p. 47; and Edward Wilmot Blyden, 'The Liberian Scholar', in *Black Spokesman*, p. 267.

20 David Levering Lewis's *W.E.B. Du Bois: Biography of a Race, 1868–1919* (New York, 1993) and *W.E.B. Du Bois: The Fight for Equality and the American Century, 1919–1963* (New York, 2001) together provide an excellent and detailed biography. Du Bois's 'The Suppression of the African Slave-trade to the United States of America, 1638–1870', along with several of his most famous and popular works, can be found in the W.E.B. Du Bois volume of the Library of America (New York, 1986).

21 W.E.B. Du Bois, *The Negro*, intro. John K. Thornton, in *The Oxford W.E.B. Du Bois*, ed. Henry Louis Gates, Jr. (Oxford, 2007), pp. 8, 9 and 11–12; W.E.B. Du Bois, *Black Folk Then and Now: An Essay in the History and Sociology of the Negro Race*, intro. Wilson Moses, in *The Oxford W.E.B. Du Bois*, ed. Henry Louis Gates, Jr. (Oxford, 2007), pp. 12–13 and 16–19; and W.E.B. Du Bois, *The World and Africa: An Inquiry into the Part Which Africa Has Played in World History*, intro. Mahmood Mamdani, in *The Oxford W.E.B. Du Bois*, ed. Henry Louis Gates, Jr (Oxford, 2007), pp. 64, 65, 67 and 68.

22 Du Bois, *The Negro*, pp. 13–14 and 19; Du Bois, *Black Folk Then and Now*, pp. 11, 12 and 16; Du Bois, *World and Africa*, pp. 69, 75 and 79.

23 Du Bois, *Black People Then and Now*, p. 18; and Du Bois, *World and Africa*, pp. 74–6. For a concise overview of the concept and historiography of the Hamitic Hypothesis, see P. S. Zachernuk, 'Hamitic Hypothesis', in *A Global Encyclopedia of Historical Writing*, ed. D. R. Woolf, 2 vols (New York, 1998), vol. I, pp. 395–6. More detailed studies of the Hamitic Hypothesis are Edith Sanders, 'The Hamitic Hypothesis: Its Origin and Function in the Time Perspective', *Journal of African History*, X/4 (1969), pp. 521–32; and Philip S. Zachernuk, 'Of Origins and Colonial Order: Southern Nigerian Historians and the "Hamitic Hypothesis", c. 1870–1970', *Journal of African History*, XXXV/3 (1994), pp. 427–55.

24 Keita, *Race and the Writing of History*, pp. 76–7; Du Bois, *The Negro*, pp. 8, 11, 15, 19, 35–6, 52 and 58; and Du Bois, *World and Africa*, pp. 63–7.

25 Du Bois, *The Negro*, pp. 13, 40 and 48; Du Bois, *Black Folk Then and Now*, p. 11; and Du Bois, *World and Africa*, pp. 65, 79 and 88–9.

26 Adeleke, *Afrocentrism*, p. 90; and Walker, *We Can't Go Home Again*, pp. xix–xx.

27 George G. M. James, *Stolen Legacy: The Greeks were not the Authors of Greek Philosophy, but the People of North Africa, commonly called the Egyptians* (1954; repr., 1988), pp. 4, 7, 14, 70 and 153; Shavit, *History in Black*, pp. 142–3 also comments on the contradiction that the Egyptians did not write their wisdom down in books but the Greeks looted the Egyptian libraries.

28 James, *Stolen Legacy*, pp. 27–40; Mary Lefkowitz, *Not Out of Africa: How Afrocentrism Became an Excuse to Teach Myth as History* (New York, 1996), pp. 91–121; and Howe, *Afrocentrism*, pp. 66–7.

29 James, *Stolen Legacy*, pp. 14, 17, 42, 45 and 46; Luciano Canfora, *The Vanished Library: A Wonder of the Ancient World* (Berkeley, CA, 1990); Peter Marshall Fraser, *Ptolemaic Alexandria*, 3 vols (Oxford, 1972); Peter Green, *Alexander to Actium: The Historical Evolution of the Hellenistic Age* (Berkeley, CA, 1990), especially pp. 80–91; and Edward Alexander Parsons, *The Alexandrian Library: Glory of the Hellenic World, its Rise, Antiquities, and Destruction* (Amsterdam, 1952).

30 James, *Stolen Legacy*, pp. 41–130.

31 Howe, *Afrocentrism*, p. 188.

32 Suzanne Marchand, 'Leo Frobenius and the Revolt against the West', *Journal of Contemporary History*, XXXII/2 (1997), pp. 166–9; W.E.B. Du Bois, *The*

Negro, p. 26.; W.E.B. Du Bois, *The World and Africa*, p. 51n; Howe, *Afrocentrism*, pp. 48, 116, 120n, 167–8, 177 and 236; and Walker, *We Can't Go Home Again*, pp. 26–31. For a brief study of Frobenius see Janheinz Jahn, *Leo Frobenius: The Demonic Child* (Austin, TX, 1974).

33 Howe, *Afrocentrism*, pp. 165–6; Walker, *We Can't Go Home Again*, p. 35; and Adeleke, *Afrocentrism*, p. 89.

34 Cheikh Anta Diop, *The African Origin of Civilization* (Chicago, IL, 1974), pp. ix, xiv, 45; *The Peopling of Ancient Egypt and the Deciphering of Meroitic Script: Proceedings of the Symposium Held in Cairo from 28 January to 3 February 1974* (Paris, 1978), especially the discussions on pp. 73–103; Cheikh Anta Diop, 'Origin of the Ancient Egyptians' and 'Annex', in *General History of Africa*, vol. II: *Ancient Civilizations of Africa*, ed. G. Mokhtar (Berkeley, CA, 1981), pp. 27–83.

35 Cheikh Anta Diop, *Civilization or Barbarism: An Authentic Anthropology* (Chicago, IL, 1991), chapters 1–4. It first appeared in French as *Civilisation ou barbarie* (Paris, 1981).

36 For a concise overview of the current thinking on the dating of the Thera eruption, see 'Minoan Eruption' in Wikipedia, accessed 8 March 2016. For a more detailed and technical account see Walter L. Friedrich et al., 'Santorini Eruption Radiocarbon to 1627–1600 BC', *Science* (28 April 2006), p. 548; S. W. Manning et al., 'Chronology for the Aegean Late Bronze Age, 1700–1400 BC', *Science* (28 April 2006), pp. 565–9; Michael Balter, 'New Carbon Dates Support Revised History of Ancient Mediterranean', *Science* (28 April 2006), pp. 508–9; and Felix Höflmayer, 'The Date of the Minoan Santorini Eruption: Quantifying the "Offset"', *Proceedings of the 6th International Radiocarbon and Archaeology Symposium*, ed. E. Boaretto and N. R. Rebollo Franco, *Radiocarbon*, LIV/3–4 (2012), pp. 435–48.

37 Howe, *Afrocentrism*, pp. 166–9, 178 and 180–81; Russell G. Schuh, 'The Use and Misuse of Language in the Study of African History', *Journal of Modern African Studies*, XXV/1 (1997), pp. 36–81; and Kevin MacDonald, 'Cheikh Diop amd Ancient Egypt in Africa', in *Ancient Egypt in Africa*, ed. David O'Connor and Andrew Reid (London, 2003), pp. 93–105.

38 Diop, *Civilization or Barbarism*, especially pp. 231–376.

39 Howe, *Afrocentrism*, pp. 187–9. Quote on p. 189.

40 For good summaries of the Afrocentric ideology see Adeleke, *Afrocentrism*, pp. 12–13; Howe, *Afrocentrism*, pp. 231–2; and Shavit, *History in Black*, pp. ix–x.

41 Howe, *Afrocentrism*, pp. 50 and 60.

42 Ibid., p. 68; and Walker, *We Can't Go Home Again*, p. 4.

43 Constance Irwin, *Fair Gods and Stone Faces* (New York, 1963); Ivan van Sertima, *They Came Before Columbus* (New York, 1975); Ivan van Sertima, ed., *African Presence in Early America* (New Brunswick, NJ, 1992); Ivan van Sertima, *Early America Revisited* (New Brunswick, NJ, 1998); Walter Bower, *Scotichronicon*, ed. D.E.R. Watt (Edinburgh, 1993), vol. I, pp. 27–45; and

Gerald Massey, *A Book of the Beginnings*, vol. I: *Egyptian Origins in the British Isles* (London, 1881). Also see Hornung, *Secret Lore of Egypt*, p. 186.

44 Herodotus, *The Histories*, in *The Landmark Herodotus: The Histories*, ed. Robert B. Strassler (New York, 2007), pp. 119–21; Plato, *Phaedo*, in *The Dialogues of Plato*, trans. Benjamin Jowett (Chicago, IL, 1952), p. 247b; and Orosius, *Seven Books of History*, pp. 36–7.

45 Diop, *African Origins of Civilization*, pp. 7–9; Shavit, *History in Black*, pp. 148–9; Walker, *We Can't Go Home Again*, pp. xx–xxi; and Toby Wilkinson, *The Rise and Fall of Ancient Egypt* (New York, 2010), pp. 18–20.

46 Stuart Tyson Smith, 'Race', in *The Oxford Encyclopedia of Ancient Egypt*, ed. Donald B. Redford, vol. III (Oxford, 2001), pp. 111–16; H. W. Fairman, 'Ancient Egypt and Africa', *African Affairs*, LXIV (Special Issue, 1965), p. 69; Shavit, *History in Black*, pp. 149–50; Ann Macy Roth, 'Building Bridges to Afrocentrism: A Letter to My Egyptological Colleagues', in *The Flight from Science and Reason*, ed. Paul R. Gross, Norman Levitt and Martin W. Lewis (New York, 1996), p. 315; Donald R. Redford, *From Slave to Pharaoh: The Black Experience of Ancient Egypt* (Baltimore, MD, 2004), pp. 5–6; Diop, *African Origin*, chapters 1 and 2; Diop, *Civilization or Barbarism*, Chapter Two, particularly pp. 65–8; and Walker, *We Can't Go Home Again*, pp. 50–51.

47 Roth, 'Building Bridges to Afrocentrism', pp. 315–16.

48 Keita, *Race and the Writing of History*, pp. 27–40 and 178; Lerone Bennett, *Before the Mayflower: A History of Black America, 1619–1964* (New York, 1975), pp. 6–7; and Hornung, *Secret Lore of Egypt*, p. 187.

49 Anthony T. Browder has a website IKG Cultural Resource Center at www.ikg-info.com. One of its links take readers to the tours conducted by Browder.

50 The gallery of the posters can be viewed at the Budweiser website. The documentary can be accessed at www.youtube.com. John Henrik Clarke (1915–1998) was an autodidact Afrocentrist scholar. Despite not having a school diploma let alone an accredited PhD, Clarke was a University professor at Hunter College from 1969 to 1986 and also taught at Cornell College. He was a leader of the African American scholars who seceded from the African Studies Association in 1968 to found the African Heritage Studies Foundation. In Afrocentrist circles he is considered a historian, not an Egyptologist, but based on his work on the Egyptian posters in the 'Great Kings and Queens of Africa' series, he might better be considered a fabulist. For an excellent explanation of why Cleopatra was not black see Walker, *We Can't Go Home Again*, pp. 55–7.

51 Marnie Hughes-Warrington, *Revisionist Histories* (London, 2013), pp. 50–51; and Roger Barnes, *Heru Son of Ausar* (Moriches, NY, 1993).

52 Adeleke, *Afrocentrism*, pp. 12–13; Howe, *Afrocentrism*, pp. 2, 32–3, 68 and 231–2; and Shavit, *History in Black*, pp. ix–x.

53 Howe, *Afrocentrism*, pp. 2, 153 and 232; Shavit, *History in Black*, pp. 26, 154, 157, 166 and 194; and Walker, *We Can't Go Home Again*, pp. xvii and 37–8.

54 David O'Connor and Andrew Reid, 'Introduction: Locating Ancient Egypt in Africa', in *Ancient Egypt in Africa*, ed. O'Connor and Reid (Walnut Creek, CA, 2003), p. 8; and Hornung, *Secret Lore of Egypt*, pp. 187–8.

55 Walker, *We Can't Go Home Again*, pp. xxix–xxx, 3, 41 and 77; Shavit, *History in Black*, pp. 260–61; Howe, *Afrocentrism*, pp. 110–11; O'Connor and Reid, 'Introduction: Locating Ancient Egypt', p. 8; and Michael Rowlands, 'The Unity of Africa', in *Ancient Egypt in Africa*, pp. 39–40.

56 Howe, *Afrocentrism*, pp. 125, 165, 180 and 183–5; *The Peopling of Ancient Egypt and the Deciphering of Meroitic Script: Proceedings of the Symposium Held in Cairo from 28 January to 3 February 1974*, especially the discussions on pp. 73–103; and C. Loring Brace et al., 'Clines and Clusters versus "Race": A Test in Ancient Egypt and the Case of a Death on the Nile', in *Black Athena Revisited*, ed. Mary R. Lefkowitz and Guy MacLean Rogers (Chapel Hill, NC, 1996), pp. 158–62.

57 Robin Walker, *When We Ruled: The Ancient and Medieval History of Black Civilizations* (Baltimore, MD, 2011), p. 284. For newspaper coverage by the *Dallas Morning News* of the controversy, see Anne Belli, 'Group Blasts Chief of Ramses Exhibit', 16 March 1989; Dan Shine, 'Egyptian Defends Exhibit', 17 March 1989; Lawrence E. Young, 'Egyptian: Ramses was Black', 29 March 1989; and 'Ramses Protest Planned', 6 April 1980. Coverage also appeared in the *Washington Post*, 'Egypt Says Ramses II Wasn't Black', 23 March 1989; and *St Paul Pioneer Press*, 'Egypt Wants No Part of Racial Issue', 26 March 1989; Walker, *We Can't Go Home Again*; and John H. McWhorter, *Losing the Race: Self-sabotage in Black America* (New York, 2000).

Twelve: Egyptomania and Fiction

1 H. P. Lovecraft, 'Under the Pyramids', in *The Thing on the Doorstep and Other Weird Stories*, ed. S. T. Joshi (New York, 2001), p. 68.

2 Agatha Christie, *Death on the Nile* (1937; London, 2001), pp. 145–6.

3 Edward Said quoted in Christopher Frayling, *The Face of Tutankhamun* (London, 1992), p. 276.

4 Gustave Flaubert's *Salammbô* (1862), set in Carthage, and Mika Waltari's *The Etruscan* (1955) are among the relatively few exceptions.

5 Charlotte Booth, *The Myth of Ancient Egypt* (Stroud, 2011), p. 202; Erik Hornung, *The Secret Lore of Egypt: Its Impact on the* West (Ithaca, NY, 2001), p. 63; Michael Rice and Sally MacDonald, 'Introduction: Tea with a Mummy: The Consumer's View of Egypt's Immemorial Appeal', in *Consuming Ancient Egypt*, ed. Sally MacDonald and Michael Rice (London, 2003), p. 11; and Tim Schadla-Hall and Genny Morris, 'Ancient Egypt on the Small Screen: From Fact to Faction in the UK', in *Consuming Ancient Egypt*, p. 195.

6 See pp. 152–3 and 208–9 of this book.

7 See pp. 215–16 of this book; David Huckvale, *Ancient Egypt in the Popular Imagination: Building a Fantasy in Film, Literature, Music, and Art* (Jefferson, NC, 2012), pp. 101–3, 139–42, and 155–6; Anatole France, *Thaïs*, trans. Basia Gulati and intro. Wayne C. Booth (Chicago, IL, 1976).

8 See pp. 213–14 and 231–4 of this book; Huckvale, *Ancient Egypt in the Popular Imagination*, pp. 159–62 and 180; and Richard Marsh, *The Beetle: A Mystery* (1897; London, 2008).

9 Matthew Bernstein, 'Introduction', in *Visions of the East: Orientalism in Film*, ed. Matthew Bernstein and Gaylyn Studlar (New Brunswick, NJ, 1997), p. 4; Antonia Lant, 'The Curse of the Pharaoh, or How Cinema Contracted Egyptomania', in *Orientalism in Film*, pp. 79–80 and 83; Leslie Halliwell, *The Dead that Walk: Dracula, Frankenstein, the Mummy, and Other Favourite Movie Monsters* (New York, 1988), p. 207; James Steffin, 'The Eyes of the Mummy', at www.tcm.com; James Steffin, 'The Loves of Pharaoh', at www.tcm.com; and the Wikipedia article on 'The Loves of Pharaoh'.

10 Simon Louvish, *Cecil B. DeMille and the Golden Calf* (London, 2007) is a good biography of DeMille that places his films *Cleopatra* and *The Ten Commandments* in the contexts of when they were produced.

11 Jon Solomon, *The Ancient World in the Cinema* (New Haven, CT, 2001), pp. 142–58; and Sam Serafy, 'Egypt in Hollywood: Pharaohs of the Fifties', in *Consuming Egypt*, ed. Sally MacDonald and Michael Rice (London, 2003), pp. 84–6.

12 Bruce Feiler, *America's Prophet: Moses and the American Story* (New York, 2009); Jan Assmann, *Moses the Egyptian: The Memory of Egypt in Western Monotheism* (Cambridge, MA, 1997); Solomon, *Ancient World in the Cinema*, pp. 159–60; and '"Racist" Casting Claim for Ridley Scott's *Exodus*', at www.stuff.co.nz, accessed 11 March 2016.

13 Lucy Hughes-Hallett, *Cleopatra: History Dreams, and Distortions* (New York, 1991), pp. 133–4, 217 and 252; *The Inferno of Dante*, trans. Robert Pinksy (New York, 1994), p. 49, Canto V, line 55; and Mary Hamer, 'Timeless Histories: A British Dream of Cleopatra', in *Visions of the East*, pp. 272–5.

14 Hughes-Hallett, *Cleopatra*, pp. 269 and 292; Hamer, 'Timeless Histories', pp. 272–5; and Solomon, *Ancient World in the Cinema*, pp. 63–7.

15 *Hughes-Hallett, Cleopatra, pp. 266–94; Solomon, Ancient World in the Cinema*, pp. 67–75; and *Cleopatra: 50th Anniversary* DVD (2013). And the two following paragraphs.

16 Huckvale, *Ancient Egypt in the Popular Imagination*, pp. 38–9; Solomon, *Ancient World in the Cinema*, pp. 75, 78, 294–5; See also the Wikipedia articles for *Cleopatra* (1970), *Antony and Cleopatra* (1972) and *Carry on Cleo*, accessed 11 March 2016.

17 Margaret George, *The Memoirs of Cleopatra* (New York, 1997); Huckvale, *Ancient Egypt in Popular Imaginations*, p. 220; for the *Cleopatra* miniseries see the Wikipedia article, accessed 11 March 2016; Solomon, *Ancient World*

in the Cinema, p. 78; for *Rome* the TV series see the Wikipedia article, accessed 11 March 2016; Colleen McCullough, *The October Horse* (New York, 2002); Colleen McCullough, *Antony and Cleopatra* (New York, 2007); Maria Dahvana Headley, *Queen of Kings: A Novel of Cleopatra, the Vampire* (New York, 2011); and for Angelina Jolie as Cleopatra see the articles at www.lifeandstylemag. com and www.movienewz.com/cleopatra, accessed 11 March 2016.

18 Sigmund Freud, *Moses and Monotheism* (New York, 1967) and Dominic Montserrat, *Akhenaten: History, Fantasy and Ancient Egypt* (London, 2000), pp. 139, 140, 145, 148, 156–7, 162 and 167.

19 Thomas Mann, *Joseph and His Brothers*, trans. John E. Woods (New York, 2005); Erik Hornung, *The Secret Lore of Egypt: Its Impact on the West* (Ithaca, NY, 2001), p. 196; Mika Waltari, *The Egyptian*, trans. Naomi Walford (New York, 1949); and Naguib Mahfouz, *Akhenaten: Dweller in Truth* (New York, 2000).

20 Huckvale, *Ancient Egypt in the Popular Imagination*, pp. 28–9; Solomon, *Ancient World in the Cinema*, pp. 243–56; Montserrat, *Akhenaten*, p. 163; and Serafy, 'Egypt in Hollywood', pp. 77, 80 and 86.

21 Huckvale, *Ancient Egypt in the Popular Imagination*, pp. 30–31; Solomon, *Ancient World in the Cinema*, pp. 250–51; and Serafy, 'Egypt in Hollywood', pp. 82–3.

22 Naguib Mahfouz, *Three Novels of Ancient Egypt: Khufu's Wisdom, Rhadopis of Nubia, Thebes at War*, trans. Raymond Stock, Anthony Calderbrank and Humphrey Davies (New York, 2007).

23 For information on Wilbur Smith see his website at www.wilbursmithbooks. com; for information on individual titles see www.amazon.com; also see information concerning Wilbur Smith at www.fantasticfiction.co.uk; and his interview with the *Daily Telegraph* (14 September 2014) concerning his new Egyptian novel *Desert God* at www.telegraph.co.uk.

24 For information on Christian Jacq see the Wikipedia article and www.fantasticfiction.co.uk, accessed 11 March 2016. Additional information on individual titles can be found in the book descriptions provided by Amazon. com. Information on Jacq's newest series is available from www.amazon.fr. Stephanie Thornton, *Daughter of the Gods* (New York, 2014) and Stephanie Dray, *Lily of the Nile* (New York, 2011), *Song of the Nile* (New York, 2011) and *Daughter of the Nile* (New York, 2013).

25 Huckvale, *Ancient Egypt in Popular Culture*, pp. 28–30; Solomon, *Ancient World in the Cinema*, pp. 250–51; the Turner Classic Movies website's entry for *The Valley of the Kings*; Brian Fagan, *The Rape of the Nile: Tomb-robbers, Tourists, and Archaeologists in Egypt* (Wakefield, RI, 1992), pp. 291–5; and C. W. Ceram, *Gods, Graves, and Scholars: The Story of Archaeology* (New Yorik, 1967), pp. 152–75. MGM secured the use of Ceram's copyright for *Valley of the Kings*. Robin Cook's *Sphinx* was published in 1979.

26 Huckvale, *Ancient Egypt in the Popular Imagination*, pp. 1–2, 7 and 142–3.

27 Ibid., p. 58.

28 Ibid., pp. 11–16; Carter Lupton, '"Mummymania" for the Masses: Is Egyptology Cursed by the Mummy's Curse?', in *Consuming Egypt*, ed. Sally MacDonald and Michael Rice (London, 2003), pp. 24, 31, 33–4 and 37; and Halliwell, *Dead That Walk*, pp. 199–207.

29 Lupton, 'Mummymania', p. 36; and Halliwell, *Dead that Walk*, p. 212.

30 Huckvale, *Ancient Egypt in the Popular Imagination*, pp. 20–28; and Halliwell, *Dead That Walk*, p. 192. The synopses of the four films are based on my viewing of the films. Halliwell provides more detailed synopses.

31 Halliwell, *Dead that Walk*, pp. 231–9; and Huckvale, *Ancient Egypt in the Popular Imagination*, pp. 39–43.

32 Halliwell, *Dead that Walk*, pp. 239–40, did not like either *Blood from the Mummy's Tomb* or *The Awakening*; Huckvale, *Ancient Egypt in the Popular Imagination*, pp. 43–8.

33 Anne Rice, *The Mummy or Ramses the Damned* (New York, 1989); and Huckvale, *Ancient Egypt in the Popular Imagination*, pp. 143 and 221.

34 Lupton, 'Mummymania', pp. 45–6.

35 Huckvale, *Ancient Egypt in the Popular Imagination*, pp. 49–51.

36 Montserrat, *Akhenaten*, p. 162; and Rita Rippetoe, 'Lynda S. Robinson and Lauren Haney: Detection in the Land of Mysteries', in *The Detective as Historian: History and Art in Historical Crime Fiction*, ed. Ray B. Browne and Lawrence A. Kreiser, Jr. (Bowling Green, OH, 2000), pp. 11–13.

37 Booth, *Myth of Ancient Egypt*, p. 28; Huckvale, *Ancient Egypt in the Popular Imagination*, pp. 48–9; and Agatha Christie, *Death on the Nile* (1937; London, 2001), pp. 145–6.

38 For commentary on the novels of Davis, Roberts and Saylor, see Terrance L. Lewis, 'John Maddox Roberts and Steven Saylor: Detecting in the Final Decades of the Roman Republic'; and Peter Hunt, 'Lindsey Davis: Falco, Cynical Detective in a Corrupt Roman Empire', in *The Detective as Historian*, pp. 22–31 and 32–44.

39 Gary Hoppenstand, 'Elizabeth Peters: *The Last Camel Died at Noon* as Lost World Adventure Pastiche', in *Detective as Historian*, pp. 293–305; Elizabeth Peters and Kristen Whitbread, *Amelia Peabody's Egypt: A Compendium* (New York, 2003).

40 See the Wikipedia article on Anton Gill, accessed 11 March 2016.

41 Rippetoe, 'Lynda S. Robinson and Lauren Haney', pp. 19–20 and the Wikipedia article for Lauren Haney.

42 Ibid., pp. 13–17 and the Wikipedia article for Lynda S. Robinson, accessed 11 March 2016.

43 The article on Paul C. Doherty in Wikipedia. See also his website at www. paulcdoherty.com. For comments on one of Doherty's series set in medieval England, see Edward L. Meek, 'P. C. Doherty: Hugh Corbett, Secret-agent and Problem-Solver', in *The Detective as Historian*, pp. 76–84.

44 Nick Drake's article in Wikipedia, accessed 11 March 2016.

Postscript

1 See 'American Pharoah' and 'Pioneerof the Nile' in Wikipedia, accessed 14 September 2015.

2 *Tut* miniseries, information available at www.imdb.com, accessed 14 September 2015.

3 Oliver Moody, 'Is Nefertiti in King Tut's Tomb too? A British Expert Claims to have Found Signs of a Secret Room Behind a Hidden Door', *The Times* (London), 11 August 2015, p. 3; Jacob Wirtschatter, 'Researchers: Nefertiti May be in Tut's Tomb', www.usatoday.com; Caroline M. Rocheleau, 'Has Nefertiti's Tomb been Discovered', www.archaeologistsdiary.wordpress. com; 'Egypt Panel Approves Using Radar to Find Nefertiti Tomb', www. phys.org; and 'Egypt says 90 percent Chance of Hidden Rooms in Tut Tomb', 28 November 2015, www.msn.com (all accessed 29 March 2016).

4 See also Peter Hessler, 'Scans of King Tut's Tomb Reveal New Evidence of Hidden Rooms', *National Geographic*, 17 March 2016; 'Tomb Radar: King Tut's Burial Chamber Shows Hidden Rooms', *New York Times*, 17 March 2016.

5 'Ben Carson: Egyptian Pyramids were Grain Stores, not Pharaohs' Tombs', 5 November 2015; and 'Egypt Antiquities Officials Scoff at Carson's Pyramid Claims', 10 November 2015, www.msn.com.

SELECT BIBLIOGRAPHY

Adkins, Lesley and Roy, *The Keys of Egypt: The Obsession to Decipher Egyptian Hieroglyphs* (New York, 2000)

Bierbrier, Morris, *Who Was Who in Egyptology*, 4th revd edn (London, 2012)

Booth, Charlotte, *The Myth of Ancient Egypt* (Stroud, 2011)

Burleigh, Nina, *Mirage: Napoleon's Scientists and the Unveiling of Egypt* (New York, 2007)

Carrott, Richard G., *The Egyptian Revival: Its Sources, Monuments, and Meaning, 1808–1858* (Berkeley, CA, 1978)

Curl, James Stevens, *The Egyptian Revival: Ancient Egypt as the Inspiration for Design Motifs in the West* (London, 2005)

Curran, Brian, *The Egyptian Renaissance: The Afterlife of Ancient Egypt in Early Modern Italy* (Chicago, IL, 2007)

—, Anthony Grafton, Pamela Long and Benjamin West, *Obelisk: A History* (Cambridge, MA, 2009)

Day, Jasmine, *The Mummy's Curse: Mummymania in the English-speaking World* (London, 2006)

Ebeling, Florian, *The Secret History of Hermes Trismegistus: Hermeticism from Ancient to Modern Times* (Ithaca, NY, 2007)

Fagan, Brian M., *The Rape of the Nile: Tomb Robbers, Tourists, and Archaeologists in Egypt* (Wakefield, RI, 1992)

Fowden, Garth, *The Egyptian Hermes: A Historical Approach to the Late Pagan Mind* (Princeton, NJ, 1993)

Francaviglia, Richard V., *Go East, Young Man: Imagining the American West as the Orient* (Logan, UT, 2011)

Frayling, Christopher, *The Face of Tutankhamun* (London, 1992)

Herodotus, *The Landmark Herodotus: The Histories*, ed. Robert B. Strassler (New York, 2007)

Hornung, Eric, *The Secret Lore of Egypt: Its Impact on the West* (Ithaca, NY, 2001)

Howe, Stephen, *Afrocentrism: Mythical Pasts and Imagined Homes* (London, 1998)

Huckvale, David, *Ancient Egypt in the Popular Imagination: Building a Fantasy in Film, Literature, Music, and Art* (Jefferson, NC, 2012)

Humbert, Jean-Marcel, Michael Pantazzi and Christine Ziegler, *Egyptomania: Egypt in Western Art, 1730–1930* (Ottawa, 1994)

—, and Clifford Price, eds, *Imhotep Today: Egyptianizing Architecture* (London, 2003)

Irwin, Robert, *Dangerous Knowledge: Orientalism and Its Discontents* (Woodstock, NY, 2008)

Iversen, Erik, *The Myth of Egypt and Its Hieroglyphs in European Tradition*, (1963; repr. Princeton, NJ, 1993)

Jeffreys, David, *Views of Ancient Egypt Since Napoleon Bonaparte: Imperialism, Colonialism and Modern Appropriations* (2003; repr. Walnut Creek, CA, 2011)

Jordan, Paul, *Riddles of the Sphinx* (New York, 1998)

Lehner, Mark, *The Complete Pyramids* (London, 1992)

Luckhurst, Roger, *The Mummy's Curse: The True History of a Dark Fantasy* (Oxford, 2012)

MacDonald, Sally, and Michael Rice, eds, *Consuming Ancient Egypt* (London, 2003)

Montserrat, Dominic, *Akhenaten: History, Fantasy and Ancient Egypt* (London, 2000)

O'Conner, David, and Andrew Reid, eds, *Ancient Egypt in Africa* (2003; repr. Walnut Creek, CA, 2011)

Ray, John, *The Rosetta Stone and the Rebirth of Ancient Egypt* (Cambridge, MA, 2007)

Redford, Donald B., ed., *The Oxford Encyclopedia of Ancient Egypt*, 3 vols (Oxford, 2001)

Romer, John, *The Great Pyramid: Ancient Egypt Revisited* (Cambridge, 2007)

Said, Edward, *Orientalism* (New York, 1979)

Shavit, Yaacov, *History in Black: African-Americans in Search of an Ancient Past* (London, 2001)

Shaw, Ian, ed., *The Oxford History of Ancient Egypt* (Oxford, 2000)

Stolzenberg, Daniel, *Egyptian Oedipus: Athanasius Kircher and the Secrets of Antiquity* (Chicago, IL, 2013)

Strathern, Paul, *Napoleon in Egypt* (New York, 2008)

Trafton, Scott, *Egypt Land: Race and Nineteenth-century American Egyptomania* (Durham, NC, 2004)

Tyldesley, Joyce, *Egypt: How a Lost Civilization was Rediscovered* (Berkeley, CA, 2005)

Ucko, Peter, and Timothy Champion, eds, *The Wisdom of Egypt: Changing Visions Through the Ages* (London, 2003)

Verner, Miroslav, *The Pyramids: The Mystery, Culture, and Science of Egypt's Great Monuments* (New York, 2001)

Walker, Clarence, *We Can't Go Home Again: An Argument about Afrocentrism* (Oxford, 2001)

Wilkinson, Toby, *The Rise and Fall of Ancient Egypt* (New York, 2010)

Yates, Frances, *Giordano Bruno and the Hermetic Tradition* (1964; repr. Chicago, IL, 1991)

Zivie-Coche, Christiane, *Sphinx: History of a Monument* (Ithaca, NY, 2002)

ACKNOWLEDGEMENTS

Ancient Egypt and Egyptomania are fascinating topics and Egyptomania is a never-ending story. I am writing these acknowledgements the day after I saw an advertisement for a forthcoming movie, *Gods of Egypt*, a fantasy film based on the god Set's struggle with his fellow deities Horus and Osiris, along with some endangered mortals helping out the hapless Egyptians. With that sort of plot, special effects will abound. It's too early to say much more.

I would like to thank some people for their help on this project and if I have forgotten someone, I hope they will forgive me. First, I would like to thank the people of Reaktion Books. Michael Leaman, the publisher, has been a great support for this project and has also been very patient with a book that went well past its deadline and well beyond its word limit. His forbearance is greatly appreciated. I would also like to thank Amy Salter, Harry Gilonis and Becca Wright for their good and conscientious work on this book. Harry, in particular, had to deal with an author who had a very incomplete understanding of the necessary specification for an electronic illustration.

The Athens State University library staff have been very supportive of my research, particularly Robert Burkhardt, Barbara Burks and Judy Stinnett. Robert and Barbara have now started happy retirements. Their gain is the university community's loss. Judy Stinnett, as inter-library loan librarian, has patiently obtained all sorts of strange and weird books and articles for me. I would like to thank Brandon Lunsford, archival services librarian at Johnson C. Smith University, for generously providing the picture of George G. M. James. I would also like to thank Joan Kleinknecht, the librarian of the Scottish Rite of Freemasonry Supreme Council's library in Washington, DC. She generously supplied me with copies of various articles published in some hard-to-find historical journals published by the Freemasons. I would also like to thank the staff of the Freemason's Hall in Fort Wayne, Indiana, for a wonderful tour of that fascinating building.

Ann Marie Lang, Blake Denton, Susan Owen and Joy Bracewell read parts of the manuscript and made helpful suggestions. Kelton Riley heroically read the whole manuscript and helped to identify typos, awkward sentences and opaque statements. In particular, I want to acknowledge the help and support of Richard Francaviglia. He read the manuscript and made numerous invaluable suggestions for how to improve clarity and organization and provided some very helpful references. Richard and I possess a mutual interest in the study of pseudo-historical ideas in popular culture and sometimes in academe, and the phenomenon of orientalism as well. Finally I would like to thank my wife, Twylia, for bearing with me in my constant lumbering through libraries, museums and bookstores for evidence of Egyptomania. She is a wonderful travelling companion, even if she did find Egypt hot, dusty and simply not to her taste.

PHOTO ACKNOWLEDGEMENTS

The author and publishers wish to express their thanks to the below sources of illustrative material and/or permission to reproduce it. Some locations of artworks or artefacts are given below in the interests of brevity.

Alexandria National Museum: p. 47; courtesy the author: pp. 8, 22, 173, 179, 188, 254, 375; from [John Barrow], *A New Geographical Dictionary: Containing a Full and Accurate Account of the Several Parts of the Known World, as it is Divided into Continents, Islands, Oceans, Seas, Rivers, Lakes, &c. The Situation, Extent, and Boundaries, of all the Empires, Kingdoms, States, Provinces, &c. In Europe, Asia, Africa, and America* . . . 2 vols (London, 1759–60): p. 93; photo C. M. Battey: p. 312; The British Museum, London: p. 164; photo A. S. Campbell: p. 12; photo Corbis: p. 344; photo Dmitrismirnov: p. 62; from Ignatius Donnelly, *Atlantis: The Antediluvian World* (New York, 1882): p. 287; from Amelia Edwards, *A Thousand Miles Up the Nile* (London, 1891): pp. 182, 202; from Elbert Eli Farman, *Along the Nile with General Grant* (New York, 1904): p. 207; photo Ginabovara: p. 250; photo Giorgio-monteforti: p. 142; photo William Henry Goodyear, courtesy Brooklyn Museum Archives: p. 232; photo Patrick Gray: p. 98; from the *Illustrated London News*, vol. XCIV, no. 2608 (20 April 1889): p. 219; photo INTERFOTO/S'ammlung Rauch/Mary Evans Picture Library: p. 175; photo Internet Archive Book Images: p. 219; J. Paul Getty Museum, Los Angeles (reproduced courtesy Getty Trust Open Content Program): p. 122; courtesy of Johnson C. Smith University archives, Charlotte, North Carolina: p. 316; photo Melchior Küsel: p. 247; Library of Congress, Washington, DC (Prints and Photographs Division): pp. 12, 153, 168, 225, 257, 287, 312, 320; photo Los Angeles County Museum of Art: pp. 36, 109; photo Mary Evans Picture Library: pp. 117, 161; photo Nesnad: p. 339; from John Clark Ridpath, *Ridpath's Universal History: An account of the origin, primitive condition and ethnic development of the great races of mankind, and of the principal events in the evolution and progress of the civilized life among men and nations, from recent and authentic sources,* . . . vol. X (Cincinatti, OH, 1892/6): p. 98; from *La Sainte Bible*, illustrated by Gustave Doré (Tours, 1866): p. 58; photo F. W. Schmidt: p. 278; from Giorgio de Sepibus, *Romani*

INDEX